To my Wife

THE BEGINNINGS OF NATURALISM
IN AMERICAN FICTION

The American Institute in the University of Upsala

ESSAYS AND STUDIES
ON AMERICAN LANGUAGE AND LITERATURE

Edited by
S. B. LILJEGREN

In Cooperation with
O. S. Arngart, Frank Behre, and Eilert Ekwall

IX

THE BEGINNINGS OF NATURALISM IN AMERICAN FICTION

A Study of the Works of Hamlin Garland, Stephen Crane, and
Frank Norris with Special Reference to Some European Influences

1891—1903

By

LARS ÅHNEBRINK

NEW YORK: RUSSELL & RUSSELL · INC.
1961

PS
371
A2
1961

PREFACE

Scholars generally agree that naturalism in the United States came of age in the writings of Theodore Dreiser, whose first novel, *Sister Carrie* (1900), is a fairly typical work of the movement. As early as the nineties, however, there was substantial experimentation in naturalism. Although it is true that some critics, such as Oscar Cargill, Robert E. Spiller, and Vernon Louis Parrington, have in brief accounts classified Stephen Crane and Frank Norris as, to a greater or lesser degree, disciples of Zola, and that a few have linked Hamlin Garland with naturalism, no extensive study of the subject, neither in itself, nor with reference to its European sources has been published. In consequence it is worth while to examine this subject in detail.

Scholarly works on the individual authors dealt with in this book are comparatively few. There is no complete biography or critical study of Garland; Eldon C. Hill's unpublished dissertation supplies chiefly biographical data on the early Garland. Thomas Beer's impressionistic biography is still the only full-length study of Crane. Scholars have, however, given more attention to Norris. Since Franklin Walker brought out his life of Norris in 1932, three additional books on that author have been published: Ernest Marchand's critical study of Norris's writings, and Marius Biencourt's and my own studies of Norris's indebtedness to Zola. Part of my monograph has, in revised form, been incorporated in the present work.

I have confined myself to an analysis of Garland, Crane, and Norris, since they seem to be the first important American writers to have been obviously influenced by naturalism. Moreover, I have discussed mainly those writings of the three authors which are clearly naturalistic or exhibit traces of naturalism. Other works by these authors have as a rule been dealt with only in so far as they throw light on the writers' development or shift of attitude. The study has been limited to fiction, since that was the chief mode of expression of the authors analyzed. The investigation covers the period running from 1891, the date of publication of Garland's first book of short stories, *Main-Travelled Roads*, to 1903, the date of publication of Norris's last novel, *The Pit*.

In an attempt to define the writers' positions in the emergence of American naturalism, attention has been paid to relevant social, philosophical, and literary aspects of life in the United States during the period between the Civil War and the turn of the century. In addition, the analysis has been extended to the authors' literary creeds, choice of theme and method, use of setting, and type of characterization. As the title indicates, I have been particularly concerned with foreign influences, French, Russian, and Scandinavian, my study of which has been limited mainly to related ideas, characters, episodes, and particulars. Thus there are noted several specific features and qualities of the type of naturalism exhibited in the writings of the three authors which set it off from French naturalism. In the chapters on French influences I have used, for purposes of consistency, French versions of the works concerned, in spite of the fact that translations—often toned down and abridged—may have been used by the American writers. English translations have, as a rule, been used for the works of Russian authors and of Ibsen.

In the eighties and nineties the American writers whose aim was a faithful reproduction of everyday life commonly referred to themselves as "realists." At the same time American writers and critics were generally employing the terms "realism" or "new realism" for French naturalism as it entered the United States. This led to a confusion of terminology, which, not limited to those two decades, has, to some extent, persisted to this day. A definition of the terms "realism" and "naturalism" as used in this book therefore is necessary. *Realism* is a manner and method of composition by which the author describes *normal, average life* in an accurate and truthful way (exemplified in Howells' *The Rise of Silas Lapham*). *Naturalism*, on the other hand, is a manner and method of composition by which the author portrays *life as it is in accordance with the philosophic theory of determinism* (exemplified in Zola's *L'Assommoir*). In contrast to a realist, a naturalist believes that man is fundamentally an animal without free will. To a naturalist man can be explained in terms of the forces, usually heredity and environment, which operate upon him.

*

I am greatly indebted to my teacher, Professor S. B. Liljegren, University of Upsala, who, in 1945, suggested this study and since then has helped with constant advice and encouragement. His stimulating suggestions and unfailing interest can never be adequately acknowledged. For valuable criticism of part of the manuscript by Professor Kenneth B. Murdock, Harvard University, I express my sincere gratitude. His aid in various matters I shall not readily forget. During my studies in America I had the privilege of meeting many distinguished scholars in the field of American literature, whose kind interest and help I greatly appreciate. In addition to Professor Murdock, I should like to mention Professor Willard Thorp, Princeton University, who helped me in various ways during my stay in Princeton; Professor Robert E. Spiller, University of Pennsylvania, with whom I discussed several problems relative to American naturalism; Professor Thomas H. Johnson, Lawrenceville School, Lawrenceville, N.J., who helped to locate some of my sources; Professor Herbert F. West, Dartmouth College; Professor Harry H. Clark, University of Wisconsin; Professor Tremaine McDowell, University of Minnesota; and Professor Garland Greever, University of Southern California. Special thanks are due to Professor Eldon C. Hill, Miami University, Ohio, for his hospitality and several kindnesses during my stay in his home, where he made available to me his extensive Garland material. For valuable assistance in many ways I express my thanks to Mr. Vilas Johnson, Mr. Franklin J. Meine, Mr. Vincent Starrett, and Mr. Ames C. Williams. I must also gratefully recognize the kindness, assistance, and criticism of Professor Franklin Walker and Dr. Imogene Walker, Mills College and University of California, respectively. Professor Gunnar Tideström, University of Upsala, has kindly read the chapter on "The Influence of Ibsen" and given me valuable suggestions. I offer my warm thanks also to several persons who have suggested stylistic and other revisions, particularly to Professor Andrew Hilen, University of Washington, Mrs. Carol King, and Mr. Carl L. Anderson.

I take pleasure in acknowledging two valuable grants-in-aid awarded me by the Rockefeller Foundation: one in 1946, which helped to finance the academic year of 1946–7 spent in the United States collecting the material for this book; the other in 1948, which helped to bring this work to an early completion. My sincere thanks are also due to the American Scandinavian Foundation and to Dr. Henry Goddard Leach, its former president.

I am greatly indebted to the courtesy of the staffs of libraries, especially the Doheny Library in the University of Southern California, where I was given access to the extensive Garland Collection which enabled me to present fresh material on my subject, Princeton University Library, Newark Public Library, New York Public Library, Dartmouth College Library, Newberry Library, and Upsala University Library. For permission to use and quote from Garland's books and unpublished material my thanks are due to Mrs. Constance Garland Doyle and Mrs. Isabel Garland Lord. I am especially grateful to Mrs. Jeanette (Charles N.) Black, Frank Norris's widow, for the privilege of an interview in 1947 and for permission to print Appendix F, 1; to Mrs. Kathleen (Charles G.) Norris for permission to print Appendix F, 2; and to Miss Mildred Howells for permission to quote from *Life in Letters of William Dean Howells* and from some unpublished letters of W. D. Howells. I am grateful also to Doubleday & Co., Macmillan Co., and Alfred A. Knopf, who have granted me permission to quote from copyrighted material. Finally I cannot fully express the debt I owe to my wife, Fil. lic. Erna Åhnebrink, whose enthusiastic co-operation has been of great service to my work in all its stages.

Uppsala, April, 1950.

Lars Åhnebrink.

CONTENTS

CHAPTER I

THE AMERICAN SCENE

SOCIAL, PHILOSOPHICAL, AND LITERARY BACKGROUND

During the decades that followed the Civil War swiftly-moving
changes took place in the national life of the United States which
transformed American civilization to a marked degree, demanding
new ways of living and thinking and a revaluation of established
codes of life. The postwar decades saw the emergence of what
is commonly called "modern America."[1] Of the manifold forces
that helped to create the economic, social, and cultural transformation three factors were of particular importance: industrialism and
the rise of the city, the westward movement of settlement and the
closing of the frontier, and science and the new philosophy of life
based upon science.[2]

While the war-stricken South[3] still suffered from the consequences of the conflict, the North experienced great changes
through industrialism.[4] Gradually America became an industrial
nation, the war itself giving impetus to the factory system. The
coming of industrialism to America was somewhat delayed, mainly
because of the rivalry of Great Britain—where it had already come of

---

[1] Allan Nevins, *The Emergence of Modern America, 1865–1878* (New York,
1944) in *A History of American Life*, VIII.

[2] Walter Fuller Taylor, *A History of American Letters* (New York, 1936), pp.
241 ff. See also Ralph Leslie Rusk, *The Literature of the Middle Western Frontier* (2 vols., New York, 1925).

[3] Harold Underwood Faulkner, *American Political and Social History* (New
York, 1946), pp. 371 ff. See also Sidney Andrews, *The South since the War*
(Boston, 1866), Whitelaw Reid, *After the War: A Southern Tour* (Cincinnati,
1866), and W. L. Fleming, *Civil War and Reconstruction in Alabama* (New York,
1905).

[4] C. D. Wright, *The Industrial Evolution of the United States* (New York,
1902).

age—and because of lack of suitable transportation facilities and an adequate currency, yet, by the turn of the nineteenth century, the United States had risen to a leading position in an industrialized world. Factories emerged over a large area; first they were concentrated in the big cities in the Northeast, but they rapidly pushed westwards. Transcontinental railroads were built and new labor-saving machinery and other inventions helped to hasten the development. The foremost industries in the postwar years were steel, meat-packing, and oil. The effects of industrialism were many and far-reaching. Among other things it gave rise to a new hierarchy of financial giants[1] and at the same time it created an industrial proletariat made up of individuals who were mere cogs in a machine, insignificant beings subjected to a standardized order. Another consequence of industrialism was the rise[2] of big cities. The lure of the city, where limitless opportunities were supposed to exist, was increased by the loneliness of country life and the drudgery of farm work.

The seventies and eighties with their variegated and artificial life and nation-wide corruption have been appropriately termed *The Gilded Age* after Mark Twain's and Charles Dudley Warner's novel. President Grant's administration particularly, was involved in many national scandals.[3] Among the financiers who in those decades accumulated large fortunes, were Jay Gould, Cornelius Vanderbilt, Leland Stanford, Collis P. Huntington, Andrew Carnegie, John D. Rockefeller, Gustavus F. Swift, Jay Cooke, and J. Pierpont Morgan. Most of these men rose from poverty and small beginnings to worldly splendor and wealth; their idea of success was largely material, and their ethics may perhaps be summed up in the words of the young Rockefeller, "I'm bound to be rich! Bound to be rich!" Great capitalists, comparatively small in number, controlled banks, credit, railroads, coal, iron, and other key industries in a rich and expanding nation. Old

---

[1] See G. F. Redmond, *Financial Giants of America* (2 vols., Boston, 1922), Gustavus Myers, *History of the Great American Fortunes* (3 vols., Chicago, 1910), and Ida M. Tarbell, *History of the Standard Oil Company* (2 vols., New York, 1904).

[2] See A. M. Schlesinger, *The Rise of the City, 1878–1898* (New York, 1933) in *A History of American Life*, X.

[3] Henry Adams' novel *Democracy* (New York, 1880) reveals the corruption and intrigues in the political circles of Washington.

values and morals tended to collapse and an increasing materialism gradually gained ground. Lured by the spectacle of prosperity and free land and in answer to the heavy demands of industry upon the labor market, immigrants[1] in ever increasing numbers flooded the United States in the seventies, eighties, and nineties. Scandinavians, Germans, Italians, and people of other nationalities poured into the eastern seaports and formed distinctive groups or sections in great cities or pushed westward and established their own communities and settlements. The influx of immigrants, composed mostly of illiterate masses from the backwash of Europe, created particular problems in those cities where industrialism had already attracted a great part of the rural population. Since labor was cheap, the workers had to live in the worst sections of the cities, toward which hordes of immigrants were also pouring. As early as 1870 the slum[2] had become a terrible institution and up to the end of the century conditions grew steadily worse. The slums of New York, Philadelphia, and Boston were notorious. One of the worst nests of crime and disease was the New York Bowery, the locale of some of Stephen Crane's naturalistic tales. The slums were made up of cheap, unsafe, wooden shacks or brick houses lacking proper sanitation and adequate heating and mostly filled to overflowing with underpaid workers, women and children. Saloons, gambling dens, and disreputable places of amusement were numerous. How bad conditions actually were may be judged from an editorial in the 1892 *Arena*.

The dead sea of want is enlarging its borders in every populous centre. The mutterings of angry discontent grow more ominous. Rights denied the weak through the power of avarice, have brought us face to face with a formidable crisis which may yet be averted if we have the wisdom to be just and humane. But the problem cannot be longer sneered at as inconse-

---

[1] See J. R. Commons, *Races and Immigrants in America* (New York, 1920) and G. M. Stephenson, *A History of American Immigration, 1820–1924* (New York, 1926).

[2] See Edith E. Wood, *The Housing of the Unskilled Wage Earner* (New York, 1919) and Maurice Parmelee, *Poverty and Social Progress* (New York, 1916). For housing and slum conditions in New York City see also Jacob A. Riis, *How the Other Half Lives* (New York, 1890). It may be of interest to note that both Hamlin Garland and Stephen Crane knew Riis. See Garland, *Roadside Meetings* (New York, 1930), p. 329.

quential. It is no longer local; it affects and threatens the entire body politic. ... To-day no thoughtful person denies that this problem is one of grave magnitude. Last year, according to the court records, there were 23,895 warrants for eviction issued in the city of New York. In 1889 the published statistics show that over 7,000 persons died in the work-houses, insane asylums, and hospitals of the same city. More than one person in every five who passed from life died in some public institution. 3,815, or almost one person in every ten who died found his last resting-place in the Potter's Field.[1]

Social workers made attempts at securing relief for these people who lacked even the bare necessities of life. B. O. Flower, the editor of the progressive *Arena*, wrote in 1892: "*Abolish special privileges, monopoly* in transportation and *speculation in land*, and plutocracy will be shorn of its Samsonian locks. Of course, there are other reforms needed, but these seem to me basic and of prime importance; and in compassing these, greater liberty and more healthful freedom will be enjoyed by the people, while justice to all the people will be approached as never before."[2] In contrast to the tenement dwellers, the leisure class, the *nouveaux riches*, displayed a life of wealth and abundance.

The passing of the Homestead Act of 1862, which granted a quarter section (160 acres) of free land to *bona fide* settlers, after a preliminary period of occupation, gave great impetus to the westward movement of settlement. This process was speeded by new discoveries of minerals, by the building of the transcontinental railroads, and by the influx of a large body of immigrants, who rapidly filled up the last frontier,[3] that territory between the settled areas along the Pacific and a westward moving frontier line, which by 1850 ran from eastern Minnesota south through Nebraska, Kansas, and Arkansas to Texas. To encourage the building of transcontinental railroads Congress adopted the policy of conferring upon the railroad companies lavish land grants including a "right of way and alternate sections on each side of the track."[4] The first transcontinental line—the Union Pacific—was completed in 1869. Others followed and the last decades of the century

---

[1] "Uninvited Poverty," *Arena*, V (March, 1892), 523.

[2] "Two Hours in the Social Cellar," *Arena*, V (April, 1892), 656.

[3] F. L. Paxson, *The Last American Frontier* (New York, 1910).

[4] Faulkner, *op. cit.*, p. 427.

saw a tremendous railroad expansion.[1] By various methods of propaganda the railroads encouraged settlement in the vast, unpopulated areas of the West. Pamphlets telling future settlers of free land and reduced fares were circulated. Thousands of settlers, lured by the vision of free land, poured into the last frontier area. True, a great number of them received their land by virtue of the Homestead Act, but because the land laws were rather liberal and legislatures often corrupt, corporations bought up land through their agents by commuting at $1.25 an acre and sold it to homesteaders for many times that amount. Particularly in the Middle West fraudulent speculation in public land flourished and farmers became easy victims of crooked agents and land sharks. Moreover the railroad companies charged heavy rates to transport the products of the farmers who, on the other hand, received a very low price for them. Actually the settlers were in the grip of a complex of forces, including land agents, local middlemen, railroad officials, and Wall Street businessmen that gouged them from all sides. The following description of a farmer selling a load of corn may be given as an illustration of conditions in the Middle West:

> One forenoon a man went past here with a load of sixty bushels of corn. As he returned in the afternoon, I asked him how much he had got for his load of corn. He held up two pairs of boy's boots, and said that his sixty bushels of corn, and $1 in cash, had just purchased them. It took at least seven days' labor of a man and team to raise that corn, and another long day to haul it to market, to say nothing of interest on the farmer's investment and other expenses.[2]

In many cases the farmer had to ask for a loan with his home as security, and if he was unable to pay off his debt in time, he had to sell his farm or leave it. Other factors helped to make life intolerable. Farming itself meant hard toil for man and woman from sunup to sundown. Few pleasures were to be had in isolated areas, where there were heat and dust in summer and bliz-

---

[1] Cf. J. P. Davis, *The Union Pacific Railway* (Chicago, 1894), W. F. Gephart, *Transportation and Industrial Development in the Middle West* (*Columbia Univ. Studies*, XXXIV, No. 1, 1909), and Slason Thompson, *A Short History of American Railways* (Chicago, 1925).

[2] Edward W. Martin, *History of the Grange Movement* (San Francisco, 1874), pp. 364–5.

zards in winter. Droughts, locust pests, and prairie fires sometimes devastated a promising crop. A trip to a neighboring town, a country fair, a circus, or a barn dance were longed-for events in the monotonous life of the farmer on a bleak Dakota prairie. In dejection many a ruined man had to take the backward trail East, realizing the truth of the slogan, "In God we trusted, in Kansas we busted." Revolt against these conditions and particularly against the railroads flared up among the Middle Western farmers in the seventies and eighties. To protect their interests they united and one of their earliest organizations, the Grange,[1] got control of the state legislatures in the Middle West. The Grange, however, soon collapsed; and later the Greenback and Populist parties took up the cause of the farmers.

Such conditions destroyed the optimism of the settlers and a mood of bitterness and despair took its place. The change of temper may also be traced back to the fact that by 1890 the frontier was practically gone, for the supply of free land was exhausted. Frederick Jackson Turner, who has called attention to the significance of the frontier in molding the American character, described the effect of the disappearance of the frontier in the following terms:

> This, then, is the real situation: a people composed of heterogeneous materials, with diverse and conflicting ideals and social interests, having passed from the task of filling up the vacant spaces of the continent, is now thrown back upon itself, and is seeking an equilibrium. The diverse elements are being fused into national unity. The forces of reorganization are turbulent and the nation seems like a witches' kettle.[2]

The period after the Civil War was also the era of the organized feminist movement, which had its inception in 1848 at the Women's Rights Convention held at Seneca Falls, N.Y. The debate on the woman question increased especially after 1890 when the National American Woman Suffrage Association was formed.[3]

---

[1] S. J. Buck, *The Granger Movement* (*Harvard Historical Studies*, XIX, 1913). Hamlin Garland's *A Spoil of Office* (Boston, 1892) treats of this organization.

[2] Quoted by Faulkner in *op. cit.*, p. 417.

[3] For full account of the suffrage struggle, see Elizabeth Cady Stanton *et al.*, *History of Woman Suffrage* (6 vols., New York, 1881–1922). For the woman question, see also Nevins, *op. cit.*, pp. 335–43 with bibliography p. 427. Cf. also pp. 80–2 of the present study.

In a consideration of the changes that reshaped America in the latter part of the century the impact of science seems to have been of considerable importance. After the close of the Civil War new ideas of man and man's place in the universe began to take root in the United States, challenging the validity of established truths and traditional ways of thinking. The concept that the universe was a static creation of God was superseded by the belief in a constantly changing universe. Man was no longer a free, ethical being, but an individual devoid of free will and helpless in the grip of mechanical causes and effects. Even before the publication of *The Origin of Species* (1859), scholars were aware of the principle of the transformation of species, and works such as Sir Charles Lyell's *Principles of Geology* (1832) and Robert Chambers' *Vestiges of Creation* (1844) paved the way for the evolutionary hypothesis.[1] It was primarily *The Origin of Species* and *The Descent of Man* (1871) that contributed to the intellectual unrest in the last third of the century. Darwin's followers saw the consequences of his theory of evolution when extended to include human life, and the belief that man's ancestor was "a hairy quadruped, furnished with a tail and pointed ears, probably arboreal in habits," offered implications, the effects of which were difficult to predict. In applying evolution to society and thus proving the validity of a process already at work, Herbert Spencer, Darwin's most eminent co-worker and the originator of the expression "the survival of the fittest," enriched the study of sociology. His vogue in America during the last decades of the century almost transcended that of Darwin. He was widely read and his ideas helped to change the outlook of many rising authors and intellectuals. Struggling writers such as Hamlin Garland, Theodore Dreiser, and Jack London have told us of the impact Spencer and other evolutionists had on their minds. Garland wrote of his years in Boston:

---

[1] Richard Hofstadter, *Social Darwinism in American Thought, 1860–1915* (Philadelphia, 1945), p. 2. Valuable material for the impact of Darwinism on American thought is also furnished by Merle Curti, *The Growth of American Thought* (New York, 1943). See also Bert J. Loewenberg, "Darwinism Comes to America 1859–1900," *Mississippi Valley Historical Review*, XXVIII (1941), 339–69.

I read both day and night, grappling with Darwin, Spencer, Fiske, Helmholtz, Haeckel,—all the mighty masters of evolution whose books I had not hitherto been able to open. . . .
Herbert Spencer remained my philosopher and master. With eager haste I sought to compass the 'Synthetic Philosophy.' The universe took on order and harmony . . . It was thrilling, it was joyful to perceive that everything moved from the simple to the complex—how the bow-string became the harp, and the egg the chicken. My mental diaphragm creaked with the pressure of inrushing ideas. My brain, young, sensitive to every touch, took hold of facts and theories like a phonographic cylinder, and while my body softened and my muscles wasted from disuse, I skittered from pole to pole of the intellectual universe like an impatient bat.[1]

Darwinism probably found congenial soil in postwar America. "With its rapid expansion, its exploitative methods, its desperate competition, and its peremptory rejection of failure, post-bellum America was like a vast human caricature of the Darwinian struggle for existence and survival of the fittest."[2] In the rising age of *laissez-faire* capitalism, Darwinism seemed to justify the ethics of ruthless magnates. The law of the survival of the fittest was applied to society, to business transactions, to almost everything; and many capitalists believed, like Spencer, that the struggle for existence and war were factors desirable and even necessary to human life in their elimination of weaker species. A successful business transaction which crushed a rival firm, was but an illustration of the struggle for existence and the survival of the fittest. Perhaps never before had a rising plutocracy been justified in its ethical standards and ways of living by a simpler and more appropriate philosophy. James J. Hill, the railroad king, once asserted that "the fortunes of railroad companies are determined by the law of the survival of the fittest"[3] and John D. Rockefeller addressed a Sunday-school class in the following words:

The growth of a large business is merely a survival of the fittest. . . . The American Beauty rose can be produced in the splendor and fragrance which bring cheer to its beholder only by sacrificing the early buds which grow up around it. This is not an evil tendency in business. It is merely the working-out of a law of nature and a law of God.[4]

---

[1] *A Son of the Middle Border* (New York, 1917), pp. 322–3.

[2] Hofstadter, *op. cit.*, p. 30.

[3] *Highways of Progress* (New York, 1910), p. 126.

[4] Quoted in William J. Ghent, *Our Benevolent Feudalism* (New York, 1902), p. 29.

Another factor which may have facilitated the acceptance of Darwinian ethics in America was the mood of despair and unrest felt during and after the Civil War. To those in whom the war shook the faith in a loving and all-forgiving God, the Darwinian philosophy offered a plausible solution. Moreover, "To those already inclined to cynicism or despair," remarked David F. Bowers, "the Darwinism interpretation of war as another instance of the ever present struggle for existence seemed to provide overwhelming confirmation, and was readily accepted in this spirit."[1]

The number of American followers of Darwin and Spencer grew rapidly in the postwar decades. Two American intellectuals especially, John Fiske and Edward Livingston Youmans, became popularizers of the new ideas. Together with Asa Gray, the Harvard botanist, and others, they fought untiringly the evolutionary battle in the United States. A visit by Thomas Henry Huxley to America in 1876, when he delivered an address at the opening ceremonies of the Johns Hopkins University, and a visit by Spencer in 1882 undoubtedly stimulated the increasing interest in evolutionary thought.

Although America seemed congenial to the new trends of thought, there were at least two strongholds which offered considerable resistance: the universities and especially the church. Up to the Civil War much American thinking had been religious even in the centers of learning, but after it the evolutionary doctrine became gradually influential in leading universities because of the conversion of scientists to the new ideas. The opposition of the church continued throughout the postwar decades. Religious leaders soon realized that evolution constituted a direct threat to Christianity by undermining people's faith in revealed religion and at the same time by destroying the values of Christian ethics. The church was plunged into a crisis,[2] the outcome of which was uncertain.

The clergy were also affected by new criticisms of the Bible by scholars. In Germany, for instance, David Friedrich Strauss published his famous *Das Leben Jesu* (Germ. ed., 1835), in which

---

[1] "Hegel, Darwin, and the American Tradition," in *Foreign Influences in American Life*, ed. by David F. Bowers (Princeton, 1944), p. 160.

[2] See Arthur M. Schlesinger, "A Critical Period in American Religion, 1875-1900," *Massachusetts Historical Society Proceedings*, LXIV (1932), 523-47.

he attempted to prove that the gospel narrative had a mythical origin and growth. Popularizers of Biblical criticism won a large audience in the United States. A book like Washington Gladden's *Who Wrote the Bible?* (1891) was widely read. These circumstances no doubt helped to pave the way for a growing acceptance of evolution among liberal clergymen, who, toward the close of the century, in the social gospel movement saw a field of work more appropriate to the spirit of the modern era.

Although evolution was openly denounced by large groups of people, others preferred some kind of compromise. Men like Asa Gray made attempts at reconciling science with religion. In others again, the new doctrines caused bewilderment and despair and created a philosophy of doubt and uncertainty. The general unrest of the time and the broadening of American horizons by the scientific spirit were pictured in an editorial in the *Arena:*

> Nothing is more apparent at the present time than the rapid growth of the revolutionary spirit in almost every department of thought. ... To the thoughtful student of man's progress who believes in the ever onward march of life, the present conflict is rich in promise. He notes the significant fact that the general unrest and signs of growth are along the whole line of human development. ...
>
> In the religious world, there is in progress a wonderful quickening of conscience, a determined revolt against the old-time accepted letter of the law, against form, right, dogma, and ostentation, which, while they may awe the ignorant, necessarily offend the cultured; ...
>
> This religious revolution now assumes such gigantic proportions that it can justly be compared to the Reformation, which in the sixteenth century was regarded with such universal indignation and alarm by the dominant thought of the age. In all civilized countries the same spirit of growth and unrest is visible, yet, at the present time America seems to be the storm centre.[1]

Gradually the temper of American thought changed.[2] Two factors are particularly significant when one attempts to trace the origin of this change in attitude: one group of people emerging from the ranks of evolutionary optimists began to disbelieve in the ability of science to solve all the problems of the universe; another group, to whom religion had been the lodestar of life,

---

[1] "The Broadening Horizon of Civilization. The Unrest of the Hour," *Arena*, V (May, 1892), 775-6.

[2] Cf. p. 6.

felt, owing to the implications of Darwinism, the foundations of their belief crumble away. Of other factors, not referred to before, which helped to create a darkening outlook on life—traditional optimism and idealism were, however, strong—the possible impact of the philosophy of Schopenhauer and the writings of Flaubert, Maupassant, Hardy, and others, should not be overlooked.

It is difficult to ascertain to what degree the new ideas of man and the universe dissolved the established beliefs of the common man. Catchwords like "the struggle for existence," "the survival of the fittest," and "the human beast" certainly penetrated into the popular mind. On the whole, however, it is perhaps safe to assume that Darwinism in the United States was primarily an interest of the intellectual elite. Business men and laboring people, with few exceptions, must have got it second-hand. In divulging the findings of science and in interpreting evolution and the mood of the closing nineteenth century, literature itself, native as well as foreign, no doubt played a significant role.

The Civil War gave a fatal blow to romanticism and Emersonian idealism. The war revealed man as no divine creature of Emersonian make and this world appeared as no work of a loving God. Moreover, before the close of the century many writers of the older generation who upheld the old tradition were dead. Thoreau, Hawthorne, and Emerson were gone; Melville and Lowell died in 1891, Whitman and Whittier in 1892, and Holmes in 1894. The younger generation grew up in an America vastly different from that of Emerson. The intellectual climate of America with its postwar problems, industrial and agrarian issues, and evolutionary doctrines favored a realistic outlook. To the new generation life was no roseate dream but a hard, everyday struggle for existence. Prevailing conditions were less congenial to romanticism, and an inevitable, gradual change toward realism was felt.

The dominant literary form of expression of the new era was the novel, which seemed best to reflect the variegated phases of modern life. Poetry, with the exception of Emily Dickinson's, struck a minor note, and the drama was dominated by the sentimental-romantic tradition until James A. Herne and others began experimenting with realistic problem plays of the Ibsen type in the early nineties.

The last quarter of the century may perhaps best be characterized as a battle[1] between romanticism and realism in American letters. In an article entitled "The New Battle of the Books" a critic spoke of this struggle:

> For a long time a wordy war has raged in the magazines and the newspapers between the so-called realists and romanticists. In "Harper's Monthly" Mr. Howells has for years been asserting the importance of novels that keep close to the facts of life; and the critics and criticasters have daily attacked his teaching and practice as materialistic and debasing, as disregarding "the depth, variety, and beauty of life."[2]

In 1889 Edgar Saltus voiced the vacillation of the writers between two opposite approaches to literature. "The ambitious writer," he wrote, "has on one side of him a corpse still warm, in whose features he recognizes Romanticism; on the other is that silk stocking filled with mud which is the emblem of the Naturalists. But somewhere near at hand are tombs marked Dostoïevsky, Flaubert, Eliot."[3]

Native optimism and traditional romanticism were, however, deeply rooted in the American mind and realism made but slow headway. The last frontier, with its spirit of optimism and self-reliance, and an expanding America with seemingly limitless resources favored a romantic outlook and helped to delay the trend toward realism. "The West," said Hamlin Garland, "had become the Golden West, the land of wealth and freedom and happiness." The West was fabulous, mythical, hopeful. "Vast sweeps of untracked prairies, whose grasses waved like a sea; lakes in whose depths cool groves were mirrored; droves of elk and deer and antelope; rushing rivers on whose banks stood vine-decked cottages—these were the sunny vistas of the songs' pictures."[4]

Although predominantly realistic in tone, subject matter, and treatment, the local color movement, which dominated the literary scene in the seventies and reached its peak in the eighties and slowy exhausted itself in the nineties, betrayed a taste for the

---

[1] See Chap. VI.

[2] George Pellew, "The New Battle of the Books," *Forum*, V (July, 1888), 564.

[3] "The Future of Fiction," *North American Review*, CXLIX (November, 1889), 584.

[4] Preface to *Jason Edwards* (Boston, 1892).

quaint and the picturesque. This movement, spurred on by Bret Harte's *The Luck of Roaring Camp* (1870), was very influential, and groups of writers quickly responded to it and began writing about the locale in which they lived and worked, chronicling its history, folklore, and setting, and recording the habits, speech, and mannerisms peculiar to the people of the region. Various geographical sections were discovered and exploited as fictional material. "The vital movement," wrote Percy H. Boynton, "started with a fresh and vivid treatment of native American material, and it moved in a great sweeping curve from the West down past the Gulf, up through the southeastern states into New England, across to the Middle West, and back into the Ohio Valley until every part of the country was represented by its exposition."[1] Besides Bret Harte, Mark Twain and Joaquin Miller wrote of the West; Joel Chandler Harris, Lafcadio Hearn, George Washington Cable, and others interpreted the South. A vanishing New England culture sharply distinct from the robust and expanding West was fictionized by such writers as Sarah Orne Jewett and Mary Wilkins Freeman. By creating new centers of letters this nation-wide movement contributed to the overthrow of the literary supremacy of New England.

William Dean Howells, the leader of the realistic revolt in America, was not untouched by the movement. To his contemporaries, his moving from Boston to New York in the eighties was symbolic of the change of literary centers. In an article entitled "The Literary Movement in New York"[2] in the November 1886 issue of *Harper's Monthly*, George Parsons Lathrop mentioned among other authors living in the metropolis Edmund Clarence Stedman, R. H. Stoddard, E. Fawcett, R. W. Gilder, John Burroughs, Julian Hawthorne, E. P. Roe, and Hjalmar Hjorth Boyesen.

The alert and rising Middle West also claimed attention as a literary center, for a group of authors appeared there, Edward Eggleston, E. W. Howe, Joseph Kirkland, and Hamlin Garland among them. "Centres of art production are moving westward," wrote Garland in 1894, "that is to say, the literary supremacy of the East is passing away. ... Racial influences are at work, and

---

[1] *A History of American Literature* (New York, 1919), p. 412.

[2] George Parsons Lathrop, "The Literary Movement in New York," *Harper's Monthly*, LXXIII (November, 1886), 813–33.

changes in literary and social ideals are hastening a far-reaching subdivision, if not decentralization, of power."[1] Garland predicted also in a boastful mood that Chicago would rival New York as a literary market place, "a publishing center which by reason of its geographical position would be more progressive than Boston, and more American than Manhattan."[2]

Gradually American literature began to reflect the changes wrought in America by the rise of industrialism, the advance of science, the westward march of settlement, and the closing of the frontier. Writers keenly sensitive to the currents of the day were stirred by the new tides of thought. Poets like Sidney Lanier, William Vaughn Moody, and Walt Whitman, as well as the humorist Mark Twain,[3] all illustrate to various degrees the impact of science on their thinking. The implications of evolution on theology were voiced, for instance, in America in Margaret Deland's *John Ward, Preacher*, and in England in Mrs. Humphry Ward's *Robert Elsmere*, both of which appeared in 1888.[4]

In an atmosphere dominated by big business and crass materialism, disillusioned intellectuals found themselves rootless. Henry James and F. Marion Crawford became expatriates and fell into "that melancholy process of vibration between two continents in which an increasingly large number of persons pass a great part of their lives; their hearts and affections being wholly in neither."[5] Most writers, however, faced the America of the machine age and some of them grappled with the vital issues of the day and attacked the new order. As early as 1873 *The Gilded Age* showed the spirit of the time in its exposure of political corruption in Washington. Other literary works reflecting the corruption of the age are J. W. De Forest's *Honest John Vane* (1875), Albion W. Tourgée's *Figs and Thistles* (1879), and Henry Adams' *Democracy* (1880). Even Walt Whitman in his *Democratic Vistas* (1871) protested

---

[1] *Crumbling Idols* (Chicago and Cambridge, 1894), p. 147.

[2] *A Son of the Middle Border*, p. 457.

[3] Cf. *What Is Man?* (1906) and *The Mysterious Stranger* (1916).

[4] Of these books and Olive Schreiner's *The Story of an African Farm* George Parsons Lathrop wrote: "It was significant that the three novels of the year 1888 which most aroused the readers of English ... came from the pens of women." "Audacity in Women Novelists," *North American Review*, CL (May, 1890), 611.

[5] *Nation*, XIX (July 16, 1874). Quoted in Nevins, *op. cit.*, p. 254.

against the false values of the Gilded Age, against "the scrofu-
lous wealth, the demonism of greed," although eventually pre-
serving his faith in democracy. With the gradual disappearance
of the frontier, "the Eldorado of the home-seeker," an optimistic
mood was slowly giving way to a somber outlook increased by
the hapless conditions of the farmers. The plight of the farmers
gave particular sting to the harsh realism of Hamlin Garland.
Problems of labor and capital, industrialism, and economics entered
the novel in such works as T. B. Aldrich's *The Stillwater Tragedy*
(1880), John Hay's *The Bread-Winners* (1884), and Henry F.
Keenan's *The Money-Makers* (1885). This was also the age of
Henry George, the advocate of the single tax, who formulated
his economic and social theories in *Progress and Poverty* (1879)
and in *Social Problems* (1884), while Edward Bellamy in his *Looking
Backward* (1888) gave a strong impetus to Utopian romance in
his picture of a Utopia of collectivism.

The dominant figures in American realism during the last
quarter of the century, Henry James and W. D. Howells, whose
realism was partly inspired from abroad, felt the social and economic inquietude of the time. James ventured only once into
social reform in *The Princess Casamassima* (1886), but in at least
half a dozen novels Howells touched upon various social and economic problems caused by an industrialized world. On the whole,
however, their interests focused on issues other than social and
economic. Howells emphasized ethical and moral problems, while
James, a forerunner of the stream of consciousness method, was
more interested in psychological aspects and the technique of
the novel. Both drew from life around them for inspiration. Both
pleaded for a novel which should be honest, sincere, and true
to life, and both exercised a great influence on their generation.
Howells, particularly in his capacity of editor, was something of
an oracle to rising authors. The kind of realism[1] that these writers,
although vastly different in temperament and attitudes, aimed at
was generally restrained in tone, and, in some of their works,
the naturalistic experimenters of the nineties revolted against
this timidity.

In tracing the origin of American realism a recent critic advanced the opinion that "Realism in America, whatever it owed to

---

[1] Cf. also pp. 128–35.

contemporary skepticism and the influence of Darwinism, poured sullenly out of agrarian bitterness, the class hatreds of the eighties and nineties, the bleakness of small-town life, the mockery of the nouveaux riches, and the bitterness in the great new proletarian cities."[1] All these factors undoubtedly contributed to the shift from romanticism to realism in American letters. Another factor of importance was the influence of European realistic and naturalistic writings. Translations[2] of modern French, Russian, Scandinavian, and German literature poured in increasing numbers into the United States between the close of the Civil War and the turn of the century.[3] A critic in 1887 asserted that "Translations from the French have given place to paraphrases from the Russian, the Flemish, and even the Icelandic. We are promised a posthumous work from the Flemish of Hendrik Conscience, the novels of Tolstoi, Dostoyevsky, and Gogol are first among the literary fashions, and now we have the Icelandic idyl, 'Sigrid.'"[4] Another writer, Maurice Thompson, observed that

Just now we are trying to be French; yesterday we were cultivating the Russians; last week the English had us under their thumbs. Daudet and Maupassant, despite Mr. Howells's eloquent plea for Tolstoï, are influencing (to a surprising degree) the currents of American fiction at this moment, while Scott and Thackeray and Dickens are powerless. It would be interesting and deeply instructive if all thinking Americans could see with absolute vision just how this Latin influence has reached the centres of taste in the United States. ... Naturally the fiction that we read shapes in some degree the fiction that we write.[5]

In the light of the great and solid writings from abroad, the native literature of America seemed thin and flat to some contemporary critics. The *Dial* said in 1884 that American fiction of the day betrayed "an ignorance of all that is highest in life, a calm, self-satisfied acceptance of a petty standard. So long as fiction is felt by a large majority of persons to be nothing more than a

---

[1] Alfred Kazin, *On Native Grounds* (New York, 1942), p. 16.

[2] A factor which markedly increased the activity in the translation of foreign writers in the nineties was the passing of the international copyright law of 1891.

[3] See Chap. III.

[4] "Current American Literature," *North American Review*, CXLV (August, 1887), 216.

[5] "Foreign Influence on American Fiction," *North American Review*, CXLIX (July, 1889), 118.

means of amusement, just so long will it present these as its main characteristics."[1] Another critic, after an analysis of *Anna Karenina*, *War and Peace*, and *Salammbô* complained: "As we turn from the strong meat of such works as these to the pastry of the homemade fiction, there is a painful sense of the limitations of American novelists."[2] One writer accused immigration of having dried up American literature,[3] while Hjalmar Hjorth Boyesen in an article entitled "Why We Have No Great Novelists" assumed that American literature was poor because American authors were writing for young girls and not for men and women. He wrote:

The average American has no time to read anything but newspapers, while his daughters have an abundance of time at their disposal, and a general disposition to employ it in anything that is amusing. The novelist who has begun to realize that these young persons constitute his public, naturally endeavors to amuse them. He knows, in a general way, what ladies like, and as the success of his work depends upon his hitting their taste, he makes a series of small concessions to it, which, in the end, determine the character of his book. He feels that he is conversing with ladies and not with men. . . .

This silence concerning all the vital things of life, and the elaborate attention paid to things of small consequence, I believe to be the most serious defect in the present American fiction. The strong forces which are visibly and invisibly at work in our society, fashioning our destinies as a nation, are to a great extent ignored by our novelists. Politics, for instance . . . is, out of deference to the ladies, rarely allowed to invade our novels.[4]

Boyesen went on to say that the novelist's final judge was "the young American girl. She is the Iron Madonna who strangles in her fond embrace the American novelist; the Moloch upon whose altar he sacrifices, willingly or unwillingly, his chances of greatness. . . . When, however, we read a novel like Tolstoï's 'Anna Karénina' or Daudet's 'Le Nabab,' we appreciate, perhaps, the difference between a literature addressed to girls and a literature intended for men and women."[5]

---

[1] *Dial*, VI (July, 1884), 68.

[2] "Recent Fiction," *Dial*, VII (May, 1886), 14.

[3] Sidney G. Fisher, "Has Immigration Dried up Our Literature?" *Forum*, XVI (January, 1894), 560–7.

[4] *Forum*, II (February, 1887), 616–17.

[5] *Ibid.*, p. 619.

In 1891 a conservative critic observed that though "great books are not being written by Americans at the moment," idealism was the prevalent mood among American writers:

It is a healthy atmosphere in which literary men work in this country; an atmosphere which makes it possible to be serious without being pessimistic; to believe in something and enjoy something without becoming Philistine in view and taste. Mr. Howells' latest story, "An Imperative Duty," is an admirable illustration of art dealing with a question of tragical possibilities and yet holding it off from the first heat of feeling so as to preserve sanity of mood and a true sense of relation with the general order of things.[1]

Richard Burton, too, spoke in 1895 of the healthful, decent tone in American letters, asserting that "the negative spirit, the cynic mood, and the manner of the realist or the pessimist belong, with us, rather to the critics than to the creators. . . ."[2]

However, as early as 1882 certain "dangerous tendencies" were evident in the American novel. Some recent novels, said a critic in the *Dial*, afforded "conspicuous illustrations of a certain dangerous tendency which is becoming too common in our fiction, and of which every virtuous reader must be concerned to discover alike the meaning and the cause."[3] The supposedly dangerous American novels were Constance Fenimore Woolson's *Anne*, George Parsons Lathrop's *An Echo of Passion*, and Frances Hodgson Burnett's *Through One Administration*. The nationalistic magazine, *America*, felt it its duty to denounce un-American fiction. Anna Farwell De Koven wrote:

The American race has many faults and many limitations, but as a rule, it is honest and clean in instinct and independent in action. Recently, however, the proverbial national weakness, *imitativeness*, is leading to a most grievous departure from the straight path. . . . Edgar Saltus, with his crisp, epigrammatic style, manufactured out of anglicized French words, characteristic of Balzac and Gautier, his pessimistic philosophy and most defective morals stands at the head of the list, and Amélie Rives, Mrs. Atherton, and Miss Daintrey fill up the catalogue and substantiate

---

[1] Hamilton Wright Mabie, "A Year's Literary Production," *Forum*, XII (February, 1892), 800.

[2] "The Healthful Tone for American Literature," *Forum*, XIX (April, 1895), 256.

[3] R. O. Beard, "A Certain Dangerous Tendency in Novels," *Dial*, III (October, 1882), 110.

the accusation. ... it is time that there should be some protest[1] against such writers, and against a literature which is so thoroughly un-American and so causelessly impure.[2]

In general, however, American realism in the seventies and eighties was largely genteel in tone, mostly aloof from the homely and painful realities of life, with the rare exceptions of a few works dealing with changing conditions and attitudes in an industrialized America. In the nineties two reactions set in against this tradition, which had been exemplified particularly by Howells: one expressed itself in a harsher realism, an experimental naturalism; the other in the historical romance stimulated by the popularity of Stevenson, by a burst of enthusiasm accompanying the war with Spain, and by a desire to escape the bitter realities of a disillusioned age. Realism in America was making good headway when it was almost submerged by the vogue of the romantic-historical novel, which, spurred on in 1880 by Lew Wallace's *Ben-Hur*, reached its peak in the nineties. A critic in the *Bookman* remarked in 1899—the memorable year of Frank Norris's *McTeague*—that "morbid realism ... was swept out of sight five or six years ago by the sudden on-rush of works of ideality and romance."[3] Serious writers had to fight hard to make themselves heard at a time when books such as S. Weir Mitchell's *Hugh Wynne* (1897), Charles Major's *When Knighthood Was in Flower* (1898), Mary Johnston's *To Have and to Hold* (1900), Winston Churchill's *Richard Carvel* (1899) and George Barr McCutcheon's *Graustark* (1901) were the fashion of the day.

To sum up: A scientific-industrialized America with its economic and social issues was less in harmony with a romantic attitude toward life. Idealism and romanticism faded in a period which called not for dreams or wishful thinking, but for truth and exactness. Gradually the temper of the time changed. Creative writers turned

---

[1] Protests against the new tendencies came also from James Lane Allen. See the Preface to his *Summer in Arcady* (New York and London, 1896).

[2] "Un-American Fiction," *America*, II (June 6, 1889), 305–6.

[3] *Bookman*, IX (June, 1899), 356. "Zola has ceased to be called 'maître,'" wrote William R. Thayer, "or to be imitated by disciples; ... We violate no confidences in declaring that Realism in fiction is passing away." The following popular writers were mentioned: Caine, Doyle, Zangwill, Weyman, Crockett, Du Maurier, Stevenson, Crawford, Scott, and Kipling. "The new Story-Tellers and the Doom of Realism," *Forum*, XVIII (December, 1894), 470–80.

more and more to realistic prose to record "modern America," and especially in the works of Howells and James realism in America made good headway.

When the naturalistic experimenters of the nineties began to subject American society to a searching scrutiny they reinforced and widened tendencies already implicit in the American tradition. A strong impetus to a new technique and a new way of writing seems, however, to have come from Europe which contributed to the gradual emancipation of American literature from many conventions and prejudices. French naturalism, which, in addition to the realism of Turgenev, Tolstoy, and Ibsen, was destined to prove a major force in this liberation, swept almost like an epidemic over Europe, and in the closing decades of the nineteenth century reached the United States, inspiring authors like Hamlin Garland, Stephen Crane, and Frank Norris.

CHAPTER II

NATURALISM IN FRANCE

TOGETHER WITH
SOME NOTES ON ITS ADOPTION IN ENGLAND, SCANDI-
NAVIA, AND GERMANY. RUSSIAN REALISM

Naturalism[1] is a term somewhat loosely applied to the literary movement that may be said to have taken its inception from Flaubert's *Madame Bovary* (1857) and developed in the works of the brothers Goncourt, Zola, Daudet, Maupassant, and others. Zola became the champion of the new literary tendencies. After 1870 this movement took on the dignity of a naturalistic school of letters which greatly influenced French literature in the seventies and eighties. When in 1877 Zola achieved his success with *L'Assommoir*, naturalism was gaining rapid headway and the ten years between the publication of this novel about the lower classes and *La Terre* (1887) marked the climax of the movement in France. As early as 1884, however, a reaction set in, for in that year J.-K. Huysmans, Zola's friend and at first a faithful disciple of naturalism, published his famous *A Rebours*, in which he abjured his allegiance to the school. In 1887 there appeared the well-known *Manifeste des Cinq*, in which five of Zola's former disciples repudiated naturalism, or, more correctly, the Zolaism and bestiality of *La Terre*.

French naturalism, which exerted a certain influence on the literatures of other countries, developed out of the realism of the reign of Louis-Philippe and of the second Empire. It was a logi-

---

[1] Essential for this chapter were, besides Zola's critical writings (see p. 125), P. Martino, *Le Naturalisme français* (1870–1895) (Paris, 1930) and Poul Levin, *Den naturalistiske Roman* (Copenhagen and Christiania, 1907). See also Johan Mortensen, *Från Röda Rummet till sekelskiftet* (Stockholm, 1918), pp. 5–47, Vernon Louis Parrington, *Main Currents in American Thought* (New York, 1930), III, 323–34, and Hans Röhl, *Der Naturalismus* (Leipzig, 1927).

cal outgrowth of nineteenth century thought in the realm of letters. Great discoveries in the natural sciences affected the intellectual outlook of the century—the leading idea was evolution—and offered new visions and new prospects to mankind. The mid-century discoveries seemed revolutionary. Traditional thinking about man and the universe was challenged. The scientific tendencies of the period were characterized by a repudiation of previously accepted propositions and by a reliance on observation, experience, and facts; the century may be described as analytic, intellectual, and interrogative, in search of truth and exactness. Science put its imprint on it and became a sort of fetish which people worshiped for it seemed to offer a solution of the riddles of the universe. Nothing occult or transcendental existed; spiritual and organic phenomena were equally deduced from matter; natural laws were omnipotent and controlled everything; matter was the entire reality. Science invaded many fields of learning and rapid changes were effectuated through its impact on philosophy, religion, politics, belles-lettres, etc. In the field of religion, for instance, it threatened the supremacy of orthodoxy. The metaphysical school of philosophy was partly superseded by positivism, and realism received a new tenor, a new substance of ideas, which eventually led to naturalism. The basic philosophy of literary naturalism was deterministic and positivistic and consequently the naturalists focused their interests on the external reality. Darwin's interpretation of the mechanism of the universe, the positivism of Comte, and Marx's socialism were adopted by the naturalistic school. Mill, Spencer, Buckle, Huxley, Haeckel, and other scholars substantially influenced the new generation. The new scientific, philosophical, and social ideas were merged in the naturalistic novel and gave to it its specific character.

The scientific method of the natural sciences was applied to fields where emotion, speculation, and imagination predominated. For instance, Renan, an intimate friend of Berthelot, the chemist, used it in writing of religion. Claude Bernard's *Introduction à l'étude de la médecine expérimentale* (1865) did much to establish medicine as an exact science and he successfully advocated an experimental method. Upon this book Zola founded *Le Roman expérimental*, which demanded a literature governed by science and in which he used the same method as the scientist. By substituting for the word "doctor" the word "novelist," he could make his meaning clear and give to the work of art the rigidity of a scientific truth. He formulated the theory of naturalism and illustrated it in his gigantic study of degeneracy, *Les Rougon-Macquart.* To him literature, like medicine, was no longer an art; it was a science. By applying the method of the scientist to literature, he hoped to raise the novel to the level of science, since to him and to others of his time the voice of science was ultimate truth. He based his ideas on the theories of Taine, who became the philosopher and theorist of naturalism. His theories about the causes of human actions and particularly his doctrines of *race,* *milieu,* and *moment* challenged traditional conceptions of man; these ideas were, of course, mainly derived from Darwin. Taine reduced psychology to physiology and the study of character to the study of temperament, and he applied his positivistic formula to literary criticism. He taught moreover that the physical milieu constantly affected the individual, who was subjected to the rigidity of determinism.[1] Zola reduced Taine's doctrines to the study of heredity and milieu, the two basic factors which, to him, fundamentally transformed and reshaped human destinies.

Zola and other naturalists introduced into the novel a pseudo-scientific terminology. Many naturalistic novels were saturated with scientific terms and technical detail; the brothers Goncourt spoke of "la méthode anatomique," and the novel was nothing but "une analyse," "une étude," "un cas pathologique." In *Les Rougon-Macquart* Zola's intentions were purely scientific, for he stated explicitly in the preface to *La Fortune des Rougon* (1871) that he wanted to "expliquer" the development of a family through the "analyse" based upon "des documents" and that "l'hérédité" had its laws as "la pesanteur." The method of clinical dissection was successfully used in *Madame Bovary* by Flaubert, who, a doctor's son, said: "Je me suis moi-même franchement disséqué au vif en des moments peu drôles."[2] Scientific methods and beliefs became of great importance to the contents and the technique of the naturalistic novel. It became "un roman documentaire," based solidly on physical reality and crammed with facts and

---

[1] Martino, *op. cit.*, p. 21.

[2] Quoted by Sten Linder in *Ernst Ahlgren i hennes romaner* (Stockholm, 1930), p. 166. Cf. also Flaubert, *Correspondance* (Paris, 1920), III, 168.

24

data actually seen and experienced. The naturalistic writer was to seek the truth in the spirit of a scientist, for Zola and his followers did not admit of anything occult; reality, hard and brutal as it was, had to be described with exact minuteness of detail. The naturalist was to collect "human documents" and make a series of preliminary studies, sketches, etc., before he set about doing the real work.[1] This involved careful preparation and endless toil; Zola was a great worker and his slogan was: "Travaillez, tout est là!" Imagination and plot were reduced to a minimum.

The result was both beneficial and detrimental to the novel. On the one hand it increased the sense of fidelity to reality and observed facts. Successful handling of the documents Zola exhibited, for instance, in *L'Assommoir* and *Germinal*. On the other hand he often went to extremes and created such distortions of reality as *La Faute de l'abbé Mouret* and *Le Ventre de Paris*. The naturalist had learnt from Taine that the milieu was of primary importance in the life of the individual and as a result much of the space was given to the description of setting. Furthermore, the French writers had a predilection for a certain kind of setting. Usually their stories took place in great industrial cities, preferably in the slums, which were exposed without mercy. Sometimes the descriptions expanded into accurate surveys of an epoch and became veritable documents of historical value. The naturalists liked to paint the ugly details of modern civilization. With scientific zeal they chose exact localities and used exact names, etc., for, according to Zola, the naturalistic novel was to be "la reproduction exacte de la vie." The study of the milieu was to be carried out methodically and objectively so that the novelist might reproduce it accurately.

Because of their scientific pretensions the naturalists felt free to choose for their study or analysis any subject however brutal or revolting. They excused their audacity and frankness and their lack of restraint and taste by resorting to the mystic word "science." As early as 1865 Taine had given the naturalistic writer certain fundamental doctrines:

---

[1] In *Les Romanciers naturalistes* in *Œuvres complètes* (50 vols., Paris, 1927-9), XLII, 307-9, Zola described in detail Daudet's method of novel writing. This edition will hereinafter be referred to as *Œuvres*.

Du roman à la critique et de la critique au roman, la distance aujourd'hui n'est pas grande. Si le roman s'emploie à montrer ce que nous sommes, la critique s'emploie à montrer ce que nous avons été. L'un et l'autre sont maintenant une grande enquête sur l'homme, sur toutes les variétés, toutes les situations, toutes les floraisons, toutes les dégénérescences de la nature humaine. Par leur sérieux, par leur méthode, par leur exactitude rigoureuse, par leurs avenirs et leurs espérances, tous deux se rapprochent de la science.[1]

In following this advice the novelists enlarged the scope and field of their work to embrace what seemed to them the entire man and the entire reality—that is, the entire natural and physical reality. The naturalists took up subjects earlier shunned or prohibited, such as prostitution, free love, social misery of many sorts, and burning questions of the day; they held the convenient belief that "La morale n'avait plus rien à faire avec la littérature, pas plus qu'avec la science"[2] and that "Le vice et la vertu sont des produits comme le vitriol et le sucre."[3] The lower classes, the masses became heroes and heroines of grim tales, and the new subject matter was treated of with a sincerity and brutality uncommon before.

While the novels of the brothers Goncourt may be labeled analytical monographs, describing single topics, the novels of Zola and Daudet portrayed society at large. Zola, for instance, chose large subjects; he wanted to present a vast tableau of French society during the second Empire and pictured the political world, the financial world, the world of pleasure, and groups such as laborers, peasants, soldiers, etc. This was exactly what Taine had suggested: "une grande enquête sur l'homme, sur toutes les variétés." Balzac's *La Comédie humaine* was of course Zola's immediate model. Occasionally he was inebriated by his descriptions and everything took on a gigantic, exaggerated form: ". . . il anime un des détails, pour en faire une sorte de symbole, et du coup tous les autres enflent, deviennent énormes; pendant une page, ou deux, l'auteur, obéissant à un emballement lyrique, oublie son dessein, si souvent répété, de n'écrire que des 'procès-verbaux.'"[4] The

---

[1] Martino, *op. cit.*, p. 23.

[2] *Ibid.*

[3] Preface to Taine's *Histoire de la littérature anglaise* (Paris, 1863).

[4] Martino, *op. cit.*, pp. 77–8.

mine in *Germinal*, for instance, became a living monster that devoured the miners.

Whereas in Flaubert, the brothers Goncourt, and some of their followers, the aim was fundamentally esthetic, in a naturalist like Zola the purpose was predominantly social and humanitarian. Flaubert and Maupassant were strictly objective, whereas Zola's objectivity was tinged with indignation. In this he deviated from strict naturalism, which claimed to be an objective study of life without any *Tendenz*. The naturalist was to be "as cold as a vivisectionist at a lecture," abstain from comment, never show his own personality, and never turn to the reader for sympathy. A classic illustration of this attitude was the description of the death scene in *Madame Bovary*, which Flaubert carried out with the detachment of a physician, for he believed that "le grand art est scientific et impersonnel." The naturalistic novel should not satirize nor preach, but only describe human life objectively; the naturalist should draw no conclusions because the conclusions were implicit in the material. Despite its so-called objectivity naturalism was critical of society. Zola, especially, had a reformer's zeal. He believed that society was responsible for all the misfortunes that befell the French people; he criticized violently "ce régime politique détesté," and associated the doctrine of naturalism with the Republican idea. He was a moralist and depicted repulsive scenes in order to arouse disgust for vice. He wanted to know why there were drunkards and harlots. He aimed his most violent attacks at the French bourgeoisie, devoting whole books to the criticism of this class of society, but, in general, his criticism was leveled at society at large. He saw flagrant class-distinctions, fathomless corruption, intellectual ambiguity, and moral rottenness, all of which he wanted to disclose and hold up for opprobrium. At heart, he was an optimistic Utopian, whose temperament clashed with the naturalistic formula, while naturalists like Flaubert[1] and Maupassant were misanthropists and pessimists who saw little hope for mankind.

Zola believed that, just as the animals were transformed by the surroundings to which they adapted themselves, the individual man was refashioned by the environment in which he lived. The individual could not be separated from the milieu that surrounded

---

[1] I refer, of course, only to the author of *Madame Bovary*.

and molded him; it bound and enclosed him and he was unable to extricate himself. "Nous estimons," wrote Zola, "que l'homme ne peut être séparé de son milieu, qu'il est complété par son vêtement, par sa maison, par sa ville, et sa province; et, dès lors, nous ne noterons pas un seul phénomène de son cerveau ou de son cœur, sans en chercher les causes ou le contre-coup dans le milieu."[1] In order to demonstrate their hypotheses, Zola and his disciples selected men and women on whom the influence of the environment easily put its imprint: weak and passive characters, who were afflicted by an hereditary taint and who submissively responded to, and were affected by, their milieu.

In the preface to *La Fortune des Rougon* Zola wrote:

Je veux expliquer comment une famille, un petit groupe d'êtres, se comporte dans une société, en s'épanouissant pour donner naissance à dix, à vingt individus, qui paraissent, au premier coup d'œil, profondément dissemblables, mais que l'analyse montre intimement liés les uns aux autres. L'hérédité a ses lois, comme la pesanteur.

Je tâcherai de trouver et de suivre, en résolvant la double question des tempéraments et des milieux, le fil qui conduit mathématiquement d'un homme à un autre homme.

These ideas concerning the influence of heredity and milieu, mainly derived from Taine, Claude Bernard, and Prosper Lucas, were basic pillars of Zola's naturalistic creed, and it was upon them that he built *Les Rougon-Macquart*. The fallacy of his arguments has been exposed by more than one critic, but to him, in the early seventies, they seemed true and unassailable. Man was a product generated by the struggle for life and was transformed by his surroundings. Thus, coal-miners grew crook-backed, heavy-built, anemic, brutal, wishing only to eat, to drink, and to sleep. The influence of heredity was of equal importance to the naturalistic writer and Zola founded *Les Rougon-Macquart* on "une mère affectée d'une tare nerveuse et un père alcoolique," and his novels show, like most naturalistic works, a process of dissolution and degeneration.

The naturalists extended the study of character to embrace the entire physical man with all his physical impulses and instincts and, in their emphasis on instincts and hidden, unconscious urges and the role these phenomena play in human life, they contributed

---

[1] *Le Roman expérimental* in *Œuvres*, XLI, 186.

to a deeper understanding of man. Too often, however, the novelists went to extremes. By stressing the Darwinian concept of man and his affinity with organic nature and the influence of heredity and environment on the individual, they identified him with the brute controlled by instincts, particularly sex.

The characters preferred by the French naturalists belonged to the lower classes. The heroes and heroines were workers, harlots, drunkards, servant-maids, forlorn creatures, and mass-individuals. They were generally portrayed as indolent and dull, devoid of free will and purpose, sensual, and often abnormal, the products of a certain milieu and a certain kind of work; but they were seldom pictured as evil. Usually they were depicted with shocking and sensual detail as creatures dominated by their instincts. Besides types with strong physiques the naturalists preferred characters of excitable and neurotic temperaments, and often these traits were merged into one character. The novelists' portraiture of character became superficial; they painted types instead of individuals, and since psychology was reduced to physiology, they were apt to view merely the animality and the primitiveness of man. Man was devoid of a soul and of higher ethical motives; he was a helpless creature determined by heredity and environment. Consequently the characters were not ethically responsible for their actions, they were pawns driven by outer forces or inner urges; moral checks were always lacking. The principle of free will was denied and man was the victim of forces beyond his control. The universe was controlled by the mechanistic laws of causation and the struggle for life was tragic in its hopelessness. The individual did not have confidence in religion or social government; everywhere vice, malice, wickedness, "les tares héréditaires, la misère" stared him in the face. The outcome of life was usually hopeless sorrow, sometimes stolid resignation; often there was no other end than annihilation.

The frank portrayal of sex was particularly characteristic of French naturalism. Love was generally depicted as a physical craving like hunger and thirst, irresistible, a natural force that blindly struck its victim. This was in conformity with the naturalists' belief in the importance of the instincts and desires of man and their denial of free will and the capacity of the individual to control natural urges. Love was no longer ethically or intellectually conditioned, but was reduced to sexual desire. The ideal concept of love was swept away before the naturalistic one.

The naturalistic conception of nature denounced the traditional, romantic, and symbolic view that conceived of nature as a living, incarnate entity. Nature should be studied and reproduced objectively and truthfully. The novelist chose phenomena which had an everyday, close-to-the soil, and often repulsive effect on the reader; sounds became noises and odors bad smells. Climatic changes and the processes of nature were faithfully chronicled: heavy rains, supreme heat, growth, fructification, etc. The evolutionary doctrine placed man in a new and intimate affinity with the vegetative and the animal kingdom and in conformity with this concept the naturalist was apt to paint phenomena which directed one's attention toward the earth. Parallels between man, plant, and animal are often met with in naturalistic fiction. Take for instance the simultaneous births of a child and a calf in the opening chapter of *La Terre*, which illustrates the essence and quality of Zola's naturalism.

In spite of the fact that the naturalistic formula was both doctrinaire and extreme, and although the naturalistic school in France soon weakened, in the eighties naturalism as a literary movement, pregnant with the spirit and ideas of its age, and possessing an almost volcanic force, began to be felt in the literatures of other European countries, where it was adopted and transformed in conformity with tradition and prevailing taste. It opened up new paths to the delineation of man and nature and helped to break down prejudices and conventions.

In England it[1] played a less significant role than in France and was adopted in a less extreme form probably because of the strong Victorian tradition of convention and decorum. Its chief exponents, George Moore and George Gissing, often softened the effect of their portrayals of slums and outcasts with sentiment and pity. Moore's most typically naturalistic novel in the manner of *L'Assommoir*, *A Mummer's Wife* (1885), carried the significant epigraph: "Change the surroundings in which man lives, and,

---

[1] See William C. Frierson, *L'Influence du naturalisme français sur les romanciers Anglais de 1885 à 1900* (Paris, 1925) and William York Tindall, *Forces in Modern British Literature, 1885-1946* (New York, 1947), pp. 145-84.

in two or three generations, you will have changed his physical constitution, his habits of life, and a goodly number of his ideas." Another of Moore's powerful, naturalistic novels, *Esther Waters* (1894), is the depressing tale of a servant girl and her illegitimate child. Gissing's dismal novels of the slums and the lower classes, for instance *The Unclassed* (1884) and *The Nether World* (1889), treat of the sordid material typical of naturalism: viciousness, brutality, poverty, and prostitution. George Meredith transformed naturalism to an affirmation of life, whereas Thomas Hardy saw no hope for humanity and his somber work was a plea for the negation of life. His characters were helpless victims of deterministic forces, as well as subjects of chance or fate, doomed to inevitable catastrophe.[1]

Georg Brandes helped to introduce naturalism to the Scandinavian countries, where it became aligned with social issues and ethical problems. In Denmark particularly J. P. Jacobsen— *Fru Marie Grubbe* (1876; Eng. tr., *Marie Grubbe*, 1917) and *Niels Lyhne* (1880; Eng. tr., 1896)—and Herman J. Bang were influenced by the movement. Such Norwegian writers as Hans Jæger, Christian Krohg, Arne Garborg, and Amalie Skram experimented with naturalistic techniques. Ibsen's *Gengangere* (1881; Eng. tr., *Ghosts*, 1885) may also be said to have been in part influenced by the movement. In Sweden especially some of the works of August Strindberg—*Röda rummet* (1879; Eng. tr., *The Red Room*, 1913) and *Fröken Julie* (1888; Eng. tr., *Miss Julia*, 1912)—exhibit naturalistic tendencies.

In Germany the impact of French naturalism was felt particularly after 1880. In the early years of the movement the lyric played a certain part through Arno Holz only to be superseded later by the drama. Gerhart Hauptmann wrote *Die Weber* (1892; Eng. tr., *The Weavers*, 1899) and Hermann Sudermann contributed several plays, among which the best known are *Die Ehre* (1889; Eng. tr., *Honor*, 1915) and *Heimat* (1893; Eng. tr., *Magda*, 1896).

Even before the emergence of French naturalism, Russia had

---

[1] Among other English writers who seem to have been influenced by naturalism Hubert Crackanthorpe and above all Arthur Morrison ought to be mentioned. The latter is known for his *Tales of Mean Streets* (1894) and *A Child of the Jago* (1896) concerned with the slums and their victims viewed with detachment mingled with humor.

produced three great writers who were destined to make valuable contributions to the world's literature: Turgenev, Dostoevsky, and Tolstoy.[1] Russian realism has many points in common with French naturalism; practitioners of both aimed at an accurate and true portrayal of contemporary setting and character; but there are also striking differences, primarily in the attitude toward and the treatment of material. Whereas many French naturalists were like vivisectionists, cold and indifferent, the Russian realists viewed their characters with compassion and pity. The Russians were, in general, less—if at all—interested in the human animal and the theories of heredity and environment, stressing instead the significance of adverse fate. In *Le Roman expérimental* Zola stated explicitly that he was a determinist and not a fatalist. Both determinists and fatalists, of course, denied free will, but there was a vast difference between the two attitudes. "Le fatalisme," said Zola quoting Claude Bernard, "suppose la manifestation nécessaire d'un phénomène indépendant de ses conditions, tandis que le déterminisme est la condition nécessaire d'un phénomène dont la manifestation n'est pas forcée."[2] On the whole, in the French naturalistic novel the action proceeded logically toward its inevitable ending, whereas in the Russian realistic novel, particularly in that of Turgenev and above all that of Dostoevsky, the action proceeded illogically through the influence of chance, fate, or circumstances.

The great Russian realistic novels were primarily psychological with a profound penetration into the human soul. Turgenev, a born aristocrat and an aesthete, was among the first to make Russian fiction of this sort known in Europe; he possessed a keen understanding of his country and its problems. He portrayed the culture of Russia before 1862 as that of a land of "superfluous

---

[1] It has seemed necessary to include a brief section on Russian realism because of its popularity in the eighties (see pp. 34–8) and because of the influence that Turgenev and Tolstoy seem to have exerted on Garland, Crane, and Norris (see Chaps. XII, XIII), who, however, to judge from my own research, appear to owe no noticeable debt to Dostoevsky. In this chapter I have focused the interest on French naturalism and dealt with Russian realism *after* the French movement, despite the fact that Russian realism emerged earlier than naturalism in France. In the following chapter, on the other hand, a more or less chronological treatment has seemed appropriate.

[2] *Œuvres*, XLI, 31. For Zola's use of chance, see pp. 248–9, 265.

men." He spent almost half of his life abroad and this helped him to view his material with detachment; he was no moralist, but a disinterested onlooker, an analyst, and above all a supreme artist. The theme on which he focused his interest was admirably synthesized by the character Potugin in *Smoke* (1867; Eng. tr., 1868): "Man is weak, woman is strong, opportunity all-powerful."[1] This motif was repeated in practically all his novels: Rudin and Bazarov, the heroes of *Rudin* (1856; Eng. tr., 1873) and *Fathers and Sons* (1862; Eng. tr., 1867) are illustrations of failure. The strong woman is represented, for example, by Elena in the novel entitled *On the Eve* (1860; Eng. tr., 1871). Turgenev is also famous for his lyric pictures of the Russian countryside, his subtlety of touch, and the pictorial quality of his soft and sinuous prose.

There is a vast distance between the refined world of Turgenev and the chaotic one of Dostoevsky. Although both portrayed Russian life, the world of Dostoevsky was filled with misery, anguish, madness, and crime. He was a philosopher, a moralist, painter of the poor, the sick, the demented, whose souls he probed and analyzed with profound understanding; like Tolstoy he was a Slavophile and believed in Russia and her future. His fame rests chiefly on four novels: *Crime and Punishment* (1866; Eng. tr., 1886), *The Idiot* (1868; Eng. tr., 1887), *The Possessed* (1871–2; Eng. tr., 1914), and *The Brothers Karamazov* (1879–80; Eng. tr., 1912), and his characters may roughly be divided into three groups[2]: the saint represented by Prince Myshkin in *The Idiot*, the culprit as portrayed by Stavrogin in *The Possessed*, the mixed type possessing both constructive and destructive elements, both noble and evil instincts as exemplified by Raskolnikov in *Crime and Punishment*. Unlike the slowly deteriorating characters of the French naturalists, those of Dostoevsky were usually ruined by sudden catastrophe. He viewed suffering humanity, humble souls struggling desperately for survival, with sympathy.

The third of the great Russians was Tolstoy, whose gradual evolution to a reformer and preacher was excellently drawn in his autobiographical works, *Childhood, Boyhood,* and *Youth* (1852–7;

---

[1] *Smoke* (Mod. lib. ed., New York, n.d.), p. 121.

[2] Hildegard Bennewitz, *Die Charaktere in den Romanen Joseph Conrads* (Greifswald, 1933), p. 47.

Eng. tr., 1886). His panoramic view of Russian society during the times of the Napoleonic wars in *War and Peace* (1865–9; Eng. tr., 1886) is classic. He was at heart a reformer endowed with a strong social sense and vast sympathy for the poor and the humble. He hated war and his descriptions of battles were filled with the moanings and lamentations of the wounded; his terrible scenes of blood and revolting detail swept away the glamour of war. In *Anna Karenina* (1875–7; Eng. tr., 1886) Tolstoy attacked adultery; he led Anna Karenina inevitably toward destruction, for he was a believer in the holiness of matrimony, in decent living and the sanctity of the family. Tolstoy began by viewing passion as something primitive, sensual, poetic even; he ended, however, by regarding it as something perverse, as for instance in *The Kreutzer Sonata* (1890; Eng. tr., 1890).

To sum up: Literary naturalism was an outgrowth of nineteenth century thought and involved the application of scientific methods to literary creation. The chief theorist of the movement was Taine who helped to formulate its underlying philosophy. Beginning with *Madame Bovary*, the new literary tendencies took on the dignity of a naturalistic school mainly through the works of such writers as the brothers Goncourt, Zola, Daudet, and Maupassant. Zola, by no means a consistent naturalist, advocated an experimental method in *Le Roman expérimental*. Particularly in the eighties creative writers in other European countries, for instance England, Denmark, Norway, Sweden, and Germany, became responsive to naturalism. Prior to the emergence of naturalism in France, Russia had produced three major realistic writers—Turgenev, Tolstoy, and Dostoevsky—who made lasting contributions to the world's literature.

Gradually during the latter part of the nineteenth century the rich and variegated literature of Europe began to be known and to enrich the cultural and intellectual life of the United States. When French naturalism eventually took root in America in the nineties, it was not an isolated cultural movement or wave, for it was accompanied and even preceded by other influences and forces, primarily from Russia and Scandinavia, that were to play decisive parts in the genesis, development, and general character of literary naturalism in the United States.

CHAPTER III

ASPECTS OF EUROPEAN REALISTIC AND NATURALISTIC LITERATURE IN AMERICA PRIOR TO 1900

RUSSIAN, FRENCH, ENGLISH, SCANDINAVIAN, AND GERMAN

In the late eighteen sixties the American reader, familiar with the idealistic writings of the transcendentalists and other romantic works, was probably shocked by the distinctively modern spirit found in Turgenev's *Fathers and Sons*[1] with its new subject matter, treatment, and underlying pessimistic philosophy. This novel seemed to indicate that a new era was about to dawn; it revealed some of the changes in the attitude toward science and the outlook on life which were taking place. During the next decade many of Turgenev's novels and short stories were translated into English and made available for American readers.[2] W. D. Howells and Thomas Sergeant Perry were among the first to greet the new literature with understanding and insight. In the eighties, the United States were almost inundated with Russian literature, and the American interest in it culminated in a veritable "craze" for Russian literature embracing not only the great masters such as Pushkin, Gogol, Turgenev, Tolstoy, and Dostoevsky, but also a number of lesser figures. Tolstoy seems to have been the most popular Russian writer in America during the eighties and nineties, superseding even Turgenev.

The year 1886 is a landmark in the American interest in Rus-

---

[1] First American translation in 1867.

[2] See Royal A. Gettmann, *Turgenev in England and America* (Urbana, Ill., 1941), pp. 187–8. See also p. 315 of the present study.

sian literature.[1] Joseph Kirkland, who was then working on his first realistic novel, *Zury*,[2] which appeared in the following year, was an admirer of Russian literature, and in 1886 he wrote an article for the *Dial* called "Tolstoï, and the Russian Invasion of the Realm of Fiction." He discussed *Childhood, Boyhood, Youth*, and *War and Peace* (Part III).

These Russian novels mark an era in literature. The romantic and the realistic are engaged in a life-and-death struggle. It is their Waterloo, and lo, in the eastern horizon appears a Blücher, with a force which must decide the battle in favor of realism. The Old Guard hurls itself on the foe—it is taken in flank and must perish if it cannot surrender. It seems that for the present literary generation the victory is won and the war virtually over. Photographic exactitude in scene-painting— phonographic literalness in dialogue—telegraphic realism in narration —these are the new canons for the art of fiction ... Such books as Tolstoï's make the careful observer suspect that unless English fiction can shake off some of the iron trammels that bind it, it must yield all hope of maintaining its long-held supremacy.[3]

The *Literary World* for October 2, 1886, devoted a column to the reviewing of *The Great Masters of Russian Literature in the 19th Century*. The reviewer declared: "M. Dupuy's charming little book on the three great masters of modern Russian fiction— Gogol, Turgénief, Tolstoï—is here brought before readers of English. ..." And he added:

Compared with such realism the brutality of Zola is forever intolerable. The difference is that in the most realistic of the Russian novels, from Gogol to Dostoyevsky, the characters are men and women, however degraded; ... they are human and not animated embodiments of the cardinal sins. In a word, the Russian masters describe the world they see with sympathetic appreciation; Zola and his compeers content themselves with the revolting externals of vice. There are not wanting

---

[1] Note also that Ernest Dupuy's *The Great Masters of Russian Literature in the 19th Century* (Fr. ed., 1885), E. M. de Vogüé's *Le Roman russe* (Eng. tr., 1887), and J. F. Hapgood's *Epic Songs of Russia* appeared in 1886. The interest in Russia and Russian literature was so strong that an American writer even wrote a novel of Russian life: Sophie Radford de Meissner, *The Terrace of Mon Désir: A Novel of Russian Life* (Boston, 1886). It was published anonymously. Cf. p. 36.

[2] See p. 56.

[3] "Tolstoï, and the Russian Invasion of the Realm of Fiction," *Dial*, VII (August, 1886), 81. Note also Kirkland's own war novel, *The Captain of Company K* (1891), an unheroic treatment of war.

signs which indicate a distinct tendency toward realism in English and American fiction; let us hope, in spite of the "irony of truth" which Mr. Davidson[1] finds in the Rougon-Macquart chronicle, that it will be the poetic realism of Turgénief and Tolstoï rather than the brutalizing naturalism of Zola.[2]

A literary survey of the year 1886 also described the great invasion of Russian literature in the United States:

> The interest in Russian literature, especially fiction, marked by a number of translations, has amounted to a positive and noticeable feature of the year, and deserves a separate mention by itself at this point. This movement probably had its springs first in the charming novels of Henry Gréville, and second, and more powerfully in the somber writings of Tourgénief, which gave the attention of English readers a strong set in the direction of Tourgénief's compatriots.[3]

The article made special mention of the following authors and books: Tolstoy's *My Religion, Childhood, Boyhood, Youth, War and Peace*, and *Anna Karenina*, Tchernuishevsky's *Vital Question; or, What Is to Be Done*, Dostoevsky's *Crime and Punishment*, Gogol's *Taras Bulba* and *Dead Souls*, and finally Dupuy's *The Great Masters of Russian Literature in the 19th Century*. The article concluded:

> All these have been American publications, to which may be added an American writer's Russian novel, "The Terrace of Mon Désir," and Miss Hapgood's "Epic Songs of Russia"; while in England there has also been published a translation of Lermontoff's "A Hero of Our Time." This infusion of the Russian element has perceptibly colored the year's current and imparted a taste thereto which is not to be missed. ... Besides the appetite for Russian fiction ... there has been a marked interest in French and Spanish authors, illustrated by the translations of Balzac, Flaubert, and Feuillet, of Valera's "Pepita Ximenez" and of Valdés's "The Marquis of Peñalta." The German stream has been drier than for some years.[4]

---

[1] See p. 38 n. 3.

[2] "Masters of Russian Literature," *Literary World*, XVII (October 2, 1886), 327. In the *Dial* of March and May 1886 parts I and II of *War and Peace* were briefly discussed and a short sketch was given of the author.

[3] "The World's Literature in 1886. A General Survey. I. The United States and England ... The Russian Infusion," *Literary World*, XVII (December 25, 1886), 480.

[4] *Ibid.*, pp. 481-3.

While Flaubert's *Salammbô* was given a decidedly unfavorable review in the *Literary World*,[1] the same magazine, in the same month, spoke favorably of Dostoevsky's *Crime and Punishment*.[2] In December of 1886, while reviewing *Crime and Punishment* for the *Dial*, William Morton Payne declared that after the infusion of Russian literature, America was at last prepared to recognize the unique power of Dostoevsky. He added:

An attempt was made several years ago to introduce Dostoyevsky to English readers, but it was not very successful. A "craze" for Russian literature was doubtless just as possible then as now, but Dostoyevsky was hardly the author to inaugurate the fashion. He was too terribly in earnest to interest a public accustomed to derive sustenance from the current novels of society. . . . In a word he flung aside the literary conventionalities, and wrote of what men actually said and thought and felt. Now that the strangeness of the Russian literature is giving away before an increasing familiarity with its masterpieces, we are better prepared for such a writer as Dostoyevsky—prepared to feel with him and to recognize his almost unique power.[3]

In the following year, 1887, a critic observed that "the taste for translations of foreign fiction seems to be on the increase." He continued: "The interest in Russian fiction is still being 'exploited' by our literary workers, and now that the greater writers, from Gogol to Tolstoï have been presented to us, it is but natural for a long train of the lesser ones to follow."[4] And in the *Dial* another critic confirmed this statement. "Vladimir Korolénko," the notice read, "is a new writer for English readers, but, being a Russian, he is sure of a hearing in the present curiously excited condition of the reading public."[5]

Probably more than any other Russian writer Tolstoy continued to attract an unusual amount of interest for at least another decade, a fact which was, in some measure, due to his so-called conversion—

---

[1] The reviewer affirmed: ". . . we can say, with all sincerity, that it would be far better had *Salambô* [*sic*] never passed into English literature." *Literary World*, XVII (October 16, 1886), 349.

[2] Review of *Crime and Punishment: A Russian Realistic Novel*. *Literary World*, XVII (October 30, 1886), 364–5.

[3] "Recent Fiction," *Dial*, VII (December, 1886), 190.

[4] *Dial*, VIII (July, 1887), 68–9.

[5] Review of Tolstoy's *A Russian Proprietor and Other Stories*. *Dial*, IX (March, 1888), 269.

38

the realistic novelist turned religious reformer. There were, of course, many who were shocked by the bold and sometimes repulsive details found in his work, but his vogue continued. "Tolstoi's name is on every tongue," affirmed one C. A. Bartol. "The great Russian author is a sort of literary Napoleon for the day. He startles the world from its propriety. Every book he writes is a moral volcano. . . . Mr. Wanamaker and Mr. Anthony Comstock pronounce Tolstoi's writing indecent and foul."[1]

This same year, 1886,[2] in which was exhibiting a "craze" for Russian literature, was important also because it marked a growing change[3] in the attitude of the United States toward Zola and his

---

[1] "Tolstoi and 'The Kreutzer Sonata,'" *Forum* X (November, 1890), 264–5. See also F. W. Farrar, "Count Tolstoi's Religious Views," *Forum*, VI (December, 1888), 337–49 and Sara A. Hubbard's review of Tolstoy's *My Confession* and *The Spirit of Christ's Teaching*. *Dial*, VIII (October, 1887), 125–7. In his introduction to *Sebastopol* (New York, 1887) Howells voiced his admiration for Tolstoy, who was "the human being with whom at this moment I find myself in the greatest intimacy; not because I know him, but because I know myself through him; because he has written more faithfully of the life common to all men, the universal life which is the most personal life, than any other author whom I have read. This merit the Russian novelists have each in some degree; Tolstoï has it in pre-eminent degree, and that is why the reading of 'Peace and War,' 'Anna Karenina,' 'My Religion,' 'Childhood,' 'Boyhood, and Youth,' 'Scenes at the Siege of Sebastopol,' 'The Cossacks,' 'The Death of Ivan Illitch,' 'Katia,' and 'Polikouchka,' forms an epoch for thoughtful people. In these books you seem to come face to face with human nature for the first time in fiction. All other fiction at times *seems* fiction; these alone seem the very truth always." Pp. 5–6. The quotation gives evidence of the great number of Tolstoy's works available in English in 1887.

[2] In his well-documented study *Zola aux États-Unis* (Providence, R.I., 1943) Albert J. Salvan stated: "De 1850 à 1865, intérêt croissant pour la littérature française. Critique favorable et défavorable de Dumas, Balzac, George Sand et Victor Hugo. En 1878 les trois auteurs dont les romans en français sont le[s] plus populaires sont Henry Gréville, George Sand et Victor Cherbuliez." P. 11. Cf. also J. L. Motley, "Novels of Balzac," *North American Review*, LXV (July, 1847), 108 and Benjamin Griffith, *Balzac aux États-Unis* (Paris, 1931). Cf. also *Cahiers des langues modernes*. I. *Romanciers Américains contemporains*, ed. by Henri Kerst (Paris, 1946). "Il semble que Balzac ait été lu en entier bien avant 1885, date où commence à paraître la première traduction *in extenso* de Katherine Wormeley, par des Américains qui allaient chaque année en France, se tenaient au courant des modes nouvelles et pratiquaient les langues étrangères." Pp. 18–19.

[3] One incident which may have contributed to the change of attitude toward Zola in 1886 was a speech delivered by Professor Thomas Davidson before

work. Before 1886 the reception of Zola in America had been hostile. The venomous attacks by literary critics are typified by such outbursts as the following taken at random: "It is a story for demi-reps and drunkards of the most debased kind"—"the realism of filth is a degradation of art"—"vital with blood and force"— "A Filthy Book"—"Zola's Stink Pot"—"the microscopic examination of a pailful of sewage."[1] But "L'année 1886," wrote an American critic, "est une période décisive en ce qui concerne la réputation de Zola aux États-Unis,"[2] and "Pendant la période qui va de 1886 à 1903, nous allons trouver une acceptation croissante des excès du naturalisme au nom de la morale."[3] No Russian, nor any other foreign or native writer, had met with such opposition as Zola did in America.

There were numerous translations of works by French writers in the eighties and nineties—not only by such masters as Balzac, Flaubert, the brothers Goncourt, Zola, Daudet, and Maupassant,[4] but also by lesser writers—and of all these Zola was the author most frequently discussed in literary magazines; and his fame was equaled among other continental authors only by that of Tolstoy. "Entre 1878 et 1900," Salvan observed, "trente et une maisons américaines ont publié environ cent quatre-vingts éditions des différents ouvrages de Zola."[5] Works by Huysmans were not introduced to America until the nineties.[6]

What seemed to have shocked the American critics and the

---

the Concord School of Philosophy in the spring of 1886. Speaking of Socrates' irony he said, "I can think of only four other men whose irony has the same characteristic—Aristotle, Jesus, Goethe and Zola." To link Zola with Jesus caused a great stir in those days. *Literary World*, XVII (August 7, 1886), 264.

[1] Salvan, *op. cit.*, pp. 38 n., 68 n.

[2] *Ibid.*, p. 83.

[3] *Ibid.*, p. 85. In this survey particular stress is laid on Zola because of his influence on Garland, Crane, and Norris. For the discussion of Zola and America see also C. R. Decker, "Zola's Literary Reputation in England," *PMLA*, XLIX (December, 1934), 1140–53 and Herbert Edwards, "Zola and the American Critics," *American Literature*, IV (May, 1932), 114–29.

[4] Speaking of the popularity of the short story in the nineties W. D. Howells observed: "The vogue that Maupassant's tales in the original or in versions have enjoyed may have had something to do with it." Introduction to Hamlin Garland's *Main-Travelled Roads* (Chicago and New York, 1898), p. 2.

[5] Salvan, *op. cit.*, p. 73.

[6] See p. 310.

reading public most was the bold treatment of sex in French fiction. Howells—otherwise sponsor of modern European literature—was particularly sensitive to overt treatments of sex in literature. In 1884 Lorado Taft, the sculptor, made the following comment on French art, a comment which was equally applicable to French literature.

... We do not want modern French art, with its littleness and license. We are not a nation of libertines.

But we do want its perfection of technique, its wonderful drawing, in its intense realism, that takes one outdoors when he paints a landscape, and keeps him there until it is done. We can have no characteristic American art until we have learnt that same fidelity to nature. Why, if our prairies could only be painted as they really are, what wonder and admiration they would excite among those trained to appreciate faithful transcripts of nature! ... Millet was great ... What a privilege it is to be an American![1]

This statement may be regarded as typical of the period.

It was but natural that the outspoken description of the life of the French peasants in *La Terre* should shock American readers. A reviewer in the *Critic* was of the opinion that

As a story, we cannot conceive of anybody's finding it interesting; it is dull, slow, unpleasant and bestial; but as a study, one reads between the lines and is filled with pity and a wholesome sense of warning. "Zola" has become a synonym for everything that is bad; and when a suspicion of profligacy, sensuality, and riotous bestiality appears in other work, we are wont to shrink from the suggestion of "an American Zola." But it is safe to say that the American Zolas have never based their sensuality and bestiality on any such ground as a revelation or a warning or an impulse to pity, as may be perceived by the careful reader of Zola himself.[2]

Somewhat more than a decade later, in a laudatory article[3] on Zola, Howells was able to see some values if not beauty in such a book as *La Terre*.

---

[1] *Proceedings of the Art Union of Central Illinois. Practical Art in Illinois.* Address delivered before the Art Union of Central Illinois, at its annual meeting in Decatur, May 21-2, 1884, by Lorado Taft. For Garland's attitude toward sex, see pp. 205 ff.

[2] *Critic,* XII (May 26, 1888), 255–6.

[3] W. D. Howells, "Émile Zola," *North American Review,* CLXXV (November, 1902), 587–96.

If Tolstoy's conversion stimulated the American interest in the Russian writer, it was Zola's stubborn attitude in the Dreyfus affair that contributed to his increased fame in the United States. A writer in *Ainslee's Magazine* said that the "conclusion of the Zola trial has been a relief. It is possible that Zola has done more to leave an enduring name in history by this action than by all the reputation which has come to him as a novelist."[1]

In the eighties and nineties a group of English writers, to a certain extent influenced by French naturalism and Russian realism, headed by such figures as Gissing, George Moore, Hardy, and others, were also being read and debated in the United States. The year 1888 seems of particular interest, since it saw the American publication of at least three significant English books: Thomas Hardy's *Wessex Tales*, Olive Schreiner's *The Story of an African Farm*,[2] and Mrs. Humphry Ward's *Robert Elsmere*. These books were frequently commented upon in American magazines. Thomas Hardy seems to have been a force in America particularly in the nineties, and he may have influenced the American local color school, and rising realists learned perhaps some of their techniques of story writing from him.[3] To those who considered the realism of Howells and James superficial, Hardy loomed as a master who dared to write almost as Zola did. Gissing[4] and George Moore[5] were presented to the American public by the *Bookman* in 1895. As early as 1894, however, the *Chap-Book* commented as follows upon *Esther Waters*:

I think Mr. Quiller-Couch is right about "Esther Waters," it is the greatest novel England has produced since "Tess." Mr. George Moore may well congratulate himself, for his work is one to be proud of. It is not a pleasant story: it is really not a nice story, but it is great. I mean great in the sense that Zola's work is great—a conscientious study of low and oftentimes disgusting life. That Mr. Moore is conscientious in "Esther Waters" I think no one can deny. Working under the influences of Balzac and along the lines of Zola and Verga, he has written a powerful story and, notwithstanding its naturalism and the disapproval of English newsdealers, it is very moral. That's the strange thing, nowadays.

---

[1] William Hale, "Émile Zola as a National Figure," *Ainslee's Magazine*, I (April, 1898), 65–6.

[2] First published in England in 1883.

[3] See Carl J. Weber, *Hardy in America* (Waterville, Me., 1946).

[4] See *Bookman*, I (May, 1895), 225.

[5] "The Rise of Mr. George Moore," *Bookman*, I (June, 1895), 322–4.

The self-constituted judges of the world's morality always pick out for their condemnation the most moral things. One remembers how they talked about "Ghosts" and "The Second Mrs. Tanqueray," and now —it is "Esther Waters."[1]

One of George Moore's defenders in the United States was Harry Thurston Peck. Thomas Beer was of the opinion that "He helped Mr. Moore to become an idol of American writers ... They have not been able to imitate his delicate, running sentences that escape monotony by the turn of a word, a gull's whirl in the fog, but they learned about women from him."[2] The nineties also saw the publication of a great number of slum stories by English writers. Typical works include Arthur Morrison's *Tales of Mean Streets* (1894) and *A Child of the Jago* (1896), Edward W. Townsend's *Chimmie Fadden, Major Max, and Other Stories*, Henry W. Nevinson's *Slum Stories of London*, Rudyard Kipling's "The Record of Badalia Herodsfoot" in *Many Inventions* (1893), Somerset Maugham's *Liza of Lambeth* (1897), and Richard Whiteing's *No. 5 John Street* (1899).

The increased use of the short story as a literary form in the nineties may be explained partly by the popularity of the tales of Kipling[3] and the rise of innumerable magazines.

Among those who contributed to the introduction of modern Scandinavian literature in America, Hjalmar Hjorth Boyesen and William Dean Howells[4] ought to be mentioned. In a number of magazine articles and in several books[5] the Norwegian-born scholar and novelist Boyesen favored the cause of such writers as Ibsen, Kielland, Björnson, and others. His own fictional works,

---

[1] "Notes," *Chap-Book* (July 1, 1894), p. 95.

[2] *The Mauve Decade* (Garden City, N. Y., 1926), pp. 119–20. H. T. Peck was "the first American who treated Huysmans, Mallarmé, Prévost, Sudermann and Hauptmann to more than a passing paragraph of uneasy regard. . . . His apostolate for Zola was continuous." *Ibid.*, pp. 196–7.

[3] Cf. also the following statement in the *Literary World*, XXII (1891): "Mr. Kipling has been the prodigy of the year, but his permanent place yet remains to be determined. Count Tolstoy's 'Kreutzer Sonata' displaced 'Looking Backward' as the reigning sensation." P. 24. This refers to the year 1890.

[4] See pp. 48–9.

[5] See for example his *Essays on German Literature* (New York, 1892), *A Commentary on the Writings of Henrik Ibsen* (New York, 1894), and *Essays on Scandinavian Literature* (New York, 1895).

to a certain extent written under the inspiration of the great Scandinavian masters, particularly Ibsen, as well as his contributions to American criticism have been almost overlooked by scholars dealing with this period in American literature. In an article written in 1887 and entitled "Why We Have No Great Novelists," Boyesen spoke of the barrenness of American literature and seized the opportunity to speak of some representatives of the modern trend in Scandinavian literature. "Björnson," he asserted, "has recently published a novel ('Flags Are Flying in Harbor and City') in which he introduces successively four generations of the same family, for the purpose of illustrating the psychological and physiological laws of heredity in their mutual interdependence, and enforcing the moral lessons which are involved therein. Alexander Kielland diagnoses with dispassionate serenity and truth the hidden diseases of the body social, and by his keen and biting satire arouses against himself a storm of denunciation."[1] In 1888 a critic declared in a review of Ibsens *The Pillars of Society and Other Plays* that the lack of virility charged against current American literature could not be imputed to the contemporary literature of Scandinavia.[2] W. D. Howells gave a laudatory review of the book in *Harper's Monthly*. Because of its importance for this study as well as for the light it throws on the native American drama, the review is worthy of being quoted at length:

One's reserves one nearly always has, and in coming to praise even such powerful work as Henrick [*sic*] Ibsen's dramas (of which the reader may now get three in English in the cheap and pretty Camelot editions) one must own that there is often more of type than of character in his personages, and that the reality of the action is sometimes strained to an allegorical thinness. Nevertheless the effect is not much less than tremendous, especially in that play called *Ghosts* where the sins of the father are visibly visited upon the son. Life is made a little difficult by the contemplation of the far-reaching suggestion of this simple action: it appears that you are not only to live rightly for your own sake, but for your children's sake, in whom your vices and evils will walk the earth

---

[1] *Forum*, II (February, 1887), 622. Several of Björnson's books were brought out in America in English translations in the eighties. For his visit to the United States, see H. Eitrem, "Bjørnstjerne Bjørnsons Amerikaferd i 1880–81," *Edda*, XXIX (1929), 165–206.

[2] *Critic*, XIII (November 3, 1888). The Ibsen volume included the following three plays: *The Pillars of Society, Ghosts, An Enemy of Society*. It was this book that made such a deep impression on Hamlin Garland. See p. 364.

long after you are under it. This was hinted by the prophets aforetime, science has since affirmed it, and again the poets are burning it into tough human consciousness. We have already spoken of Björnson in his dealing with the same problem, and now one may learn how forcibly his great fellow-laureate handles it. Ibsen's other subjects are *The Pillars of Society*, in which we see how the precious superstructure which we are so zealous to "save" from time to time is propped upon an inwardly rotten respectability; and *The [sic] Enemy of Society*, who tries to set right a dangerous evil in his little town, and has his windows broken by his more public-spirited fellow-citizens for his trouble, and stands outcast and alone where he had been idolized before. All three of the plays are bitter with the most caustic irony, which is all the more mordant because it is so just. The literary quality is peculiar. The action opens so tamely, so flatly, that it seems to you impossible to go on with a thing like that; but at the same moment you find yourself in the grip of a curiosity which intensifies to the most poignant interest, and holds you spell-bound to the end.

These dramas are played in Europe. We fancy them offered to the fat optimism that goes to our theatres only to be "amused"; but what our average audiences would have to say of them we will not fancy. Nothing, though, need prevent the reader from setting up a scene for them in his own imagination; and if he likes to know something of the man who wrote them, and who lives in willing exile from the narrow social conditions of home, we commend him to the essay of Georg Brandes (published by Putnams), and to the interesting paper of Mr. Edmund Gosse in the *Fortnightly* for February.[1]

Another Ibsen admirer, Hamlin Garland, wrote a commendatory article on "Ibsen as a Dramatist" for the June, 1890, *Arena*, in which he commented on the current American drama. "The drama of the day," he asserted, "is in a transition stage. . . . In this transition stage the works of Henrik Ibsen are coming to have great significance."[2] Then he proceeded to a discussion of Ibsen's dramas and found that *An Enemy of Society* was the most radical in form and subject of the six dramas he had read. Garland made particular mention of *A Doll's House, Ghosts, Rosmersholm*, and *Pillars of Society* and he added: "Ibsen is a great herald, his dramas lead to the future."[3]

The following statement taken from an article by Wilbur L.

---

[1] "Editor's Study," *Harper's Monthly*, LXXVIII (May, 1889), 984-5.

[2] *Arena*, II (June, 1890), 72.

[3] *Ibid.*, p. 81. See also Garland's *Crumbling Idols*, pp. 99-118. Cf. Chap. XIV of this study.

Cross on Ibsen's *Brand* is revelatory of the growing fame of Ibsen in America in the nineties:

Ibsen's social dramas are becoming very well known among us. Scholars and critics read them and find in them a new and original dramatic form; the fashionable world reads one of them and talks about them all. Their tendency is usually condemned both in the review and in the drawing-room, and indeed he is a very bold thinker who in our society will defend the *denoûement* of *A Doll's House*. . . . But among English readers, judging from recent criticisms of Ibsen, it [*Brand*] is known only by name. Hence we hope a welcome service will be performed by presenting here its outline.[1]

An indication of the increasing familiarity with Ibsen's dramas was also the publication of some burlesques on his plays in 1893. A writer in the *Dial* said of *Mr. Punch's Pocket Ibsen:* " 'Rosmersholm,' 'A Doll Home,' 'Hedda Gabler,' and 'The Wild Duck' are thus presented in revised forms, while in 'Pill-Doctor Herdal' we have rather a reverent attempt to tread in the footprints of the Norwegian dramatist, than a version of any actually existing masterpiece."[2]

Concerning the attitude toward Ibsen and his plays in general and the subject of Ibsen in America, Annette Andersen observes:

Not only in his own land, Norway, but also in Germany, England, France, and other European countries, many of his plays met a strong opposition that grew more intense with the ideas presented in *A Doll's House* and *Ghosts*. But by 1889 the hostility towards Ibsen's plays had subsided in Germany, and five years later in England the controversy had lost at least some of its bitterness.

In America knowledge of Ibsen came chiefly from English journals which criticised early performances in London or gave reviews of the plays, as in the articles by Archer and by Gosse, which were reprinted in American periodicals as early as 1889. Even before this time, however, there had been a steadily growing interest in Ibsen and his plays. American readers of German periodicals were aware of the stir Ibsen was causing in the continental theatres, and the Scandinavians of America

---

[1] Wilbur L. Cross, "Ibsen's 'Brand,'" *Arena*, III (December, 1890), 81. See also Alfred Hennequin, "Characteristics of the American Drama," *Arena*, I (May, 1890), 700–9, Dion Boucicault, "The Future American Drama," *Arena*, II (November, 1890), 641–52, and Alfred Hennequin, "The Drama of the Future," *Arena*, III (March, 1891), 385–93. G. B. Shaw launched *The Quintessence of Ibsenism* in 1891.

[2] *Dial*, XV (July 16, 1893), 46.

had been watching in their own papers the progress of Ibsen's plays abroad.

Critics of the nineteenth century were hampered by lack of knowledge of Ibsen's plays in their entirety, for few translations were available, nor had many performances of his plays been presented to acquaint the American public with Ibsen on the stage.

After 1890 the number of articles increased, indicating greater interest in Ibsen, his personality, and life.[1]

In a survey of the year 1892 entitled "The Literary Year in Retrospect" special mention was made of the following four books: Björnson's *Flags Are Flying in Harbor and City*, Tolstoy's *Prince Serebryani*, Hardy's *Tess of the D'Urbervilles*, and Zola's *La Débâcle*.[2] During the following years the American magazines devoted more and more space to articles and reviews of Scandinavian writers. It may be worth while to give a few typical instances. Sigurd M. Wergeland had an informative article on "Modern Danish Literature, and Its Foremost Representative,"[3] in which the interest was focused on Holger Drachmann; and Björnstjerne Björnson gave an account of "Modern Norwegian Literature" in two articles for the *Forum* magazine,[4] stressing particularly the writings of Ibsen, Kielland, Jonas Lie, and Knut Hamsun. The *Chap-Book* made the following reference to August Strindberg: "His day has come and gone, and we as yet know nothing of him here."[5]

The interest of America in modern German literature waxed toward the turn of the century; the plays of Gerhart Hauptmann,[6]

---

[1] "Ibsen in America," *Scandinavian Studies and Notes*, XIV (1935–1937), 65.

[2] *Dial*, XIV (January 1 to June 16, 1893), 5. See also Boyesen's articles: "Ibsen's 'Comedy of Love,'" *Dial*, XIV (March 1, 1893), 132–4, "Ibsen's Treatment of Self-Illusion," *Dial*, XV (September 16, 1893), 137–40, and "The Drama of Revolt,"*Bookman*, I (July, 1895), 384–8.

[3] *Dial*, XIX (September 16, 1895), 135–7.

[4] *Forum*, XXI (May, 1896), 318–29 and (June, 1896), 398–413.

[5] *Chap-Book*, IV (June 15, 1896), 134. Strindberg was not widely known in America until after 1912. See John Landquist, "Strindberg i Amerika," *Nordisk Tidskrift* (1916), 216–18 and Esther Elizabeth Rapp, *Strindberg's Reception in England and America*. Unpublished diss. (Univ. of Colorado; Boulder, Colo., 1941).

[6] See J. F. Coar, "Contemporary German Literature. V. Gerhart Hauptmann's 'Führmann [*sic*] Henschel,'" *Bookman*, IX (June, 1899), 354–6 and Edward E. Hale, Jr., "The Four Best Plays of Hauptmann," *Dial*, XXVIII (June

in particular, were frequently commented upon in journals and magazines.

When the New York edition of Max Nordau's *Degeneration* was issued in 1895 it caused a stir among its American readers. A reviewer in the June, 1895, *Forum* declared in an article entitled "Are We Degenerating?" that " 'Degeneration' published a few months ago has provoked more discussion than any recent book on a similar subject."[1]

Nordau labeled Zola a "dégénéré supérieur" and accused him of being no true observer of nature, citing *Pot-Bouille* and *La Terre* as typical of his failure to observe and chronicle real life.

When considering the translations of some of the works discussed, it is important to call attention to the fact that Russian realism and French naturalism in particular were considered too strong and too intense for the American taste and the books had to be toned down and repulsive scenes had to be cut out or modified considerably in order to suit the reading public. A reviewer of Balzac's *Père Goriot* in 1885 called the free translation of the novel "vandalism." A translator of *Anna Karenina* said that he had taken the responsibility of modifying, in deference to "the squeamish taste of American novel readers", certain portions of the work. "In certain scenes," he said in his preface, "the realism is too intense for our Puritan taste; and, perforce, several of these scenes have been more or less modified in the present translation."[2] This attitude seems to have been typical of translators of certain Russian and French writers in the eighties. Zola's novels were also expurgated, of which *Une Page d'amour* (*Hélène: A Love Episode*) was the first to be translated in the United States (1878). The next year saw the publication

---

1, 1900), 430–2. They were: *The Sunken Bell, Lonely Lives, The Weavers,* and *Hannele.* Cf. also Emil Blum, "The Realistic Trend of Modern German Literature," *Arena,* VIII (July, 1893), 212–20.

[1] Charles L. Dana, "Are We Degenerating?" *Forum,* XIX (June, 1895), 458. For the discussion aroused by Nordau's book, see also an article in the *Forum,* XIX (July, 1895), 532–43 entitled "Society's Protection against the Degenerates;" E. R. W., "Where Is Literature at?" *Philistine, A Periodical of Protest,* I, No. 2 (July, 1895), William H. Carpenter, "Max Simon Nordau," *Bookman,* I (April, 1895), 157–8 and "Regeneration. A Reply to Max Nordau's 'Degeneration,' " *Literary World,* XXVII (February 8, 1896), 41–2.

[2] *Dial,* VII (May, 1886), 13–14.

of *L'Assommoir*,[1] of which the translator said in the preface that
it had been "toned down with literary ability, combined with
tact, delicacy, and refinement to suit the American reading public."
Salvan has shown that the translator had changed the novel fundamentally. He wrote: "Les scènes brutales ou pénibles telles
que les corrections que Nana reçoit de son père et l'accouchement
de Gervaise sur le paillasson de sa chambre sont, comme on pouvait
s'y attendre, adoucies considérablement."[2] The same critic added
that "Toutes les traductions de Zola, de 1878 à 1895, sont abré-
gées et modifiées."[3]

In his vindication of modern European literature Howells stood
out perhaps more than any other American writer or critic. His
knowledge of contemporary European literature was extensive. He
heralded in America the works of the great Russians, Ibsen, Zola,
Palacio Valdés, and others. In 1880, when Björnson spent the
winter in the United States, Howells gave a lunch for the Norwegian writer. In a letter to his father he said of him: "I don't
know whether you've ever heard me speak of his books; but he is
a great genius. Personally he is huge and very fair; . . . He is a
hot Republican, and just now is in disgrace at home for having
spoken disrespectfully of the king; I think he called him a don-
key."[4] Later, Björnson was to influence Howells' social outlook.[5]
When editor of the *Atlantic Monthly*, Howells published articles
on Stendhal, Dostoevsky, the brothers Goncourt, Flaubert, Zola,
Mérimée, Mistral, Alfred de Musset, Baudelaire, Gautier, Björnson, Renan, and many others. In the realism of Pérez Galdós
and Giovanni Verga he found an approach to life and literature
similar to his own. In 1890 he wrote a preface for Verga's *I
Malavoglia*. In his introduction to Pérez Galdós's *Doña Perfecta*

---

[1] *L'Assommoir, A Novel* by Émile Zola. Translated by John Stirling (Mary
Neal Sherwood) (Philadelphia: T. B. Peterson & Bros., 1879). The first British
translation of a novel by Zola was *Ladies' Paradise* (Tinsleys) which appeared
in 1883.

[2] Salvan, *op. cit.*, p. 35.

[3] *Ibid.*, p. 32. See also Malcolm B. Jones, "Translations of Zola in the
United States Prior to 1900," *Modern Language Notes*, LV (November, 1940),
520–4.

[4] *Life in Letters of William Dean Howells* (New York, 1928), I, 289–90.

[5] See George Arms, "The Literary Background of Howells's Social Criticism," *American Literature*, XIV (November, 1942), 260–76.

(1896), which he considered human and tender, he resented the influence of French naturalism found in Palacio Valdés's *La Espuma* (1890) and *La Fe* (1892).

A significant statement by Howells in 1894 is worth quoting: "In fact, these clever writers of Spain [Pérez Galdós, Juan Valera, Palacio Valdés, and Emilia Pardo Bazán] easily outclass their French contemporaries, with the exception of Zola, ranking next, in my judgment, to those of Russia."[1] Howells' attitude toward European literature was criticized by the highly nationalistic magazine *America:* "One of Mr. Howells' tenets in criticism is based on the assumption that the American taste in fiction is far below that of France, Spain, Portugal, or Russia. He has reviewed in their turn recently three alien novels, each of which he has ranked above the greatest in American literature.... Looked at from an American point of view, there is trouble for our future in this cult for alien standards of art, morals, and politics."[2]

To sum up: The growing number of translations of European realistic and naturalistic literature in the eighties and nineties undoubtedly stimulated the trend toward naturalism in American letters. In the eighties there was a vogue of Russian literature, which reached its apex about 1886. The same year saw a growing shift from the hostile attitude toward Zola and his works. In the nineties translations of Scandinavian, German, Spanish, and Italian realistic and naturalistic books also contributed to the complex of new currents and new ideas which were to enrich and influence native American literature and to advance the cause of American naturalism.[3]

---

[1] *Dial*, XVI (June 16, 1894), 372. Other critics who contributed to the introduction of European realistic and naturalistic writings in the United States include: T. S. Perry, Brander Matthews, Harry Thurston Peck, William Morton Payne, Vance Thompson, and Richard Hovey.

[2] Maurice Thompson, "The Alien Taint in Criticism," *America* (August 15, 1899), pp. 631–2.

[3] See Chaps. X–XIV.

CHAPTER IV

REALISM IN THE MIDDLE WEST

EDWARD EGGLESTON, EDGAR WATSON HOWE, AND JOSEPH KIRKLAND

The World's Columbian Exposition of 1893 brought Chicago, then chiefly noted for its stockyards and packing industries, into the national spotlight. Political and artistic leaders of the day predicted a swift and glorious development of the city. "All the near-by states," observed Garland, "were stirred and heartened by this esthetic awakening of a metropolis which up to this time had given but little thought to the value of art in the life of a community. From being a huge, muddy windy market-place, it seemed about to take its place among the literary capitals of the world."[1] This was also the year of Chicago's literary boom; writers like Harriet Monroe, Henry B. Fuller, George Ade, Finley Peter Dunne, Eugene Field, and others helped to build up the city's literary reputation. In a boastful mood Garland cried out: "Here flames the spirit of youth. Here throbs the heart of America . . ."[2] It was also in 1893 that Garland launched his significant article entitled "Literary Emancipation of the West,"[3] written in revolt against the literary overlordship of New England and heralding a new and genuinely American literature emerging in the West.

The discovery of a "Western School" of literature caused a great stir among critics. A New York writer observed:

There has been of late a general outbreak, in magazines and newspapers, of articles about culture and literature in the West, all of them

---

[1] *A Son of the Middle Border*, p. 457.

[2] *Ibid.*

[3] *Forum*, XVI (October 1893), 156–66. The article was republished in the following year in a somewhat modified form in *Crumbling Idols*, chap. x.

prophesying, and some of them professing to have discovered, a new literary school in and about Chicago. This is variously described, but the one mark upon which all the critics and prophets agree is that the literature of the West is to be absolutely novel and original. It is to cut loose entirely from forms and standards prevalent in the East and in England, and it is at last to give the genuine American "a voice."[1]

The new literature of the West emerging as a force in the nineties had roots in a native tradition. Three writers in particular were important for realism in the Middle West, and especially for Garland. Each of them produced at least one book of lasting merit and significance: Edward Eggleston with *The Hoosier School-Master* (1871), Edgar Watson Howe with *The Story of a Country Town* (1883), Joseph Kirkland with *Zury: the Meanest Man in Spring County* (1887).

Of particular pertinence to the rise of Midwest realism is the revelatory preface of *The Hoosier School-Master*, in which Eggleston stated explicitly his realistic purpose and his desire to give the West a place in American literature:

It has been in my mind since I was a Hoosier boy to do something toward describing life in the back-country districts of the Western States. It used to be a matter of no little jealousy with us, I remember, that the manners, customs, thoughts, and feelings of New England country people filled so large a place in books, while our life, not less interesting, not less romantic, and certainly not less filled with humorous and grotesque material, had no place in literature. It was as though we were shut out of good society. And, with the single exception of Alice Cary, perhaps, our Western writers did not dare speak of the West otherwise than as the unreal world to which Cooper's lively imagination had given birth.[2]

In the preface to *The Circuit Rider* (1874) Eggleston asserted that the solemn obligation of a novelist was "to tell the truth. . . . [for] no man is worthy to be called a novelist who does not endeavor with his whole soul to produce the higher form of history, by writing truly of men as they are, and dispassionately of those forms of life that come within his scope."[3] Eggleston's aim and

---

[1] "The 'Western School' of Literature," *Dial*, XV (October 16, 1893), 234.

[2] Edward Eggleston, *The Hoosier School-Master* (New York, 1889), p. 5.

[3] *The Circuit Rider* (New York, 1874), p. vii. It should be understood that realism existed in the East even before Eggleston. The local realistic tradition was far older than the works referred to here. I emphasize Eggleston's importance mainly for the rise of *Midwest* realism.

practice in writing became of importance to rising authors of the Middle West. Garland once said of him: "He is our pioneer midwest novelist, the first of a long line of writers of western and village life."[1] On another occasion the same writer, alluding to James Whitcomb Riley, Kirkland, and Howe observed that "we must not forget that Edward Eggleston was the father of us all."[2] Eggleston (1837–1902), a Methodist circuit rider from Indiana, was justly the trailmaker in finding the Midwest a subject for realistic fiction and his fame rests chiefly on *The Hoosier School-Master*, "the file-leader of the procession of American dialect novels"[3] which is still considered a minor American classic. It is interesting to note that this novel appeared in the same year as Zola's first volume of the *Rougon-Macquart* series, *La Fortune des Rougon*. The novel is a crude picture of life in backwoods Indiana about 1850 and, although the story is marred with moralizing, sentimentalism, a traditional villain and frequent caricatures—in many respects it recalls Dickens' *Oliver Twist*, particularly in its criticism of poor-house conditions and in the portrayal of the boy Shocky —it contains, nevertheless, a valuable and candid record of frontier life, its lawlessness, its revival preaching, its spelling bees, etc. The Hoosiers themselves, plain, ordinary people, are faithfully observed, though often caricatured, with their rustic manners, local customs, and racy idiom, which give to the story a sense of reality and authenticity.

Eggleston had the good fortune to be "born into an intellectual atmosphere."[4] He was well read in the classics, but he was also aware of the great thinkers of his day, for instance, Taine and Darwin. Of particular interest for this study is the fact that Eggleston shared Taine's belief that characters should be studied in relationship to their environment, and the men and women of *The Hoosier School-Master* were in part completed and explained by their environment, which made them dull, crude, and uncouth.

If I were a dispassionate critic, and were set to judge my own novels as the writings of another, I should have to say that what distinguishes

---

[1] *The Westward March of American Settlement* (1927), p. 31.

[2] *My Friendly Contemporaries* (New York, 1932), p. 131.

[3] *The Hoosier Schoolmaster* (Chicago, 1901), Preface, p. 6. Quoted by Alexander Cowie in *The Rise of the American Novel* (New York, 1948, p. 541.

[4] Eggleston, "Formative Influences," *Forum*, X (November, 1890), 280.

them from other works of fiction is the prominence which they give to social conditions; that the individual characters are here treated to a greater degree than elsewhere as parts of a study of a society—*as in some sense the logical results of the environment* ... I am mainly interested in the evolution of society.[1]

Eggleston commented on his novel, which was "dashed off in ten weeks," and on his method of treating his material, in an interesting article called "Books that Have Helped Me." He observed: "I am often asked in regard to the immediate impetus to the writing of this story [*The Hoosier School-Master*], and the answer seems paradoxical enough, I had just finished reading Taine's 'Art in the Netherlands.' Applying his maxim, that an artist ought to paint what he has seen, I tried my hand on the dialect and other traits of the more illiterate people of Southern Indiana."[2] And he continued: "A Kempis may rest where he is (on a top shelf); I would rather walk in wide fields with Charles Darwin; and above all, I would rather, if it were possible, get one peep into the epoch-making book of the next century, whatever it may be, than to go back to the best of the crypt-worshippers."[3]

Hints of Darwinian catchwords appeared also in his works. In *The Hoosier School-Master*, for instance, when Ralph Hartsook, the hero, was fighting with his lower self, Eggleston remarked: "I suppose Darwin would call it the remains of the Wild Beast."[4] Though at heart an optimist and sentimental moralist, Eggleston did not hesitate to paint with honest attention to detail some of the more sordid elements of his milieu.

Midwest realism was intensified by another writer, Edgar Watson Howe (1853–1937), a native of Indiana, in his *Story of a Country Town*. It appeared twelve years after the publication of *The Hoosier School-Master* and in the same year as Mark Twain's *Life on the Mississippi*, Zola's *Au Bonheur des dames*, and Maupassant's *Une Vie*. It is a tale filled with bitterness and *tristesse*, a grim picture of Midwestern life with its smugness, narrowness, and spiritual poverty. The book was slow to find a publisher, for seven or eight publishers rejected it. Howe, who was then an

---

[1] *Forum*, X, 286–7. Quoted by Cowie, *op. cit.* p. 549. The italics are mine.
[2] *Forum*, III (August, 1887), 584.
[3] *Ibid.*, p. 586.
[4] *The Hoosier School-Master* (New York, 1889), p. 79.

editor and owner of a small daily newspaper, the Atchison *Globe* (Kansas),[1] decided to print the novel himself. He wrote later that "the book was written almost entirely at night, on the kitchen table in the house where I still live. I had little children then, lovable and noisy, and it was my custom to retire to the kitchen for quiet, and work at the 'Story,' after a hard day's work on a daily paper."[2] It was to some extent autobiographical depicting his reminiscences of the Fairview and Twin Mounds people, who, however, were portrayed as "an average of country people on the frontier."[3] Howe asserted that "the book is mainly fiction, and was so intended. Fairview had no mill, and no tragedy."[4] Against a background of an extremely bleak and inhospi-

[1] *The Story of a Country Town* (New York, 1927). Preface, p. v.

[2] *Ibid.*, pp. vii–viii.

[3] *Ibid.*, p. viii.

[4] *Ibid.*, p. ix. Howe gave Garland some interesting information concerning the novel in an unpublished letter dated July 7, 1889. He wrote: ". . . I attended school but little during my boyhood, principally in Fairview Church, with the Meek children, whose father was named George and not 'Theodore.' Fairview Church, which was situated seven miles east of Bethany, was blown down during a heavy storm last summer. 'The Story of a Country Town' accurately represents my recollections of the Fairview neighborhood, but I came away from it when a boy of twelve. My father was the original of 'John Westlock' and he ran away, but he never came back to acknowledge his error. The woman he ran away with, however, was called 'D,' (a contraction of 'Lodema') and not 'B.' He has since deserted 'B' and is now living with another woman. He is still preaching, and a strangely erratic man of whom I know little. The 'Country Town' grossly offended him, and increased the coolness between us, although I do not believe he was ever as good a man as 'John Westlock.' Most of the other characters and incidents in the 'Country Town' are fictitious. I had an Uncle Joe, but his name was Joe Trevin, and his history was not at all like 'Joe Erring's.'

The original of 'Davy's Bend' was Brownville, Neb., a town I visited only once, during high water in the Missouri River.

I myself am the original of all the characters in the three books—at least, I sometimes fear that I am. All that they say sounds like a confession to me, and I wonder that my friends do not know it. (This in confidence.)

I wrote 'A Moonlight Boy' in five months, at night. The two other books were written in the same way. When I quit the newspaper I will write my best book, but I am successful at it, and I am afraid to give it up.

I once knew a man very like 'Tibby Cole.' His name was E. D. Coe, and he lived at Golden, Colorado. I have attended his conventions and band[?] concerts frequently; in fact, I sang in his conventions, and played a cornet in his band. His widow lives at Golden . . ."

table prairie district out West, Fairview, where the sun was never bright and where the cold shadow of a gray church spread and enveloped symbolically all the houses and their inhabitants like a curse, there were enacted two dramas, the disappearance of the Rev. John Westlock and his subsequent deterioration, and the murder of Clinton Bragg and the murderer's suicide. Like their environment the people were hard, stern, and grim; there was no humor, delight, or happiness to make life easier for them; no tree, no bush to give life and add color to this bleak and gloomy landscape; everywhere there was lack of beauty and ideals; only hatred, bitterness, disillusion, and tragedy remained. Like Eggleston and Taine, Howe made the environment and the work responsible for the rough and uncouth manners of the people. One of the characters, Mr. Briggs, remarked:

> "Those of us who live in the country . . . cannot be particular. Our clothing, our food, and our ways are rough, but substantial and honest. We have other matters to look after. We may have our ambitions like other men, but they are dwarfed and bent by holding the plow, and pitching the hay."[1]

Consequently the people became slow and ignorant; they were all lonely and friendless, unhappy and discontented. "There never was a happy man in Fairview," said one of them.[2] The women were badly treated and sometimes deserted, and the children did not love their parents. Kind words were seldom heard and joyous faces were seldom seen. One of the chief sources of the misery of the people was religion, a dogmatic and narrow Methodism. It was incarnate in the grave and silent character of the Rev. John Westlock, endowed with stubbornness and severity. In the portrayal of his decline, his elopement with a slovenly widow and consequent disintegration, Howe pronounced an anathema against this kind of religion. These bleak and critical pictures of the narrow life of a small Midwestern community anticipated Stephen Crane's *Whilomville Stories* (1900), Edgar Lee Masters' *Spoon River Anthology* (1915), and Sinclair Lewis' *Main Street* (1920). Despite its Dickensian types, Gothic paraphernalia, melo-

---

[1] *The Story of a Country Town*, p. 74. The loneliness and bleakness of the prairie was also a favored theme in Garland's works.

[2] *Ibid.*, pp. 92-3.

dramatic passages, and stereotyped dialogue Howe wrote a book of real power and depth.

It is probably misleading to say that he helped create a "new literary mood."[1] Nor should his novel be recognized "as a significant pioneering work of naturalistic fiction."[2] His aim and method was not Zola's or that of any other naturalist. The book is mainly an important contribution to the anti-romantic realism of the eighties, and as such it blazed the trail for the early works of Garland in the following decade.

When *Zury* saw publication in 1887—the year of Harold Frederic's *Seth's Brother's Wife*,[3] Zola's *La Terre* and *Le Manifeste des Cinq*—Joseph Kirkland (1830–94), the son of a woman writer, Caroline Kirkland, was nearly sixty years old, living as a successful lawyer in "plutocratic grandeur" in Chicago. The novel may be classified as a forerunner of that harsher brand of realism which contributed to the rise of naturalism, since it achieved a more truthful realism than its predecessors. As one critic put it, "Edward Eggleston's 'Hoosier Schoolmaster' had gone so far into humor as to approach burlesque, and Ed Howe's 'Story of a Country Town' had overemphasized grimness and spiritual depression."[4] Kirkland wrote two more realistic novels, *The McVeys* (1888), a sequel to *Zury*, and *The Captain of Company K* (1891), which is a forerunner of Crane's *The Red Badge of Courage* in its unheroic portrayal of war. Kirkland's realism stemmed to some extent from Howe and Eggleston; mainly perhaps from the latter, judging from what Kirkland once told Garland: "I am

---

[1] Robert E. Spiller *et al.*, *Literary History of the United States* (New York, 1948), II, 794.

[2] James D. Hart, *The Oxford Companion to American Literature* (New York, 1944), p. 339.

[3] It should be noted here that this book, which Garland reviewed in 1887 (see p. 70) probably exerted a considerable influence on him. *Seth's Brother's Wife* is an anti-romantic study of the hard, depressing life on a New York State farm. With unflinching realism Frederic described the loneliness and meanness of farm life, its unrelieved physical strain, its mental barrenness, its futility and its deadening effects on the people, who were molded to its sordid patterns. The men grew mean and coarse and the women were enslaved and bitter by the hopeless toil or suffered from marriage to men who were beneath them intellectually.—A similar denunciation of rural life was voiced by Garland in such books as *Main-Travelled Roads*, *Jason Edwards*, and *Prairie Folks*. See pp. 82–6.

[4] *Newberry Library Bulletin*, No. 3 (December, 1945), p. 3.

afraid my eyes were fixed on Eggleston's 'Hoosier Schoolmaster'
and 'The Circuit Rider' as examples to be improved upon."[1] And
in a letter to Garland dated June 7, 1887, Kirkland wrote: "I used
Howe's 'Annals of a Country Town'[2] as an example—and a warning." He was fairly well read in classic and modern literature; he
admired Tolstoy, Daudet, and above all Hardy, on one of whose
novels he declared that he modeled *Zury*. In the preface Kirkland wrote:

> If a critic shall say, "This novel is a palpable imitation of Thomas
> Hardy's *Far from the Madding Crowd;* an attempt to reproduce, on
> American soil, the unflinching realism of the picture given by that re-
> markable work, of English low life down in actual contact with the soil
> itself," then the writer will be satisfied. He will know that he has hit
> his mark, or at least come near enough to make his aim evident.[3]

In an unpublished letter to Louise C. Shuler dated July 18, 1887
Kirkland spoke of his admiration for Hardy, Tolstoy, and Daudet.
"How well it pays to write *the truth,* unadorned and undisguised!
I was very uncertain as to the possibility of making my homely
subject interesting—so sordid, unhandsome, unromantic, even
malodorous to the cultivated and refined olfactories—and lo! from
Italy to California come welcome recognitions of the 'touch of
nature.' ... I like the Englishman Thomas Hardy very much.
I think his 'Far from the Madding Crowd' a remarkable work.
Tolstoï is excellent—so is much of Daudet."[4]

Zury is the candid picture of the drab lives of Zury Prouder,
a typical Western man, molded by a severe and sordid environment, and of Anne McVey and her two illegitimate children.
"All the characters in 'Zury,' " Kirkland once told Garland in an
unpublished letter, "have their prototypes in my down-state acquaintances. The book is as true as I could make it. Many of
its incidents are literally exact."[5] In the *Transcript*, Garland
gave *Zury* a laudatory review, which gave rise to a profitable
relationship between him and Kirkland:

---

[1] Garland, *Roadside Meetings*, p. 111.

[2] The correct title is *The Story of a Country Town*.

[3] Weber is not aware of Kirkland's avowed debt to Hardy. See Weber, *op.
cit.*, chap. xi.

[4] Published by the permission of the Newberry Library.

[5] *Roadside Meetings*, p. 111.

... The writers of the West had not (and have not now) risen to the full knowledge of the fact that the realistic study of their actual surroundings was their only salvation from utter conventionality ... But the full revelation of the inexhaustible wealth of native American material, and wealth in a section hitherto considered barren and hopeless of art materials, will come to the Eastern reader with the reading of "Zury"... The book is moreover likely to have a very great influence upon any Western writer who is planning a new novel. To say that Joseph Kirkland has written the most realistic novel of American interior society is to state the simple fact. It is as native to Illinois as Tolstoï's "Anna Karénina" or Tourgénieff's "Fathers and Sons" are to Russia ... "Zury" is unsurpassed, in some respects, by any story of American rural life hitherto written, and I am much mistaken if the author does not take a high place at once in the estimation of American critics. ...[1]

Kirkland went a step beyond Eggleston and Howe in blazing the trail for a faithful portrayal of Midwestern life. His immediate successor was Hamlin Garland.

To sum up: It is something of an exaggeration to speak of *The Hoosier School-Master*, *The Story of a Country Town* and *Zury* as milestones in American letters, and it is not quite accurate to call any one of them a precursor of naturalism unless, erroneously, we call such realists as Howells and James precursors of naturalism. What the authors of these books aimed at was, it seems to me, a *realistic* treatment of certain aspects of Middle Western life. Eggleston, Howe, and Kirkland were all *realists*. The two first mentioned were less so, I believe, than Kirkland, since a strain of sentimentality (in Eggleston) and of Gothic terror (in Howe) marred their work. Kirkland achieved a greater sense of reality, but, on the whole, he did not go beyond the border of Howells' realism. The reason why I have stressed their importance here is that, in their realistic descriptions of the *Middle West*, they were forerunners of Garland, who, in my opinion, is one of the first[2]

---

[1] "Zury, The Meanest Man in Spring County," *Boston Evening Transcript* (Monday, May 16, 1887).

[2] Henry B. Fuller has at times been labeled a precursor of naturalism on account of his two realistic Chicago novels, *The Cliff-Dwellers* (1893) and *With the Procession* (1895). Theodore Dreiser regarded these novels as "the birth cries of naturalism in this country." Quoted in Harry Hartwick, *The Foreground of American Fiction* (New York, 1934), p. 87. A recent critic, Alexander Cowie, asserted that naturalism perhaps began with Fuller's *The Cliff-Dwellers*. *Op.*

important American writers to have been influenced by literary naturalism.[1]

cit., p. 749. These statements need, however, some qualification. Crane's *Maggie* was also published in 1893, and before that date Garland had portrayed prairie and city life in a manner considerably closer to the methods of literary naturalism than Fuller.

[1] See "Zola and Garland," pp. 233–49.

CHAPTER V

EMERGENCE OF NATURALISM

In the nineties a small group of American writers came more or less close to naturalism in technique and view of life. The most important were Hamlin Garland, Stephen Crane, and Frank Norris.[1] Although these writers were to an extent inspired by European models,[2] the native realistic tradition, no doubt, exerted a considerable influence on them. As has already been touched upon, Garland's predecessors were, as regards Midwest realism, Eggleston, Howe, and Kirkland,[3] and, in his turn, he may have influenced both Crane and Norris.[4] Garland, who was ten years

---

[1] Among other prose writers prior to 1904, who, at least in some of their work, in one way or other, may have been influenced by naturalism, the following ought to be mentioned: Hjalmar Hjorth Boyesen, Abraham Cahan, Kate Chopin, Laura Daintrey, Margaret Deland, Edgar Fawcett, Harold Frederic, Alice French, I. K. Friedman, Ellen Glasgow, Robert Grant, E. F. Harkins, Robert Herrick, Grace King, Alfred Henry Lewis, Will Payne, David Graham Phillips, William Sydney Porter, Julian Ralph, Amélie Rives, Edgar Saltus, Robert Shackleton, Stanley Waterloo, Edith Wharton, Hervey White, Brand Whitlock, Stephen French Whitman, and Harry Leon Wilson. See Bibliography.
In 1900 Dreiser launched his naturalistic *Sister Carrie* and in the same year appeared London's collection of short stories, *The Son of the Wolf.* Although both of these writers may easily be linked with Garland, Crane, and Norris, they belong, it seems to me, to a later period and consequently I shall not consider their early work in this study. For Frederic and naturalism see Charles Child Walcutt, "Harold Frederic and American Naturalism," *American Literature,* XI (March, 1939), 11–22. Frederic's relationship with naturalism needs, however, a more extensive investigation and I am preparing a study on this particular problem.
[2] See Chaps. X–XIV.
[3] See p. 52.
[4] Since my purpose has been to investigate the relationships of the three writers to certain European authors, I have not dealt with the equally interesting question of these writers' connections with each other and with Howells, James, Frederic, and other American writers.

older than Norris and eleven years older than Crane, was, moreover, for some time a friend of both. He met Crane in the summer of 1891 at the Seaside Assembly at Avon-by-the-Sea, N. J., where Garland gave a series of lectures on American literature.[1] Crane was then a reporter for the *New York Tribune.* The two men met many times afterward[2] and in various ways Garland helped and encouraged Crane, who readily admitted his debt to Garland. In an undated letter to a friend, Lily Brandon, he called Howells and Garland his "literary fathers."[3]

Garland's first reference to Norris seems to be the following entry in his unpublished diary for February 28, 1899:

> Left on 1 P.M. train for Chicago. Read all the way to Syracuse a long novel "McTeague" by Frank Norris. A fine study of the squalid but not altogether sordid life of San Francisco. . . .[4]

He did not meet Norris, however, until January 1900,[5] from which date they were good friends until the latter's death in 1902.[6] Norris may have met Garland through the Hernes.[7] The Garland and Norris families frequently visited each other in New York. In some of the letters which Garland and Norris exchanged they commented on each other's work. Although impressed by Garland, Norris criticized some points in *Her Mountain Lover* and in *The Captain of the Gray-Horse Troop,* and Garland, despite his admiration for Norris, accused him of imitating Zola. Norris's debt to Garland is, it seems, obvious in *The Octopus.*[8]

---

[1] See Appendix, pp. 442–3.

[2] For material on Garland's acquaintance with Crane see Garland's *Roadside Meetings,* pp. 189–206 and his article "Stephen Crane as I Knew Him," *Yale Review,* N.S. III (April, 1914), 494–506.

[3] I am indebted to Ames W. Williams for this information. See also p. 152.

[4] *McTeague* appeared in February, 1899.

[5] Garland, *Companions on the Trail,* p. 10.

[6] Cf. the following entry in Garland's unpublished diary on the occasion of the death of Frank Norris, October 25, 1902. ". . . He filled a large part in my life and thought. . . . He stood tall and he looked out widely on the world. For one so young his view of social movements and forces was singularly large—almost epic. . . . He was a man of great laughter—of short, pithy speech—humorous, almost always deeply sympathetic."

[7] Cf. p. 72.

[8] The central theme of *The Octopus* is similar to that in Garland's story "Under the Lion's Paw" in *Main-Travelled Roads.* See p. 203.

Crane and Norris met only once, on board the tug "Three Friends" in connection with the Cuban war. They were both reporters and the author of *McTeague* seems to have had little to say to the author of *Maggie* and *The Red Badge of Courage*. Their attitude toward each other was one of reserve. Later on, Norris probably had Crane in mind when he drew the following portrait of a journalist:

It will be long before I forget the picture which the Young Personage made while at work upon his "stuff." Table there was none, and the plunging of the boat made it out of the question to write while sitting in a chair. The correspondents took themselves off to the cabin and wrote while sitting in their bunks. The Young Personage was wearing a pair of duck trousers grimed and fouled with all manner of pitch and grease and oil. His shirt was guiltless of collar or scarf and was unbuttoned at the throat. His hair hung in ragged fringes over his eyes. . . . His dress-suit case was across his lap and answered him for a desk. Between his heels he held a bottle of beer against the rolling of the boat, and when he drank was royally independent of a glass. While he was composing his descriptive dispatches which some ten thousand people would read in the morning from the bulletins in New York, I wondered what the fifty thousand who had read his war novel and have held him, no doubt rightly, to be a great genius would have said and thought could they have seen him at the moment.[1]

Crane was pleased with *McTeague*, but he considered it too moral.[2] Still he asked William Heinemann, the London publisher, to buy Norris's next novel.[3] Norris watched Crane's rapidly rising star with interest, and no doubt with envy, and commented occasionally on his writing.[4]

---

[1] Franklin Walker, *Frank Norris: A Biography* (Garden City, N.Y., 1932), pp. 179–80.

[2] Beer, *Sephen Crane*, p. 226.

[3] *Ibid.*, p. 231.

[4] The earliest reference to Crane's work made by Norris is perhaps his review of *Maggie* and *George's Mother* in the *Wave* of July 4, 1896. See p. 105. *George's Mother* is also mentioned in the short story "His Sister" published in the *Wave* of November 28, 1896, and in 1897 there appeared Norris's parody of *The Red Badge of Courage*. See p. 112 n. 2. See also Norris's critical article about Crane's London reporting, "Crane in London," in the *Wave* of September 18, 1897.

1. HAMLIN GARLAND 1860–1940

Hamlin Garland[1] was born on September 14, 1860, on a farm near West Salem, Wis., and when he was eight years of age, the family crossed the Mississippi and settled in Winnesheik County, Iowa. Next year, they moved out on the unploughed prairies of Mitchell County, Iowa, the scene of some of the stories in *Main-Travelled Roads*. Hamlin's father, Richard H. Garland, a native of Maine, was a stern and domineering character, a good storyteller, an atheist, and a migrant by nature, who seems to have been in a state of constant physical and spiritual unrest. His wife, Isabel McClintock, a native of Ohio, was a gay and tenderhearted woman, imaginative and fond of music, from whom no doubt Hamlin inherited some of his artistic bent.

Even as a boy Hamlin had to do a man's work on the farm, ploughing, sowing, and threshing. Although he was a robust, healthy, ordinary boy, he was sensitive by temperament, and gradually developed an intense dislike of farm life. No doubt his childhood impressions influenced his mind and character and furnished material for his early fiction. In an unpublished letter to E. W. Howe, dated July 2, 1886, Garland wrote: "I was born in Wisconsin and grew up in a troublesome manner on the great Iowa prairies."

If the hard work on the farm at times made the boy feel bitter and sullen, nature was his compensation. The rolling prairies, the gorgeous sunsets, and the teeming life of the vast plains, all appealed strongly to the youth in his quest for beauty on the farm, and helped to create the poetic conception of nature which is felt in many of his early works.

---

[1] In this study I have been concerned only with Garland's realistic and naturalistic works, which represent his best writings of the nineties. Material for this chapter is drawn from Garland's *Roadside Meetings* (New York, 1930), *Companions on the Trail* (New York, 1931), *A Son of the Middle Border* (New York, 1917), *A Daughter of the Middle Border* (New York, 1921), and especially from his unpublished notebooks, diaries, and numerous letters. Eldon C. Hill's unpublished dissertation, *A Biographical Study of Hamlin Garland from 1860 to 1895* (Ohio State Univ.; Columbus, Ohio, 1940), was also helpful. Since Garland's reminiscences contain numerous errors as to date, names, and particulars, they have been used with caution.

In those days, books were scarce on the Border,[1] for, besides the Bible, some Sunday School books, and the McGuffey readers, few books were to be found in the barren little houses on the prairie.[2] True, there were Beadle's dime novels, and Hamlin delighted in Old Sleuth's stories, *Lady Gwendoline's Dream*, and *Buckskin Joe*. In 1871, in the pages of *Hearth and Home*, Hamlin read his first chronicle of everyday life, *The Hoosier School-Master*, which impressed him greatly. "This book," he wrote in his reminiscences, "is a milestone in my literary progress as it is in the development of distinctive western fiction ..."[3] The boy was, however, still under the spell of romantic fiction, and his mind was filled with tales of Indians, scouts, renegades, dukes, and duchesses. Scott, in particular, and American imitators of Scott fascinated him, and he read *Ivanhoe* many times "with the most intense pleasure."[4]

On his fifteenth birthday he received a copy of *Paradise Lost* which, however, did not impress him very much. He was more interested in the Chicago paper which reported some of the lectures of Robert Ingersoll, the well-known agnostic. There seems to have been no religious crisis in Garland's life, for the faith in which he and his father "had been reared had already grown dim, and under the light of Ingersoll's remorseless humor most of our superstitions vanished."[5]

In 1876 Garland entered the Cedar Valley Seminary at Osage, Iowa, from which he was graduated four years later. He called the years at the seminary his "gateway to the sun," for to him they meant freedom from the hay fork and the hoe, they opened up new vistas and stirred vague longings for an intellectual life. They revealed to the ambitious youth an entirely new world, the

---

[1] See, e.g. Clara Martin Baker, "Books in a Pioneer Household," *Journal of the Illinois State Historical Society*, XXXII (September, 1939), 261–87. See also Robert R. Hubach, "Illinois, Host to Well-known Nineteenth Century Authors," *ibid.*, XXXVIII (December, 1945), 446–67 and John T. Flanagan, "The Middle Western Historical Novel," *ibid.*, XXXVII (March, 1944), 7–47.

[2] Garland once told Eldon C. Hill in an interview that he gained his "first knowledge of Shakespeare, Tennyson, Dickens, Hawthorne, Longfellow, Whittier, Poe, Bryant and scores of other authors from McGuffey's readers." Quoted by the permission of Eldon C. Hill.

[3] *A Son of the Middle Border*, p. 115.

[4] *Ibid.*, p. 120.

[5] *Ibid.*, p. 192.

world of books. One day he happened to take down from a shelf
in the school library a little red volume called *Mosses from an
Old Manse*. He took the book home, and Hawthorne immediately
cast his spell upon him. The impression this book made on the
eighteen-year-old Garland is evident from the following passage
taken from an unpublished manuscript "My Literary Inspirations":

There were two of these volumes and I not only read them, I absorbed
them, pondered them, dreamed them. As Eggleston had taught me
the humor and pathos of the near at hand, so Hawthorne taught me the
mystical qualities of the town-pumps, the fire-place and the rose. He
became my literary hero, I read everything I could find of his work—
and I read all the comments upon his life and character which came my
way. ... I perceived that his artistry was immensely higher than that
of Eggleston and yet there was a kinship between them. They made
literature of American themes.

The subjects which Garland enjoyed most at the seminary
were the natural sciences, history, philosophy, literature, French,
and German.[1] He seems to have acquired at least a reading
knowledge of these languages.

In 1881 his parents moved to Ordway, Brown County, S. D.
Meanwhile, Hamlin did odd jobs; he was a book agent, clerk, and
lecturer. In 1882 together with his brother he tramped through
the Eastern states and worked as a carpenter in Illinois and Massachusetts. On his return West, he taught school in Grundy
County, Ill., and in 1883 took up a claim in McPherson
County, S. D., where he stayed for a year. While working in his
father's store, Garland, in accordance with his plan to become a
teacher, read eagerly Chambers' *Encyclopaedia* and Green's *Short
History of the English People* and made a careful outline of Taine's
History of English Literature.

In the fall of 1884, after having sold his claim, he went to Boston
with approximately one hundred and thirty dollars in his pocket
to qualify for teaching. Boston was then the literary center of
America, although challenged by New York, and Garland responded
quickly to the intellectual surge of the city, which Oliver Wendell
Holmes called "the Hub of the Universe."[2] Garland took up his

---

[1] I am indebted to Eldon C. Hill for this information.

[2] See George P. Lathrop, "Literary and Social Boston," *Harper's Monthly*,
LXII (February, 1881), 381–98; also Lilian Whiting, "Literary Boston," *Cosmopolitan*, X (December, 1890), 205–16.

quarters in a "hall bedroom" near the Public Library, and he lived sparingly on twenty dollars a month, devoting from ten to fourteen hours a day to study. He read such American classics as Emerson, Hawthorne, Whittier, and Longfellow, but he was also immersed in the scientific writings of Darwin, Spencer, Haeckel, Helmholtz, and Fiske, which helped to make him a confirmed evolutionist.[1] In one of his unpublished notebooks dated October 16, 1884, Garland quoted the following lines under the headline *Darwin*: "Man expresses his passions in common form with the brute. In fact man betrays his animal origin as clearly in his brute actions as in brute formation." And he added rather boastfully: "Therein Mr. Darwin confirms what I have argued for years. And I am glad to have such a man upon my side. Expression can be reasoned out and systematized for it has certain obvious laws at its root." His notebooks also reveal that he made a summary of Sidney Lanier's *The English Novel* (1883), outlined the history of French literature, and transcribed some of Emerson's

---

[1] See also p. 8. Note also the following entry in Garland's unpublished notebook dated May 15, 1885, under the heading *Spencer*: "Spencer's *Studies in Sociology* I have just read. It is a work preparatory to the great work upon which he is now at work. The thought most prominent in my mind as I lay down the book is how he riddles our petty ideas of society and the state. In his statement of the biases toward a one-sided view of the world he lays open the whole hidden machinery which moves us like puppets upon a wire. How ridiculous we will look to men a century hence with the hypothesis of evolution already grandly stated, yet men cling to the follies and nonsense of special dispensation and a carpenter God." Cf. also what Garland wrote later in life of his years in Boston: "From my meals I returned to my table in the library and read until closing time . . . I became an evolutionist in the fullest sense, accepting Spencer as the greatest living thinker. Fiske and Galton and Allen were merely assistants to the Master Mind whose generalizations included in their circles all modern discovery." *A Son of the Middle Border*, pp. 323-4. And again:

"These were growing days! I had moments of tremendous expansion, hours when my mind went out over the earth like a freed eagle, but these flights were always succeeded by fits of depression as I realized my weakness and my poverty. Nevertheless I persisted in my studies.

Under the influence of Spencer I traced a parallel development of the Arts and found a measure of scientific peace. Under the inspiration of Whitman I pondered the significance of democracy and caught some part of its spiritual import. With Henry George as guide, I discovered the main cause of poverty and suffering in the world, and so in my little room, living on forty cents a day, I was in a sense profoundly happy." *Ibid.*, p. 331.

works, for instance the essay "Self-Reliance." He often attended lectures and went frequently to see Edwin Booth, the great Shakespearean actor, at the theater. He became acquainted with Moses True Brown, director of the Boston School of Oratory, and was first a pupil and later an instructor at this school.

During the years 1885–89, he taught private classes in literature and lectured in and about Boston. One of his earliest projects was a series of lectures entitled "The Evolution of American Thought,"[1] based chiefly on Spencer, Whitman, and De Tocqueville. He lectured on a great variety of topics: Booth, Hugo,[2] Browning, Swinburne, Shakespeare, Lanier, Turgenev, Whitman, Impressionism, the drama, the modern novel in Germany and America, the local novel, etc., using Taine's method of explaining the authors as influenced by *race, milieu,* and *moment.*[3] He also delivered a great number of lectures on Henry George's land theories. The reading of *Progress and Poverty* together with his own experiences in the Middle West had made him an enthusiastic single-taxer. In fact, Garland's interest in the single tax movement was in important factor in his early career as a writer.

Thanks to Garland's unpublished notebooks, diaries, and letters, it is possible to trace his early activities as a lecturer and emerging writer. In 1885 he studied eagerly modern literature and soon began lecturing on literary and political topics. At one of his lectures he met Charles E. Hurd, literary editor of the *Boston Evening Transcript,* who later called his attention to James Whitcomb Riley, Joseph Kirkland, Ibsen, and Björnson.[4] Garland's

---

[1] This series of lectures go under different titles in his books and MSS, for instance: "The Development of American Ideals," "The Development of English Ideals," and "The Evolution of American Ideals."

[2] Cf. B. O. Flower, "Some Social Ideals Held by Victor Hugo," *Arena,* X (June, 1894), 104–9.

[3] See lecture, p. 440. Cf. also the following entry in one of his early notebooks. Under the headline *Grant Allen* Garland wrote: "Man like every other organism lives surrounded by an environment. Environment acts upon the organism and organism upon the environment. . . ." Garland may have had in mind such scientific books by Allen as *Physiological Aesthetics* (1877) and *The Evolutionist at Large* (1881). Later Alien had a temporary *succès de scandale* on account of his treatment of the sex problem in *The Woman Who Did* (1895).

[4] *A Son of the Middle Border,* p. 391. Garland wrote of Hurd later: ". . . in his gentle way he influenced me more than any other of my acquaintances

reading of Ibsen's dramas was of great importance to the rising author. In 1885 he also made the acquaintance of John J. Enneking and other American disciples of French Impressionism,[1] who may have stimulated his own use of an impressionistic technique. During the following year he made definite attempts at story writing, as his letters to E. W. Howe reveal, but lectures and classes interfered. He had established himself as a critic in a small way, and he wanted to become an essayist on literary topics. He wrote critical articles on Hugo, Scott, Dickens,[2] and other authors, which were printed in the *Transcript*. These articles, which were often crude and presumptuous, boldly stated his honest and often radical opinions concerning literary gods, and he was consequently critized by conservative writers. But his greatest ambition was to become a writer of fiction, and in a notebook dated March 3, 1886, there is a reference to a story of his called "Rise of Boomtown," which, however, was never printed.

From his arrival in Boston he eagerly read classic and contemporary literature, and his notebooks and letters reveal that, by 1886, he was probably familiar with most of the American classics and with a great number of contemporary American writers, such as, Howells, James, Whitman, Howe, Eugene Ware, Lanier,

at this time." *Roadside Meetings*, p. 32. Cf. also: "Instructed by Howells, we had read the novels of Valdés, Tolstoy, and Flaubert. Now, through William Archer, we studied the dramas of Ibsen and Björnson." *Ibid.*, p. 67. See also the following entry in Garland's notebook, May 15, 1885, under the headline *Björnson: Mansana*. "This is by all odds the most vigorous of the novels of Björnson that I have read. While *Arne* gives many touches of peasant life it is a more easily successful work. Having an intrinsic interest apart from the artistic construction put into it. ... *Mansana* is splendidly drawn in his psychological entanglements. ..." Garland added that Björnson's style as translated reminded him of that of Joaquin Miller. An American translation of *Arne* appeared in 1881, and *Captain Mansana and Other Stories* was brought out in 1882 by a New York publisher. They were reissued in 1884 and 1890 in a three-volume edition of Björnson's *Works*. In another notebook, 1885–6, Garland mentioned Kielland's *Garman and Worse*. An English translation of this novel appeared in London in 1884.

[1] Cf. Theodore Child, "A Note on Impressionist Painting," *Harper's Monthly*, LXXIV (January, 1887), 313–15.

[2] His attitude toward Dickens is seen in a letter dated February 25, 1934: ". . . as a student of fiction in Boston, I ridiculed his exaggerations and deplored his characters—for that was the fashion among the younger critics. Today . . . I feel something resembling awe as I confront the throngs of Dickens' characters."

Riley, Edgar Fawcett, Mary Wilkins Freeman, and Sarah Orne Jewett. In 1886 Howells began his "Editor's Study" for *Harper's Monthly*, and the fight between romanticism and realism was in full swing. Although a confirmed anti-romantic, in 1886 Garland considered the realism of Howells and James rather superficial and conventional.[1] He pleaded for a deeper kind of realism, exemplified, for instance, in the novels of the German writer, Friedrich Spielhagen, whom he studied carefully. In his notebooks he mentioned particularly *Lady Clara de Vere*, *Problematic Characters*, *Quisiana; or, Rest at Last*, *Hammer and Anvil*, and *Through Night to Light*. Among other German writers whom he enjoyed reading were: Auerbach, Heyse, Hackländer, Freytag, Heine,[2] Streckfuss, Sudermann, and Nordau, to whose *Conventional Lies of Society* (1884) Garland referred with admiration. His interest in aesthetic theory increased when Eugène Véron's *Æsthetics* fell into his hands about 1886.[3] Hugo was one of his early favorites,[4] and before 1890, as may be inferred from his notebooks, he was also acquainted with some of the works of George Sand,[5] Balzac, and Zola. There is, however, no evidence that he was vitally impressed by naturalistic reading.[6]

In the late eighties and early nineties Garland was a radical in literature and politics, and a faithful disciple of Spencer. His

---

[1] See Garland's lecture notes to "The Modern Novel in Germany and America," p. 445. For Garland's critical attitude toward Howells, see also the notebook dated May 15, 1885, in which he wrote: "Howells considered one of the greatest of our present writers, though attempting to show the 'Undiscovered Country' gives us never an insight into the inner world." A similar attitude toward Howells as well as James is evident in the notebook dated March 3, 1886. See also p. 139.

[2] Garland said of Heine in the notebook dated October 16, 1884: "He is almost the only writer who can make German light and readable. He is the best prosaist, even better than Goethe."

[3] Cf. p. 139 and Appendix, p. 433.

[4] Cf. Garland's entry in the notebook dated October 16, 1884, under the headline *Hugo's Man Who Laughs*. "I lay down this book with its closing sentence ringing in my ear. . . . What a magician is this man . . . Glorious Hugo . . . standing on a height above us we cannot fully estimate him."

[5] Cf. also Garland's entry in the notebook dated October 16, 1884: "George Sand's *Mauprat* is a powerful work. . . . She excels in the psychological, and therein has some resemblance to George Eliot." Garland also mentioned Jane Austen's *Persuasion* and *Pride and Prejudice*.

[6] See pp. 141-3.

earlier somewhat hostile attitude toward Howells changed by 1887, for late in January of that year he wrote a laudatory review of Howells' *The Minister's Charge* for the *Transcript.* Of other noteworthy reviews written for the the same paper in 1887, those of Kirkland's *Zury* and Harold Frederic's *Seth's Brother's Wife* should be mentioned. Besides his critical writing, Garland also wrote prose sketches and poetry, and was engaged in outlining a play, in which he intended to act himself. Garland's interest in Russian literature, especially in the works of Turgenev and Tolstoy, was great in 1887 and subsequent years, as is evident from the mention of their works in his notebooks and elsewhere. *Anna Karenina, Fathers and Sons,* and *Smoke* were some of his favorites. In his notebook dated 1885–6 Garland listed under the headline *Russian Literature:* "Turgenev, Tolstoy, Dostoevsky, and Stchedrin." By this time, Garland had also read some of the works of Hardy and other British realists and naturalists. He was later acquainted with some of the novels of Pérez Galdós and Palacio Valdés.

Of importance for Garland's development as an author was no doubt the influence which Howells exerted on his writing. Garland met Howells for the first time in June of 1887 at Lee's Hotel, Auburndale. This meeting marked the beginning of a friendship which lasted until Howells' death in 1920. Concerning his probable debt to Howells, Garland wrote of this period:

I wrote and rewrote, inspired by Howells, whose flexible yet always beautiful style I greatly admired. I had no wish to imitate him—my expression must be my own—but the care, the judgment, the taste which were so evident in every line that he published, held me to my resolution.[1]

In 1887 after almost three years in Boston, Garland made the first of a series of trips to the West, and this, together with the encouragement of Joseph Kirkland, made him turn definitely to the writing of fiction. A good portrait of the twenty-seven-year-old newspaper reporter from Boston was drawn by Kirkland in an unpublished letter to his family dated July 4, 1887.

Hamlin Garland spent Saturday night and Sunday forenoon with me. Enthusiast—country-boy—farmer's son—largely self-educated—wants to reform the literature of our country! Reconstruct it on re-

---

[1] *Roadside Meetings,* p. 121.

alistic basis. Hates Lowell, Holmes and the other fossil representatives of classicism. Loves Walt Whitman and Howells and Howe and Miss Baylor and *me*. He has a great work on hand, "Literary Democracy," apotheosis of common people. Wants me to devote myself to literature even at the sacrifice of business.[1]

Another of Garland's contemporaries, Joseph Edgar Chamberlin, penned the following picture of the young radical from the prairies:

> In appearance, in the '80's, Garland was a young man of certain singularities, but of great beauty. He was of medium height, of supple figure, with abundant brown hair, and wore a rather long, brown beard, that gave him a sort of apostolic appearance. His grave, meditative manner heightened this apostolic effect. He would have made an excellent model for John, the Beloved Disciple. A very young man then he had the weight of studious centuries on his excellent square shoulders. Also he had joined the Anti-Poverty Society, and espoused the doctrines of Henry George; and he deeply felt the sorrows of the disinherited laboring man. I doubt if ever Garland has been as serious in his life as he was in 1887 or if he ever will be again.[2]

During his trip to the Middle West in the summer of 1887, Garland was struck by the loneliness of the prairie, the endless toil of the people, the hopelessness and futility of the life led by the worn-out farmers and farmers' wives. He saw the vast plains and the human mites against them in a new light, apparently colored by his reading:

> My study of Spencer, Whitman and other[s] of the great leaders of the world, my years of absorbed reading in the library, my days of loneliness and hunger in the city had swept me into a far bleak land of philosophic doubt where even the most daring of my classmates would hesitate to follow me.[3]

His mood of bitterness and indignation at the social system, under which the farmers labored, craved an outlet and he asked himself:

> "Why have these stern facts never been put into our literature as they have been used in Russia and in England? Why has this land no storytellers like those who have made Massachusetts and New Hampshire illustrious."[4]

---

[1] Published by the permission of the Newberry Library. Garland met Whitman in October 1888.

[2] "Hamlin Garland—The Hardy of the West" in *Hamlin Garland* (pamphlet), p. 10.

[3] *A Son of the Middle Border*, p. 357.

[4] *Ibid.*, p. 356.

Garland returned to the East in the fall of the same year with
material for stories, which he was eager to tell. During this trip
to the West he wrote the first draft of the poem "Color in the
Wheat," and the story "Mrs. Ripley's Trip," based on a tale
which his mother had told him.[1] He even tried to sell some of
his sketches and stories to various magazines, but they were
rejected, because, as it seemed, they were too crude, or too bitter,
or too true to life.

In 1888 Garland succeeded in placing some sketches, articles,
and poems in *Harper's Weekly* and the *American*. A letter to
him from Kirkland, dated February 13, 1888, gives evidence of
Garland's creative activity. "Three novels[2] at once under way ..."
In 1888 he had also begun working on a play entitled *Under the
Wheel*.

Garland saw James A. Herne's domestic drama *Drifting Apart*[3]
late in 1888 or early in 1889. He met the actor-playwright in
1889 as can be inferred from letters exchanged between them
and an instant friendship, equally profitable to both, sprang
up between them. "My happiest days in Boston were associated
with the Hernes," he wrote once.[4] Not only did Garland write
two plays himself, *Under the Wheel* and *A Member of the Third
House* (never printed as a play), but he also was active in the
creation of a new American drama, and in the establishment of
the first of the "Little Theaters" in America.[5] He wrote Eldon
C. Hill in 1939:

---

[1] *A Son of the Middle Border*, pp. 371–2.

[2] One was "Rise of Boomtown."

[3] After seeing *Drifting Apart* Garland sent Herne the following undated
letter printed in a circular: "I want to write and thank you for the very great
pleasure I took in your play, 'Drifting Apart.' It was at once a surprise and
an inspiration. A surprise to find such work done by a man whose very name
was unfamiliar to me; an inspiration, because I said he is a product of the
new spirit of truth. Perhaps, without knowing it, you are linked with the new
school of genuine realists; not the realists of the tank-drama and the fire-engine,
but the school of artists who are trying to depict the essentials of the life common to us all of to-day. ...

In such moments we feel what Valdés meant when he said, 'There are no
trivial things, absolutely. Values are relative; that which is trivial to one, is a
great fact to another; the death of a child, for example.' "

[4] *Roadside Meetings*, p. 72.

[5] See Appendix, pp. 451–3.

With regard to my work in promoting the drama, it is worthy of note, I think, that I drew up the first suggestion for an "Independent Theater" in Boston, and that for nearly twenty years[1] I worked with Howells, Herne and Brander Matthews along these lines. By way of articles, lectures and letters to the Transcript and other papers I clamored for a drama that should be true to our way of life and be filled by characters of our own place and time.[2]

He also helped to put the Ibsen-inspired play *Margaret Fleming*[3] on the stage at Chickering Hall, Boston, in 1891. Garland's brother, Franklin, was in the cast and Garland himself served as "Man in Front" for six weeks. Herne and Garland read and commented on each other's plays and on June 4, 1889, Herne wrote Garland:

... thank you for your offered aid in rewriting "Drifting Apart," but let me try first what I can accomplish. I rewrote the parts of Percy and Mary on Sunday—worked hard all day. I never did such hard work—or rather I never found writing such hard work. It didn't seem to come, I had to *think* it all out—*all day* and 7 pages—and my day's work is usually 30 pages. Katharine C. says it is fine work, but I'm going over it again. If I do make fine work of it, it will be a reflection of Hamlin Garland and his mentorship. I never saw my faults, conspicuous as I know they must be to others. I could not see them, until you made them so clear. I shall take the 1st and 3rd acts with me and when I have them as perfect as *I* can get them I'll ask you to read them.

This seems to indicate that Garland had a hand—if not in the writing—at least in the revision and perfection of *Drifting Apart*. To a certain extent, Garland probably contributed to Herne's evolution from melodramatist to realist, for at the time of their acquaintance (1889) Garland was familiar with some of the writings of Ibsen, Zola, Hardy, Turgenev, and Tolstoy. Garland even succeeded in converting the Hernes to the single tax ideas. On June 12, 1889, Herne wrote Garland: ". . . we are single taxers from the *feet up*." Garland's paramount interest in the single tax[4] found expression in his play *Under the Wheel* and in the short

---

[1] This is an exaggeration. Garland met Herne in 1889 and Herne died in 1901.

[2] Published by the permission of Eldon C. Hill.

[3] See pp. 453–5. Cf. also "An Epoch-Marking Drama," *Arena*, IV (July, 1891), 247–9.

[4] To Garland the single tax implied far more than merely a system of taxation. He said in 1891: "Beginning on the solid earth, it [the single tax]

story "Under the Lion's Paw," which were both completed in
1889. In theory, Garland was not a socialist, but occasionally
he discussed socialism with Howells, who leaned far more than
Garland toward socialism. Garland wrote once: "I have never
been a socialist—as you [Professor Leonard] may have guessed
from a reading of my book—and the work of Lenin and Trotsky
would have cured me if I had been. I am an individualist in
theory, Browning, Ibsen, Whitman are more nearly my masters
than Marx and Lenin. I hate despotism in the socialists as I hate
it in the kaisers." Concerning early influences on his social thinking Garland wrote in 1935:

... Henry George was a powerful influence, much more so than Bellamy, William Morris or Shelley. Shelley never influenced me in economic ways. His lyric poetic note was his main appeal to me. I had
very little interest in his long poems. Lanier was a powerful influence
in several ways and so was Whitman. Howells I have fully acknowledged.
Without doubt Henry George opened my eyes to the chasm between the
rich and the poor. Bernard Shaw once told me that Henry George liberated him, and long before Bellamy, *Progress and Poverty* influenced
... us.

Some of Garland's reading and literary interests in the years 1888
and 1889 are shown in the following transcript from a notebook
dated 1888–9:

Books to Be Read at Once:
Ibsen's book of dramas.[1]

---

mounts through 'Free Trade, Free Production, Free Land, Free Men!' to the
highest conception of truth and right. It is a road leading to a land in whose
serene air vices die and virtues bloom." "A New Declaration of Rights," *Arena*,
III (January, 1891), 162.

[1] For some of the titles I supply additional information: Henrik Ibsen, *The
Pillars of Society and Other Plays*. Camelot Series. No. 31 (New York, 1888).
Cf. also Garland's library p. 426; Mrs. Humphry Ward, *Robert Elsmere* (New
York, 1888); Olive Schreiner (Ralph Iron), *The Story of an African Farm* (New
York, 1888), first published in London, 1883; Opie Read, *Len Gansett* (Boston,
1888); Edward Waldo Emerson, *Emerson in Concord: A Memoir* (Boston, 1889);
Kalevala: The National Epic of Finland. Tr. into English verse by J. M. Crawford. 2 vols. (New York, 1886; London, 1888); I. F. Hapgood, ed., *Epic Songs
of Russia* (New York, 1886). It is probable that Garland had the French version
in mind, *Le Roman expérimental* (Paris, 1880). We know that Garland had a
reading knowledge of French. See p. 65. Cf. also Émile Zola, *The Experimental
Novel, and Other Essays*. Tr. by B. M. Sherman (New York, 1894). For Véron
and Kielland see pp. 69, 67 n. 4 respectively.

"Robert Elsmere," Mrs. Ward.
"Story of an African Farm," Schreiner.
"Len Gansett," Opie Read.
"Emerson" by Emerson.
"Poems" of Jones Very.
"Poems" of Ellery Channing.
"Poems" of Paul Heyse.
Wagner, "On Conducting."

Books to Buy:

Kalevala.
Book of Kings. Chandos Classics.
"Epic Songs of Russia," Hapgood.
Zola's "Experimental Novel."
Véron.
Björnson.
Ibsen.
Turgenev.
Hugo.
Kielland.

Significant for this study are the references to Zola, Turgenev, and Ibsen at this early date. Concerning his reading in the eighties and nineties, Garland wrote Hill in 1938: "I read and weighed nearly every book published each year in America."[1] The statement is of course an exaggeration, but on the whole Garland seems to have been an omnivorous reader and even before 1890 he was fairly well acquainted with American and European literature, classic as well as modern.

In 1890 he met the editor of the *Arena*, B. O. Flower, who published his play, *Under the Wheel*,[2] which also appeared during the same year in book form. Flower not only printed some of Garland's early work, but also sent him on a tour to the West to investigate labor and farm conditions. On November 21, 1890, Garland sent Herne the following enthusiastic letter:

Things is [*sic*] boomin' here. These Flowers are "Corkers" ... I've accepted the editorial management of a "Single-Tax Department"—and so it goes! ... Gods! Aint we livin' in great days? ... B. O. Flower and

---

[1] Printed by the permission of Eldon C. Hill.

[2] In 1892 the play was republished in a novelized form as *Jason Edwards* and will be dealt with in the following as a novel.

I are getting chums. He's one o' my kind. Dont smoke, chew, drink . . .
He's indefatigable . . . He's concentrated moral purpose.

And behind him stands that brother of his pouring out money wherever needed . . . . I'm going to go west to listen mainly.

Flower pushed Garland on in many ways. He exhorted him not
to suppress his realism and urged him to be as frank and outspoken as he wanted. Flower's patronage of Garland and other
sincere writers should be remembered,[1] for with the probable exception of the *Arena* American magazines[2] of the time were slow
to sponsor young, radical writers.

Before we proceed in our investigation of Garland's early works
it is necessary to examine more closely some of the immediate
conditions or issues of the day which may help to explain Garland's writings—and, to an extent, also both Crane's and Norris's. Current events were reflected in certain periodicals,[3] of
which the *Arena* was a leading exponent of progressive and re-
formative thought and a forum for the discussion of social and
economic questions. David H. Dickason has found that the
"advanced liberal thought" of the *Arena* embraced

advocacy of governmental relief of unemployment by a public works
building program; the right of labor to organize and to strike; municipal
slum-clearance and construction of low-cost housing units; federal or
state control of the liquor traffic; reform of the prison system with an
extension of industrial training; and governmental ownership of natural
monopolies. In addition, the *Arena* antedated the muckrakers by ten
years in its attacks on corruption in the trusts; and also championed such
diverse movements as feminism, the eradication of child labor, and mod-
ernization of the nation's school system.[4]

---

[1] See David H. Dickason, "Benjamin Orange Flower, Patron of the Realists,"
American Literature, XIV (May, 1942), 148–56.

[2] *The Yellow Book* had a great number of American imitators, which spon-
sored new writers and new techniques. These magazines were, however, of
short duration and exercised little influence on the reading public at large. The
following ten were mentioned in the *Literary World* for February 8, 1896: *The
Chap-Book, The Bibelot, The Philistine, The Lark, The Bauble, The Horn-Book,
Book-Talk, The Olio, The Fly Leaf,* and *Miss Blue Stocking.*

[3] Social topics and other current events were dealt with in such magazines
as the *Nation*, the *North American Review*, the *Independent*, the *Outlook*, *Scribner's, McClure's*, the *Cosmopolitan*, the *Standard*, and the *Forum*.

[4] "Benjamin Orange Flower, Patron of the Realists," *American Literature*,
XIV (May, 1942), 148 n. 6. The *Arena* had a circulation of over one hundred
thousand. *Ibid.*, p. 149.

Let us first focus our interest on a few of the subjects mentioned. The slums in certain large cities, as in New York, Boston, Philadelphia, and Chicago, grew worse toward the end of the century.[1] In a series of editorials and articles in the early nineties Flower exposed the "Cancer Spots in Metropolitan Life" and illustrated how people were victimized by social conditions or adverse fate.

On one night last February, *one hundred and twenty-four* destitute homeless men begged for shelter in the cells; of this number *sixty-eight were native born Americans.* The station was so crowded, that in *one cell, eight by nine and a half feet, fourteen men passed the night,* some standing a part of the night, while others lay packed like sardines. After a time, those on the floor exchanged places with the poor creatures who had been standing. The following incident related [in a book entitled *Chicago's Dark Places*] is as typical as it is pathetic: An old man, cold, homeless, destitute, not knowing where to lay his head, was seen to take a shovel and deliberately break a window in a store opposite a police station. He was immediately arrested. "What did you do that for?" demanded the officer. " 'Cos I was hungry and cold and knew if you got me I could have food and shelter." He was taken care of *after* he had broken the law. There is something radically wrong with social conditions which compel men who find every avenue from exposure and starvation closed, to become law-breakers in order to live.[2]

Note the following episode:

One laboring man being interrogated by one of the commissioners who gathered the facts for the author of this work [*Chicago's Dark Places*], replied to the question, "What can you say for those who won't work, who are commonly called the 'bums of society'?" in such a thoughtful and suggestive way that I give his words verbatim.

"Let me ask, What is a bum? As a rule, you will find him to be a creature degraded by circumstances and evil conditions. Let me illustrate. A man loses his job by sickness or some other unavoidable cause. He seeks work, and I have shown you how difficult it is to find it. He fails time and time again. Is there any wonder that he grows discouraged, and that, picking up his meals at the free lunch counter, sleeping in the wretched lodging houses, associating with the filthy and degraded, he, step by step, drifts further away from the habits of integrity and industry that used to be a part of himself? He sinks lower and lower until, overcome by circumstances, he is at the bottom of the social ladder,—at once a menace and a disgrace to the city. Instead of blaming and condemning him, poor fellow, we should look at the circumstances that made him what he is, and endeavor to remedy them."[3]

---

[1] See pp. 3-4.

[2] Flower, "Cancer Spots in Metropolitan Life," *Arena*, IV (November, 1891), 761-2.

[3] *Ibid.*, p. 762.

Two factors especially contributed to the misery in the slum areas: the low theaters and music halls, and above all the saloons, "the black plague of nineteenth century life,"[1] according to Flower. The debate on the "saloon curse" in tenement areas was carried on with vigor and militancy in newspapers and magazines.[2] Garland and Crane, both contributors to the *Arena*,[3] and acquainted

[1] *Ibid.*, p. 766. Cf. also the following articles by Flower: "A Present-Day Tragedy," *Arena*, X (June, 1894), 115–16; "Wellsprings and Feeders of Immorality," *Arena*, XI (December, 1894), 56–70; "Social Conditions as Feeders of Immorality," *Arena*, XI (February, 1895), 399–412; "They Have Fallen into the Wine Press: Some Facts Illustrating the Onward March of Uninvited Poverty," *Arena*, IX (February, 1894), 384–99. Flower and others, "The Tenement House Curse," *Arena*, IX (April, 1894), 659–84, with bibliography bearing on this subject, pp. 683–4; William P. McLoughlin, "Evictions in New York's Tenement Houses," *Arena*, VII (December, 1892), 48–57; Eva McDonald Valesh, "The Tenement House Problem in New York," *Arena*, VII (April, 1893), 580–6.

[2] Vol. I of the *Arena* (December, 1889–May, 1890) contained four articles on the "Rum Problem." The one, written by Henry George, *Arena*, I (January, 1890), 196–208, begins: "For years the liquor question has been largely and widely discussed in the United States. . . . Intemperance is a grave evil." See also Vols. II, III, VII, and VIII of the *Arena*. For an account of the liquor problem, see Nevins, *op. cit.*, pp. 335 ff.; also Daniel Dorchester, *The Liquor Problem in All Ages* (New York, 1888); D. L. Colvin, *Prohibition in the United States* (New York, 1926); and E. H. Cherrington, ed., *Standard Encyclopaedia of the Liquor Problem* (Westerville, Ohio, 1924–30).

[3] Garland contributed the following articles and stories to the *Arena:* "Ibsen as a Dramatist," *Arena*, II (June, 1890), 72–82; "Under the Wheel. A Modern Play in Six Scenes," *Arena*, II (July, 1890), 182–228; "The Return of a Private," *Arena*, III (December, 1890), 97–113; "A New Declaration of Rights," *Arena*, III (January, 1891), 157–84; "The Test of Elder Pill," *Arena*, III (March, 1891), 480–501; "A Prairie Heroine," *Arena*, IV (July, 1891), 223–46; "An Evening at the Corner Grocery. A Western Character Sketch," *Arena*, IV (September, 1891), 504–12; "Mr. and Mrs. Herne," *Arena*, IV (October, 1891), 543–60; "Uncle Ripley's Speculation," *Arena*, V (December, 1891), 125–35; "A Spoil of Office: A Story of the Modern West," *Arena*, V (January, 1892), 253–68; *Arena*, V (February, 1892), 376–400; *Arena*, V (March, 1892), 495–522; *Arena*, V (April, 1892), 619–44; *Arena*, V (May, 1892), 749–74; *Arena*, VI (June, 1892), 104–32; "The Alliance Wedge in Congress," *Arena*, V (March, 1892), 447–57; "Under the Dome of the Capitol. A Prose Etching," *Arena*, VI (September, 1892), 468–70; "The West in Literature," *Arena*, VI (November, 1892), 669–76; "The Future of Fiction," *Arena*, VII (April, 1893), 513–24; "A Human Habitation," *Arena*, IX (December, 1893), 130; "The Land Question, and Its Relation to Art and Literature," *Arena*, IX (January, 1894), 165–75; "The Single Tax in Actual Application," *Arena*, X (June,

through personal experiences with the slums, were further stimulated to use them as settings by this popular discussion.

A problem closely linked with that of the slum was the influence
of the environment on the individual. A writer in the *Arena* of
1891 gave the following illustration:

Take, for example, a boy brought up in the slums around Tomkins
Square, in New York City. From his earliest childhood he is of necessity
familiar with all manner of wickedness; the best dressed women of his
neighborhood are fallen women; the boys who have the most money to
spend are those who lead vicious lives; the brightest house is the saloon.
New York City is the metropolis of vice as she is of trade, and every vice
in the long catalogue of sin has a representative practitioner among the
varied nationalities that swarm her slums. I am told by the most eminent
of her Police Justices that there is no known vice of ancient or modern
times that has not, some time or other, been recorded in her police court
records as an offence committed. Can a child spend his life amid such
environment without being, both in body and brain, affected by it? For
a child to grow up virtuous in such a locality is little less than a miracle—
and the day of miracles has passed.

If a child is born and bred to manhood in such environment, he has no
choice but to become wicked. He is not free to choose good from evil.
He has no discriminating sense of right and wrong. His moral responsibility is *nil*. What little conscience he may have inherited is soon blunted
and lost. He has no conscious remorse—no self contempt for his wickedness. He is beyond reformation; for his brain has been shaped by the
thoughts which his environment necessarily engenders, until it is incapable of willing virtue—just as the feet of certain Chinese women are put
in clamps until they are permanently deformed and incapable of loco-
motion.[1]

The theme illustrated here is a favorite one in naturalistic
fiction. It is the grim story of an individual, apparently devoid
of free will, molded by his environment, to which his responsiveness
may have been facilitated by inherited propencities for drink,
etc. Such a theme lead to a consideration of the existence of
free will, a question made popular by the growing interest in he-

1894), 52–8; and "A Woman in the Camp: A Christmas Sketch," *Arena*, XI
(December, 1894), 90–7.

Crane's contributions consisted of two proletarian sketches: "An Ominous
Baby," *Arena*, IX (May, 1894), 819–21 and "The Men in the Storm," *Arena*,
X (October, 1894), 662–7.

[1] Arthur Dudley Vinton, "Morality and Environment," *Arena*, III (April,
1891), 574.

redity[1] during the last decades of the nineteenth century. Interest in the subject is extensively shown in the works of Garland, Crane, and Norris.[2]

A serious agrarian question in the eighties and nineties was the plight of the farmers, particularly those of the Middle West.[3] Since Garland was a farmer's son, it is but natural that he was keenly alive to the situation, as some of his own books and articles illustrate, *Main-Travelled Roads*, for instance, *Jason Edwards*, and *A Spoil of Office*.

Garland was also aware of the plight of the farmers' wives, who took their place in the growing struggle for the emancipation of woman. In the last decades of the century the movement for woman's rights grew in strength and activity,[4] as is evinced by a

---

[1] See, for instance, A. M. Holmes, "Heredity and Environment," *Arena*, IX (April, 1894), 571–81; Helen H. Gardener, "Environment; Can Heredity Be Modified?" *Arena* X (July, 1894), 145–52; B. O. Flower, "Early Environment in Home Life," *Arena*, X (September, 1894), 483–93; same author, "The Right of the Child Considered in the Light of Heredity and Prenatal Influence," *Arena*, XIII (July, 1895), 243–62; Sydney Barrington Elliot, "Prenatal Influence," *Arena*, IX (March, 1894), 417–26; Helen H. Gardener, "Heredity: Is Acquired Character or Condition Transmittable?" *Arena*, IX (May, 1894), 769–76; this article deals with theories of heredity held by Lamarck, Darwin, and Weismann; M. Louise Mason, "Prenatal Influence," *Arena*, X (September, 1894), 545–6; and J. J. Morrissey, "Hereditary Influences and Medical Progress," *Arena*, XVII (January, 1897), 283–92.

[2] See pp. 184 ff.

[3] See pp. 5–6. See also J. R. Dodge, "The Discontent of the Farmer," *Century Magazine*, XLIII (January, 1892), 447–56; Alfred R. Wallace, "The Social Quagmire and the Way Out of It," *Arena*, VII (March, 1893), 395–410; and W. D. McCrackan, "The Farmer and the Land," *Arena*, IX (April, 1894), 625–31.

[4] Much was also done: women's colleges founded (Vassar in 1861, Smith in 1871), co-education introduced (first at Oberlin in 1834), property law changed, etc. Feminism was particularly strong on the West coast. For the discussion see, for instance, F. Benedict Herzog, "On Higher Education for Women," *Century Magazine*, XXVI (1883), 157–8; Jos. Rodes Buchanan, "The Cosmic Sphere of Woman," *Arena*, I (May, 1890), 666–81; Frances E. Willard, "The Woman's Cause Is Man's," *Arena*, V (May, 1892), 712–25; Sara A. Underwood, "A Woman's Case," *Arena*, VI (August, 1892), 334–60; Mary A. Livermore, "Women's Clubs—A Symposium," *Arena*, VI (August, 1892), 362–88; Cora Maynard, "The Woman's Part," *Arena*, VII (March, 1893), 476–86; James L. Hughes, "The Last Protest against Woman's Enfranchisement," *Arena*, X (July, 1894), 201–13; Josephine K. Henry, "The New Woman of

rapid survey of magazine articles, which also considered marriage[1]
and divorce problems[2] and gave special attention to dress reform
struggles.[3] B. O. Flower introduced an editorial for the 1891
Arena: "The constantly broadening sphere of woman's influence
is to me the most hopeful and important sign of our times. The
era of woman has dawned, bearing the unmistakable prophecy
of a far higher civilization than humanity has ever known."[4]
A woman writer remarked: "Leading thinkers among women of
broad culture have long been pleading for the freedom of woman,
urging her right to education, wages, and suffrage on an equality
with man."[5] Finally, in an article in 1893 B. O. Flower commented on the dress question:

---

the New South," *Arena,* XI (February, 1895), 353–62; Annah Robinson Wat-
son, "The Attitude of Southern Women on the Suffrage Question," *Arena,* XI
(February, 1895), 363–9; Helen H. Gardener, "Shall Women Vote?" *Arena,*
XV (December, 1895), 67–79; Anna Edith Updegraff Hilles, "Woman in
Society To-Day," *Arena,* XVI (July, 1896), 263–75; and Susan B. Anthony,
"The Status of Woman, Past, Present, and Future," *Arena,* XVII (May, 1897),
901–8. I have stressed the debate in the *Arena* because Garland was a con-
tributor to that magazine and one of the first American writers to portray the
"New Woman." See also the chap. on "The American Woman" in Arthur
Meier Schlesinger, *The Rise of the City,* pp. 121–59. For satires on the "new
woman," see Burton Harrison's novel *A Bachelor Maid* (New York, 1894) and
Robert Grant's *Unleavened Bread* (New York, 1900).

[1] See, for instance, the discussion in the *Cosmopolitan,* VI (November, 1888),
93–6 in the column "Live Questions. Is Marriage a Failure?" See also Hiram
M. Stanley, "Our Civilization and the Marriage Problem," *Arena,* II (June,
1890), 94–100.

[2] See an editorial on "The Divorce Problem in the United States" in the
Arena, V (December, 1891), 136–44. See also Schlesinger's comment in *op.
cit.,* p. 154: "The growing absorption of women in interests outside the home,
whether as social butterflies or as bread-winners or reformers, seemed to some
a sufficient explanation of the waning sanctity of the marriage relation. Whatever the reason there could be no doubt as to the fact. With sixteen thousand
divorces granted in 1878, the number rose to nearly twenty-nine thousand in
the year 1888 and to almost forty-eight thousand in 1898."

[3] Frances E. Russell, "Freedom in Dress for Women," *Arena,* VIII (June,
1893), 70–7; Hattie C. Flower, "The Rational Dress Movement," *Arena,* IX
(February, 1894), 305–26; and Ellen Battelle Dietrick, "Male and Female Attire
in Various Nations and Ages," *Arena,* X (August, 1894), 353–65.

[4] "The Era of Woman," *Arena,* IV (August, 1891), 382.

[5] Frances E. Russell, "Woman's Dress," *Arena,* III (February, 1891), 352.

The systematic crusade for the introduction of a rational dress for woman, which is being carried on under the auspices of the Dress Committee of the National Council of Women, is a part of a far greater conflict which the best thought of our age has made possible, and which marks the last quarter of the nineteenth century as the dawning time of woman's era."[1]

Indubitably the discussion and the actual victories won for woman in society influenced writers like Garland and Norris, for the "new woman" type appears frequently in their works.[2]

In his first collection of short stories, *Main-Travelled Roads* (1891), containing six realistic and naturalistic stories of the Middle West and representing perhaps Garland's main literary achievement, he voiced some of the issues mentioned above, namely, marriage, the emancipation of woman, and the agrarian situation. The stories pictured the drab, hapless life of Midwest farmers, who struggled heroically but gained few of life's comforts. Although Garland was in sympathy with these unhappy people, particularly with the women, he succeeded on the whole in retaining the artist's point of view without moralizing or preaching. In these impressionistic stories the author came close to naturalism in his choice of subject matter and characters, and in his emphasis on social determinism. Critics in the Middle West leveled an instant attack at the book, because of the ugly picture it gave of life on the farm. Eastern reviewers were on the whole friendly, and Howells wrote:

The stories are full of those gaunt, grim, sordid, pathetic, ferocious figures, whom our satirists find so easy to caricature as Hayseeds, and whose blind groping for fairer conditions is so grotesque to the newspapers and so menacing to the politicians. They feel that something is wrong, and they know that the wrong is not theirs. The type caught in Mr. Garland's book is not pretty; it is ugly and often ridiculous; but it is heart-breaking in its rude despair.[3]

---

[1] "Parisian Fashionable Folly Versus American Common Sense," *Arena*, VIII (June, 1893), 130.

[2] See pp. 220–8, 361 ff.

[3] Introduction to *Main-Travelled Roads*, p. 4. B. O. Flower said of the stories: "With the boldness of Tolstoi, with the originality in treatment of Ibsen, and with a wealth of tenderness, love, and humanity far exceeding either, Mr. Garland has in 'Main-Travelled Roads' given a work destined, I believe, to hold a permanent place in our literature, and to be one of the most characteristic and valued contributions of the new school known as Impressionism." *Arena*, IV (August, 1891), xvii.

The following year (1892) saw the publication of four of Garland's books, namely *Jason Edwards, A Member of the Third House, A Little Norsk,* and *A Spoil of Office.*[1] Of great interest and importance for this study is *Jason Edwards,*[2] which described tenement life in Boston and settlers' life in the fictitious Boomtown in the Middle West. Jason Edwards, a mechanic-farmer, and his wife and daughters had to leave Boston when conditions became unbearable because of their poverty, and hopefully they set out for the "Golden West" in quest of free land. But land was no longer free, for it was in the hands of land sharks, and the Edwards were as unfortunate as in Boston. Finally nature combined with society to defeat them. A hailstorm destroyed the wheat, and Jason was paralyzed in his shattered house. Defeat was everywhere, for Jason had failed in the West, too. Disillusioned he went back to Boston to live with his daughter Alice, who had been torn for years between marriage and her wish to have a career of her own, and her sense of duty to her parents. When there was no way out for her parents, she eventually gave in and promised to marry Walter Reeves, her patient suitor.

The novel is perhaps Garland's closest approach to naturalism. The Boston slum was depicted with a naturalist's care for significant and unpleasant detail. But despite the vice and brutality

---

[1] The novels will be dealt with in the order given above, since Garland filed copyright on *Jason Edwards* on January 4, on *A Member of the Third House* on March 3, on *A Little Norsk* on June 18, and on *A Spoil of Office* on October 30. See Hill, *op. cit.*, p. 145.

[2] Later in life Garland wrote somewhat apologetically of the novel: " 'Jason Edwards' ... is of value only as an indication of the bitter and accusing mood of that day, a time of parlor socialists, single-taxers, militant populists, Ibsen dramas, and Tolstoyian encyclicals against greed, lust, and caste." *Roadside Meetings*, p. 126. That *Jason Edwards* grew out of experiences actually observed, is affirmed by the following statement made by Garland in an interview for the *Los Angeles Herald*, November 27, 1892, when he and his parents visited the city during a trip to California:

"When I deal with farm life it is from what I know, and all the incidents spoken of in this work I have been through with myself.

There is a mystic quality connected with free land, and it has always allured men into the West. I wanted to show that it is a myth. I have desired to deal with the American workingman when his livelihood was cut off. I have made an active study of the iron workers and have talked with men who had pursued the more elusive paradise, but who had returned without finding it." Quoted by Hill, *op. cit.*, pp. 148–9.

of the surroundings, the Edwards were not morally affected by
them. Like Jane Snowdon, the heroine of Gissing's *The Nether
World* (1889), Alice, somewhat idealized, was unsullied by the
slums.[1] Alice was no Nana or Gervaise; on the contrary, with her
physical and moral strength she heralded a new type: the independent, modern woman.

In his next novel, *A Member of the Third House*, Garland continued his exposure of the evils of American society.[2] From the
slums of Boston and the conditions of the farmers in the Middle
West he turned to the political life of big cities. In the character
of Wilson Tuttle, in some ways the author himself, Garland drew
a portrait of a man who stood for truth, justice, and honesty in
the midst of corruption and political nefariousness.

A Little Norsk grew out of Garland's adventure in a blizzard when
holding down his claim in 1883. The novelette relates how two
bachelors, pioneers in South Dakota, took care of a small Norwegian
girl, Elga, whose parents had frozen to death in a snowstorm.[3]
She grew up with them, they sent her to school, and although
both were in love with her, they married her to one of her school
friends, Will Kendall, whom she thought she loved. He died,
however, after having displayed his dishonest character. The
story ends with the prospect that one of the bachelors would

[1] Cf. Zola's Lalie in *L'Assommoir* and Crane's Maggie pp. 255 ff.

[2] Flower, who read the play version, wrote Garland on September 3, 1890:
"I am not, however, certain that you do not lay yourself and your publishers
liable notwithstanding your preface, because you graphically portray so many
individuals that will be readily recognized, then passing from that without changing your characters you picture individuals which in the first part of the play
are well known personages as being criminals ... I think it would be a most
wise thing to have the opinion of Attorney-general Waterman on the drama be
fore it is published, as he would be able to speak, I think, authoritatively as
to whether it would render you or the publishers in any way liable." This reveals how close he kept to his models. Garland said of the novel in the interview
for the *Los Angeles Herald*: "*The Member of the Third House* really sprang ob-
scurely from experiences in Chicago and Boston and certain transactions in
Washington some three or four years ago. It is probable that Boston contributed
the largest part." Quoted by Hill, *op. cit.*, p. 149.

[3] Garland wrote Eldon C. Hill in 1935 that except for the incident of the
death of Elga's mother the book was "purely fictional." Garland said of the
story in the interview for the *Los Angeles Herald*: "*A Little Norsk* is really a
statement of the problem of two modern men in their relation to each other
and in relation to a motherless girl." Quoted by Hill, *op. cit.*, p. 149.

marry Elga and take care of her baby. The realism of the early part of the book describing the blizzard is vivid. The latter part, on the other hand, is conventional with its happy ending, and it lacks the force and originality of the first chapters. The story is an early attempt at a psychological novel, heralding *Rose of Dutcher's Coolly*, rather than an exposé of social conditions.

In *A Spoil of Office*,[1] a political novel, Garland described the

[1] A critic in the *Mexican Herald* spoke favorably of the book, adding: "Mr. Garland has done work worthy of the great Russian writers of our day . . . He has something to say and he knows how to say it, for not only does he observe with a Zolaesque fidelity but he paints with broad, free strokes a picture of contemporary America." (Undated clipping in the Garland file.) It is interesting to note that Garland was compared with Zola and the Russians. Garland said of the novel in the interview for the *Los Angeles Herald* quoted above:

"The idea in the *Spoil of Office* was to treat of the West and its great political movements and revolutions as they would stand related to a young man of political ambitions like Bradley Talcott. The whole book deals with things and events as seen from this young man's center. I tried to take him through a development of a farm hand whose opportunities had been meager and who did not realize his power of development, on through many changes, up to his life in congress—that is, to apparent success.

His success, however, from my point of view, consisted in his keeping himself clean and unspotted in his public life, so full of temptations. The climax of his life, in my estimation, came in his rise to a comprehension of the altruism which was expressed throughout by Ida Wilbur. While it is a political novel, it is a political novel as the veritist would make it . . . The book is full of problems, the inordinate growth of cities, the apparent thinning out of the rural population and other problems. In this book I have no mouthpiece, I aim to have it an actual work and having it an actual scene of the West. . . . While I am a reformer I want to be an artist and I do not aim to teach obviously but teach rather as light instructs us." Quoted by Hill, *op. cit.*, p. 149. It should also be remembered that the novel contains many autobiographical elements. In some ways, the development of Bradley Talcott was Garland's own and many of the ideas expressed by Ida Wilbur were no doubt the author's own.

On September 14, 1892 Howells wrote from Ohio the following letter to Garland: ". . . I read *A Spoil of Office* as soon as I got it, and I meant long ago to have told you how much I liked it. The story interested me greatly; your hero was simply and strongly studied; I knew him and felt him from the first to last. It was brave of you to take a Woman's Righter for a heroine; but Nettie Russel was worth a lot of her for human nature; Nettie was *fine*, and awfully true. I think you have got very close to the *Life of classes and kinds* as well as persons; the book is new in that, and I am proud of it for that reason. At first I did not like your seeming to change in favor of the Democracy against Republicanism; when I saw that this was not final I was consoled.—I read every word of the book." Quoted by Hill, *op. cit.*, pp. 145-6.

evolution of Bradley Talcott from a hired man to a politician in Washington, a development largely due to the influence of an emancipated woman, Ida Wilbur.[1] Moreover, Garland advocated the Populist party, woman's rights, and honesty in politics. The marriage question was also debated in this novel so crammed with social issues, some of which had already been dealt with in his earlier work.

It should be remembered that the book was written at the suggestion of B. O. Flower, who may in part be responsible for its overt propaganda. But it is perhaps misleading to blame Flower for having turned Garland a propagandist. Although Flower and the *Arena* stimulated Garland's inherent moralism and strong ethical outlook, it should not be overlooked that it was Flower who helped *launch* Garland as a writer.

Prairie Folks, a companion volume to *Main-Travelled Roads*, was brought out in 1893, when Garland moved to New York, where he often saw Crane and occasionally Howells and the Hernes. It contains nine stories of Western life, some of which were completed in the late eighties. They are, on the whole, not so bitter and pessimistic as those of the earlier volume, but they, too, deal with the harshness of farm life and the primitiveness of human nature. Some of the narratives have fine delineations of distinctively Western characters. The story "Sim Burns's Wife" illustrating a marital problem—Lucretia Burns's vain struggle to liberate herself from a dwarfing marriage—comes close to naturalism in technique and ideas. In 1893, Garland collected most of his verse and published it in book form as *Prairie Songs*. Garland's literary manifesto, *Crumbling Idols*,[2] appeared in 1894, in which, with youthful enthusiasm, he advocated veritism and Western art

---

[1] Cf. Annie L. Diggs, "The Women in the Alliance Movement," *Arena*, VI (July, 1892), 161–79. It is probable that the prototype of Ida Wilbur was some such woman as those portrayed in this article, for Garland made her a member of the Alliance movement.

[2] For a full discussion of this book, see pp. 135 ff. Walter Blackburn Harte wrote of Garland in the *Chicago Inter Ocean* for February 18, 1894: ". . . I had a conversation in Hamlin Garland's new quarters in New York, the other day . . . his study is a plainly furnished room, with a few portraits of some favorite contemporaries on the wall—among others Ibsen, Tolstoi, Walt Whitman, W. D. Howells and Enneking, the Boston painter . . ."

and literature and was rather abused, particularly by Eastern critics.[1]

Speaking of *A Spoil of Office* in November, 1892, Garland told an interviewer: "I do not expect to write another political novel. I aim not to repeat, and as my ideas in this respect have been stated, it is improbable that I will ever write of politics again. I expect some time to treat of Chicago, and of university life, also."[2] The Chicago novel was started about 1893 and the bulk of it was written during the following year when Garland established his headquarters in Chicago. Appearing in 1895, entitled *Rose of Dutcher's Coolly*, it represents Garland's best attempt at a psychological novel. The book described with a good deal of frankness the evolution of Rose from a happy child of nature to a mature, emancipated woman undecided whether to choose a career or marry. Artistically the former part of the novel is superior to the latter, for, as long as Rose remained in the West, she retained a certain naturalness, vitality and innocent charm, which she gradually lost, when Garland transferred her to Chicago. At the same time, Garland's interest in Rose diminished and he became more and more preoccupied with the message he wanted to convey, i.e. that a woman should have a career of her own and marriage should be an intellectual companionship based on mutual freedom and responsibility. Because of the audacity with which he described the stirrings of sex in Rose, he was for some time the subject of a widespread controversy, and was much criticized by reviewers.[3]

In 1897 appeared *Wayside Courtships*, a volume of short stories, in which Garland, on the whole in a lighter vein, dealt with problems treated of in his earlier stories: the quest for an intellectual life, the revolt against farm conditions, the emancipation of woman, and the problem of marriage. See, for instance, "A Stop-Over at Tyre," which, however, ends on a pessimistic note.

During the following year *Ulysses S. Grant* was published. The research required for this book demanded much energy and

---

[1] On May 30, 1894, Howells sent Garland the following encouraging note: "You are getting plenty of abuse from the critics these days, but you are getting respect, too. They all know there is an honest man inside your book, and a strong one. You go further than I do, but you are in the right way, and you will arrive! You *have* arrived, in fact." *Life in Letters of William Dean Howells*, II, 51.

[2] Quoted by Hill, *op. cit.*, p. 150.

[3] See p. 207.

creative power.[1] To get a change of milieu and to collect new material for stories, he joined the gold rush for the Klondike in Alaska. From Glenora, B.C., he wrote to his brother on July 22, 1898:

> We have made 1000 miles of hell's own trail. No danger, but discomforts many. I am as hard as nails. I walked and led my horse 150 miles, wallowing in the river, going to bed with wet feet for twenty days. No sun, no game, no flowers, no fruit, no dry land. I lost one of my six horses . . .
>
> I am writing of the trail a short story.—Hope to make an acceptable thing of it. It was a tremendous experience.

The result of this trip was *The Trail of the Goldseekers* (1899), a book in prose and verse. In the same year appeared *Boy Life on the Prairie*, a charming description of his early experiences in the Middle West. According to one of his notebooks some of the sketches in this book were written in 1887 or 1888.

By 1900, in shifting the locale of his stories from the Middle West to the Rocky Mountain region, Garland, the realist, turned romanticist. Signs of a change of attitude and subject matter had been perceivable even as early as 1891 after his first trip to the Mountains, and his writings in the early nineties are not wholly devoid of romantic and sentimental elements. Of the factors which contributed to Garland's metamorphosis, the following should be mentioned: The antagonism which met his stories of the plains, particularly in the Middle West, irritated and depressed him, and

---

[1] In one of his notebooks Garland made the following comment on *Grant* dated April 20, 1897: "I have now been at work for more than a year at the above task. It is still a mighty theme and interests me but I am not sure that I ought to give so much of the best and most creative period of my life to this work. I fear that the inspiration I now have for new work will come less often each year. I think I shall not be able to give my whole time to this work."

Garland had trouble with this book, and on January 24, 1897, Howells wrote him: "This is very interesting, and lets one see the man plainly. But it lacks texture, and compared with your work in fiction I find a poorness in the diction which I do not like. No doubt you feel the McClures sitting on your head, but you must be good and strong in spite of them. Read Taine's 'French Revolution' a little and see how he *packs* his material, and yet makes every word tell. You ought to have put that long Fishback interview into your own language. The effect of it is to cheapen your page as it now stands. How could a newspaper have done worse?" Unpublished letter in the University of Southern California Library.

so he turned with relief and joy to the Rocky Mountain area and its heroic and romantic types. His books had not sold very well because of their unpleasant material, and therefore he began to write romances in the hope of securing a material success. In addition, many of his friends were shocked by the sordidness of his stories which they found too depressing. They wanted a little more romance and optimism in his narratives. Numerous letters to that effect from Richard Watson Gilder, Eugene Ware, Stanley Waterloo, and others may have affected Garland's attitude. Gradually his reforming zeal disappeared and only occasionally did he deliver any lectures on the single tax.[1] The ardent reformer of the late eighties and early nineties had mellowed and turned a conventional writer.[2]

2. STEPHEN CRANE 1871–1900

The report which, in 1891, Crane wrote on Garland's lecture at Avon-by-the-Sea on "The Local Novel" struck the lecturer as unusually correct and precise in view of the fact that it was written by a young reporter.[3] Two years later Garland had another occasion to praise the New York newspaperman. One day, the mail brought him a volume in yellow paper wrappers, *Maggie: A Girl of the Streets*, by Johnston Smith. It bore the following note in Crane's fine, upright script: "The reader of this book must inevitably be shocked, but let him keep on till the end, for in it the writer has put something which is important."[4] Garland, who had himself explored the Boston slums and described them in *Jason Edwards*, and was then living in Harlem, immediately recog-

---

[1] Cf. the following entry in his diary for September 22, 1899: "Chicago. — On the way home I stopped into the Single Tax Club for a few minutes. It stirred something in me—something not altogether pleasant. I still regard the system as the best yet devised. It is vital in a sense, but it no longer seems so vital as some other things. I do not now expect it to do more than modify thought. Once I thought it might change our way of living. So it will, but long hence probably . . ."

[2] Garland married Zulime Taft in 1899. For Garland's other work, see pp. 421–3. He devoted his last years mainly to reminiscent writing and psychic research. He died in his Hollywood home on March 5, 1940.

[3] *Roadside Meetings*, p. 189.

[4] *Ibid.*, p. 191. Cf. also p. 191.

nized the sincerity and honesty of Crane's grim picture of the New York Bowery. In the November 1893 issue of the *Arena*, Garland reviewed *Maggie* together with Paul Bourget's novel *Cosmopolis* under the heading "An Ambitious French Novel and a Modest American Story."[1]

This [*Maggie*] is of more interest to me, both because it is the work of a young man, and also because it is a work of astonishingly good style. It deals with poverty and vice and crime also, but it does so, not out of curiosity, not out of salaciousness, but because of a distinct art impulse, the desire to utter in truthful phrase a certain rebellious cry. It is the voice of the slums. It is not written by a dilettante; it is written by one who has lived the life . . . It gives the dialect of the slums as I have never before seen it written—crisp, direct, terse. It is another locality finding voice.

It is important because it voices the blind rebellion of Rum Alley and Devil's Row. It creates the atmosphere of the jungles, where vice festers and crime passes gloomily by, where outlawed human nature rebels against God and man.[2]

Otherwise, the book remained practically unnoticed, and only a few copies were sold. It was Crane's maiden effort, and it proved a complete failure.

Crane was born on November 1, 1871, in Newark, N.J., the fourteenth and last child of a Methodist clergyman. His parents were both college graduates, devoted Methodists, who wrote articles on religious subjects. At nine years of age Crane lost his father. "After my father died," he wrote later, "mother lived in

---

[1] Garland erroneously dates his review June, 1893, in *Roadside Meetings*, p. 199. Ames W. Williams and Vincent Starrett repeat the mistake in *Stephen Crane: A Bibliography* (Glendale, Calif., 1948), p. 14. For Garland's literary beliefs in the early nineties it may also be of interest to quote what he said of Bourget's novel: "This latest of Bourget's novels is of the sort that America can get along very well without. It has some excellences (unfortunately), just enough to get a reading, though it will be dull to those to whom most French novels are a stale story well told. It is a singular thing that French writers should confine themselves so largely to morbid sexuality and to criminal classes. They make unpardonably dull books, because there is so little real life in them. Most of them are pathological, as Nordau called it, diseased, not healthy. . . . It is not salacious; it is only a study of the abnormal pursued in the evident belief that there is more human nature in crime and vice than in the commonplace, wholesome action of men and women. This is a mistake from my point of view." *Arena*, VIII (November, 1893), xi–xii.

[2] *Ibid.*, p. xii. Note Garland's avoidance of the words "realism" and "naturalism."

and for religion. We had very little money."[1] The sensitive and precocious boy grew up in an atmosphere of poverty and religious zeal. Whereas Methodism soon lost its grip on the youth, poverty followed him throughout his adventurous life. At thirteen or fourteen, mainly through the influence of his brother William,[2] he began questioning the tenets which his mother preached with great enthusiasm at home and at prayer meetings. Gradually he became a sceptic and later in life he occasionally attacked religion.

Crane's schooling was varied and rather desultory. Between 1882 and 1888 he went to school at Asbury Park, N.J., where his family had moved in 1882, and between 1888-90 he attended Pennington Seminary at Pennington, N.J., and the Hudson River Institute at Claverack, N.Y., a military school famous for its Methodist tradition. In September 1890 he entered Lafayette College with the class of '94, where he completed one term, and joined the Delta Upsilon Fraternity. "The Faculty of Lafayette," asserts Beer, "remembered Stephen as a towheaded, pleasant boy who preferred boxing to study."[3] Finally he transferred to Syracuse University, where he stayed from January until June, 1891. The only grade on record from this college is an A in English literature. In later years Crane wrote that "When I was at school few of my studies interested me, and as a result I was a bad scholar ... I was always very fond of literature, though."[4] Crane's brother Townley secured for him the post of correspondent to the *New York Tribune* in Syracuse, and occasionally he wrote articles and sketches for it and for the *Detroit Free Press*. He assured his classmates that "the police court was the most interesting place in Syracuse."[5] The following letter demonstrates his attitude toward college:

I did little work at school but confined my abilities, such as they were, to the diamond. Not that I disliked books, but the cut-and-dried curriculum of the college did not appeal to me. Humanity was a more interesting study. When I ought to have been at recitations I was studying

---

[1] Thomas Beer, *Stephen Crane* (Garden City, N.Y., 1927), p. 49. I am greatly indebted to this book for the chapter on Crane's life and career.

[2] See Crane letter quoted by Beer, *op. cit.*, p. 50.

[3] Beer, *op. cit.*, p. 55.

[4] J. Henry Guntzer, Jr., "A Memorial to Stephen Crane," *Delta Upsilon Quarterly* (January, 1922), p. 37.

[5] Beer, *op. cit.*, p. 57.

faces in the streets, and when I ought to have been studying my next day's lessons I was watching the trains roll in and out of the Central Station. So, you see, I had, first of all, to recover from College; I had to build up, so to speak.[1]

In the summer of 1891, a few months after his mother's death, he left Syracuse, thus ending for good his formal education.

Of his early work for the press, Crane wrote in later years:

When I was about sixteen, I began to write for the New York newspapers, doing correspondence from Asbury Park and other places. Then I began to write special articles and short stories for the Sunday papers and one of the literary syndicates, reading a great deal in the meantime and gradually acquiring a style.[2]

How much Crane actually had read when he left college, is impossible to ascertain. According to his biographer, he was then acquainted with some of the works of Tolstoy, who "was the world's foremost writer,"[3] and whose work he kept on admiring throughout his life. A Canadian lady gave him a copy of *Sebastopol*. Moreover, he read Flaubert's *Salammbô*, but he "did not think very well of the Carthaginian princess but this was better than the English could do."[4] Nor did he like Robert Louis Stevenson. Crane was then not familiar with the work of Henry James.

On leaving college, Crane had to confront the hardships and privations of a bitter struggle for life. But he was young, enthusiastic, and happy to be out of college, for after all, life not books was the thing that counted, and he wanted to become a writer. While continuing his occasional newspaper work, he immersed himself in the New York Bowery. With wonder and sympathy Crane saw the tide of human misery flow past him:

---

[1] John N. Hilliard, "Letters from Stephen Crane," *New York Times Literary Supplement* (July 14, 1900), p. 467. For brief studies of Crane's schooling, see Claude Jones, "Stephen Crane at Syracuse," *American Literature*, VII (March, 1935), 82–4; Lyndon U. Pratt, "The Formal Education of Stephen Crane," *American Literature*, X (January, 1939), 460–71; and Harvey Wickham, "Stephen Crane at College," *American Mercury*, VII (March, 1926), 291–7.

[2] Guntzer, *op. cit.* Beer emphasizes perhaps too much Crane's supposedly limited reading when observing that he "seldom read books." Beer, *op. cit.*, p. 112.

[3] Beer, *op. cit.*, p. 55. Cf. p. 96 of the present study.

[4] *Ibid.*, p. 55.

gamblers, outcasts, prostitutes, vice in every form. Once he got a black eye in a saloon brawl and on another occasion he saw a dance hall

wrecked by a gang of sailors from the Brooklyn Navy Yard who had been wrongfully expelled. There was a notorious procurer and that girl was supposed to be the daughter of a wealthy family somewhere uptown who came here for the curious pleasure of attracting suitors and then making them quarrel while she went to refuge in the shadow of some policeman.[1]

Out of his experiences in the East Side slums and the reading of Zola[2] came *Maggie* (1893), which Crane had to pay to have published. It was perhaps one of the first books in American literature to deal with the slums from a naturalist's point of view.[3] There was no moralizing or explicit teaching in the book and it offered no solution. Although the writer was in sympathy with the heroine, he remained detached and the book ended on a pessimistic note. In brief it was the tragic story of Maggie, her love, seduction, and death by drowning. The narrative was told in a series of short and vivid impressionistic scenes, in which sordid and brutal details were amassed to such a degree as to occasionally surpass even Zola's *L'Assommoir* in cumulative effect.

At the time when Crane wrote his slum stories, the Bowery was generally regarded either as a quaint, picturesque section which attracted sightseers, or as a plague spot, which reformers and propagandists made vain attempts to remove.[4] Crane, however, told his story without biased comment. An interesting letter of 1896 gives information about his purpose in *Maggie* and about his attitude toward the Bowery:

Mrs. Howells was right in telling you that I have spent a great deal of time on the East Side and that I have no opinion of missions. That —to you—may not be a valid answer since perhaps you have been informed that I am not very friendly to Christianity as seen around town. I do not think that much can be done with the Bowery as long as the . . . (blurred) . . . are in their present state of conceit. A person who thinks himself superior to the rest of us because he has no job and no pride

[1] *Ibid.*, pp. 80-1.
[2] Cf. Chap. X.
[3] Cf. *Jason Edwards* where the slums were part of the setting.
[4] See pp. 77-9. Cf. also Julian Ralph, "The Bowery," *Century Magazine*, XLIII (December, 1891), 227-37. See also pp. 3-4 of this study.

and no clean clothes is as badly conceited as Lillian Russell.[1] In a story of mine called 'An Experiment in Misery' I tried to make plain that the root of Bowery life is a sort of cowardice. Perhaps I mean a lack of ambition or to willingly be knocked flat and accept the licking. The missions for children are another thing and if you will have Mr. Rockefeller give me a hundred street cars and some money I will load all the babes off to some pink world where cows can lick their noses and they will never see their families any more. My good friend Edward Townsend—have you read his 'Daughter of the Tenements'?—has another opinion of the Bowery and it is certain to be better than mine. I had no other purpose in writing 'Maggie' than to show people to people as they seem to me. If that be evil, make the most of it.[2]

Meanwhile Crane lived at times with a noisy gang of struggling artists in the Art Students' League building at 143 East 23rd Street in New York City. They were often hard up and lived four in one room, where they cooked over a gas stove, ate frankfurters and rye bread, drank beer, smoked stale tobacco, played poker, painted on towels, slept on the floor and dreamt "blood-red dreams of fame." Probably his association with artists, many of whom had studied in Paris, exerted an influence on the young writer. He not only acquired a painter's point of view,[3] but some of his views of life may have been derived from his contact and discussions with this group of painters.

Maggie won for Crane the friendship of Garland and Howells. Frequently Crane walked to Garland's flat in Harlem where Garland entertained and encouraged him and occasionally lent him some money. By 1893, Crane was described as a starving writer, reeking with stale cigarette smoke and dressed in a long, shabby, gray ulster. His mood was bitter and sullen. Garland introduced him to Howells, who "went sedately mad" over *Maggie* and invited Crane for dinner. *The Black Riders* (1895), Crane's first book of poetry, is believed to have been composed after this

---

[1] An actress whom Crane disliked.

[2] Beer, *op. cit.*, pp. 140–1.
Concerning his attitude toward socialism, Crane tells us that at some time he "was a Socialist for two weeks but when a couple of Socialists assured me I had no right to think differently from any other Socialist and then quarrelled with each other about what Socialism meant, I ran away." Beer, *op. cit.*, pp. 205–6.

[3] Note that the hero of the semi-autobiographical novel, *The Third Violet* (1897), is an impressionist painter. For the life of the studios, see *ibid.*, pp. 131 ff.

meeting, at which Howells read some of Emily Dickinson's poems aloud.[1] Crane's poems, some of which are reminiscent of French symbolist poetry, were in free rhythm, with no rhymes, and they expressed disillusion and bitterness at the false values of the world. In general the reviews were hostile, but a critic in the *Bookman* wrote:

> On the whole, Mr. Crane's work has traces of *Entartung*, but he is by no means a decadent, but rather a bold—sometimes too bold—original, and powerful writer of eccentric verse, skeptical, pessimistic, often cynical; and one who stimulates thought because he himself thinks. It is no exaggeration to say that the small volume that bears his name is the most notable contribution to literature to which the present year has given birth.[2]

---

[1] Beer, *op. cit.*, p. 119. *The Black Riders* was dedicated to Garland, who wrote in one of his own copies of the book on November 18, 1924: "I saw Crane set down some of these lines while sitting at my desk. Evidently they were composed subconsciously and (as he said) needed only to be drawn off by way of his pen's point. Hamlin Garland."

One of the painters with whom Crane was acquainted in those years was Corwin Knapp Linson, who in 1926 told Garland of his early association with Crane: "For it was in those early years in New York, while struggling for a place and an identity as an artist, that I became associated with Stephen Crane. He just about lived in my studios, first on W. 22nd, then on 30 and Broadway, 40th St. and finally up on 8th Ave., and we had one thing in common, among many others, a persistently empty pocket, but, as well, one purpose alike, an individual devotion to our elected work.

Even here I might be tedious, but I just want to tell you how much you meant to him in encouragement and stimulation. You may never have realized it. Once when I found him in a little room somewhere in the 30's or 40's near 6th Ave., with his toes almost out of his shoes, he seemed not to be aware of that little trouble at all, but said at once "I've been up to see Garland, CK (he pronounced it 'Ceek'). He tells me I am a genius! That's what he said 'Genius' " not boastfully, but with a happy lingering over the word, feeding on it, hugging his elation to himself. I am certain, Mr. Garland, that you and Howells had more to do with the vitality of his morale in those days than any others whomsoever. I knew others to whom he took his work, but "Howells" and "Garland" were names frequently on his lips, furnishing him peculiar delight."

[2] "New Books," *Bookman*, I (May, 1895), 254. The review of the book of poems in the *Philistine*, I (June, 1895), 27, ends with this amusing passage: "This was Mr. Howells proving that Ibsen is valuable and interesting. It is to be hoped that Mr. Crane will write another poem about him after his legs have been worn off." The reference to Ibsen is of interest in this connection.

The theme of war, occasionally used in *The Black Riders,* was to be the motif of most of Crane's subsequent books. In 1895[1] appeared *The Red Badge of Courage,* his most important war narrative and perhaps his greatest achievement. In spite of the shift of background from the New York slums of *Maggie* to the imagined battlefields of Chancellorsville in this war story, Crane did not change his focus of interest: the individual in his relationship to society and the group. Since he wrote the novel without any personal experience of war,[2] it may be worth while investigating what books he read or may have had access to at this period. Beer has it that *The Red Badge of Courage* was written on a dare after Crane had dipped into a translation of *La Débâcle.* No doubt even before the composition of *Maggie,* he was familiar with some of Zola's work. Once he wrote of *Nana:*

... this girl in Zola is a real streetwalker. I mean, she does not fool around making excuses for her career. You must pardon me if I cannot agree that every painted woman on the streets of New York was brought there by some evil man. Nana, in the story, is honest.[3]

Crane admired Zola's sincerity and honesty, but he ranked Tolstoy as "the supreme living writer of our time..."[4] He liked both

---

[1] The publication of the novel was somewhat delayed, because early in 1895 Crane was sent across the country to write stories of the Southwest and Mexico for Irving Bacheller's Syndicate. Although the novel was offered to and accepted by the publishers in December 1894, it was not brought out until October, 1895. See letter of Victor S. Sicilia to Max J. Herzberg, August 19, 1932, in the Newark Public Library, N.J.

[2] Note the following passage taken from a letter which he wrote in England. The letter begins with references to the reviewers of *The Red Badge of Courage:*

"They all insist that I am a veteran of the Civil War, whereas the fact is, as you know, I never smelled even the powder of a sham battle. I know what the psychologists say, that a fellow can't comprehend a condition that he has never experienced, and I argued that many times with the Professor. Of course, I have never been in a battle, but I believe that I got my sense of the rage of conflict on the football field, or else fighting is a hereditary instinct, and I wrote intuitively; for the Cranes were a family of fighters in the old days, and in the Revolution every member did his duty. But, be that as it may, I endeavoured to express myself in the simplest and most concise way. ..." "Some Letters of Stephen Crane," *Academy,* LIX (Aug. 11, 1900), 116.

[3] Beer, *op. cit.,* p. 148.

[4] Introduction by Thomas Beer to Vol. VII, xiii, of *The Work of Stephen Crane,* ed. by Wilson Follett (12 vols., New York, 1925–27). This edition will hereafter be referred to as *Work.*

Anna Karenina[1] and *War and Peace*,[2] although he resented their length and didacticism. Crane may also have read Bierce's *Tales of Soldiers and Civilians* (1891) and *Can Such Things Be?* (1893), or looked into Frank Wilkeson's *Recollections of a Private Soldier in the Army of the Potomac* (1887), or Warren Goss's *Recollections of a Private* (1891). He may also have seen some of the numerous Civil War articles with illustrations that were running in *Harper's Weekly* in the eighties and early nineties. He possibly read *Corporal Si Klegg and His Pard* (1887) by Wilbur F. Hinman.[3] On April 2 (1894?) he sent back *Battles and Leaders of the Civil War* to one Mrs. Armstrong with the following note:

> Thank you very much for letting me keep these so long. I have spent ten nights writing a story of the war on my own responsibility but I am not sure that my facts are real and the books won't tell me what I want to know so I must do it all over again, I guess.[4]

Moreover, Crane had talked with many veterans of the Civil War, and his brother William was an expert on the strategy of the battle of Chancellorsville—the protracted battle of *The Red Badge of Courage*. From these and other sources Crane created a war story which revealed his extraordinary power of probing the mind of a raw recruit. The novel told of the reactions of an unexperienced youth in his first battle, of his dreams, his deadly terror, and final victory over himself. The boy's soul was dissected with an anatomist's care for details, and the inner causes of his behavior were sought for with a scientist's zeal for truth.[5]

---

[1] Beer, *op. cit.*, p. 157.

[2] *Ibid.*, p. 143.

[3] See H. T. Webster's article "Wilbur F. Hinman's *Corporal Si Klegg*, and Stephen Crane's *The Red Badge of Courage*," *American Literature*, XI (November, 1939), 285-93. Crane may also have glanced at Abner Doubleday, *Chancellorsville and Gettysburg* (New York, 1882) in *Campaigns of the Civil War*, VI.

[4] Beer, *op. cit.*, p. 98. Between 1884 and 1887 the *Century Magazine* published a series of articles on the Civil War, written by both Confederate and Federate men who had taken part in it. Those articles were afterward published in four volumes as *Battles and Leaders of the Civil War* (New York, 1887-9).

[5] Vincent Starrett observes that the book "is essentially a psychological study, a delicate clinical dissection of the soul of a recruit, but it is also a *tour de force* of the imagination." Introduction to *Men, Women and Boats* (New York, 1921), p. 9.

He was viewed against a background of war: the vibration and roar of booming guns, the choking smell of gunpowder, the red flames of cracking rifles, the sound of whistling bullets, the whirling clouds of smoke, explosions and cries, dead horses and soldiers in agony, men and animals drawn helplessly into a maelstrom of desperate confusion. The book is a sample of naturalism because of its candor, its treatment of men as dominated by instincts, its pictures of masses, and its pessimistic outlook.

The Red Badge of Courage brought Crane recognition and international fame. Although America was the first country to recognize Crane's genius,[1] English critics were more lavish in their praise of the novel. One hostile review may serve as an illustration of the attitude of some American critics:

> Must we come to judge of books only by what the newspapers have said of them, and must we abandon all the old standards of criticism? Can a book and an author, utterly without merit, be puffed into success by entirely undeserved praise, even if that praise comes from English periodicals? . . . The chorus of praise in the English papers has been very extravagant, but it is noticeable that so far, at least, the American papers have said very little about the merits or demerits of the book itself . . . The book is a vicious satire upon American soldiers and American armies . . . Nowhere are seen the quiet, manly, self-respecting, and patriotic men, influenced by the highest sense of duty, who in reality fought our battles. . . . Respect for our own people should have prevented its issue in this country.[2]

Success, however, did not come until 1896. On July 22, 1896, Howells sent Garland the following note: "What a boom Crane has had! Have you read 'George's Mother'? Mrs. Howells thinks it the best of all. He's a good boy, with lots of sense . . ." And he added, evidently for comparison, "Read Abraham Cahan's 'Yekl, a Tale of the New York Ghetto.' It's fine."

George's Mother (1896) is a companion volume to *Maggie* and it exploits the same sordid material. It tells us of a young man who goes from bad to worse, victimized by a brutal environment, an oversolicitous mother, and his own inherent weakness. The

---

[1] D. Appleton & Co., "The Red Badge of Courage. A Correction," *Dial*, XX (May 1, 1896), 263.

[2] A. C. McC., "The Red Badge of Hysteria," *Dial*, XX (April 16, 1896), 227-8. See also J. L. Onderdonk, "A Red Badge of Bad English," *Dial*, XX (May 1, 1896), 263-4.

effects of drink[1] are analyzed with the same minuteness as was Henry Fleming's terror in *The Red Badge of Courage*. The story conforms to naturalism in subject matter, documentation, and detachment.

Because of the success of his Civil War story, Crane continued to write tales of war. Gradually he turned away from the material of the slums. *The Little Regiment*[2] (1896) contains six somber tales of war written more or less in the mood of *The Red Badge of Courage*. In 1897 appeared *The Third Violet*, valuable chiefly for its semi-autobiographical material. The story is based on Crane's hopeless love affair with Helen Trent in 1891, and the most interesting part of the book is the vivid account of his association with the group of impressionist painters in New York.

On December 31, 1896, Crane sailed on a filibustering trip on board the "Commodore" from Jacksonville, Fla. The vessel was, however, wrecked off the coast, and Crane was one of the few survivors who landed at Daytona, Fla. on January 3, after having spent thirty hours at sea in a ten-foot dinghy. This experience furnished him with material for one of his best short stories, "The Open Boat." Before the publication of *The Open Boat and*

[1] Crane was, no doubt, aware of the discussion going on in the *Arena* and elsewhere of the liquor and saloon problem, for his own sketch, "An Ominous Baby," *Arena*, IX (May, 1894), 819–21, appeared in the same issue as the one containing a long article by B. O. Flower and others entitled "How to Deal with the Liquor Traffic: A Symposium," *Arena*, IX (May, 1894), 827–44. It is interesting to note that one of the problems treated of in Crane's novel is the same as the one found in the following paragraph taken from an editorial in the *Arena*. "The influence of the saloon on the young is one of the most serious phases of the many-sided evils of the liquor traffic. All persons who know anything about the effect of strong drink freely indulged in, know that like opium, it weakens when it does not destroy the moral nature; it wipes out the line of moral rectitude from mental discernment; it feeds the fires of animal passion as coal feeds a furnace; it drys [sic] up the soul and shrivels the higher impulses and nobler aspirations of its victims." "The Saloon Curse," *Arena*, IV (November, 1891), 764. I am of the opinion that the social debate carried on in this magazine may, to an extent, have stimulated Crane's choice of theme. See also B. O. Flower, "Society's Exiles," *Arena*, IV (June, 1891), 37–54.

[2] Crane wrote on February 15, 1896 from Hartwood, N.Y.: "I am now finishing a novelette for S. S. McClure called 'The Little Regiment' which represents my work at its best, I think, and is positively my last thing dealing with battle." *Colophon*, Part IV (December, 1930). After *The Little Regiment* Crane wrote at least three more books of war.

Other Tales of Adventure, in 1898, Crane served as correspondent for the *New York Journal* and the *Westminster Gazette* during the Greco-Turkish War. While in Greece, he married Cora Taylor, whom he had met in Jacksonville, where she kept a house of ill-fame.

A letter from Crane to his brother William, written from London on October 29, 1897, in his financial adversity, refers to Crane's extensive travels and his attitude toward his American critics and his own work:

> I have been in England, Ireland, Scotland, Wales, France, Turkey and Greece. I have seen Italy but never trod it. . . .
>
> I am working now on a big novel.[1] It will be much longer than The Red Badge. My next short thing after the novelette (The Monster) was The Bride Comes to Yellow Sky. All my friends [who] come here say it is my very best thing. I am so delighted when I am told by competent people that I have made an advance. You know they said over here in England that The Open Boat (Scribner's) was my best thing. There seem so many of them in America who want to kill, bury and forget me purely out of unkindness and envy and—my unworthiness, if you choose. All the hard things they say of me affect me principally because I think of mine [*sic*] own people—you and Teddie and the families. . . . Your little brother is neither braggart or a silent egotist but he knows that he is going on steadily to make his simple little place and he can't be stopped, he can't even be retarded. He is coming.
>
> Sometimes I think you and old Ted worry about me and you may well worry! I have managed my success like a fool and a child but then it is difficult to succeed gracefully at 23. However I am learning every day. I am slowly becoming a man.[2]

In April, 1898, Crane left England to serve as a correspondent for the *New York World* and, later, for the *New York Journal* during the Spanish-American War in Cuba, where he frequently was at the front. In January, 1899, he left America for good and returned to England, where he made his residence in a decayed seventeenth century manor, Brede Place, Sussex. Numerous guests came to see the author of *The Red Badge of Courage* in his baronial environment. His careless living and exposure to all kinds of

---

[1] Probably *The O'Ruddy*.

[2] Reproduced here by courtesy of the Dartmouth College. The long, significant letter is printed in full in Herbert Faulkner West, *A Stephen Crane Collection* (Hanover, N.H., 1948).

dangers caused a rapid failing of his health, and on June 5, 1900, at the age of 28, he died of tuberculosis at Badenweiler, Germany.

Meanwhile, in 1899, he published two books about war, one volume of free verse, *War Is Kind*, which was less original than *The Black Riders*, and *Active Service*, a mediocre novel about his experiences as a war correspondent during the Greco-Turkish War. Crane, the social critic, appeared in the title story of *The Monster and Other Stories* (1899), which also contained the fatalistic tale "The Blue Hotel," and Crane, the child psychologist, in *Whilomville Stories* (1900). Two more war books were brought out after his death, the gloomy *Wounds in the Rain* (1900), and *Great Battles of the World* (1901). Crane's friend, Robert Barr, had to finish his last big project, an historical romance, *The O'Ruddy* (1904), which he had begun as a joke on *The Courtship of Morrice Buckler* by A. E. W. Mason.[1]

Of the many writers whom Crane met in England Joseph Conrad was perhaps the one whom he valued most.[2] In America Crane had read *The Nigger of the Narcissus* (1897), and he may have felt that there was a certain kinship in their concepts of man, and the universe, and when he came to England, he was eager to meet Conrad. The meeting took place in October, 1897, in London. Conrad tells that they talked of various things, and Crane "demanded insistently to be told in particular detail all about the Comédie Humaine, its contents, its scope, its plan, and its general significance, together with a critical description of Balzac's style."[3] Another writer whose friendship Crane appreciated was Harold Frederic.[4] Frederic, Robert Barr, and Crane used to call

---

[1] I am indebted to Ames W. Williams for this information.

[2] A proof of the friendship between the two writers is the fact that Crane gave Conrad the MS of "The Five White Mice" (published 1898), as can be seen from Conrad's note on the MS which is now in the possession of the Huntington Library.

A letter from Conrad to Garland sheds light on Crane's married life: Conrad wrote in 1922: "We were intimate with the Cranes. Their household appeared harmonious and its atmosphere quite favorable to Crane's work. She nursed him devotedly during his illnesses and during his last one succeeded to find means to take him to Switzerland in a supreme attempt to save his life."

[3] Beer, *op. cit.*, pp. 16–17.

[4] Crane even wrote an article on Harold Frederic, in which he makes favorable mention of the following books by Frederic: *Seth's Brother's Wife*, *The Lawton Girl*, *In the Valley*, *The Damnation of Theron Ware*, and *In the Sixties*. "Harold Frederic," *Chap-Book*, VIII (March 15, 1898), 358–9.

themselves the "Three Musketeers." Crane met Henry James in England, and he considered his *Portrait of a Lady* a masterpiece.[1] Oscar Wilde was in Crane's words "a mildewed chump. He has a disease and they all gas about him as though there was a hell and he came up out of it. . . . Mr. Yeats is the only man I have met who talks of Wilde with any sense. The others talk like a lot of little girls at a Sunday School party when a kid says a wicked word in a corner."[2]

Indubitably Crane was far better read in contemporary literature than his contemporaries believed him to be. That he pretended to be ignorant and illiterate is affirmed by Ford Madox Ford, one of his British contemporaries:

> To say that he was completely ignorant of Zola and Maupassant would probably be untrue. He would state at one moment, with expletives, that he had never heard of those fellows and, at the next, display a considerable acquaintance with their work.[3]

On another occasion Ford remarked:

> He [Crane] certainly always commented with knowledge on any book of Flaubert's or any short story of de Maupassant's that I happened to mention. And I can say much the same about his acquaintance with the works of James. But whether either James or the French master had any direct influence on him while he was actually writing I should not care to say. They were, however, so extremely in the air of the New York of that day that he cannot have escaped their indirect influence.[4]

To be accused of imitating French writers irritated Crane greatly. Once he wrote to James G. Huneker:

> Now I am going to wave the starry flag of freedom a little — even if you contemn the practice in one who knows not Balzac and Dostoywhat's-hisname. You Indians have been wasting wind in telling me how 'Unintrusive' and 'DELICATE' I would find English manners. I don't. It has not been the habit of people I meet at Mr. Howells or Mr. Phillips or Mrs. Sonntages to let fall my hand and begin to quickly ask me how much money I make and from which French realist I shall steal my next book. For it has been proven to me fully and carefully by authority that all my books are stolen from the French. They stand me against walls

[1] Beer, *op. cit.*, p. 157.

[2] *Ibid.*, pp. 160-1.

[3] Ford Madox Ford, *Portraits from Life* (Boston and New York, 1937), p. 35.

[4] *New York Herald Tribune, Book Supplement* (January 2, 1927), p. 6.

with a teacup in my hand and tell me how I have stolen all my things
from De Maupassant, Zola, Loti and the bloke who wrote—I forget
the book. I find nothing 'unintrusive' or 'delicate' in these goings on.
The simple rustic villagers of Port Jervis have as good manners as some
of the flower of England's literary set.[1]

And to a complete stranger he admitted:

> I am obliged to confess that I am not carnivorous about living writers.
> I have not read any of the books that you ask me to criticize except that
> of Mr. Howells, and it has disappointed me. My tastes? I do not know
> of any living author whose works I have wholly read. I like what I know
> of Anatole France, Henry James, George Moore, and several others.
> I deeply admire some short stories by Mr. Bierce,[2] Mr. Kipling,[3] and Mr.
> White.[4]

He knew Pierre Loti and the brothers Goncourt at least by name,
but when he was asked if he admired Mallarmé, he answered:
"I don't know much about Irish authors."[5] In March, 1899, he
read among other books Turgenev's *Smoke* and Du Maurier's
Peter Ibbetson.[6] He had also read some of the works of Hardy;
and H. G. Wells, he thought, had "a genius for writing of under-
class people more honestly than Charles Dickens."[7] Most of
Stevenson's work was to Crane insincere, and he did not like
Mrs. Ward's *Robert Elsmere*.[8] Of American writers besides Garland, Howells, James, and Mark Twain, he knew some of the work
of Frank Norris, R. H. Davis, and Abraham Cahan. In addition, he
liked Bret Harte's early California sketches and a few of the new
Western stories of Owen Wister and Alfred Henry Lewis.[9] As
has been said, he admired a few of Bierce's stories and of his
"Occurrence at Owl Creek Bridge" he said: "Nothing better
exists. That story contains everything."[10] Bierce himself spoke

---

[1] Beer, *op. cit.*, p. 168.

[2] Cf. p. 270 n. 1.

[3] Cf. p. 152.

[4] Introduction by Thomas Beer to Vol. VII, xiii, of *Work*.

[5] Beer, *Stephen Crane*, p. 124.

[6] *Ibid.*, p. 211.

[7] *Ibid.*, p. 231.

[8] *Ibid.*, p. 104.

[9] *Ibid.*, p. 230.

[10] Introduction by Robert H. Davis to Vol. II, xx, of *Work*. Cf. Crane
and Bierce, p. 350 n. 1, 359 n. 2.

highly of *The Red Badge of Courage* and its author: "This young man . . . has the power to feel. He knows nothing of war, yet he is drenched in blood. Most beginners who deal with this subject spatter themselves merely with ink."[1]

There are very few references to books and authors in Crane's work. In *The Third Violet* Hawker, one of the characters, observes that *Hearts at War* is a very good play.[2] Larpent in the story "Moonlight on the Snow" (1900) reads Scott's *Fair Maid of Perth*[3] and in "The Monster" a company of strollers are to play *East Lynne*.[4] In *Wounds in the Rain* there is a reference to Cervantes and Velasquez,[5] and in the story "An Old Man Goes Wooing" (1899) the old man is likened to a "stern and mournful Dante portrait."[6] Finally in the short story "The Second Generation" (1899), Kipling is mentioned, and in the same story there is also a reference to Kipling's "White Man's Burden."[7]

Crane's work, like Garland's, was, to an extent, a product of his time and experiences. His revolt was directed against the American society of his time, and the theme frequently met with in his work treats of the individual in his relation to society or the group. His development is somewhat similar to Garland's: he started out as a naturalistic delineator of the slums and ended by outlining an historical romance.

3. FRANK NORRIS 1870–1902

Among those who recognized the human values found in Crane's slum stories was a young San Francisco reporter, an admirer of Zola, Frank Norris.[8] In the spring of 1896 he had

---

[1] *Ibid.*, p. x.

[2] *Work*, III, 207.

[3] *Ibid.*, XII, 120.

[4] *Ibid.*, III, 31. Ellen Price Wood (Mrs. H. Wood) was the author of *East Lynne* (Boston, 1896).

[5] *Ibid.*, IX, 241.

[6] *Ibid.*, XI, 176.

[7] *Ibid.*, II, 236, 240. All the references to books and authors found in the works of Garland, Crane, and Norris have, of course, not been recorded.

[8] Helpful for this chapter were above all Franklin Walker, *Frank Norris: A Biography* (Garden City, N.Y., 1932), Ernest Marchand, *Frank Norris: A Study* (Stanford Univ., Calif., 1942), Marius Biencourt, *Une Influence du natu-*

joined the staff of a local magazine, *The Wave*, and in the course
of 1896 and 1897 he contributed a great number of articles and
stories to it.[1] On July 4, 1896, there appeared in the *Wave* an
unsigned review of *Maggie* and *George's Mother* written unmistakably by Norris and entitled "Stephen Crane's Stories of Life
in the Slum."

In *Maggie*, Stephen Crane has written a story something on the plan
of the episode of Nana in *L'Assommoir*. . . . I think that the charm of
his style lies chiefly in his habit and aptitude for making phrases—sparks
that cast a momentary gleam of light on whole phases of life. . . . The
author is writing . . . from the outside. Mr. Crane does not seem to *know*
his people. He does not seem to have gotten down *into* their life and to
have written from what he saw around him. His people are types, not
characters, his scenes and incidents are not particularized. . . . With
him it is the broader, vaguer, *human* interest that is the main thing, not
the smaller details of a particular phase of life.[2]

It is interesting to note that the "kinship and contrast in the
work of these two pioneers of American naturalism are both
revealed in this comment."[3] Whereas Crane was very much interested in style, Norris cared very little for it. Both owed, however, a common debt to Zola, and Norris at once saw, as he
thought, Crane's indebtedness to *L'Assommoir*.[4] By the time Norris wrote the review he had himself almost completed *McTeague*,
a novel which owes much to *L'Assommoir*.[5]

Unlike Garland and Crane, Norris grew up in a wealthy Chicago home. His father, Benjamin Franklin Norris, was a jeweler
and at the time of the birth of Frank, March 5, 1870, his busi-

ralisme français en Amérique (Paris, 1933), Lars Åhnebrink, *The Influence of
Émile Zola on Frank Norris* (Upsala, 1947), and the Introduction by Charles
Caldwell Dobie to Vol. VII of *The Complete Works of Frank Norris* (10 vols.,
Garden City, N.Y., 1928). This edition, which is used in this study, will here-
after be referred to as *Compl. Works*.

[1] The San Francisco *Wave* was a weekly magazine edited by John O'Hara
Cosgrave and established mainly to protect the interest of the Southern Pacific
Railroad. Norris usually signed his articles Frank Norris or F. N., but occa-
sionally he used the pen name Justin Sturgis or did not sign them at all.

[2] Quoted in Walker, *op. cit.*, p. 133. See also Robert E. Spiller *et al.*, *Literary History of the United States* (New York, 1948), II, 1026.

[3] Spiller *et al.*, *loc. cit.*

[4] See pp. 249 ff.

[5] See pp. 283 ff.

ness was prospering. Frank's mother was a cultivated woman, who had once been a schoolmistress in a private school outside Chicago, but had left the classroom to make her stage début at the McVickers Theater in Chicago. She soon married, however, and her career as an actress was not very long. No doubt Frank inherited some of his artistic bent and sense of the dramatic from his mother. There were two younger brothers, Lester and Charles, and the three boys enjoyed a carefree boyhood in the splendid home in Chicago. It is worth noting the differences in the backgrounds of Garland, Crane, and Norris and how it affected their writings. Yet whatever their experiences, the naturalism of the writers was, at least to a certain extent, a result of their reading of Zola,[1] Norris's more so than Garland's and Crane's.

In 1884 B. F. Norris, whose health was failing, sold the Chicago house and decided to go to California in search of a cure, taking his family with him. At first they lived in a house close to Lake Merritt, but later they moved to San Francisco and bought a famous mansion situated in the fashionable "western addition" of the city, "one block from Van Ness Avenue and two blocks from a sectional shopping district—Polk Street,"[2] which Norris was to depict in *McTeague*.

In the autumn of 1885 Norris entered a preparatory boys' school at Belmont near San Francisco, which he attended only for a year, for, unfortunately, he broke his left arm during a football match and had to leave school. During his convalescence he enjoyed reading *Ivanhoe* and *Treasure Island*. He had also become interested in drawing and he was sent to an artist, Virgil Williams, and later there was talk about art schools in London and Paris. The *Quartier Latin* became the young student's dream. In June, 1887, at the formative and most impressionable period of his life, the seventeen-year-old Frank with his father went to London to study at the Kensington School of Art. The rest of the family was left in San Francisco, but in Chicago the news of Lester's death reached them, and they had temporarily to postpone their journey. Mrs. Norris joined them and brought the youngest son with her, and the whole family set out for London.

---

[1] See Chap. X.
[2] *Compl. Works*, VII, xviii.

The stay in London was very short and soon they were established in Paris in a gloomy apartment, "that was filled with a collector's loot, the owner having been a man who went in for swords, and daggers, and cuirasses, and like implements of warfare."[1] Norris studied in the Atelier Julien and one of his teachers was Bouguereau. During his spare time he steeped himself in medievalism and read Froissart's *Chronicles*. His first bit of published writing was an article entitled "Ancient Armour" (1889), and he began to paint a picture in oil of the Battle of Crécy. When in France he learnt to read and speak French fairly well.

After a year the family returned to America, leaving the young art student in the charge of a family named Quatremain. Alone in Paris, Frank took to writing stories and sent his younger brother the copies. By chance, Frank's father came across a story and arrived at the immediate conclusion that it was high time to call his son back from Paris. His career as a painter was at an end. During the two years (1887–8) Norris spent in Paris he could not have failed to notice the literary debate going on around him. In 1887 there appeared *La Terre* and *Le Manifeste des Cinq* which caused much discussion of naturalism in magazines and elsewhere.[2] New currents and new tendencies easily influence young minds. We remember, for instance, George Moore, about a decade earlier, going to Paris with a view to studying art, but, on his return to England, devoting himself exclusively to literature, beginning his career as a disciple of Zola. Norris shows a development similar to Moore's. He, too, returned from Paris, changing the brush for the pen and finally forming his conception of literature under French influences. There is, however, no evidence that he ever read Zola in France, but it may be assumed that it was largely, directly or indirectly, because of this visit and Norris's contact with French civilization that he turned to French writers for certain models and patterns.

In 1888, Norris came back to California, and in August, 1890, he was admitted to the University of California at Berkeley, where he stayed until September 20, 1894, when he was granted an honorable dismissal. As a freshman he was an accomplished gentle-

---

[1] *Ibid.*, xxii.

[2] Cf. Matthew Josephson, *Zola and His Time* (London, 1929), pp. 311 ff.

man, wearing sideburns and talking with a Parisian accent, shocking his classmates with his independence and easy ways. He did all the things "that any normal American student does: joining a fraternity; drawing for the classbook, writing the Junior Farce, playing the banjo."[1]

Inspired by his reading of Richard Harding Davis, Kipling, Maupassant, and Bierce, Norris soon began to write short stories for student and local papers, emphasizing rapid action and surprise denouement. "Babazzouin" and "The Son of a Sheik" were published in the San Francisco *Argonaut*, in 1891, and in the same year "The Jongleur of Taillebois"[2] appeared in the *Wave*. These stories are mainly "lead-soldier romances," resulting from his interest in medievalism.

During his four years at Berkeley, Norris showed a great interest in French literature. Each term he enrolled in French courses. In his third year he attended courses on Victor Hugo and Lamartine, and in his last he was enrolled in a course "French 15" on the "realistic school" given by Professor F. V. Paget. No doubt this course stimulated the emerging writer, who, during his years at Berkeley, began to write *McTeague* under the influence of French naturalism. During the years 1892 and 1893 he enrolled in the popular courses in geology and zoology given by Professor Joseph Le Conte, who spurred on the interest in evolution among his students. The class historian of '95 wrote: "Evolution! Magic spell that opens the gate which bars the single path to all solutions! Philosopher's stone of thought, thou transmutest all base conceptions to the pure gold of truth."[3] The story "Lauth" (published in the *Overland Monthly* in March, 1893), was an immediate result of Norris's interest in Le Conte's lectures. At Berkeley Norris also enrolled in a course on medieval English poetry, which, as Franklin Walker remarked, "may have introduced him to the Germanic and Scandinavian sagas, Viking women . . ."[4]

---

[1] *Compl. Works*, VII, xxv.

[2] This horror tale was probably written under the influence of Bierce, who also contributed to the *Wave*.

[3] Franklin Walker, "Frank Norris at the University of California," *University of California Chronicle*, XXXIII, No. 3 (July, 1931), 325.

[4] Walker, *Frank Norris*, p. 57.

In 1891 he published "Yvernelle," a romantic narrative poem in three cantos written under the inspiration of Scott. Gradually, however, Norris's interest in chivalry, his love for the clang of armor and medieval heroism, gave way to other gods. During his college years he was constantly seen around the campus with a "yellow paper-covered novel of Zola in his hand."[1] "True, Richard Harding Davis leavens the lump of depressing realism. And Kipling comes along to clothe romance in khaki instead of doublet and hose. Our aspiring author even reads William Dean Howells . . . but it is Zola who has him artistically by the throat."[2]

Norris completed his four years at the University of California, but he did not graduate, nor did any one of his teachers in the English department take much interest in his work. There was a striking contrast when in the fall of 1894 he went to Harvard with the unfinished manuscript of *McTeague*, to do a year of postgraduate work. It was during this year that Norris's career began to shape itself. He enrolled in a course, "English 22," given by Professor Lewis E. Gates, who took an interest in Norris and encouraged him. As a recognition, *McTeague*, when published, was dedicated to Gates. "English 22," in which Norris received an A, "called for a short daily theme and a long fortnightly one,"[3] and he handed in excerpts of his unfinished *McTeague*.

His Harvard experiences and the Harvard milieu offered material for another novel, *Vandover and the Brute*,[4] which was written during his year in Cambridge. It is the story of Vandover's gradual degradation and deterioration through drink and moral weakness. It is a clinical study of the effects of al-

---

[1] Charles G. Norris, *Frank Norris* (Pamphlet) (New York, 1914), p. 5.

[2] *Compl. Works*, VII, xxvi.

[3] *Ibid.* X, ix.

[4] Before the novel could be published, it had to be pruned of some details which were considered too revolting. The third chapter, a sordid picture of a drunk, was cut out; also sections previously used in *Blix* were left out. Finally Charles Norris added some five thousand words, before it was in shape to be published. It may be of interest to note that Hamlin Garland read the MS in 1914, before it was published. In the following *Vandover and the Brute* will be treated of as immediately following upon *McTeague*. The name Vandover occurs for the first time in a short story by Norris called "The Finding of Lieutenant Outhwaite," *Occident*, XX (March 13, 1891), 49–51.

cohol[1] and dissipation on the human mind. The novel conforms
to naturalism in theme, treatment, and detachment. Norris despaired of ever finding a publisher for this sordid and deeply
pessimistic picture of a young man victimized by forces beyond
his control. The first page of the manuscript carries the subtitle
"A Story of Life and Manners in an American City at the End of
the Nineteenth Century," and the year 1895. It was, however,
not published until 1914.

After the year at Harvard Norris returned to San Francisco
and, later, "in an effort to find himself" or perhaps in search of
adventure, decided to make a trip through Africa from Capetown
to Cairo. He intended to write travel sketches for a newspaper
syndicate and thus pay his expenses. About ten were written,
some of which appeared in the *San Francisco Chronicle*. They
describe life in the Transvaal, for instance "The Veldt of the
Transvaal" (1896) and "A Zulu War Dance" (1896). In Johannes-
burg he arrived in time for the Jameson Raid and with juvenile
enthusiasm joined the British forces, but he was soon captured
by the Boers and was given thirty days to leave the country. At
the same time he fell ill with an African fever, and in the spring
of 1896 returned to San Francisco in poor physical condition.

In order to recuperate he went to a mining camp in the wilds
of the California mountains. Here he also got inspiration for
the last chapters of *McTeague*, which he had apparently dropped
at Harvard after writing of the murder of Trina. After six weeks
in the High Sierras he returned to San Francisco, where he got a
position on the *Wave*.[2] The book was completed, but did not
find a publisher until 1899, after Norris had been recognized
in the East through *Moran of the Lady Letty* (1898), served on
the staff of the McClure Company and entered the service of
Doubleday, Page and Co.

Norris's reading, up to the time of the publication of his sea story,
may be said to have been intensive rather than extensive. Indeed,

---

[1] Cf. the theme of Crane's *George's Mother*. Norris's novel exposed the lax
morale of American university life. See also B. O. Flower, "Present Day Tendencies and Signs of the Times. Low Ethical Ideals in Our Higher Educational
Centres. Bacchanalian Revels in Modern University Life." *Arena*, VII (February, 1893), 371–7.

[2] Walker, *op. cit.*, p. 129.

this may be said also of his later reading. From his references to authors and books in his early articles, especially those in the *Wave*, it is possible to get some idea of his literary tastes. His greatest interest seems to have been in French writers—an interest which lasted throughout his life. He not only read Hugo, Balzac, Flaubert—*Madame Bovary* was one of his favorites—Maupassant, Daudet, and Zola, but he also translated pieces from French writers for the *Wave*.[1] Zola, however, was the writer he enjoyed most. In an article "Zola as a Romantic Writer" he mentioned or referred to the following novels by Zola: *Lourdes, Rome, Germinal, L'Œuvre, La Bête humaine, La Débâcle,* and *Le Rêve*.[2] Curiously enough he omitted *L'Assommoir,* a novel which influenced him greatly at this time.

At Harvard he also enjoyed reading French authors, for on April 4, 1895, he borrowed from the library Daudet's *Jack,* which may have influenced *Vandover and the Brute*. Moreover, at Harvard he read Pierre de Bourdeille's *Des Dames,* Zola's *Nouveaux Contes à Ninon,* and Edmond and Jules de Goncourt's *Germinie Lacerteux,* all in French.[3] His early interest in Stevenson was kept alive by reading *New Arabian Nights,* and he also enjoyed reading Howells' *A Woman's Reason* and George Eliot's *Middlemarch.*

Stevenson and Kipling are also referred to in his writing. In 1896, reviewing a book of modern city life in India, *His Honour and a Lady* by Sarah Jeanette Duncan, Norris remarked:

It is impossible not to compare this elaborate study of Indian society with the rapid *ébauches* of Mr. Kipling flung off at white heat, crammed

---

[1] See "Fifi" by Léon Faran. Transl. by F. N. *Wave,* XVI, No. 4 (January 23, 1897), 5; "Not Guilty" by Marcel L'Heureux. Transl. by Justin Sturgis. *Wave,* XVI, No. 25 (June 19, 1897), 5; "The Story of a Wall" by Pierre Loti. Transl. by F. N. *Wave,* XVI, No. 35 (August 28, 1897), 13, and "An Elopement" by Ferdinand Bloch. Transl. from the French by F. N. *Wave,* XVI, No. 52 (December 25, 1897), 13.

[2] *Wave,* XV, No. 26 (June 27, 1896), 3. Concerning authorship, see p. 156 n. 4.

[3] Willard E. Martin, Jr., "Frank Norris's Reading at Harvard College," *American Literature,* VII (May, 1935), 203–4. Note also that Norris borrowed Thomas Fillebrown, *A Text-book of Operative Dentistry* (1889), Erasmus Wilson, *A System of Human Anatomy* (1851), and Gallus Thomann, *Real and Imaginary Effects of Intemperance* (1884). *Ibid.,* p. 204.

with living, breathing things, with no execrable "literary finish" to hide the true, honest grain of human life underneath.[1]

Norris also successfully imitated Kipling's style.[2]

In 1896 he reviewed Arthur Morrison's *Chronicles of Martin Hewitt:*

Mr. Morrison's collection surprises me. That the man who wrote "Tales of Mean Streets" could descend to such crude, unoriginal, really amateurish compositions as these "Chronicles" is not to be explained. . . . You lay down the "Chronicles" with a feeling of indignation.[3]

Norris's interest in slum stories is shown by the fact that in his story, "His Sister," he gives the following list of tenement dwellers: "There's Chimmie Fadden, there's Cortlandt Van Bibber, there's Rags Raegen, there's George's Mother, there's Bedalia [*sic*] Herodsfoot, and Gervaise Coupeau and Eleanor Cuyler."[4]

Darwin and Spencer are referred to in the Kiplingesque story "A South Sea Expedition."[5] Dickens and Scott continued to

[1] *Frank Norris of "The Wave"* (San Francisco, 1931), p. 143. First printed in the *Wave* of July 18, 1896. Concerning the reason that Norris was drawn to Kipling and his work, Franklin Walker remarked: "It is most natural that Frank Norris should have been attracted to Kipling, for the latter expressed those talents and ideas closest to his own nature. Here was a writer only five years older than Norris, wedding romance and realism, turning out stories of his own locale, proclaiming the attractiveness of the machine age, spreading the doctrine of the indomitable fighting spirit of the Anglo-Saxon. Here was a man who radiated energy, who wrote with intensity, and whose philosophy of life accepted rather than rejected. Here was a writer who gained his effects by objective portrayal of life 'in the raw.' To the reader wearied of American fiction, with its triple streams of historical novels, sentimental romances, and local-color vignettes, the freshness and vitality of Kipling's portrayal of the life about him acted like a tonic." *Op. cit.*, p. 68.

[2] Norris's cleverness to imitate various styles is excellently illustrated in his parodies of Kipling, Crane, Bret Harte, Davis, Bierce, and Anthony Hope printed in the *Wave* of December 24, 1897 and reprinted in *Frank Norris of "The Wave,"* pp. 77–100. The six parodies carry the following titles: I. The 'Ricksha that Happened by R–d K–g; II. The Green Stone of Unrest by S–n Cr--e; III. A Hero of Tomato Can by B–e H–te; IV. Van Bubble's Story by R–d H–g D–s; V. Ambrosia Beer by A–e B–e; VI. I Call on Lady Dotty by An–y H–pe.

[3] *Frank Norris of "The Wave,"* p. 142. First published in the *Wave* of July 18, 1896.

[4] *Ibid.*, p. 39. First published in the *Wave* of November 28, 1896. Of particular interest is Norris's reference to characters by Townsend, Davis, Crane, Kipling, and Zola. Gervaise Coupeau is of course the heroine of *L'Assommoir.*

[5] *Compl. Works*, X, 88.

fascinate him and he liked some stories of Bret Harte and Bierce. In 1897, he knew about Maeterlinck and Ibsen, for both are mentioned in articles in the *Wave*.[1]

In 1898, *McClure's* sent Norris to Cuba with the Shafter Expedition to report on the Spanish-American War. Like Crane whom he met on board the "Three Friends," he was under fire during most of the campaign. Out of his experience came the powerful sketch entitled "Comida: An Experience in Famine" (1899). But very soon Norris had to leave Cuba, for there was a recurrence of the African fever, and again he nearly succumbed. In bad health he returned to San Francisco and then proceeded to New York.

Moran of the Lady Letty, the first one of his novels to be published, appeared in September, 1898. It is an alluring romance of the sea filled with realistic and naturalistic details. Norris contrasted effectively a strong, primitive woman, reminiscent of those of the Old Norse sagas, with an over-civilized type of man Ross Wilbur. Their strange adventures at sea were told in the manner of Stevenson's *The Wrecker*. Norris completed the novel while it was running serially in the *Wave*.[2] On the whole Norris looked upon the book as a "corking good story." Among those who gave it favorable reviews was the literary editor of the *Louisville Times*, Isaac F. Marcosson, who throughout Norris's career remained his eager advocate and received some of his finest letters. The first of them demonstrates admirably Norris's literary ambitions:

Thank you very much indeed for your encouraging review of 'Moran of the Lady Letty.' It is very flattering for an absolutely new and unknown story-writer to be treated so generously. However, I hope to be less new and more known before many years. I do not think, though, that I shall ever write another story of adventure. When I wrote 'Moran' I was, as one might say, flying kites, trying to see how high I could go without breaking the string. However, I have taken myself and my work much more seriously since then and in my next novel—I think it will go out in the spring—I have tried to do something really worth while. . . .

I have great faith in the possibilities of San Francisco and the Pacific Coast as offering a field for fiction. Not the fiction of Bret Harte,

---

[1] *Frank Norris of "The Wave*," pp. 127, 157. Concerning Norris's saga interest, see pp. 382 ff.

[2] The story ran serially from January 8 until April 19, 1898.

however, for the country has long since outgrown the 'red shirt' period. The novel of California must be now a novel of city life, and it is that novel I hope some day to write successfully.[1]

Howells, too, wrote an appreciative review of *Moran*,[2] and on December 31, 1898, Norris thanked him with special pleasure because Howells had praised him for daring "to attempt the bold and unconventional." In his letter Norris also referred to his novel of San Francisco tentatively called "The People of Polk Street," of which he wrote: "It is as naturalistic as Moran was romantic and in writing it I have taken myself and the work very seriously."[3]

McTeague, which appeared in February 1899, does bear the stamp of a writer who has taken himself and his work seriously. The novel may be called a consciously naturalistic manifesto. It is a study of two temperaments under the pressure of heredity and environment. The title is taken from the hero of the book, a strong, heavy-built, stupid, self-made San Francisco dentist. He gets acquainted with Trina Sieppe, a cousin and intimate friend of Marcus Schouler, with whom she "keeps company." Marcus and McTeague are the best of friends, they occupy the same table at the car conductors' coffee-joint, where they meet at every meal. McTeague, too, is in love with her, and after some time Marcus gives her up to him. Then Trina wins five thousand dollars in a lottery. He marries her, and some years of happiness follow. Trina has invested her money in a firm. The hereditary desire for saving rises strong within her and by care and deception she increases her fortune. She cannot curb her instinct for thrift, for it is stronger than herself. McTeague is forbidden to practice dentistry, because Marcus, his former rival, makes known his lack of either diploma or license. Gradually disintegration begins. McTeague and Trina move to a wretched house, and McTeague is thrown into idleness and begins to drink. As he has no money and Trina refuses to give him any, he becomes mean and churlish. Trina, too, grows miserable, caring only for her savings, and both decline rapidly. In the

---

[1] Isaac F. Marcosson, *Adventures in Interviewing* (New York, 1923), pp. 232–4. Norris's "next novel" was *McTeague*.

[2] See *Literature*, III (December 17, 1898), 577–8.

[3] Reproduced by courtesy of the Harvard Library.

subplot we meet Zerkow, a Jewish junk collector, who marries a half-mad housemaid, Maria Macapa. He is fascinated by her quaint preoccupation with a service of gold plate and by marrying her he hopes he will find the treasure. His useless searching drives him insane, and he murders her in cold blood. The next day his body is found floating in the bay. Meanwhile McTeague and Trina grow more and more wretched, and one day McTeague deserts her. As a result of his brutality she has to have two fingers amputated and is forced to give up her work. She becomes a scrubwoman. McTeague returns, however, murders her and, taking her money, seeks refuge in the mountains. He goes back to the Big Dipper mine, where he was once a car-boy. His sixth sense warns him, however, that danger is approaching, and he leaves the mine two days before the sheriff and his deputies reach it. In an attempt to cross Death Valley in his flight from justice, he meets Marcus, who is searching for him. In the struggle in the sunburnt alkali desert, McTeague kills Marcus, but before the latter dies, he manages to handcuff their wrists together. McTeague, too, is thus doomed to die in the desert.

As is evident from this outline, the novel adheres rather closely to the naturalistic pattern. It is, perhaps, the most important American novel of the nineties which employs *in extenso* a naturalistic technique.[1] *McTeague*, modeled on *Thérèse Raquin* and *L'Assommoir*,[2] is naturalistic in theme, subject matter, treatment, and ideas.

The attitude of the reviewers was rather hostile, although they admitted the strength and power of the book. The review in the *Outlook* was typical:

It is a misfortune that he should have devoted so much skill and virility to the description of a life so essentially without spiritual significance, and so repulsive in its habit and quality. There is a touch of idealism in the relations of the two elderly lovers who appear in the story; otherwise the reader is immersed in a world of bald and brutal realism from

---

[1] Cf. Oscar Cargill, *Intellectual America: Ideas on the March* (New York, 1941), p. 97. The publishers felt constrained to print the following apologia at the end of the first edition of *McTeague*: "It may as well be stated at the outset that this is a harsh, almost brutal story. It deals with a class of people who are beyond question 'common,' and the author is far too conscientious an artist not to depict them as they really are. . . ."

[2] See pp. 277 ff.

beginning to end, and is brought into association with none whose vulgarity and brutality is unrelieved by higher qualities. . . . It is to be hoped that Mr. Norris will find subjects better worthy of his power.[1]

A critic in the *Argonaut* was rather insolent:

. . . seven tenths of the story the normal reader will peruse with a mixture of depression and disgust. We have heard Zola called '*Apôtre de ce qui pue.*' Similarly, Mr. Norris riots in odors and stenches. He might have changed his sub-title and called his book 'McTeague: A Study in Stinks.'[2]

Some magazines demonstrated their opposition by keeping silence. The *"Nation,* the *Atlantic Monthly,* and the 'big three,' *Harper's, Scribner's* and the *Century,* ignored *McTeague."*[3]

Among the critics who rose in defense of the book were Howells and Marcosson, who had both spoken favorably of *Moran.* Howells looked upon *McTeague* as a remarkable book, comparing it with the works of Zola, but he deplored its melodramatic ending. He wrote:

. . . It is saying both too much and too little to say that Mr. Norris has built his book on Zolaesque lines, yet Zola is the master of whom he reminds you in a certain epical conception of life. He reminds you of Zola also in his lingering love of the romantic, which indulges itself in the end in an anticlimax worthy of Dickens. He ignores as simply and sublimely as Zola any sort of nature or character beyond or above those of Polk street in San Francisco, but within the ascertained limits he convinces you, two-thirds of the time, of his absolute truth to them. He does not, of course, go to Zola's lengths, breadths, and depths; but he goes far enough to difference his work from the old-fashioned American novel. . . .

Mr. Norris has, in fact, learned his lesson well, but he has not learned it all. His true picture of life is not true, because it leaves beauty out. Life is squalid and cruel and vile and hateful, but it is noble and tender and pure and lovely, too. By and by he will put these traits in, and then his powerful scene will be a reflection of reality; by and by he will achieve something of the impartial fidelity of the photograph. In the meantime he has done a picture of life which has form, which has texture, which has color, which has what great original power and ardent study of Zola give, but which lacks the spiritual light and air, the consecration which the larger art of Tolstoy gives. It is a little inhuman, and it is distinctly

---

[1] Quoted by Walker, *op. cit.,* pp. 223–4.

[2] *Ibid.,* p. 224. The full title of the novel is: *McTeague: A Story of San Francisco.*

[3] Walker, *op. cit.,* p. 225.

not for the walls of living-rooms, where ladies of the family sit and the children go in and out. This may not be a penalty, but it is the inevitable consequence of expansion in fiction.[1]

Norris probably followed Howells' advice to bring in light and beauty, for his subsequent books are more humane and lighter in tone and touch than the gloomy and depressing *McTeague*.[2]
Having read Howells' review Norris wrote from New York City:

> Need I say how pleased and delighted I am over your review of *McTeague* in this last number of *Literature*. It has encouraged me more than anything that has ever been said of my work. I believe, too, you were quite right in saying that it was not the whole truth, and that the novel that is true to life cannot afford to ignore the finer things. I agree in every one of your criticisms always excepting the anticlimax, the "death in the desert" business. I am sure that has its place.[3]

And in answer to Marcosson's appreciation of *McTeague*, Norris wrote on March 14, 1899:

> ... I was very much afraid you would not approve of my dentist, and am rather uncertain as to his reception by the G. P. But so far the critics have been unusually good to me. ...
> What pleased me most in your review of 'McTeague' was the 'disdaining all pretensions to style.' It is precisely what I try most to avoid. I detest 'fine writing,' 'rhetoric,' 'elegant English,'—tommyrot. Who cares for fine style! Tell your yarn and let your style go to the devil. We don't want literature, we want life.
> You saw every point I tried to make in 'McTeague' and didn't misunderstand where many other critics have been thick-witted enough.[4]

Garland, who read *McTeague* in February 1899, sent Norris a note of appreciation, to which Norris replied:

> Thank you so very much for your very encouraging letter about McTeague which I have just received and read. I value very highly indeed the congratulations you were kind enough to extend to me and sincerely hope I shall always merit your appreciation in the matter of my work in the future.[5]

---

[1] "A Case in Point," *Literature*, I (March 24, 1899), 241-2. Quoted by Walker, *op. cit.*, pp. 227-8.

[2] The unmarketability of *Vandover and the Brute* may also have contributed to Norris's change of attitude.

[3] Mildred Howells, *op. cit.*, II, 102.

[4] Marcosson, *op. cit.*, pp. 234-5. G. P. stands for "general public."

[5] Unpublished letter pasted in Garland's copy of *McTeague*. Cf. p. 61.

The winter of 1898–9, which Norris spent in New York as
a publisher's reader, was in many ways troublesome for him. He
was not a successful reader, sometimes lacked money,[1] and occasionally despaired about his literary career. A letter, dated May 7,
1899, to Mr. and Mrs. Ernest Peixotto gives evidence of his
feelings:

... when will we all be together again, and will I ever forget how
much you both helped to make this hard winter of '98–99 easy for me.
What I should have done without you I honestly don't know, because
there were times when the whole thing was something of a grind and
it didn't seem worth while to go on at all. Well, somehow one does pull
through—with such help as yours.[2]

As a contrast to the tragic and somber *McTeague* there appeared in September, 1899, the delightful and joyous *Blix*, the
story of Norris's wooing[3] and struggle for literary recognition.
On March 14, 1899, he informed Marcosson of his purpose in
writing *Blix*:

It is as different from 'McTeague' as 'McTeague' was different from
'Moran.' It is essentially a love story. But what I have tried to do was
to turn out a love story that should not slop over. No sentimentality
—everything healthy and clean and natural. 'Blix' does not belong to
any 'school' so far as I can see. It's not naturalism and it's not romanticism; it's just a story. Nothing very violent happens. There are no
disagreeable people in it and it finishes—to my notion—happily.

I'm not so sure but what 'McTeague' could have happened in any
big city anywhere. But it would be absolutely impossible for 'Blix' to
have occurred anywhere else but San Francisco. It is more intimately
Californian than anything I have ever done. There is no dirt in it, none
of the grime and grabble of the Polk Street business, unavoidable as they
were.[4]

Blix contains some interesting information about Norris's reading.
There are, for instance, several references to Kipling. Describing

---

[1] Since the separation of Norris's parents in 1894 the economic situation
of the Norris family changed considerably. Moreover, in New York, Norris
was homesick for California. See letter dated March 22, 1899 from Norris
to Mrs. Davenport. See Walker, *op. cit.*, p. 209.

[2] Ernest Peixotto, "Romanticist Under the Skin: Frank Norris," *Saturday
Review of Literature*, IX (May 27, 1933), 613–14.

[3] In the fall of 1896 Norris met Jeanette Black at a ball and on January 12,
1900 they were married, and later one child, a daughter, was born to them.

[4] Marcosson, *op. cit.*, p. 234–5.

his work on the San Francisco *Daily Times* (read the *Wave*),
Condy (read Norris) admits that he had had "an inoculation of
the Kipling virus, had suffered an almost fatal attack of Harding
Davis, and had even been affected by Maupassant."[1] He men-
tions Kipling's *Life's Handicap*, *Plain Tales from the Hills*, *Many
Inventions*, and *The Seven Seas*.[2]

Norris's interest in polar exploration found expression in the
rather uneven novel *A Man's Woman*, published in February,
1900. The book, composed immediately after the Spanish war,
tells of Ward Bennett's futile attempt to reach the North Pole.
Norris's chief interest, however, was focused on the clash between
the indomitable wills of Bennett and Lloyd Searight, a nurse, with
whom he was in love. Walker rightly observes that there are "two
notes running through this novel written during a period of reaction: the pervading air of the sick-room tainted with the vitiating
warmth of malarial fever; and the emphasis on the gruesome and
horrible which reflects memories of a boy who had recently slept under boards glazed with human blood and seen soldiers writhe in
the base hospitals outside of Santiago."[3] Norris himself did not
consider the novel very successful. He wrote to Marcosson:

It's a kind of theatrical sort with a lot of niggling analysis to try to
justify the violent action of the first few chapters. It is very slovenly
put together and there are only two real people in all its 100,000 words.
It's different from my other books, but it's the last one that will be, if
you understand what I mean. I am going back *definitely* now to the style
of MacT. and stay with it right along. I've been sort of feeling my way
ever since the 'Moran' days and getting a twist of myself. Now I think
I know where I am and what game I play the best. The Wheat series
will be straight naturalism with all the guts I can get into it.[4]

An idea as "big as all out-doors" was in Norris's mind. *The
Epic of the Wheat* had been conceived and in a burst of enthusiasm
he wrote Howells:

[1] *Compl. Works*, III, 10.
[2] *Ibid.*, pp. 38, 52, 65, 127. There are also references to Shakespeare (pp. 95,
117, 122, 124), Browning (pp. 103, 151), Lafcadio Hearn (p. 50) and the sentence
"Most couples would have 'drifted apart'" (p. 44) echoes James A. Herne's
Drifting Apart.
[3] Walker, *op. cit.*, p. 215.
[4] Marcosson, *op. cit.*, pp. 237-8.

I have the idea of another novel or rather series of novels buzzing in my head these days. I think there is a chance for somebody to do some great work with the West and California as a background, and which will be at the same time thoroughly American. My idea is to write three novels around the one subject of *Wheat*. First, a story of California (the producer), second, a story of Chicago (the distributor), third, a story of Europe (the consumer) and in each to keep to the idea of this huge Niagara of wheat rolling from West to East. I think a big epic trilogy *could* be made out of such a subject, that at the same time would be modern and distinctly American. The idea is so big that it frightens me at times but I have about made up my mind to have a try at it.[1]

The Octopus (April, 1901), *The Pit* (January, 1903), were the first two volumes of the trilogy; and *The Wolf*, which was to have been the third, was never written. The central theme of the series is the Wheat, displayed as a vast symbol, a huge, impersonal life force.

The Octopus marks the beginning of a new phase in Norris's writings. His scope broadened and his concern was less with individual than with social problems. The change of attitude was partially due to his own maturity and his emerging interest in the conflicts and debates of his times, particularly between capital and labor, and between the plutocracy and the people. It must be remembered, however, that Norris was more interested in these conflicts and issues because they afforded material for dramatic stories than because he was concerned with reform and social justice.

Norris spent much time in the preparation and writing of *The Octopus* and was glad when it was completed. On September 13, 1900 he wrote his friend Marcosson:

The Squid is nearing conclusion. Hooray! I can see the end. . . . I know that in the masses I've made no mistake. You will find some things in it that—for me—are new departures. It is the most romantic thing I've ever done. One of the secondary sub-plots is pure romance—oh, even mysticism, if you like, a sort of allegory—I call it the allegorical side of the wheat subject—and the fire in it is the Allegory of the Wheat. The movement of the whole business is very slow at first—don't really get under weigh till after the first 15,000 words (it's about 200,000 words long), then, with the first pivotal incident it quickens a bit, and from there on I've tried to accelerate it steadily till at the last you are—I hope— just whirling and galloping and tearing along till you come *bang!* all of

---

[1] Mildred Howells, *op. cit.*, II, 102-3.

a sudden to a great big crushing END, something that will slam you right between your eyes and knock you off your feet—all this I *hope* for. *Sabe?* There will be about twenty characters in the book, ten really important, ten (about) secondary and five or six mere supers. In the front matter I am going—maybe—to insert a list of *dramatis personæ* and—this *surely* —a map of the locality.[1]

The scene of the novel is the fertile San Joaquin Valley in Southern California in the early eighties, and the picture of the growing and harvesting of wheat is vivid. A group of farmers are involved in a struggle to resist the encroachments of the Pacific and Southwestern Railroad, whose unofficial agent is S. Behrman. Through him the railroad trust influences prices and rates. In order to protect their interests, the farmers form a league against the railroad, but all is in vain, and in an armed clash many of the rebellious farmers are killed and their families are thrown into poverty. Magnus Derrick becomes insane; Behrman dies in the hold of a ship, where, symbolically, he is smothered by the wheat itself. The novel was based on an actual conflict between a group of farmers and a railroad trust.[2]

Although *The Octopus* contains many romantic elements, it is naturalistic in theme, treatment, and deterministic philosophy. It is a sociological novel which presents graphically the life and problems of the San Joaquin farmers, but Norris's attitude toward the issues involved is not consistent throughout the book. He sympathizes with the farmers and the 'reds,' but he finds excuses even for the railroad, a fact which somewhat disturbs the unity of the book, unless it is realized that Norris felt that both the railroad and its enemies were victims of forces they could not control. Norris's concern was primarily artistic and not ethical. (Cf. Garland's story "Under the Lion's Paw.") In the clash between the farmers and the railroad he saw mainly an issue of great dramatic quality, less a social evil which should be removed. Perhaps also an attempt at achieving objectivity and detachment had something to do with his apparently inconsistent attitude toward the problems involved.

In general the reviewers pronounced *The Octopus* a novel of great power. Some critics objected to Norris's seeming partisan-

---

[1] Marcosson, *op. cit.*, pp. 238–9.

[2] See Walker, *op. cit.*, pp. 246 ff. See also pp. 173–6 of the present study.

ship with the 'reds,' others to the romantic flaws and the voluptuousness in the portraiture of women. Many criticized his debt to Zola, and Howells asserted that *The Octopus* was "an epic of Zolaesque largeness." Granted its defects he considered it "a great book, simple, sombre, large, and of a final authority as the record of a tragical passage of American, of human events, which, if we did not stand in their every-day presence, we should shudder at as the presage of unexampled tyrannies."[1]

The Octopus contains some significant references to books and authors which may help us to understand certain aspects of the novel. Annixter now and then read a chapter of *David Copperfield*, and Magnus' wife enjoyed reading *Marius the Epicurean*, *The Essays of Elia*, *Sesame and Lilies*, and *The Stones of Venice*.[2] There are also references to Byron, Bryant, Goethe, Schiller, Bakunin, *Beowulf*, *The Nibelungen*, *The Roman de la Rose*, and Daudet's *Tartarin de Tarascon*. Judging from the following quotation it is probable that Norris had read some of the political and social thinkers of his day: Presley [read Norris] "flung aside his books of poems—Milton, Tennyson, Browning, even Homer—and addressed himself to Mill, Malthus, Young, Pushkin, Henry George, Schopenhauer."[3]

Compared with *The Octopus*, *The Pit* is a conventional novel lacking the former's verity and power. The subject was less interesting to Norris than that of its predecessor, which had more humane implications. *The Pit*[4] describes a "deal" in the Chicago wheat pit. The hero, Curtis Jadwin, is a famous speculator who succeeds in gaining a temporary corner in wheat, but is beaten by the immense production of new crops in the West. Meanwhile he has married Laura Dearborn. She drifts into an affair with an artist, Sheldon Corthell, while Jadwin spends most of his time at the Board of Trade. After Jadwin's crash, Laura realizes

---

[1] "Editor's Easy Chair," *Harper's Monthly*, CIII (October, 1901), 825.

[2] *Compl. Works*, I, 57.

[3] *Ibid.*, II, 23.

[4] The novel was probably inspired by Joseph Leiter's colossal failure in 1898. Another famous capitalist, Charles T. Yerkes, whose name echoes Norris's Curtis, may also have been a probable source of inspiration. Yerkes inspired such novelists as Fuller, Will Payne, Herrick, and Dreiser. The matrimonial crisis described in the novel was, to a certain degree, based on that of Norris's parents. See p. 118 n. 1.

that, after all, she loves him, and the book ends with their setting out on a journey westward to face a new life.

The naturalistic technique in this novel is evident particularly in the scenes describing the Board of Trade and the furious battle in the wheat pit. As a story of the rise and fall of a business man it is a companion-piece to Howell's *The Rise of Silas Lapham* and Fuller's *The Cliff-Dwellers*.

Norris's premature death on October 25, 1902, following an appendicitis operation, ended his short literary career. The last volume of *The Epic of the Wheat*, *The Wolf*, was to have dealt with a European famine relieved through American wheat. Its locale was intended to be Genoa.

Norris's later reading seems to have followed more or less the lines established before he published *Moran of the Lady Letty*. French writers continued to interest him, especially Zola, Flaubert, and Hugo, but he also found La Rochefoucauld interesting and his "Salt and Sincerity"[1] seems to owe a great deal to the French writer. In *The Responsibilities of the Novelist* (1903), a book of critical writings, where he mentions a great many writers, he refers with respect to Bourget, Dumas, and Maeterlinck. Hardy, too, is praised and Tolstoy, whose *Anna Karenina* he mentions, is called "incontestably great."[2] Dreiser's *Sister Carrie* and Conrad's *Lord Jim* were two major discoveries for Norris when he was a reader for Doubleday. Among American writers besides Dreiser he thought that Harold Frederic, Robert Herrick, and Owen Wister showed promise.

Those who knew Norris testify that he was generous and affectionate and had unusual charm and magnetism. Garland, who greatly admired him wrote:

My record describes him as 'a stunning fellow—an author who does not personally disappoint his admirers. He is perilously handsome, tall and straight, with keen brown eyes and beautifully modeled features. His face is as smooth as that of a boy of twenty, but his hair is almost white. I have never known a more engaging writer. He is a poet in appearance, but a close observer and a realist in his fiction.[3]

---

[1] *Compl. Works*, VII, 193–226.

[2] *Ibid.*, p. 33.

[3] *Companions on the Trail*, pp. 103–4. As an illustration of their acquaintance the following unpublished letter written by Norris to Garland from a New Jersey hotel in 1901 may be quoted here: "I am destined to be forever at cross

And Harry Thurston Peck made the following comment on Crane and Norris:

I never met a less blood-boultered Banquo than poor little Mr. Crane. He is inoffensive as a lamb, and Mr. Norris is extremely like him in manner, albeit he has none, or too little, of Mr. Crane's humour. The author of the terrible 'McTeague' is a pleasant, cultivated young gentleman, inclined to be obstreperous—and humourless—in arguments on realism, but in every other respect a very pleasant boy.[1]

Norris's development as a writer went through three phases: he began as an author of naturalistic novels of character (*McTeague*, *Vandover and the Brute*); in an attempt to find himself he went through a period of transition in which he emphasized moral values (*A Man's Woman*), and he ended by writing more or less sociological novels from a deterministic point of view (*The Octopus*, *The Pit*).

To sum up: In Garland the robustness of his pioneer temperament was mingled with a strong moral pathos. His demand for freedom, his sense of justice and honesty, and his quest for an intellectual life found utterance in his revolt against social conditions particularly in the Middle West. Compared with Garland's ethical outlook, that of Crane and Norris appears, in the main, aesthetic, born of greater interest in art than in reform. But they were, in their way, ethically conscious and in sympathy with the poor, the oppressed, and the outcast. Despite differences in temperament and background the three writers were, however, alike in that they dared to write "the bold and the unconventional," thus contributing to the widening of the sphere of American letters.

---

purposes with you and to appear always in the most unfavorable light. Did you finally get a copy of the Squid. The first one I sent you—not knowing your residence address was returned to me with its accompanying letter from Collier's Weekly. Another one went to West Salem Saturday. May I not expect your latest in return? Though I don't deserve it. Thank you very kindly for your invitation to visit you in Chicago. My wife and I expect to be there in September of this year and we shall certainly give ourselves the pleasure of looking you up."

[1] Beer, *The Mauve Decade*, pp. 190-1.

CHAPTER VI

LITERARY CREDOS

The new conception of the universe demanded a new literature based upon and governed by science. Truth, sincerity, honesty, and objectivity became the catchwords of the writers of the day. The new literature revolted against the traditional forms of expression, and in a series of manifestos, in prefaces, articles, pamphlets, and books the writers expounded and defended their methods and theories. Before Zola launched his handbook of naturalism, *Le Roman expérimental*, the brothers Goncourt had already brought out their *Idées et sensations* in 1866. Undoubtedly the debate caused by naturalism reached its climax in the eighties when Zola brought out a series of books expounding his theories[1]: *Mes Haines* (1879), *Le Roman expérimental* (1880), *Le Naturalisme au théâtre* (1881), *Nos Auteurs dramatiques* (1881), *Les Romanciers naturalistes* (1881), *Documents littéraires* (1881), and *Une Campagne* (1882). In 1888 Maupassant published *Pierre et Jean* containing an interesting essay entitled "Le Roman,"[2] in which he laid down criteria for the writing and judging of fiction. In England Walter Besant set down rules for creative writing in *The Art of Fiction*[3] (1884). In two more essays, "The Candour of English Fiction" (*New Review*, 1890) and "The Science of Fiction" (*New Review*, 1891), he further discussed his views on English letters. George Moore, a disciple of Zola, told in *Confessions of a Young Man* (1888) of the impression made upon him when reading an article by Zola on naturalism.[4]

---

[1] See also a list of his prefaces and speeches in *Œuvres*, L, 392–4.

[2] First written for the Paris *Figaro* in the fall of 1887. The essay was a development of ideas expressed in earlier articles by Maupassant. It advocated a psychological novel in the manner of Bourget.

[3] It was mainly a plea for the novel that amused.

[4] George Moore, *Confessions of a Young Man* (New York, 1901), p. 63. Cargill wrote of the book: ". . . countless Americans learned all they know about

In 1894 an American translation of *Le Roman expérimental* was issued under the title of *The Experimental Novel.* And in 1898 Tolstoy's attack on art, literature, and music, *What Is Art?*, caused a great stir among American writers and critics.

In the nineties the new literature and the new literary theories were also much debated in literary journals and magazines and elsewhere throughout the United States. The new tendencies in literature called forth both defenders and attackers. During the nineties and even after, the discussion of literary theories was confusing because of the looseness of terms used. In general, in the eighties and nineties the movement usually called naturalism went under the name of realism, but readers of, for instance Zola and Howells, recognized in these two writers vastly different exponents of "realism." A critic in the *Dial* of April, 1895, voiced this confusion in an article called "The Allotrophy of 'Realism.' " The writer observed:

> Discouraging indeed to the mere student of text-books, this apparent confusion of terms seems to indicate that the word "realism" (whether or not with the approval of its chief promotors) is obtaining a wider and deeper meaning. Ten years ago it meant that "a novel should have neither plot, nor beginning, nor end." The realistic novel was then "the novel of the bare fact," photographic, rather than a portraiture, in the delineation of character. This now should go, perhaps, by the name of naturalism.[1]

In an article in the *Forum* the school of Zola was called the *realistic* school *par excellence*, and an essay by Emil Blum in the *Arena* of July, 1893, on German naturalists carried the title "The Realistic Trend of Modern German Literature." In order not to be linked with Zola's type of writing Garland used the words *veritism* and *veritist*.[2] When some one labeled Zola a realist, Norris would cry out angrily that Zola was no realist but a romanticist,

---

Impressionism, Decadence, and Naturalism from this book, and some few were stimulated by it to inquire further into the subjects there scanned and to acquire a sounder knowledge of them." *Ideas on the March*, p. 79. See also Moore's *Impressions and Opinions* (1891), G. B. Shaw's *The Quintessence of Ibsenism* (1891), *The Sanity of Art* (1895), *The Perfect Wagnerite* (1898), and Oscar Wilde's *Intentions* (1891).

[1] George Merriam Hyde, "The Allotrophy of 'Realism,' " *Dial*, XVIII (April 16, 1895), 231–2.

[2] See pp. 138 ff.

in order to distinguish Zola's writings from the "teacup realism" of Howells.[1] A distinction between realism and naturalism was given by Albion W. Tourgée in an article entitled "The Claim of 'Realism.'"

... the "realist" strives to maintain his exclusive right to the claim that he is the only truth-teller in fiction by drawing a line betwixt himself and the so-called "naturalist." The real distinction may be stated in a sentence. The "realist" keeps to what he deems a middle course ... Truth, he says, does not lie midway between extremes, but embraces the antipodes. The absence of vice or virtue is not life, but the union and contrast of them. So what the "realist" so carefully avoids, the "naturalist" paints with unflagging zeal. Nothing is too high or too low, too fair or too foul, for him. He paints vice in the nude and virtue in its loveliest colors. M. Zola is the type of the "naturalists"; Mr. Howells the head of the "realists."[2]

While in France in the early eighties the fight for naturalism was at its highest, in America in the seventies, eighties, and nineties a group of writers were fighting the battle for realism.[3] These writers, to a certain extent inspired by European realism and naturalism and probably spurred on by the discussion provoked by French naturalism, attempted to expound, explain, and defend the new attitudes toward life, art, and literature. In this battle against traditional romanticism, not only such established writers as Henry James and W. D. Howells took part, but also the naturalistic experimenters of the nineties.

An obvious manifestation that the old school was vanishing and a new era was about to dawn was exhibited in the parodies and attacks that Mark Twain aimed at romanticism.[4] More direct attacks on romanticism and an advocacy of realism or veritism—in Norris's case, Zolaesque naturalism—came from a group of writers who set forth their literary credos in essays and books. I have included a brief section on James' realistic theory and a

---

[1] See p. 157.

[2] *North American Review*, CXLVIII (March, 1889), 386.

[3] Cf. William C. Frierson, "The English Controversy over Realism in Fiction," *PMLA*, XLIII (June, 1928), 533–48. See also Herbert Edwards, "Howells and the Controversy over Realism in American Fiction," *American Literature*, III (November, 1931), 237–48.

[4] See S. B. Liljegren, *The Revolt against Romanticism in American Literature as Evidenced in the Works of S. L. Clemens* (Upsala, 1945).

longer one on Howells' in order to show the similarity to and the continuity of some of the literary theories of these two writers and those of Garland, Crane, and Norris. At the same time a tendency, though vague and inconsistent, away from the realism of James and Howells toward naturalism came gradually to the fore, at least in the case of Norris.

1. HENRY JAMES AND *THE ART OF FICTION*. 1884

Stimulated by a pamphlet by Walter Besant, Henry James published "The Art of Fiction" in 1884.[1] In this essay he expressed his literary theories and pleaded for realism and freedom for the artist to paint all life. He defended the French writers, particularly Zola, "to whose solid and serious work no explorer of the capacity of the novel can allude without respect..."[2]

The chief ideas laid down in the essay may be grouped under five different headings: *A Definition*. "A novel," asserted James, "is in its broadest definition a personal, a direct impression of life: that, to begin with, constitutes its value, which is greater or less according to the intensity of the impression. But there will be no intensity at all, and therefore no value, unless there is freedom to feel and say."[3] *The Importance of Reality*. James maintained that the air of reality was the chief virtue of a novel on which its other merits depended.[4] The writer ought to attempt to produce the illusion of life. *The Sphere of the Novel*. The novel should treat of all aspects of life. James asserted that "the province of art is all life, all feeling, all observation, all vision. ... it is all experience. That is a sufficient answer to those who maintain that it must not touch the sad things of life..."[5] *The Question of Morality*. Questions of art were questions of execution, whereas questions of morality were "quite another affair."[6] He

---

[1] James' essay appeared together with Besant's in W. Besant, *The Art of Fiction* (Boston, 1884).

[2] James, "The Art of Fiction," in *American Critical Essays*, ed. by Norman Foerster (London, 1930), p. 185.

[3] *Ibid.*, p. 163.

[4] *Ibid.*, p. 168.

[5] *Ibid.*, p. 176.

[6] *Ibid.*, p. 182.

attacked Besant's praise of prudence in the English novelists, an attack which also embraced the American writers, stating that in "the English novel ... there is a traditional difference between that which people know and that which they agree to admit that they know, that which they see and that which they speak of, that which they feel to be a part of life and that which they allow to enter into literature."[1] Thus, James pleaded for a more liberal attitude toward sex in literature. *Advocacy of Objectivity and Sincerity.* He considered that the only condition which he could think of attaching to the composition of a novel was that it must be sincere.[2]

2. W. D. HOWELLS AND *CRITICISM AND FICTION.* 1891

From 1886 to 1892, when directing the critical department of *Harper's Monthly* called the "Editor's Study," Howells conducted a campaign for realism in American letters. In 1891 he published a book of literary theory entitled *Criticism and Fiction*,[3] largely ideas expressed earlier in the *Harper's* column. In the eighties and nineties when realism was struggling to make itself heard, it was almost overrun by the vogue for historical romances. Traditional idealism and romanticism yielded but reluctantly to the

---

[1] *Ibid.*, pp. 182–3.

[2] *Ibid.*, p. 184.

[3] Further material for the discussion of Howells' literary credo can be found in *My Literary Passions* (1895), *Impressions and Experiences* (1896), *Heroines of Fiction* (1901), and *Literature and Life* (1902). For the present study it has been necessary to concentrate on *Criticism and Fiction*, which is Howells' chief contribution to the literary debate of the period.

It is interesting to note that most of the books on literary theory were of pocket-size, beautifully printed and neatly bound. See for instance Howells' *Criticism and Fiction*, F. Marion Crawford's *The Novel: What It Is*, and Garland's *Crumbling Idols* (1894).

In the discussion of the battle for realism and the objections of the romancers to realism, E. Marchand in his book on Norris is somewhat confusing, because he makes no clear distinction between realism and naturalism. He seems to be unaware of the fact that most of these attacks were aimed at French naturalism rather than against Howellsian realism. See point 1 of the objections to realism: "It was indecent." P. 4. This can hardly be said of Howells' realism. Howells suffered greatly from these criticasters, because "realism" in the nineties implied realism and naturalism. See Marchand, *op. cit.*, pp. 4 ff.

attacks of the realist. Counterattacks were launched by stubborn romancers like Maurice Thompson and F. Marion Crawford, whose *The Novel: What It Is* (1893) was mainly a plea for the novel that entertained. Conservative critics accused Howells, the leader of American realists, of dullness and triviality. Consequently it was but natural that Howells, in his struggle for realism, first turned against what he considered to be its chief enemy, romanticism.

The romances of Scott and imitations thereof had long held the field when Howells delivered his attack on romanticism in fiction. He had by then written about twenty novels, most of them in the realistic manner which he advocated in *Criticism and Fiction*. He rebelled against romanticism in no uncertain terms. He asserted that "In criticism it is his [the realist's] business to break the images of false gods and misshapen heroes, to take away the poor silly toys that many grown people would still like to play with."[1] He went on to say that it was not possible for the realist to respect such literary monsters as Jack the Giant-killer or Puss in Boots, the convict Vautrec or the Marquis de Montrivaut, for when Balzac created the two last-mentioned characters "he was not realistic, he was romantic."[2] Howells, who was an admirer of Balzac and his art, condemned the romantic paraphernalia of *Le Père Goriot*, the untrue, exorbitant feelings of Goriot, and the romantic exaggerations frequently found in Balzac's works, especially in his heroes. But Balzac was excused because he wrote during a period when the battle for realism was not yet won and when the romantic tradition was preponderantly strong.

Howells did not show any indulgence toward the long-winded historical tales of Scott. Although he admitted that they still could amuse young people, he complained of the diffuse and clumsy style, of the tedious descriptions, and the tiresome moralizing on every page. What was true of Scott was also true of another great master, Goethe, whom, however, he considered "greater than Scott in being less romantic..."[3]

Deploring the fact that romanticism still lingered in England

---

[1] *Criticism and Fiction*, p. 16.
[2] *Ibid.*, p. 17.
[3] *Ibid.*, p. 22.

despite the novels of Thomas Hardy, Howells maintained that English literature had declined, because of the careless writings of Scott, Bulwer-Lytton, Dickens, and others. As he disapproved of certain classical literature, declaring that only parts of it were still alive, he did not appreciate novels which were intended solely to amuse and offered no food for thought. The novel of escapism did not attract the realist of *A Modern Instance*. He said of the novel which aimed merely to entertain:

No sordid details of verity here, if you please; no wretched being humbly and weakly struggling to do right and to be true, suffering for his follies and his sins, tasting joy only through the mortification of self, and in the help of others; nothing of all this, but a great, whirling splendor of peril and achievement, a wild scene of heroic adventure and of emotional ground and lofty tumbling . . .[1]

He proclaimed, moreover, that the critics were unable to judge the new literature, for their minds were too strongly fixed in the romantic tradition. The American critics were biased and intolerant and they judged creative art from personal preferences only; instead their business should be to classify and analyze rather than to blame and praise. His views of the critics are reminiscent of those expressed by Maupassant in the preface to *Pierre et Jean*. The French writer also found that critics were inclined to praise or blame a work of art and to judge it according to their own taste and personal conception of art. In order to deserve the title, a critic should be nothing but "un analyste sans tendances, sans préférences, sans passions, et, comme un expert en tableaux, n'apprécier que la valeur artiste de l'objet d'art qu'on lui soumet."[2] It is possible that both writers arrived at their attitudes toward critics independently, but it is perhaps safe to assume that Howells knew of Maupassant's essay and may have found his own views expressed and verified by the French writer.

While denouncing the romantic school of literature, Howells advocated a kind of realism, which he found in larger measure in Mark Twain, Henry James, George Eliot, Tolstoy, Turgenev, Pérez Galdós, and Giovanni Verga than in the French naturalists. "Unconsciously I have always been," Howells once wrote, "as

---

[1] *Ibid.*, p. 106.

[2] *Pierre et Jean* (New York, 1936), p. xxxv.

much of a realist as I could," and he defined realism as follows: "Realism is nothing more and nothing less than the truthful treatment of material . . ."[1] The only requirement of realism was *truthfulness*. To be true to life, was the first principle of realism. Truth above all, claimed Howells: "I confess that I do not care to judge any work of the imagination without first of all applying this test to it. We must ask ourselves before we ask anything else, Is it true?—true to the motives, the impulses, the principles that shape the life of actual men and women?"[2] The same quest for truth in fiction was also a salient point in *Le Roman expérimental*, in which Zola demanded of the novel the rigidity of a scientific truth. This feature was also emphasized in Maupassant's "Le Roman," in which he observed that there had come "une école réaliste ou naturaliste qui a prétendu nous montrer la vérité, rien que la vérité et toute la vérité."[3]

According to Howells, realistic literature should be "simple, natural and honest." It should not concern itself with the "romantic exaggeration" nor with the filth and squalor of Zola's naturalism. For the realist was stimulated "not by vain shows and shadows and ideals, but by realities, in which alone the truth lives."[4] Nothing in life was insignificant to the realist, but he was mainly interested in the commonplace, the average, and the trivial. The normal was what counted most in life and literature. Garland once wrote of Howells:

> Howells intends to treat of the average, the commonplace, to celebrate the normal men and women of America. He aims at being true to his time and place. Like Whitman he has no need of themes of feudalism. In his quiet way he is quite as revolutionary. His realism is not that of the French. Zola is not a realist as Howells uses the term, for the reason that he treats, not of the average but of the abnormally criminal classes. He deals too largely with phenomenal cases, with the animal traits in men. This is truth of a certain sort but it has no kinship with the realism of Howells, and is very far from the ideal of Whitman. Decorum, decency and humour were the characteristics of the average American as Whitman observed him and these qualities are in the novels of Howells. The majority of men are not libertines or thieves, nor the majority

---

[1] Howells, *op. cit.*, p. 73.

[2] *Ibid.*, p. 99.

[3] Maupassant, *op. cit.*, p. xxxvi. Cf. also the same emphasis on truth in Garland and Norris.

[4] Howells, *op. cit.*, p. 16.

of women conscienceless even in Paris. In his war upon the romantic
school with the super-human and ideal characters, Zola and his followers
have gone to the opposite extreme.[1]

Howells' interest was, as Alfred Kazin summarized it, "in the
domesticities of society, homely scenes and values, people meeting
on trains, ships, and at summer hotels . . . friendly dinners, the
furrows of homespun character, housekeeping as a principle of
existence . . . Howells had therefore no reason to think of realism
as other than simplicity, Americanism, and truth."[2] His realism
was a quiet realism depicting the commonplace, clean American
life as he saw and understood it, seemingly devoid of theft, murder,
adultery, and the like. Moreover, his realism was selective, but
selective on a sound, philosophic basis, on a definite, reasoned
theory: What was most common and most usual, was most real,
according to Howells. The naturalist, however, frequently dealt
with the uncommon, the abnormal, selecting that because it fitted
his theory of life; the realist should, ideally, have no theory.
Anything that *was*, was real; what was most common, therefore,
not the abnormal, was his material. If the sordid in a given time
and place was most common, then it was real and the realist used
it; if it was not most common, as it was in the world Howells
wrote about, then the realist did not use it. The naturalist, however, always used it, because he had a theory according to which
life was sordid and mean, conditioned by material and biological
forces.

Although an admirer of Flaubert's *Madame Bovary* and Dostoevsky's *Crime and Punishment* and of Tolstoy's *Anna Karenina*
Howells did not wish American novelists to utilize such tragic
themes. As is seen in his novels and in his critical works, he was
the confirmed realist who found naturalism false to his theory
of realism. In *Criticism and Fiction* he stated clearly his views
on naturalism, which seem to have been similar to those of Palacio Valdés, who "has some words of just censure for the French
naturalists . . . He [Valdés] sees the wide difference that passes
between this naturalism and the realism of the English and
Spanish; and he goes somewhat further than I should go in con-

---

[1] "William Dean Howells." Typewritten MS, undated.
[2] *On Native Grounds*, p. 8.

demning it."[1] Howells maintained that French naturalism was good as long as it depicted French life, but it did not belong in America. It was too dreary, too tragic, to attract the American apostle of the cheerful average.

One of the chief principles of realistic and naturalistic fiction was the quest for objectivity.[2] Howells turned particularly against the lack of objectivity shown by Balzac in some of his works and remarked of him: "He felt obliged to construct a mechanical plot, to surcharge his characters, to moralize openly, and baldly; he permitted himself to 'sympathize' with certain of his people, and to point out others for the abhorrence of his readers. This is not so bad in him as it would be in a novelist of our day."[3]

Although his realism seems to have been partly inspired by his extensive reading of European literature, Howells aimed above all at an *American*[4] realism portraying American characters and American scenes. America was the canvas on which the artists and writers painted; it furnished the material, while Europe provided certain patterns, models, and techniques. He urged writers to use the American language in their works, to call, for instance, an elevator an elevator and so on. American realism should be distinguished from realism elsewhere, since America herself was different from the old countries of Europe. It was quite inconceivable, asserted Howells, that an American author should write such a deeply tragic novel as *Crime and Punishment*,[5] for America was prosperous and well-ordered, and very few American authors had had experiences, similar to those of Dostoevsky, and he added that "whoever struck a note so profoundly tragic in American fiction would do a false and mistaken thing—as false and as mistaken in its way as dealing in American fiction with certain nudities which the Latin peoples seem to find edifying."[6] The novelist should

---

[1] Howells, *op. cit.*, p. 59.

[2] By objectivity I mean objectivity *in technique*, i.e. an avoidance of direct explanatory or didactic intervention by the writer. Both realists and naturalists try to be objective in technique.

[3] Howells, *op. cit.*, p. 20.

[4] Cf. Benjamin T. Spencer, "The New Realism and a National Literature," *PMLA*, LVI (1941), 1116–32.

[5] Dreiser's *An American Tragedy* (1925) may be called "An American Crime and Punishment."

[6] Howells, *op. cit.*, p. 128.

depict conditions that were particularly American. "Our novelists, therefore, concern themselves with the more smiling aspects of life, which are the more American, and seek the universal in the individual rather than the social interests."[1] He went on to say that death and sickness abounded in America too, but they were in the very nature of things and could not be helped, nor were they "peculiarly American, as the large, cheerful average of health and success and happy life is."[2]

A group of young radical writers whose experiences of American life were at variance with Howells', went a step beyond his realism, which they thought too gentle and quiet. Although their theories of literature in many respects recalled his, their practice no doubt marked a definite advance toward naturalism.

3. HAMLIN GARLAND AND *CRUMBLING IDOLS*. 1894

When Garland launched his literary manifesto he had, no doubt, thoroughly absorbed most of Howells' convictions as expressed in *Criticism and Fiction*. Valuable suggestions afforded perhaps also Emerson and Whitman and the prefaces to Eggleston's novels. Moreover, he may have depended upon certain critical theories of French and German thinkers, particularly Taine, Nordau, and Spielhagen. Véron's *Æsthetics* meant much to him. He was also aware of *Le Roman expérimental*.[3]

The themes running through Garland's manifesto were the inadequacy of the old masterpieces as models for modern literature, a demand for originality, and Americanism. He wrote in the preface to his critical essays:

I believe in the living, not the dead. The men and women around me interest me more than the saints and heroes of other centuries. . . .

Youth should be free from the dominion of the dead; therefore I defend the individual right of the modern creative mind to create in the image of life, and not in the image of any literary master, living or dead.[4]

In his advocacy of freedom from masters and insistence on creativity and on a distinctly American literature Garland

---

[1] *Ibid.* p. 128.
[2] *Ibid.* p. 129.
[3] See p. 75.
[4] *Crumbling Idols*, p. viii.

echoed Emerson's ideas in *The American Scholar*[1], the American declaration of intellectual independence. He also echoed Emerson's rhetorical style; particularly the author's foreword recalls the rhetoric of Emerson's address.

Garland was a zealous reformer and fought his battle for veritism with great enthusiasm, inspired, it seems to me, by the efforts of Howells. He criticized Sheridan and Scott, as Howells had done; he maintained, moreover, that the so-called classics were mostly worthless reading and attracted only the bookish few, and he turned against the British domination of American literature. He believed with Emerson that "Our day of dependence, our long apprenticeship to the learning of other lands, draws to a close. The millions that around us are rushing into life, cannot always be fed on the sere remains of foreign harvests."[2] As has been pointed out, Howells, too, urged the novelist to break the bonds of tradition. The American universities were considered strongholds of conservatism in literature and art. Howells felt this and so did Garland and both condemned these bulwarks of conservative tradition. Howells observed:

There is probably no chair of literature in this country from which the principles now shaping the literary expression of every civilized people are not denounced and confounded with certain objectionable French novels, or which teaches young men anything of the universal impulse which has given us the work, not only of Zola, but of Tourguéneff and Tolstoï in Russia, of Björnson and Ibsen in Norway, of Valdés and Galdós in Spain, of Verga in Italy.[3]

In *Crumbling Idols* Garland echoed Howells:

It can almost be stated as a rule without an exception that in our colleges there is no chair of English literature which is not dominated by conservative criticism, and where sneering allusion to modern writers is not daily made. The pupil is taught to worship the past, and is kept blind to the mighty literary movements of his own time. If he comes to understand Ibsen, Tolstoy, Björnson, Howells, Whitman, he must do it outside his instruction.[4]

---

[1] In *Roadside Meetings* Garland admitted his indebtedness to Emerson. Speaking of the ideas in his book of essays he observed: "In all this I was re-stating Emerson, of course, but my words had some power of their own." P. 260.

[2] *Essays* (New York, 1945), p. 308.

[3] Howells, *op. cit.*, p. 28.

[4] *Crumbling Idols*, p. 9.

Not only were the universities centers of conservatism, but the critics molded by these institutions were equally bound by the traditional approach to literature. They admonished the writers to take Shakespeare, Dickens, and Scott as their models and to look to Greece and Rome for inspiration; from the past alone could true and great literature be learnt. "The free untrodden paths do not lie in the direction of the past," pronounced Garland. "Shakespeare and Molière are to be ignored *as models* ... The undue worship of Shakespeare or any other dramatist is fatal to individual creation."[1] Shakespeare, Dante, Milton, and Wordsworth were mere names left on the bookshelves to gather dust. Garland demanded freedom from all masters, not merely a change of masters. "The American realist should stand for a liberated art. If this means emancipation from Shakespeare, or Scott, or Hugo, very well; but we should not argue for a change of masters. We should condemn with equal severity imitation of a living master like Ibsen."[2] And he added: "The fight is not between Shakespeare and Sheridan on one side, and the forces represented by Valdés and Ibsen and Howells on the other; it is the immitigable war between creative Youth and reminiscent Age. It is the rebellious demand of youth for the right to utter himself in his own way, without reference to past models."[3] While Garland rebelled against British classical literature, he also revolted against the New England school of writers who fed on the British classics. Garland was rather violent in his denunciation of the smug New England spirit and spoke in favor of the traditionless West. According to Garland New York, like Boston was too near London; it was no longer America.[4] Like Howells, he accused American literature of imitativeness. A new, native literature was, however, emerging in the virile West ousting the idols of the East and the British classics. Garland pleaded for Chicago as a literary center: "In the West there is coming into expression and literary influence the great Scandinavian and Germanic element to which the traditions of English literature are very weak and unimportant, and to whom Boston and New York are of small account."[5]

Garland's aim in *Main-Travelled Roads* was, it seems to me,

[1] *Ibid.*, p. 88. [2] *Ibid.*, p. 89. [3] *Ibid.*, p. 91.
[4] *Ibid.*, p. 154. [5] *Ibid.*, p. 147.

mainly to present a protest against the romantic portrayal of the Middle West. This purpose was clearly stated in the dedication of the book which reads as follows: "To my father and mother whose half-century pilgrimage on the main-travelled road of life has brought them only toil and deprivation, this book of stories is dedicated by a son to whom every day brings a deepening sense of his parents' silent heroism." On the following page he voiced his anti-romantic concept of the rural West:

> The main-travelled road in the West (as everywhere) is hot and dusty in summer, and desolate and drear with mud in fall and spring, and in winter the winds sweep the snow across it; but it does sometimes cross a rich meadow where the song of the larks and bobolinks and black-birds are tangled. Follow it far enough, it may lead past a bend in the river where the water laughs eternally over its shallows.

> Mainly it is long and wearyful [sic] and has a dull little town at one end, and a home of toil at the other. Like the main-travelled road of life it is traversed by many classes of people, but the poor and the weary predominate.

All Garland's early stories were exemplifications of this concept of the West, and in order to make the picture as complete as possible he desired to paint all aspects of life and to pay particular consideration to the description of the milieu, for he believed with Taine that a distinctive literature sprang from a description of environment acting upon the individual. "In order to present the realities of that life," Garland once wrote, "I put in the storm as well as the sun. I included the mud and manure as well as the wild roses and the clover."[1] Garland's tone, in his delineation of the people and the conditions of the West, was harsher than Howells' treatment of the "smiling aspects of life." But at the same time it was not the brutal naturalism of Zola. In order to avoid confusion with these two exponents of so-called "realism," Garland, as has been said above, used the word "veritism" and "veritist." In an early notebook dated 1886, Garland attacked what he called the conventional realism of Howells and James. A sounder form of realism which was true to modern life, he found in the writings of Friedrich Spielhagen.

> There is a great cry of Realism among certain classes of men today which involves a very great mistake ... Realism as advocated [by

---

[1] *Roadside Meetings*, p. 179.

Spielhagen] means a study of the manners and customs of the present age and as such has a very great meaning but as carried out by the writers above-mentioned [Howells and Henry James] is an absurd characterization of very weak work. Those men chronicle conventional trifles mainly. They no more give a real idea of this life of ours than a painter gives an idea of the landscape by painting the grasses with painstaking care. Their realism is of such character that to understand this age through their works would require as much reading and generalization as to judge of the present without any aid. They generalize nothing. They represent conventional personages not types. They study no great psychological movement . . . They seem to know passion only when it is conventional, or clothed in conventional forms.[1]

This was a somewhat strong outburst against the realistic leaders of America of the day. Later, as has been noted, Garland came to champion Howells in articles and lectures.[2] In *Crumbling Idols* he sympathized with Howells.

In a letter to Eldon C. Hill dated February 14, 1939, Garland explained how he came to use the word "veritism." He wrote:

You ask about my use of the word veritist. I began to use it in the late[3] nineties. Not being at that time a realist in the sense in which the followers of Zola used it, I hit upon the word veritist which I may have derived from Véron.[4] In truth I was an impressionist in that I presented life and landscape as I personally perceived them but [since] I sought a deeper significance in the use of the word, I added a word which subtended verification. I sought to verify my impressions by comparing impressions separated by an interval of time. I thought to get away from the use of the word realism[5] which implied predominant use of sexual vice and crime in the manner of Zola and certain of the German novelists.[6] For the most part, the men and women I had known in my youth were normal,

---

[1] Garland's unpublished notebook dated Jamaica Plain, March 3, 1886.

[2] See also "A Spoil of Office" in the *Arena*, V (April, 1892), 622.

[3] It should be an earlier date for the term was used in an interview in 1892 (p. 85 n.) and in *Crumbling Idols* (1894).

[4] Eugène Véron, *Æsthetics*. Transl. by W. H. Armstrong (London and Philadelphia, 1879). Cf. also the following statement by Garland: ". . .I had adapted Veritism as the word which best described my theory, a word which I gained from reading Eugène Véron's 'Esthetics' and Max Nordau's savage 'Conventional Lies'" *Roadside Meetings*, p. 32. The word "veritism" may also have been derived from the Italian "verismo." Cf. Paul Arrighi, *Le Verisme* (Paris, 1937).

[5] In the nineties the word "realism" often implied pornography. A title like *Nana. A Realistic Novel* was occasionally interpreted as *Nana. A Pornographic Novel*.

[6] For instance Hauptmann, Sudermann, and others.

hardworking and decent in work and action. Their lives were hard, unlovely, sometimes drab and bitter but they were not sexual perverts.

As a veritist, I argued that one could be as real and as true in presenting the average man and woman as in describing cases of incest, adultery and murder. I found as Whitman told me he had found in the life of the average American, a certain decorum and normality. As a veritist I have recorded my perceptions.[1]

The influence of Véron on Garland's literary credo was probably of great importance. Garland's much-thumbed copy of Véron's Æsthetics is full of annotations, comments and marginalia. Before the word "Introduction" (p. v) Garland had written in pencil: "This book influenced me more than any other work on art. It entered into all I thought and spoke and read for many years after it fell into my hands about 1886. Hamlin Garland." According to the marginalia in Garland's copy he found many parallels between Véron and Whitman, Zola, Nordau, Posnett. Véron, too, stressed the importance of sincerity in the novel and freedom for the writer to express himself. Like Garland, the French critic attacked the past and urged the novelist to avoid imitation. Probably many of the ideas laid down by Véron were absorbed by Garland and in more or less modified form went into his little book of critical essays.[2]

In a lecture manuscript probably written in the early nineties Garland explained the task of the veritist: "I use the word veritist because the word realist no longer suffices. The veritist chooses for his subject the probable, the normal." Moreover, the veritist portrayed native themes and he was not interested in historical romances nor in superficial love stories. He did not shrink from describing the sordid elements of life, but he kept the right proportions. The veritist was not supposed to imitate any one, he was free from models, living and dead. The veritist depicted life, and his sources of inspiration were life and nature. The veritist stated the truth and nothing but the truth. The following was, according to Garland, the essence of veritism: "'Write of those things of which you know most, and for which you care most. By so doing you will be true to yourself, true to your locality, and true to your time.'"[3] Truth and

---

[1] Published by Eldon C. Hill's permission.

[2] I intend to investigate this particular problem in a separate study.

[3] *Crumbling Idols*, p. 35.

sincerity were important elements in the literary make up of Garland, as they were in James' and Howells'. According to Garland, the veritist was mainly interested in the present, in the modern man and woman, and he depicted the wholesome and the average. He concerned himself with the pure love of healthy men and women and avoided undue preoccupation with sex. In addition, the veritist discredited plots and formal complications and dealt with "life face to face, and swiftly and surely and always from the individual artist's standpoint."[1]

In a newspaper interview on February 18, 1894, for the *Chicago Inter Ocean*, Garland explained his literary point of view:

> I believe in relating a man's work to life and to the simple principles of style, like simplicity, clearness, genuineness, and the like ... The modern artist dealing with the modern man and modern conditions— that is, the modern, serious, thinking, human artist, is not trying to handle the beautiful all the time, to give a false interpretation of life which shall compel people to say how beautiful it is. But he deals with significance.

He went on to say that he aimed at portraying the average farmer, renter, and hired man, to picture their life as it actually was, "to put in the proper proportion of dusty days, rainy days, the proper proportion of terrible toil and pleasuring." He admitted that he saw the beauty of nature, but just the same he had to picture the pain and squalor beneath the surface.

Not only did Garland rebel against the domination of classical British literature and the literature of the East, but he also turned against the advocates of French naturalism. Although he was a confirmed evolutionist who read and admired the works of Darwin and Spencer and a political reformer and humanitarian to boot, he did not appreciate the naturalism of Zola, evolutionist and reformer.[2] His theory of veritism led him to decry the French school of naturalistic fiction.

Visiting an exhibition of modern French art in 1893 at the Chicago Fair, he jotted down his impressions in his notebook for that year. He observed: "There was the same deep-seated unwholesomeness here that one finds in their literature, the morbid

---

[1] *Ibid.*, p. 94.

[2] But in Garland's early notebooks and lecture notes Balzac and Zola were referred to with respect. Cf. MS of "The Literature of Democracy." P. 449. See also Chap. X.

seeking of effect at any cost . . . Naked . . . female figures. Morbid
sexuality everywhere . . . It was a great disappointment. Against
it our painters will stand well for they will be wholesome and
sane in their art."

In an undated manuscript "The Novel of Life," he discussed
the merits of veritism, attacking Zola's naturalism. He remarked:
"Zola is not a veritist . . . I am not a believer in the French
'realists.' They are too largely concerned with vice and crime.
They slander the human race."

In the same manuscript he complained repeatedly of the morbidity of modern French literature,[1] and he praised Howells
for being a "clean" writer: "Howells more than any other of
our writers, has demonstrated that a public exist for a sane and
wholesome novel. But it still remains true of almost all fiction of
America and indeed of the world, that it treats of the morbid, the
diseased, the criminal, rather than the healthy."

Again and again he stated the opinion that veritism must not
be mixed up with naturalism.[2] His desire was to stand apart
from the movement, and he took care to point out that he personally was not to be identified with the French naturalists. He
had tested naturalism, but its frank exposure of humanity was
too unreserved to satisfy the radical but rather prudish mind of
the young Garland. In an undated but probably late manuscript
he sided with Howellsian realism:

In advocating veritism I am not to be understood as apologizing for
the so-called realists of our day. In fact they are not realists from Howells'
point of view. They are indeed imitators of the French who seem to us
to be sex-mad . . . No nation can endure and transact business whose
citizens are as depraved as those set forth by Zola or his feeble imitators
here in America.

This revolt against Zola's naturalism was also evident in *Crumbling Idols*. When he repeatedly asserted that veritism "will not
deal with crime and abnormities, nor with diseased persons,"[3]
we may assume that he alluded to French naturalism. When de-
fining veritism he was eager to point out that it did not include
"the study of murderers, insane or criminal classes," as did Zola's

---

[1] Cf. p. 90 n. 1.
[2] Cf. Chap. X.
[3] *Crumbling Idols*, p. 28.

La Bête humaine, Germinal, and other French naturalistic work. Garland's comments show that he desired to stand apart from the naturalist movement which to him meant a preoccupation with sexuality, vice, and crime. In later years he turned more and more against naturalism as exploited abroad and in America and became a militant anti-naturalist.

Zola was one of the first critics to note that the novel was the form, *par excellence,* of the modern age. The spirit of the age, with its need of exact truth, deserted the stage, where, according to Zola, too much conventionality hampered it, and embraced the novel, whose field he considered limitless. Other critics were aware of this development.[1] In the United States the novel was the predominant literary form in the eighties and nineties, the only rival being perhaps the short story. Many writers, for instance Garland and Crane, preferred the novelette.

One of the theories propounded by Garland in *Crumbling Idols* was that literature should be native, i.e. free from all foreign models. American literature had not depicted the life of the American people but had imitated foreign models, particularly British ones. American art, to be enduring and worthy, must be original and creative, he maintained, not imitative. The vast expanse of the American continent lay before the writer teeming with stories to be written. The Middle West and the Far West, particularly, had no literature of their own. The lumbering districts of Washington and Oregon together with California with its splendid scenic views and gorgeous vistas offered material for numerous stories. Why did not these areas have a literature of their own? Garland suggested two reasons: first, lack of market, and second, lack of perception. The market had been saturated with British classics and romances or cheap imitative American novels, and the writers who ought to deal with the American scene had been busy making a living, toiling day and night, that

---

[1] Cf. Garland's lecture "The Epic of the Age—the Novel." See Appendix, p. 439. See also an article in the *North American Review,* CLXXV (September, 1902), 289-98, entitled "Will the Novel Disappear?" by James Lane Allen, Howells, Garland, Hamilton W. Mabie, and John Kendrick Bangs. This article was a refutation of a statement by Jules Verne, who had advanced the opinion that the novel would disappear. See also Richard Burton's article "The Predominance of the Novel," *Dial,* XVI (June 16, 1894), 354-6.

their senses had been dulled. And even worse, the critics and teachers had taught the young to imitate, not to create. He lamented that the life of the wide prairies of the West was not yet portrayed in literature, "a life that was unlike any ever seen on the earth . , ."[1] Time and again Garland stressed the fact that American themes abounded: ". . . there is a great heterogeneous, shifting, brave population, a land teeming with unrecorded and infinite drama."[2] But there was hope for the future of American literature, for a group of young writers were at work on native themes and they were not imitators of false gods but studied life and conditions which had long been familiar to them.

Concerning the scope of fiction Garland, like Crane, advanced the opinion that the novel should be short.[3] Moreover, he maintained that the short story comprising from 6,000 to 20,000 words was the most perfect form of writing. Many of his stories shaped themselves into tales numbering from 15,000 to 20,000 words. They were really novelettes. *A Little Norsk* might serve as an illustration of what he meant by a short novel or a novelette.

"It is a settled conviction with me," Garland asserted in his book of essays, "that each locality must produce its own literary record..."[4] After the enumeration of some of the principal representatives of the local color movement, G. W. Cable, Mary Wilkins Freeman, Joseph Kirkland, Harold Frederic, and others, he declared: "It is precisely the same movement which is going on

---

[1] *Crumbling Idols*, p. 14.

[2] *Ibid.*, p. 15. Being asked once to name the characteristically American books that could not have been written by a non-American, Garland mentioned particularly: Whittier's *Snow-Bound*, Lowell's *Biglow Papers*, Whitman's *Leaves of Grass*, Eggleston's *Hoosier School-Master*, Bret Harte's *The Argonauts of North Liberty*, Joaquin Miller's *Songs of the Sierras*, Mark Twain's *Roughing It*, Howells' *The Rise of Silas Lapham* and *A Modern Instance*, Mary Wilkins Freeman's *A Humble Romance and Other Stories*, James Whitcomb Riley's dialect verse, and George Ade's *Artie*. This list is in the University of Southern California Library.

[3] It is probable that Turgenev's short novels served as a model. Cf. section on "Turgenev and Garland," pp. 317 ff. Cf. also the following statement by Howells in a letter to Charles Dudley Warner dated April 1, 1877: "I still don't agree with you that a novel need be long in order to be great. . . . The man who has set the standard for the novel of the future is Tourguénief . . ." *Life in Letters of William Dean Howells*, I, 232.

[4] *Crumbling Idols*, p. 22.

in Norway, Holland, Hungary,—all over Europe, in fact."[1] Modern literature was full of local color and it was the local color element that put the Norwegian and Russian literature "almost at the very summit of modern novel writing,"[2] while English and French literature occupied the second place as to truth and sincerity. What was, then, local color? According to Garland it meant that "the writer spontaneously reflects the life which goes on around him."[3] And he defined it as follows: *Local color in a novel means that it has such quality of texture and back-ground that it could not have been written in any other place or by any one else than a native.*[4] Within the bounds of the local color novel there was even room for such a stark piece of naturalism as Norris's *McTeague*, considered by Garland to be one of the best novels of California, and the naturalistic *Sister Carrie* by Dreiser, which caused Garland to ask if Dreiser was a native Chicagoan.[5]

The novels of the past were often given to discussion and comment upon the action; the modern novels, on the other hand, were less obvious in their methods.[6] The novel of the future "will put its lessons into general effect rather than into epigrams. Discussion will be in the relations of its characters, not on quotable lines or paragraphs."[7] The new literature was not concerned with explaining why the characters acted as they did; instead in the modern novel the action spoke for itself. Comment was superfluous. The elaborate explanations and clarifications of the doings of the characters in Dickens and Balzac belonged to the past, whereas the modern age and modern literature demanded the objectivity of the scientist. In his notebook for 1894 Garland said of the novel: "It should not preach, it should exemplify." In a letter to Gilder dated October 2, 1889, concerning Garland's story "Prairie Heroine," Garland wrote:

All you say is very true—Prairie Heroine in some phases is a little too obviously preaching. My tendency is to present things concretely

---

[1] *Ibid.*, p. 34.

[2] *Ibid.*, p. 58. It should be remembered that Garland admired such writers as Ibsen, Björnson, Kielland, and Tolstoy.

[3] *Crumbling Idols*, p. 62.

[4] *Ibid.*, p. 64.

[5] See unpublished letter of Dreiser to Garland, January 8, 1903.

[6] *Crumbling Idols*, pp. 50–1.

[7] *Ibid.*, p. 51.

and let others find the preaching. I knew when I did that final section that it was falling off from the artistic standpoint—but I wanted to 'let the light in' as Walt Whitman asked me to do. I wanted to give hope, somehow.[1]

In the manuscript of "The Novel of Life" he also maintained that the artist "should delineate rather than preach . . . Dickens, Thackeray not merely exemplified the life they hated, they preached whole pages about it . . . Condemn the preaching in Dickens and Thackeray as well as in Tolstoy and Hardy. I am willing to admit that direct personal statement in a novel is bad art."

Although, theoretically, Garland condemned preaching in literature, most of his early writings were filled with the spirit of the reformer, and some tales composed in the heat of his anger were in the main propaganda.

With regard to his aim of writing in 1889, Garland alleged that "truth was a higher quality than beauty, and that to spread the reign of justice should everywhere be the design and intent of the artist."[2] The fact that the novelist should adhere to the strictest objectivity in technique did not prevent him from having a definite purpose in mind when writing. According to Garland the novel ought to have a purpose. In his notebook for 1894 he wrote as follows: "The novel should instruct as life instructs. It should not preach, it should exemplify. It should cure evils by flinging the whole light of art upon them." And in "The Novel of Life" he said that the veritist had a purpose at bottom: he should criticize present conditions. He continued: "Everywhere the novel is opposed to caste, to privilege, to tyranny of church and state. Tolstoi, Björnson, Kielland, Sudermann, Valdés, Howells, all stand for a higher thought and purer altruism." Speaking of the veritist in *Crumbling Idols* Garland remarked that he aimed to "hasten the age of beauty and peace by delineating the ugliness and warfare of the present."[3] He summed up his attitude in the following terms:

The realist or veritist is really an optimist, a dreamer. He sees life in terms of what it might be, as well as in terms of what it is; but he writes of what is, and, at his best, suggests what is to be, by contrast. He aims

---

[1] Published by courtesy of the New York Public Library.

[2] *A Son of the Middle Border*, p. 374.

[3] *Crumbling Idols*, p. 52.

to be perfectly truthful in his delineation of his relation to life, but there is a tone, a color, which comes unconsciously into his utterance, like the sobbing stir of the muted violins beneath the frank, clear song of the clarionet; and this tone is one of sorrow that the good time moves so slowly in its approach.[1]

Not until the emergence of the realistic and particularly the naturalistic novel in America as elsewhere, did American fiction become distinctly democratic, i.e. a literature treating of the lower classes of society with an emphasis on the common man. Garland's ideas of democracy were derived from a variety of sources—names such as Emerson,[2] Whitman, Taine, Spencer, De Touqueville, Posnett, Véron, Nordau, Spielhagen, and Ibsen were found in the manuscript notes of his lecture on "The Literature of Democracy." It is, however, safe to assume, considering Garland's admiration for Whitman, that *Democratic Vistas* was one of Garland's major sources of inspiration.

In *Crumbling Idols* he proclaimed that the literature of the future would be democratic, that is, it would concern itself with the lives of common people and be read by the man in the street. There was a persistent demand for better literature, but, although people read trash, it was well that they read:

The lower ranks of Western readers, as everywhere, devour some millions of tons of romantic love-stories, or stories of detectives or Indians. . . .

These facts . . . are signs of life, and not of death. It is better that these people should read such things than nothing at all.[3]

Garland also turned against the East, accusing it of being aristocratic, and voiced his belief that the original utterance of the American democracy would come from the West. He was particularly outspoken in his belief in democracy in "The Literature of Democracy:"

I assert that the history of intellectual America for the last century is a history of the growth and dominance of ideas born on democratic social conditions . . . Tell us of *the people* in France, in Germany, in Denmark, plead for our advancement in Russia and in Spain. Sound the call for the peoples' enfranchisement, the leveling of ranks. Ad-

---

[1] *Ibid.*

[2] Howells' and Garland's emphasis on the average and the normal is reminiscent of Emerson's "the low and the common."

[3] *Crumbling Idols*, p. 8.

vocate justice, mercy, equality before the law. Paint the customs, the multitudinous acts, emotions and concerns of the modern man till sympathy widens like a sea, till we shall indeed know each other as if face to face, till sharing each other's burdens we march shoulder to shoulder up the heights to brotherhood and liberty.

In answer to this call from the thinking classes of the people came splendid warriors like Hugo, satirists like Thackeray, humorists and sentimentalists like Dickens. Björnson and Ibsen in the North, Auerbach, Spielhagen and Freytag in Germany, Tourgénief, Gogol and Tolstoy in Russia, Galdós and Valdés in Spain, Balzac, Daudet and Zola, all belong to this mighty movement which is to overturn all other values and ideals. On they march like a conquering march.

In George Eliot the common people found their greatest delineator. . . . In the person of Hugo their greatest advocate.[1]

In his early work Garland wrote about plain people but his stories became hardly what he had hoped for: a literature *about* and *for* the people.

In denouncing romantic fiction, Howells also attacked the conservatism of the critics and their inability to appreciate modern trends in literature. Garland, too, assaulted conservative critics and deplored their lack of understanding of the new spirit in literature. His attacks were more violent in tone than those of Howells. He lashed the critics' dependence upon old familiar models. "They are timidly negative when not partisanly conservative. They can safely praise Ruskin and Carlyle, and repeat an old slur on Browning or Whitman."[2] They could not judge the value of modern literature, because they were too dependent upon the taste of the conservative East. The conservatism which marred the outlook of almost any critic, was a danger to the new literature, observed Garland, since it fostered literary hypocrites who worked insincerely in the old manner indicated by the critics. And yet, the best critics of Europe had been waiting for modern American literature: "Posnett, Dowden, Taine, Véron, Freiligrath, Björnson, every critic who has perceived the forward movement of all art, has looked for a new conception, a new flavor, a new manner in American literature."[3] Garland remarked that despite the opposition of the critics the new literature

---

[1] Cf. Appendix, pp. 448–50.
[2] *Crumbling Idols*, pp. 10–11.
[3] *Ibid.*, p. 165.

was well on its way and admonished the writers not to despair; soon they would find an audience for their work, for the future of American literature was one of great promise.

One of the most interesting chapters in Garland's manifesto is the one treating of impressionism in painting. As a visitor to the World's Fair in Chicago in 1893, he was aware of the immense growth of impressionistic or open-air painting. Like the veritist, he asserted, the impressionist must be an iconoclast. "Here, as everywhere, there are the two parties,—the one standing for the old, the other welcoming the new."[1] The impressionists revolted against classic, romantic, and symbolic subjects and attacked mythological painting and false idealism. The fundamental idea of impressionism, according to Garland, was that "a picture should be a unified impression. It should not be a mosaic, but a complete and of course momentary concept of the sense of sight."[2] The impressionist strove to represent "in color an instantaneous effect..."[3] In nature the coloring of objects was a pure illusion, for no color existed by itself, sunlight being the only creative source of color in nature.

Of more interest, however, was Garland's concept and use of impressionism in literature. In a novel written in an impressionistic technique one scene succeeds the other consecutively.[4] In addition, the descriptive passages are reduced to a minimum, say a few graphic sentences, and much space is given to dialogue. Garland was one of the first writers in America to use the impressionistic technique in his work. According to his own statement, he received his "first idea of colored shadows from reading one of Herbert Spencer's essays ten years ago. I then came to see blue and grape-color in the shadows on the snow. By turning my head top-side down, I came to see that shadows falling upon yellow sand were violet, and the shadows of vivid sunlight falling on the white of a macadamized street were blue, like the shadows on snows."[5] In an undated letter to one Mr. Briggs, Garland affirmed that he was "an impressionist—not a realist." In his early

---

[1] *Crumbling Idols*, p. 139.
[2] *Ibid.*, p. 122.
[3] *Ibid.*
[4] See *Main-Travelled Roads*.
[5] *Crumbling Idols*, p. 129.

stories he used an impressionistic technique probably stimulated by Spencer, French impressionist painters, and their American disciples, such as Childe Hassam, John S. Sargent, and John J. Enneking. Enneking was one of his early friends in Boston.

A principal distinction between impressionism and Zola's naturalism can be briefly explained as being primarily a matter of technique. Zola and his followers were eager to have all objects of a scene carefully and minutely recorded, everything had to be told, one feature after the other, every detail being equally stressed. When Zola described a street or a harbor or a railroad station, he devoted page after page to the enumeration of every object that met his eye; nothing was too unimportant to be left out of the picture.[1] The impressionist on the other hand was able to create a similar impression with two or three phrases. The result was not a photographic representation but a personal impression of nature. Although the techniques used by a naturalist like Zola and impressionists like the Goncourts were different from each other, the underlying philosophy was the same: a deterministic philosophy based upon the scientific thought of the nineteenth century. The brothers Goncourt popularized the impressionistic style in France, and Garland and Crane were two early exponents of impressionism in American literature.

Garland's theory of veritism shows that he was substantially a *realist*—not a naturalist—and a realist very much after the manner of Howells. In practice, however, Garland went a step beyond Howells' realism toward naturalism.[2]

4. STEPHEN CRANE AND HIS LITERARY CREDO

Crane[3] revolted not only against the social conditions of his time, but also against the smug complacency of the genteel tradition and the conventional standard of American literature. Sentimentalism, melodrama, and romanticism were alien to his conception of life. He wanted "art straight," nearness to life, and

---

[1] There are impressionistic passages also in Zola's works.

[2] For the influence of Zola, see pp. 233 ff.

[3] Material for a discussion of Crane's literary theories is scarce. Besides hints in his works, there exist a few letters and at least one article which give some information on his credo.

personal honesty. Like Keats, he voiced the belief that a work of art was not born without pain. Of *The Red Badge of Courage* he once wrote:

It was an effort born of pain—despair, almost; and I believe that this made it a better piece of literature than it otherwise would have been. It seems a pity that art should be a child of pain, and yet I think it is. Of course, we have fine writers who are prosperous and contented, but in my opinion their work would be greater if this were not so. It lacks the sting it would have if written under the spur of a great need.[1]

In an interview[2] with W. D. Howells for the *New York Times* dated October 28, 1894, Crane demonstrated his allegiance to the realistic forces in the battle for realism. The article was entitled: "Fears Realists Must Wait. An Interesting Talk with William Dean Howells. The Eminent Novelist Still Holds a Firm Faith in Realism, but Conserves a Doubt If Its Day Has Yet Come. He Has Observed a Change in the Literary Pulse of the Country Within the Last Few Months—A Reactionary Wave" (Signed Stephen Crane). In the interview Howells was reported as saying that the novel should have an intention, but should not preach. To write merely to amuse the people was unworthy of any writer. "It is the business of the novel," maintained Howells, "to picture the daily life in the most exact terms possible, with an absolute and clear sense of proportion."[3] Crane—he called himself "the other man"—observed that there seemed to have been a change in the literary attitude of the country within the last four months. "Last winter for instance, it seemed that realism was about to capture things, but then recently I have thought that I saw coming a sort of a counter wave, a flood of the other—a reaction in fact."[4] Crane was perhaps thinking of the flood of historical romances that submerged America in the nineties.

In an undated letter to a friend of his, written about 1896, he told how he came to join the realistic forces in American literature. Crane wrote:

You know, when I left you, I renounced the clever school in literature. It seemed to me that there must be something more in life than to sit

---

[1] *The Red Badge of Courage* (Mod. lib. ed., New York, n. d.), pp. xvi–xvii.
[2] Reprinted in *Americana*, XXXVII, 270–4.
[3] *Ibid.*, p. 272.
[4] *Ibid.*, p. 270.

and cudgel one's brains for clever and witty expedients. So I developed all alone a little creed of art which I thought was a good one. Later I discovered that my creed was identical with the one of Howells and Garland and in this way I became involved in the beautiful war between those who say that art is man's substitute for nature and we are the most successful in art when we approach the nearest to nature and truth, and those who say—well, I don't know what they say . . . they can't say much but they fight villainously and keep Garland and I out of the big magazines. Howells, of course, is too powerful for them.

If I had kept to my clever Rudyard Kipling style the road might have been shorter but, oh, it wouldn't be the true road. The two years of fighting have been well spent. And now I am almost at the end of it. This winter fixes me firmly. We have proved too formidable for them, confound them.[1]

This letter shows that Crane helped to fight the battle for realism in America together with his admired leaders, Howells and Garland, and his literary theories, too, conform in many respects to those advanced by the two writers. Above all he considered truthfulness the most important principle. The author should be true to himself and true to the life that surrounded him. "I decided," wrote Crane once, "that the nearer a writer gets to life the greater he becomes as an artist. . ."[2] And he summed up his aim in writing as follows: ". . . most of my prose writings have been towards the goal partially described by that misunderstood and abused word, realism."[3] In his work he aimed at accuracy and truth and requested "personal honesty" of himself and other writers. His purpose was to achieve nearness to life, but life can evade us and Crane realized his inability to record it truthfully. In his "War Memories" he wrote: "'But to get the real thing!' . . . 'It seems impossible! It is because war is neither magnificent nor squalid; it is simply life, and an expression of life can always evade us. We can never tell life, one to another, although sometimes we think we can.'"[4]

Some time after the publication of *The Red Badge of Courage* Crane wrote the following letter which demonstrates what a conscientious artist he was:

---

[1] Unpublished letter of Crane to Miss Lily Brandon. Reproduced by the permission of Ames W. Williams.

[2] *The Red Badge of Courage* (Mod. lib. ed.), p. xvi.

[3] *Ibid.*

[4] *Work*, IX, 201.

The one thing that deeply pleases me in my literary life—brief and inglorious as it is—is the fact that men of sense believe me to be sincere. *Maggie*, published in paper covers, made me the friendship of Hamlin Garland and W. D. Howells; and the one thing that makes my life worth living in the midst of all this abuse and ridicule is the consciousness that never for an instant have those friendships at all diminished. Personally I am aware that my work does not amount to a string of dried beans— I always calmly admit it. But I also know that I do the best that is in me, without regard to cheers or damnation. When I was the mark for every humorist in the country, I went ahead; and now, when I am the mark for only 50 per cent of the humorists of the country, I go ahead, for I understand that a man is born into the world with his own pair of eyes, and he is not at all responsible for his quality of personal honesty. To keep close to my honesty is my supreme ambition. There is a sublime egotism in talking of honesty. I, however, do not say that I am honest. I merely say that I am as nearly honest as a weak mental machinery will allow. This aim in life struck me as being the only thing worth while. A man is sure to fail at it, but there is something in the failure.[1]

Howells, Garland, Crane, and Norris, all working for the liberation of American literature, are linked together in their demand for truth and sincerity in the writer.

In Crane's interview with Howells quoted above, the latter maintained that the novel should have an intention, but it should never preach. Crane held the same idea in a letter to a friend written immediately after the success of his first war novel:

I have been very careful not to let any theories or pet ideas of my own creep into my work. Preaching is fatal to art in literature. I try to give to readers a slice out of life; and, if there is any moral or lesson in it, I do not try to point it out. I let the reader find it for himself. The result is more satisfactory to both the reader and myself. As Emerson said: "There should be a long logic beneath the story, but it should be kept carefully out of sight."[2]

On these grounds he objected to the preaching of Tolstoy, although, otherwise, he was a warm admirer of his art. "I confess," wrote Crane in 1897, "that the conclusions of some of his novels, and the lectures he sticks in, leave me feeling that he regards his genius as the means to an end."[3] *Anna Karenina* was "too long

---

[1] "Some Letters of Stephen Crane," *Academy*, LIX (August 11, 1900), 116.
[2] *Ibid.*
[3] *Work*, VII, xiii.

because he has to stop and preach but it's a bully book."[1] He also considered the didacticism of *War and Peace* and *Sebastopol* out of place in a work of art. He even advanced the opinion that *McTeague* was too moral.[2]

As has been said Crane, like Garland, advocated the short novel and he demonstrated it in such works as *Maggie* and *George's Mother*. After a reading of *Nana* he wrote: "Zola is a sincere writer but—is he much good? He hangs one thing to another and his story goes along but I find him pretty tiresome."[3] Crane acknowledged the sincerity of Zola's work, but found his scope in the novel too broad. He also turned against the unwieldy bulk of *War and Peace* and remarked that Tolstoy "could have done the whole business in one third of the time and made it just as wonderful. It goes on and on like Texas."[4] Crane even considered *The Red Badge of Courage* too long. Neither did he approve of the length of Hardy's novels. "Mr. Hardy . . . impresses me as a gigantic writer who 'overtreats' his subjects."[5]

Garland and Norris, too, as will be seen later, maintained that the people were the best judges of literature. In *The Third Violet* a character held the opposite view, probably Crane's own. A discussion was going on between Oglethorpe and Hollanden (read Crane):

> Oglethorpe contended that the men who made the most money from books were the best authors. Hollanden contended that they were the worst. Oglethorpe said that such a question should be left to the people. Hollanden said that the people habitually made wrong decisions on questions that were left to them. "That is the most odiously aristocratic belief," said Oglethorpe.
>
> "No," said Hollanden, "I like the people. But, considered generally, they are a collection of ingenious blockheads."[6]

It is difficult to ascertain Crane's attitude toward and understanding of French naturalism, since he did not advance any

---

[1] Beer, *Stephen Crane*, p. 157.

[2] *Ibid.*, p. 226.

[3] *Ibid.*, p. 148.

[4] *Ibid.*, p. 143.

[5] *Work*, VII, xiv. Mark Twain's novels were also too long to attract Crane, who observed that 400 pages of humor was too much. *Work*, VII, xiv. This is not really a criticism of length, but of tone.

[6] *Work*, III, 166-7.

opinion on the subject, as far as I have been able to make out. He spoke, however, as has been said, with qualified praise of Zola whose sincerity he admired.

Crane's literary credo, although expressed only in occasional fragments, has points in common with that of James, Howells, and Garland and demonstrates that, in theory, he was a *realist*—not a naturalist. In practice, however, he went beyond the realism of James and Howells and the veritism of Garland in such naturalistic stories as *Maggie* and *George's Mother*.

5. FRANK NORRIS AND *THE RESPONSIBILITIES OF THE NOVELIST. 1903*

Norris's contribution to the critical debate consisted of a series of essays and articles written mostly after the publication of *The Octopus* (1901), when he had secured a reputation as a novelist. The essays[1] were brought together and published, unedited, after Norris's death in 1903. Critics and reviewers pointed out many deficiencies and incongruities in them. True, the essays are uneven in quality and value, but they throw light on his work and constitute, in the main, a defense for Norris's romantic Zolaism as exemplified in his own work. The articles, which were written to satisfy a demand by editors, were composed in great haste, and this fact may in part account for many of the inconsistencies and obscurities found in them.

In these essays Norris revolted against the cheap, sentimental

---

[1] Most of these essays were first published in various magazines from 1901 to 1903. Two critics, Biencourt and Marchand, have analyzed Norris's literary theories at length. Biencourt's discussion is more complete and systematic than Marchand's, but it is somewhat one-sided. In general, Biencourt believes that when two ideas or points of view are identical or similar in Norris and Zola, Zola is the only conceivable source of Norris's ideas. Biencourt, like Marchand, is apt to forget Norris's probable indebtedness to the critical theories laid down by James, Howells, and Garland, all of whom, however, probably derived some of their ideas from the group around Zola.

Parrington called *The Responsibilities of the Novelist* "the textbook of the young naturalists." *Main Currents of American Thought*, III, 188. Howard Mumford Jones and Ernest E. Leisy said that it "became the pronunciamento of the new school of naturalism." *Major American Writers* (New York, 1935), 1501.

romance, the historical novel, and the supremacy of the "New England School" of writing, just as Garland and Crane had done. While attacking the historical novel Norris admitted, however, that Scott was an admirable writer, but his imitators were only profiteers. Their sole aim was to make money,[1] and they were content to prostitute American literature with their cheap volumes. Like Garland, he was aware of the great changes that were taking place in American literature. "Such an overturning of old gods and such a setting up of new ones, such an image-breaking, shrine-smashing, relic-ripping carnival I doubt has ever been witnessed . . . It has been a sort of literary Declaration of Independence."[2] He perceived that such writers as Irving, Holmes, Lowell, and Hawthorne were losing their grip on the mind of the American reader, and he delighted in the thought that the overlordship of New England, which "for too long dominated the entire range of American fiction," no longer was a menace to a free, non-imitative American literature. Garland had attacked the Eastern school of traditionalists, accusing them of imitating British classics and of being narrow and aristocratic in their outlook. Norris went a step further when maintaining that there had been no school of American writers, writing on native themes; the "New England School" was not American.[3]

In at least two articles, "Zola as a Romantic Writer"[4] and "A Plea for Romantic Fiction,"[5] Norris stated clearly what he understood by the terms "realism" and "naturalism." Realism was to Norris the kind of fiction that confined itself to the type of normal, ordinary life. It was moreover "respectable as a church and proper as a deacon . . ."[6] It was minute, and it stul-

---

[1] Crane, too, turned against the literary moneymakers. See p. 154. Cf. also Norris's article "Fiction-Writing as a Business," in *Compl. Works*, VII, 121–6. Cf. Zola's "L'Argent dans la littérature" in *Le Roman expérimental. Œuvres*, XLI, 129–62.

[2] *Compl. Works*, VII, 105.

[3] This is a violent exaggeration.

[4] Unsigned editorial in the *Wave*, XV, No. 26 (June 27, 1896), 3. There is no doubt that Norris wrote this article. The inherent ideas, the intimate knowledge of Zola's works, the style, everything points to Norris as the author.

[5] *Compl. Works*, VII, 163–8. This article repeats many of the ideas laid down in the earlier essay.

[6] *Ibid.*, p. 164.

tified itself. It was the commonplace tale of commonplace people; it noted only the surface of things, the smaller details of everyday life, small passions, restricted emotions, the excitement of an afternoon call, the drama of a broken teacup. According to Norris, this kind of realism was best exemplified in the novels of Howells.

Norris revolted against this realism and against Howells' concept of life, for to Norris life was more than mere externals, and literature implied more than a "meticulous presentation of teacups, rag carpets, wall paper and hair-cloth sofas..."[1] It was also "the unplumbed depths of the human heart, and the mystery of sex, and the problems of life, and the black, unsearched penetralia of the soul of man."[2] To chronicle this type of life realism did not suffice. Only "Romance" could take cognizance of variations from the type of normal, everyday life, for, to Norris, romance went deeper than realism; it was "an instrument with which we may go straight through the clothes and tissues and wrappings of flesh down deep into the red, living heart of things."[3] Romance might even treat of the sordid elements of human life. This kind of romance, was, according to Norris, best illustrated in the novels of Zola. It followed that he equated naturalism, or rather Zolaism, with romance, and according to this definition Zola was no realist; on the contrary, he was "the very head of the Romanticists."[4] That "Zola should be quoted, a realist, and as a realist of realists, is a strange perversion," asserted Norris.[5] Naturalism, he said in 1896, had a vague meaning, but naturalism, as understood by Norris, was "but a form of romanticism after all,"[6] it was not an inner circle of realism. If one observed the methods employed by the so-called realists—Howells, for instance—and Zola, it was easy to see the difference. Howells' characters "lived across the street from us," they were ordinary and *bourgeois* and behaved well like most people. Turning to the characters of *Les Rougon-Macquart* Norris found they lived in a world of their own. And he continued:

---

[1] *Ibid.*, p. 167.
[2] *Ibid.*, pp. 167–8.
[3] *Ibid.*, p. 163.
[4] *Ibid.*, p. 164.
[5] *Wave*, XV, No. 26 (June 27, 1896), 3.
[6] *Ibid.*

The naturalist takes no note of common people, common in so far as their interests, their lives, and the things that occur in them are common, are ordinary. Terrible things must happen to the characters of the naturalistic tale. They must be twisted from the ordinary, wrenched out from the quiet, uneventful round of every-day life, and flung into the throes of a vast and terrible drama that works itself out in unleashed passions, in blood, and in sudden death. The world of M. Zola is a world of big things; the enormous, the formidable, the terrible, is what counts; no teacup tragedies here. Here Nana holds her monstrous orgies, and dies horribly, her face distorted to a frightful mask; Étienne Lantier, carried away by the strike of coal miners of *Le Voreux* . . . is involved in the vast and fearful catastrophe that comes as a climax of the great drama; Claude Lantier, disappointed, disillusioned, acknowledging the futility of his art after a life of effort, hangs himself to his huge easel; Jacques Lantier, haunted by an hereditary insanity, all his natural desires hideously distorted, cuts the throat of the girl he loves, and is ground to pieces under the wheels of his own locomotive; Jean Macquart, soldier and tiller of the fields, is drawn into the war of 1870, passes through the terrible scenes of Sedan and the Siege of Paris, only to bayonet to death his truest friend and sworn brother-at-arms in the streets of the burning capital.

Everything is extraordinary, imaginative, grotesque even, with a vague note of terror quivering throughout like the vibration of an ominous and low-pitched diapason. It is all romantic, at times unmistakably so, as in *Le Rêve* or *Rome*, closely resembling the work of all modern romanticists, Hugo. We have the same huge dramas, the same, enormous scenic effects, the same love of the extraordinary, the vast, the monstrous, and the tragic.

Naturalism is a form of romanticism . . .[1]

That Norris believed naturalism to be but a form of romanticism —in opposition to Howells' realism—was also exemplified by most of his work, in which romantic elements are mingled with naturalistic ones.

Norris pleaded for romance, which as I take it, stands for Zolaism, and exhorted young writers not to study the mere surface of things; instead they should break away from Howells' realism and study the deeper human passions in the manner of Zola and other naturalists.

"To be true is the all-important business," Norris maintained. "Paint the horse pea-green if it suits your purpose."[2] Truth,

---

[1] *Ibid.* Cf. letter to Marcosson (p. 118) where Norris contrasts naturalism and romanticism.

[2] *Compl. Works*, VII, 174.

declared Norris, was not the same as accuracy; one could be true
to life and at the same time grossly inaccurate. He believed that
probability was better than reality. This idea was advanced in
the short story entitled "His Sister," published in the *Wave* of
November 28, 1896, in which the following conversation took
place between Strelitz, a writer, and his mother: "'But that's a
true story,' exclaimed Mrs. Strelitz. [The story was "Condition
of Servitude."] 'That really happened.' 'That don't help matters
any if it don't read like real life,' he returned . . . 'It's not the
things that have really happened that make good fiction, but the
things that read as though they had.'"[1] Probability was also
stressed by Norris in an editorial in the *Wave*:

> . . . Fiction is what seems real, not what is real.
> But for all this, the story writer must go to real life for his story . . . .
> The complications of real life are infinitely better, stronger and more
> original than anything you can make up. . . . Writers and mosaicists
> alike select and combine. . . .
> Someone objects at this point: What about imagination? What about
> fancy? What about invention? There is no such thing as imagination. . . .[2]
> you can't imagine anything that you have not already seen and observed.[3]

Balzac, and after him James and Maupassant, had declared
that "Le vrai peut quelquefois n'être pas vraisemblable." The
novelists "devront souvent corriger les événements au profit de
la vraisemblance et au détriment de la vérité . . . Le réaliste, s'il
est un artiste, cherchera, non pas à nous montrer la photographie
banale de la vie, mais à nous en donner la vision plus complète,
plus saisissante, plus probante que la réalité même."[4]

To gain the knowledge of truth one should turn to "life itself,
the crude, the raw, the vulgar." "Life was better than literature.
To live was better than to read; one live human being was better
than ten thousand Shakespeares; an act was better than a thought,"
asserted Norris's spokesman, Condy, in *Blix*.[5]

Norris, too, pleaded for objectivity in technique. The novelist

---

[1] *Frank Norris of "The Wave,"* p. 34.

[2] This was one of the shocking ideas in *Le Roman expérimental*.

[3] Justin Sturgis, "Fiction Is Selection," *Wave*, XVI, No. 37 (September 11, 1897), 3.

[4] *Pierre et Jean*, p. xxxix.

[5] *Compl. Works*, III, 124.

must not become a preacher; instead he ought to remain the artist. "Do not preach, exemplify," was Howells' slogan. "The preaching, the moralizing," wrote Norris, "is the result not of direct appeal by the writer, but is made—should be made—to the reader by the very incidents of the story."[1] Comment was superfluous, for if the author made a scene appear terrible to the reader he needed not "say in himself or in the mouth of some protagonist, 'It is terrible!' "[2] Truth set forth with the deepest sincerity on the part of the writer together with the strictest objectivity; these were salient points in Norris's literary credo, which he illustrated to the best of his ability in his writings. Life, as he understood it, should be depicted in all its varying phases. Unlike Howells and Garland, he was eager to proclaim that the sincere writer should pry into all the different problems of life, sound the depths of the human heart, as well as the mystery of sex, and study the normal as well as the abnormal.

Like Zola, Spielhagen, Garland, and others, Norris advanced the opinion that the novel was the epic of the age. "Each age speaks with its own peculiar organ," he asserted.[3] *Macbeth*, for instance, was representative of the Elizabethan period.

To-day is the day of the novel. In no other day and by no other vehicle is contemporaneous life so adequately expressed; and the critics of the twenty-second century, reviewing our times, striving to reconstruct our civilization, will look not to the painters, not to the architects nor dramatists, but to the novelists to find our idiosyncrasy.[4]

Because the novel was the great expression of modern life, the novelists had great responsibilities. Two points were particularly important to them: first, the novel should be about and for the people; second, the novel should be *American.*

As has been pointed out earlier, Garland pleaded for a purely American novel and demanded a truthful picture of American life and particularly of rural Western life as opposed to romantic and sentimental portrayals of America and the frontier. Norris expressed the same idea. He mentioned the fact that Cooper's tales were written in conformity with the romantic traditions of

---

[1] *Compl. Works*, VII, 23.
[2] *Ibid.*, p. 188.
[3] *Ibid.*, p. 4.
[4] *Ibid.*

his time and did not give a truthful picture of the West. In fact, he claimed that the West was presented only in dime novels. He demanded an American epic delineating the honest, vigorous pioneer who blazed the trail through the wilderness and won the boundless prairies from the Indians. In the conquest of the West, he perceived the possibilities of an American epic, a "neglected epic," as he himself put it. Garland had written: ". . . my hopes and ambitions for the West arise from absolute knowledge of its possibilities. I want to see its prairies, its river banks and coules, its matchless skies, put upon canvas."[1] Likewise Norris saw the possibilities for the American writer to exploit the American scene: "A whole Literature goes marching by, clamouring for a leader and a master hand to guide it."[2] Not only did the Middle West offer innumerable themes, but also the Far West, particularly the big cities, abounded with materials for stories. He wrote in 1896:

". . . just think, in a great city like this,[3] with thousands and thousands of people, all with wholly different lives and with wholly different interests—interests that clash. Just think of the stories that are making themselves every hour, every minute. There must be hundreds and hundreds of stories better than anything ever yet written only waiting for some one to take them down. Think of how near you may have come to an interesting story and never know it."[4]

Unlike Garland, who believed that the purpose of the novelist was to depict his own province, Norris declared that if the local colorists were great enough, they would become universally acknowledged and then cease to be local, as, for instance, Tolstoy. Local colorists like Bret Harte, G. W. Cable, and Eggleston were not deep enough, not penetrating enough in their analysis. If they were so they should "at least strike the universal substratum. . ."[5] Norris demanded a national, epic novel, but since America—although a union—was not yet a unified whole, it was too early to hope for a national epic or "The Great American Novel." Since the novelists did not see humanity as a "conglomerate whole," as

---

[1] *Crumbling Idols*, p. 36.
[2] *Compl. Works*, VII, 39.
[3] The scene of action of the story was New York.
[4] *Frank Norris of "The Wave,"* p. 37.
[5] *Compl. Works*, VII, 67.

for instance Shakespeare did, they should be sectional, limited to their own circumscribed areas.[1]

What the anemic American novel needed above all was vitality. "Vitality is the thing, after all," exclaimed Norris. Simplicity, too, was of great importance. Biencourt paralleled Norris's urge for simplicity with Zola's demand for "un style fort, solide, simple, humain."[2] It is, however, more probable that, if this idea was not original in Norris, he echoed Tolstoy's views in *What Is Art?*[3] Both authors attacked the artificiality of modern art and quoted at length from the Bible to illustrate simplicity in art and literature.

Concerning the structure of the novel, much could be learned from the great masterpieces, observed Norris. The narrative should move slowly up to the climax, and the pivotal event should be carefully built up from the very beginning. The catastrophe should come unexpectedly like an explosion and bring the novel to a dramatic ending.

Although there was not yet, according to him, an American school of fiction, Norris, like Garland, prophesied a glorious future for American letters: "The school of fiction, American in thought, in purpose, and in treatment will come in time, inevitably."[4] The American muse, a child of the people, would bring American literature to an ultimate and complete success.

Norris's emphasis on an *American* novel may in part be traced to his nationalism, which, toward the end of the century, received an impetus as a result of the conflict with Spain and the further rise of American imperialism.

Most of Zola's novels may be called *romans à thèse*, but that does not imply that Zola drew any conclusions from his works. His intention was to show that his works carried their conclusions with them. Norris, too, advocated the purpose novel, but he warned against preaching. He, moreover, exhorted the writer to draw his material from life and present it without comment. He believed that every novel must do one of three things:

---

[1] *Ibid.*, p. 151.

[2] Biencourt, *op. cit.*, p. 65 n. 27.

[3] Cf. also the similarities between Tolstoy's and Norris's ideas of democracy and art and literature. See Marchand, *op. cit.*, pp. 11 ff.

[4] *Compl. Works*, VII, 151.

tell something, show something, and prove something. In the first group he placed *The Three Musketeers* and in the second *Romola*. The third group which he held to "be the best class proves something, draws conclusions from a whole congeries of forces, social tendencies, race impulses, devotes itself not to a study of men but of man. In this class falls the novel with the purpose, such as *Les Misérables*."[1] As an example of the purpose novel, in which the artistic elements were not outdone by the tendency of the story, he mentioned the novels of Hardy. *Fécondité* by Zola served to exemplify the contrary. "The purpose for which Zola wrote the book ran away with him."[2] This book was nothing but a sermon on the fruitfulness of women. Although the writer was boiling with indignation at some injustices which he was writing about, as an artist, however, "his sufferings must be for him a matter of the mildest interest."[3] In *The Octopus* he exhibited a certain degree of sympathy for the people, but this was never carried out fully and constituted only an undercurrent of the novel.[4] The clash between the ranchers and the railroad in California was to Norris in the main "good material." And he added: "He would see a story in it, a good scene, a great character. Thus the artist. What he would do, how he would feel as a man is quite a different matter."[5]

Norris also turned against those who declared that the novel with a purpose was depressing and of no value. He maintained that if there were crime, poverty, and injustice in life, there was even greater cause for its appearance in literature.

In *Crumbling Idols* Garland stated that it was better for the people to read trash than not to read at all.[6] Norris voiced the same idea. Speaking of the people, he affirmed that "they do not understand Henry James, but be glad they even care for 'The Duchess' and 'Ouida.' "[7] Out of their reading of cheap literature would come their appreciation of the modern novel. Like Zola,

---

[1] *Ibid.*, pp. 21–2.

[2] *Ibid.*, p. 24.

[3] *Ibid.*

[4] A critic like Granville Hicks is prone, it seems, to overemphasize Norris's sociological interest. For title see Bibliography.

[5] *Compl. Works*, VII, 25. Cf. *The Octopus*.

[6] See p. 147.

[7] *Compl. Works*, VII, 81.

and Hardy, Norris maintained that one found human nature more undisguised among the lower classes than among the wealthy ones. This view was also stated in the preface to *Les Frères Zemganno* (1879) by the brothers Goncourt. Zola elaborated this idea in *Le Roman expérimental*, where he declared that "un homme du peuple est plus facile à étudier et à peindre qu'un gentilhomme. . . . L'homme du peuple se livre tout de suite, tandis que le monsieur bien élevé se cache sous le masque épais de l'éducation."[1] Likewise, Norris went to the poor communities in search of material for his stories. In one of his early works he observed: "For more than two hours young Strelitz [read Norris] roamed idly from street to street. Now in the theater district, now in the slums and now in the Bowery. As a rule he avoided the aristocratic and formal neighborhoods, knowing by instinct that he would be more apt to find undisguised human nature along the poorer unconventional thoroughfares."[2]

Norris proclaimed, moreover, that "no art that is not in the end understood by the People can live or ever did live a single generation."[3] The novelist wrote for the people; therefore he had to present the whole truth and nothing but the truth, for it was essential that "the People hear, not a lie, but the Truth."[4] Marchand has proved Norris's debt to *What Is Art?* for some of his ideas on democracy in art and literature.[5] But he was apparently unaware of the fact that Norris was also, of course, acquainted with and perhaps indebted to certain ideas of democracy as expressed by Garland. Both Tolstoy and Norris believed that art and literature should be for and about the people, both defended popular taste and advanced the opinion that literature that was not understood by the people would perish. "In the last analysis the People are always right," concluded Norris. The muse was no trickster, she was a teacher and a child of the people and the novel was a

great force, that works together with the pulpit and the universities for the good of the people, fearlessly proving that power is abused, that

---

[1] *Œuvres*, XLI, 219.
[2] *Frank Norris of "The Wave,"* p. 38.
[3] *Compl. Works*, VII, 6.
[4] *Ibid.*, p. 7.
[5] See Marchand, *op. cit.*, p. 11 ff. Cf. also Whitman.

the strong grind the faces of the weak, that an evil tree is still growing in the midst of the garden, that undoing follows hard upon unrighteousness, that the course of Empire is not yet finished, and that the races of men have yet to work out their destiny in those great and terrible movements that crush and grind and rend asunder the pillars of the houses of the nations.[1]

Norris's literary theory, like Crane's, has points in common with that of James, Howells, and Garland, but he revolted overtly against Howells' realism and pleaded for naturalism, or Zolaism, which to him, was but a form of romanticism.

To sum up: It is perhaps true that realism in America had few literary models, but it is an exaggeration to assert that it had "virtually no theory," as Kazin says.[2] The writers who fought for realism and naturalism in America—some of them not too strong in critical theory—were fairly unanimous concerning some principles of their credos, for example, their insistence on truth, objectivity in technique, and sincerity; in practice, however, they deviated greatly from their individual literary theories because of differences in temperament, experiences, and attitudes toward and concept of life. In the last analysis it should be remembered that the literary theories discussed above, which demonstrated that Garland and Crane were realists, and Norris a Zolaesque naturalist, were perhaps of less importance in the struggle for realism and naturalism than the realistic and naturalistic works themselves. The aspiring writer learned more about naturalism from Zola's novels than from *Le Roman expérimental*. After reading *Crumbling Idols* in 1894, John Burroughs summed up the point excellently by urging Garland to be creative instead of critical: "The talk about art does not signify much: *make a work* that tells."[3]

---

[1] *Compl. Works*, VII, 26.
[2] *On Native Grounds*, p. 14.
[3] Quoted by Eldon C. Hill, *op. cit.*, p. 193.

CHAPTER VII

THEME AND METHOD OF PREPARATION

It is a well-known fact that the French naturalists' choice of subjects marked a widening of the field of fiction. Chiefly they chose such aspects of life as had been shunned or considered unworthy of artistic treatment. Some of them had been treated of by earlier writers, but the latter had dealt with them in a more or less romantic or sentimental way. The naturalists, on the other hand, presented them with audacity and frankness. Theoretically, all subjects were of equal importance, but in practice they selected themes that fitted the naturalistic interpretation of the world. They wrote about modern themes drawn from faithful observation of contemporary life. The French naturalists had a predilection for subjects like the awakening of sex, the physical side of love, free love, prostitution, all kinds of social misery, pathological cases, etc. They preferred mostly analyses of character like *Germinie Lacerteux* or social studies like *Germinal*. Zola especially liked big themes: mines, railroads, markets, department stores, etc.[1]

The American experimenters in naturalism also dealt with new topics, thus broadening the scope of American fiction. If they dealt with old themes, they treated of them in a new way. Poor people were, for instance, no longer described in the manner of Dickens. Marital incompatibility—an old theme—was treated of in a new and daring way. Zola, Tolstoy, Turgenev, Ibsen, and others provided new models.

Some of the subjects preferred by French naturalists were also dealt with by the American writers, who, however, applied them to American material, and in the process adapted them to American conditions. Prostitution, for instance, was touched upon in *Mag-*

---

[1] Just as Zola made the department store the central idea in *Au Bonheur des dames*, E. F. Harkins in *The Schemers* (1903) took as his theme an American department store.

gie, _Vandover and the Brute_, and _The Octopus_, all of which also used the common naturalistic motif of seduction.[1] Vandover and Trina in _McTeague_ may be called pathological cases, and the physical side of love and the awakening of sex were insisted upon in _Rose of Dutcher's Coolly_, _McTeague_, and _The Octopus_.

The desire to expose social conditions and social evils—common in naturalistic fiction—was most evident in Garland. The corruption of the political world was, for instance, revealed in _A Member of the Third House_, but in this book Ibsen[2] rather than French naturalism served as a model. The bad conditions of the farmers were probably best described in _Main-Travelled Roads_ and _Jason Edwards_. Garland's pictures of hog-killing, cornhusking, threshing, and harvesting in the prairie West were new in American letters, at least as regards treatment. The Bowery had not been used as a background for naturalistic stories before Crane. In the Far West Norris saw great possibilities for naturalistic fiction; new themes abounded, for no American writer had described this vast area in the manner of Zola. In applying Zola's method to American material, Norris aimed at creating novels that would be at the same time distinctly modern and genuinely American. Both Norris and Zola possessed a certain epic quality which found expression in their choice of large subjects. Zola had built the gigantic edifice of _Les Rougon-Macquart_, which described "l'histoire naturelle et sociale d'une famille sous le second Empire." He had moreover written _Les Trois Villes_ and completed three volumes of _Les Quatre Évangiles_. These large novels evidently stimulated Norris, for he, too, projected a trilogy, _The Epic of the Wheat_. His vision of American life was epic and especially in _The Octopus_ he succeeded in grasping some of the spirit and essence of the America of his day. C. Hartley Grattan wrote in 1929 of this novel:

The men and women are distinctly American, and it should be said, in spite of the conflicting influences to which Norris was subjected, he never deviated from the essential American pattern of life he was at the moment recording. The large and fertile abundance of the life of these American

---

[1] The seduction motif was also characteristic of early sentimental and romantic novelists. The manner of treatment, however, was different.

[2] Both Ibsen and Zola were social critics, but their attitudes were different. Essentially Ibsen criticized moral evils, whereas Zola criticized material evils.

peasants is unmistakably American. No one could for a moment confuse them with Russians, Reymont's Poles, Zola's Frenchmen, Hamsun's Norwegians, Hardy's Englishmen, Sudermann's Germans, or even with Suckow's German-Americans. They are Americans of the old British stock.[1]

Like Balzac and Zola, Norris aimed at painting a vast canvas of contemporary America. In *McTeague* he depicted the lower middle class, in *Vandover and the Brute* the artist's life, in *The Octopus* the farmer's, and in *The Pit* that of the big business man.

Some of these studies of character and social conditions may well be called *romans documentaires*. They demanded a serious preparation, and a careful collecting of material was necessary before the novelist could begin to write. Imagination played a minor role; instead the emphasis was on the methodical and scientific study of the setting, the characters, and problems involved. Garland, Crane, and Norris had at least partially learned the naturalistic technique of documentation and careful study of physical reality.[2]

In *Comment Émile Zola composait ses romans*, Henri Massis gave a detailed analysis of the method used by Zola in composing his novels. Zola himself said in the preface to *La Fortune des Rougon* that "Depuis trois années, je rassemblais les documents de ce grand ouvrage..."[3]

He studied manuals, scientific works, read articles in newspapers and journals and consulted people well versed in the subject on which he intended to base his book. Furthermore, he sought direct personal experience. Before writing *La Bête humaine*, for instance, he rode in a locomotive to study technical details, to feel the warmth from the boiler and the draught from outside, and to observe the landscape passing by at a rapid speed. When one compares his *Note sur mon voyage en locomotive* with parts of the completed novel, it is interesting to see how closely he followed his notes. He even lived for some time in miserable conditions in order to feel the pressure of economic difficulties and to learn how to describe accurately the life of the poor.[4] He annotated carefully

[1] "Frank Norris," *Bookman*, LXIX (July, 1929), 509.
[2] See Chap. X, "The Influence of Zola."
[3] *Œuvres*, II, 8.
[4] Zola had experienced poverty during his years as a struggling writer in Paris. See Josephson, *op. cit.*, pp. 42 ff.

every impression and when he had collected all necessary documents, he sat down to write, and when the last page of his dossier was consumed his novel was ready.

Turning from Zola to the American writers we note a certain similarity of method. This does not necessarily imply that they learnt their technique from French naturalism. It is also possible that the methods of American journalism and the scientific orientation of nineteenth century European thought were as responsible as Zola or other naturalists for this technique.[1] They were, however, like Zola, anxious to get the right atmosphere, the correct terms, the authentic details and the exact setting for their novels and stories. Garland was a farmer's son and had actually lived as a farmer before he wrote *Main-Travelled Roads* and in order to write the political and economic novels *A Spoil of Office* and *A Member of the Third House* he went to the Middle West and to Washington, D.C., to study the actual conditions and to collect notes. Crane had carefully absorbed life in the Bowery, before he wrote his slum stories, and Norris, whose method of preparation comes closest to that of Zola, knew well San Francisco and particularly the Polk Street environment, before he composed *McTeague*.

Both Garland and Norris used notebooks, in which they gathered material, jotted down impressions, sketches, ideas, well-turned

---

[1] Harold Frederic successfully employed the naturalistic technique of documentation in his novel *The Damnation of Theron Ware* (1896), for the preparation of which he needed five years. Of his method he wrote in 1896: "After I had got the people of my novel grouped together in my mind, I set myself the task of knowing everything they knew. As four of them happened to be specialists in different professions, the task has been tremendous. For instance, one of them is a biologist, who, among other things, experiments on Lubbock's and Darwin's lines. Although these pursuits are merely mentioned, I got up masses of stuff on bees and the cross-fertilization of plants. I had to teach myself all the details of a Methodist minister's work, obligations, and daily routine, and all the machinery of his church. In the case of Father Forbes, who is a good deal more of a pagan than a simple-minded Christian, and loves luxury and learning, I had to study the arts he loves as well as his theology. I have waded in Assyriology and Schopenhauer, pored over palimpsests and pottery, and in order to write understandingly about a musician who figures in the story, I bored a professional friend to death to get technical, musical stuff." *Bookman*, III (July, 1896), 384. After all this preparation the book wrote itself.

sentences, possible titles of books, etc. In one of his notebooks called "Notes and Hints" Garland wrote short sketches and stories; one is entitled "A Storm on the Lake" (dated Chicago 1893) and was later used in *Rose of Dutcher's Coolly*, and another is an outline of a novel called "Going Home." Some of Garland's notes are of particular interest for this study, because they show his early interest in slum conditions. In his notebook, begun on October 16, 1884, he jotted down the following impressions from a walk in the Boston slums:

Curious Places. Walk down Federal Street. Curious store. Window full of filthy bird cages. Doves mostly. Bantam chickens. Inside dirty floor sawdusted. Enormous, great, brindled mastif tied to a sort of counter ... Shop dirty ... Little further on streets became dirtier and swarming with children. Ragged, nearly naked. Slatternly mothers ... Saw pretty girl looking from a terribly dirty and dilapidated window. Sweet face a vivid contrast to the squalor and filth, dressed in a grayish colored dress. Some dozens of men full of drink. A terrible revolution it would be to some of the aristocracy of Boston to study these parts of Boston.

In the following somber, proletarian sketches worthy of reproduction *in extenso*, Garland gives evidence of a naturalistic impressionism anticipating Crane.

Two Pictures

(Poverty's Child)

In the brilliant sun a woman walked, a basket slung at her back, a child astride her hip.

The street was lined with lovely cottages in the midst of velvety lawns.

Robins called from the pink and green radiance of apple trees in bloom. The white of pear trees dazzled the eyes.

And in the cool sweet air, wearily trudging from house to house, the smell of darkness and disease about her, the miserable mother walked — her face white, her hopeless eyes dark as night, a ragged shawl draping her unkempt hair.

Her slow eyes gazed lifelessly from side to side but the thin faced babe astride her hip held a limp dandelion in his little fist and blinked curiously at the shaven lawns.

Hamlin Garland.

(Childhood)

In the heart of the city the Court lay, a bit of Colonial life, battered, unkempt and falling to decay. Small wooden houses with sides to the street, narrow brick walks meshing of telegraph wires over-head.

A few sickly trees stood about before the swayed and settling roofs.
In the pale November sunlight two little girls were playing . . .
They were playing busily in a corner where some few leaves had drifted
to form a carpet for their bare and blue-veined little feet.

Their clothing was merely rags. Their arms protruded from their
grimy sleeves their hair was tangled above their eyes like the mane of
wild cattle.

One of them rose with an air of dignity and pride. Her attitude was
fine and graceful.

"I'll be the lady," she said, "and you can call upon me."

Hamlin Garland.[1]

In his notebook marked "Summer 1892" there is the following
outline of a story called "A Radical Father."

A Radical Father. Story of a man who had two daughters. He hated
the weaknesses and pettinesses of women and was determined to make
them different. They wore pantalons and plain skirts. Rode astride.
He put snakes before them. Taught them to handle bugs and snakes.
Talked to them on sexual affairs. He made them wear heavy boots and
to go without gloves. But they were beautiful for all. They could not
escape his supremacy after so long a time. His control was absolute.
They were wild after men. This is how they expressed it, "When my
man comes along."

When writing a story of penitentiary conditions, Garland was
even locked up overnight in a narrow steel cell next to one occupied by a murderer, for he wanted to know how it really felt to
be in jail. In an undated letter he wrote one Mr. Briggs: "My
methods of work are these: to go directly from my home in the
city to the Rocky Mountains and then plunge at once into the
life I am to write about. By these . . . means I secure clean-cut
impressions of costumes and customs." And on another occasion
he wrote one Mr. Sill:

First I make copious notes while on the trail and among the Indians.
I take down the actual (translated) conversation of the red people. I
sit with them around the fire in their tuques and have their songs and
prayers interpreted to me as they go on. I do not trust to my memory
so far as the basic facts are concerned. These notes, however, I do not
use literally. I seldom refer to them—but the mere effect of writing them
down seems to organize them in my mind.

Often I strike out a paragraph which takes form in my mind and set

---

[1] From an early unpublished MS signed by Garland. Undated.

down in my note-book as a key-note or color-note which is to govern a chapter. Sometimes as in making studies for "The Gray Horse" I plan a chapter or set down a scrap of conversation.[1]

The similarity of Garland's method to that of Zola is obvious, but there is a difference as to the way they used their notes. Garland was primarily an impressionist in technique, whereas Zola preferred a descriptive method.

Garland tried to keep close to the spoken word, and his dialogues were on the whole accurate and true to life. In 1894, he informed a journalist: "When I have the first rough draft written I read it to an expert typewriter and fill in the details as I read. The sound of my own voice keeps me very close to absolute colloquialisms, for I refer everything to my ear, and so avoid all stereotyped conversations."[2]

Whether Crane ever used a notebook has been doubted by scholars. Edwin Valentine Mitchell, however, has shown that Crane actually used a notebook.[3] In addition, he, too, had a time of preparation, before he set about writing. He soaked himself in the milieu he wanted to write about. He was a good observer and he talked with and listened to workers, bartenders, street girls, and the like, as the case needed. Even during his college days he could be found

lurking about the police court watching the prisoners being brought in for minor offenses. Crime seemed to hold a great fascination for him and his curiosity frequently led him into contact with the lower strata of city civilization. He gloried in talking with shambling figures who lurked in dark door-ways on deserted slum streets, and his love for adventure constantly kept his feet on the illy-lighted thorofares honeycombing the city.[4]

When on his way to report on the Spanish-American War he arrived at Ponce, Porto Rico, Crane suddenly disappeared from his friends. But they knew where to find him—"in a back-street

---

[1] This quotation, taken from an undated letter, refers to his later work, but we may safely assume that his early method was substantially the same.

[2] Walter Blackburn Harte, "Hamlin Garland—A Virile New Force in Our Literature," *Chicago Inter Ocean* (February 18, 1894).

[3] *The Art of Authorship* (New York, 1935), pp. 69–70.

[4] Thomas E. Martin, "Stephen Crane: Athlete and Author," *Argot*, III (March, 1935), 1–2.

cantena, with the wastrels of Ponce—drunkards, drabs, and tin-horn gamblers."[1] Crane may also have learnt some of his uncanny insight into the slum life of New York City from his colleagues on morning newspapers, with whom it was his custom to eat now and then. The following letter of inquiry sent by Crane to the New Jersey Historical Society shows his desire to get information about the subject he wanted to write about:

> I am about to attempt a novel upon Revolutionary times in the Province of New Jersey, and I would be very glad if you could tell me the titles of some of the books on the manners and customs of the times in the Province. I am particularly interested in Elizabethtown.[2]

Turning to Norris we realize that his notebook was his greatest treasure, for Charles G. Norris informs us that keeping it taught Frank Norris

> the difference between seeing life subjectively and objectively. No one, he believed, could become a writer, until he could regard life and people, and the world in general, from the objective point-of-view,— until he could remain detached, outside, maintain the unswerving attitude of the observer.[3]

Norris wrote in *Blix:*

> He [Condy] "went in" for accuracy of detail; held that if one wrote a story involving firemen one should have, or seem to have, every detail of the department at his fingers' ends, and should "bring in" to the tale all manner of technical names and cant phrases.[4]

A fair illustration of Norris's method is his preparation for *The Octopus.* Norris based his novel on an actual feud between the railroad and the California farmers which culminated in the Mussel Slough affair of 1880, in which seven men were killed. Perhaps the assault leveled at American railroads in the nine-

---

[1] Introduction by Charles Michelson to *Work*, XII, xviii.

[2] Printed in the *Newark Sunday Call* of June 17, 1923.

[3] *Frank Norris*, p. 8.

[4] *Compl. Works*, III, 10. The medical details in *McTeague* and *A Man's Woman* were supplied by Albert J. Houston, a medical student and close friend of Norris's. Norris even visited an operating room in a hospital to get information how to describe the excision of a hip joint. Captain Joseph Hodgson helped him with Arctic details in *A Man's Woman*, and Harry Rhodes informed Norris about navigation. George D. Moulson explained all the technicalities involved in a "deal" in wheat.

ties, coming to a climax in the Pullman strike of 1894, stimulated Norris to take up the problem between the railroad and the farmers. The Southern Pacific, commonly called The Octopus,[1] figured much in the newspapers from 1892 until 1895. In April, 1899, in order to get "le milieu matériel" Norris went to California, where he stayed for about four months. The following excerpt from a letter dated April 5, 1899, and written before his departure for the West to his college friend Harry Wright shows his serious preparation for *The Octopus:*

It involves a very long, a very serious, and perhaps a very terrible novel. It will be all about the San Joaquin wheat raisers and the Southern Pacific, and I guess we'll call it The Octopus—catch on? I mean to study the whole question as faithfully as I can and then write a hair-lifting story. There's the chance for the big, epic, dramatic thing in this, and I mean to do it thoroughly—get at it from every point of view, the social, agricultural, and political—just say the last word on the R. R. question in California. I am going to study the whole thing *on the ground* and come back here in the winter and make a novel out of it.[2]

He collected material on the Mussel Slough affair in the Mechanics' Library in San Francisco and in the files of the *San Francisco Chronicle*. At the suggestion of Ernest Peixotto, he visited the Santa Anita Rancho (San Benito County), where he stayed for about a month studying the growth and harvesting of wheat and meeting some of the prototypes of the characters of *The Octopus*. He also attended a barn dance, an episode which he used with success in the novel. A woman living at the Santa Anita Rancho told him numerous stories of early California, which he used for *The Octopus*. He also spent several weeks on Gaston Ashe's ranch in Monterey County, but he seems to have spent little time in the San Joaquin Valley in his search for material. Walker believes that he "visited the town of Tulare, which he pictures as Bonneville." Moreover,

he possibly attended a rabbit drive, which he used as a feature of the valley life, but he created the country of *The Octopus* by ingeniously transferring a section of San Benito County to the lower San Joaquin,

---

[1] Apparently Norris used for the title of his novel a name which was in current use. The term was already used in Stewart Denison's *An Iron Crown: A Tale of the Great Republic* (Chicago, 1885). Consequently Zola did not inspire the title. Cf. Biencourt, *op. cit.*, p. 207.

[2] Walker, *op. cit.*, p. 244.

in the process flattening out the hills, enlarging the estates, and moving a Spanish mission over the Coast Range. Thus he concentrated his California.[1]

Norris even interviewed Collis P. Huntington, who, it seems, was the prototype of Shelgrim.

With all his notes and fresh impressions of California he went back to New York in the fall of 1899 and set about writing his novel. In the manner of Zola he even made short biographies of his *Dramatis Personae*[2] and drew a map of the locale of the book. During the writing of the novel he often ran into difficulties in regard to technicalities. For the political details, which gave Norris considerable trouble, he received help from Harry Wright and Marcosson. In November, 1899, he wrote Marcosson:

If you have been involved in politics recently, perhaps you can give me a pointer or two. I am in a 'political muddle' myself in 'The Octopus,' the first of my set of three novels on the wheat question, which I have just started. You know this involves, in California, the fight between the farmers of the San Joaquin and the Southern Pacific Railroad. I was out there this summer getting what stuff I needed but I did not think I should need political notes. *Now*, I find that I do, and should have found out a good deal about politics and political 'deals' but I want to find out more. . . .[3]

And on September 13, 1900, when *The Octopus* was nearing conclusion, he again wrote to his friend, telling him of his method of preparation:

It is the hardest work I ever have done in my life, a solid year of writing and four months' preparation—bar two months—and *I* think the best thing far and away I ever did. You've no idea of the outside work on it. I've been in correspondence with all kinds of people during its composition, from the Traffic Manager of a Western railroad to the sub-deputy-assistant of the Secretary of Agriculture at Washington. Also in connection with it all, I've helped run and work a harvester in the San Joaquin—that is, I've helped on the sacking-platform—but of course you don't know where that is.[4]

The naturalistic technique of documentation was successful in *The Octopus*. In describing the fertile San Joaquin, Norris suc-

---

[1] Walker, *op. cit.*, pp. 248-9.
[2] See Appendix, pp. 262 ff.
[3] Marcosson, *op. cit.*, p. 237.
[4] *Ibid.*, p. 238.

ceeded in catching something of the essence of America, its vitality and freshness, its romance, and its tragedy. Harlan Hatcher said of the novel:

> Frank Norris got into this book not only the spirit of the robber barons, the tough frontiersmen, the lawless drifter and fortune hunter, the educated men from eastern colleges, and violent transmutation of fortune, but also some of the romance of empire-building, of panting locomotives on the Western plains, and of the lingering beauty of the golden prairies and the excitement of young love.[1]

To sum up: To record certain aspects of industrial America an expansion of the field of American letters was inevitable. Themes like the conflict between capital and labor, the corruption of politics, and the slums of big cities were dealt with in a new and daring way. To give an illusion of reality these subjects often demanded a thorough documentation and at least Garland and Norris took pains to collect extensive notes for their writings.

---

[1] *Creating the Modern American Novel* (New York, 1935), p. 16.

CHAPTER VIII

SETTING

In conformity with the belief that the milieu[1] molded the individual, the French naturalists emphasized setting and by making it as elaborate and exhaustive as possible they thought that they could understand and explain man and his actions in a better and more exact way than before. Zola, for instance, described with great patience and thoroughness streets, houses, rooms, furniture, etc. Dialogue and action were given comparatively little space in order to make room for detailed descriptions, which at times degenerated into tiresome enumerations of plants, odors, etc., revealing his pseudo-scientific zeal. The general impression of his elaborate and abundant descriptions was a vast canvas teeming with tumultuous, vibrating life.

Although, in general, the three American writers chose different parts of the United States as background for their works—Garland wrote largely about the Middle West, Crane about New York, and Norris about California—their approaches and attitudes were fairly similar.

As has been touched upon, Zola and other French naturalists frequently used great cities or rather city slums as setting. Likewise, the American writers utilized cities as backgrounds for their work, and they, too, described slum districts. Boston was partly the setting of *Jason Edwards*, and New York served as a background for Crane's impressionistic pictures. When composing

---

[1] In this chapter I have limited myself to a description of the exterior milieu (e.g. country, town), the background or setting of a story. In the discussion of the influence of the milieu on the characters in the following chapter I have used the word "milieu" in a wider sense, namely to denote not only the exterior milieu, but also the interior milieu (e.g. house, room) and the social milieu (e.g. trade, relatives, friends). For the discussion of terms, see Joan Yvonne Dangelzer's *La Description du milieu dans le roman français de Balzac à Zola* (Paris, 1938), pp. 7–8.

McTeague Norris was aware of the fact that to be able to inter-
pret modern California, he had to write a novel of city life. As
a result he laid *McTeague* in San Francisco, which also served as
a background for *Blix*, partly for *Moran of the Lady Letty* and
Vandover and the Brute, and to a less degree for *The Octopus*. *The
Pit* was staged in Chicago, where also the action of the latter part
of Garland's *Rose of Dutcher's Coolly* took place.

The three writers did not refrain from including sordid details
in their descriptions of setting. Their descriptive passages were
mostly based on facts, and to increase the sense of reality they
imparted to their pictures all kinds of sounds, colors, and odors.
To that effect they also frequently referred to localities with their
exact names.

The Boston milieu which Garland preferred to describe in
Jason Edwards was not the fashionable part of the city, but the
tenement area around the ironically named Pleasant Avenue
with its noise and squalor. This district was pictured with its
vice and general sordidness in the manner of Zola in *L'Assommoir*.[1]
In *Rose of Dutcher's Coolly* Garland did not depict the slum sections of Chicago particularly, but, nevertheless, he included sordid details. The terrible noise, the soot-laden air and the filth
irritated him. Moreover, the city had a peculiar smell, a "rotten,
piney, turpentiney smell..."[2] Crane, too, was apt to dwell on the
seamy side of city life. His Bowery pictures showed the misery
and degradation of humanity in New York's worst sections.[3] New
York itself was to him frightening with its towering buildings and
narrow streets, where the incessant human strife went on as in a
chasm. Like Garland and Crane, Norris employed tenement areas
as background for some of his work, and he often had recourse
to revolting and brutal detail in the manner of Zola.[4]

Concurrent with this more or less naturalistic description of the
city, there was felt an apparent tendency at romanticizing it. This
was particularly true of Garland and Norris. Lyric pictures of

[1] Since the three writers appear to owe a considerable debt to Zola with
regard to their use of city slums as background, it has seemed necessary to deal
more fully with that particular setting in the chapter on the influence of Zola.
See pp. 237 ff.

[2] *Rose of Dutcher's Coolly*, p. 167.

[3] See pp. 251 ff.

[4] See pp. 284 ff.

Chicago at sunset and at night contrasted effectively with those depicting its squalor. Moreover, the city was to Garland an escape from the loneliness and mental barrenness of the country, an intellectual and cultural center that he idealized. The following quotation shows how the vast and terrifying Chicago took on beauty when love had entered Rose's heart:

There were moments when it seemed the most splendid presence in the world—at sunset, when the river was crowded with shipping and the great buildings loomed up blue as wood-smoke, and almost translucent; when the brick walls grew wine-colored; when the river was flooded with radiance from the western sun, and the great steamers lay like birds wearied and dreaming after a long journey.

Sometimes, too, at night, when she came out of the concert hall and saw the glittering twin tiaras of burning gold which the Great Northern towers held against the blue-black, starless sky, two hundred feet above the pavement; or when in the early evening she approached the mountainous Temple, luminous and sparkling with electric lights, lifting a lighted dome as airy as a bubble three hundred feet into the pale sapphire of the cloudless sky—the city grew lofty.

The gross, the confused in line, the prosy in color, disappeared at such moments, and the city, always vast, took on grace and charm and softened to magnificence; became epic, expressing in prophecy that which it must attain to; expressed the swift coming in of art and poetry in the lives of the western world-builders.[1]

Norris, too, romanticized Chicago, which was to him a symbol of America. In this city the spirit of the United States was felt primarily in its force, energy, and tumultuous life:

The Great Grey City, brooking no rival, imposed its dominion upon a reach of country larger than many a kingdom of the Old World. For thousands of miles beyond its confines was its influence felt. Out, far out, far away in the snow and shadow of northern Wisconsin forests, axes and saws bit the bark of century-old trees, stimulated by this city's energy. . . . Her force turned the wheels of harvester and seeder a thousand miles distant in Iowa and Kansas. Her force spun the screws and propellers of innumerable squadrons of lake steamers crowding the Sault Sainte Marie. For her and because of her all the Central States, all the Great Northwest roared with traffic and industry; sawmills screamed; factories, their smoke blackening the sky, clashed and flamed; wheels turned, pistons leaped in their cylinders; cog gripped cog; beltings clasped the drums of mammoth wheels; and converters of forges belched into the clouded air their tempest breath of molten steel.[2]

---

[1] *Rose of Dutcher's Coolly*, pp. 291–2.
[2] *Compl. Works*, IX, 57.

And again:

It was Empire, the resistless subjugation of all this central world of the lakes and the prairies. Here, midmost in the land, beat the Heart of the Nation, whence inevitably must come its immeasurable power, its infinite, infinite, inexhaustible vitality. Here, of all her cities, throbbed the true life—the true power and spirit of America; gigantic, crude with the crudity of youth, disdaining rivalry; sane and healthy and vigorous; brutal in its ambition, arrogant in the new-found knowledge of its giant strength, prodigal of its wealth, infinite in its desires. In its capacity boundless, in its courage indomitable; subduing the wilderness in a single generation, defying calamity, and through the flame and the débris of a commonwealth in ashes, rising suddenly renewed, formidable, and Titanic.[1]

San Francisco, too, was somewhat idealized by Norris. Although in *McTeague* he showed a predilection to depict the ugliness, grotesqueness, and brutality of San Francisco, in *Blix* and *Moran of the Lady Letty*, on the other hand, he described the idyllic side of the city, its peculiar beauty, its gay life and colors, and its invigorating winds from the Pacific.

Whereas in his writings Crane showed little interest in nature and the countryside, both Garland and Norris depicted rural settings and rural life with insight and feeling. Earlier than Garland, Howe, Kirkland, and others had described the dreariness and loneliness of the Middle West. To their grim pictures Garland added a number of impressionistic scenes, in which he stressed the desolation and solitude of the prairie West. Because his chief desire was to strip this section of the country of some of its false glamour by depicting it as it really was, he was perhaps at times liable to overemphasize its gloom and ugliness. Moreover, the majority of his pictures of the Middle West and frontier life savor of his bitterness and indignation at the social conditions of the farmers and at the indifference, even hostility of nature toward man. Frequently this indignation was expressed by contrasting the farmer's bondage to labor with the tranquil blue sky and the glorious sunsets.

Garland liked to depict the prairie from various angles. It was desolate and drear in spring, hot and dusty in summer, and cold and swept by snows and blizzards in winter.[2] Sometimes, to be

---

[1] *Ibid.*, pp. 57-8.
[2] Cf. p. 138.

sure, on a fine summer's afternoon it could be "wonderfully beautiful."

It was about five o'clock in a day in late June, and the level plain was green and yellow, and infinite in reach as a sea; the lowering sun was casting over its distant swells a faint impalpable mist, through which the breaking teams on the neighboring claims ploughed noiselessly, as figures in a dream. The whistle of gophers, the faint, wailing, fluttering cry of the falling plover, the whir of the swift-winged prairie-pigeon, or the quack of a lonely duck, came through the shimmering air. The lark's infrequent whistle, piercingly sweet, broke from the longer grass in the swales near by. No other climate, sky, plain, could produce the same unnamable weird charm. No tree to wave, no grass to rustle, scarcely a sound of domestic life; only the faint melancholy soughing of the wind in the short grass, and the voices of the wild things of the prairie.[1]

In his many descriptions of the plain Garland achieved a poetic vision comparable to Turgenev's in *A Sportman's Sketches*.[2]

The beautiful lakes, the serene sky, the gorgeous sunsets, the few groves of oak and the fields of barley and wheat could, however, only temporarily dispel the triviality and endless drudgery of life in the Middle West. To him the farms were humble and desolate, standing unshaded and unsheltered on the immense plain. The interior of the houses was in keeping with the exterior: small rooms, wooden chairs, bare walls, and no books.

California with its prosperity, fertility, tumultuous life, and vigorous people—as Norris saw it—afforded a striking contrast to the bleak Middle West depicted by Garland. The robustness, the vitality, the grandeur of America were often stressed in Norris's pictures of California, and the motifs from the Far West seemed to have called forth what was best in Norris. The Far West was to him the world's frontier of romance, inhabited by a new race, a hardy, brave, passionate, empire-building people, primitive, brutal, without fear like the West itself.

In *McTeague* he drew remarkable pictures of Death Valley and the mountains, but rural California was best portrayed in *The Octopus*. In broad strokes he painted the valley, the plain, the mountain, the ranch, and the range. Repeatedly and using the same terms time and again he depicted the fertility and the infinite vastness of the San Joaquin Valley. With his epic vision he con-

---

[1] *Main-Travelled Roads*, pp. 140–1.
[2] See also "Turgenev and Garland," p. 320.

centrated on the gigantic sweep of fertile land and had little to say about flowers, animals, birds, insects, etc. He described the valley in various lights and in various seasons always emphasizing its fruitfulness.

To sum up: Garland, Crane, and Norris were all eager to reproduce the American setting in an accurate and truthful way. Their concept of the milieu was to a certain degree deterministic, that is, they transformed the setting into a force which had a considerable influence on the characters, as will be illustrated in the following chapter. Concurrent with a desire to expose the evils of big cities there ran a stream of idealism and lyricism at least in Garland and Norris. Garland had a tendency to idealize the city as an intellectual and cultural center, whereas the country to him spelled banality and mental barrenness. In general, to Crane and Norris, and at times also to Garland, the city was a nest of sin and vice, where young girls like Maggie and Minna Hooven went from bad to worse. Like the French naturalists the three writers occasionally employed the slums as background for their work and included sordid and brutal details. We may assume that they owed some of their frankness, desire for exposé, and descriptive technique to the French naturalists, particularly to Zola.[1]

---

[1] See Chap. X.

CHAPTER IX

CHARACTERS

1. SOME NOTES ON TECHNIQUE

For the most part, Garland and Crane rarely gave elaborate descriptions of the physical appearances of their personages, using instead but few significant adjectives or succinct phrases. This is particularly true of Crane, who described, for instance, the Swede in "The Blue Hotel" as "burly," and George Kelcey in *George's Mother* as simply "a brown young man." Like Zola, Norris was, however, more elaborate in his physical descriptions. Thus McTeague was frequently referred to as a giant with an immense square-cut head, a salient jaw, a shock of yellow hair, huge hands—the hands of the old-time car-boy—and a characteristic saying, "You can't make small of me." Trina had a pale round face suggestive of anemia, with narrow, half-open eyes, and a tiara of royal, black hair. When Maria in *McTeague* was asked about her name, she had always the same answer, "Maria-Miranda-Macapa—Had a flying squirrel an' let him go."[1] The Other Dentist in *McTeague* had the following attributes, "a poser, a rider of bicycles," "a courser of greyhounds, wearing salmon-pink neckties and astonishing waistcoats." In the same novel Miss Baker was always preparing tea, and Old Grannis was binding his pamphlets. In *The Octopus* Annixter had a passion for violent discussion, and when cornered he entrenched himself behind the remark, "Yes, that's all very well. In some ways it is and then again in some ways, it isn't."[2] Angèle Varian in the same novel had "the Egyptian fullness of the lips," and Hilma's voice was

---

[1] *Compl. Works*, VIII, 18.

[2] Cf. William Bacon's habitual remark in Garland's story "Elder Pill, Preacher," " 'Sometimes he is an' then agin he ain't.' " *Prairie Folks*, p. 34. See also Appendix, pp. 462 ff.

low in pitch and of a velvety huskiness. Mrs. Wessels in *The Pit* was always counting something, passers-by, photographs, dancing couples, or pews in a church.[1]

It was typical of the three authors that, in the portrayal of character, they used to a considerable degree sordid and brutal detail and pictured men and women devoid of grace and beauty. This is Lucretia Burns in Garland's story "Sim Burns's Wife":

> Lucretia Burns had never been handsome, even in her days of early girlhood, and now she was middle-aged, distorted with work and child-bearing, and looking faded and worn as one of the boulders that lay beside the pasture fence near where she sat milking a large white cow. . . .
> It was a pitifully worn, almost tragic face—long, thin, sallow, hollow-eyed. The mouth had long since lost the power to shape itself into a kiss, and had a droop at the corners which seemed to announce a breaking-down at any moment into a despairing wail. The collarless neck and sharp shoulders showed painfully.[2]

In his war stories Crane dwelled on the ugly detail:

> The orderly sergeant of the youth's company was shot through the cheeks. Its supports being injured, his jaw hung afar down, disclosing in the wide cavern of his mouth a pulsing mass of blood and teeth. And with it all he made attempts to cry out. In his endeavour there was a dreadful earnestness, as if he conceived that one great shriek would make him well.[3]

Norris also used sordid and grotesque details, as in his description of McTeague asleep:

> [Trina] saw his red, congested face; the huge mouth wide open; his unclean shirt, with its frayed wristbands; and his huge feet encased in thick woollen socks. . . . Sprawled at full length upon the bed, the dentist snored and snored, stupefied, inert, his legs wide apart, his hands lying palm upward at his sides.[4]

2. THE PROBLEM OF FREE WILL

According to genuine naturalists, man has no free will; either external or internal forces, environment or heredity control him and determine his behavior, for which he is not responsible. This

---

[1] *Compl. Works*, IX, 6, 101, 104, 171.

[2] *Prairie Folks*, pp. 101–2.

[3] *Work*, I, 186.

[4] *Compl. Works*, VIII, 256–7.

belief is called determinism and is fundamental in naturalism. There are, of course, different stages of determinism, because a writer may not be a confirmed determinist, but a determinist only to a certain degree. All determinists believe, of course, in the *existence* of the will, but the will is often enslaved on account of various reasons.

In the United States determinism was slow to take root, for native optimism and individualism helped to check its progress and acceptance.[1] In the American fiction of the nineties the problem of free will was, however, deepened and intensified by another doctrine, that of fatalism.[2] Garland, Crane, and Norris responded in various ways to the problem of free will. Unlike Zola, who was a confirmed determinist and refused to accept fatalism,[3] they accepted both determinism and fatalism as forces which at times controlled man's will, and in some of their writings the two concepts were intertwined. Both beliefs led, of course, to the denial of free will.

The American writers who had observed how the human "insect" was ground under the granite wheels of industrialism were prone to reject the freedom of the will. Certain factors, such as native optimism, moralism, and a possible influence of Ibsen's individualism and psychology of will, may perhaps have helped to counterbalance a complete surrender to a denial of free will.[4]

Garland's study of such determinists as Taine and Darwin had taught him that man had no free will. In addition, personal experiences in the Middle West and his contact with literary determinism had confirmed him in his belief that man's will was enslaved. Unlike the French naturalists he did not express this belief by means of depicting degeneration or degradation; none of his principal characters was ruined by sensuality, drink, or debauchery in a depressing slum environment. Instead, he showed how the desolate prairie and the toil made almost beasts of individuals

---

[1] For the discussion of free will, see pp. 79–80.

[2] Fatalism is here taken as a term denoting the use of chance or fate as it is exemplified in the works of Turgenev, Dostoevsky, and Hardy. According to them human life was not regulated by natural laws, but was made irrational and illogical through the operation of inevitable chance. Se also pp. 315 ff.

[3] See p. 31.

[4] See Chap. XIV.

who were hard-working and morally unimpeachable. The dreary milieu put its imprint upon them and they grew insensitive and indifferent. The women in particular felt the loneliness, desolation, and spiritual poverty of the West, and to those who were unable to rebel successfully against the hard conditions, the lot was bitter. Not only did the dismal environment harden the people, but the endless, often hopeless toil tended to make the farmers stupid, callous, and selfish, and their wives plain, dull, and careworn. They had to cope with the environment; if they failed they were eliminated. The following quotation, in which Garland echoes Darwin, well summarizes the concept:

A fine nature must either adapt itself to its hard surroundings or die. Men who toil terribly in filthy garments day after day and year after year cannot easily keep gentle; the frost and grime, the heat and cold will soon or late enter into their souls. The case is not all in favor of the suffering wives, and against the brutal husbands. If the farmer's wife is dulled and crazed by her routine, the farmer himself is degraded and brutalized.[1]

A few succeeded in overcoming the influence of the environment but, in spite of their toil, it was impossible for the majority to liberate themselves from its effects or to cast aside the bondage of poverty which society had imposed upon them. Most of the characters in *Main-Travelled Roads* felt "the irrevocableness of living, the determinate, unalterable character of living."[2] They had no free choice, no free will; a rigorous determinism ruled their lives.

On the whole, in the three writers determinism was less a matter of heredity than one of social conditions, and it was, therefore, sometimes colored by indignation at the oppression of the individual by society. According to one of his principles—the effect of heredity was another—Zola portrayed his characters as primarily the victims of social conditions; and for the most part the American writers, consciously or unconsciously, followed in his footsteps. To them existing economic and social conditions were often such that they enslaved man's will, destroyed his belief in moral and ethical values, and brought him to defeat and ruin. The inability of the individual to resist social pressure led in-

---

[1] *Prairie Folks*, p. 137. See also *Main-Travelled Roads*, p. 40.
[2] *Main-Travelled Roads*, p. 48.

evitably to a somber view of life. The poor farmer on the inhospi-
table plain was helpless, "'Just like a fly in a pan of molasses.
There ain't any escape for him. The more he tears around the
more liable he is to rip his legs off.' "[1] The view of life as a futile
striving, because of intolerable social conditions, was shown particularly in *Main-Travelled Roads* and *Jason Edwards*. It was a
myth, an illusion, to believe that the farmers of the Middle West
were free; instead they were in the grip of unscrupulous land
sharks. To Timothy Haskins and his family in "Under the Lion's
Paw" there was no way out after the land agent, because of the
improvements Haskins himself had made, had doubled the price
of the farm, on which they had lived and toiled like slaves for
three years. He could not pay five hundred dollars rent a year,
nor could he afford to buy the farm. Thus, a striving family
became the victim of a bad social system, and the specter of home-
lessness loomed over them:

> There is no despair so deep as the despair of a homeless man or woman.
> To roam the roads of the country or the streets of the city, to feel there
> is no rood of ground on which the feet can rest, to halt weary and hungry
> outside lighted windows and hear laughter and song within—these are
> the hungers and rebellions that drive men to crime and women to shame.[2]

In *Main-Travelled Roads* Garland expressed his belief in social
determinism, but there were also traces of fatalism which were
given even greater prominence in *Jason Edwards*, where fatalism
and determinism were both used to illustrate the denial of free
will. In this novel determinism was employed more or less in
the Zola fashion. Set in a slum district, some of the minor characters were by heredity and environment, destined to ruin.

Reeves "seemed to see more of the hideous future of these
people, these young people born for a prison or a brothel in so
many cases."[3] Garland's determinism was also colored by social
indignation in this novel; the factory workers were portrayed as
prisoners without possibilities of ever freeing themselves from
their hopeless conditions. To denote their kinship with the animals they were also given almost ape-like traits; one of the laborers was described as "a curious combination of timid face, re-

---

[1] *Ibid.*, p. 118.
[2] *Ibid*, p. 223.
[3] *Jason Edwards*, p. 90.

treating chin, narrow, brainless skull, but tremendous power and endurance."[1]

In the social determinism illustrated in *Jason Edwards*, the bondage of the will was again emphasized. Edwards, the steady, hard-working mechanic-farmer, was ruined by social and economic conditions: in Boston rent went up and wages down; in the Middle West land was no longer free, and despite ferocious labor he was unable to keep poverty away. His struggles were hopeless, for life seemed to conspire against him. Disillusioned, filled with a sense of futility, he had to take the back trail to the East. Garland's depiction of Edwards' failure was a verification of the fact that there was no free will, no choice. " 'A man once jumped over-board because he wanted to. It was a free choice—only the ship was on fire—that's about as much free choice as Edwards had.' "[2]

Adding to his utter helplessness and despair and emphasizing his frustration, fatalism combined with determinism to accomplish his ruin: " 'God and man has joined hands to break me down,' " sighed Edwards.[3] A severe drought having all but killed his wheat, he prayed for rain; but instead of rain there came a devastating hailstorm that completed the destruction of his property and paralyzed himself, whereas his neighbor's wheat was not damaged at all. Fate struck the final blow at the man who had earlier been so sorely afflicted by social conditions.

A Member of the Third House, in which Garland voiced no determinism, shows a marked change in the author's attitude. In this novel, Garland expressed by means of Senator Ward a belief in the freedom of the will and man's ability to control forces. Ward was afflicted with a strong propensity for drink, inherited from his father who, although a good man, had been a drunkard; and in his fraternizing with party politicians in offices "reeking with liquor," the inborn appetite came almost to master him. Ward was, moreover, a weakling. In spite of these handicaps he did not, however, go from bad to worse in the fashion of Coupeau in *L'Assommoir*; instead his better self triumphed over the factors which, according to the naturalists, should inevitably have

---

[1] *Ibid.*, p. 74.

[2] *Ibid.*, p. 103.

[3] *Ibid.*, pp. 205–6.

brought him to ruin. Ward lost his senatorship and his social connections, it is true, but he won a moral victory over self.[1]

Traces of determinism were, however, evident in *Prairie Folks*, the tone of which was less somber than that of the earlier stories. Sim Burns and his wife were victims of social conditions and a hapless, brutalizing toil. The inherited consequences of fruitless labor could be seen in their children. In the bent shoulders of the eldest ones they could see "the beginnings of deformity that would soon be permanent."[2]

In *Rose of Dutcher's Coolly* Garland showed that a woman who possessed a certain amount of vitality and will power was able to triumph over sexual desire and a depressing environment. Rose was in many ways an exceptional girl, superior to her fellow women in character and moral power. In this novel Garland was no longer a determinist; instead he believed in the freedom of the will. Moreover, his interest had shifted from the type and the social group to the individual. Rose "was not a victim . . . She was quite evidently a proud, strong woman . . ."[3]

In his early stories Garland portrayed man as a victim of forces beyond his control. Sometimes fate or chance interfered to emphasize the bondage of the will, and increased the feeling of futility and frustration. Then his attitude toward the problem of the will changed with a shift of his thematic interest. Man was, after all, responsible for his success or failure in life. Even if the conditions of society were at times adverse and bore hard on the individual, it was man's duty to rise above a depressing environment and to try to control the forces which otherwise would have crushed him or brought him to degradation. Thus Garland shows a clear development in his thinking.

Like Garland, Crane, too, adopted a deterministic view of life, but in contrast to both Garland and Norris,[4] who gradually adopted the belief that it was possible for man to triumph over the forces which threatened him with ruin, Crane seems to have held, throughout his life, that man's will was enslaved. He did not portray a single character possessing genuine freedom of the will

---

[1] Cf. Chap. on Ibsen, p. 375.
[2] *Prairie Folks*, p. 130.
[3] *Rose of Dutcher's Coolly*, p. 133.
[4] See pp. 221 ff.

in the manner of Rose. Crane was fundamentally a psychologist, and his psychology was largely naturalistic; that is, he was interested in the psychological process, in instinctive emotions and reactions, which lay beyond will and consciousness. To show this he created characters who were mostly poor, hungry, and terror-stricken; outcasts and strangers in the world, helpless and insecure and unable to assert themselves in the struggle for life.

In considering the elements which seem to have formed Crane's pessimistic view of man, one should not overlook two probable sources—besides personal experiences, temperamental idiosyncrasies, and American social conditions: French determinism and Russian fatalism.[1] Whether Schopenhauer's doctrines of the negation of the will and passive meditation contributed to the shaping of Crane's view of life remains to be investigated.

A deterministic view of life was particularly evident in *Maggie* and *George's Mother*. Like Zola, Crane believed that heredity and milieu influenced man's actions to a considerable degree. Heredity was a determining factor, a force which struck man blindly. The Biblical statement that "the sins of the fathers shall be visited upon the heads of the children, even unto the third and fourth generation of them that hate me," called forth the following outburst from Crane:

> Well, then, I hate Thee, unrighteous picture;
> Wicked image, I hate Thee;
> So, strike with Thy vengeance
> The heads of those little men
> Who come blindly.
> It will be a brave thing.[2]

Jimmie's and Maggie's parents were both confirmed drunkards, veritable beasts when drunk, but the hereditary propensity for drink, so strong in Jimmie, did not come to the fore in Maggie. Eventually, however, the Bowery environment pervaded with vice victimized both of them. In accordance with the pattern of French naturalists Jimmie degenerated rapidly into a drunkard and fighter. He grew up among quarrels, blows, and vice and his home was a "reg'lar livin' hell." As a young man he believed in nothing, was afraid of nothing, and maintained an attitude of con-

[1] See Chaps. X and XIII.
[2] *Work*, VI, 44.

tempt toward his environment. He was involved in rows, frequently got himself arrested and had affairs with women. He had no respect for the world, for his study of life in the gutter had divested him of all idols and ideals. There was only one possible result of a life so handicapped from its beginning by heredity and environment.

The fate of Maggie was even more tragic than that of Jimmie, because she was a victim rather than a product of her environment. Crane's purpose in *Maggie* was probably to show the malevolence of all men and the indifferent and negative attitude of society to the individual, whose ruin was of no consequence to it. She was described as passive and innocent and possessing inherent goodness and affection. That Crane had a definite thesis in his story was confirmed by what he wrote on a copy of the novel which he presented to the Rev. Thomas Dickson:

> It is inevitable that this book will greatly shock you, but continue, pray, with great courage to the end, for it tries to show that environment is a tremendous thing in this world, and often shapes lives regardlessly. If one could prove that theory, one would make room in Heaven for all sorts of souls (notably an occasional street girl) who are not confidently expected to be there by many excellent people.[1]

Like most naturalistic characters, Jimmie and Maggie were described as weak and uncomplicated, and their intellectual limitations were revealed by their meager vocabulary and by Jimmie's habit of showing his emotional intensity by cursing. Following the naturalistic literary pattern, and in order to illustrate the doctrine of the influence of heredity and milieu, Crane placed weak and submissive characters afflicted with evil heredity and easily imposed upon, in a slum environment. To these characters life was a never ceasing struggle, composed of hardships and insults; they were helpless and alone in a hard and brutal world. Their ruin was as inevitable as if brought about by a natural law. There was no hope and no free will. Maggie, who was idealistically conceived—a rose in a mud-puddle, unsullied by the slums—exemplified a naturalistic decline. After her seduction she became a prostitute. The process of degeneration set in and was followed by inevitable suicide as a result of environmental and social pres-

---

[1] *Bookman*, I (May, 1895), 229.

sure. Her process of degradation was given relief by Crane's irony. When Maggie had gone to the bad, her drunken and beastly mother meditated as follows:

"An' wid all d' bringin'-up she had, how could she?" moaningly she asked of her son. "Wid all d' talkin' wid her I did an' d' t'ings I tol' her to remember. When a girl is bringed up d' way I bringed up Maggie, how kin she go teh d' devil?"[1]

A deterministic view of life was also voiced in *George's Mother*. The environment was similar to that in *Maggie*, and the characters were equally passive and easily imposed upon. George Kelcey, the hero, was a daydreamer, an escapist, who felt a stranger in the world. Just as in *Maggie*, environment acted as a natural force upon him and brought him to destruction. He had no will even to protest against the forces which drove him down; he was doomed to fail. He succumbed easily to the lure of saloons and of idleness, for he felt that drunkards and outcasts were his fellow men and drinks his antidote to a hostile world. An over-solicitous mother and her religious activity, together with a corrupted environment, contributed to his ruin.

In his proletarian stories Crane was largely a social determinist. A bitter denunciation of society appeared in "An Experiment in Misery," in which the multitude of buildings and particularly the skyscrapers of the metropolis were used as symbols of a nation that forced its "regal head into the clouds, throwing no downward glances; in the sublimity of its aspirations ignoring the wretches who may flounder at its feet."[2] Instead of taking care of the unemployed and the homeless, society was indifferent and suffered them to go wrong. To the derelicts in the City Hall Park who sat on the benches which were "sanctified by traditions of their class," the noise of the city came vaguely, but it spelled no hope to them, only despair and futility, for society was oblivious of them.

In the same story the sound of a snoring man in a miserable house became symbolic of the revolt of a whole class of people against the existing social conditions. It was "the protest of the wretch who feels the touch of the imperturbable granite wheels, and who then cries with an impersonal eloquence, with a strength

---

[1] *Work*, X, 191. Cf. also chap. on Zola, pp. 260–1.
[2] *Work*, XI, 34.

not from him, giving voice to the wail of a whole section, a class, a people."[1] The protest was directed not only against the social injustice of the metropolis but against that of the whole universe. Characters like Maggie and Kelcey felt in particular the world's ungratefulness and indifference. They were out of place in their world. "They were possessed of various virtues which were unappreciated by those with whom they were commonly obliged to mingle; they were fitted for a tree-shaded land where everything was peace."[2] In their misery and poverty, such wretches found solace and relief in the company of their like.

In the story "A Desertion" Crane pictured a terror-stricken soul, an innocent little shopgirl thrown helplessly upon the world. Returning home one evening she found her father, her only protection, dead at the table. What would be the fate of the poor girl? Crane hints that it will be the street. Who was to blame? Society or life itself? Crane did not furnish an answer to the question. Perhaps he had no answer.

Frequently in Crane the fates of the characters appear to be arbitrarily contrived rather than to rise logically from the deterministic forces of heredity and environment. As a matter of fact, determinism and fatalism were also mingled in his work. Perhaps nowhere was man's tragedy brought to light in a more lucid and direct way than in Crane's sketches of individuals beaten by an inexorable fate. "Strange and still strange are the laws of fate," he said in "A Man and—Some Others."[3] The operation of fate was perhaps best illustrated in "The Blue Hotel"[4] and "The Open Boat."

Henry Fleming in *The Red Badge of Courage* was a pawn, too, governed by his instincts and uncontrollable forces, and so were most of his fellow soldiers. He had no free will; he was a nameless unit moved by implacable forces, together with other nameless units. He realized that he could not escape from his regiment, for "there were iron bars of traditions and law on four sides. He was in a moving box."[5] War was a complex machine in which the soldiers

---

[1] *Ibid.*, p. 28.
[2] *Work*, X, 35.
[3] *Work*, XII, 70.
[4] See pp. 358–9.
[5] *Work*, I, 48.

had become entangled, and the army was a gigantic trap, serving as the instrument of fate. The soldiers moved aimlessly around according to no rule or pattern. Confusion, terror, and anxiety were everywhere. An attack was a blind and despairing rush toward a vague and dimly felt enemy hidden somewhere behind a cloud of smoke from spluttering rifles. Some men fell, "struck down by other men who, perhaps half a mile away, were aiming at somebody else."[1] Blind forces were supreme and man was caught in their grip.

Crane followed the creed of the naturalists in denying the freedom of the will, and illustrated it in his naturalistic stories of the Bowery. For the most part his characters did not know why they were doomed to fail. Some had possibly been lacking in moral power, courage, and will to succeed, and had therefore been eliminated in the struggle for existence. Others were perhaps not to be blamed morally; social conditions, natural laws, or fate had brought them to their tragic end. In general his characters were of the unfit, unable to assert themselves. There was no room, no foothold for them, only despair and frustration in a world wherein the battle was to the strong, and the weak and humble were trampled down.

Norris adopted Zola's tenet that the individual was a product of heredity and environment, and illustrated the doctrine in a number of short stories and in some of his novels. Like Garland and Crane, he accepted fatalism in addition to determinism, and wove both into the fabric of his works. Thus he showed man devoid of free will, helpless in the face of biological and social forces, or a victim of fate.

Biological determinism was illustrated in three vividly painted sketches, veritable studies in heredity, entitled "Little Dramas of the Curbstone."[2] The scene of the first drama was a street outside a clinic to which a mother had brought her sick child. The woman led her son, who was blind and an idiot:

Blind and an idiot, absolute stagnation, life as unconscious as that of the jelly-fish, an excrescence, a parasitic fungus in the form of a man, a creature far below the brute. The last horror of the business was that he never moved; he sat there just as his mother had placed him, his mo-

---

[1] *Work*, II, 189.
[2] *Compl. Works*, IV, 19–25.

tionless, filmy eyes fixed, his jaw dropped, his hands open at his sides, his hat on wrong side foremost. He would sit like that, I knew, for hours —for days, perhaps—would, if left to himself, die of starvation, without raising a finger. What was going on inside of that misshapen head —behind those fixed eyes?[1]

This monster of a child was the victim of heredity. "Heredity . . . father a degenerate, exhausted race, drank himself into a sanitarium,"[2] was the doctor's comment on the case.

The second drama concerned a humble little group of mankind, a poor old woman with her two girls, one about ten, the other about six or seven years of age. The little group was walking slowly along the street. Now and then, however, the youngest girl collapsed and had to be carried by her patient, worn-out mother. The girl was a paralytic, the result of hereditary affliction.

The actor of the third drama was a young man of eighteen or nineteen years who preferred to go to prison rather than return home with his mother. Nothing was said about heredity in this cryptic and somber sketch, but from the concluding paragraph quoted below it can be inferred that Norris looked upon the youth and the children of the other stories as victims of heredity:

And as I went along I wondered where was the father of that young fellow who was to spend his first night in jail, and the father of the little paralytic girl, and the father of the blind idiot, and it seemed to me that the chief actors in these three Little Dramas of the Curbstone had been somehow left out of the programme.[3]

In the short story "A Case for Lombroso"[4] Norris contrasted two individuals of different temperaments. One was a fine young Harvard man named Stayne who was a " 'torrowbred' to his very boots," a man of strength, honesty, and courage; the other

---

[1] *Ibid.*, p. 21.

[2] *Ibid.*

[3] *Ibid.*, p. 25.

[4] Note the use of the word "case" in the title. The story seems to be a variation of the theme of Zola's *Thérèse Raquin*. Norris adopted Zola's theory that there existed a number of temperaments, particularly the sanguine and the nervous one, and a combination of these opposite temperaments spelled ruin to the persons concerned. Stayne corresponded to Laurent and Cresencia to Thérèse. The story was first published in the San Francisco *Wave* (April 11, 1897) and reprinted in *Compl. Works*, X, 35-42. Cf. also Chap. X.

a degenerate girl, Cresencia Hromada, tall and fair and of the oldest and purest Spanish blood. "She had come of a family of unmixed blood, whose stock had never been replenished or strengthened by an alien cross. Her race was almost exhausted, its vitality low, and its temperament refined to the evaporation point. To-day Cresencia might have been called a degenerate."[1] Cresencia loved Stayne with a desperate, furious passion, a passion which was abnormal and which revealed all the degenerate characteristics of her stock. She could not explain her passion; it was a disease, a kind of insanity, from which she was not able to free herself. Stayne, when brought into contact with the degenerate Spanish girl, developed, rather curiously, into a brutal villain, all the inherent evil characteristics of his nature coming to light. The two opposite temperaments—one healthy and sound, the other nervous and degenerate—clashed and, like the two jars of Æsop's fable, "floating helplessly in ungovernable currents, crashed together. That of the finest clay shivered and sank at once—the other, of coarser fibre, settled slower to its ruin."[2]

The sketch "Suggestions: III, Brute" is an illustration of the influence of environment and trade upon man, and may be quoted *in toto*:

> He had been working all day in a squalid neighbourhood by the gas works and coal yards, surrounded by lifting cranes, pile drivers, dredging machines, engines of colossal, brutal strength, where all about him were immense blocks of granite, tons of pig iron; everything had been enormous, crude, had been huge in weight, tremendous in power, gigantic in size.
>
> By long association with such things he had become like them, huge, hard, brutal, strung with a crude, blind strength, stupid, unreasoning. He was on his way home now, his immense hands dangling half-open at his sides; his head empty of thought. He only desired to be fed and to sleep. At a street crossing he picked up a white violet, very fresh, not yet trampled into the mud. It was a beautiful thing, redolent with the scent of the woods, suggestive of everything pretty and delicate. It was almost like a s[i]mile-made flower. It lay very light in the hollow of his

---

[1] *Compl. Works*, X, 36.

[2] *Ibid.*, p. 40. A typical case of atavism appeared in the short story "A Reversion to Type." *Compl. Works*, IV, 43–50. One day Paul Schuster got drunk, and the alcohol unleashed terrific inherited tendencies and turned him into a beast. Hereditary themes were also found in "Son of a Sheik." *Compl. Works*, IV, 68–74 and "A Caged Lion." *Compl. Works*, IV, 94–103.

immense calloused palm. In some strange way it appealed to him, and blindly he tried to acknowledge his appreciation. He looked at it stupidly, perplexed, not knowing what to do; then instinctively his hand carried it to his mouth; he ground it between his huge teeth and slowly ate it. It was the only way he knew.[1]

The story illustrated also a kind of mental abnormality—rather common in naturalistic writings—that was reflected in certain coercive actions or instinctive behavior patterns.

But it was not only in his short stories and sketches that Norris voiced his determinism; at least three of his novels are also primarily deterministic: *McTeague*, *Vandover and the Brute*, and *The Octopus*. In the first two, the determining forces were largely heredity and environment, whereas in the latter social conditions and natural laws victimized the characters and enslaved their wills. Furthermore, in *McTeague* and *Vandover and the Brute*, fate[2] played a certain role in the lives of the characters and contributed to their degradation. Many of Norris's personages such as McTeague, Trina, Vandover, Mrs. Hooven, and Magnus Derrick illustrated a typically naturalistic decline. In *McTeague* he reduced psychology to physiology and studied two temperaments in conflict with each other. As a faithful Zola adherent, he was anxious to describe as fully as possible the milieu (exterior, interior, and social) that surrounded McTeague, for the milieu completed and explained him and his behavior. No detail, however tedious, seemed irrelevant. Hence the many descriptions of Polk Street and its people, of visits to the theater and the Mechanics' Fair, of excursions to Schuetzen Park, etc. Life was a drudgery; McTeague could not free himself from his environment which made him dull and brutal. But the Polk Street milieu was not actually a determining force in the life of McTeague until catastrophe befell him in the form of a letter from the authorities forbidding him to practice. After that he took to drink and his hereditary affliction, namely, his propensity for drink, became more and more evident. In this connection it is worth while calling attention to the fact that McTeague originally was molded by an environment other than that of Polk Street, the wild Placer County

region of California. His work as a car-boy at the Big Dipper
Mine, where he had trundled the heavy cars of ore in and out of
the tunnel under the direction of his father, together with the
untamed region of Placer County had put their indelible imprint
on him. Like his native mountains, McTeague was silent, wild,
massive and gigantic. This is a description of the mountain area
with its primeval forces which helped to mold the dentist:

Here and there the mountains lifted themselves out of the narrow river
beds in groups like giant lions rearing their heads after drinking. The
entire region was untamed. In some places east of the Mississippi nature
is cosy, intimate, small, and homelike, like a good-natured housewife.
In Placer County, California, she is a vast, unconquered brute of the
Pliocene epoch, savage, sullen, and magnificently indifferent to man.[1]

Norris said explicitly in the following quotation that these colossal
and savage mountains were reflected in McTeague's own nature,
physically as well as mentally:

The still, colossal mountains took him back again like a returning prodigal, and vaguely, without knowing why, he yielded to their influence
—their immensity, their enormous power, crude and blind, *reflecting themselves in his own nature*, huge, strong, brutal in its simplicity.[2]

In McTeague the influences of heredity and environment were
intertwined and, under certain conditions, the one called forth the
other. His responsiveness to the Polk Street surrounding was
favored by his dull and passive temperament. In his physical
appearance he was like a huge, enormously strong, brainless ape:

... McTeague was a young giant, carrying his huge shock of blond
hair six feet three inches from the ground; moving his immense limbs,
heavy with ropes of muscle, slowly, ponderously. His hands were enormous, red, and covered with a fell of stiff yellow hair; they were hard
as wooden mallets, strong as vises, the hands of the old-time car-boy.
Often he dispensed with forceps and extracted a refractory tooth with
his thumb and finger. His head was square-cut, angular; the jaw salient,
like that of the carnivora.[3]

His mental equipment corresponded well with his physique:
"McTeague's mind was as his body, heavy, slow to act, sluggish.

---

[1] *Compl. Works*, VIII, 322.
[2] *Ibid.*, p. 329. Italics are mine.
[3] *Ibid.*, p. 3.

Yet there was nothing vicious about the man. Altogether he suggested the draught horse, immensely strong, stupid, docile, obedient."[1] Another factor which contributed to his tragedy was his inherited tendency to drink, for he was the son of an alcoholic father, and an inherited evil flowed in his veins.

The determining forces, heredity and environment, did not play the same dominating role in Norris's novel as they did in *L'Assommoir*, for Trina and Marcus Schouler contributed also to the tragic fate of the dentist. In addition, fate brought McTeague and Trina together, and fate gave them five thousand dollars, which became Trina's misfortune and which helped to ruin both of them.

The other characters of the novel, it must be added, were not colored by their environment to the same degree as McTeague. Trina's devolution and tragic death were due more to her inherited passion for saving and to its consequences than to her immediate surroundings. Her ancestors on both sides were German-Swiss peasants, and "A good deal of peasant blood still ran undiluted in her veins, and she had all the instinct of a hardy and penurious mountain race—the instinct which saves without any thought, without idea of consequence—saving for the sake of saving, hoarding without knowing why."[2]

In *Vandover and the Brute* Norris mingled biological determinism and fatalism. Like *McTeague* this novel was a study of temperament, wherein physiological phenomena, instincts, nerves, etc., rather than the soul were analyzed. The pressure of different surroundings acting on a pliable temperament became fatal in the life of Vandover. "In a suitable environment," Norris asserted, "Vandover might easily have become an author, actor, or musician, since it was evident that he possessed the fundamental *afflatus* that underlies all branches of art. As it was, the merest chance decided his career."[3] The Darwin-inspired novel may also be called a study in human variation, in atavism, in reversion to type, for gradually Vandover stripped off the veneer of civilization and became more and more like a beast. His character

---

[1] *Ibid.*
[2] *Ibid.*, pp. 116–17.
[3] *Compl. Works*, V, 9.

was transformed into increasingly simple forms by a continual process of reduction:

> Vandover sank to the grade of these people at once with that fatal adaptability to environment which he had permitted himself to foster throughout his entire life, and which had led him to be contented in almost any circumstances. It was as if the brute in him were forever seeking a lower level, wallowing itself lower and lower into the filth and into the mire, content to be foul, content to be prone, to be inert and supine.[1]

This example of evolution, or more correctly devolution, was probably a result of Norris's interest in Darwinism and evolutionary thought. Darwinian ideas and catchwords were scattered throughout his books, but they were perhaps most numerous in this novel.

Around Vandover, Norris grouped two young men, Charlie Geary and Dolliver Haight. Geary, Vandover's opposite, pushing, selfish, and domineering, represented the survival of the fittest. Haight, on the other hand, timid, but kind and intelligent became the sport of fate, and his life as well as Vandover's illustrated the doctrine of no free will, with the difference that Vandover was the victim largely of deterministic forces, and Haight of fate. Geary alone had the strength to triumph over environment and the good fortune to escape adverse chance. Norris probably intended to exemplify different concepts of the will in these various characters.

The milieu which transformed Vandover consisted, to begin with, of his friends. Geary, for instance, influenced him in a negative way. Because of Vandover's yielding disposition, he submitted easily to Geary's dictatorship, became indolent and avoided his duties in the conviction that his friend would pull him out of any difficulties into which he might fall.

After his removal to San Francisco, Vandover again easily adapted himself to the new environment. He had gone through Harvard without contracting any other vices than "a vague distaste for responsibility, and an inclination to shirk disagreeable duties."[2] As his character gradually changed, the brute within him came more and more to the fore. Despite his passivity there was, however, some volitional power left in Vandover, which he

---

[1] *Ibid.*, p. 278.

[2] *Ibid.*, p. 22.

used in his struggles with his lower self. But stronger forces, heredity, environment, and fate, inevitably pulled him down. He was thrown helplessly upon the world; nothing and nobody could help him. Not even religion could afford him any solace. Caught in a vast labyrinth with no chance of ever finding the way out, he lost in the struggle for life because he was not fit, because he was too weak and had to perish. Geary, on the other hand, survived, for he was strong and fit and able to crush weak Vandover. "Every man for himself ... the weakest to the wall, the strongest to the front," was his motto.[1] Thus Geary did not hesitate to sacrifice his college friend to gain an advantage in the struggle for existence. The last phases of Vandover's decline were like the slow decay of a withering plant. Note the use of botanic vocabulary:

> He had arrived at a state of absolute indifference. He had so often rearranged his pliable nature to suit his changing environment that at last he found that he could be content in almost any circumstances. He had no pleasures, no cares, no ambitions, no regrets, no hopes. It was mere passive existence, an inert, *plantlike vegetation*, the moment's pause before the final decay, *the last inevitable rot*.[2]

In many respects, Vandover's life may be compared to that of a plant, and the stages of his development were those of a plant: growth, maturity, and decay. As, according to Darwin, a plant developed certain variations within its species when removed from one habitat to another, in like manner, Vandover gradually changed according to the different environments that acted upon him.[3]

Moran in *Moran of the Lady Letty* was first molded by Norwegian mountains; then, in the manner of McTeague, she was transplanted to another milieu, but one which was in harmony with her temperament: the vast, mighty ocean, now calm and undisturbed, now furious and untamed. The new surroundings together with her hard work aboard the ship completed and explained her character; even her body seemed to suggest the ocean and the winds. In Moran the environment did not act as a determining force in her life; instead her will reigned supreme.

---

[1] *Ibid.*, p. 288.

[2] *Ibid.* p. 244. Italics are mine.

[3] Cf. O. Holmberg, "Darwinistisk människoteckning. Anteckningar till 'Fru Marie Grubbe,'" *Studier tillägnade Efraim Liljeqvist, I* (Lund, 1930), 535–64.

In contradistinction to Vandover, whose will was enslaved, Norris described in *Blix* how a weak and passive character, Condy, was able to triumph over his paralysis of will and his inherent passivity thanks to a vigorous woman. A *"strong* man—strong in everything—is the grandest thing in the world," asserted Blix[1]; and gradually a male force developed in Condy, "a certain *strength* he had not known before, came swiftly into being."[2] Thus Norris illustrated his belief that women exerted a good influence on men. This view was evident in almost all his work. Trina, for example, influenced McTeague for the better, at least at one phase of his life; and Moran, who was a glorification of primitivism, strength and will, helped to make a man of Wilbur.

A remarkable apotheosis of will was displayed in *A Man's Woman*, in which Bennett was able to defy nature in the Arctic region. In him the Darwinian doctrine of the survival of the fittest merged with an Ibsenian cult of individualism and stubbornness of will.[3] Like Bennett, Lloyd, too, possessed a strong will and a high moral purpose. Temporarily Bennett's strength was conquered, not by external forces, but by fate and his "very self's self." In the end, however, his will was supreme and he won a moral victory over self.

In *The Octopus*, Norris was predominantly a social determinist, illustrating how social and economic conditions crushed a whole group of people. A typical case was Dyke. He was a steady, sober, and good-looking fellow who had worked faithfully for the Pacific and Southwestern Railroad for over ten years as an engine driver, and even risked his life for the company during a strike. But when hard times came along and wages were reduced, the company made no exception in his case. Because he would not work for starvation wages he was forced to leave his job. He then went into the hop-raising business, financing the venture by mortgaging his crop and homestead. With prospects of a bumper crop, Dyke cherished good hopes for the future till suddenly the railroad raised the freight on hops from two to five cents. Under

---

[1] *Compl. Works*, III, 57. Norris's interest in Darwinism was linked with the Kiplingesque cult of the strong man and the Anglo-Saxon race.

[2] *Ibid.*, p. 146. Cf. the development of the spoiled son of a millionaire into a strong and virile man in Kipling's *Captain Courageous* (1897).

[3] See pp. 391 ff.

contract to deliver his crop, he was ruined, for the new rate consumed all his profits. His life was wrecked by the policy of the railroad, the insatiable octopus. He had hoped for justice and fair treatment, but he met only high tariff rates and sneers from the railroad officials:

> His energy, industry, and foresight had been sound. He had been merely the object of a colossal trick, a sordid injustice, a victim of the insatiate greed of the monster, caught and choked by one of those millions of tentacles suddenly reaching up from below, from out the dark beneath his feet, coiling around his throat, throttling him, strangling him, sucking his blood. For a moment he thought of the courts, but instantly laughed at the idea. What court was immune from the power of the monster? Ah, the rage of helplessness, the fury of impotence! No help, no hope—ruined in a brief instant—he a veritable giant, built of great sinews, powerful, in the full tide of his manhood, having all his health, all his wits.[1] Part II, chap. 2, p. 241

Then followed his slow, but inevitable collapse—an honest man struck down and wrecked by the power of the railroad. The steps of his degradation led downward from drunkenness and theft to murder, a decline frequently found in naturalistic works.

The railroad contributed also to the ruin of the ranchers of the San Joaquin valley. Annixter, Harran Derrick, Hooven, Osterman, and Broderson were all brought to an untimely death, and Magnus Derrick was demented. Like Haskins in Garland's story they were under the lion's paw; they were crushed under the wheels of the railroad trust. Moreover, the consequences of the armed clash were far-reaching for the stricken families. A case in point was Mrs. Hooven and her daughters. After a long and terrible *via dolorosa* Mrs. Hooven died of starvation on a street in San Francisco with her half-dead child in her arms, and the eldest daughter, Minna, was brought to a life of shame and ruin.

Norris did not, however, blame the railroad officials for the tragedies; conditions, natural forces, not men, were responsible *nonsense* for what had happened, as Shelgrim, the head of the railroad, informed Presley:

> "... You are dealing with forces, young man, when you speak of Wheat and the Railroads, not with men. There is the Wheat, the supply. It must be carried to feed the People. There is the demand. The Wheat is one force, the Railroad, another, and there is the law that governs

---

[1] *Compl. Works*, II, 67.

them—supply and demand. Men have only little to do in the whole business. Complications may arise, conditions that bear hard on the individual—crush him maybe—*but the Wheat will be carried to feed the people* as inevitably as it will grow. If you want to fasten the blame of the affair at Los Muertos on any one person, you will make a mistake. Blame conditions, not men."[1]

Natural forces contributed also to the defeat of Jadwin, the financial superman of *The Pit*. Despite his strength it was impossible for him to control the wheat. He, too, was driven by forces, in the face of which he was helpless. He could not corner the wheat; instead the wheat cornered him. He happened to stand between two sets of circumstances which made him do what he did. Even Titans of the world, who were thought to be the fittest to survive, were relentlessly crushed when they challenged the laws of nature:

... demand and supply, these were the two great laws the Wheat obeyed. Almost blasphemous in his effrontery, he had tampered with these laws, and had roused a Titan. He had laid his puny human grasp upon Creation and the very earth herself, the great mother, feeling the touch of the cobweb that the human insect had spun, had stirred at last in her sleep and sent her omnipotence moving through the grooves of the world, to find and crush the disturber of her appointed courses.[2]

Norris's attitude toward the problem of free will was far from consistent throughout his work. Some of his characters possessed freedom to choose between alternatives and were capable of moral decisions; but others, and those were in the majority, were portrayed as devoid of free will.

3. SEX

The works of the French naturalists, who were prone to reduce love to sexuality, were notorious for their shocking and obtrusive treatment of sex. Like hunger and thirst, the sex impulse was looked upon as an urge which had to be satisfied. Although the American experimenters of the nineties were more conservative in their concept of love and more reticent in their treatment of sex, they too admitted that sex was an instinct that played a consid-

---

[1] *Ibid.*, p. 285.
[2] *Compl. Works*, IX, 358.

erable part in human life. Each of them wrote at least one book in which the handling of sex was particularly bold for the period: *Rose of Dutcher's Coolly*, *Maggie*, and *McTeague*, respectively.

In *Crumbling Idols* as well as elsewhere, Garland voiced his distaste for uncalled-for treatment of sex in modern literature and art. As an evolutionist he protested against this tendency, which he called a return to "monkey morality" rather than progress. He was particularly disgusted at the sexuality of contemporary French art and belles-lettres. He spoke of "sterile French sexualism," and of American society plays that appeared to be "sexually diseased, precisely as in the French novel..."[1] French novelists seemed to find "healthy human feeling a bore," and to scent a "suggestive situation with the nostrils of a vulture."[2] At the Exhibition of modern French art in 1893, he was shocked at the nudity of the models finding "morbid sexuality" everywhere.[3] Like Howells, he believed, because his aim in writing

---

[1] *Crumbling Idols*, p. 86.

[2] *Ibid.*

[3] See pp. 141–2. In later years Garland's attitude toward sex in literature and art became still more conservative and he warred against the "pornographic school of writers." In a letter dated February 5, 1934, he wrote to Floyd Logan: "We are sex-mad—from my point of view—but I am aware that these incidents are considered necessary in an advanced literature. To me—as an evolutionist—they are a return to the life of the animals who are supposed to be lower on the scale of life.

My sadness comes not from a sense of my own failure but from the fear that my life will go out in an age of chaos and debasement. It may be that I am all wrong and that women will be happier passing from man to man as men have passed from woman to woman but it is revolting to me...." Some years later, on April 16, 1939, he informed August Derleth: "I have given up reading fiction. I find it so preoccupied with the animal side of sex life that I do not venture to open any modern novel. It would seem that virtuous women no longer interest novelists or dramatists. I am bored by the glorified prostitute and the girl libertine—bored and saddened." Finally, to be linked with Dreiser, one of the "pornographic writers," displeased Garland very much. On March 2, 1920 [?] he wrote, but did not send, the following unfinished letter to Carl Van Doren: "I appreciate the very great compliment involved in your mentioning me in your lectures as one of the side-lines. I am grateful for any remembrance now—but I do not see how you can find any connection between Dreiser and myself. I am an old fogy. I believe in marriage, the home, prohibition, censorship, the single tax and many other isms that are now discredited by the 'young' writers of fifty. I have always hated obscenity, tales of vice and crime, and jokes about the chastity or modesty of women. I

was to depict the normal life of honest men and women, that sex in literature, if treated of at all, should be touched upon in a decorous way. To the veritist, love was only a part of life and far from the most important. Sex should be given its proper place, the place it had in the lives of the hard-working, average American, no more and no less.

Garland illustrated this theory in most of his writings. In his early stories of the Middle West he revolted against the romanticists' glorification of love, and pictured it as devoid of beauty. To that end he preferred to portray men and women who were past their early youth and worn out by their toil, and in whose lives love played practically no part. Sim Burns in the story "Sim Burns's Wife" illustrates Garland's unromantic and unidealistic conception of love:

No grace had come or ever could come into his life. Back of him were generations of men like himself, whose main business had been to work hard, live miserably, and beget children to take their places when they died.

His courtship had been delayed so long on account of poverty that it brought little of humanizing emotion into his life. He never mentioned his love-life now, or if he did, it was only to sneer obscenely at it. He had long since ceased to kiss his wife or even speak kindly to her. There was no longer any sanctity to life or love. He chewed tobacco and toiled on from year to year without any very clearly defined idea of the future. His life was mainly regulated from without.[1]

Apparently, both the romantic and the natural sides of love—that is, both the romanticist's and the naturalist's concept of love—were to him a falsification of life.

The year after his denunciation of sexuality in his literary mani-

---

have never written about vice or crime. My stories are hard and rude and sordid but not in the beastly sense. I have never held with the pornographic school and my most advanced notions in 'Crumbling Idols,' as you know, had nothing to do with the glorification of sexual promiscuity. I am an individualist but my notions of liberty do not include license.

The pornographic school of writing is as old as the Cro-Magnon Man—or older. It is so old and so hackneyed in theme that I have no interest in it. My attempt has been to treat of themes which are characteristic of my age and of America. It is so easy to write stories of sexual 'irregularities.' I have tried to keep close to the normal, decent, hard-working folk of my day. The other kind of thing pays better but I could never quite bring myself to it."

[1] *Prairie Folks*, p. 109.

festo, there appeared *Rose of Dutcher's Coolly*, in which the frank handling of sex contrasted with his earlier treatment of love. The novel brought forth a storm of protest against its author. A typical example was John Burroughs, who wrote Garland on February 14, 1896:

... I think you make the sex of Rose too pronounced: one expects her to turn out a regular man devourer. I think all prurient suggestions in a story are to be avoided, especially when the hand of the author is so conspicuous as in this story. This morbid sex-consciousness is one of the diseases of the age. At least this feature of your book strikes me as unfortunate. It is extraneous and plays no part in the story. In such a master as Ibsen the sex problem is vital and plays a part and one is not offended. It must be inevitable or not at all. I do not think Zola a safe guide in such matters. In one of his books a man gets up in the morning, puts his head out of the window for a sniff of fresh air, when his nose is regaled with the stink of human excrement. Why put that in, even if true? The nasty, the stinking, the obscene are not to go in unless they are vital and the action demands them, then I never flinch. I do not think young girls are ever lecherous. Young men have a vague attraction for them; but it is only the perfume of sex as it were ...[1]

As Burroughs suggested, the handling of sex in *Rose of Dutcher's Coolly* reminds us more of Zola than of Ibsen. Like the French writer in *La Joie de vivre*, Garland pictured the awakening of sex in a young girl, and love, as a physiological phenomenon, an instinct, which demanded an outlet. But the moralist remained strong in the son of the prairies, for, although he recognized sex as a force in human life, he maintained that man should, and was able to, control his sexual urges. This is, of course, the very opposite of the naturalists' concept and literary use of sex. To them, as has been pointed out earlier, love was a natural force that struck blindly, and man was not morally responsible for his actions.

---

[1] A few more quotations may be given:

A critic in the *New York Tribune* (April 19, 1896) wrote for instance: "His style is turgid, strained, and forced; his psychology materialistic and vicious. Life to him is a series of purely physical and psychological sensations closely identified with sex." Quoted by Hill, *op. cit.*, p. 202.

William Morton Payne found the novel "characterized by several noticeable defects, such as an obtrusive didacticism, a repulsive lack of reticence concerning those details of the sex problem that it should be the first principle of wholesome art to avoid, and a style that is often slovenly." *Dial*, XX (February 1, 1896), 80.

Like Albine in *La Faute de l'abbé Mouret*, Rose was a primitive child of nature, full of animal life. She identified herself with nature, the seasons, the growth of plants; and to her the mating of animals, birth, and death held no secrets. Sound and healthy, she had an animal's instincts and urges. Garland stressed repeatedly her primitiveness and animality and, although the facts of life confronted her in various ways, she was not disturbed by them:

> She learned early the signs which pass in the country to describe the unnamable and covert things of human life. She saw them scrawled on the fences, on school-house doors, and written on the dust of the road. There was no escaping them. The apparently shameful fact of sex faced her everywhere.
>
> And yet through it all she lived a glad, free, wholesome life.[1]

Gradually she began to feel vague stirrings of sex when she met her friend Carl:

> She felt a terrible hunger, a desire to take his head in her arms and kiss it. Her muscles ached and quivered with something she could not fathom. As she resisted she grew calm, but mysteriously sad, as if something were passing from her forever. The leaves whispered a message to her, and the stream repeated an occult note of joy, which was mixed with sorrow.
>
> The struggle of wild fear and bitter-sweet hunger of desire—this vague, mystical perception of her sex, did not last with Rose.[2]

Desire had awakened within the young girl, and to illustrate the significance of the phenomenon in Rose, Garland said that "it was the beginning of her love-life. It was the second great epoch of her life."[3]

Rose grew up to be a sensual young woman, and, when at a circus she observed a handsome athlete, she was immediately attracted by his naked majesty which "appealed to her pure wholesome awakening womanhood, with the power of beauty and strength and sex combined."[4] Rose was no sexless, sweet heroine clinging helplessly to a strong man. Nor was she, on the other hand, a naturalistic example of degeneration like Nana, a victim

---

[1] *Rose of Dutcher's Coolly*, p. 19.

[2] *Ibid.*, p. 26.

[3] *Ibid.*

[4] *Ibid.*, p. 50.

of her instincts. Unfailingly her moral and intellectual power saved her when temptation came, for within her complex character, Rose possessed, besides her pronounced sexual desire, an unusual forcefulness of will and brains.

Because of her sexuality Rose was akin to the naturalistic type of woman, but, because of her high ethical and intellectual standard and power to control her desire, she was at the same time a protest against this type. Her many intellectual interests and her platonic love for the athlete were among the factors which "enabled her to escape the clutch of mere brute passion . . ."[1] But when spring came her sexual urge was intensified. The parallelisms between man and nature, frequently used as a theme in naturalistic work, for example, in *La Faute de l'abbé Mouret* and *La Terre*, is illustrated in the following quotation:

> Something elemental stirred in her blood as the leaves came out. The young men took on added grace and power in her eyes. When they came before her in their athletic suits, strong and joyous, her eyes dreamed and her heart beat till the blood choked her breathing.
>
> Oh, the beautiful sky! Oh, the shine and shade of leaves! Oh, the splendor of young manhood! She fought down the dizziness which came to her. She smiled mechanically as they stood before her with frank, clear eyes and laughing lips, and so, slowly, brain reasserted itself over flesh, and she, too, grew frank and gay.[2]

Rose overcame, however, the temptations of sex, for "something drawn from generations of virtuous wives and mothers, saved her from the whirlpool of passion."[3] And Garland added:

> . . . some hidden force rose up to dominate the merely animal forces within. Some magnificent inheritance of organic moral purity.
>
> She was saved by forces within, not by laws without. Opportunities to sin always offer in every hour of every life. Virtue is not negative, it is positive; it is a decoration won by fighting, resisting. This sweet and terrible attraction of men and women toward each other is as natural and as moral as the law of gravity, and as inexorable. Its perversion produces trouble. Love must be good and fine and according to nature, else why did it give such joy and beauty?[4]

Although Garland admitted that sex was an instinct, a desire, which played a decisive part in human life, he was not amoral in

---

[1] *Ibid.*, p. 52.
[2] *Ibid.*, pp. 99–100.
[3] *Ibid.*, p. 104.
[4] *Ibid.*, p. 110.

his judgements. He believed that man should, and was able to, control his desire, for in Garland the moralist was stronger than the naturalist.

In *Maggie* it was the theme rather than the treatment of sex that was shocking to the American reader of the nineties.[1] Crane did not describe the awakening of sex in Maggie, and the seduction was mentioned only in passing. Nothing whatever was said of her sexual desire, if she ever had one. She idealized Pete, whom she envisioned as a knight. He was to her "the ideal man. Her dim thoughts were often searching for far-away lands where the little hills sing together in the morning. Under the trees of her dream-gardens there had always walked a lover."[2] Maggie was portrayed as an innocent girl seduced by a villain. After the seduction she was heart-broken and lost her self-reliance, but she did not feel she was a bad woman. Although she was forced into prostitution she remained pure, and had none of the sensual qualities of Nana's who reveled in vice. Maggie was a victim of a taboo-ridden society and the male sex-hunger.

In the character of Pete, the seducer, Crane illustrated the thesis that a careless gratification of the male desire led to the destruction of an innocent girl if circumstances were favorable.

In *The Responsibilities of the Novelist* Norris expressed the opinion that it was the duty of the serious writer to explore "the unplumbed depths of the human heart, and the mystery of sex ... and the black, unsearched penetralia of the soul of man."[3] Accordingly Norris tried to probe the human instincts, and in so doing paid particular attention to sex throughout his works. Like Garland and Crane, he too was rather reticent in his treatment of sexual behavior. To him sex was often synonymous with "vice." Like Zola he preferred to depict the awakening of sex, which he dealt with more or less frankly in, for instance, McTeague, Trina, Moran, and Vandover. In *McTeague* love was looked upon as a physiological phenomenon which struck blindly as a natural force. McTeague and Trina could not help being drawn to each other. When Trina felt the awakening sexual urge, she was

---

[1] As is well known, the book was privately printed, and neither publisher nor author dared to put his name on its cover.

[2] *Work*, X, 159.

[3] *Compl. Works*, VII, 167-8.

frightened, for to her, love was a desire which she could not escape. As in Rose the awakening of sex in Trina was looked upon as something natural and pure:

> When McTeague had all at once caught her in his huge arms, something had leaped to life in her—something that had hitherto lain dormant, something strong and overpowering. It frightened her now as she thought of it, this second self that had wakened within her, and that shouted and clamoured for recognition. And yet, was it to be feared? Was it something to be ashamed of? Was it not, after all, natural, clean, spontaneous? Trina knew that she was a pure girl; knew that this sudden commotion within her carried with it no suggestion of vice.[1]

But while sex was natural in Trina it was something impure, an inherited evil in McTeague. To illustrate this inconsistent concept of sex we need only quote the following passage:

> What was this perverse, vicious thing that lived within him, knitted to his flesh?
> Below the fine fabric of all that was good in him ran the foul stream of hereditary evil, like a sewer. The vices and sins of his father and of his father's father, to the third and fourth and five hundredth generation, tainted him. The evil of an entire race flowed in his veins.[2]

Once awakened, the sexual instinct in both Trina and McTeague became a natural force which clamored for recognition. The desire—Norris generally used the terms "the animal," "the brute," "the second self," "the evil instincts"—became gradually irresistible; but moral scruples held back the dentist, and the gratification of his sexual desire did not take place until after the marriage ceremonies.

In the lives of McTeague and Trina "love" spelled a curse, for the "mysterious instincts" that bound them irrevocably together ultimately caused their destruction. The stages of McTeague's "love" of Trina went from brutal desire, to gratification of desire, satiety, indifference, cruelty, sadism, and, finally, murder. Sex as a destructive force was also given considerable prominence in *Vandover and the Brute* where, as in McTeague, it was looked upon not as a natural instinct but as a vice, a lower self. McTeague, Trina, and Vandover were Norris's most typical studies of natu-

---

[1] *Compl. Works*, VIII, 77.
[2] *Ibid.*, p. 27.

ralistic degeneration. In all of them the sex impulse was described as a dominant, destructive element at a certain moment of their lives.

In his later books Norris's concept of sex changed radically. After having been a fundamentally physiological phenomenon in *McTeague*, sex became a moral and ennobling emotion in *The Octopus* and *The Pit*. The naturalistic psychology of desire gave way to a moralistic psychology of will. Laura in *The Pit* preferred Jadwin to Corthell because the former attracted her as an individual, a human being, whereas the latter stirred only the sexual side of her character. Trina irresistibly followed her instincts, whereas Laura, although she, too, experienced the sexual urge, was able to control it. As in Rose her forcefulness of will triumphed over her desire.

In *A Man's Woman* the problem of sex played practically no part; instead the emphasis was laid on the will power of Lloyd Searight and Ward Bennett. Hilma in *The Octopus*, on the other hand, became a symbol of fruitfulness, and in her as in Annixter love had an ennobling effect. Like Zola's Albine, Hilma was a healthy child of nature, full of animal life. At first Annixter felt merely a sexual desire for Hilma, but gradually his desire changed into love and self-sacrifice. Love was no longer, as in *McTeague*, an evil; it became "all the sweetness of life, all the great vivifying eternal force of humanity . . ."[1]

Norris's concept of sexual selection was probably colored by Darwinian thought. In the choice of partner, woman, like the female animal, selected the male who was the strongest and most attractive. This belief was perhaps best illustrated in *The Pit*, where Laura rejected both Sheldon Corthell and Landry Court, and eventually chose Jadwin because he was the strongest. Moran gave herself up to Wilbur only after he had conquered her in a hand-to-hand battle; and Trina yielded to the strange desire of being conquered and subdued. Lloyd Searight, too, had to give herself up to Ward Bennett, because she was a woman and consequently a weaker species.[2] In a way, both Bennett and Lloyd were perhaps an illustration of sexual selection. The strong preferred the strong: "What a pair they were, strong, masterful both, in-

---

[1] *Compl. Works*, II, 82. Cf. p. 343 n. 3.

[2] Cf. also pp. 386 ff.

solent in the consciousness of their power."[1] After the woman
had chosen her partner, she submitted docilely to the male force,
as the female animal to the male.

The restraint which Norris showed in his handling of sex in
human beings was less marked in his description of the earth
as a living monster with strong sexual urges. The earth, "the
nourisher of nations, the feeder of an entire world," was a symbol
of fruitfulness, and Norris liked to speak of its period of reproduction, "its pains of labour" and "the fruit of its loins."[2] Ploughing
was described as a sexual act, for which the earth seemed to be
panting:

The heroic embrace of a multitude of iron hands, gripping deep into
the brown, warm flesh of the land that quivered responsive and passionate
under this rude advance, so robust as to be almost an assault, so violent
as to be veritably brutal. There, under the sun and under the speckless
sheen of the sky, the wooing of the Titan began, the vast primal passion,
the two world-forces, the elemental Male and Female, locked in a colossal embrace, at grapples in the throes of an infinite desire, at once terrible
and divine, knowing no law, untamed, savage, natural, sublime.[3]

The American writers analyzed above portrayed sex in terms intended to give as little offense as possible to their readers. A certain delicacy of touch was evident in their work; except for some
brutality in McTeague there was no exposure of sexual details as
in the French writers. In some cases, however, both Garland and
Norris portrayed woman with a certain amount of sensuality and
eroticism. The scenes of seduction in Maggie, Vandover and the
Brute, and The Octopus were mentioned only in passing. Garland
never treated of such scenes. To a certain degree, Garland and
Norris admitted sex as a physiological and deterministic force in
human life, but in both writers the psychology of desire was mingled
with a psychology of will. None of them was able to free himself
of his moral bias; they were moralists under the skin and liable
to look upon sex as a vice. But the fact that the physical side of
love, the awakening of sex, etc., were portrayed, particularly in
woman, was a daring venture, and it is hardly to be doubted that
they owed some of their audacity to French naturalism.[4]

---

[1] *Compl. Works*, VI, 34.

[2] *Ibid.*, I, 11–12.

[3] *Ibid.*, pp. 125–6. Cf. *La Terre*.

[4] See Chap. X.

4. THE BEAST IN MAN

Popular among French naturalists was the post-Darwinian belief that man was fundamentally an animal[1]; his actions therefore
depended essentially upon physiological phenomena. Although
human nature had evolved conscious behavior, under certain conditions the thin veneer of civilization cracked, and man reverted
to his elemental stage. Occasionally, environment was so terrible
that it completely dehumanized the people living in it. More
often, however, man revealed his animal origin as the result of a
sudden crisis, a fight, for instance. Alcoholism and sexual urges
also often roused the "brute" within man and made him revert
to a stage of primitivism and elementalism.

Garland was acquainted with evolutionary thought[2] and references to Darwin and the theory of evolution are to be found here
and there in his early works.[3] Like the French naturalists he depicted man's kinship with the animal, going as far as to portray
the factory workers in *Jason Edwards* with ape-like characteristics.[4]
But it was by man's emotional nature more often than by his physique that Garland illustrated his thesis. In "A Branch-Road" in
Main-Travelled Roads the fight for a woman aroused the brute within
Young and Will. The latter's passion, which was described as
his "worst self," was intense and called forth a conflict between
his evil nature and his better self. When Young was angry, Garland said that the "wolf" rose in him,[5] and when Will, in a fit of
jealousy, wrote a letter to Agnes, his fiancée, it "came from the
ferocity of the mediæval savage in him."[6] Similarly William Bacon,
in the story "Elder Pill, Preacher," was known as an honest, temperate man until something carried him off his balance; then Garland demonstrated Bacon's kinship with his animal ancestors. A
quarrel transformed him into a "grizzly bear" with a "raucous
snarl," and he fought with "his eyebrows working up and down,

---

[1] This belief was, of course, not confined to French naturalists—it was a
common factor everywhere in the Western world in scientific and social thought.
La Bête humaine should, however, not be overlooked.

[2] See p. 166.

[3] See p. 186.

[4] See pp. 187–8.

[5] *Main-Travelled Roads*, p. 27.

[6] *Ibid.*, p. 36.

his hands clenched into frightful bludgeons, his breath rushing through his hairy nostrils."[1] And again: "He was like a wild beast excited to primitive savagery by the smell of blood."[2] In the story "A Division in the Coolly," Garland portrayed two men who were fighting with each other like frantic beasts. In the heat of fury they returned to an animal state. Note Garland's use of nouns denoting animals:

> Jim's face flamed into a wild wrath. His lips lifted at the corners like a wolf's as he leaped the fence with a wild spring and lunged against Bill's breast. The larger man went down, but his great arms closed about his assailant's neck with a bear-like grip. Jim could neither rise nor strike; with a fury no animal could equal he pressed his hands upon Bill's throat and thrust his elbow into his mouth in the attempt to strangle him. He meant murder.[3]

Steve in the story "Saturday Night on the Farm" is a good illustration of how alcohol unleashed the brute within man. When drunk he became a beast with rolling eyes and enormous strength, and his rage was a wild, unreasoning fury.[4]

Usually the hard toil on the farm brutalized man, and Sim Burns and his wife, for example, were portrayed as dumb brutes little above the animal level.

Like Norris,[5] Garland portrayed man at war with his brute instincts, but with the difference that man was able, as a rule, to control his lower self. Haskins in "Under the Lion's Paw" is an illustration. When in a fit of anger and "transformed into an avenging demon,"[6] he was about to murder Butler, the land shark, with a fork, he was able to control himself, release his grip on the weapon, and let it fall to the ground.

Man's kinship with all nature, and brute nature in particular, was also exemplified in some of Crane's works. In a crisis, for example, man behaved fundamentally as an animal. The most typical instance is perhaps Henry Fleming in *The Red Badge of Courage*. Struck with fear a squirrel quickly ran away when Henry

---

[1] *Prairie Folks*, p. 47.

[2] *Ibid.*, p. 46.

[3] *Other Main-Travelled Roads*, p. 233.

[4] *Prairie Folks*, p. 158. For other instances of the beast in man, see *ibid.*, pp. 162, 164, 221.

[5] See pp. 216 ff.

[6] *Main-Travelled Roads*, p. 228.

threw a pine cone at it. Nature had given him a sign, and he acted in accordance with his animal instincts. Thus, Henry tried to justify his cowardice by reflecting on the behavior of animals in a similar situation. Moreover, in the heat of battle the soldiers became animals developing "teeth and claws," and Henry, furious as a wounded wolf in front of a relentless enemy set his teeth "in a cur-like snarl."[1] When the fight was over, Henry "had been an animal blistered and sweating in the heat and pain of war."[2] In another story we see how a man, when fighting a snake, reveals his hereditary savagery:

> And now the man went sheer raving mad from the emotions of his forefathers and from his own. He came to close quarters. He gripped the stick with his two hands and made it speed like a flail. The snake, tumbling in the anguish of final despair, fought, bit, flung itself upon this stick which was taking its life.[3]

Partly as a result of his interest in Darwinism or in popular interpretations of the evolutionary theory, Norris chose to portray primitive characters. Man was, according to him, rather close to the ape, a point he chose to emphasize by his physical descriptions of certain characters. McTeague's physical and mental characteristics were little above the level of his savage ancestors.[4] Ward Bennett in *A Man's Woman* was also a primitive type:

> He was an enormous man, standing six feet two inches in his reindeer foot-nips and having the look more of a prize fighter than of a scientist. Even making allowances for its coating of dirt and its harsh, black stubble of half a week's growth, the face was not pleasant. Bennett was an ugly man. His lower jaw was huge almost to deformity, like that of the bull-dog, the chin salient, the mouth close-gripped, with great lips, indomitable, brutal. The forehead was contracted and small, the forehead of men of single ideas, and the eyes, too, were small and twinkling, one of them marred by a sharply defined cast.[5]

The beachcombers in *Moran of the Lady Letty* were of the lowest type of men known to Wilbur, the hero: "The faces were those of a higher order of anthropoid apes: the lower portion—jaws, lips,

---

[1] *Work*, I, 147.
[2] *Ibid.*, p. 200.
[3] *Ibid.*, XI, 248.
[4] See pp. 198-9.
[5] *Compl. Works*, VI, 2.

and teeth—salient; the nostrils opening at almost right angles, the eyes tiny and bright, the forehead seamed and wrinkled—unnaturally old. Their general expression was one of simian cunning and a ferocity that was utterly devoid of courage."[1]

In almost all of Norris's works references to the brute within man occur. When the instinct of self-preservation was roused, man often disclosed his animal parentage. The cold, the ice, and the hardships of the Arctic region turned Bennett's men into beasts. While thought and reason dwindled in their brains, the primitive instincts of the animal—"to eat, to sleep, to be warm"—came to possess them more and more. In the wreck of the *Mazatlan*, everyone on board thought only of saving himself; none had the least thought for anyone else: "It was the primitive animal instinct, the blind adherence to the first great law, an impulse that in this moment of excitement could not be resisted."[2] And again: "It was the animal in them all that had come to the surface in an instant, the primal instinct of the brute striving for its life and for the life of its young."[3] The strange sixth sense that stirred in McTeague, warning him that danger was ahead, was also described as a purely animal instinct that clamored for recognition and obedience.[4]

When his rage was aroused, he became a different man, and in his fight with Marcus, for example, his wrath was a kind of obsession, an evil mania, which turned him into a beast. At the sight of blood dropping from his ear, the dentist turned wild:

The brute that in McTeague lay so close to the surface leaped instantly to life, monstrous, not to be resisted. He sprang to his feet with a shrill and meaningless clamour, totally unlike the ordinary bass of his speaking tones. It was the hideous yelling of a hurt beast, the squealing of a wounded elephant. He framed no words; in the rush of high-pitched sound that issued from his wide-open mouth there was nothing articulate. It was something no longer human; it was rather an echo from the jungle.[5]

In a like manner, the sight of blood, after Lauth had killed one of his enemies, awoke all the animal savagery within him: "In the

---

[1] *Compl. Works*, III, 248.
[2] *Ibid.*, V, 112.
[3] *Ibid.*, p. 122.
[4] *Ibid.*, VIII, 331.
[5] *Ibid.*, pp. 200–1.

twinkling of an eye the pale, highly cultivated scholar, whose life had been passed in the study of science and abstruse questions of philosophy, sank back to the level of his savage Celtic ancestors. His eyes glittered, he moistened his lips with the tip of his tongue, and his whole frame quivered with the eagerness and craving of a panther in sight of his prey."[1] The exhilaration of killing, the joy of battle, and the human brute aroused were also illustrated in Wilbur, in whom, at the sight of his smitten enemy, "the primitive man, the half-brute of the stone age, leaped to life,"[2] thrilling his muscles "with a strength they had not known before."[3]

When drunk, man was liable to unleash his animal brutality, as is illustrated by Schuster[4] and, especially, by McTeague and his father. Every Sunday McTeague's father became "an irresponsible animal, a beast, a brute, crazy with alcohol."[5] And in McTeague himself the alcohol roused the brute and goaded him to evil.[6] The sexual desire was also able to call forth the beast in man. In McTeague and in Vandover it stirred the "evil instincts" which were so close to the surface.

Norris was particularly interested in the conflict between the lower and better selves of man. That conflict constituted, for example, the theme of *Vandover and the Brute*. Such a problem, of course, never existed for pure naturalists, to whom man was nothing but an animal. But Norris was no consistent naturalist. To him man was constantly fighting against the brute impulses which tried to force him down. In this struggle, however, man was seldom the victor; the brutal instincts reigned supreme both in Vandover and in McTeague. To Norris, man in the brute state was apparently no happy animal, for he viewed Vandover with disillusioned eyes.

5. INSIGNIFICANCE OF MAN IN THE MODERN UNIVERSE

As has been pointed out, Garland, Crane, and Norris portrayed man as able, at certain critical moments of his life, to augment

---

[1] *Compl. Works*, X, 119.
[2] *Ibid.*, III, 285.
[3] *Ibid.*
[4] See p. 196 n. 2.
[5] *Compl. Works*, VIII, 2.
[6] *Ibid.*, p. 261.

his physical power by an apparent relapse to savagery, and to triumph over an enemy or any other obstacle that came in his way. Viewed in a larger context, however, against the vastness and infinity of the universe, man was but an atom, a gnat, incapable of playing a significant role in the world at large. Even his little rebellions against the universe were doomed to fail, for he could not change or disturb the laws that regulated life; on the contrary he was entirely subservient to them.

In their writings, Garland, Crane, and Norris stressed repeatedly man's insignificance in the world. They frequently reduced man to an "infinitesimal insect," a "gnat," an "atom," a "mole," an "ant," or a "speck in the sun." This view may have been deduced from the theory of evolution, but it is worth noting that American social conditions of the period also helped to emphasize man's insignificance and helplessness in an industrialized world. In great cities like New York and Chicago, with their towering buildings and bustling life, man felt keenly his littleness and unimportance. At times a skyscraper or a bridge became symbolic of society's indifference toward the human ant. From Brooklyn Bridge, Reeves in "Under the Wheel" looked down on New York:

Over me soared and sung those stupendous cables, the marvel of man's skill, etched on the sky, delicate as a spider's web. I stood there looking down at the sea of grimy roofs, a lava-like, hideous flood of brick and mortar, cracked, and seamed, and monstrous for its lack of line or touch of beauty, a modern city. I saw men running to and fro like ants, lost in the tumult of life and death struggle. I saw pale girls sewing there in dens reeking with pestilence. I saw myriads of homes where the children could play only in the street or on the sooty roof, colonies of hopeless settlers sixty feet from their mother earth. And over me soared the bridge to testify to the inventive genius of man.[1]

A similar attitude was expressed by Crane in "An Experiment in Misery," but with less outspoken social indignation.[2] In *The Pit* Norris, too, voiced the idea that society, the city, ignored the individual, who was crushed and annihilated "with such horrible indifference."[3]

In the face of the universe, man was but a withered blade of grass moved to and fro by the storm. George Kelcey in *George's*

---

[1] *Arena*, II (July, 1890), 189.
[2] See p. 192.
[3] *Compl. Works*, IX, 58.

Mother "felt like a man of paper, blown by the winds,"[1] and Henry Fleming recognized his insignificance when an officer spoke of him and his regiment as if he referred to a broom.[2] In "The Open Boat" Crane expressed the belief that nature regarded man with complete indifference. The four shipwrecked men of the story were heading for the beach when they observed a tower:

This tower was a giant, standing with its back to the plight of the ants. It represented in a degree, to the correspondent, the serenity of nature amid the struggles of the individual—nature in the wind, and nature in the vision of men. She did not seem cruel to him then, nor beneficent, nor treacherous, nor wise. But she was indifferent, flatly indifferent.[3]

Garland had already expressed the same idea in *Jason Edwards*, where, after the devastating hailstorm, the sun rose again on a serene and glorious landscape, and Reeves felt "the force of Nature's forgetfulness of man. She neither loves nor hates. Her storms have no regard for life. Her smiling calms do not recognize death. Sometimes her storms coincide with death, sometimes her calms run parallel to men's desires. She knows not, and cares nothing."[4] Nature's forgetfulness and indifference to man was voiced also by Norris. After meeting the railroad president, Presley meditated:

... there was no malevolence in Nature. Colossal indifference only, a vast trend toward appointed goals. Nature was, then, a gigantic engine, a vast Cyclopean power, huge, terrible, a leviathan with a heart of steel, knowing no compunction, no forgiveness, no tolerance; crushing out the human atom standing in its way with nirvanic calm, the agony of destruction sending never a jar, never the faintest tremor through all that prodigious mechanism of wheels and cogs.[5]

6. THE NEW WOMAN

The type of woman most frequently met with in naturalistic writings—such as Madame Bovary, Gervaise, Nana, or Trina—was generally weak, passive, often neurotic and hysterical, dominated

---

[1] *Work*, X, 61.

[2] *Ibid.*, I, 155.

[3] *Ibid.*, XII, 55-6.

[4] *Jason Edwards*, p. 182. See also *Prairie Folks*, pp. 138-9.

[5] *Compl. Works*, II, 286.

by heredity and environment, ruled by passions and instincts, and lacking will power and brains. In marked contrast to this type was the new woman, the modern woman, or the emancipated woman as she was also called. She possessed a will of her own and dominated men instead of being dominated by them.

Both Garland and Norris adopted the new type of a strong and self-reliant woman, and portrayed her career in their works. It is probable that the debate on the feminist movement in the late eighties and nineties stimulated their use of this type.[1] The American woman, particularly the pioneer woman of the West, was strong, independent, and self-reliant. The freedom of the West offered women new careers: they taught school, took care of the sick, and even did men's work on the farm. The hard, dangerous conditions of the frontier fostered independence and courage in both men and women. It is interesting to note that two of the early writers who delineated this strong woman in American fiction were Western born. Garland, son of the Middle Border, was partly inspired to depict the heroism of the pioneer woman by his own experiences on the frontier, where he saw the toil and fortitude of his mother and other women.[2] And Norris, born in Chicago and raised in the Far West, was also aware of the independence of the American woman gained through working side by side with her husband.[3]

Through his literary friends in Boston and through his reading of Ibsen, Björnson, and Turgenev, Garland was well aware of the new woman as a character in belles-lettres, and with the zeal of a reformer he sat down to describe an independent woman who revolted against convention and the narrowness and bleakness of life on the prairies. In *Crumbling Idols* Garland spoke with admiration of the powerful and dominant women created by Ibsen; his sole reservation was that Ibsen probably created too many remarkable women to be absolutely true to his time and country.[4]

The modern woman as presented by Garland can be studied

---

[1] See pp. 6, 80–2.
[2] See pp. 63 ff.
[3] Norris's mother was in many ways a "new woman." See Walker, *op. cit.*, p. 44.
[4] *Crumbling Idols*, p. 115.

in almost all of his early work. In the preface to *Under the Wheel* Garland stated his purpose explicitly: "I have also aimed at setting forth in a modest way the growing desire of the modern woman to stand as an individual beside man. Alice Edwards, in a dim, searching way, is walking toward the light, as I see her. In rejecting charity and demanding justice she is voicing the expanding personality of the modern man and woman." In the novelized version of the play, *Jason Edwards*, Garland portrayed Alice as an emancipated, strong, and determined young woman, who was averse to abandoning her own career because of marriage. In *Main-Travelled Roads*, as is well known, he had depicted the farmer's wife as bitter and worn out, with little hope of ever bettering her position.

An emancipated young woman also played an important role in *A Spoil of Office*. Ida Wilbur was, prior to the creation of Rose, perhaps one of Garland's most typical and fully developed new women. She was the hero's unattainable ideal and the motivating force in all his actions. "She had come to him as the right woman comes sometimes to a man, and thereafter his whole life is changed."[1] Ida was truly emancipated, a social reformer and a radical lecturer who delivered addresses on "The Real Woman-Question," and discussed modern literature, Ibsen, and Howells. She was in fact Garland himself, the radical and the humanitarian; she was his spokesman and an outlet for his revolutionary and reformatory zeal, for his advocacy of freedom and equal rights for women. She pleaded for the emancipation of women, and drafted her declaration of independence:

"I claim the right to be an individual human being first and a woman afterwards. Why should the accident of my sex surround me with conventional and arbitrary limitations? I claim the same right to find out what I can do and can't do that a man has. Who is to determine what my sphere is—men and men's laws or my own nature? These are the vital questions. I deny the right of any man to mark out the path in which I shall walk. I claim the same right to life, liberty, and the pursuit of happiness that men are demanding."[2]

---

[1] *Arena*, V (January, 1892), 261. *A Spoil of Office* was first serialized in the *Arena*.

[2] *Ibid.*, V (March, 1894), 515. Note Garland's use of the words of the American Declaration of Independence. Cf. p. 376.

Ida advocated the same social and political rights for women as for men, and claimed personal independence in married life. Consequently Garland did not stress the physical differences of the sexes. He wanted woman to be looked upon first as an individual and secondly as a woman.[1] Ida was portrayed as a beautiful and magnetic woman, though sexually cold and indifferent. Her mind was set upon making a career, and she had no time for love-making; she was a heretic and a suffragist, a female radical endowed with Garland's own ideas and ideals.

In another of his novels, Garland presented a more human and, from a literary standpoint, much more valuable character— Rose, the modern woman of *Rose of Dutcher's Coolly*. In contrast to his other new women, for instance Ida Wilbur, who like some of Ibsen's heroines—Nora, Hedda Gabler, and others—possessed a certain intellectual coldness, Rose was a full-blooded and passionate woman. Like Ida she had to fight for her social and personal rights. The novel described Rose's struggle for an education, for greater activity and personal freedom, her sexual stirrings, her concessions to convention, and her intellectual unrest. Even as a child she showed an independent and brave spirit; she was not easily frightened, and she was not superstitious, as were her playmates; she was unconventional, primitive, and vital, possessing a good deal of common sense. Instead of falling a victim to her passions, she mastered them. At the university she became a successful student. Gradually her mental horizon broadened and, like Garland, she emerged from her studies a confirmed determinist. Her intellectual emancipation was completed. Before she was able to settle in Chicago as an independent writer, she had rebelled at the dreary conditions of the prairies and against her father, who was brought up in the old tradition and could not understand her.[2]

The main problem in the novel was, however, that of the conflict between career and marriage, a problem which Garland solved in a somewhat romantic way. A passionate beauty, Rose did not lack suitors, but in accordance with the ethics of the new woman she did not want to marry, to be dependent; rather she wished to concentrate on her own career. Moreover, she did not want to

[1] See Chap. XIV.
[2] Cf. pp. 327-8.

marry a man intellectually inferior to her. While still a young girl she had declined an offer to marry a man who was not her mental equal. To Rose, as to most of the new women, marriage meant giving up a promising career; and, according to Garland, a woman should not marry before thirty. When Rose eventually married, she chose a man who considered his wife's career equally important to his own. "She did not look to marriage as a safe harbor," observed Garland. "Neither had she regarded it as an end of all individual effort, as many of her companions unequivocally had done."[1] Rose was a proud, strong, and independent woman who turned to a prospective husband with hopes of respect and understanding rather than of mere financial support. When she did receive from the man she loved an offer of marriage which included a declaration of independence for her in her married life, both as an individual and as woman,[2] she accepted it, because it appealed to her whole nature, "to her intellectual part as well as to her material self; an offer of companionship uttered this time by a voice which had no tremor in it."[3]

Frank Norris, too, although an avowed disciple of Zola, incorporated this new type of woman[4] in his more or less naturalistic novels. She was the heroine of at least three of his books, *Moran of the Lady Letty*, *Blix*, and *A Man's Woman*. Whereas Garland's concept of woman was that of the emancipated woman demanding freedom, independence, and equal rights, Norris's new woman was also conscious of her duties as a wife. As the title denotes, the heroine of *A Man's Woman* belonged to the man; she voluntarily gave up her own career to accompany her husband, to guide and encourage him in his work. Norris stressed the physical as well as the mental differences between man and woman, and pointed out that woman was constitutionally the weaker one; but, like Ibsen and Turgenev, he maintained that, despite her physical weakness, she was mentally and morally the stronger. Moran was a strong, determined, primitive woman, possessing great physical

---

[1] *Rose of Dutcher's Coolly*, p. 132.

[2] See also Chap. XIV.

[3] *Rose of Dutcher's Coolly*, p. 334.

[4] Norris even used masculine names for some of his heroines: Turner Ravis, Travis Bessemer, Lloyd Searight, Sidney Dyke, etc. See Marchand, *op. cit.*, p. 108 n.

strength and valor like the undaunted women of the Old Norse sagas. She easily dominated the men who came to know her; her independence was absolute, she was a thing apart. Her exaggerated McTeague-like proportions, her hugeness, her brawny muscles, her coarse skin, her skill in sailing and in battle, her long fair hair recalled a Valkyrie. But, despite her primitiveness, she may also be called a representative of the modern women, for she worked for a living on her father's boat and took the same pride in her profession as did Ida Wilbur in *A Spoil of Office*. In the moment of danger she displayed her independence and superiority over the men, and was prepared bravely to meet any danger. "She was herself again, savage, splendid, dominant, superb in her wrath at their weakness, their cowardice."[1] Moran did not have to struggle for her independence because she had enjoyed personal freedom and independence since childhood. Sailing with her father on the Seven Seas, dressed in men's clothes, and doing the same work as men, she had even acquired the habit of eating with her knife and drinking an occasional tumbler of whisky. In all, she was a marked contrast to the naturalistic woman as well as to the conventional Victorian woman of the drawing room. In her way, she was far more emancipated than Ida or Rose. As a primitive woman sailor, she was completely free from convention and the bonds of civilization. While Garland's Rose was described as a primitive child of nature only in her youth, Moran remained so until her violent death. Like a true emancipated woman, she paid little attention to love and marriage. To Wilbur, the weak, overcivilized society gentleman, she was "almost, as one might say, without sex—savage, unconquered, untamed, glorying in her own independence, her sullen isolation."[2] In the fight between them, he realized that it was not Moran herself that he fought; "it was her force, her determination, her will, her splendid independence, that he set himself to conquer."[3] Finally conquered, she acknowledged Wilbur's superiority and was ready to marry him. Having become dependent upon Wilbur after the fight, she lost her strength and will to self-defence. Wilbur himself developed rapidly into a powerful man,

---

[1] *Compl. Works*, III, 222.
[2] *Ibid.*, p. 229.
[3] *Ibid.*, p. 287.

and together they were about to set out upon new voyages far from civilization when Moran was brutally murdered.

A similar theme of a physically strong woman helping her weak and irresolute lover to become a determined and forceful character was also to be found in *Blix*. Although of great physical power, Travis Bessemer or "Blix," as she was also called, lacked Moran's kinship with the Valkyries of the Old Norse sagas. She was a serious and well-to-do girl who, when she recognized its shallowness and futility, renounced the society life of San Francisco. In contrast to Trina and the degenerate characters met with in naturalistic works, there was nothing extraordinary about Blix; Norris was eager to stress her healthy average:

> She impressed one as being a very normal girl: nothing morbid about her, nothing nervous or false or over-wrought. You did not expect to find her introspective. You felt sure that her mental life was not at all the result of thoughts and reflections germinating from within, but rather of impressions and sensations that came to her from without.[1]

Like Moran, Blix was unintellectual but had a cherished desire to study medicine. Both were tall "as most men" and of a heavy build, large-boned, deep-chested, and extremely vital, radiating a healthy animality. Blix was, however, a more human and womanly type, with a highly developed maternal instinct. Exerting a wholesome influence on the hero, who lacked determination and force, she gradually persuaded him to refrain from his bad habit of gambling, and encouraged him in his writing. At the same time she revealed herself as a truly emancipated woman when she announced her decision to go to New York to take up medicine. The following statement has the ring of the career woman:

> "... But why shouldn't I have a profession just like a man—just like you, Condy? You stop and think. It seemed strange to me when I first thought of it; but I go thinking about it and talking it over with Papum, and I should *love* it. I'd do it, not because I would have to do it, but because it would interest me. Condy, you know that I'm not a bit strong-minded, and that I hate a masculine, unfeminine girl as much as you do."[2]

But the decision did not make Blix slacken her efforts to encourage Condy to become more energetic and forceful. It was her efforts along these lines which occasioned him to exclaim: "'You're the

---

[1] *Ibid.*, p. 4.
[2] *Ibid.*, p. 103.

kind of girl that are [*sic*] the making of men. By Jove, you'd back
a man up, wouldn't you? You'd stand by him till the last ditch."[1]
This was exactly what Lloyd Searight did in *A Man's Woman.*
The character of Blix was in many respects a preliminary study for
the more complex and elaborate character of Lloyd. Finally it
might be added that Blix, too, was called a man's woman, for
Condy said of her: "'But, Blix, you're—you're—the finest woman
I ever knew. You're a *man's* woman, that's what you are.'"[2]

Lloyd Searight was a professional woman, and through hard
and exacting work she had acquired great skill in doing the work
she had chosen, that of a nurse. Tall and of athletic build, obstinate and wilful, she was a strong, energetic and dominant type
and, like Moran and Blix, possessed physical beauty.[3] As a nurse
she was successful and independent, despite the fact that she had
taken up hard and serious work only to satisfy her desire to be
worthy of the man, an Arctic explorer, whom she loved. Although
a woman of means, she had broken away from conventional society
to take training. She was proud of her profession and eager to do
her very best. "Succeed she would and must. Her inborn obstinacy, her sturdy refusal to yield her ground, whatever it should be,
her stubborn power of resistance, her tenacity of her chosen course,
came to her aid as she drew swiftly near to the spot whereon the
battle would be fought."[4] Like Moran, Lloyd gave up her independence only after a fight with the man she loved. In Lloyd's
case, however, there was no hand-to-hand encounter but an emotional struggle of equal violence. In her silent struggle with
Bennett, her steadfastness weakened, her independence melted
away, and she realized that he was the stronger, and that it was
her love for him that made her a brave woman. "He had been
her inspiration; he had made her want to be brave and strong and
determined, and it was because of him that the greater things of
the world interested her. She had chosen a work to be done
because he had set her an example."[5] And she reproached her-

---

[1] *Ibid.*, p. 105.

[2] *Ibid.*, p. 144.

[3] She was, however, at times seized by nervous attacks in the manner of
Trina, Vandover, Jadwin, and others. See *Compl. Works*, VI, 46–7.

[4] *Compl. Works*, VI, 105.

[5] *Ibid.*, pp. 146–7.

self because she had not set about her work with the true spirit
of the emancipated woman. She had hoped to win her lover by
revealing herself as a strong, independent, professional woman,
worthy of a giant like Bennett. Instead she became aware of her
ultimate dependence upon the man she loved. Thereafter she
was ready to follow him, even to give up her career in order to
be his help and inspiration. "Was not this her career, after all,
to be his inspiration, his incentive, to urge him to the accomplishment of a great work? Now, of the two, she was the stronger."[1]
Such was Norris's ideal of a truly emancipated woman.

7. PESSIMISM AND OPTIMISM

Broadly speaking, in the latter part of the nineteenth century
two opposite currents of thought affected the intellectual outlook
of Europe: evolutionary optimism and pessimism. In America,
the impact of evolution, the consequences of industrialism, and
the influence of European deterministic and fatalistic literature
may have affected, to some degree, traditional optimism, but,
as we shall see, native optimism still held its sway to a considerable extent.

A reading of such books as *Jason Edwards, George's Mother*,
or *McTeague* does not give a hopeful picture of American life. In
these books social conditions were bad, and society frequently
defeated the individual, who saw little hope for the future. Despite man's honesty and moral purpose, despite his attempts
to control forces, he was beaten; his struggles and efforts were in
vain, for the laws of the universe were omnipotent and inexorable. Although the human insect at times rebelled, he was inevitably crushed, and the world went on indifferently.

Were then Garland, Crane, and Norris pessimists? Did they
believe that life was futile and that there was no hope for the
individual? Actually Garland's determinism and pessimism were
fairly superficial, and originated primarily from his social indignation. Despite his somber picture of American society with its corruption and injustice, he believed in reform and social betterment,
and a reformer and a moralist can never be called a pessimist.

---

[1] *Ibid.*, p. 207.

His most pessimistic books were *Main-Travelled Roads* and *Jason Edwards*, but, although these ended in despair and resignation with no ray of hope, they were written by a man who was an idealist burning with a keen sense of justice and with an ardent hope for a quick relief for the poor and the helpless. He believed in progress, in the ultimate righteousness of man, and in man's ability to create his own destiny.

Crane, on the other hand, was more of an artist than a reformer. There were, however, traces of moralism in his works, for instance in "The Monster." He pictured America and American life as he saw it, unadorned and without bias. The picture was drawn in dark colors, for conditions were often degrading and man helpless. Nor did he give any indication of faith in a change of the existing conditions, for he was suspicious of social programs, and he refused to believe in the doctrine of progress. Life was mean, a trap, and there was not much hope for man in a world in which he was controlled either by natural laws or by chance. In some of Crane's stories there was evidence that man could work his way through despair and confusion to trust and stability. A ray of hope was felt, for example, toward the end of *The Red Badge of Courage*. In many of his stories, however, there was no other end than annihilation. Crane was no optimist; rather was he a disillusioned artist in a world of enigmas. His dark outlook originated in part from his own temperament and his experiences, but it is also probable that the post-Darwinian concept of man and man's insignificance in the universe emphasized and strengthened his feeling of life's futility and man's despair and frustration. His ultimate symbol for human life was four shipwrecked men in an open boat, "pulling at the oars through the night, waiting and watching for the dawn to break on an unknown shore..."[1]

Norris's pessimism, it seems to me, was rather superficial and largely literary, for it did not spring from his own temperament. He had no definite and consistent view of life, for his outlook —as far as it was revealed in his works—changed easily according to different sources of inspiration.[2] At heart he was a writer who, like Zola, possessed a genuine joy of living. His most pessimistic books, *McTeague* and *Vandover and the Brute*, were hardly repre-

---

[1] *Work*, III, xxii.

[2] See Chaps. X and XIV.

sentative of his temperament. *The Octopus*, on the other hand, with its mixture of romanticism and naturalism, was perhaps more typical of his mind and art. Inherent in this novel was, as in Norris himself, a delight in action, color, and life itself. If Norris was a pessimist, he was a pessimist on the surface, for under the skin he was a true optimist.

The ending of *The Octopus* probably gives a clue to his optimism. There he advanced the opinion that an individual at times had to be sacrificed for a universal good:

... the individual suffers, but the race goes on. Annixter dies, but in a far-distant corner of the world a thousand lives are saved. The larger view always and through all shams, all wickednesses, discovers the Truth that will, in the end, prevail, and all things, surely, inevitably, resistlessly work together for good.[1]

Those were the words of a disciple of Spencer; the law of the survival of the fittest was a law that sometimes bore hard on the individual but was of the greatest importance for the race. Like Spencer and his followers Norris saw only the group, the nation, the world as the unit of survival, favoring the belief that the species counted for more than the individual.

This doctrine was also voiced in Norris's last novel, in the scene where Laura and Corthell discussed Darwinism. Laura remarked: "The individual—I, Laura Jadwin—counts for nothing. It is the type to which I belong that's important, the mould, the form, the sort of composite photograph of hundreds of thousands of Laura Jadwins. . . . One must help building up only the permanent things. Then, let's see, the individual may deteriorate, but the type always grows better. . . . Of course the type is more important than the individual."[2] Like Zola Norris was an evolutionary optimist. Moreover, in *The Octopus* his optimism found expression in an apotheosis of the vitality of America, its bustling life and its young, vigorous race.

To sum up: In some of the works of Garland, Crane, and Norris was expressed the naturalistic doctrine that man lived in a mechanistic, deterministic world. These authors rejected the traditional belief that man was divine, a creature of God; instead they looked

---

[1] *Compl. Works*, II, 361.
[2] *Ibid.*, IX, 234-5.

upon man as an insignificant being, ruled by forces beyond his control. Man was akin to all nature, and to illustrate this belief they occasionally portrayed him as a beast. Yet even as they admitted man's relationship with the animals, they did not equalize man and animal. Man was a higher being than the beasts, and his better self was in constant struggle with his lower self, his animal nature. This dualism of human nature was emphasized by Garland and Norris. In the manner of the French naturalists they also admitted that the instincts played a considerable part in human life and, in their portrayal of sexual desire, at least Garland and Norris gave evidence of boldness and audacity. Since a rigorous determinism (heredity, environment, social, or economic conditions) governed man's actions, he was devoid of free will and consequently not responsible for his behavior. This concept of man was fundamental in naturalism and different from that usually embraced by realists, who believed that man was a free ethical being responsible for his own judgments.

None of the three writers analyzed was consistent in his view of man. Garland and Norris were definitely less so than Crane. Characters possessing free will—such were especially Garland's and Norris's new women—were set off against those who were victims of conditions or natural laws. Man was conceived both as a pawn and a free ethical being; as an animal ruled by his instincts and a human being capable of moral decisions. Like the French naturalists, Crane and Norris pictured a process of degradation, a gradual decline of their characters, who moved downward, sinking deeper and deeper socially and morally. This was particularly true of some of Crane's and Norris's characters. Garland, on the other hand, did not depict a process of deterioration. His men and women were often defeated, but they were not morally or ethically degraded. In general the three authors felt sympathy for the helpless and beaten individuals portrayed by them. Garland in particular viewed his unfortunate women and ill-fated men with pity and compassion. Although Crane and Norris tried to be objective, they could not help sympathizing with the victims of society. Their men and women were sometimes types, occasionally romantic abstractions like Alice and Maggie, or grotesques like McTeague or symbols like Angèle; a few were fully imagined and independently alive. In their concept of man these writers were typical of their time and period, during which new and old ideas were set against each other. Although they did not fully accept a naturalistic concept of man, they shared some of the beliefs of man essential to naturalism. Whereas Crane was a disillusioned writer who saw little hope for man in this world, Garland and Norris were at heart evolutionary optimists, who believed in progress, in the future of America, and in the ultimate prevalence of truth, justice, and happiness.

CHAPTER X

THE INFLUENCE OF ZOLA

In 1893 Zola completed his gigantic *Les Rougon-Macquart*, and many of the twenty volumes found American translators shortly after their publication in France.[1] Before Garland brought out his first book, most of the *Rougon-Macquart* novels were published —among them *L'Assommoir* (1877) and *La Terre* (1887). *Le Docteur Pascal*, the last volume of the series, appeared in the same year as *Maggie*. Zola was at work on his unfinished *Les Quatre Évangiles*, when *Moran of the Lady Letty* was published.

Zola was the French writer who was most frequently discussed and commented upon in America in the eighties and nineties,[2] and he was perhaps the one who exerted a more substantial influence on the American experimenters in literary naturalism than any other French author. In various ways and to varying degrees the works of Garland, Crane, and Norris exhibit similarities in technique, philosophy, and motifs to Zola's works. In the following pages an attempt is made to trace some of these resemblances.

1. ZOLA AND GARLAND

Even before 1890 Garland seems to have been acquainted with some of Zola's works.[3] Except for a few early favorable comments on the French writer, Garland's attitude toward him was rather hostile.[4] Nevertheless, in some of his early books Garland was probably affected by Zola's writings. The only critic, as far as I know, who has considered a probable influence of Zola on Garland is Salvan,

---

[1] See Salvan, *op. cit.*, pp. 189 ff.
[2] See p. 39.
[3] See pp. 69, 75, 140, 449.
[4] See p. 142.

who devotes a few pages in *Zola aux États-Unis* to this problem.[1] His treatment, however, is rather superficial and, in many ways, unsatisfactory. Thus he does not take up for discussion either *Main-Travelled Roads* or *Jason Edwards*.

La Terre, Zola's well-known portrayal of farm life, had a vogue in the years during which *Main-Travelled Roads* was written.[2] We may probably assume that Garland, who was an omnivorous reader, was familiar with the book, which treated of a subject similar to the one on which he was at work. It seems likely in view of his past experiences, that, in this novel, Garland found some of his own views and ideas stressed and confirmed. Both writers wanted to strip rural life of the glamour and false sentimentality which had characterized most of the earlier descriptions of country life. Both aimed at depicting farm life as they saw it, without avoiding unpleasant details. Garland, of course, never went to the excesses of Zola; the American farmers—as Garland depicted them—were never so bestial or sexually perverted as Zola's. It is true that there was meanness and brutality in Garland's peasants, but there was never obscenity.

In *La Terre* Zola revolted against the idealistic, Rousseau-inspired concept of rural life. The following picture was to him a false one:

> —"Heureux laboureur, ne quitte pas le village pour la ville, où il te faudrait tout acheter, le lait, la viande et les légumes, où tu dépenserais toujours au delà du nécessaire, à cause des occasions. N'as-tu pas au village de l'air et du soleil, un travail sain, des plaisirs honnêtes? La vie des champs n'a point son égale, tu possèdes le vrai bonheur, loin des lambris dorés; et la preuve, c'est que les ouvriers des villes viennent se régaler à la campagne, de même que les bourgeois n'ont qu'un rêve, se retirer près de toi, cueillir des fleurs, manger des fruits aux arbres, faire des cabrioles sur le gazon . . ."[3]

His aim in *La Terre* was to avoid those pleasant descriptions of farm life which abounded in sentiments "de simplicité, de vertu, de bonheur parfait, telles qu'on les trouve dans les petits contes

---

[1] Salvan, *op. cit.*, pp. 157–60.

[2] See Salvan, *op. cit.*, pp. 88 ff.

[3] *Œuvres*, XVI, 84. In contrast to Zola, in Garland—as in Hardy—the problem was how to get away from the soil. Cf. Tolstoy who advocated a return to nature.

moraux pour les enfants."[1] Like Zola, Garland did his best to divest his reader of any sentimental notions he might have of the happy and healthy life led by the farmers; like the French writer he wanted to refute Rousseau's slogan: "Back to nature." Garland wrote:

He [Howard McLane] thought of the infinite tragedy of these lives which the world loves to call peaceful and pastoral. His mind went out in the aim to help them. What could he do to make life better worth living? Nothing. They must live and die practically as he saw them to-night.[2]

Furthermore, both writers portrayed the farm wife in dark colors. It was she who worked like a galley-slave to take care of husband and children, to keep the house clean, and to help with the chores whenever she could. Her life was endless toil from beginning to end, and as a result she became dull and indifferent from overwork, a mere brute. This is Zola's description of a farmer's wife molded by her work and environment:

La mère hocha sa tête tremblante. Ah! oui, bon sang! elle avait travaillé, elle aussi, plus qu'un homme bien sûr! Levée avant les autres, faisant la soupe, balayant, récurant, les reins cassés par mille soins, les vaches, le cochon, le pétrin, toujours couchée la dernière! Pour n'en être pas cre-vée, il fallait qu'elle fût solide. Et c'était sa seule récompense, d'avoir vécu: on n'amassait que des rides, bien heureux encore, lorsque, après avoir coupé les liards en quatre, s'être couché sans lumière et contenté de pain et d'eau, on gardait de quoi ne pas mourir de faim, dans ses vieux jours.[3]

Garland described a woman marked by toil as follows:

Julia Peterson, faint with fatigue, was toiling back and forth between the corn-rows, holding the handles of the double-shovel corn-plough, while her little brother Otto rode the steaming horse. Her heart was full of bitterness, her face flushed with heat, and her muscles aching with fatigue. The heat grew terrible.... All these things, if she saw them, only threw her bondage to labor into greater relief.
... The corn must be ploughed, and so she toiled on, the tears dropping from the shadow of the ugly sun-bonnet she wore. Her shoes, coarse and square-toed, chafed her feet; her hands, large and strong, were browned, or, more properly, *burnt*, on the backs by the sun. The horse's harness, "*creak*-cracked" as he swung steadily and patiently forward, the moisture pouring from his sides, his nostrils distended.[4]

---

[1] Œuvres, XVI, 97.
[2] Main-Travelled Roads, p. 122.
[3] Œuvres, XVI, 83.
[4] Main-Travelled Roads, pp. 153–4.

And again:

> Haskins worked like a fiend, and his wife, like the heroic woman that she was, bore also uncomplainingly the most terrible burdens. They rose early and toiled without intermission till the darkness fell on the plain, then tumbled into bed, every bone and muscle aching with fatigue, to rise with the sun next morning to the same round of the same ferocity of labor.[1]

In addition to some general resemblances in the concept of farm life, which may have been accidental,[2] but which are worth mentioning nevertheless, Garland seems to have used at times a descriptive technique reminiscent of Zola's. Garland's pictures of dirty and ill-smelling men and gloomy, careworn women were painted, in the manner of Zola, with great attention to unpleasant detail.[3]

Zola's elaborate descriptions of such meals as the wedding feast and the goose dinner in *L'Assommoir*, are justly famous,[4] and in *Main-Travelled Roads* there are, it seems, echoes of these feasts. Take for instance the following passage:

> Potatoes were seized, cut in halves, sopped in gravy, and taken *one, two!* Corn cakes went into great jaws like coal into a steam-engine. Knives in the right hand cut meat and scooped gravy up. Great, muscular, grimy, but wholesome fellows they were, feeding like ancient Norse, and capable of working like demons. They were deep in the process, half-hidden by steam from the potatoes and stew, in less than sixty seconds after their entrance.... She redoubled her exertions to please him, and by so doing, added to the amusement of the crowd that gnawed chicken-bones, rattled cups, knives and forks, and joked as they ate with small grace and no material loss of time.[5]

And again:

> Wheelock gripped a chicken-leg imperturbably, and left it bare as a toothpick with one or two bites at it. His face shone in two clean sections

---

[1] *Ibid.*, p. 220.

[2] Garland may, no doubt, have arrived at his concept of farm life independently. This is most probable in view of his past experiences. Zola and others, e.g. Frederic in *Seth's Brother's Wife*, may, however, have served as literary models. Cf. also Auerbach's dark portrayals of farm life in *Schwarzwälder Dorfgeschichten* (New York, 1882), a book which is mentioned in one of Garland's notebooks.

[3] Cf. *Main-Travelled Roads*, pp. 85–6. See also Lucretia Burns, p. 184 of this study.

[4] Cf. pp. 274–5.

[5] *Main-Travelled Roads*, pp. 18–19.

around his nose and mouth. Behind his ears the dirt lay undisturbed. The grease on his hands could not be washed off.[1]

Since Garland grew up among farmers in the Middle West, it is probable that he had observed such gluttonous and primitive eating habits. Nevertheless, there is a possibility that Zola may in part have inspired Garland's technique when depicting these meals.

In *Jason Edwards* Garland came rather close to the methods of Zola in *L'Assommoir*. Both novels may be called *des romans ouvriers*, and Zola and Garland alike portrayed the misfortunes of a typical laborer under the pressure of bad social conditions.[2] Garland not only laid his own novel in the slums of a big city, but he also followed Zola's technique of describing slum streets, depicting their teeming life at various times of the day and from various angles. Zola's descriptions of the awakening of "le boulevard de la Chapelle" and his portrayal of the surging life of "la rue de la Goutte-d'Or" are well known.

Zola began his description of "le boulevard de la Chapelle" as it appears at dawn, when the street is empty, devoid of people and naked in the gray light of early morning; it was then shown as it appears a few hours later, filled with laborers hurrying to factories and mills, soon followed by a horde of underpaid shopgirls. At noon the saloon on the street corner is crowded with workers eating their lunch, drinking and laughing over their coarse jokes, while ragged women nurse their dirty, crying children on nearby benches.[3]

Turning to Garland's novel we note that he, too, devoted considerable space to descriptions of slums.

---

[1] *Ibid.*, p. 21.

[2] It should be noted, however, that the Edwards family were unsullied by the slums, in contrast to the other tenement dwellers. Furthermore, fate also contributed to the tragedy of the Edwards. It must not be understood that it was solely because of Zola's novel of the Paris slums, *L'Assommoir*, that Garland took up a similar subject. Garland, stimulated by the popular discussion of slum conditions carried on in magazines, based his novel on his own experiences in the Boston slums. See p. 170. But with regard to the literary execution he seems to have used Zola's novel as a model. *L'Assommoir* may have appealed to him because Zola, in a new way, described conditions and social evils which Garland, the reformer, wanted to expose.

[3] For full quotation, see pp. 284-5.

Pleasant Avenue may be compared with "le boulevard de la Chapelle" or "la rue de la Goutte-d'Or." We note the same emphasis on sordidness and squalor, and the same desire to expose human misery and degradation. This is Pleasant Avenue on a sultry afternoon:

> It was about five o'clock of a stifling hot day on Pleasant Avenue. Ironically bitter, the nàme of the street seemed now, like many another old-time name in Boston.
> The sun had gone out of it, but the heat still pulsed from the pavements and breathed from the doors and open windows of the four-story brick and wooden buildings, rising like solid walls on each side of the stream of human life which filled the crevasse with its slow motion.
> Children, ragged, dirty, half-naked and ferocious, swarmed up and down the furnace-like street, swore and screamed in high-pitched, unnatural, animal-like voices, from which all childish music was lost. Frowzy women walking with a gait of utter weariness, aged women, bent and withered, and young women soon to bring other mouths and tongues and hands into this frightful struggle, straggled along the side-walks, laden with parcels, pitifully small, filled with food.
> Other women and old people leaned from the open windows to get a breath of cooler air, frowns of pain on their faces, while in narrow rooms foul and crowded, invalids tortured by the deafening screams of the children, and the thunder of passing teams and cars, and unable to reach the window to escape the suffocating heat and smell of the cooking, turned to the wall, dumbly praying for death to end their suffering.[1]

When dusk came, the street took on a different aspect in both books. It became the meeting-place of the inhabitants of the tenements. Drunken men lingered in groups on the pavements outside the saloons, women quarreled in the doorways, and children played in the middle of the street. An atmosphere of vice and human misery permeated the entire area. Young girls carried on their flirtations while pacing up and down the street. Take for instance this scene from "la rue de la Goutte-d'Or":

> Les yeux vifs, coulant de minces regards par le coin pincé des paupières, elles voyaient tout, elles renversaient le cou pour rire, en montrant le gras du menton. Dans les gros éclats de gaîté, lorsqu'un bossu passait ou qu'une vieille femme attendait son chien au coin des bornes, leur ligne se brisait, les unes restaient en arrière, tandis que les autres les tiraient violemment; et elles balançaient les hanches, se pelotonnaient, se dégingandaient, his-

---

[1] *Jason Edwards*, pp. 24-5. Cf. also Zola's picture of "la rue de la Goutte-d'Or" on a hot June afternoon. *Œuvres*, VIII, 142-3.

toire d'attrouper le monde et de faire craquer leur corsage sous leurs formes naissantes. La rue était à elles.[1]

Street urchins and young men surrounded the girls, exchanging frivolous remarks with them.

Puis, quand elles s'arrêtaient, en affectant de suffoquer, la gorge renversée et palpitante, on pouvait chercher, il y avait bien sûr par là une de leurs connaissances, quelque garçon du quartier; et elles marchaient languissamment alors, chuchotant et riant entre elles, guettant les yeux en dessous. Elles se cavalaient surtout pour ces rendez-vous du hasard, au milieu des bousculades de la chaussée. De grands garçons endimanchés, en veste et en chapeau rond, les retenaient un instant au bord du ruisseau, à rigoler et à vouloir leur pincer la taille. Des ouvriers de vingt ans, débraillés dans des blouses grises, causaient lentement avec elles, les bras croisés, leur soufflant au nez la fumée de leurs brûle-gueule. Ça ne tirait pas à conséquence, ces gamins avaient poussé en même temps qu'elles sur le pavé.[2]

Vice was everywhere. When darkness came, the jokes were likely to become obscene.

Et elles [Nana and Pauline] riaient, amusées, sans un dégoût, plus roses et comme sur leur fumier naturel. Autour d'elles, les gros mots partaient, des ordures toutes crues, des réflexions d'hommes soûls. C'était leur langue, elles savaient tout, elles se retournaient avec un sourire, tranquilles d'impudeur, gardant la pâleur délicate de leur peau de satin.[3]

Garland gave a similar picture of the street at dusk. Observe the resemblance in atmosphere to Zola's description.

The street was again crowded with people, but differently—they had eaten their suppers, young and old, and now in the falling dusk, were out of doors to get a little rest and fresher air. It was not and could not be fresh air. The children were playing still, but a little less wildly. Girls of fifteen or seventeen, hardly more than children, were promenading up and down the streets, chatting among themselves and exchanging dubious sentences with groups of young men and boys standing in the doorways, insolent and noisy, boys with savage, cruel, sneaking mouths, and evil eyes. Many of these young people, already old in vice, were talking horribly and laughing senselessly, as they stood in dark nooks and doorways, while their toil-worn and weary mothers were working within doors, clearing away the supper dishes, or putting the younger children to bed, having

---

[1] Œuvres, VIII, 366.

[2] Ibid., p. 367.

[3] Ibid., pp. 367–8.

neither time nor patience to watch over their grown-up sons and daughters.

The older men smoked on stolidly, as they sat on the door-steps, filling the street with poisonous smoke. Some of them sauntered down to the saloon on the corner, and some were talking politics in the middle of the street. Most of them paid very little attention to Reeves, but the girls snickered as he passed. One or two said, "Ah, there!" in that indescribable tone which is both a jest and an invitation.[1]

Note in particular that Garland, too, described how young girls carried on overt flirtations with men on the sidewalks. Like Zola, Garland stressed the general atmosphere of vice and poverty of the district which infected all life, turning young men into criminals and young girls into prostitutes. Garland asserted that the street was "a hot, unwholesome alley, swarming with vicious and desperate life—a horribly ugly, graceless, badly-lighted alley, poison-tainted, vice-infected."[2] Garland's denunciation of social conditions was as indignant and as violent as Zola's.

An important feature of the tenement section was the saloon.[3] It played a significant part in L'Assommoir, in which Zola aimed at describing "la déchéance du travailleur parisien sous la déplorable influence du milieu des barrières et du cabaret."[4] McBreen's corner saloon on Pleasant Avenue, although mentioned only in passing, may be compared with Colombe's saloon at the corner of "la rue des Poissoniers" and "le boulevard de Rochechouart."

Having described the street in various lights and from various angles, Zola went on to depict the exterior of the tenement houses. With exhaustive detail the author painted the dismal structure of the huge house on "rue de la Goutte- d'Or," stressing its ugliness and decay. In fact, it was likened to a ruin:

... la maison avait cinq étages, alignant chacun à la file quinze fenêtres, dont les persiennes noires, aux lames cassées, donnaient un air de ruine à cet immense pan de muraille.[5]

And again:

Les fenêtres sans persienne montraient des vitres nues, d'un vert glauque d'eau trouble. Certaines, ouvertes, laissaient pendre des matelas à car-

[1] *Jason Edwards*, pp. 89–90.
[2] *Ibid.*, p. 91.
[3] For the discussion of the "saloon curse," see p. 78.
[4] *Œuvres*, VIII, 461.
[5] *Ibid.*, p. 44.

reaux bleus, qui prenaient l'air; devant d'autres, sur des cordes tendues, des lignes séchaient, toute la lessive d'un ménage, les chemises de l'homme, les camisoles de la femme, les culottes des gamins; il y en avait une, au troisième, où s'étalait une couche d'enfant, emplâtrée d'ordure. De haut en bas, les logements trop petits crevaient au dehors, lâchaient des bouts de leur misère par toutes les fentes.[1]

After noting its dirt-gray paint falling off in shreds and its shabby prison-like walls, Zola proceeded to describe the interior of the building, at the same time portraying the people occupying its many rooms and corridors, and recording carefully the various noises and smells. Vice had put its stamp on these people who were destined to a tragic end by the influence of heredity and environment. Zola described this house, in which the Lorilleux family lived, by letting Coupeau take his sweetheart, Gervaise, on a visit to the tenement which she had not seen earlier. The device gave Zola an excellent opportunity to record the sordid details in a graphic way:

En effet, l'escalier B, gris, sale, la rampe et les marches graisseuses, les murs éraflés montrant le plâtre, était encore plein d'une violente odeur de cuisine. Sur chaque palier, des couloirs s'enfonçaient, sonores de vacarme, des portes s'ouvraient, peintes en jaune, noircies à la serrure par la crasse des mains; et, au ras de la fenêtre, le plomb soufflait une humidité fétide, dont la puanteur se mêlait à l'âcreté de l'ognon cuit. On entendait, du rez-de-chaussée, au sixième, des bruits de vaisselle, des poêlons qu'on barbotait, des casseroles qu'on grattait avec des cuillers pour les récurer. Au premier étage, Gervaise aperçut, dans l'entrebâillement d'une porte, sur laquelle le mot: *Dessinateur*, était écrit en grosses lettres, deux hommes attablés devant une toile cirée desservie, causant furieusement, au milieu de la fumée de leur pipes. Le second étage et le troisième, plus tranquilles, laissaient passer seulement par les fentes des boiseries la cadence d'un berceau, les pleurs étouffés d'un enfant, la grosse voix d'une femme coulant avec un sourd murmure d'eau courante, sans paroles distinctes; et elle put lire des pancartes clouées, portant des noms ... On se battait au quatrième: un piétinement dont le plancher tremblait, des meubles culbutés, un effroyable tapage de jurons et de coups; ce qui n'empêchait pas les voisins d'en face de jouer aux cartes, la porte ouverte, pour avoir de l'air.[2]

Garland followed the same procedure. After having portrayed the street and its people, he went on to depict the tenement house

[1] *Ibid.*, p. 45.
[2] *Ibid.*, p. 53.

in which the Edwards family lived. Its squalid interior was described in the manner of Zola. Garland described a young couple, Alice and her suitor Reeves, on their way to a tenement house—in this case Alice's home—which equaled in squalor and general decay the one depicted by Zola:

> They turned in at last at one of the cave-like apertures opening upon the narrow walk, and passed into a hall which led straight through to the foul-smelling yard and alley behind.
>
> There were two families on each floor, and as the doors were open, the smells of cooking food were mingled into an indescribable hot stench— boiled beef, onions, cabbage, fried pork and the smell of vile coffee. Babies were squal[l]ing, loud-voiced women, worried with their cares and bad-tempered from weariness, were scolding and slapping the children who ran in and out with a prodigious clatter, and shrieking and squalling. . . .
>
> The room they entered was the usual living-room of the average mechanic, except that it had a carpet and piano, as if it laid claim to the name of parlor. But the table, partly spread for supper, told that it was also the dining-room. The furniture was of very humble sort, and was a peculiar mixture of old-fashioned pieces and bargains at the shoddy furniture-rooms of the city.
>
> . . . The windows of the side, the only windows, looked out upon another similar tenement, across a narrow side street, along which boomed and thundered passing teams loaded with heavy plates of iron, or with immense flapping loads of lumber. Venders of fruit were crying loudly and unmusically. It was very close and unwholesome . . . From the street foul odors and the boom of travel. Overhead some one was tramping heavily. In the hall the children fought and screamed, and clattered up and down the stairs.[1]

Note particularly the fact that the two writers emphasized the foul-smelling stenches, the noises, the fighting, and the general atmosphere of human misery.

We have observed that both Zola and Garland used the device of describing a tenement house by letting a person pay a visit to the place in question. This procedure was repeated when Zola outlined "la fabrique de boulon et de rivets" in *L'Assommoir*, and when Garland depicted the steelmill in *Jason Edwards*. Both writers had a character visit the factory, and in both novels the visitors, Gervaise and Jason Edwards, had to walk through a horrible district full of dilapidated houses, rickety sheds, and dreary workshops. Thus the authors had ample opportunity to

---

[1] *Jason Edwards*, pp. 28–30.

display the sordid milieu in which the workers had to live, and to voice their social discontent. This is Gervaise on her way through the slums to the factory:

La fabrique de boulons et de rivets devait se trouver par là, dans ce bout de la rue Marcadet, elle ne savait pas bien où; d'autant plus que les numéros manquaient souvent, le long des masures espacées par des terrains vagues. C'était une rue où elle n'aurait pas demeuré pour tout l'or du monde, une rue large, sale, noire de la poussière de charbon des manufactures voisines, avec des pavés défoncés et des ornières, dans lesquelles des flaques d'eau croupissaient. Aux deux bords, il y avait un défilé de hangars, de grands ateliers vitrés, de constructions grises, comme inachevées, montrant leurs briques et leurs charpentes, une débandade de maçonneries branlantes, coupées par des trouées sur la campagne, flanquées de garnis borgnes et de gargotes louches. Elle se rappelait seulement que la fabrique était près d'un magasin de chiffons et de ferraille, une sorte de cloaque ouvert à ras de terre, où dormaient pour des centaines de mille francs de marchandises, à ce que racontait Goujet. Et elle cherchait à s'orienter, au milieu du tapage des usines; de minces tuyaux, sur les toits, soufflaient violemment des jets de vapeur; une scierie mécanique avait des grincements réguliers, pareils à de brusques déchirures dans une pièce de calicot; des manufactures de boutons secouaient le sol du roulement et du tic tac de leurs machines.[1]

Walking to the factory Jason passed through a neighborhood which was equally bad, a street lined with sheds and ramshackle workshops:

Edwards' daily walk was down a narrow street, a drear, desolate, gray crevice, hot and joyless. The hot, dusty gray of the cobble-stones, the brown-gray of the sidewalks, the sullen drab of the houses which lined the way, forming a desolate searing attack upon the eyes, unrelieved by any touch of coolness, harmony or grace.

. . . A street lined with tumble-down sheds in which rags were picked over; sheds where blacksmiths toiled at horse-shoeing or sharpening picks; sheds alternating with vacant lots, with "Free Dump" cards appearing there, showing that some speculator was not averse to having his lot graded for him.

Frightful stenches were abroad along this street, offal wagons passed, heavy drays with clashing, clanging loads of iron rolled slowly along, drawn by three horses tandem. The railway side-tracks and shops were here, and the sound of engines starting and stopping, coupling and jerking, was a daily, hourly tumult.

Shops and foundries of various kinds were located here on this low ground, and along the cindery paths, hot as ashes in the sun, sticky in the

---

[1] Œuvres, VIII, 167–8.

rain, a dreary procession of workmen like Jason Edwards plodded sullenly, slouching for the most part with little of the lightness and joy which the morning should possess.[1]

Then followed a procession of workingmen, similar to that of the first chapter of *L'Assommoir*:

Men with ragged, grimy coats, with dinner-pails in their hands and pipes in their mouths, went to their work, as prisoners to the tread-mill. They had no interest in their tasks, they were working in general to live and feed their children. They were not like craftsmen, but convicts in their joyless walk.[2]

Both Zola and Garland gave exhaustive descriptions of the interior of the factory with its huge whirling machines, terrible noises, and maddening hot air, in which the men had to work all day long.

Here follows Zola's account:

Il [Goujet] la [Gervaise] conduisit à droite, dans un autre hangar, où son patron installait toute une fabrication mécanique. Sur le seuil, elle hésita, prise d'une peur instinctive. La vaste salle, secouée par les machines, tremblait; et de grandes ombres flottaient, tachées de feux rouges. Mais lui la rassura en souriant, jura qu'il n'y avait rien à craindre; elle devait seulement avoir bien soin de ne pas laisser traîner ses jupes trop près des engrenages. Il marcha le premier, elle le suivit, dans ce vacarme assourdissant où toutes sortes de bruits sifflaient et ronflaient, au milieu de ces fumées peuplées d'êtres vagues, des hommes noirs affairés, des machines agitant leurs bras, qu'elle ne distinguait pas les uns des autres. Les passages étaient très étroits, il fallait enjamber des obstacles, éviter des trous, se ranger pour se garer d'un chariot. On ne s'entendait pas parler. Elle ne voyait rien encore, tout dansait. Puis, comme elle éprouvait au-dessus de sa tête la sensation d'un grand frôlement d'ailes, elle leva les yeux et s'arrêta à regarder les courroies, les longs rubans qui tendaient au plafond une gigantesque toile araignée, dont chaque fil se dévidait sans fin; le moteur à vapeur se cachait dans un coin, derrière un petit mur de briques; les courroies semblaient filer toutes seules, apporter le branle du fond de l'ombre, avec leur glissement continu, régulier, doux comme le vol d'un oiseau de nuit. Mais elle faillit tomber, en se heurtant à un des tuyaux du ventilateur, qui se ramifiait sur le sol battu, distribuant son souffle de vent aigre aux petites forges, près des machines. Et il commença par lui faire voir ça, il lâcha le vent sur un fourneau; de larges flammes s'étalèrent des quatre côtés en éventail, une collerette de feu dentelée, éblouissante, à peine teintée d'une pointe de laque; la lumière

---

[1] *Jason Edwards*, pp. 68–70.
[2] *Ibid.*, p. 70.

était si vive, que les petites lampes des ouvriers paraissaient des gouttes d'ombre dans du soleil. Ensuite, il haussa la voix pour donner des explications, il passa aux machines: les cisailles mécaniques qui mangeaient des barres de fer, croquant un bout à chaque coup de dents, crachant les bouts par derrière, un à un; les machines à boulons et à rivets, hautes, compliquées, forgeant les têtes d'une seule pesée de leur vis puissante; les ébarbeuses, au volant de fonte, une boule de fonte, qui battait l'air furieusement à chaque pièce dont elles enlevaient les bavures; les taraudeuses, manœuvrées par des femmes, taraudant les boulons et leurs écrous, avec le tic-tac de leurs rouages d'acier luisant sous la graisse des huiles. Elle pouvait suivre ainsi tout le travail, depuis le fer en barre, dressé contre les murs, jusqu'aux boulons et aux rivets fabriqués, dont des caisses pleines encombraient les coins. Alors, elle comprit, elle eut un sourire, en hochant le menton; mais elle restait tout de même un peu serrée à la gorge, inquiète d'être si petite et si tendre parmi ces rudes travailleurs de métal se retournant parfois, les sangs glacés, au coup sourd d'une ébarbeuse. Elle s'accoutumait à l'ombre, voyait des enfoncements où des hommes immobiles réglaient la danse haletante des volants, quand un fourneau lâchait brusquement le coup de lumière de sa collerette de flamme. Et, malgré elle, c'était toujours au plafond qu'elle revenait, à la vie, au sang même des machines, au vol souple des courroies, dont elle regardait, les yeux levés, la force énorme et muette passer dans la nuit vague des charpentes.[1]

And again:

Cependant, les autres ouvriers tapaient aussi, tous à la fois. Leurs grandes ombres dansaient dans la clarté, les éclairs rouges du fer sortant du brasier traversaient les fonds noirs, des éclaboussements d'étincelles partaient sous les marteaux, rayonnaient comme des soleils, au ras des enclumes. Et Gervaise se sentait prise dans le branle de la forge, contente, ne s'en allant pas.[2]

This is Garland's description of the foundry:

As Edwards looked in at the foundry door on his way back, about five o'clock, men were "pouring." It was a grewsome sight. With grimy, sooty shirts, open at the throat, in a temperature of deadly heat, they toiled like demons. There was little humanity in their faces, as the dazzling metal threw a dull-red glow on them.

Here and there, with warning shouts, they ran, bent like gnomes, with pots of shining, flame-colored liquid lighting their grimy faces. Here toiled two stalwart fellows, with a huge pot between them; with hoarse shouts they drew up beside a huge "flask" or moulding-box. The skimmer pushed away the slag, the radiant metal leaped out and down into the sand, sending spurts of yellow-blue flame out of a half-hundred crevices.

---

[1] *Œuvres*, VIII, 177–8.
[2] *Ibid.*, p. 171.

There was a man calking the next flask with wet sand. He paid no attention to the pot of deadly liquid, which passed close enough to singe his hair. A little further on, another man was knocking off the clamps that held the flask together. Everywhere was heat, the smell of burning wood, gases, steam, and the sight of leaping, exploding, shining metal.

Edwards looked up at Jerry, who stood beside the furnace, stripped almost to the skin, in a heat that would kill a man unaccustomed to it, heaving scraps of iron into the horrible cauldron, which he was obliged to stir occasionally with a long bar.[1]

We observe the similarities between the two passages: both writers pictured the toiling laborers and their hard work with emphasis on sordid and technical detail, with a view to exposing the bad conditions under which the laborers had to work.

The similarities between Garland's novel and *L'Assommoir* are particularly noticeable in the first part of *Jason Edwards*, where the locale was the Boston slums. In the second part of the novel, which was laid in the prairies of the West, Garland may have been stimulated by another of Zola's novels, namely *La Terre*. As a matter of fact, there is an episode in *Jason Edwards*, which may be compared with one in *La Terre*, i.e. the description of the hailstorm and its effects.

In *La Terre* Zola described how a sixty-year-old, unsuccessful farmer, Mouche, lay paralyzed from a fatal stroke in his decayed house. Meanwhile a terrible hailstorm broke out, smashed the windows of his house, and demolished his vineyard, which was the family's chief means of subsistence. The paralyzed man, who lay helplessly on the earthen floor of the kitchen during the storm, was attended by his two daughters. This is Zola's portrayal of the devastating storm:

—La grêle! la grêle!
Saisies, révoltées et blêmes sous le fléau, elles regardaient. Cela dura dix minutes à peine. Il n'y avait pas de coups de tonnerre; mais de grands éclairs bleuâtres, incessants, semblaient courir au ras du sol, en larges sillons de phosphore; et la nuit n'était plus si sombre, les grêlons l'éclairaient de rayures pâles, innombrables, comme s'il fût tombé des jets de verre. Le bruit devenait assourdissant, une mitraillade, un train lancé à toute vapeur sur un pont de métal, roulant sans fin. Le vent soufflait en furie, les balles obliques sabraient tout, s'amassaient, couvraient le sol d'une couche blanche.

---

[1] *Jason Edwards*, pp. 76–7. Cf. p. 83 n. 2.

—La grêle, mon Dieu! ... Ah! quel malheur! ... Voyez donc! de
vrais œufs de poule!

Elles n'osaient se hasarder dans la cour, pour en ramasser. La violence
de l'ouragan augmentait encore, toutes les vitres de la fenêtre furent
brisées; et la force acquise était telle, qu'un grêlon alla casser une cruche,
pendant que d'autres roulaient jusqu'au matelas du mort.[1]

A similar episode of an equally destructive storm is found
in *Jason Edwards.* Over the prairies of the Middle West there
came suddenly a hailstorm with great violence, accompanied with
thunder as in *La Terre.* To the luckless Jason the storm spelled
ruin. At the beginning of the storm Jason had a stroke, was
brought into the house, and laid on the floor by his two daughters.
The house was badly battered by the storm, the windows were
smashed, the doors broken, and the roof was carried away
by its terrible onslaughts. The portrait of the ill-fated Jason
lying on the floor of his storm-beaten house, while his harvest
was being destroyed by merciless nature, is just as tragic as that
of the stricken Mouche in *La Terre.* The difference is, however,
that Mouche was paralyzed before the storm started and died
in the midst of it, whereas Jason was hit during the storm itself
and did not die, but remained an invalid for the rest of his life.
Garland described the storm as follows:

It came drifting along the plain with incredible speed, shimmering like
snow. A hissing, roaring sound now grew upon the ear, the wheat was
trampled by the coming storm. ...

The next moment, before he [Jason] could turn to Alice, the storm-
wind rushed upon them, carrying away the roof of the kitchen and dashing
out every window, filling the room with floods of water and rebounding
hailstones. In the deafening, distracting tumult, Linnie and her mother
saw Edwards put his hand to his head and sink slowly to the ground,
with Alice clinging to him.

... Somehow, in the midst of that horrible crackling roar, in the midst
of the incessant glare of the lightning, while the wind and hail dashed
out the window-panes and flooded the floor with water, she dragged
the unconscious man across the sill and closed the door.

It seemed hours to her as she sat there drenched and white, looking
down at the gray head dabbled in the water, as if it were blood, while she
rubbed the cold hands and temples.

The wind tore through the house, stripping the curtains from the windows, and the pictures and little ornaments from the walls, littering the

---

[1] *Œuvres,* XVI, 113.

floor with broken glass. It seemed as if the roof would be torn from their heads, and all be left naked to the storm.[1]

After the storm, which was over as suddenly as it had come, stillness and quiet fell, but the effect of the hailstorm was equally ruinous to both families. Zola pictured the destruction as follows:

Ah! quel ravage désolait ce coin de terre! quelle lamentation montait du désastre, entrevu aux lueurs vacillantes des lanternes! Lise et Françoise promenaient la leur, si trempée de pluie, que les vitres éclairaient à peine; et elles l'approchaient des planches, elles distinguaient confusément, dans le cercle étroit de lumière, les haricots et les pois rasés au pied, les salades tranchées, hachées, sans qu'on pût songer seulement à en utiliser les feuilles. Mais les arbres surtout avaient souffert: les menues branches, les fruits, en étaient coupés comme avec des couteaux; les troncs eux-mêmes, meurtris, perdaient leur sève par les trous de l'écorce. Et plus loin, dans les vignes, c'était pis, les lanternes pullulaient, sautaient, s'enrageaient, au milieu de gémissements et de jurons. Les ceps semblaient fauchés, les grappes en fleur jonchaient le sol, avec des débris de bois et de pampres; non seulement la récolte de l'année était perdue, mais les souches, dépouillées, allaient végéter et mourir ... Peu à peu, tous s'emportaient; était-ce possible de perdre, en un quart d'heure, le fruit d'un an de travail?[2]

And this is Garland's description of the effects of the hailstorm:

The plain looked deliciously cool and moist, the lark's clear piping was heard in a kind of thanksgiving note, and only a practised eye could see the terrible effect of the hailstorm on the wheat.

Where it had stood tall and yellow and hot an hour ago, it now lay broken, beaten to the ground, wet, tangled and twisted into knots. It was mangled beyond any possible recovery; escaping the drouth, it was now trampled into the muddy earth.[3]

Chance dealt the final blow to the Mouche family as well as to the Edwards. The storm had hit them hardest, while their

---

[1] *Jason Edwards*, pp. 167–70. This episode was no doubt based on Garland's own experiences in the Middle West where storms occasional lydestroyed a promising crop. Concerning Jason's stroke, it should be noted that Garland may have had in mind his own mother who was paralyzed in the summer of 1889. See chap. "My Mother Is Stricken" in *A Son of the Middle Border*, pp. 396–409. These assumptions, if true, do not necessarily exclude an influence of Zola, who, it seems, stimulated Garland in his use and dramatization of actual experiences.

[2] *Œuvres*, XVI, 115–16.

[3] *Jason Edwards*, pp. 171–2.

neighbors had suffered very little or not at all. Even in the works of Zola, the so-called confirmed determinist, chance played a certain role. He wrote in regard to the ill-fated Mouche family: "Qu'avaient-ils fait pour être punis de la sorte? Ni sécurité, ni justice, des fléaux sans raison, des caprices qui tuaient le monde."[1]

Finally it may be added that both families felt the catastrophe to be a punishment from God. In both books, however, God was challenged by insignificant man. This is from *La Terre*:

Brusquement, la Grande, furibonde, ramassa des cailloux, les lança en l'air pour crever le ciel, qu'on ne distinguait pas. Et elle gueulait:
— Sacré cochon, là-haut! Tu ne peux donc pas nous foutre la paix?[2]

In like manner Alice scorned Heaven. Looking at the prostrate figure of her father she said bitterly: "'See what God has done!'"[3] This scorn was also exemplified by the dead Mouche whose one eye refused to close but stared blindly upward, and by Jason, whose eyes—as he lay unconscious—stared defiantly toward the serene sky that had caused his tragedy.

2. ZOLA AND CRANE

It has been noted that Crane was acquainted with at least two of Zola's works, namely *Nana* and *La Débâcle*,[4] and that he considered Zola an honest writer although he found him "pretty tiresome." Critics have linked Crane with Zola,[5] but there has been no one, it seems, who has considered in any detail Crane's debt to the French writer. Parrington wrote that *The Red Badge of Courage* "was a *tour de force*, inspired by Zola's *Le débâcle* [sic], but more by Tolstoi—*War and Peace* and perhaps *Sebastopol*."[6] Spiller asserted that "There is no doubt that he [Crane] took direct inspiration from these French realists [Maupassant and Flaubert], and even more certainly from Zola, for *L'Assommoir* probably

---

[1] *Œuvres*, XVI, 116. Zola's ill-fated Mouche recalls somewhat Turgenev's Bazarov in *Fathers and Sons*. For Jason Edwards and Bazarov see pp. 321–2.

[2] *Œuvres*, XVI, 116.

[3] *Jason Edwards*, p. 179.

[4] See p. 96.

[5] We remember that Norris noted Crane's debt to *L'Assommoir*. See p. 105.

[6] Parrington, *op. cit.*, III, 328.

provided the plot for *Maggie*, and *La Débâcle* bears a close resemblance to *The Red Badge of Courage* . . . His work shows the stamp of European naturalism . . ."[1] Salvan,[2] finally, listed some likenesses between *Maggie* and *L'Assommoir*:

> Certaines ressemblances avec l'ouvrage de Zola peuvent être signalées. D'abord le milieu où se passe l'histoire, quartier populaire d'où les personnages ne sortent guère. Des scènes entières rappellent *L'Assommoir*. Les promenades aux musées de Maggie et de Pete ont la même qualité comique que la visite au Louvre de la noce de Coupeau. Le bal public où Pete montre en différentes occasions ses belles manières et ses faiblesses trop humaines rappelle le Café-Concert où Lantier emmena un jour Gervaise. Le roman de Maggie est, comme *L'Assommoir*, l'histoire de la déchéance et de la mort d'une héroïne pour laquelle le lecteur ne peut se défendre d'éprouver une immense pitié.
>
> En outre, la technique de Stephen Crane se rapproche de celle de Zola. Il dissimule du mieux possible sa sympathie envers ses personnages. Le langage qu'il leur prête est l'argot et la prononciation de la Bowery. . . .[3]

Concerning *La Débâcle* and *The Red Badge of Courage* Salvan was more uncertain: "Dans la question toujours délicate d'établir un rapport d'influence définie entre Zola et Stephen Crane, nous sommes forcés de rester sur une note évasive."[4] Salvan's treatment of Crane's probable debt to Zola does not seem satisfactory. As the quotations indicate, he pointed out some similarities between *L'Assommoir* and *Maggie*, but he did not give sufficient evidence of Crane's supposed indebtedness to Zola. Furthermore, he did not even take into consideration a possible inspiration from Zola in such a naturalistic novel as *George's Mother*.

It is above all in Crane's slum stories that the kinship between Zola and Crane is felt. We know that Crane had steeped himself in the Bowery atmosphere, and that he drew directly from his experiences for stories[5]; nevertheless a few of Zola's novels seem to have been a source of inspiration and a literary model for some of Crane's own stories. It is probable that Crane's reading of Zola confirmed in part what he saw and felt about life in the New York

---

[1] Spiller *et al.*, *op. cit.*, II, 1022.

[2] Salvan, *op. cit.*, pp. 160–6.

[3] *Ibid.*, p. 162.

[4] *Ibid.*, p. 164.

[5] See pp. 92–3. Note also the discussion of the slums in the early nineties. See pp. 77–80.

slums. Beer has it that *Maggie* "was not absolute reporting. He [Crane] had invented its small plot and only two incidents of the story were from the life—the fight in the saloon and the destruction of Maggie's lambrequin by her mother."[1] If this is true, then it is even more likely that Crane may have drawn on his reading for inspiration.

Actually, *Maggie* comes close to the theme and method of *L'Assommoir*. Both authors described a good woman's way toward ultimate destruction, and both told their stories with frankness and objectivity, yet with a certain degree of sympathy for their heroines.[2] The slum environment together with a weak temperament was in part responsible for the inevitable catastrophe; both novels gave evidence of the curse of alcohol not only for the individual but for society at large.

The two writers not only laid their stories in the slums of great cities—Paris and New York—but they were also eager to depict these areas in an accurate and truthful fashion. When discussing Zola and Garland, we observed how extensively Zola portrayed the locale of the story, the milieu of the characters (exterior, interior, and social). Crane appears to have used a similar technique. It is probably no mere coincidence that he opened his tale by describing a street scene, just as Zola had done in *L'Assommoir*. Crane introduced the atmosphere of the slum district by depicting a fight between the ragged urchins of Rum Alley and Devil's Row.[3] Moreover, he sketched the sordid area close to the harbor—"squat ignorant stables," laborers unloading a scow at a dock by the river, and "a worm of yellow convicts" crawling slowly along an island.[4] Then he proceeded to describe in greater detail the tenement house where Maggie lived. It is worth noting that Crane, like Zola and Garland, delineated the tenement by letting two of his characters enter the building:

Eventually they [Jim and his father] entered a dark region where, from a careening building, a dozen gruesome doorways gave up loads of babies

---

[1] Beer, *op. cit.*, p. 98.

[2] Note also both writers' attempt at recording the vulgar language of their characters.

[3] Note the symbolic use of the names of the streets: Zola's "rue de la Goutte-d'Or" and Crane's "Rum Alley."

[4] *Work*, X, 138.

to the street and the gutter. A wind of early autumn raised yellow dust
from cobbles and swirled it against a hundred windows. Long streamers
of garments fluttered from fire-escapes. In all unhandy places there
were buckets, brooms, rags, and bottles. In the street infants played or
fought with other infants or sat stupidly in the way of vehicles. Formidable women, with uncombed hair and disordered dress, gossiped while
leaning on railings, or screamed in frantic quarrels. Withered persons,
in curious postures of submission to something, sat smoking pipes in
obscure corners. A thousand odours of cooking food came forth to the
street. The building quivered and creaked from the weight of humanity
stamping about in its bowels.[1]

The passage should be compared with Zola's description of the
tenement house on the "rue de la Goutte-d'Or".[2] We note the same
emphasis on gloom, decay, and general misery; the atmosphere is
equally vulgar and revolting in both cases. The imagery of the
last sentence of the quotation has a Zolaesque flavor.

The two rooms occupied by the Johnsons were on a par with
those in which the Coupeau family lived after they had to give up
the laundry. Everything gave evidence of lack of taste, poverty,
and general decay. The neighbors gossiped, quarreled, and drank.
The Johnson household was not a happy one. Both parents were
confirmed drunkards, who fought with each other regularly and
beat their children, Maggie, Jim, and Tommie, at every opportunity. The home was a "reg'lar livin' hell." The following passage gives an idea of the milieu in which the three children grew
up. One evening Mr. Johnson returned home drunk, and began
a fight with his wife, who was in a similarly vicious mood:

There was a crash against the door, and something broke into clattering
fragments. Jimmie partially suppressed a yell and darted down the stair-
way. Below he paused and listened. He heard howls and curses, groans
and shrieks—a confused chorus as if a battle were raging. With it all
there was the crash of splintering furniture. The eyes of the urchin
glared in his fear that one of them would discover him.

Curious faces appeared in doorways, and whispered comments passed
to and fro. "Ol' Johnson's playin' horse agin."

Jimmie stood until the noises ceased and the other inhabitants of the
tenement had all yawned and shut their doors. Then he crawled upstairs

---

[1] *Ibid.*, pp. 141–2.

[2] See pp. 240–1. Cf. also the similarity between Crane's and Garland's
descriptions of the tenements. Note, for instance, the "gruesome doorways."
See p. 242 of this study.

with the caution of an invader of a panther's den. Sounds of laboured breathing came through the broken door-panels. He pushed the door open and entered, quaking.

A glow from the fire threw red hues over the bare floor, the cracked and soiled plastering, and the overturned and broken furniture. In the middle of the floor lay his mother asleep. In one corner of the room his father's limp body hung across the seat of a chair.

The urchin stole forward. He began to shiver in dread of awakening his parents. His mother's great chest was heaving painfully. Jimmie paused and looked down at her. Her face was inflamed and swollen from drinking. Her yellow brows shaded eyelids that had grown blue. Her tangled hair tossed in waves over her forehead. Her mouth was set in the same lines of vindictive hatred that it had, perhaps, borne during the fight. Her bare red arms were thrown out above her head in an attitude of exhaustion, something, mayhap, like that of a sated villain.[1]

The passage may be compared with Zola's description of the homecoming of the drunkard Bijard. Both episodes illustrate admirably the demoralizing effect of alcohol on the mind of the individual. Note that neither Zola nor Crane actually described the fight as seen; both implied by means of sounds that a battle was going on. The devastating effects of the fight were then disclosed to the reader by the writers in scenes that are similar in tone and general atmosphere. Both depicted the two combatants[2] prostrate on the floor in the midst of their wrecked pieces of furniture.

En arrivant rue de la Goutte-d'Or, elle [Gervaise] trouva toute la maison bouleversée. Ses ouvrières avaient quitté l'établi, et étaient dans la cour, à regarder en l'air. Elle interrogea Clémence.

—C'est le père Bijard qui flanque une roulée à sa femme, répondit la repasseuse. Il était sous la porte, gris comme un Polonais, à la guetter revenir du lavoir ... Il lui a fait grimper l'escalier à coups de poing, et maintenant il l'assomme là-haut, dans leur chambre ... Tenez, entendez-vous les cris.

Gervaise monta rapidement. Elle avait de l'amitié pour Mme Bijard, sa laveuse, qui était une femme d'un grand courage. Elle espérait mettre le holà. En haut, au sixième, la porte de la chambre était restée ouverte,

---

[1] *Work*, X, 149–50. Crane's elaborate description of a saloon (*ibid.*, pp. 181 ff.) should be compared with Zola's detailed description of Colombe's "assommoir." *Œuvres*, VIII, p. 33 ff.

[2] Note the difference between the two wives. Mme Bijard was a naturally good and hard-working woman, who never beat her children and who took to drinking as an antidote to her husband's viciousness, while Mrs. Johnson was a slovenly woman who did not care at all for her family.

quelques locataires s'exclamaient sur le carré, tandis que Mme Boche, devant la porte criait:

—Voulez-vous bien finir! ... On va aller chercher les sergents de ville, entendez-vous!

Personne n'osait se risquer dans la chambre, parce qu'on connaissait Bijard, une bête brute quand il était soûl. Il ne dessoûlait jamais, d'ailleurs. Les rares jours où il travaillait, il posait un litre d'eau-de-vie près de son étau de serrurier, buvant au goulot toutes les demi-heures. Il ne se soutenait plus autrement, il aurait pris feu comme une torche, si l'on avait approché une allumette de sa bouche.

—Mais on ne peut pas la laisser massacrer! dit Gervaise toute tremblante.

Et elle entra. La chambre, mansardée, très propre, était nue et froide, vidée par l'ivrognerie de l'homme, qui enlevait les draps du lit, pour les boire. Dans la lutte, la table avait roulé jusqu'à la fenêtre, les deux chaises culbutées, étaient tombées, les pieds en l'air. Sur le carreau, au milieu, Mme Bijard, les jupes encore trempées par l'eau du lavoir et collées à ses cuisses, les cheveux arrachés, saignante, râlait d'un souffle fort, avec des oh! oh! prolongés, à chaque coup de talon de Bijard. Il l'avait d'abord abattue de ses deux poings; maintenant, il la piétinait.

—Ah! garce! ... ah! garce! ... ah! garce! ... grognait-il d'une voix étouffée, accompagnant de ce mot chaque coup, s'affolant à le répéter, frappant plus fort à mesure qu'il s'étranglait davantage. ...

Quand Bijard eut rencontré une chaise et se fut étalé sur le carreau, où on le laissa ronfler, le père Bru aida Gervaise à relever Mme Bijard.[1]

Moreover, in both books the terrible scene was witnessed by the frightened children:

The small frame of the ragged girl was quivering. Her features were haggard from weeping, and her eyes gleamed with fear. She grasped the urchin's arm in her little trembling hands and they huddled in a corner. The eyes of both were drawn, by some force, to stare at the woman's face, for they thought she need only to awake and all the fiends would come from below. They crouched until the ghost mists of dawn appeared at the window, drawing close to the panes, and looking in at the prostrate, heaving body of the mother.[2]

And this is the Bijard children:

Et, pendant toute cette tuerie, Gervaise voyait, dans un coin de la chambre, la petite Lalie, alors âgée de quatre ans, qui regardait son père assommer sa mère. L'enfant tenait entre ses bras, comme pour la protéger, sa sœur Henriette, sevrée de la veille. Elle était debout, la tête serrée dans une coiffe

[1] *Œuvres*, VIII, 198–200.
[2] *Work*, X, 150–1.

d'indienne, très pâle, l'air sérieux. Elle avait un large regard noir, d'une fixité pleine de pensées, sans une larme.[1]

The passages quoted indicate that the milieu in which Maggie and Jim grew up was like that in which the Bijard children had to live. It is probable that the Bijard household[2] served to some extent as a model for Crane's description of the Johnson family. Further and even more definite evidence seems to confirm such an assumption. Père Bijard was a drunkard, a sadist, an unmitigated beast who, on the rare occasions when he worked, always had a bottle of alcohol beside him from which he took large draughts. When intoxicated he was extremely cruel, and he managed to kill both his good, hard-working wife and his little daughter Lalie[3] by systematic ill-usage. This brute of a father seems to have been in Crane's mind when creating the Johnsons, particularly Mrs. Johnson. She was, in fact, as beastly and degraded as Bijard when drunk; and both were drunk most of the time and succeeded in terrifying their children to the same degree. In both characters, who were portrayed with indignant exaggeration, the authors denounced the alcoholist in no uncertain terms.

Originally, the Johnson and the Bijard family had had three children,[4] respectively, the eldest of whom were daughters, Maggie and Lalie. The girls resemble each other in certain respects. Both were idealized. Despite the fact that they lived in the slum sections of the city, they were unsullied by their environment. In that respect Maggie stood in marked contrast to her brother Jim who, in the typical pattern of naturalistic writing, followed in the footsteps of his father and became a drunkard in the manner of Coupeau, whose father had also been a drunkard. Moreover, despite the fact that the girls were often hungry and still more often beaten by their drunken parents, they remained incredibly kind and patient. They were almost like saints; terrified, but inured by many previous

---

[1] Œuvres, VIII, 199–200.

[2] The Coupeau household, particularly in its decay, may perhaps also have served as a model. Note that Coupeau beat his children, Nana and Étienne, on several occasions. Mrs. Johnson's degeneration has points in common with that of Gervaise.

[3] In Maggie Tommie died, presumably of ill-usage.

[4] Note that the Coupeau family consisted of three children, Claude, Étienne, and Nana.

experiences of the same kind, they witnessed with resignation the fights between their parents. When her mother died, Lalie, aged eight, took care of the house and the two small children, Henriette and Jules. In like manner Maggie acted as the little mother of Jim and Tommie when Mrs. Johnson was in jail, or too drunk to be able to take care of her family. In the scene in which the reader first encounters the little girl Maggie, she is portrayed as looking after Tommie, a "red, bawling infant."[1] The following passage describing Lalie is equally true of Maggie: "Toujours tendre et dévouée malgré ça [the ill-usage], d'une raison au-dessus de son âge, remplissant ses devoirs de petite mère, jusqu'à mourir de sa maternité, éveillée trop tôt dans son innocence frêle de gamine."[2]

One episode, in particular, seems to give further support to these likenesses. When one day Bijard returned home dead drunk as usual, Lalie was so panic-stricken that she happened to break a cup. There followed a terrible scene. Bijard brought out a whip and used it mercilessly in his drunken madness:

Une légère écume lui venait aux lèvres, ses yeux jaunes sortaient de leurs trous noirs. Lalie, affolée, hurlante, sautait aux quatre angles de la pièce, se pelotonnait par terre, se collait contre les murs; mais la mèche mince du grand fouet l'atteignait partout, claquant à ses oreilles avec des bruits de pétard, lui pinçant la chair de longues brûlures. Une vraie danse de bête à qui on apprend des tours. Ce pauvre petit chat valsait, fallait voir! les talons en l'air comme les gamines qui jouent à la corde et qui crient: Vinaigre! Elle ne pouvait plus souffler, rebondissant d'elle-même ainsi qu'une balle élastique, se laissant taper, aveuglée, lasse d'avoir cherché un trou. Et son loup de père triomphait, l'appelait vadrouille, lui demandait si elle en avait assez et si elle comprenait suffisamment qu'elle devait lâcher l'espoir de lui échapper, à cette heure.[3]

A similar scene, although somewhat differently handled, is found in Crane's novel, where Maggie's mother, after having quarreled with her husband, and after many draughts from a "yellow-brown bottle," gave her daughter a terrible beating because the latter happened to smash a plate.

Maggie broke a plate.
The mother started to her feet as if propelled. "Good Gawd!" she howled. Her glittering eyes fastened on her child with sudden hatred.

---

[1] *Work*, X, 142.
[2] *Œuvres* VIII, 346.
[3] *Ibid.*, pp. 345–6.

The fervent red of her face turned almost to purple. The little boy ran to the halls, shrieking like a monk in an earthquake. He floundered about in darkness until he found the stairs. He stumbled, panic-stricken, to the next floor.

An old woman opened a door. A light behind her threw a flare on the urchin's face. "Eh, child, what is it dis time? Is yer fader beatin' yer mudder, or yer mudder beatin' ye fader?" . . .

Jimmie and the old woman listened long in the hall. Above the muffled roar of conversation, the dismal wailings of babies at night, the thumping of feet in unseen corridors and rooms, and the sound of varied hoarse shoutings in the street and the rattling of wheels over cobbles, they heard the screams of the child and the roars of the mother die away to a feeble moaning and a subdued bass muttering.[1]

The quotations illustrate how an insignificant mishap called forth the bestiality of Bijard and Mrs. Johnson under the influence of drink. The difference is, however, that there is no evidence that Mrs. Johnson was a sadist in the manner of Bijard, although we may suspect that she was just as cruel. It has already been noted that Lalie was eventually beaten to death, whereas Maggie left her home to encounter a fate which in its way was equally tragic.

For Maggie's development from child to a young girl, Crane seems to have found another model in *L'Assommoir*, namely Nana. Like Nana, Maggie was pretty and a most rare product of a tenement district. Of both girls it may be said with equal justice that they "blossomed in a mud-puddle."[2] They differed, however, in that Nana "était dans le vice comme un poisson dans l'eau,"[3] while Maggie was basically innocent. In addition, Maggie lacked Nana's sensuality. Two episodes, especially, link the girls together. When Nana was fifteen she took a position in a workshop where artificial flowers were made. Likewise, Maggie went to work in a collar-and-cuff factory. The descriptions of the workplaces display fundamental similarities as well as typical dissimilarities. In both establishments the workers were women, and in both places the environment was equally demoralizing. Zola emphasized particularly the moral decay of the women workers, while Crane showed more restraint and merely hinted at it. Crane wanted, it seems, to demonstrate that factories turned human

---

[1] *Work*, X, 146–7.
[2] *Ibid.*, p. 156.
[3] *Œuvres*, VIII, 375.

beings into machines, and that everything worked against Maggie, whose ruin was thus justified. This is Mme Tireville's workshop:

Vrai! Nana complétait à l'atelier une jolie éducation! Oh! elle avait des dispositions, bien sûr. Mais ça l'achevait, la fréquentation d'un tas de filles déjà éreintées de misère et de vice. On était là les unes sur les autres, on se pourrissait ensemble; juste l'histoire des paniers de pommes, quand il y a des pommes gâtées. Sans doute, on se tenait devant la société, on évitait de paraître trop rosse de caractère, trop dégoûtante d'expressions. Enfin, on posait pour la demoiselle comme il faut. Seulement, à l'oreille, dans les coins, les saletés marchaient bon train. On ne pouvait pas se trouver deux ensemble, sans tout de suite se tordre de rire, en disant des cochonneries. Puis, on s'accompagnait le soir; c'étaient alors des confidences, des histoires à faire dresser les cheveux, qui attardaient sur les trottoirs les deux gamines, allumées au milieu des coudoiements de la foule. Et il y avait encore, pour les filles restées sages comme Nana, un mauvais air à l'atelier, l'odeur de bastringue et de nuits peu catholiques, apportée par les ouvrières coureuses, dans leurs chignons mal rattachés, dans leurs jupes si fripées qu'elles semblaient avoir couché avec. Les paresses molles des lendemains de noce, les yeux culottés, ce noir des yeux que Mme Lerat appelait honnêtement les coups de poing de l'amour, les déhanchements, les voix enrouées, soufflaient une perversion au-dessus de l'établi, parmi l'éclat et la fragilité des fleurs artificielles. Nana, reniflait, se grisait, lorsqu'elle sentait à côté d'elle une fille qui avait déjà vu le loup. Longtemps, elle s'était mise auprès de la grande Lisa, qu'on disait grosse; et elle coulait des regards luisants sur sa voisine, comme si elle s'était attendue à la voir enfler et éclater tout d'un coup. Pour apprendre du nouveau, ça paraissait difficile. La gredine savait tout, avait tout appris sur le pavé de la rue de la Goutte-d'Or. A l'atelier, simplement, elle voyait faire, il lui poussait peu à peu l'envie et le toupet de faire à son tour.[1]

And this is Crane's description of the factory:

The air in the collar-and-cuff establishment strangled her. She knew she was gradually and surely shrivelling in the hot, stuffy room. The begrimed windows rattled incessantly from the passing of elevated trains. The place was filled with a whirl of noises and odours. She became lost in thought as she looked at some of the grizzled women in the room, mere mechanical contrivances sewing seams and grinding out, with heads bent over their work, tales of imagined or real girlhood happiness, or of past drunks, or the baby at home, and unpaid wages. She wondered how long her youth would endure. She began to see the bloom upon her cheeks as something of value. She imagined herself, in an exasperating future, as a scrawny woman with an eternal grievance.[2]

---

[1] *Ibid.*, pp. 372–3.
[2] *Work*, X, 169.

With the appearance of a suitor, vague dreams of a life of splendor loomed before the two girls. Soon they wearied of their jobs. Meanwhile conditions in their homes became unbearable, their parents being drunk almost every day. It should be remembered that, as their degradation proceeded, Coupeau and Gervaise spent the evenings at the saloon or fighting in the dismal little room that was now their home. The climax was reached one Saturday. When Nana returned home from work, she found her parents completely drunk and the room in great disorder. Unable to stand this kind of life any longer, she went away to join her lover:

Un samedi, Nana trouva en rentrant son père et sa mère dans un état abominable. Coupeau, tombé en travers du lit, ronflait. Gervaise, tassée sur une chaise, roulait la tête avec des yeux vagues et inquiétants ouverts sur le vide. Elle avait oublié de faire chauffer le dîner, un restant de ragoût. Une chandelle, qu'elle ne mouchait pas, éclairait la misère honteuse du taudis.

— C'est toi, chenillon? bégaya Gervaise. Ah bien! ton père va te ramasser!

Nana ne répondait pas, restait toute blanche, regardait le poêle froid, la table sans assiettes, la pièce lugubre où cette paire de soûlards mettaient l'horreur blême de leur hébétement. Elle n'ôta pas son chapeau, fit le tour de la chambre; puis, les dents serrées, elle rouvrit la porte, elle s'en alla.

— Tu redescends? demanda sa mère, sans pouvoir tourner la tête.
— Oui, j'ai oublié quelque chose. Je vais remonter... Bonsoir.[1]

Crane has a similar motivation for Maggie's flight from her home. Jim had been fighting with his drunken mother, and the room was in a chaotic upheaval. Then Pete, Maggie's lover, appeared in the midst of the debris, and Maggie, unable to stand the strain of the environment any more, abandoned her home:

He [Jim] was leaning against the wall and swearing. Blood stood upon bruises on his knotty forearms where they had scraped against the floor or the walls in the scuffle. The mother lay screeching on the floor, the tears running down her furrowed face.

Maggie, standing in the middle of the room, gazed about her. The usual upheaval of the tables and chairs had taken place. Crockery was strewn broadcast in fragments. The stove had been disturbed on its legs, and now leaned idiotically to one side. A pail had been upset and water spread in all directions.

The door opened and Pete appeared. He shrugged his shoulders. "Oh,

[1] Œuvres, VIII, 382–3.

gee!" he observed. He walked over to Maggie and whispered in her ear: "Ah, what d'hell, Mag? Come ahn and we'll have a outa-sight time."

The mother in the corner upreared her head and shook her tangled locks. "Aw, yer bote no good, needer of yehs," she said, glowering at her daughter in the gloom. Her eyes seemed to burn balefully. "Yeh've gone t' d' devil, Mag Johnson, yehs knows yehs have gone t' d' devil. Yer a disgrace t' yer people. An' now, git out an' go ahn wid dat doe-faced jude of yours. Go wid him, curse yeh, an' a good riddance. Go, an' see how yeh likes it." . . .

The woman on the floor cursed. Jimmie was intent upon his bruised forearms. The girl cast a glance about the room filled with a chaotic mass of *débris*, and at the writhing body of her mother.

"Git th' devil outa here."

Maggie went.[1]

In fact, Mrs. Johnson forced her daughter to leave home by her own outrageous conduct, just as the parents did in Nana's case.

When the parents realized that their daughters had "gone to the bad," their reactions were similar. In spite of their own questionable morality both Gervaise and Coupeau looked upon themselves as innocent and virtuous, and considered Nana "une morveuse qui se mêlait de déshonorer la famille!"[2] They stated that they were not responsible for their daughter's tragedy; instead Nana was a disgrace to her parents. Note Zola's irony:

Oui, ce chameau dénaturé [Nana] lui [Gervaise] emportait le dernier morceau de son honnêteté dans ses jupons sales. Et elle se grisa trois jours, furieuse, les poings serrés, la bouche enflée de mots abominables contre sa garce de fille. Coupeau, après avoir roulé les boulevards extérieurs et regardé sous le nez tous les torchons qui passaient, fumait de nouveau sa pipe, tranquille comme Baptiste; seulement quand il était à table, il se levait parfois, les bras en l'air, un couteau au poing, en criant qu'il était déshonoré; et il se rasseyait pour finir sa soupe.[3]

Like Zola, Crane was ironic in his treatment of the indignant mother, who had assumed an attitude of injured innocence. In fact, Crane's irony seems even more poignant than Zola's.

"May she be cursed for ever!" she shrieked. "May she eat nothin' but stones and deh dirt in deh street. May she sleep in deh gutter an' never see deh sun shine again. D' bloomin'—"

"Here now," said her son. "Go fall on yerself, an' quit dat."

---

[1] *Work*, X, 176–7.
[2] *Œuvres*, VIII, 377.
[3] *Ibid.*, p. 383.

The mother raised lamenting eyes to the ceiling. "She's d' devil's own chil', Jimmie," she whispered. "Ah, who would t'ink such a bad girl could grow up in our fambly, Jimmie, me son. Many d' hour I've spent in talk wid dat girl an' tol' her if she ever went on d' streets I'd see her damned. An' after all her bringin'-up an' what I tol' her and talked wid her, she goes teh d' bad, like a duck teh water."[1]

When eventually it became known that Maggie had committed suicide, her mother was as self-conceited as was Gervaise. Despite her own moral degradation Mrs. Johnson passed judgment on her daughter, a fundamentally good woman, who had gone wrong through no fault of her own.[2]

It has been said above that Maggie as a child resembled Lalie, and that as a young girl she had points in common with Nana. It is probable that Crane had Gervaise Coupeau in mind when he created the last phase of Maggie's life. The downfall of Maggie is related to that of Gervaise. Temperamentally, the two women belonged to the same type. They were basically good, but weak and easily imposed upon. Both Gervaise and Maggie possessed a naive, romantic concept of their lovers, which facilitated their seductions.[3]

Elle [Gervaise] n'était point coureuse du tout; les hommes l'ennuyaient; quand Lantier l'avait prise, à quatorze ans, elle trouvait ça gentil, parce qu'il se disait son mari et qu'elle croyait jouer au ménage. Son seul défaut, assurait-elle, était d'être très sensible, d'aimer tout le monde, de se passionner pour des gens qui lui faisaient ensuite mille misères. Ainsi, quand elle aimait un homme, elle ne songeait pas aux bêtises, elle rêvait uniquement de vivre toujours ensemble, très heureux.[4]

To Maggie, Pete was the "ideal man," a "knight." In reality, both Lantier and Pete were good-for-nothings, veritable dandies and lady-killers, who later deserted the women seduced by them.

---

[1] *Work*, X, 179.

[2] After a time both Nana and Maggie returned home, but were soon forced to leave again—Maggie for good, Nana only to return.

[3] The following was the reason for Gervaise's downfall: "C'est arrivé comme ça arrive toujours, vous savez. Je n'étais pas heureuse chez nous; le père Macquart, pour un oui, pour un non, m'allongeait des coups de pied dans les reins. Alors, ma foi, on songe à s'amuser dehors. . . ." *Œuvres*, VIII, 17. This was also the reason why Nana and Maggie left home and were seduced.

[4] *Œuvres*, VIII, 38.

One episode[1] in particular links Gervaise with Maggie. Toward
the end of *L'Assommoir* there is a scene depicting Gervaise, starving
and degraded, walking aimlessly up and down the streets, accosting
several men in the manner of a prostitute.
On a cold, snow-swept evening we see Gervaise, forlorn and
desperate, pacing the streets. Note the constrast between the
woman's dejection and the atmosphere of pleasure and wealth
around her:

Gervaise reprit lentement sa marche. Dans le brouillard d'ombre fu-
meuse qui tombait, les becs de gaz s'allumaient; et ces longues avenues,
peu à peu noyées et devenues noires, reparaissaient toutes braisillantes,
s'allongeaient encore et coupant la nuit, jusqu'aux ténèbres perdues de
l'horizon. Un grand souffle passait, le quartier élargi enfonçait des cor-
dons de petites flammes sous le ciel immense et sans lune. C'était l'heure,
où d'un bout à l'autre des boulevards les marchands de vin, les bastrin-
gues, les bousingots à la file, flambaient gaîment dans la rigolade des pre-
mières tournées et du premier chahut. La paie de grande quinzaine emplissait le trottoir d'une bousculade de gouapeurs tirant une bordée. Ça
sentait dans l'air la noce, une sacrée noce, mais gentille encore, un com-
mencement d'allumage, rien de plus. On s'empiffrait au fond des gargotes; par toutes les vitres éclairées, on voyait des gens manger, la bouche
pleine, riant sans même prendre la peine d'avaler. Chez les marchands
de vin, des pochards s'installaient déjà, gueulant et gesticulant. Et un
bruit du tonnerre de Dieu montait, des voix glapissantes, des voix grasses,
au milieu du continuel roulement des pieds sur le trottoir. "Dis donc!
viens-tu becqueter? . . . Arrive, clampin! je paie un canon de la bouteille
. . . Tiens! v'là Pauline! ah bien! non, on va rien se tordre!" Les portes
battaient, lâchant des odeurs de vin et des bouffées de cornet à pistons.
On faisait queue devant l'Assommoir du père Colombe, allumé comme
une cathédrale pour une grand'messe; et, nom de Dieu! on aurait dit une
vraie cérémonie, car les bons zigz chantaient là-dedans avec des mines de
chantres au lutrin, les joues enflées, le bedon arrondi. On célébrait la
sainte Touche, quoi, une sainte bien aimable, qui doit tenir la caisse au
paradis. Seulement, à voir avec quel entrain ça débutait, les petits rentiers,
promenant leurs épouses, répétaient en hochant la tête qu'il y aurait bi-
grement des hommes soûls dans Paris, cette nuit-là. Et la nuit était très
sombre, morte et glacée, au-dessus de ce bousin, trouée uniquement par
des lignes de feu et des boulevards, aux quatre points du ciel.[2]

---

[1] The visit which Pete and Maggie paid to the museum (*Work*, X, 170) is
reminiscent of that of Coupeau and Gervaise. *Œuvres*, VIII, 77 ff. Moreover,
Crane's "hilarious hall" (pp. 194 ff.) recalls Zola's "café-concert." Pp.
276 ff. Cf. Salvan, *op. cit.*, p. 162.

[2] *Œuvres*, VIII, 428-9.

Crane has a similar scene in the next to last chapter of his novel. When Maggie saw no way out she was, like Gervaise, forced to walk the streets. There is the same contrast between the heroine's gloomy mood and desperate need on the one hand, and the atmosphere of pleasure and wealth radiating from the places of amusement on the street on the other. The methods used by Zola and Crane in depicting the episodes are almost identical. At times even Crane was prone to become fairly elaborate in his descriptions:

Upon a wet evening, several months later, two interminable rows of cars, pulled by slipping horses, jangled along a prominent side street. A dozen cabs, with coat-enshrouded drivers, clattered to and fro. Electric lights, whirring softly, shed a blurred radiance. A flower-dealer, his feet tapping impatiently, his nose and his wares glistening with rain-drops, stood behind an array of roses and chrysanthemums. Two or three theatres emptied a crowd upon the storm-swept sidewalks. Men pulled their hats over their eyebrows and raised their collars to their ears. Women shrugged impatient shoulders in their warm cloaks and stopped to arrange their skirts for a walk through the storm. People who had been constrained to comparative silence for two hours burst into a roar of conversation, their hearts still kindling from the glowings of the stage.

The sidewalks became tossing seas of umbrellas. Men stepped forth to hail cabs or cars, raising their fingers in varied forms of polite request or imperative demand. An endless procession wended toward elevated stations. An atmosphere of pleasure and prosperity seemed to hang over the throng, born, perhaps, of good clothes and of two hours in a place of forgetfulness.

In the mingled light and gloom of an adjacent park, a handful of wet wanderers, in attitudes of chronic dejection, were scattered among the benches.

A girl of the painted cohorts of the city went along the street. She threw changing glances at men who passed her, giving smiling invitations to those of rural or untaught pattern and usually seeming sedately unconscious of the men with a metropolitan seal upon their faces. Crossing glittering avenues, she went into the throng emerging from the places of forgetfulness. She hurried forward through the crowd as if intent upon reaching a distant home, bending forward in her handsome cloak, daintily lifting her skirts, and picking for her well-shod feet the dryer spots upon the sidewalks.

The restless doors of saloons, clashing to and fro, disclosed animated rows of men before bars and hurrying bar-keepers. A concert-hall gave to the street faint sounds of swift, machine-like music, as if a group of phantom musicians were hastening.[1]

---

[1] *Work*, X, 208-9.

Both Gervaise and Maggie spoke to several men, but no one paid any attention to them as they walked from lighted avenues into dark alleys. Everything seemed hopeless to them. They felt superfluous,[1] because no one seemed to care for them or would listen to their entreaties. When Gervaise was forced to walk the streets, she made the following gloomy reflection, which might also have been uttered by Maggie: "Cette fois, c'était fini. Pas un fifrelin, plus un espoir, plus que de la nuit et de la faim. Ah! une belle nuit de crevaison, cette nuit sale qui tombait sur ses épaules!"[2] However, Gervaise's end was not yet to come, for she was saved temporarily from starvation by her friend Goujet, whom she happened to meet on the street. Maggie, on the other hand, had no friends, no one who cared for her. She was alone in a world which ignored her, and thus she directed her steps toward the river.

The tragedy of Gervaise and Maggie was that, despite their moral lapses, they were naturally good and virtuous women, whose ruin was brought about by the brutal impact of circumstances and environment on weak temperaments.

Some of the parallels recorded here may have been accidental, but taken together they confirm the assumption that Crane was indebted to *L'Assommoir* in his first novel as to plot, characterization, technique, episodes, and particulars. Despite the borrowings, almost always used with restraint, *Maggie* bears the unmistakable stamp of Crane's individual temperament, his conciseness, brevity, and artistry.

Since it is obvious that *Maggie* owes a considerable debt to *L'Assommoir*, one may suspect that Zola also exerted an influence on Crane's next novel, *The Red Badge of Courage*, a war novel like *La Débâcle*. This assumption seems to be supported by the fact that, when Crane wrote his novel, he had no firsthand experience of war. It is therefore plausible that he had recourse in part at least to literary sources. Both Parrington and Spiller believed—as referred to above—that Crane's war novel owed something to *La Débâcle*, whereas Salvan was more uncertain.[3]

---

[1] Cf. Gervaise's reflection before she died: "La terre ne voulait pas d'elle . . ." *Œuvres*, VIII, 457.

[2] *Ibid.*, p. 421.

[3] See pp. 249–50 of this study.

A comparison between the two novels reveals various similarities, some of which grow, out of the general similarity of theme.[1] Both books are grim narratives of war, and are to a large extent devoted to a prolonged military engagement. Their total effect is similar: they illustrate the horror of war, its bloodshed and confusion, its lack of glamour and heroism. War is, moreover, seen from the point of view of a group of soldiers, and their emotions and reactions—generally unheroic ones—are analyzed with a directness and candor equaled perhaps only by Tolstoy's frank and penetrating portrayals of war.

In addition to the similarities mentioned, the heroes of both books, Maurice and Henry Fleming, also have some points in common, although, in my opinion, Henry is probably more closely related to Volodia in *Sebastopol*[2] than to Maurice. Both Zola and Crane, as well as Tolstoy before them, depicted an unheroic type of soldier in marked contrast to the conventional concept of previous war heroes. The type was somewhat differently conceived of by Tolstoy and Zola, but Crane seems to have drawn on both writers for his portrait of Henry. Maurice, a young intellectual somewhat reminiscent of Rudin[3], enrolled in a burst of enthusiasm as a volunteer in the 106th infantry regiment. He fancied heroic deeds on the battlefield, but he soon discovered that war was far from heroic, quite the reverse in fact. Similarly, Henry was a young volunteer in the 104th regiment, and equally enthusiastic about the supposed glory of war. He, too, came to realize the difference between reality and dreams. Both experienced the drudgery and monotony of camp-life, the forced inactivity before battle and the suspense of waiting for the enemy, and finally the dreadful reality of war itself.

---

[1] The task of establishing Zola's influence on Crane's novel is a difficult one, especially because Crane and perhaps Zola, too, seem, to an extent, to have been inspired by Tolstoy's war narratives. In addition to similarities in tone and general effect, at least two incidents in Zola's novel, the execution and the conflagration, have their counterparts in *War and Peace*. For Crane's debt to Tolstoy, see Chap. XIII. It should be remembered that Crane had read *The Downfall* (*La Débâcle*) (see p. 96), which was brought out simultaneously in France and America in 1892, two years before Crane completed his own war novel. See p. 96 n. 1.

[2] See pp. 347–51.

[3] Maurice, dying by chance on a barricade, recalls Rudin, who was killed by a random bullet on a Parisian barricade.

When Maurice was about to fight his first battle he was seized with fright.[1] The clamor of war appalled him, and he was on the point of running away when Jean, a fellow soldier, detained him. This is Zola's picture of Maurice's panic and attempted flight:

> Le feu redoublait, la batterie voisine venait d'être renforcée de deux pièces; et, dans ce fracas croissant, la peur, la peur folle s'empara de Maurice. Il n'avait pas eu d'abord cette sueur froide, cette défaillance douloureuse au creux de l'estomac, cet irrésistible besoin de se lever, de s'en aller au galop, hurlant. Sans doute, maintenant, n'y avait-il là qu'un effet de la réflexion, ainsi qu'il arrive chez les natures affinées et nerveuses.[2]

Henry, too, was seized with panic, experienced the same deadly terror, and felt the same anguish which made Maurice want to run away. The difference is, however, that Henry actually ran away; nor is the quality of their terror the same. In Maurice, fear was little more than the common battle-sickness, whereas in Henry it was a psychological problem,[3] which could only be solved when he had overcome his dread and had developed into a truly heroic soldier.[4]

There are other instances that link Maurice with Henry. When they were about to fire their guns for the first time, they acted in a similar fashion. As has been mentioned, they fired before any orders had been given, merely to hear the comforting bang of the rifles. Both fired at random, aiming at the outskirts of the forest in front of them. This is the passage describing Maurice's first shot:

Maurice, le premier, déchargea le sien [le chassepot]. Jean, Pache, Lapoulle, tous les autres l'imitèrent. Il n'y avait pas eu d'ordre, le capitaine voulut arrêter le feu; et il ne céda que sur un grand geste de Rochas, disant la nécessité de ce soulagement. Enfin, on tirait donc, on employait donc ces cartouches qu'on promenait depuis plus d'un mois, sans en brûler une seule! Maurice surtout en était ragaillardi, occupant sa peur, s'étourdissant des détonations. La lisière du bois restait morne, pas une feuille ne bougeait, pas un Prussien n'avait reparu; et l'on tirait toujours sur des arbres immobiles.

... Et Maurice, et tous les autres, s'enrageaient, brûlaient leur poudre,

---

[1] This is, of course, the normal reaction of most raw recruits before their first battle.

[2] *Œuvres*, XX, 234.

[3] Cf. Volodia's attitude before battle. See pp. 347–8.

[4] Cf. Volodia's development. See p. 349.

à fusiller le bois[1] lointain, où tombait une pluie[2] lente et silencieuse de petites branches.[3]

And this is Crane's version of a similar situation:

The captain of the company had been pacing excitedly to and fro in the rear. . . . His talk was an endless repetition. "Reserve your fire, boys —don't shoot till I tell you—save your fire—wait till they get close up—don't be damned fools—"

Perspiration streamed down the youth's face, which was soiled like that of a weeping urchin. He frequently, with a nervous movement, wiped his eyes with his coat sleeve. His mouth was still a little way open.

He got the one glance at the foe-swarming field in front of him, and instantly ceased to debate the question of his piece being loaded. Before he was ready to begin—before he had announced to himself that he was about to fight—he threw the obedient, well-balanced rifle into position and fired a first wild shot. Directly he was working at his weapon like an automatic affair.[4]

Note that in both cases the engagement was opened by way of the accidental shot fired by Maurice and Henry respectively.

Moreover, like Zola, Crane described his hero as dominated by animal instincts, in accordance with the formula of literary naturalism. This is Henry in the midst of battle, portrayed like an animal at bay:

The youth cried out savagely at this statement. He crouched behind a little tree, with his eyes burning hatefully and his teeth set in a cur-like snarl. The awkward bandage was still about his head, and upon it, over his wound, there was a spot of dry blood. His hair was wondrously tousled, and some straggling, moving locks hung over the cloth of the bandage down toward his forehead. His jacket and shirt were open at the throat, and exposed his young bronzed neck. There could be seen spasmodic gulpings at his throat.[5]

In addition to the resemblances recorded above, there are a few other episodes that link the two novels together. Both open with descriptions of the armies in bivouac. The enemy had not

---

[1] Henry, too, fired at the woods, a fact which started a general shooting: ". . . he fired an angry shot at the persistent woods. This action awakened the men. . . . They . . . at once commenced firing." *Work*, I, 161–2.

[2] Cf. a similar image in Crane's novel after the crash of a shell: "It [the shell] landed in the grove, and, exploding redly, flung the brown earth. There was a little shower of pine needles." *Ibid.*, p. 58.

[3] *Œuvres*, XX, 235–6.

[4] *Work*, I, 63–4.

[5] *Ibid.*, p. 147.

yet been encountered, and the camps were full of rumors as to when and where the battle was going to take place. The soldiers were anxious to grapple with the mysterious enemy, but hitherto there had been no opportunity. There was a common feeling of frustration in both armies, and the generals were called incompetent by the soldiers, who had tired of the futile marching and the current disorder.

Another episode is the incident of the knapsacks.[1] The situation is similar in both books. Having marched a good deal one day, the soldiers were tired and began to hope for food and rest. A bridge was crossed, and yet the soldiers were forced to march on despite sore feet and empty stomachs. When no pause was granted they began stealthily to drop their knapsacks, and in *La Débâcle* they dropped their rifles, too, Zola thereby indicating the disorganization and the lax morale of the French army. In Crane's novel it was only the knapsacks that the tired soldiers left behind. Both writers made the observation that the soldiers hid their knapsacks carefully, as if they intended to return and get them later. But Crane's motivation for the leaving of the knapsacks was the very opposite of Zola's. Crane's soldiers stripped themselves of things they could dispense with; but, because they were eager to fight, they kept their rifles.

The men had begun to count the miles upon their fingers, and they grew tired. "Sore feet an' damned short rations, that's all," said the loud soldier. There was perspiration and grumblings. After a time they began to shed their knapsacks. Some tossed them unconcernedly down; others hid them carefully, asserting their plans to return for them at some convenient time. . . . Presently few carried anything but their necessary clothing, blankets, haversacks, canteens, and arms and ammunition. "You can now eat and shoot," said the tall soldier to the youth. "That's all you want to do."[2]

There is still another incident worth mentioning. When in *La Débâcle* the battle was practically lost, Maurice together with his friend Jean took refuge in a forest close to the battlefield. Here

---

[1] *Ibid.*, pp. 46–7; and *Œuvres*, XX, 35.

[2] *Work*, I, 46–7. Observe that Crane, like Zola, described the army as a monster, a huge, crawling worm. "A moment later the regiment went swinging off into the darkness. It was now like one of those moving monsters wending with many feet . . . the backs of all these huge crawling reptiles." *Ibid.*, p. 38. And again: "They were like two serpents crawling from the cavern of the night." *Ibid.*, p. 39.

the enemy fire was devastating, for the forest was crowded with soldiers trying to escape. The air was filled with the groans of the wounded, cannon balls splintered the trees above their heads, and the crashing sound of falling trees augmented the roar of battle. Zola described the forest as a human being, alive, writhing in its last agony. The trees themselves seemed to encircle Maurice with their boughs, as if they wished to detain him. However, he went through the wood unmolested, whereas most of his fellow soldiers were either wounded or killed in the horrible slaughter:

Dès les premiers pas, tous sentirent qu'ils entraient dans un enfer; mais ils ne pouvaient reculer, il fallait quand même traverser le bois, leur seule ligne de retraite. A cette heure, c'était un bois effroyable, le bois de la désespérance et de la mort. Comprenant que des troupes se repliaient par là, les Prussiens le criblaient de balles, le couvraient d'obus. Et il était comme flagellé d'une tempête, tout agité et hurlant, dans le fracassement de ses branches. Les obus coupaient les arbres, les balles faisaient pleuvoir les feuilles, des voix de plainte semblaient sortir des tronc fendus, des sanglots tombaient avec les ramures trempées de sève. On aurait dit la détresse d'une cohue enchaînée, la terreur et les cris de milliers d'êtres cloués au sol, qui ne pouvaient fuir, sous cette mitraille. Jamais angoisse n'a soufflé plus grande que dans la forêt bombardée.

Tout de suite, Maurice et Jean, qui avaient rejoint leurs compagnons, s'épouvantèrent. Ils marchaient alors sous une haute futaie, ils pouvaient courir. Mais les balles sifflaient, se croisaient, impossible d'en comprendre la direction, de manière à se garantir, en filant d'arbre en arbre. Deux hommes furent tués, frappés dans le dos, frappés à la face. Devant Maurice, un chêne séculaire, le tronc broyé par un obus, s'abbatit, avec la majesté tragique d'un héros, écrasant tout à son entour. Et, au moment où le jeune homme sautait en arrière, un hêtre colossal, à sa gauche, qu'un autre obus venait de découronner, se brisait, s'effondrait, ainsi qu'une charpente de cathédrale. Où fuir? de quel côté tourner ses pas? Ce n'étaient, de toutes parts, que des chutes de branches, comme dans un édifice immense qui menacerait ruine et dont les salles se succéderaient sous des plafonds croulants. Puis, lorsqu'ils eurent sauté dans un taillis pour échapper à cet écrasement des grands arbres, ce fut Jean qui manqua d'être coupé en deux par un projectile, qui heureusement n'éclata pas. Maintenant, ils ne pouvaient plus avancer, au milieu de la foule inextricable des arbustes. Les tiges minces les liaient aux épaules; les hautes herbes se nouaient à leurs chevilles; des murs brusques de broussailles les immobilisaient, pendant que les feuillages volaient autour d'eux, sous la faux géante qui fauchait le bois. A côté d'eux, un autre homme, foudroyé d'une balle au front, resta debout, serré entre deux jeunes bouleaux. Vingt fois, prisonniers de ce taillis, ils sentirent passer la mort.[1]

---

[1] *Œuvres*, XXI, 341-2.

Crane created a similar episode, as intense and dramatic as Zola's. When Henry believed the battle was lost, he fled into a nearby forest. At first it seemed quiet and peaceful to the harassed soldier, for the sounds of the battle could not be heard. But as he went further in, it took on an aspect as menacing[1] and dangerous as the one in *La Débâcle*. Henry met just one dead soldier, the sight of whom left him numbed with horror, whereas Maurice had met dying and dead soldiers at every step.

The ground was cluttered with vines and bushes, and the trees grew close and spread out like bouquets.... The creepers, catching against his legs, cried out harshly as their sprays were torn from the barks of trees. The swishing saplings tried to make known his presence to the world. He could not conciliate the forest. As he made his way, it was always calling out protestations. When he separated embraces of trees and vines the disturbed foliages moved their arms and turned their face leaves toward him. He dreaded lest these noisy motions and cries should bring men to look at him.[2]

And again after the meeting with the dead man, who, he feared, would rise and pursue him, Henry, like Maurice, imagined that the forest made attempts to detain him as if it were a human being.

Sometimes the brambles formed chains and tried to hold him back. Trees, confronting him, stretched out their arms and forbade him to pass. After the previous hostility this new resistance of the forest filled him with a fine bitterness. It seemed that Nature could not be quite ready to kill him.[3]

Finally, despite the grim presentations of war, both novels end on an optimistic note. Symbolically, the sun broke through the clouds bringing a ray of hope to man. In *La Débâcle*:

Jean, plein d'angoisse, se retourna vers Paris. A cette fin si claire d'un beau dimanche, le soleil oblique, au ras de l'horizon, éclairait la ville immense d'une ardente lueur rouge. On aurait dit un soleil de sang, sur une mer sans borne. ...[4]

---

[1] It reminds us also of Bierce's tale "What I Saw of Shiloh" in *Battle Sketches* (London, 1930), pp. 9–39. Cf. also the animated forest in Norris's story "The Jongleur of Taillebois." *Compl. Works*, X, 3 ff.

[2] *Ibid.*, p. 81–2.

[3] *Ibid.*, p. 86.

[4] *Œuvres*, XXI, 585.

And in *The Red Badge of Courage*:

It rained. The procession of weary soldiers became a bedraggled train, despondent and muttering, marching with churning effort in a trough of liquid brown mud under a low, wretched sky. Yet the youth smiled, for he saw that the world was a world for him, though many discovered it to be made of oaths and walking-sticks. . . .

Over the river a golden ray of sun came through the hosts of leaden rain clouds.[1]

It seems probable that *La Débâcle* served as a model for *The Red Badge of Courage* for some matters of structure and tone as well as for certain episodes. Crane was, however, far from being an imitator of Zola's novel. Instead, with his vivid imagination and sensitive mind, he dealt with war in his own artistic way, though influenced by his reading.

Like *Maggie*, Crane's second novel of the New York slums bears the stamp of Zola. Apart from being an analysis of the conflict between two generations,[2] *George's Mother*,[3] like *L'Assommoir*, may be called a study in drink and the effects of drink on the individual. The degeneration of George Kelcey is perhaps Crane's most elaborate portrayal of a process of deterioration in the manner of Coupeau and Gervaise.

The Bowery, the locale of the story, was presented with a naturalist's care for unpleasant detail. Crane opened his book with a full description of a street and its teeming life on a rainy afternoon. A young laborer was seen plodding along the avenue on his way home, carrying his lunch-pail under his arm. Attention should be called to the opening chapter of *L'Assommoir*,[4] where Zola depicted a similar street and a group of laborers on their way to their jobs. In the manner of Zola, Crane then proceeded to describe the immediate milieu which surrounded George Kelcey and his mother.

---

[1] *Work*, I, 199–200. Zola and Crane differed in their concepts of war. The French writer looked upon war as a necessity, an indispensable means of purification of the peoples—a belief deduced from Darwinism—whereas Crane, like Tolstoy, regarded war as a horrible and meaningless slaughter.

[2] Cf. pp. 328–30.

[3] For the title cf. *Nana's Mother* (*L'Assommoir*) and *Nana's Brother* (*Germinal*). See Salvan, *op. cit.*, pp. 190–1. Cf. the discussion of the slums and the effects of drink in the *Arena*. See p. 79.

[4] See pp. 284–5. Cf. also the discussion of the street scene in *Jason Edwards*. Pp. 238–42.

By a series of vivid pictures he called forth the tenement area, its foul-smelling back yards and alleys, its decayed houses, and its miserable inhabitants who were for ever quarreling and fighting. It may perhaps suffice here to quote the following passage describing Bleecker's lodgings as an illustration of the milieu:

Bleecker lived in an old three-storeyed house on a side street. A Jewish tailor lived and worked in the front parlour, and old Bleecker lived in the back parlour. A German, whose family took care of the house, occupied the basement. Another German, with a wife and eight children, rented the dining-room. The two upper floors were inhabited by tailors, dressmakers, a pedlar, and mysterious people who were seldom seen. The door of the little hall bedroom, at the foot of the second flight, was always open, and in there could be seen two bended men who worked at mending opera-glasses. The German woman in the dining-room was not friends with the little dressmaker in the rear room of the third floor, and frequently they yelled the vilest names up and down between the balusters. Each part of the woodwork was scratched and rubbed by the contact of innumerable persons. In one wall there was a long slit with chipped edges, celebrating the time when a man had thrown a hatchet at his wife. In the lower hall there was an eternal woman, with a rag and a pail of suds, who knelt over the worn oil-cloth. Old Bleecker felt that he had quite respectable and high-class apartments.[1]

This passage may be compared with Zola's picture of the huge, gruesome tenement on the "rue de la Goutte-d'Or."[2] Symbolically, in *George's Mother* a brewery dominated the view; moreover, as in *L'Assommoir*, the area boasted a great number of saloons which were portrayed like monsters, whose open mouths devoured the laborers and then spewed them out late at night. Or again, the saloon was like a canker which infected the entire region. Note, for instance, Zola's gloomy reflection in *L'Assommoir*:

L'alambic, sourdement, sans une flamme, sans une gaîté dans les reflets éteints de ses cuivres, continuait, laissait couler sa sueur d'alcool, pareil à une source lente et entêtée, qui à la longue devait envahir la salle, se répandre sur les boulevards extérieurs, inonder le trou immense de Paris.[3]

The motivation of the lure of the saloon was similar in both books. The atmosphere at home was as unpleasant to Gervaise and Coupeau as it was to George Kelcey. Consequently, the only place where they

---

[1] *Work*, X, 49.

[2] See pp. 240–1.

[3] *Œuvres*, VIII, 42.

could feel "at home" was the saloon. There, there was warmth, food, drink, forgetfulness, pleasure, and friends. Crane differed from Zola in that he stressed particularly man's utter estrangement and loneliness in life. To a romantic, weak daydreamer like Kelcey the saloon was the only place where he felt at ease and experienced social safety.

The characters of the two books, who were mostly weak and passive, lacking power to resist the lure of the saloons, were gradually molded to the unlovely pattern of their milieu. The life-stories of Coupeau and Gervaise illustrated this. And so did George Kelcey's. The stages of his decline, from a hard-working laborer to a careless good-for-nothing and a despicable drunkard, followed in the main those of Coupeau, although the last phase of Kelcey's life was never described as was that of Coupeau, who died of *delirium tremens* in a lunatic asylum. Like Coupeau, Crane's hero was at first a steady and industrious laborer who never drank anything stronger than beer. We remember that Coupeau at first never touched anything stronger than wine. Their fathers had both had fatal falls from scaffoldings. Their mothers, however, were still living. One day, on their way home from their work, they met a friend, had a drink with him at a saloon, and by degrees both drifted into bad company. There is a difference, however. The primary reason for Coupeau's alcoholism was the accident, which forced him to stay in bed for some time, and turned him into an idler. There was no such accident to account for George Kelcey's first step downward. There were, instead, many other reasons; his passive temperament, his failure in love, and his general inability to cope with life,[1] together with his mother's constant nagging, made him prefer the saloon to his home. Such drinks as wine and beer were no longer to the taste of our heroes. Coupeau preferred "eau-de-vie," while George Kelcey drank whisky. Both became more and more unwilling to work, and felt most at home among their friends at the saloon. In the two books, a gang of confirmed drunkards helped to increase the attraction of the saloon. Zola's Dickensian Bec-Salé, called Boit-sans-soif, Mes Bottes and Bibi-La-Grillade may be compared with Crane's Charley Jones, O'Connor, and Bleecker. Gradually the alcohol wrecked the lives of Coupeau and George Kelcey.

---

[1] Cf. pp. 330–1.

There is at least one episode in *George's Mother*[1] which is related to a similar one in *L'Assommoir*, namely the drinking orgy[2] which echoes the famous goose dinner in Zola's novel.[3] Both parties were described extensively, with emphasis on grotesque and brutal detail. The careful and loving preparations of the host in the one story, and of the hostess in the other, the great expectations and fine clothes of the guests, the gay atmosphere, the copious drinking (and eating in *L'Assommoir*), the singing, the recitals, the barbaric vulgarity and coarse humor—these were elements found in both scenes. Moreover, each party ended with a description of one guest lying prostrate in the midst of the debris of the room. Although it seems probable that Crane had Zola's goose dinner in mind when he depicted the party at Bleecker's, it is necessary to call attention to some differences between the two scenes. Crane's party was solely a drinking party and no women were present; nevertheless Crane showed more restraint when describing the effects of the drinks on the characters than did Zola, whose description contains much vulgarity and obscenity. There is no indecency in Crane's picture, but there is plenty of sordidness. The following quotation gives an idea of the grotesque atmosphere at Gervaise's party:

> Et le vin donc, mes enfants, ça coulait autour de la table comme l'eau coule à la Seine. Un vrai ruisseau, lorsqu'il a plu et que la terre a soif. Coupeau versait de haut, pour voir le jet rouge écumer; et quand un litre était vide, il faisait la blague de retourner le goulot et de le presser du geste familier aux femmes qui traient les vaches. Encore une négresse qui avait la gueule cassée! Dans un coin de la boutique, le tas des négresses mortes grandissait, un cimetière de bouteilles sur lequel on poussait les ordures de la nappe. Mme Putois ayant demandé de l'eau, le zingueur indigné venait d'enlever lui-même les carafes. Est-ce que les honnêtes

---

[1] Note also that Crane, in the manner of Zola, let his characters reappear in more than one book. In *George's Mother* there were also glimpses of Maggie, her mother, and Pete. The anxiety experienced by Kelcey's mother, when he stayed out late (*Work*, X, 27 ff.) recalls that felt by Gervaise in the first chapter of *L'Assommoir* when Lantier did not return home. Kelcey may also be compared with Gervaise, who developed as he did under the influence of the squalid milieu. Both were equally weak, passive and easily imposed upon, typical characters of literary naturalism. Finally the death of Coupeau's mother may be compared with that of Kelcey's mother.

[2] *Work*, X, 49 ff.

[3] *Œuvres*, VIII, 201 ff.

gens buvaient de l'eau? Elle voulait donc avoir des grenouilles dans l'estomac? Et les verres se vidaient d'une lampée, on entendait le liquide jeté d'un trait tomber dans la gorge, avec le bruit des eaux de pluie le long des tuyaux de descente, les jours d'orage. Il pleuvait du piqueton, quoi! un piqueton qui avait d'abord un goût de vieux tonneau, mais auquel on s'habituait joliment, à ce point qu'il finissait par sentir la noisette. Ah! Dieu de Dieu! les jésuites avaient beau dire, le jus de la treille était tout de même une fameuse invention! La société riait, approuvait, car, enfin, l'ouvrier n'aurait pas pu vivre sans le vin, le papa Noé devait avoir planté la vigne pour les zingueurs, les tailleurs et les forgerons. Le vin décrassait et reposait du travail, mettait le feu au ventre des fainéants; puis, lorsque le farceur vous jouait des tours, eh bien! le roi n'était pas votre oncle, Paris vous appartenait. Avec çà que l'ouvrier échiné, sans le sou, méprisé par les bourgeois, avait tant de sujets de gaîté, et qu'on était bien venu de lui reprocher une cocarde de temps à autre, prise à la seule fin de voir la vie en rose! Hein! à cette heure, justement, est-ce qu'on ne se fichait pas de l'empereur? Peut-être bien que l'empereur lui aussi était rond, mais ça n'empêchait pas, on se fichait de lui, on le défiait bien d'être plus rond et de rigoler davantage. Zut pour les aristos! Coupeau envoyait le monde à la balançoire. Il trouvait les femmes chouettes, il tapait sur sa poche où trois sous se battaient, en riant comme s'il avait remué des pièces de cent sous à la pelle. Goujet lui-même, si sobre d'habitude, se piquait le nez. Les yeux de Boche se rapetissaient, ceux de Lorilleux devenaient pâles, tandis que Poisson roulait des regards de plus en plus sévères dans sa face bronzée d'ancien soldat. Ils étaient déjà soûls comme des tiques. Et les dames avaient leur pointe, oh! une culotte encore légère, le vin pur aux joues, avec un besoin de se déshabiller qui leur faisait enlever leur fichu; seule, Clémence commençait à n'être plus convenable. Mais, brusquement, Gervaise se souvint des six bouteilles de vin cacheté; elle avait oublié de les servir avec l'oie; elle les apporta, on emplit les verres.[1]

Crane pictured the drinking orgy in similar terms:

The invaluable O'Connor brought forth a man who could play the mouth-organ. The latter, after wiping his instrument upon his coat-sleeve, played all the popular airs. The men's heads swayed to and fro in the clouded smoke. They grinned and beat time with their feet. A valour, barbaric and wild, began to show in their poses and in their faces, red and glistening from perspiration. The conversation resounded in a hoarse roar. The beer would not run rapidly enough for Jones, so he remained behind to tilt the keg. . . . The glasses, mugs, and cups travelled swift and regular, catching orange reflections from the lamp-light. Two or three men were grown so careless that they were continually spilling their drinks.[2]

---

[1] *Ibid.*, pp. 223-4.
[2] *Work*, X, 53.

And again:

The air hung heavy and stifling with the odours of tobacco, men's breaths, and beer half filling forgotten glasses. There was ruck of broken tumblers, pipes, bottles, spilled tobacco, cigar-stumps. The chairs and tables were pitched this way and that way, as after some terrible struggle. In the midst of it all lay old Bleecker, stretched upon a couch in deepest sleep, as abandoned in attitude, as motionless, as ghastly, as if it were a corpse that had been flung there.[1]

Both authors were apparently interested in the psychology of drinking. By recording the gradual changes of effect which the alcohol exerted on the individual, they were able to give a picture of the mentalities of the human brute which was both mercilessly true and revolting. When drunk, man as Zola and Crane saw him sloughed off the thin veneer of civilization and revealed his animal nature.[2]

---

[1] *Ibid.*, p. 58. Other works by Crane which also bear the stamp of Zola, particularly in the choice of milieu and sordid detail, include: "An Experiment in Misery," "The Men in the Storm," notably in the representation of crowds, "A Desertion," "A Dark Brown Dog," and "The Scotch Express," in which the engine was described in terms of "la Lison" in *La Bête humaine*: "The monster [the locomotive] roared suddenly and loudly, and sprang forward impetuously. A wrong-headed or maddened draught-horse will plunge in its collar sometimes when going up a hill. But this load of burdened carriages followed imperturbably at the gait of turtles. They were not to be stirred from their way of dignified exit by the impatient engine. ... In starting this heavy string of coaches, the engine breathed explosively. It gasped, and heaved, and bellowed; once, for a moment, the wheels spun on the rails, and a convulsive tremor shook the great steel frame." *Work*, XI, 152–3. And again: "This valkyric journey on the back of the vermilion engine, with the shouting of the wind, the deep, mighty panting of the steed, the grey blur at the track-side, the flowing quicksilver ribbon of the other rails, the sudden clash as a switch intersects, all the din and fury of this ride, was of a splendour that caused one to look abroad at the quiet green landscape and believe that it was of a phlegm quite beyond patience. It should have been dark, rain-shot, and windy; thunder should have rolled across its sky. ... Without those finely firm hands on the bridle, the engine might rear and bolt for the pleasant farms lying in the sunshine at either side. ... The dragon is insatiate. The fireman is continually swinging open the furnace door, whereat a red shine flows out upon the floor of the cab, and shovelling in immense mouthfuls of coal to a fire that is almost diabolic in its madness. The feeding, feeding, feeding goes on until it appears as if it is the muscles of the fireman's arms that are speeding the long train. An engine running over sixty-five miles an hour, with five hundred tons to drag, has an appetite in proportion to this task." *Ibid.*, pp. 157–9. For the description of "la Lison" see p. 299 of this study.

[2] Cf. pp. 214 ff.

3. ZOLA AND NORRIS

We know that Norris was well acquainted with many of Zola's novels,[1] and that he looked upon the French writer as his avowed master.[2] In an article entitled "Why Women Should Write the Best Novels" he wrote in a manner which suggests he himself had faced the problem he was describing:

But the fascination of a great story-writer—especially upon the young, untried little story-writer—is strong, and before the latter is well aware he is taking from the big man that which he has no right to take. He is taking his code of ethics, his view of life, his personality, even to the very incidents and episodes of his story. He is studying literature and not life.[3]

Norris's debt to Zola[4] may be traced, at least to some extent, in all his novels, but it is fully apparent in four novels: *McTeague*, *Vandover and the Brute*, *The Octopus*, and *The Pit*. These novels have one feature in common: all depict the slow but inevitable course of man toward destruction—a common naturalistic pattern. Different elements contributed to the disintegration of the characters, but, as in Crane's works, usually social conditions, heredity, and circumstances were the principal factors conducive to their ruin. Norris had probably learnt this by reading Zola's novels, a source which he used extensively but almost always with judiciousness and moderation.

Two of Zola's novels, *Thérèse Raquin*[5] and *L'Assommoir*, seem to have been Norris's chief literary models for *McTeague*. In the

---

[1] See p. 111.

[2] See p. 461.

[3] *Compl. Works*, VII, 180.

[4] Biencourt has already treated of Norris's debt to Zola in an extensive and, on the whole, well-documented study. Nevertheless, for purposes of consistency and completeness, it has seemed advisable to include a section on Zola's influence on Norris; and for purposes of convenience, instead of making a summary of Biencourt's chief results, I have included some revised chapters of my monograph *The Influence of Émile Zola on Frank Norris*. Whenever opinions differ, this fact has been recorded in the footnotes. Marchand and Salvan follow, for the most part, Biencourt. For Norris's debt to Maupassant, see Biencourt, *op. cit.*, pp. 78, 92–3.

[5] Neither Biencourt nor any other scholar of Norris has, it seems, been aware of Norris's debt to *Thérèse Raquin*, which is fundamental for the understanding of *McTeague*.

preface to *Thérèse Raquin* Zola wrote about his aim in writing the novel:

> Dans *Thérèse Raquin*, j'ai voulu étudier des tempéraments et non des caractères. Là est le livre entier. J'ai choisi des personnages souverainement dominés par leurs nerfs et leur sang, dépourvus de libre arbitre, entraînés à chaque acte de leur vie par les fatalités de leur chair. Thérèse et Laurent sont des brutes humaines, rien de plus. J'ai cherché à suivre pas à pas dans ces brutes le travail sourd des passions, les poussées de l'instinct, les détraquements cérébraux survenus à la suite d'une crise nerveuse. Les amours de mes deux héros sont le contentement d'un besoin; le meurtre qu'ils commettent est une conséquence de leur adultère, conséquence qu'ils acceptent comme les loups acceptent l'assassinat des moutons; enfin, ce que j'ai été obligé d'appeler leurs remords, consiste en un simple désordre organique, en une rébellion du système nerveux tendu à se rompre. L'âme est parfaitement absente, j'en conviens aisément, puisque je l'ai voulu ainsi.
>
> On commence, j'espère, à comprendre que mon but a été un but scientifique avant tout. Lorsque mes deux personnages, Thérèse et Laurent, ont été créés, je me suis plu à me poser et à résoudre certains problèmes: ainsi, j'ai tenté d'expliquer l'union étrange qui peut se produire entre deux tempéraments différents, j'ai montré les troubles profonds d'une nature sanguine au contact d'une nature nerveuse. Qu'on lise le roman avec soin, on verra que chaque chapitre est l'étude d'un cas curieux de physiologie. En un mot, je n'ai eu qu'un désir: étant donné un homme puissant et une femme inassouvie, chercher en eux la bête, ne voir même que la bête, les jeter dans un drame violent, et noter scrupuleusement les sensations et les actes de ces êtres. J'ai simplement fait sur deux corps vivants le travail analytique que les chirurgiens font sur des cadavres.[1]

Norris's purpose in *McTeague* was similar. Like Zola, he did not want to portray characters, but to study temperaments. Both authors chose to depict two different temperaments and to record the influence which they exerted on each other.[2] The parts played by Thérèse and Laurent correspond in many ways to those of Trina and McTeague, with the important and significant difference, however, that Zola described a case of adultery and a subsequent ill-fated marriage, whereas Norris only depicted an unhappy marriage. In both cases, the influence which the one temperament exerted on the other became fatal, and led to the characters' slow but inevitable destruction.

Besides the fact that the fundamental ideas of the two books are

---

[1] *Œuvres*, XXXIV, viii–ix.

[2] Cf. the short story "A Case for Lombroso." See pp. 195–6 of this study.

similar, a close analysis reveals other resemblances. The exterior portraits of Thérèse[1] and Trina exhibit points of similarity: each of them had an attractive, lithe figure, big, expressive eyes, a face of striking paleness contrasted by a mass of black hair. Mentally they were also alike; both were of a nervous disposition, hysterical, unbalanced, and abnormal. Beneath the quiet surface Thérèse was extremely passionate. Her sexual urge was her predominant characteristic, whereas Trina's chief idiosyncrasy, despite her temporary passionate outbursts, was greed.[2] The two women's emotions, resulting from their nervous temperaments, oscillated from one extreme to another. Moments of calmness and placid quietude alternated with spells of violent outbursts of passion. The women's passions and nervous crises frightened the men. This is Laurent's attitude:

Tous ses instincts de femme nerveuse éclatèrent avec une violence inouïe; le sang de sa mère, ce sang africain qui brûlait ses veines, se mit à couler, à battre furieusement dans son corps maigre, presque vierge encore. Elle s'étalait, elle s'offrait avec une impudeur souveraine. Et, de la tête aux pieds, de longs frissons l'agitaient.

Jamais Laurent n'avait connu une pareille femme. Il resta surpris, mal à l'aise. ... Les sanglots, les crises de Thérèse l'epouvantèrent presque ...[3]

And this is McTeague's reaction:

During the first months of their married life these nervous relapses of hers had alternated with brusque outbursts of affection when her only fear was that her husband's love did not equal her own. Without an instant's warning, she would clasp him about the neck, rubbing her cheek against his ... Those sudden outbursts of affection on the part of his little woman, outbursts that only increased in vehemence the longer they lived together, puzzled rather than pleased him.[4]

Against these small, nervous, and easily roused women both writers set huge and indolent men: Zola the sanguine and somewhat sluggish Laurent, and Norris the phlegmatic McTeague. Both

---

[1] It is worth noting that in *Thérèse Raquin* (cf. also *Madeleine Férat*) Zola focused his interest on *two* characters. In the *Rougon-Macquart* series, on the other hand, Zola usually depicted a great number of people dwarfed by a depressing milieu.

[2] Cf. Balzac's *Eugénie Grandet*.

[3] *Œuvres*, XXXIV, 36–7.

[4] *Compl. Works*, VIII, 161–2. For McTeague's bewilderment in regard to and fear of Trina's outbursts of affection, see also *ibid.*, pp. 160 and 215.

Laurent and McTeague belonged to a primitive type of man, in whom the lower, animal instincts predominated; both were young giants, angular, with enormous hands, heavy muscles, and bull-like necks; both were of great strength and their movements and mentalities were slow. Thérèse examined Laurent and found him

un grand gaillard, carré des épaules ... Elle contemplait avec une sorte d'admiration son front bas, planté d'une rude chevelure noire, ses joues pleines, ses lèvres rouges, sa face régulière, d'une beauté sanguine. Elle arrêta un instant ses regards sur son cou; ce cou était large et court, gras et puissant. Puis elle s'oublia à considérer les grosses mains qu'il tenaient [*sic*] étalées sur ses genoux; les doigts en étaient carrés; le poing fermé devait être énorme et aurait pu assommer un bœuf. Laurent était un vrai fils de paysan, d'allure un peu lourdes [*sic*] le dos bombé,les mouvements lents et précis, l'air tranquille et entêté. On sentait sous ses vêtements des muscles ronds et développés, tout un corps d'une chair épaisse et ferme. Et Thérèse l'examinait avec curiosité, allant de ses poings à sa face, éprouvant de petits frissons lorsque ses yeux rencontraient son cou de taureau.[1]

McTeague was portrayed in similar terms (see p. 198 of this study). To illustrate the strength of their heroes, Zola said that Laurent could have killed a bull with his fist, whereas Norris asserted that McTeague had once "knocked down a half-grown heifer with a blow of his fist between the eyes ..."[2] Moreover, Laurent loved to sit in a warm room, slowly digesting his meal, smoking his pipe and drinking his "gloria à trois sous." And "Il aurait voulu bien manger, bien dormir, contenter largement ses passions ..."[3] McTeague's only pleasures were "to eat, to smoke, to sleep, and to play upon his concertina,"[4] and he loved to sit in his "Dental Parlours" drinking his beer and smoking his huge porcelain pipe while his food digested. Whereas Laurent was depicted as a sluggard possessing a craving appetite for women, McTeague was portrayed as a hard-working though immensely stupid dentist who had nothing erotic about him.[5]

---

[1] *Œuvres*, XXXIV, 25–6.
[2] *Compl. Works*, VIII, 196.
[3] *Œuvres*, XXXIV, 28.
[4] *Compl. Works*, VIII, 2.
[5] It seems necessary to call attention to some other possible sources of inspiration for McTeague. Biencourt has rightly pointed out the similarities of mentalities and professions between Charles Bovary and McTeague. *Op. cit.*, pp. 194–5. It should be remembered, however, that Camille in *Thérèse Raquin* may also have been an inspiration for McTeague's slow temperament. Camille,

Circumstances willed that these men of strong physique and slow temperaments come under the influence of nervous women. Laurent was drawn to Thérèse with the same deterministic necessity as McTeague was drawn to Trina. Here is Zola's couple:

La nature et les circonstances semblaient avoir fait cette femme pour cet homme, et les avoir poussés l'un vers l'autre. A eux deux, la femme,

---

it should be noted, is, in some respects, reminiscent of Charles Bovary. On the other hand, we may call attention to other likenesses between *Madame Bovary* and *McTeague*. In addition to general similarities of tone, it should be noted that Homais, the druggist in Flaubert's novel, had infringed the law by not having a diploma to practice medicine. McTeague, as is well known, had no diploma to practice dentistry. Moreover, in each book the men, Charles and McTeague, gave evidence of their stupidity when taking the women, Emma and Trina, to the theater. The incidents are equally amusing in both books. Finally, Emma's attitude toward her husband has points in common with Trina's.—Walker believes that Jimmie White, one of Norris's friends, was in many ways the prototype of McTeague (Walker, *op. cit.*, p. 63), and Marchand states categorically that "Norris borrowed McTeague's great strength and stature, his blond hair, his customary docility, his occasional blind rages, his elephant trumpetings, his concertina, melancholy tunes, canary and all, from Goddedaal, Swedish mate of the brig *Flying Scud* in Stevenson's *The Wrecker*'' (Marchand, *op. cit.*, p. 107 n.). To a certain extent both of these critics are right, for, evidently, Norris used a number of sources for McTeague, borrowing one trait here and another there. Some of McTeague's characteristics were probably based on the author's personal reactions to and observations of the unusual display of strength exhibited by such athletes as Jimmie White, but still more were derived from literary sources. The parallels between McTeague and Goddedaal enumerated by Marchand are striking and seem indisputable. Nor can the parallels be accidental, since we know that Norris was a great admirer of Stevenson's works, and an entire novel, *Moran of the Lady Letty*, was in part written under the inspiration of Stevenson. Norris's interest in Darwinism and in the Old Norse sagas may also have contributed to the creation of this type. But, nevertheless, one of the main sources from which Norris derived McTeague and, perhaps, this muscular type of hero so common in his works, was no doubt the novels of Zola. A few more parallels seem to support this assumption. McTeague and Coupeau (*L'Assommoir*) have some features in common: both had a prominent chin and obstinate hair standing on end. Coupeau had "La mâchoire inférieure saillant . . . Sa grosse chevelure frisée se tenait tout debout." *Œuvres*, VIII, 34. Goujet (*L'Assommoir*) was a giant like McTeague with a square-cut head, immense strength, and feeble intellect: "Goujet était un colosse de vingt-trois ans . . . d'une force herculéenne. . . . La tête carrée, la chair alourdie par le rude travail du marteau, il tenait des grosses bêtes: dur d'intelligence, bon tout de même." *Œuvres*, VIII, 110-11. Cabuche (*La Bête humaine*) was another of Zola's giants with "des poings énormes, des mâchoires

nerveuse et hypocrite, l'homme, sanguin et vivant en brute, ils faisaient un couple puissamment lié. Ils se complétaient, se protégeaient mutuellement.[1]

This is Norris's:

Their undoing had already begun. Yet neither of them was to blame. From the first they had not sought each other. Chance had brought them face to face, and mysterious instincts as ungovernable as the winds of heaven were at work knitting their lives together.[2]

In the beginning, both women, owing to their nervous and alert tempers, succeeded in rousing the sluggish mentalities of their husbands. Later, the influence of the women became destructive, for both men, from having been dull and slow but fairly harmless, developed into brutal murderers. Actually, it was Thérèse's passion for Laurent that drove him to murder Camille, her husband. Similarly, it was chiefly Trina's greed which made McTeague murder her. Of course, the characters influenced each other mutually. The stages of the married life of each couple went from irresistible passion to satiety, hatred, and violent death. They destroyed each other's lives. Laurent was in part responsible for Thérèse's tragedy. Likewise, McTeague was partly the cause of Trina's ruin.

Prior to the violent death of the two couples, the husbands displayed their viciousness and brutality by beating their wives, who took abnormal pleasure in having pain inflicted upon them. Thérèse's masochism is illustrated in the following paragraph:

---

de carnassier." *Œuvres*, XVIII, 359. In the same novel Jacques, the engine-driver, was described as a twenty-six-year-old fellow "de grande taille, très brun, beau garçon au visage rond et régulier, mais que gâtaient des mâchoires trop fortes." *Ibid.*, p. 38. Finally in *La Terre* Buteau, too, had "des mâchoires puissantes de carnassier," reminiscent of McTeague's "jaw salient, like that of the carnivora." Another of McTeague's characteristics, repeated constantly, was his enormous hands, "the hands of the old-time car-boy." This seems to be but an echo of the constant mentioning in *La Bête humaine* of Roubaud's hands in expressions like these: "ses poings d'ancien homme d'équipe se serraient, comme au temps où il poussait des wagons." *Œuvres*, XVIII, 12. Or "l'homme aux grosses mains qui, autrefois, avait poussé des wagons." *Ibid.*, p. 24. Or again, "Il lui [Séverine] aurait sorti le cœur, de ses doigts gourds d'ancien ouvrier." *Ibid.*, p. 26.

[1] *Œuvres*, XXXIV, 45.
[2] *Compl. Works*, VIII, 78.

Laurent, ivre, rendu furieux par les tableaux atroces que Thérèse étalait devant ses yeux, se précipitait sur elle, la renversait par terre et la serrait sous son genou, le poing haut.

—C'est cela, criait-elle, frappe-moi, tue-moi ... Jamais Camille n'a levé la main sur ma tête, mais toi, tu es un monstre.

Et Laurent, fouetté par ces paroles, la secouait avec rage, la battait, meurtrissait son corps de son poing fermé. A deux reprises, il faillit l'étrangler. Thérèse mollissait sous les coups; elle goûtait une volupté âcre à être frappée; elle s'abandonnait, elle s'offrait, elle provoquait son mari pour qu'il l'assommât davantage. C'était encore là un remède contre les souffrances de sa vie; elle dormait mieux la nuit, quand elle avait été bien battue le soir.[1]

And this is Trina's perverted love for her brutal husband:

As time went on, McTeague's idleness became habitual. He drank no more whiskey than at first, but his dislike for Trina increased with every day of their poverty, with every day of Trina's persistent stinginess. At times—fortunately rare—he was more than ever brutal to her. He would box her ears or hit her a great blow with the back of a hairbrush, or even with his closed fist. His old-time affection for his "little woman," unable to stand the test of privation, had lapsed by degrees, and what little of it was left was changed, distorted, and made monstrous by the alcohol. ...

And in some strange, inexplicable way this brutality made Trina all the more affectionate; aroused in her a morbid, unwholesome love of submission, a strange, unnatural pleasure in yielding, in surrendering herself to the will of an irresistible, virile power.

Trina's emotions had narrowed with the narrowing of her daily life. They reduced themselves at last to but two, her passion for her money and her perverted love for her husband when he was brutal. She was a strange woman during these days.[2]

Apart from the leading idea, two different temperaments which clashed with each other, and apart from certain character traits no doubt suggested by *Thérèse Raquin*, *McTeague* resembles *L'Assommoir* as regards plot[3] and episodes. The opening scenes

---

[1] *Œuvres*, XXXIV, 204.

[2] *Compl. Works*, VIII, 263-4. Cf. the same trait exhibited in Maria Macapa. *Ibid.*, p. 264.

[3] Before Gervaise's marriage to Coupeau she had been the mistress of Lantier, who, however, deserted her and ran away with another woman. Similarly in *McTeague*, prior to Trina's marriage with McTeague she had "kept company" with Marcus, who, however, gave her up to McTeague and left San Francisco to take a job on a cattle ranch. The marriage of Gervaise and Coupeau has points in common with that of Trina and McTeague. The wedding in *McTeague*

of the two novels resemble each other, although the atmosphere is different—in Norris's novel it is one of comfort and peace, whereas in Zola's it is mingled with anguish. In *L'Assommoir* Gervaise sat by her window looking down into the street, noticing the stores and shops, and observing various groups of workers on their way to their jobs. It was early morning and the town was waking up. This is "le boulevard de la Chapelle":

... elle [Gervaise] retourna s'accouder à la fenêtre ... Il y avait là ... un défilé sans fin d'ouvriers allant au travail, leurs outils sur le dos, leur pain sous le bras. ... On reconnaissait les serruriers à leurs bourgerons bleus, les maçons à leurs cottes blanches, les peintres à leurs paletots ... à la porte des deux marchands de vin qui enlevaient leurs volets, des hommes ralentissaient le pas. ...

Gervaise s'entêta encore à la fenêtre pendant deux mortelles heures, jusqu'à huit heures. Les boutiques s'étaient ouvertes. Le flot de blouses descendant des hauteurs avait cessé. ... Aux ouvriers avaient succédé les ouvrières, les brunisseuses, les modistes, les fleuristes, se serrant dans leurs minces vêtements, trottant le long des boulevards extérieurs; elles allaient par bandes de trois ou quatre, causaient vivement, avec de légers

---

cost 200 dollars and that in *L'Assommoir* 200 francs, and both couples had to make up the deficit. After some time they were able to pay their debts, and then, like all happily married people, the two couples began to dream of a house of their own. Of course, the house they wanted was occupied, but at last they came across "une trouvaille," "an ideal home," situated not far from their places of work. But in the midst of this happiness, the peripeteia came like a thunderbolt from a clear sky: in *McTeague*, a letter from the authorities informed the hero that he had to give up practicing, because he had no diploma from a dental college; and in *L'Assommoir*, an accident happened to Coupeau, who fell from the roof of a house. In both cases, the accidents befell the heroes, who had to give up their jobs. This circumstance contributed to their ultimate ruin. Coupeau, formerly temperate and industrious, became unwilling to work and began to spend his time in saloons. McTeague, too, grew idle, and the day usually ended with some half dozen glasses of whisky at Joe Frenna's saloon. Earlier neither of the men had tasted strong drink. To support the families the women had to work and, although both couples moved into cheaper and cheaper lodgings, it was hard to make both ends meet. Finally the two women became scrubwomen. The reappearance of the old lovers, Lantier and Marcus, contributed also to the catastrophe.

Another parallel shows that Lantier was involved in politics, as was Marcus in *McTeague*. Early in *L'Assommoir* we learn that Lantier "s'occupe beaucoup de politique." He talked "du mal de cette crapule de Bonaparte." *Œuvres*, VIII, 6. In Norris's novel Marcus dazzled McTeague with his stock of half-truths of political economy—"phrases he had caught at some of the ward 'rallies' and 'ratification meetings.'" *Compl. Works*, VIII, 11.

rires et des regards luisants jetés autour d'elles. ... Puis, les employés étaient passés ... des jeunes gens efflanqués ... de petits vieux ... Et les boulevards avaient pris leur paix du matin; les rentiers du voisinage se promenaient au soleil; les mères, en cheveux, jupes sales, berçaient dans leurs bras des enfants en maillots, qu'elles changeaient sur les bancs; toute une marmaille mal mouchée, débraillée, se bousculait, se traînait par terre, au milieu de piaulements, de rires et de pleurs.[1]

Norris introduced Polk Street in the same manner, by letting McTeague walk up to the window, observing the street with its corner drug stores, barber shops, cheap restaurants, and its procession of workers. This is the awakening of Polk Street:

Bull-like, he heaved himself laboriously up, and, going to the window, stood looking down into the street. ...

On week days the street was very lively. It woke to its work about seven o'clock, at the time when the newsboys made their appearance together with the day labourers. The labourers went trudging past in a straggling file—plumbers' apprentices, their pockets stuffed with sections of lead pipe, tweezers, and pliers; carpenters, carrying nothing but their little pasteboard lunch baskets painted to imitate leather; gangs of street workers, their overalls soiled with yellow clay, their picks and long-handled shovels over their shoulders; plasterers, spotted with lime from head to foot. This little army of workers, tramping steadily in one direction, met and mingled with other toilers of a different description ... all along the street could be seen the shop keepers taking down their shutters.

Between seven and eight the street breakfasted. ... A little later, following in the path of the day labourers, came the clerks and shop girls, dressed with a certain cheap smartness, always in a hurry, glancing apprehensively at the power-house clock. Their employers followed an hour or so later—on the cable cars for the most part—whiskered gentlemen with huge stomachs, reading the morning papers with great gravity; bank cashiers and insurance clerks with flowers in their buttonholes.

At the same time the school children invaded the street, filling the air with a clamour of shrill voices, stopping at the stationers' shops ...

Towards eleven o'clock the ladies from the great avenue a block above Polk Street made their appearance, promenading the sidewalks leisurely, deliberately. They were at their morning's marketing. They were handsome women, beautifully dressed.[2]

There seems to be no reason to doubt that Norris had *L'Assommoir* in mind when composing the first chapter of *McTeague*. Norris, like Zola, described the laborers coming in a line, and then

---

[1] *Œuvres*, VIII, 4–8.
[2] *Compl. Works*, VIII, 4–6.

followed a detailed enumeration of different categories of workers, and then employers, wealthy gentlemen, ladies, and children. One category was added to the file by Norris, namely the newsboys, who appeared at the same time as the workers. Zola's description of the street is perhaps more graphic and artistic than Norris's, because the former depicted the street and its people by letting Gervaise, in agony, from her window try to catch sight of her belated husband on the boulevard. There is no such motivation in Norris's scene.

Zola appears to have been an inspiration also for other episodes. The description of the marriage ceremony in L'Assommoir resembles in many ways the marriage scene in McTeague.[1] The atmosphere during the wedding in both novels was rather unecclesiastical. The ceremony was performed at lightning speed "pendant une absence du bon Dieu." Irritating noises heightened the impression of secularity. Zola gave the following picture of the ceremony:

... l'église s'emplissait du piétinement des sacristains, du vacarme des chaises remises en place. On devait préparer le maître-autel pour quelque fête, car on entendait le marteau des tapissiers clouant des tentures. Et, au fond de la chapelle perdue, dans la poussière d'un coup de balai donné par le bedeau, le prêtre à l'air maussade promenait vivement ses mains sèches sur les têtes inclinées de Gervaise et de Coupeau, et semblait les unir au milieu d'un déménagement, pendant une absence du bon Dieu, entre deux messes sérieuses.[2]

And Norris described the attendant noises as follows: "Outside the noises of the street rose to the windows in muffled undertones, a cable car rumbled past, a newsboy went by chanting the evening papers; from somewhere in the building itself came a persistent noise of sawing."[3]

Moreover, in L'Assommoir the haphazard ceremony was over quite abruptly, leaving behind a sense of disappointment:

Et les formalités, la lecture du Code, les questions posées, la signature des pièces, furent expédiées si rondement, qu'ils se regardèrent, se croyant volés d'une bonne moitié de la cérémonie. . . . Quand la noce eut de nouveau signé sur un registre, à la sacristie, et qu'elle se retrouva en plein

---

[1] Cf. pp. 305–6.
[2] Œuvres, VIII, 70.
[3] Compl. Works, VIII, 142.

soleil, sous le porche, elle resta un instant là, ahurie, essoufflée d'avoir été menée au galop.

—Voilà! dit Coupeau, avec un rire gêné.

Il se dandinait, il ne trouvait rien là de rigolo. Pourtant, il ajouta:

—Ah bien! ça ne traîne pas. Ils vous envoient ça en quatre mouvements ... C'est comme chez les dentistes: on n'a pas le temps de crier ouf! ils marient sans douleur.

—Oui, oui, de la belle ouvrage, murmura Lorilleux en ricanant. Ça se bâcle en cinq minutes et ça tient bon toute la vie ...[1]

Norris followed the same procedure:

> All at once the ceremony was over before anyone expected it. ... She [Trina]—perhaps McTeague as well—felt that there was a certain inadequateness about the ceremony. Was that all there was to it? Did just those few muttered phrases make them man and wife? It had been over in a few moments, but it had bound them for life. Had not something been left out? Was not the whole affair cursory, superficial? It was disappointing.[2]

By depicting the wedding in such a hasty and worldly fashion, the writers, at all events Zola, intended to give a satirical picture of the servants of the church. Moreover, in both novels the ceremonies became symbolic of coming evil.

Furthermore, the feasts following upon the wedding ceremonies exhibit many similar points. The dinner was announced in the following casual way in L'Assommoir: "Ah! zut! cria Coupeau, mettons-nous à table."[3] And in McTeague: "'To der table!' commanded Mr. Sieppe."[4] The guests took their seats in a haphazard manner while making a tremendous noise. In L'Assommoir:

> Alors, la noce, très égayée, s'attabla avec un grand bruit de chaises. Gervaise était entre Lorilleux et M. Madinier, et Coupeau, entre Mme Fauconnier et Mme Lorilleux. Les autres convives se placèrent à leur goût, parce que ça finissait toujours par des jalousies et des disputes, lorsqu'on indiquait les couverts. Boche se glissa près de Mme Lerat.[5]

And in McTeague: "The company sat down with a great clatter, Trina at the foot, the dentist at the head, the others arranged themselves in haphazard fashion. But it happened that Marcus

---

[1] Œuvres, VIII, 69–70.
[2] Compl. Works, VIII, 142–3.
[3] Œuvres, VIII, 85.
[4] Compl. Works, VIII, 144.
[5] Œuvres, VIII, 85.

Schouler crowded into the seat beside Selina, toward which Old Grannis was directing himself."[1] In *L'Assommoir* there were two waiters at the table, and in *McTeague* the guests were attended by Maria Macapa and a hired waiter from a restaurant. In Zola's novel the glutton's role played by Mes-Bottes corresponds to that of Heise in *McTeague*, though on a minor scale. In *L'Assommoir* Mme Boche and mère Coupeau took care of the children during the meal, and in Norris's novel it was Miss Baker who looked after the boys. The atmosphere during the dinner was vulgar, grotesque even, in both novels. Plates of food were brought in and quickly devoured. Everybody ate and drank for the sake of eating and drinking. The air was acrid, heavy with cooking and perspiration. Norris depicted the dinner in a manner closely related to Zola's:

For two hours the guests ate; their faces red, their elbows wide, the perspiration beading their foreheads. All around the table one saw the same incessant movements of jaws and heard the same uninterrupted sound of chewing. Three times Heise passed his plate for more roast goose. Mr. Sieppe devoured the calf's head with long breaths of content-ment; McTeague ate for the sake of eating, without choice; everything within reach of his hands found its way into his enormous mouth. . . . Soon the room became very warm, a faint moisture appeared upon the windows, the air was heavy with the smell of cooked food. . . .

As the evening wore on, the gas and two lamps were lit. The company were still eating. The men, gorged with food, had unbuttoned their vests. McTeague's cheeks were distended, his eyes wide, his huge, salient jaw moved with a machine-like regularity; at intervals he drew a series of short breaths through his nose. Mrs. Sieppe wiped her forehead with her napkin. . . .

At last that great supper was over, everything had been eaten; the enorm-ous roast goose had dwindled to a very skeleton. Mr. Sieppe had reduced the calf's head to a mere skull; a row of empty champagne bottles— "dead soldiers," as the facetious waiter had called them—lined the mantel-piece. Nothing of the stewed prunes remained but the juice, which was given to Owgooste and the twins. The platters were as clean as if they had been washed; crumbs of bread, potato parings, nut-shells, and bits of cake littered the table; coffee and ice-cream stains and spots of congealed gravy marked the position of each plate. It was a devastation, a pillage; the table presented the appearance of an abandoned battlefield.[2]

---

[1] *Compl. Works*, VIII, 144–5.

[2] *Ibid.*, pp. 146–9. It has been noted earlier that Garland and Crane were also influenced by Zola's descriptions of meals, but none of them, not even Crane in his picture of a drinking orgy, came as close to Zola's method as did Norris. See pp. 236–7, 274–6.

This picture given by Norris of the supper is strongly reminiscent of the wedding feast in *L'Assommoir*, as well as of the famous goose dinner in the same novel. The goose appeared also in Norris's novel. The goose dinner in *L'Assommoir* ended with singing, and Mme Lerat sang "L'enfant du bon Dieu" in a melancholy way; similarly, in *McTeague* the guests intoned "Nearer, My God, to Thee," but "They sang in very slow time. The song became a dirge, a lamentable, prolonged wail of distress."[1] It should, however, be pointed out that Norris, in contradistinction to Zola, carefully avoided all indecencies and obscene allusions.

In addition to similarities of characterization, plot, and episodes between *McTeague* and Zola's two novels, there are also affinities between the subplot of *McTeague* and an incident in *La Bête humaine*. The general motive underlying the subplot was avarice. Zerkow married Maria Macapa only to be able to listen again and again to her story of a set of gold plates, hoping to find it some day, for Maria had told Zerkow that she had hidden it somewhere. He believed that the treasure was to be found in his junk shop, and he searched for it everywhere, night and day, but in vain. Finally he murdered his wife. The handling of this subplot may have been suggested by an episode in *La Bête humaine*, where a signalman, named Misard, lived with his wife, Phasie, to whom a legacy of a thousand francs had been given by her father. She had hidden it and refused to hand it over to her husband. Slowly he poisoned her to death. Although he searched everywhere, he was not able to find the treasure. After the death of his wife, Misard employed an old woman of the neighborhood, La Ducloux, to help him, and in the end she induced him to marry her by pretending that she had discovered the secret hoard. The motive underlying both episodes was greed. The hidden treasure, real or not, was never found, despite frantic searching. The description of the maniacal seeking for the lost treasure is similar in both books. This is Misard's pursuit: "Je [Flore] l'ai entendu, la nuit, qui tapait dans tous les murs."[2] And again: ". . . il [Misard] se mit à quatre pattes . . . Plusieurs carreaux étaient descellés, il les arracha. Rien, toujours rien!"[3] "Et un bruit inaccoutumé lui ayant fait prêter

---

[1] *Ibid.*, p. 150.
[2] *Œuvres*, XVIII, 43.
[3] *Ibid.*, p. 279.

l'oreille, elle comprit que Misard, avec une pioche, était en train
de fouiller le sol battu de la cuisine."[1] Zerkow was as maniacal
as Misard in his seeking:

> And at night Maria would sometimes wake to find Zerkow gone from
> the bed, and would see him burrowing into some corner by the light of
> his dark lantern ... "I'll find it. It's here somewheres, hid somewheres
> in this house." ... "I woke up about an hour ago," Maria explained, "and
> Zerkow wasn't in bed; maybe he hadn't come to bed at all. He was down
> on his knees by the sink, and he'd pried up some boards off the floor and
> was digging there."[2]

These quotations seem to confirm the assumption that Norris may
in part have been inspired by La Bête humaine for his subplot.
As to the half-mad greaser's obsession with the set of a hundred
golden plates, Norris may have heard such a story and found it
suitable for his novel. Then he linked it with the Zola episode,
but gave the story a more dramatic ending through the cruel
murder of Maria and the suicide of Zerkow.[3]

The influence of Zola is predominant in McTeague and shows
that Norris consciously aimed at adapting Zola's naturalistic
method to native American material.

Vandover and the Brute, written during Norris's year at Harvard, when he was at work on *McTeague*, reveals similar sources
of inspiration. Charles G. Norris said of *Vandover and the Brute*
that "The influence of Émile Zola is evident throughout the
story."[4] This is true, for in technique and characterization Norris's novel presented similarities with Zola's works. Like *L'As-*

---

[1] *Ibid.*, p. 285.

[2] *Compl. Works*, VIII, 208–10.

[3] Norris was perhaps also indebted to Zola for the symbolism of *McTeague*.
See Frederic Taber Cooper, *Some American Story Tellers* (London, 1912),
pp. 309 ff. Biencourt has noted most of the parallels recorded here between
McTeague on the one hand and *L'Assommoir* and *La Bête humaine* on the
other, but our emphasis is in many cases different; whereas Biencourt has
devoted only three lines (*op. cit.*, p. 197) to the important parallels between the
opening scenes of *McTeague* and *L'Assommoir*, I have considered them worthy
of a more elaborate treatment. In addition, Biencourt has noted parallels which
seem to me less convincing, for instance, those between Trina and Catherine
Maheu (*op. cit.*, pp. 196–7), and those between Maria Macapa and Sidonie
Macquart (*op. cit.*, p. 198).

[4] *Compl. Works*, V, vii.

sommoir and *McTeague*, the novel told of the slow but inevitable decay and degradation of the individual.

Not only does the title of *Vandover and the Brute* recall that of *La Bête humaine*, but the theme is also reminiscent of that of Zola's book: the fierce struggle within man between his better and lower self. In the end, the lower self, the brute, won the battle. Generally, the brute in Vandover never became so violent, so homicidal, as in the characters of *La Bête humaine*. But the main idea of the evil brute stirring in man was pivotal in both novels.

Vandover's disintegration[1] was brought about primarily because his personality was too flexible, too easily imposed upon. His yielding disposition led him to submit to the dictatorship of stronger friends. Vandover had the same pliable nature as Gervaise in *L'Assommoir*, whom he resembles in many respects. Like her, Vandover was able to adapt himself easily to new environments, which gradually molded him in accordance with their unlovely patterns. Circumstances, too, conspired against them. Gervaise "se sentait prise d'une sueur devant l'avenir et se comparait à un sou lancé en l'air retombant pile ou face, selon les hasards du pavé."[2] This was true also of the ill-fated Vandover. In the end their weak temperaments brought about their ruin.

Before Vandover reached the stage of cleaning filthy tenement apartments, he had suffered much. He had had intermittent attacks of violent terror, bordering on hysteria, and he began to fear that he was going mad. The effects of terror were elaborately described by Norris, and in many ways this description reminds us of the picture given by Zola of Thérèse and Laurent suffering from various attacks of terror and hysteria after the murder of Camille. There are, in addition, some minor parallels between Vandover and Laurent. Like Laurent, Norris's hero was of an indolent disposition: "... he loved to eat good things, he loved to be warm, he loved to sleep."[3] Both were, moreover, painters who, from various causes lost their artistic talents.[4] Whenever Laurent tried to paint a portrait, the result was always the same:

---

[1] See also pp. 199–201.
[2] *Œuvres*, VIII, 47.
[3] *Compl. Works*, V, 27. Cf. McTeague p. 280 of this study.
[4] Cf. Oswald in Ibsen's *Ghosts* and Little Billee in *Trilby*. See p. 391 n. 4.

the ghostly head of the drowned Camille. Similarly, Vandover could only paint the hideous spawns of the brute within him.[1] The effects of dissipation made Vandover insane, just as the effects of alcohol made Coupeau insane. Vandover's attacks of *lycanthropy-Mathesis* resemble the fits of Coupeau, who had "un déménagement complet, des idées de se casser la tête contre le mur, des hurlements qui empêchaient les autres malades de dormir."[2] "Vandover started up, striving to keep himself in hand, fighting against a wild desire to rush about from wall to wall, shrieking and waving his arms."[3] Vandover's dog-act was perhaps partly suggested by the terrible picture of Coupeau in the Asylum of Sainte-Anne. Compare, for instance: "Imagine-toi, je [Coupeau] voyais des rats, je courais à quatre pattes..."[4] Vandover ran "along the floor upon the palms of his hands and his toes."[5]

But whereas Coupeau died in an asylum after an attack of *delirium tremens* of more than usual violence, Vandover had a somewhat less terrible ending. To some extent, Norris seems to have been inspired by the development of Gervaise in *L'Assommoir* for his last chapter of *Vandover and the Brute*. Before her miserable death Gervaise became a scrubwoman, and to add to her humiliation she had to clean the rooms and the laundry, which earlier had belonged to herself, but had then been taken over by Virginie and Lantier. Similarly, Vandover had to clean filthy tenement cottages, built on the soil that his father and he himself formerly possessed. In *L'Assommoir*, Virginie and Lantier (old friends of Gervaise's) pointed out to Gervaise dirty spots, which she had forgotten to remove. A similar supervision occurred in *Vandover and the Brute*, where Geary (an old friend of Vandover's) and the new tenants saw to it that Vandover did his work carefully. It is worth quoting the following passages to illustrate the parallels:

---

[1] Biencourt has linked Vandover with Gervaise, but he has failed to note Vandover's debt to Laurent in *Thérèse Raquin*.

[2] *Œuvres*, VIII, 349.

[3] *Compl. Works*, V, 210.

[4] *Œuvres*, VIII, 351.

[5] *Compl. Works*, V, 242. Biencourt (p. 205) has called attention to a similar scene in *La Conquête de Plassans* (p. 327). Note also Kipling's story *The Mark of the Beast*, which may also have served as a pattern.

—Dites donc, madame Coupeau! cria Virginie qui suivait le travail de la laveuse, les lèvres pincées, vous laissez de la crasse, là-bas, dans ce coin. Frottez-moi donc un peu mieux ça! Gervaise obéit. Elle retourna dans le coin, recommença à laver. Agenouillée par terre, au milieu de l'eau sale, elle se pliait en deux, les épaules saillantes, les bras violets et raidis. ...

—Plus on met de l'huile de coude, plus ça reluit, dit sentencieusement Lantier, la bouche pleine de pastilles. ...

—Encore un peu à droite. Maintenant, faites bien attention à la boiserie ... Vous savez, je n'ai pas été très contente, samedi dernier. Les taches étaient restées.[1]

Vandover was as humiliated as Gervaise:

Suddenly the burnisher's wife came out upon the front steps, looking down into the little garden, calling for Vandover. She was not pretty; she had a nose like a man and her chin was broad.

"Say, there," she called to Vandover, "do you mean to say that you've finished inside here?"

"Yes," answered Vandover, straightening up, nodding his head. "Yes, I've finished."

"Well, just come in here and look at this."

Vandover followed her into the little parlour. Her sister was there, very fat, smelling somehow of tallow candles and cooked cabbage; near by stood the little boy still eating his bread and butter.

"Look at that baseboard," exclaimed the burnisher's wife. "You never touched that, I'll bet a hat." Vandover did not answer; he brought in the pail of water, and soaping his scrubbing brush, went down again on his hands and knees, washing the paint on the baseboard where the burnisher's wife indicated. The two women stood by, looking on and directing his movements.[2]

It is quite possible that Norris himself saw such a cleaning scene in real life, because his father had built and sold cheap flats in San Francisco. But as regards artistic composition and execution, the quotation clearly shows Norris's debt to Zola.

Finally the scene in which the vessel "Mazatlan" was wrecked reminds us of the last agony of "la Lison," the locomotive, in *La Bête humaine*. Zola gave the following picture of the engine:

La Lison, renversée sur les reins, le ventre ouvert, perdait sa vapeur, par les robinets arrachés, les tuyaux crevés, en des souffles qui grondaient, pareils à des râles furieux de géante. Une haleine blanche en sortait, inépuisable, roulant d'épais tourbillons au ras du sol; pendant que, du

---

[1] *Œuvres*, VIII, 387.

[2] *Compl. Works*, V, 305. This parallel has also been observed by Biencourt.

294

foyer, les braises tombées, rouge [*sic*] comme le sang même de ses entrailles, ajoutaient leurs fumées noires. La cheminée, dans la violence du choc, était entrée en terre; à l'endroit où il avait porté, le châssis s'était rompu, faussant les deux longerons; et, les roues en l'air, semblable à une cavale monstrueuse, décousue par quelque formidable coup de corne, la Lison montrait ses bielles tordues, ses cylindres cassés, ses tiroirs et leurs ex- centriques écrasés, toute une affreuse plaie bâillant au plein air, par où l'âme continuait de sortir, avec un fracas d'enragé désespoir.[1]

And again:

... et son âme s'en allait avec la force qui la faisait vivante, cette ha- leine immense dont elle ne parvenait pas à se vider toute. La géante éven- trée s'apaisa encore, s'endormit peu à peu d'un sommeil très doux, finit par se taire. Elle était morte.[2]

And this is the last agony of the "Mazatlan":

It was no longer the *Mazatlan*, no longer a thing of wood and iron, but some strange huge living creature that was dying there under his feet, some enormous brute that was plunging and writhing in its last agony, its belly ripped open by a hidden enemy that struck from beneath, its entrails torn out, its life-breath going from it in great gasps of steam. Sud- denly its bellow collapsed; the great bulk was sinking lower; the enemy was in its very vitals. The great hoarse roar dwindled to a long death rattle, then to a guttural rasp; all at once it ceased; the brute was dead— the *Mazatlan* was a wreck.[3]

The quotations indicate that Norris probably had "la Lison" in mind when describing the wreck of the vessel.

Three of Zola's novels, *Germinal, La Bête humaine* and *La Terre*,[4] in particular, seem to have influenced *The Octopus*. Let us first compare Norris's novel with *Germinal*. Both are studies of the ever-existing struggle between capital and labor. In Zola's novel the conflict between the miners and the mining company ended with the ruin of the former. Similarly, the conflict between the farmers and the railroad ended with the ruin of the farmers, sev- eral of whom were killed in an armed clash. It was no use for the miners and the farmers to oppose the companies backed by capital, because capital meant strength. Mme Maheu always re-

---

[1] *Œuvres*, XVIII, 294.
[2] *Ibid.*, p. 301.
[3] *Compl. Works*, V, 117-18. This parallel has not been noted by Biencourt.
[4] Biencourt, too, has focused his interest on these three novels. For back- ground of *The Octopus*, see pp. 120-1, 173-6.

peated that "on ne gagnait rien à se buter contre la Compagnie."[1]
In *The Octopus* Annixter often stated that *"You can't buck against
the railroad."*[2]

In the first chapter of *Germinal* Zola described how Étienne
Lantier, a stranger in the vicinity, was on his way toward Montsou
and, on his arrival, stopped and talked with some of the workers
in the Voreux Pit, thus introducing some of the chief characters
of the book. Norris opened *The Octopus* more or less in the same
manner, letting Presley, a poet, who stayed as a guest at Magnus
Derrick's farm and who sympathized with the ranchers, cross the
ranching country on a bicycle and meet various persons. Moreover,
both books ended in the same way. Disappointed and with broken
health, Étienne bade farewell to his friends in the village and left
for Paris. Similarly in *The Octopus*, Presley, mentally and physically
wrecked, said good-bye to his old friends in the valley and sailed
for India.

Étienne and Presley also had other likenesses. At a saloon Étienne
was brought into contact with Souvarine, an anarchist, who filled
him with the principles of anarchy. Presley, too, became interested
in an anarchist named Caraher, a saloon-keeper, who impressed
Presley with his ideas and made him a *réactionnaire*. Both Étienne
and Presley made revolutionary speeches to spell-bound audiences.
But in the end both failed in their tasks because they were at heart
outsiders.[3] Presley abandoned his socialistic ideas altogether, while
Étienne started out for Paris to take part in a communist rising.

In addition, Norris's description of the sumptuous dinner contrasted with Mrs. Hooven's *via dolorosa* in one of the last chapters
of *The Octopus* may be compared with the following episode in
Germinal. Hennebeau, general manager of the Montsou Mining
Company, and his wife gave a lunch for the Grégoires, their daughter Cécile, and Paul Négrel. Mme Hennebeau had filled her house
with expensive tapestry and magnificent furniture, "tout un luxe
d'art, dont on parla jusqu'à Lille."[4] There were "des fauteuils
Henri II, des chaises Louis XV, un cabinet italien du XVIIe

---

[1] *Œuvres*, XIV, 125.

[2] *Compl. Works*, I, 100.

[3] Biencourt has failed to note both characters' common debt to Neschdanov.
See pp. 332 ff.

[4] *Œuvres*, XIV, 214.

siècle ... Les tapis d'Orient semblaient les [the miners] lier aux pieds de leur haute laine."[1] The diningroom boasted Flemish tapestry and oak furniture. The warmth of the room was agreeable, and there was an odor of pineapple in the air. Outside, a biting December wind was blowing; moreover, a strike had started the same morning, for the conditions of the miners were unbearable. They had not even bread for themselves and their children. In addition, through an accident in the mine Maheu had been killed and his son Jeanlin had broken his legs. Consequently the Maheu family was on the brink of starvation. When the guests tasted the *hors d'œuvres*, they heard the hungry strikers' cries, and during the lunch the guests were afraid of being disturbed by the striking miners outside. "Un rond de saucisson" was served, and after the "œufs brouillés aux truffes" there appeared "des truites de rivière." A servant brought "des perdreaux rôtis" and filled the glasses with "chambertin." During the whole meal there were jokes and pleasant laughter, while the industrial crisis was discussed. When the dessert appeared, the guests altogether forgot the strike. The ladies began discussing a recipe "au sujet de l'ananas, qu'on déclara également exquis."[2] The scene illustrated the glaring contrast between the luxury of the general manager of the Monstou Mining Company and the miserable life led by their destitute miners. While the lunch went on and course followed upon course, outside the victims of the strike were clamoring for food and justice.

Let us compare this scene with a similar one in *The Octopus*. Presley accompanied the Cedarquists to a dinner with the Gerard family. Mr. Gerard was one of the vice-presidents of the P. and S.W. Railroad. In a confused daze, Presley entered the luxurious house. Then he was ushered into a large room

of excessive loftiness. Flat, rectangular pillars of a rose-tinted, variegated marble rose from the floor almost flush with the walls, finishing off at the top with gilded capitals of a Corinthian design, which supported the ceiling. ... Between the pillars around the sides of the room were hangings of silk, the design—of a Louis Quinze type—of beautiful simplicity and faultless taste. The fireplace was a marvel. ...

The windows of the room were heavily draped in sombre brocade and *écru* lace ...

---

[1] *Ibid.*, p. 229.

[2] *Ibid.*, p. 224.

Under foot, the carpet had all the softness of texture of grass; skins (one of them of an enormous polar bear) and rugs of silk velvet were spread upon the floor. .... A row of electric bulbs let into the frieze of the walls, between the golden capitals, and burning dimly behind hemispheres of clouded glass, threw a subdued light over the whole scene.[1]

The dinner was served in a superb dining room, on three sides of which "ran a continuous picture, an oil painting," representing the personages in the *Roman de la Rose.*

Against the side of the wall unoccupied by the picture stood a sideboard of gigantic size that once had adorned the banquet hall of an Italian palace of the late Renaissance. It was black with age, and against its sombre surfaces glittered an array of heavy silver dishes and heavier cutglass bowls and goblets.[2]

The dinner was excellent, from the *hors d'œuvres* to the wines of the 1815 vintage. Norris carefully enumerated the names of the French dishes served.

The effect of the dinner was heightened by the glaring contrast with the unhappy fate of the two victims of the railroad, Mrs. Hooven and her little daughter, Hilda. First, we see the pleased faces of beautiful women in elaborate toilets tasting Londonderry pheasant, *rissolettes à la Pompadour*, and sipping Château Latour in the sparkling light of electric bulbs. The next moment, we see Mrs. Hooven and her daughter, wretchedly dressed and starving, trudging along the streets numbed with pain and stomach cramps. The evening was cold, and the trade wind from off the ocean set the street lamps fluttering and dancing. Again the scene changed. Mr. Lampert, who posed as an epicure, was eating stuffed artichokes and discussing asparagus with Mrs. Gerard, who could not think of eating ordinary market asparagus "that has been fingered by Heaven knows how many hands."[3] In the street, Mrs. Hooven had fallen. Little Hilda shook her mother by the shoulder, and at last she could hear the faint words: " 'I'm sick. Go to schleep. .... Sick. .... Noddings to eat.' "[4] The two scenes changed continually, showing now a glimpse of the dinner drawing toward its end, and now a glimpse of Mrs. Hooven's last struggle for life, until ultimately

---

[1] *Compl. Works*, II, 300–1.

[2] *Ibid.*, p. 311.

[3] *Ibid.*, p. 320.

[4] *Ibid.*

the curtain fell on the words: "'My best compliments for a delightful dinner'" contrasted with "'It's no use . . . she has been dead some time—exhaustion from starvation.'"[1]

The central idea of the scenes quoted seems to be the same in both writers: extreme luxury contrasted with extreme poverty; these poor people were thrown into utter misery because of the capitalists, whose victims they were. Further, the dinner described by Norris had a refined French atmosphere. The language spoken at table was mingled with French words, for instance: *Nous voici—fin gourmet—réactionnaire—entends-tu, ma chérie, l'esprit de notre jeune Lamartine.* On three sides of the luxurious dining room in *The Octopus* there ran a large picture. In *Germinal* the lunch was served in a "salle tendue de tapisserie flamandes." Moreover, one of the guests in *Germinal* mentioned that "Il y a eu une famine dans l'Inde."[2] In *The Octopus* the Cedarquists related that they had "started a movement to send a whole shipload of wheat to the starving people in India."[3]

If it can be said that Norris derived some impulse for this episode from *Germinal*,[4] he nevertheless achieved a more artistic effect with his material than Zola. The sharp contrasts afforded by the two pictures, one light the other dark, conjured up by Norris were carefully played off against each other to a dramatic and telling climax.

Reminiscences from *La Bête humaine* are found in *The Octopus*. The descriptions of the trains, which went dashing through the landscape, making the earth quiver and shake, were doubtless inspired by Zola's vivid pictures of the trains in *La Bête humaine*.

Moreover, part of the Dyke episode was, no doubt, derived from an incident in *La Bête humaine*. When Dyke in his flight from his followers had climbed the detached locomotive, steaming on the up line at the Guadalajara station, the railroad people meant to derail the engine, but they forgot "the automatic semaphore that worked

---

[1] *Ibid.*, p. 322.

[2] *Œuvres*, XIV, 219.

[3] *Compl. Works*, II, 314.

[4] Biencourt (p. 221) has noted a similar scene in Zola's *Paris*. *Œuvres*, XXVI, 42 ff. Cf. also the scene in *L'Assommoir* depicting Gervaise starving and destitute. walking the streets. See p. 262 of this study.

simultaneously with the movement of the rails."[1] Consequently, Dyke had time to stop, and there was no accident. A similar futile attempt at derailing a train occurs in Zola's novel, where Flore tried to arrange a railroad accident in order to murder Jacques and Séverine, but she, too, forgot the automatic semaphore and no accident ensued.

Another scene, unquestionably a borrowing from *La Bête humaine*, is the picture of the released engine without a driver rushing toward "the camp of the enemy." In Zola's novel a struggle between Jacques, the engine driver, and the stoker caused the two men to fall from the engine, while the train, crowded with drunken and singing soldiers, dashed frantically along toward the frontier:

> Et la machine, libre de toute direction, roulait, roulait toujours. Enfin, la rétive, la fantasque, pouvait céder à la fougue de sa jeunesse, ainsi qu'une cavale indomptée encore, échappée des mains du gardien, galopant par la campagne rase ... et l'épouvante glaça la gare, lorsqu'elle vit passer, dans un vertige de fumée et de flamme, ce train fou, cette machine sans mécanicien ni chauffeur, ces wagons à bestiaux emplis de troupiers qui hurlaient des refrains patriotiques. Ils allaient à la guerre, c'était pour être plus vite là-bas, sur les bords du Rhin.[2]

It is worth quoting the following passage to see how closely Norris followed Zola in his animation of lifeless objects:

> The released engine, alone, unattended, drew slowly away from him [Dyke], jolting ponderously over the rail joints. As he watched it go, a certain indefinite sense of abandonment, even in that moment, came over Dyke. His last friend, that also had been his first, was leaving him. He remembered that day, long ago, when he had opened the throttle of his first machine. To-day, it was leaving him alone, his last friend turning against him. Slowly it was going back toward Bonneville, to the shops of the Railroad, the camp of the enemy, that enemy that had ruined him and wrecked him.[3]

It should also be noted that Jaques as well as Dyke referred to the locomotives as their best friends. In Zola's novel the train dashed toward the frontier, whereas in Norris's book the engine rolled toward the town of Bonneville, "the camp of the enemy."

---

[1] *Compl. Works*, II, 190. The parallel has not been noted by Biencourt.

[2] *Œuvres*, XVIII, 370.

[3] *Compl. Works*, II, 192. Biencourt has not observed this parallel. Cf. Crane's use of the same device. See p. 276.

In *The Octopus*, Norris probably aimed at painting a vast picture of rural life in the manner of *La Terre*. As a matter of fact he included a great variety of people and described their everyday life and their festivities, their pleasures and their sorrows. The epic breadth of *The Octopus*, the panoramic scenes of ploughing, sowing, and harvesting, all recall *La Terre*.[1] As the central symbol for his novel Zola chose the earth, whereas Norris took the wheat. The earth on the one hand, and the wheat on the other, caused tragedy among groups of people: "Il y avait aussi la douleur, le sang, les larmes, tout ce qu'on souffre et tout ce qui révolte, Françoise tuée, Fouan tué, les coquins triomphants, la vermine sanguinaire et puante des villages déshonorant et rongeant la terre."[2] And in *The Octopus*:

Harran dead, Annixter dead, Broderson dead, Dabney dead . . .[3]

Men—motes in the sunshine—perished, were shot down in the very noon of life, hearts were broken, little children started in life lamentably handicapped; young girls were brought to a life of shame; old women died in the heart of life for lack of food. In that little, isolated group of human insects, misery, death, and anguish spun like a wheel of fire.[4]

But in spite of all the tears, pains, and tragedies—of little consequence "dans la grande méchanique des étoiles et du soleil"— in the end the earth and the wheat triumphed. In *La Terre*:

Toujours la terre, la nourrice, serait là, qui nourrirait ceux qui l'ensemenceraient. Elle avait l'espace et le temps, elle donnait tout de même du blé, en attendant qu'on sût lui en faire donner davantage. . . . Et la terre seule demeure l'immortelle, la mère d'où nous sortons et où nous retournons, elle qu'on aime jusqu'au crime, qui refait continuellement de la vie pour son but ignoré, même avec nos abominations et nos misères.[5]

And in *The Octopus*:

But the WHEAT remained. Untouched, unassailable, undefiled, that mighty world-force, that nourisher of nations, wrapped in Nirvanic calm, indifferent to the human swarm, gigantic, resistless, moved onward in its appointed grooves. Through the welter of blood at the irrigating ditch, through the sham charity and shallow philanthropy of famine-relief com-

---

[1] Cf. the same technique used by Tolstoy in *Anna Karenina*. See also p. 343 n. 3.

[2] *Œuvres*, XVI, 516.

[3] *Compl. Works*, II, 259.

[4] *Ibid.*, p. 360.

[5] *Œuvres*, XVI, 515–16.

mittees, the great harvest of Los Muertos rolled like a flood from the Sierras to the Himalayas to feed thousands of starving scarecrows on the barren plains of India.[1]

It is probable that the optimistic note on which *La Terre* ended may to some extent account for the ray of hope toward the end of *The Octopus*.[2]

It is possible that *L'Argent* served to a certain degree as a model for Norris's novel of wheat speculation, *The Pit*. The main theme of Zola's novel is also speculation. Saccard, the hero, was irresistibly drawn toward the Bourse. He started a Universal bank, and was at first successful. He was a "Bull", and by means of advertising he succeeded in forcing up the shares of the bank to an unduly high price. The "Bears," however, began an attack on the bank, the price broke, the bank collapsed, and Saccard was ruined. Jadwin, too, was inevitably drawn into the troubled waters of the Pit. He was no longer an outsider. He turned "Bull', and by a combination of boldness and luck he established his corner. Bcause of an excessive production of wheat, he was finally beaten and ruined.

Apart from these similarities regarding plot, there are other resemblances between the two novels. The scene introducing the seething life of the Bourse was described as follows:

C'était l'heure active où la vie de Paris semble affluer sur cette place centrale, entre la rue Montmartre et la rue Richelieu, les deux artères engorgées qui charrient la foule. Des quatre carrefours, ouverts aux quatre angles de la place, des flots ininterrompus de voitures coulaient, sillonnant le pavé, au milieu des remous d'une cohue de piétons. Sans arrêt, les deux files des fiacres de la station, le long des grilles, se rompaient et se reformaient. . . . Envahis, les marches et le péristyle étaient noirs d'un fourmillement de redingotes; et, de la coulisse, installée déjà sous l'horloge et fonctionnant, montait la clameur de l'offre et de la demande, ce bruit de marée de l'agio, victorieux du grondement de la ville.[3]

---

[1] *Compl. Works*, II, 360.

[2] Cf. also the note of optimism toward the end of *Germinal*. See also p. 230 of this study.

In some instances Biencourt is liable to over-emphasize Norris's debt to Zola. Magnus Derrick, for example, owes perhaps more to Bernick in *Pillars of Society* than to père Fouan in *La Terre*. See Biencourt, *op. cit.*, p. 210. See also Chap. XIV, pp. 400–2.

[3] *Œuvres*, XIX, 19–20.

Norris set forth the surging life of the Board of Trade Building in the same way:

> It was about nine o'clock ... La Salle Street swarmed with the multitudinous life that seethed about the doors of the innumerable offices of brokers and commission men of the neighbourhood. To the right, in the peristyle of the Illinois Trust Building, groups of clerks, of messengers, of brokers, of clients, and of depositors formed and broke incessantly. To the left, where the façade of the Board of Trade blocked the street, the activity was astonishing, and in and out of the swing doors of its entrance streamed an incessant tide of coming and going. All the life of the neighbourhood seemed to centre at this point—the entrance of the Board of Trade. Two currents that trended swiftly through La Salle and Jackson streets, and that fed, or were fed by, other tributaries that poured in through Fifth Avenue and through Clarke and Dearborn streets, met at this point—one setting in, the other out. The nearer the currents the greater their speed. Men ... seemed to accelerate their pace as they approached ... young men and boys ... flung themselves panting into the entrance of the Board, were engulfed in the turmoil of the spot, and disappeared with a sudden fillip into the gloom of the interior.[1]

In the quotations we recognize the same rhythm, the same seething and roaring life of the place; both authors used similar phraseology and metaphors.

Zola depicted vividly the clamor and thunder of the Bourse: "Derrière son [Saccard] dos, la clameur de la Bourse, le bruit de marée lointaine continuait."[2] Or: "La trépidation, le grondement de machine sous vapeur, grandissait, agitait la Bourse entière, dans un vacillement de flamme."[3] Or again: "Sur la place, l'agitation avait grandi, la clameur du jeu venait battre les trottoirs grouillant de monde, avec la violence débridée d'une marée haute."[4] Norris described the terrific turmoil of the Pit in similar terms: "The roar was appalling, the whirlpool was again unchained, the maelstrom was again unleashed."[5] Or: "But again and again the clamour broke out. It would die down for an instant ... only to burst out afresh as certain groups of traders started the pandemonium again, by the wild outcrying of their offers."[6]

---

[1] *Compl. Works*, IX, 72–3.
[2] *Œuvres*, XIX, 23.
[3] *Ibid.*, p. 29.
[4] *Ibid.*, p. 45.
[5] *Compl. Works*, IX, 357.
[6] *Ibid.*, p. 377.

In the great scene depicting the final phase of the crash of
"l'universelle" in *L'Argent*, Saccard, though defeated, was described as a brave man standing in the midst of a furious throng
of people with his head erect and a smile of defiance on his lips:

A cette minute, il fut vraiment superbe, toute sa mince personne bravait
la destinée, les yeux sans un battement, le visage têtu, seul contre le flot
de désespoir et de rancune qu'il sentait déjà monter contre lui. La salle
entière bouillonnait, débordait vers son pilier; des poings se serraient, des
bouches bégayaient des paroles mauvaises; et il avait gardé aux lèvres un
inconscient sourire, qu'on pouvait prendre pour une provocation.[1]

But suddenly he could not stand this strain any longer; he felt a
mist before his eyes and his legs gave way:

Ses sens seulement s'étaient comme émoussés, il n'avait plus la sensation
du sol, il croyait marcher sur un tapis de haute laine. De même, une
brume noyait ses yeux, une clameur faisait bourdonner ses oreilles.[2]

Norris drew a similar picture of Jadwin after his failure in cor-
nering the wheat. Jadwin was still the great man, the "Great
Bull," when he, though defeated, stood in the thick of the Pit.
As proud and as defiant as Saccard, Jadwin faced a sea of roaring
people:

There in the middle of the Pit, surrounded and assaulted by herd after
herd of wolves yelping for his destruction, he stood braced, rigid, upon
his feet, his head up, his hand, the great bony hand that once had held
the whole Pit in its grip, flung high in the air in a gesture of defiance . . .[3]

But Jadwin, iron to the end, stood erect, until suddenly under
the stress of the moment he felt something snap in his brain:

The murk behind his eyes had been suddenly pierced by a white flash.
The strange qualms and tiny nervous paroxysms of the last few months
all at once culminated in some indefinite, indefinable crisis, and the wheels
and cogs of all activities save one lapsed away and ceased.[4]

Jadwin's financial crash was accompanied by a physical breakdown, whereas Saccard soon recovered, though stunned and in
a daze when leaving the Bourse.

---

[1] *Œuvres*, XIX, 354.
[2] *Ibid.*, p. 356.
[3] *Compl. Works*, IX, 376.
[4] *Ibid.*

In *L'Argent* Caroline made a visit to Mazaud, a well-known broker, who had been ruined by speculation. When she arrived at his home he had just committed suicide by shooting himself with a revolver.[1] This incident has its counterpart in *The Pit*, where Laura visited the Cresslers. She found Cressler, the dealer in grain, a ruined man, dead in an arm-chair, "and as Laura touched him the head dropped upon the shoulder and showed the bullet hole in the temple just in front of the ear."[2]

There are similarities, too, between the last scenes of the two novels. After the crash Saccard had gone to Holland, where he again had thrown himself into "une affaire collosale, le dessèchement d'immenses marais."[3] Caroline was packing in order to leave for Rome. Likewise, *The Pit* ended with the preliminaries for a journey westwards, for Jadwin, having recovered, was ready to start business anew.

It seems probable that other works by Zola also served as models for *The Pit*. In outline and technique, the first chapter of Norris's novel has points in common with that of *Nana*. In each novel there is an elaborate description of a theater performance.[4] Zola chronicled the first night of "la Blonde Vénus," and Norris depicted a performance of the Italian Grand Opera Company. The descriptions of the performances filled the first chapter of the two novels. Zola opened his chapter by stating precisely the hour and the place of the performance: "A neuf heures, la salle du théâtre des Variétés était encore vide."[5] Norris used the same procedure, for he began: "At eight o'clock in the inner vestibule of the Auditorium Theatre ..."[6] The chief characters were introduced during the two performances. Both authors described elaborately the entire representation. The descriptions of the furious throng in the vestibule, where ladies in light-colored gowns and gentlemen in black overcoats made their way through the wicket, present some similarities. Both authors mentioned the bell telling the visitors that the performance was about to begin,

---

[1] *Œuvres*, XIX, 380 ff.
[2] *Compl. Works*, IX, 350.
[3] *Œuvres*, XIX, 428.
[4] Cf. also *Madame Bovary*, pp. 254 ff.
[5] *Œuvres*, X, 7.
[6] *Compl. Works*, IX, 1.

and both described in detail the stage and what was going on there, the different acts and entr'actes. There are quotations of the singing interspersed in the description of the performance. In *Nana*, for instance: "Et elle [Nana] entama son grand air:

> *Lorsque Vénus rôde le soir* ..."[1]

And in *The Pit*: "She [the prima donna] clasped her hands imploringly, supplicating him to leave her, exclaiming from time to time:

> '*Va via, va via—*
> *Vel chieco [sic] per pietà.*' "[2]

Moreover, Zola gave the following picture of the orchestra:

A leurs pupitres, les musiciens accordaient leurs instruments, avec des trilles légers de flûte, des soupirs étouffés de cor, des voix chantantes de violon, qui s'envolaient au milieu du brouhaha grandissant des voix.[3]

Norris used the same technique when depicting the sounds of the various instruments. His description is, however, more elaborate and graphic:

They [the musicians] settled themselves in front of their racks ... Soon they began to tune up, and a vague bourdon of many sounds—the subdued snarl of the cornets, the dull mutter of the bass viols, the liquid gurgling of the flageolets and wood-wind instruments, now and then pierced by the strident chirps and cries of the violins, rose into the air dominating the incessant clamour of conversation that came from all parts of the theatre.[4]

Finally, the marriage ceremony in *The Pit* has points in common with that of *L'Assommoir*.[5] In Zola's novel a thunderstorm, impending all day long, broke loose after the ceremony, and in *The Pit* the storm accompanied the ceremony. In *L'Assommoir*: "Il faisait très beau, un soleil du tonnerre, rôtissant les rues."[6] And again: "Alors, l'orage éclata avec une extrême violence. Pendant une demi-heure, l'eau tomba à seaux, la foudre gronda sans

---

[1] *Œuvres*, X, 20.
[2] *Compl. Works*, IX, 25.
[3] *Œuvres*, X, 15.
[4] *Compl. Works*, IX, 24.
[5] Cf. Norris's use of the same episode in *McTeague*, pp. 286–9.
[6] *Œuvres*, VIII, 68.

relâche."[1] And in *The Pit*: "But the weather on the wedding day was abominable. A warm drizzle, which had set in early in the morning, developed by eleven o'clock into a steady downpour, accompanied by sullen grumblings of very distant thunder."[2] Moreover, the atmosphere during the wedding in *L'Assommoir* was unecclesiastic, as has been noted earlier in this chapter. In *The Pit*, the ceremony, which took place in an Episcopalian church, was disturbed by various noises, and the place and its entire atmosphere was as uncanonical as that of Zola's novel:

> The janitor or sexton, a severe old fellow, who wore a skull cap and loose slippers, was making a great to-do with a pile of pew cushions in a remote corner . . . Page . . . found it all strangely unfamiliar. . . . In the organ loft a tuner was at work upon the organ, and from time to time the distant mumbling of the thunder was mingled with a sonorous, prolonged note from the pipes. . . . Last of all came the clerk, osseous, perfumed, a gardenia in the lapel of his frock-coat, terribly excited, and hurrying about on tiptoe, saying "Sh! Sh!" as a matter of principle.[3]

Moreover, the ceremony was disturbed by Isabel, who had the hiccoughs and who made Page giggle. The leaden skies, the heavy downpour of rain, and the worldly atmosphere on the wedding day gave a foreboding of evil for the two couples.

To sum up: Our three authors, Crane and Norris in particular, received an important impulse to a new way of writing from the novels of Zola, to whose work they responded to varying degrees, To record their experiences, Howells' type of realism no longer sufficed. They turned to Zola, whose writings, *en vogue* in the United States in the nineties, served to some extent as a model and a liberation for them. They seem to have adopted Zola as a guide and teacher whose works probably confirmed certain of their own ideas of life and society. In his novels they learned or were supported in their beliefs that two major factors, heredity and environment, often transformed man's life fundamentally. Besides these ideas, treated of more or less independently and exemplified in the writers' choice of character and locale, they

---

[1] *Ibid.*, p. 73.

[2] *Compl. Works*, IX, 170.

[3] *Ibid.*, pp. 171–3. Biencourt has also noted Norris's debt to *L'Argent*, but he has failed to see the parallels between *The Pit* on the one hand and *Nana* and *L'Assommoir* on the other.

used certain motifs found in Zola's works, such as the street scene of the opening chapter of *L'Assommoir*. Moreover, they owed to the French writer some of their audacity and frankness, and desire to expose social conditions which victimized the individual.

Despite Garland's rather hostile attitude toward Zola, he nevertheless used some of the French novelist's works as a literary pattern. In *Main-Travelled Roads* Garland stripped rural life of its glamour and portrayed the farmers as he believed they really were, hard, brutal, and mean, just as Zola had done in a far more outspoken way in *La Terre*. In *Jason Edwards* he came close to the methods of Zola as exemplified in *L'Assommoir*—the novel which exerted an influence on our three writers—particularly in his use of the Boston slums and their degraded people as background for his story. In addition, the hailstorm episode in the second part of the novel seems to have been modeled on a similar incident in *La Terre*.

Crane's debt to Zola goes deeper, and is more extensive than Garland's. As in the case of Garland, it is primarily in the early works of Crane that the influence of Zola is most obvious. Crane's slum stories, particularly *Maggie* and *George's Mother*, and, to a less degree, his tales of war bear the stamp of Zola. *L'Assommoir* suggested not only Crane's technique of describing the Bowery in *Maggie*, but also its plot, characters, and a number of episodes. *La Débâcle* may have served in certain respects as a model for *The Red Badge of Courage*. In tone, plot, and episodes Crane's novel may be linked with Zola's. Like *Maggie*, *George's Mother* is indebted to *L'Assommoir* with regard not only to naturalistic ideas and characterization but also to the description of the milieu, the lure of the saloon, and the effects of alcohol.

Norris, whose works reveal the greatest debt to Zola of the three writers concerned, was no doubt the one who was best acquainted with Zola's works, and the one who, temperamentally, was most akin to the French master. The familiar signs of Zola's influence are found in almost all of Norris's novels, but most notably in *McTeague, Vandover and the Brute, The Octopus*, and *The Pit*. The novels which seem to have appealed particularly to Norris are: *Thérèse Raquin, L'Assommoir, Nana, Germinal, La Terre, La Bête humaine*, and *L'Argent*. Norris's aim in *McTeague* was similar to Zola's in *Thérèse Raquin*: to study two different temperaments and to record the influence they exerted on each other. Norris's novel is also obviously indebted to *L'Assommoir* for matters of plot and episodes. The subplot seems to have been modeled on an episode in *La Bête humaine*. *Vandover and the Brute* presents similarities of method and character to *Thérèse Raquin*, *La Bête humaine*, and *L'Assommoir*. *The Octopus* is indebted to *Germinal* for certain ideas, part of the plot, and characterization, to *La Bête humaine* for episodes, and to *La Terre* for suggestions of the treatment of rural life. Finally, *L'Argent* suggested points of plot, descriptive technique, and some episodes in *The Pit*, in which there occur reminiscences from *Nana* and *L'Assommoir*.

In conclusion it should be remembered that whatever the three writers owed to Zola, be it ideas, characters, certain patterns or techniques, they used them with moderation and restraint. The extreme naturalism of Zola was toned down to suit the authors' temperaments, purposes, and artistic effects.

CHAPTER XI

HUYSMANS AND FRANK NORRIS

In the preceding chapter we noted some points of resemblance between Vandover and the naturalistic type of man. We linked his pliability, constitutional weakness, and ability to adapt himself to various environments with Zola's Gervaise.[1] But Vandover's paralysis of will, his inability to act, and his failure in love as well as in other activities of life, also relate him to Turgenev's ill-fated heroes,[2] thus illustrating the kinship between the weak hero of the Russian writer and the naturalistic type. But in the complex portrait of Vandover there are traits which point beyond the Rudin as well as the naturalistic type. At a certain phase of his career, Vandover developed a taste for aesthetic refinement which links him with another literary type, that of the decadent school.

With the publication of *A Rebours* (1884),[3] a reaction—variously named symbolism, decadence, aestheticism—set in against French naturalism. It emphasized particularly the force of imagination, the need of mysticism, and the cult of beauty. With his aesthetic worship of artificiality, eccentricity, and morbidity, Huysmans, a disciple of Baudelaire, became an important force in the new tendencies. His eccentric hero, Des Esseintes, became influential in the literatures of both Europe and America.

In England, for example, Oscar Wilde wrote *The Picture of Dorian Gray* under the inspiration of Huysmans' famous novel.

---

[1] See p. 291.

[2] See p. 332.

[3] There is no evidence, so far as I know, that Norris ever read this book, but considering his great interest in French literature, it is quite probable that he was familiar with the novel. It should not be overlooked that Norris had studied art in Paris and that he had friends who acted in the manner of Vandover and Corthell. See Walker, *op. cit.*, pp. 207 ff., 279 ff. This fact, howewer, does not exclude the possibility that Norris may have been stimulated by *A Rebours* for certain aspects of his works.

In the United States the Franco-American poet, Stuart Merrill, made the first translation of Huysmans in 1890,[1] and according to F. C. Hanighen, the first American disciple of the French writer was James Huneker.[2] As early as 1895, Huneker wrote a story for the ephemeral *M'lle New York* in the hallucinative tradition of *Là-Bas*, entitled "When the Black Mass Was Heard." Among other American authors whose work bears traces of that of Huysmans, Hanighen mentioned Carl Van Vechten, Edgar Saltus, Lafcadio Hearn, and Ben Hecht. He failed, however, to notice that Norris's Vandover and Corthell are, to some extent, reminiscent of Des Esseintes.

Huysmans' hero, a wealthy nobleman, had enjoyed the fashionable life of a great city to the last drop. His life was wrecked by debauches of various kinds, and what was left to him was only a feeling of *ennui*. As a means of escape from the outer world which he despised, he created an artificial world, a hermitage, which he decorated with exotic refinement and excessive artificiality according to his own eccentric taste. There were Roman decadent paintings and rare books, exotic plants, an *orgue à bouche* and a gilt turtle set with dazzling stones. However, this unnatural life ended with the hero's nervous breakdown.

Turning to Vandover, we note that he, too, was a wealthy young man who had indulged in a series of debauches resulting in neurosis and a feeling of *ennui*. Like his French prototype, he decided to withdraw from the outer world and live a secluded life. To that effect he rented a couple of rooms in downtown San Francisco and furnished them more or less in Des Esseintes' eccentric fashion. Suddenly Vandover turned aesthete: "There did not seem to be any suitable place for the Assyrian *bas-reliefs*, and the mantelpiece was of old-fashioned white marble like the mantelpiece in Mrs. Wade's front parlour, a veritable horror. It revolted Vandover to think of putting a pipe-rack over it."[3] Vandover's rooms were like a hermitage, a retreat which he had furnished according to his own taste. "He had passed a delightful week selecting the

---

[1] F. C. Hanighen, "Huysmans' Influence in America," *Revue de littérature comparée*, XIII (1933), 174. Cf. also a brief note about Huysmans in the *Bookman*, I (June, 1895), 295–6.

[2] *Ibid.*, p. 177.

[3] *Compl. Works*, V, 151.

wall paper and the pattern for the frieze, buying rugs, screens, Assyrian *bas-reliefs*, photogravures of Renaissance portraits and the famous tiled stove with its flamboyant ornaments."[1] And the living room was furnished with almost the same care for aesthetic and eccentric detail as Des Esseintes' cottage:

> The walls were hung with dull blue paper of a very rough texture set off by a narrow picture moulding of ivory white. A dark red carpet covered with rugs and skins lay on the floor. Upon the left-hand wall, reaching to the floor, hung a huge rug of sombre colours against which were fixed a fencing trophy, a pair of antlers, a little water-colour sketch of a Norwegian fjord, and Vandover's banjo; underneath it was a low but very broad divan covered with corduroy. To the right and left of this divan stood breast-high bookcases with olive green curtains, their tops serving as shelves for a multitude of small ornaments, casts of animals by Fremilt and Barye, Donatello's lovely *femme inconnue*, beer steins, a little bronze clock, a calendar, and a yellow satin slipper of Flossie's in which Vandover kept Turkish cigarettes. . . . To the left in the angle of the room stood the Japanese screen in black and gold, and close to this a tea-table of bamboo and a piano-lamp with a great shade of crinkly red paper . . . The bay window was filled by the window-seat, covered with corduroy like the divan and heaped with cushions, one of them of flaming yellow, the one spot of vivid colour, amidst the dull browns and sombre blues of the room.[2]

Note that Vandover was as preoccupied with colors as was Des Esseintes. Like Huysmans' hero, who lived completely alone and was altogether passive except for the contemplation of the artificial beauty surrounding him and the perusal of a few pages of a decadent writer of ancient Rome, Vandover lived almost alone, doing nothing but reading a book now and then, and contemplating the beauty of his rooms.

> A new life now began for Vandover, a life of luxury and aimlessness which he found charming. He had no duties, no cares, no responsibilities. . . . His desire of vice was numbed, his evil habits all deranged; . . . he would merely have to remain inactive, impassive, and his character would of itself re-form upon the new conditions.[3]

In the manner of Des Esseintes who had his golden turtle, artificial flowers and other eccentricities with which he could while away the time, Vandover had recourse to various fads:

---

[1] *Ibid.*, p. 154.

[2] *Ibid.*, pp. 155–6.

[3] *Ibid.*, p. 157.

Vandover took his greatest pleasure while in his new quarters, delighted to be pottering about his sitting room by the hour, setting it to rights, rearranging the small ornaments, adjusting the calendar, winding the clock and, above all, tending the famous tiled stove.

In his idleness he grew to have small and petty ways. The entire day went in doing little things. He passed one whole afternoon delightfully, whittling out a new banjo bridge from the cover of a cigar-box, scraping it smooth afterward with a bit of glass. The winding of his clock was quite an occurrence in the course of the day, something to be looked forward to. The mixing of his tobacco was a positive event and undertaken with all gravity, while the task of keeping it moist and ripe in the blue china jar, with the sponge attachment, that always stood on the bamboo tea-table by the Japanese screen, was a wearing anxiety that was yet a pleasure.

It became a fad with him to do without matches, using as a substitute "lights," tapers of twisted paper to be ignited at the famous stove. He found amusement for two days in twisting and rolling these "lights" . . .

But the stove, the famous tiled stove with flamboyant ornaments, was the chiefest joy of Vandover's new life. He was delighted with it; it was so artistic, so curious, it kept the fire so well, it looked so cheerful and inviting; . . . There was hardly a minute of the day he was not fussing with it . . .[1]

The decadent or aesthetic stage of Vandover's career was not of long duration, however; his weak temperament asserted itself and gradually he sank deeper and deeper, degenerating in the manner of Gervaise.

As a literary type, Corthell, the artist of *The Pit*, may also, in some ways, be linked with Des Esseintes. Like the latter, he was a wealthy young man, sensitive by nature and of slender stature:

He was a slightly built man of about twenty-eight or thirty; dark, wearing a small, pointed beard, and a moustache that he brushed away from his lips like a Frenchman. . . . He had travelled, read, studied, occasionally written, and in matters pertaining to the colouring and fusing of glass was cited as an authority.[2]

Like Huysmans' hero, Corthell was above all an aesthete: "He passed his life gently, in the calm, still atmosphere of art, in the cult of the beautiful, unperturbed, tranquil; painting, reading, or, piece by piece, developing his beautiful stained glass."[3] Moreover, he was an artist, "soft of hand and of speech, elaborating graces

---

[1] *Ibid.*, pp. 158-9.
[2] *Ibid.*, IX, 14-15.
[3] *Ibid.*, p. 59.

of sound and colour and form, refined, sensitive, and temperamental; . . ."[1] Corthell was, however, by no means as eccentric as Des Esseintes, nor did he indulge in sexual excesses as did the Frenchman at a certain period of his life. Instead, Corthell was, in fact, remarkably passive in matters of love.[2]

What seems to have interested Norris most in *A Rebours* was probably the description of the hermitage, with the hero sitting alone by the fire in the stillness of night, reading or dreaming, surrounded by rare books, manuscripts, and beautiful, decadent paintings. Corthell was portrayed in a similar manner and in a similar environment:

Even now, perplexed as he was, he was conscious of a feeling of comfort and pleasure as he settled himself in his chair.

The lamp threw a dull illumination about the room. It was a picturesque apartment, carefully planned. Not an object that had not been chosen with care and the utmost discrimination. The walls had been treated with copper leaf till they produced a sombre, iridescent effect of green and faint gold, that suggested the depth of a forest glade shot through with the sunset. Shelves bearing eighteenth-century books in seal-brown tree calf— Addison, the *Spectator*, Junius and Racine, Rochefoucauld and Pascal hung against it here and there. On every hand the eye rested upon some small masterpiece of art or workmanship. Now it was an antique portrait bust of the days of decadent Rome, black marble with a bronze tiara; now a framed page of a fourteenth-century version of *Li Quatres Filz d'Aymon*, with an illuminated letter of miraculous workmanship; or a Renaissance gonfalon of silk once white but now brown with age, yet in the centre blazing with the escutcheon and quarterings of a dead queen. Between the windows stood an ivory statuette of the "Venus of the Heel," done in the days of the magnificent Lorenzo. An original Cazin, and a chalk drawing by Baudry hung against the wall close by together with a bronze tablet by Saint Gaudens; while across the entire end of the room opposite the fireplace, worked in the tapestry of the best period of the northern French school, Halcyone, her arms already blossoming into wings, hovered over the dead body of Ceyx, his long hair streaming like seaweed in the blue water of the Ægean.

For a long time Corthell sat motionless, looking into the fire. In an adjoining room a clock chimed the half hour of one, and the artist stirred, passing his long fingers across his eyes.[3]

Note that Norris hinted at Corthell's kinship with the decadents

[1] *Ibid.*, p. 60.

[2] Cf. the Rudin type. See pp. 315 ff.

[3] *Compl. Works*, IX, 272-3.

by stating that his room was decorated with "an antique portrait bust of the days of decadent Rome."

To sum up: Vandover was conceived as a naturalistic type illustrating the theory of the influence of environment on the individual.[1] Then, for a certain phase of his life, he was possibly modeled upon Huysmans' Des Esseintes. For his last stage he followed the naturalistic process of degeneration inspired by *L'Assommoir*.[2] In *The Pit*, Norris contrasted the strong-willed business man Jadwin with the aesthete Corthell,[3] who, to some extent, is reminiscent of Des Esseintes. Neither Vandover nor Corthell went to the excesses and eccentricities typical of Huysmans' hero, whose pronounced and bizarre hedonism has no counterpart in Norris's characters, but some of the idiosyncrasies of Des Esseintes are, it seems, easily recognizable although transplanted to, and aptly modified to suit, San Francisco and Chicago settings.

---

[1] See pp. 199–201.

[2] See pp. 292–3.

[3] Cf. also Léon in *Madame Bovary*.

CHAPTER XII

THE INFLUENCE OF TURGENEV

As has been pointed out by Gettmann in his well-documented study *Turgenev in England and America*, the United States were more responsive to the works of Turgenev than England. In the seventies and eighties most of his principal writings saw American editions: *Fathers and Sons* (1867), *Smoke* (1872), *Dimitri Roudine* (1873), *Spring Floods* (1874), *Virgin Soil* (1877), *Daughter of Russia* (1882), *Punin and Baburin* (1882), *Song of Triumphant Love* (1883), *Poems in Prose* (1883), *Annouchka* (1884), *Mumu and The Diary of a Superfluous Man* (1884), *Annals of a Sportsman* (1885), *An Unfortunate Woman* (1886), and *The Ruffian* (1887). Of English editions available during the same period, the following may be mentioned: *Liza* (1869), *On the Eve* (1871), *Virgin Soil* (1878) and *First Love, and Punin and Baburin* (1884).[1]

Turgenev's works were not only translated, but American critics and authors also helped to stimulate the interest in the Russian writer. T. S. Perry, for example, reviewer of foreign books for the *Atlantic* and the *Nation*, wrote numerous articles about Turgenev; and Howells and James spoke highly of the Russian novelist and may have helped to increase his popularity in the United States. Thus, it is evident that a large number of Turgenev's works were accessible to Garland, Crane, and Norris, before they published their first writings.

Before we enter upon a discussion of the probable influence of Turgenev on these writers, it may be advisable to comment briefly on his works. It has been pointed out earlier that the dominant theme in Turgenev's novels was that men were weak, women strong, and chance omnipotent.[2] Turgenev's long line

---

[1] See Gettmann, *op. cit.*, pp. 187–9. See also the discussion of Turgenev pp. 31–2, 34 ff.

[2] See p. 32.

of weak and wavering men—often referred to as failures[1]—includes among others, Bersenev in *On the Eve*, Litvinov in *Smoke*, Arkady in *Fathers and Sons*, Neschdanov in *Virgin Soil*, and above all Rudin in *Rudin*. The latter was portrayed as a talented and highly intelligent scholar, full of ideas and enthusiasm. He easily dominated his friends, for he was a brilliant conversationalist whose arguments carried weight, but he suffered from one major flaw: *he could not act.* It was not possible for him to transform his lofty ideas into real acts; he remained hesitant and passive. This feature came particularly to the fore whenever love was concerned. Despite his noble words and passionate nature he was unable to take the decisive step and marry the girl he believed he loved. His downfall was slow but inevitable, for he had not enough strength of mind to overcome his lethargy; by chance he was finally killed on a barricade, his death as accidental and insignificant as his life. Irresolution and fate made Rudin a failure.

Bazarov, the bitter and disillusioned nihilist in *Fathers and Sons*, resembles Rudin in many ways. They were equally intelligent and gifted, but Bazarov had not Rudin's fondness for high-flown oratory, nor his inability to act. But despite his personal courage and strong will, Bazarov was helpless, for fate was against him. He died suddenly, in the midst of his active life, of an infection caught by chance. He, too, was a failure.

Against the weak and powerless heroes Turgenev often placed strong and dominant heroines.[2] One illustration of this type was the altruistic and moderately emancipated Elena in *On the Eve*, another, the destructive and egoistic Irina in *Smoke*. Irina was a demon, a beast of prey whenever men were concerned. She loved to rouse their passion only to throw their love away "like a glove." Nevertheless men were drawn to her as to a magnet. The type includes, among others, Maria Nikolayevna in *Spring Floods*, Anna Sergeyevna (M[me] Odintsova) in *Fathers and Sons*, Valentine Mikailovna in *Virgin Soil*, and Varvara Pavlovna in *A Nest of the Gentry*.[3] In general, Turgenev's conception of woman was the reverse of that of the French naturalists. For the Russian

---

[1] See Hildegard Bennewitz, *op. cit.*, pp. 7 ff.

[2] Cf. also Karl Tiander, *Turgenjev i dansk Aandsliv* (Copenhagen and Christiania, 1913), pp. 58 ff.

[3] Ibsen has a similar type of woman in Rebecca West and Hedda Gabler.

writer, woman was essentially an individual possessed of a soul, not a being solely dominated by instincts.

Chance played an important part in Turgenev's novels.[1] An accidental infection ended Bazarov's life, and a stray bullet killed Rudin. In *A Nest of the Gentry* a notice in a Parisian paper announcing the death of Lavretzky's wife made him dream of happy days to come with Liza, whom he loved. But his exultation ceased when his supposedly dead wife suddenly returned to his house. In *Smoke*, Irina's first ball, which she attended by chance, completely altered her life.

Other characteristics of Turgenev's novels should be mentioned: his lyric conception of nature, obvious in most of his works but particularly in *A Sportman's Sketches*, and his use of dreams, premonitions, and omens.

1. TURGENEV AND GARLAND

Despite the general references to Russian literature and to Tolstoy in particular,[2] there is no mention of Turgenev in Garland's books of reminiscences. Apparently, the only reference to Turgenev in Garland's printed books is in *Crumbling Idols*, where the Russian's name occurs once.[3] Garland's notebooks and manuscript notes of the eighties, on the other hand, reveal a considerable knowledge of Turgenev.[4] Several times in that decade he referred to *Fathers and Sons;* he wrote, for example, in his notebook dated October 16, 1884:

I close "Fathers and Sons" with a profound respect for its author, and much more knowledge of Russian thought than I knew before. In this book the author has gotten deep down into the emotional stratum of human nature. He shows us the insuperable instincts of humanity in battle with Culture. Most melancholy and powerfully affecting is his main portraiture. A young man strong in his culture . . .

Turgenev's *Smoke* also commanded his attention, and his notebook dated May 15, 1885, contains the following comment:

---

[1] See p. 32.

[2] See *A Son of the Middle Border*, pp. 371, 377; *Back-Trailers of the Middle Border*, p. 79; *Roadside Meetings*, pp. 60, 67, 111–12, 117, 126, 216, 221, 250, 380, 383, 386; *Companions on the Trail*, p. 122; *Afternoon Neighbors*, p. 379.

[3] *Crumbling Idols*, p. 186.

[4] See p. 70.

This book is a merciless sarcasm against the Russian people and customs. It is gloomy, sad, disastrous. It is the bitter mood of a man who by childhood ties is urged to love the subject of his anathema. No one could more pitilessly scourge the barbarism and brutality of this savage people . . . You feel yourself in the presence of a man who is disgusted with the present and has no hopes for the future. He stands over a waste place and sees no way to make it bloom.

Garland was apparently favorably impressed by the book when he first read it, but when he reread it more than ten years later his attitude had become fundamentally negative. He finished the book on November 4, 1898, and found it "a work of splendid technique but an arid subject." Litvinov's love for a married woman made Garland indignant, and he thought the novel "hardly worth while."

In his notebook containing outlines of his lectures at the Boston School of Oratory, Garland mentioned the following novels and sketches by Turgenev: *Dimitri Roudine, Liza, Smoke, Annouchka, Poems in Prose,* and *Virgin Soil.* And in the manuscript entitled "The Literature of Democracy", he listed Björnson, Ibsen, Turgenev, Gogol, and Tolstoy side by side with Daudet and Zola.[1] "All," he said, "belong to this mighty movement which is to overturn all other values and ideas." Finally, in "The Modern Novel in Germany and America"[2] Garland remarked that Turgenev pleaded for the Russian serf, and that his analysis of character was becoming more and more psychological.[3]

Thus, Garland was acquainted with several of Turgenev's works before he published his first book, *Under the Wheel* (1890).

Garland's indebtedness to Turgenev, which apparently scholars have failed to note, may be traced, at least to some extent, in all his early work, that is, from *Under the Wheel* to *Rose of Dutcher's Coolly,* but it is perhaps most apparent in the last-mentioned novel.

What seems to have drawn Garland to Turgenev's works was partly the latter's use of the failure type of man, a type which Garland had had ample opportunity to study in the Middle West.[4] There he had seen men who were "down and out" either because of social conditions, personal shortcomings, or because of the

---

[1] See pp. 448–9.

[2] See p. 444.

[3] See also Garland's review of Kirkland's *Zury,* p. 58. Garland even devoted a lecture to Turgenev. See p. 67.

[4] See discussion of Garland's life and the plight of the farmers, pp. 71 ff.

adversity of fate. In *Main-Travelled Roads* he transplanted his experiences of the individual's struggle for a decent existence into literature.

In "Up the Coulé" we have a variety of the Bazarov type of a luckless man, beaten by fate, a failure. In this story Garland depicted two brothers, Howard McLane, a successful actor and playwright who, as Garland portrayed him, had arrived at his prominent position through sheer luck, and Grant, a forceful man and in his way as intelligent and talented as Howard, who, however, had had no chance to develop himself. He had taken over the mortgaged farm but, luckless as he was, he had not succeeded, despite tremendous toil, in keeping the old homestead. By chance, the letter which he had sent to his wealthy brother asking for money to pay the mortgage, never reached its destination. In the manner of Turgenev, Garland emphasized fate as an important factor in human life. Howard could only say: "'Circumstances made me and crushed you. That's all there is about that. Luck made me and cheated you. It ain't right.'"[1] Like Bazarov in *Fathers and Sons* Grant had fallen under the wheel of chance, never to be able to rise again. When his successful brother wanted to make amendments, it was too late; Grant summed up the situation: "'I mean life ain't worth very much to me. I'm too old to take a new start. I'm a dead failure. I've come to the conclusion that life's a failure for ninety-nine per cent of us. You can't help me now. It's too late.'"[2] It is worth noting that Garland repeatedly stressed the fact that Grant was a failure, and that his lack of success was due more to the adversity of fate, as in the case of Bazarov, than to any inherent flaw of character.

Fate also played a considerable part in the story "A Branch Road," in which a young lover, on his way to effect a reconciliation after a quarrel with his girl, was delayed by a minor accident to one of his buggy wheels.[3] He repaired the damage and proceeded on his way, but he arrived too late; the girl had left. In despair he gave up his studies and went out West; the girl married unhappily. In this story it is appropriate to speak of the "wheel of chance."

---

[1] *Main-Travelled Roads*, p. 134.
[2] *Ibid.*, p. 136.
[3] *Ibid.*, p. 33.

Besides similarities in the use of chance and the failure type, there also occur in *Main-Travelled Roads* passages of description of nature, the serene beauty and lyricism of which are reminiscent of those of Turgenev. The Russian writer's poetic delineations of the Russian steppe—often called prairie in American translations—with its flowers, its animals, its odors, and its peculiar atmosphere, must have attracted Garland, who was himself a sensitive and lyric recorder of the American prairie. Compare, for instance, Turgenev's superb tale "The Forest and the Steppe" in *A Sportsman's Sketches* with the descriptions of nature of the first story of *Main-Travelled Roads*. Both tales open with a description in gorgeous colors of a beautiful morning, and in both the moods of the characters harmonize with the glory of the new day. This is Garland's account of a "windless September dawn":

Above the level belt of timber to the east a vast dome of pale undazzling gold was rising, silently and swiftly. Jays called in the thickets where the maples flamed amid the green oaks, with irregular splashes of red and orange. The grass was crisp with frost under the feet, the road smooth and gray-white in color, the air was indescribably sweet, resonant and stimulating. No wonder the man sang! . . .[1]

And the east bloomed broader! The dome of gold grew brighter, the faint clouds here and there flamed with a flush of red. The frost began to glisten with a reflected color. The youth dreamed as he walked; his broad face and deep earnest eyes caught and reflected some of the beauty and majesty of the sky.[2]

And this is Turgenev's picture of a glorious daybreak:

. . . the rim of the sky flushes crimson; the jackdaws are heard, fluttering clumsily in the birch-trees; sparrows are twittering about the dark hayricks. The air is clearer, the road more distinct, the sky brightens, the clouds look whiter, and the fields look greener . . . And meanwhile the glow of dawn is beginning; already streaks of gold are stretching across the sky; mists are gathering in clouds over the ravines; the larks are singing musically; the breeze that ushers in the dawn is blowing; and slowly the purple sun floats upward. There is a perfect flood of light; your heart is fluttering like a bird. Everything is fresh, gay, delightful![3]

---

[1] *Ibid.*, p. 9.

[2] *Ibid.*, pp. 10–11. Even the scheme of *Main-Travelled Roads* is somewhat reminiscent of that of *A Sportman's Sketches:* both books are built up of stories grouped around the life of a country community.

[3] *A Sportman's Sketches* (London, 1895), II, 275–6. Cf. also that nature's indifference to man was stressed by both Turgenev and Garland. See, for in-

In the realistic play *Under the Wheel*, later novelized as *Jason Edwards*, Garland used these words by Bazarov as a motto: "I have fallen under the wheel." We may, therefore, reasonably expect to find in that work the influence of Turgenev, and investigation does indeed show a certain debt. The sentence quoted above was uttered by Bazarov when, dying of typhus, he realized that for him everything was over, that he had failed in the task he attempted, for death was the victor. In *Jason Edwards*, Frank Graham echoed Bazarov's words when telling Walter Reeves of the bad luck of the unhappy Edwards family: "'Well, all is —old man—if you don't help, or the Lord don't give us a good rain soon, they'll go under the wheel, sure as shootin'.'"[1]

Despite the differences in character between Bazarov, the ambitious young doctor-nihilist, and Jason Edwards, the worn-out, middle-aged mechanic-farmer, they had in common the fact that, despite their strong wills, they were both failures because, in the last instance, fate was against them. Garland repeatedly employed the word failure to denote Jason's lack of success:

"It means blight. It means that every stalk is like them"—he put his foot on the scattered straws he had thrown down. "It means failure."

"Failure! Is there no hope?"

"None—that I can see. We're squeezed out ag'in. Squeezed out of the city, and now we're squeezed out of a country of free land—I'm just about ready to quit."

"I wish I could do something to help you. It scares me to have you fail—you've been so brave."[2]

And again:

"My life is a failure—I don't know why. Don't seem 's if it was my fault. I know it ain't yours, mother. Fifty years of work—an' here we be! I've worked every well day of my life since I was ten years old; we've worked early and late, an' pinched an' saved. I never was a drinker, we ain't had the necessities of life—rent went up an' fuel went up, an' wages went down—an' here we are."[3]

---

stance, the last scene in *Virgin Soil*, where Neschdanov committed suicide, and the scene depicting the hailstorm and its terrible results in *Jason Edwards*, pp. 165–82. See also pp. 219–20 of the present study.

[1] *Jason Edwards*, pp. 129–30.

[2] *Ibid.*, p. 163.

[3] *Ibid.*, p. 165. Senator Ward in *A Member of the Third House* was also a failure.

Social determinism and fatalism were intimately intertwined in this novel.[1] Jason Edwards was the helpless victim of a pernicious social system, but it was nature and chance which completed his tragedy. As in the case of Bazarov, who by chance contracted an infection when dissecting a body of a man stricken by typhus, chance effected Jason's destruction.[2] Bedridden and waiting patiently for death, the luckless Edwards, though independently conceived and as a social type distinctly American, seems a fair replica of the doomed Bazarov in the next to last chapter of *Fathers and Sons*.

As has been said before, Turgenev usually placed weak, irresolute men against strong women. Walter Reeves, the fiancé of Edwards' daughter, is somewhat reminiscent of the Rudin type with regard to love. On the one hand he was an ambitious and energetic newspaperman; yet, when Alice, his ambitious and independent fiancée, was concerned, he was irresolute and vacillating. For years he remained excessively patient and fairly inactive in his love, waiting for Alice, who was in the Middle West, to make up her mind whether she wanted to marry him or not. The situation resembles many a one found in Turgenev's work, for instance Litvinov and Irina in *Smoke*, a weak man in love with a strong woman.

The irresolute man, wavering in matters of love, was also portrayed in *A Little Norsk*, in which Ans and Bert, two stern, hardworking, powerful, and resolute bachelors, became astonishingly passive and inactive when love was concerned. Although both were in love with Elga, they did not object to or try to prevent her marriage with a young man who turned out to be a rascal. The men were as completely under the sway of the woman as was Reeves, for their wills were as if paralyzed. In that respect they recall Litvinov, Bersenev, Sjubin, Neschdanov, and other vacillating heroes in Turgenev's works.

Bert was, moreover, to some extent a failure. Despite his endless toil on the claim, he succeeded in making no headway, and he could see no hope for the future; life seemed meaningless to him.

What was he toiling for, anyway? What mattered all this terrible tramping to and fro—was it an end or only a means? Would there ever

---

[1] See p. 187.

[2] For the hailstorm episode see pp. 246 ff.

come anything like satisfaction of desire? Life for him had been a silent, gloomy, and almost purposeless struggle. He had not looked forward to anything very definite, though vaguely he had hoped for something better.[1]

In the manner of Rudin who, after having bidden farewell to Nathalia, left everything and drifted aimlessly for some years, spending all his money, Bert, after Elga's marriage, suddenly gave up his claim, left Dakota, and traveled around the country for a couple of years. Finally he returned to Ans and the widowed Elga, poorly dressed, marked by hard toil, with exactly four dollars in his pocket, as lonely and pathetic a figure as Rudin, who was also reduced to working at odd jobs. But there is a difference between these two characters: whereas Rudin was killed on a barricade, the luckless Bert, Garland hinted, would some day get his reward, for he was looked upon as the prospective husband of Elga.[2]

In *Prairie Folks*, Elder Pill and Daddy Deering remind us of Turgenev's ill-fated men. The hero of the short story "Elder Pill, Preacher," was portrayed as a failure; with his easy flow of words and commanding personality he may perhaps be linked rather with Rudin than with Bazarov. He was essentially an able man, and he had "in him great capacity for change, for growth. Circumstances had been against his development thus far, but the time had come when growth seemed to be defeat and failure."[3]

Like Bazarov and Jason Edwards, Daddy Deering in the short

---

[1] *A Little Norsk*, p. 97. Cf. Garland's own experiences, p. 84.

[2] The bachelors, Ans and Bert, may also be compared with the friends, Bersenev and Insarov (*On the Eve*), whereas Elga is somewhat reminiscent of Elena, although she had very little of the latter's passion and devotion; both possessed, however, self-reliance and forcefulness of will. Garland once admitted that the book was purely fictional except for one episode. See p. 84 n. 3. This fact supports the belief that it may in part have been inspired by his reading.

The protagonists of *A Spoil of Office*, Ida Wilbur and Bradley Talcott, are somewhat reminiscent of Elena and Insarov in *On the Eve;* although both men were strong, their women were stronger. The sea gull episode toward the end of Turgenev's novel, giving a presentiment of the death of Elena's husband, has a replica in Garland's book, in which the flight and scream of a crane took on prophetic meaning to the hero at a crucial moment of his life.

[3] *Prairie Folks*, p. 63.

story of that name was a victim of adverse chance.[1] The former
country fiddler, who had earlier gloried in his strength and power,
swiftly succumbed to the blows of fate, and his life came to a tragic
ending. First his left hand was caught in the cogwheels of a machine, which crushed four of his fingers; then he struck his feet
with an ax and lamed himself for life.

As a matter of fact, the one accident hinged upon the other. It was the
failure of his left hand, with its useless fingers, to do its duty, that brought
the ax down upon his foot. The pain was not so much physical as mental.
To think that he, who could hew to a hair-line, right and left hand, should
cut his own foot like a ten-year-old boy—that scared him. It brought
age and decay close to him. For the first time in his life he felt that he
was fighting a losing battle.[2]

Garland's use of chance in this story relates it to *Jason Edwards*,
and is reminiscent of Turgenev's utilization of chance in *Fathers
and Sons*.

As has been touched upon, Garland's indebtedness to Turgenev
is perhaps most obvious in *Rose of Dutcher's Coolly*. Warren
Mason, the hero of the story, bears resemblances to both Bazarov
and Rudin. Mason[3] was an intellectual as was Rudin and Bazarov; he was a gifted newspaperman nearly forty years of age, interested in art and music and working on a novel, which, however, he was unable to finish because of his many interests.

In the beginning of the novel, Mason reminds one of Bazarov.
Like the hero of *Fathers and Sons*, Mason was critical, disillusioned.
His curt and somewhat irritated manner when we first meet him,
is also reminiscent of Bazarov's, but he was, like the Russian, kind
at heart despite his abrupt manner. Both were equally cynical in
their attitudes toward women. The materialistic Bazarov said of
the beautiful Mme Odintsova, whom he was later to love passion-

---

[1] "Daddy Deering" is, in its utilization of adverse chance, also reminiscent
of a short story by Tolstoy called "Polikouchka," which Garland mentioned
in one his notebooks. See also p. 343 n. 2.

[2] *Prairie Folks*, p. 220.

[3] The episode where Mason is presented to the reader for the first time,
recalls a similar scene in Turgenev. As will be remembered, Rudin was first
portrayed at a dinner given by the independent and eccentric Daria Mihailovna; Mason also appeared first at a dinner given by the emancipated woman
doctor, Isabel Herrick. Rudin's part at the dinner seems to correspond to that
of Rose, while Mason takes the part of Pigasov in *Rudin*.

ately: "'Luxurious body! ... What a study for the anatomical theatre.'"[1] And Mason, looking bored when he saw Rose, remarked: "'The girl has a fine roll of voice and a splendid curve of bust,"[2] and likened her, among other things, to "an impressionistic painting, better seen at a little distance."[3] His view was radically changed, however, when he came to know her better, just as Bazarov was forced to revise his early opinion of Mme Odintsova.

When Mason began his discussions of marriage, he shows traits that link him with Rudin. Like Rudin, he had a bent for speculating, for philosophizing, for self-analysis, and he shared Rudin's ease of invention and power of presenting a case dramatically. Thus, he was a fluent and persuasive talker, and Rose was as much impressed by Mason's smooth and melodious voice and by his flow of words, as Nathalia was by Rudin's eloquence. Mason's loquacity was revealed in two chapters, entitled "Mason Talks on Marriage" and "Mason Talks Again."

But Mason's most characteristic feature, like Rudin's, was his inability to love wholeheartedly.[4] Because of their analytic temperaments and irresolute minds, no sweeping love had ever touched their hearts. Both Rose and Nathalia, who fell in love, the one with Mason, the other with Rudin, suffered because of the men's indecision and vacillating attitude. When time came for action, Mason, in the manner of Rudin, stood irresolute, ensconsing himself behind the remark: "'You see, there are a great many considerations involved.'"[5] It was also typical of his attitude that, when he let a woman go, he rationalized it by saying it was the best thing for her: "'Is a man to have no credit for letting such a glorious creature pass him, unharmed and free?'"[6]

Toward the end of the novel Garland stressed more and more the irresoluteness of Mason's character. As has been stated, Mason was introduced as a sort of cynical and forceful Bazarov, but as the narrative proceeded he gradually took on the personality of Rudin,

---

[1] *Fathers and Sons* (Moscow, 1947), p. 81.

[2] *Rose of Dutcher's Coolly*, p. 212.

[3] *Ibid.*, p. 201.

[4] Note also that the novel was in part autobiographical. Garland did not marry until comparatively late in life. See p. 89 n. 2.

[5] *Rose of Dutcher's Coolly*, p. 269.

[6] *Ibid.*, p. 275.

whose weakness and lack of decision were especially noticeable if we compare him with Bazarov. One might with equal justice say of Rudin what Mason said of himself, if we substitute the word "realizes" for "writes": ". . . he dreams great things, but he never writes them."[1] In addition, the picture of Mason given in the following lines also links him with Rudin: "His last glance as he [Sanborn] closed the door fell upon a lonely figure lying in a low chair before the fire, and he pitied him. Mason seemed 'the great irresolute' which Isabel believed him to be; helpless to do, patient to suffer."[2]

Unlike Rudin, who so sadly perished, and Bazarov, who succumbed to the blows of fate, Mason's character underwent a remarkable change for the better. His lethargy was only a mood, and to Rose's loving eyes his cynicism seemed to be a mood, too. His transformation set in when he saw three men rescued in a terrible storm by the skill and will power of a negro. Then he made his decision: " 'Hitherto I have drifted—henceforth I *sail*,' " he asserted.[3] But despite his resolution he continued for a time to drift:

> Could he have gone to his own fireside at once, the determining letter would have been written that night, but the routine of the office, the chaff of his companions, took away his heroic mood, and when he entered a car at twelve o'clock he slouched in his seat like a tired man, and the muscles of his face fell slack and he looked like a hopeless man.[4]

And again:

> All night long he alternately mused and dozed upon the problem. He roused up at early daylight with a feeling of doom upon him. He had made a mistake. He was not fitted to be a husband—he was a poor thing, at best, who had not had energy enough to get out of a groove nor to demand adequate pay for grinding in his groove. He lacked 'push,' and had dreamed away the best years of his life, at least such parts of the years as he had saved from the merciless drive of his paper. He was pulp, squeezed dry.[5]

Then, finally, he not only made a decision but acted on it: he wrote an offer of marriage to Rose—the letter was as long and as self-critical as that of Rudin to Nathalia. As Tatiana in *Smoke* proved to be the saving angel of Litvinov, so Mason hoped that "the girl will save me from myself."[6]

[1] *Ibid.*, p. 277.   [2] *Ibid.*, p. 279.   [3] *Ibid.*, p. 305.
[4] *Ibid.*, p. 314.   [5] *Ibid.*, p. 339.   [6] *Ibid.*, p. 318.

In addition to the Turgenev-inspired portrait of Mason, Garland seems to have drawn on *Fathers and Sons* for the conflict between Rose and her father. Perhaps nowhere else in literature is the cleavage between two generations more admirably set forth than in this novel by Turgenev. We see how Arkady, together with his nihilist friend Bazarov, returns home fresh from the university to find that his world is no longer that of his father. The conflict between the younger and the older generation in Turgenev's novel probably attracted Garland because he himself had felt that he had outgrown his family intellectually.[1] Nevertheless, he felt sympathy with and understanding for his parents just as Arkady and even Bazarov did, and just as Rose did.

Like Arkady, Rose was an only child whose mother was dead. Both grew up in close companionship with their fathers. Kirsanov was, however, a man of some education, who attempted to keep pace with his son by reading the books which the boy studied. John Dutcher was an uneducated Western farmer, who toiled to send his only child to the university and, in so doing, educated her out of his world. Rose, after five years of college, returned home. Like Arkady she was met at the station by her father, who awaited her as eagerly and impatiently as Kirsanov waited for his son. In both novels the returning students rode through a landscape flooded by gorgeous sunlight. Despite the glorious weather, however, they were far from happy, for the barrier between father and child was felt from the very start. Her father's quaintness and plainness of speech surprised and puzzled Rose.

A fellow student joined her during the vacation, and the Rose-Josie couple may well be compared with Arkady-Bazarov. The contrast between Rose and Josie was striking. The former was serious and intellectual; the latter was cheerful and shallow and cared more for a dress than a book. It is interesting to compare

---

[1] When reading *Fathers and Sons* Garland possibly identified himself with Arkady, whose conflict was substantially Garland's own. Thus Turgenev's novel may have stimulated Garland to portray his own experiences. It should be remembered, however, that there was no break between Garland and his parents; instead, to judge from his letters and his reminiscences, his attitude toward his parents, especially toward his mother, was one of filial devotion. The cleavage between the younger and the older generation, an old teme, was particularly emphasized in the last decades of the nineteenth century as a result of the impact of science on modern thought.

them with the contrasting characters of the stern Bazarov and the lively Arkady, or of the quiet Bersenev and the gay, but superficial Sjubin in *On the Eve*. The girls' melancholy talk of love, during their rambling walks in overflowing meadows on a fine summer's day, recalls that of Bersenev and Sjubin in the opening chapter of *On the Eve*.

The parents in *Fathers and Sons* did their utmost to keep up with their restless children and make them wish to remain. So did John Dutcher, pathetically happy to have his daughter at home, for he hoped that Rose would marry and stay with him. Yet, the children were as impatient to get away as their fathers were desirous of having them stay. To be true to her ideals, Rose had to break away. It was a tragic moment when she told her father that she had to leave.

His eyes were opened to his fate; he [John Dutcher] saw what he had done; he had educated his daughter out of his world. Never again would she be content in the coolly beside him. He saw how foolish he had been all these years, to suppose he could educate and keep her.[1]

Like the parents in *Fathers and Sons*, Dutcher realized that the old had to give way to the young, and he acquiesced. Garland made one character say: " 'The ways of our fathers are not ours; it's tragedy either way you put it.' "[2] Thus, as in *Fathers and Sons*, the problem was left unsolved and the conflict remained.

2. TURGENEV AND CRANE

As far as I have been able to ascertain, there is no evidence that Crane read any book by Turgenev except *Smoke*, which he read in 1899.[3] We know, however, that he was a friend of Garland and Howells, who both were acquainted with Turgenev's works, and who might have introduced him to some of the writings of the Russian author in the early nineties. No scholar, it seems, has been aware of Crane's possible debt to Turgenev.

The cleavage between the younger and the older generation illustrated in *Rose of Dutcher's Coolly* was a motif also utilized by Crane in one of his short novels, *George's Mother*. True, the conflict between George Kelcey and his mother may to a certain

---

[1] *Ibid.*, p. 152. [2] *Ibid.*, p. 184. [3] See p. 103.

extent have been based on Crane's own experiences;[1] but Garland's portrayal of the conflict between Rose and her father, or Turgenev's delineation of a similar discord in *Fathers and Sons*, may perhaps also have served him as a model. Garland's novel appeared just one year before *George's Mother*, which was brought out in 1896.

Crane's portrayal of George Kelcey and his mother recalls Turgenev's description of Bazarov and his mother, Arina Vlassievna. Both Bazarov and George were only sons—George's brothers were all dead—and the sole joy of aged parents. Like Bazarov, George was morose and sullen, and both were irritated by their over-solicitous mothers. George Kelcey, a laborer, lived in the New York slums with his gentle and hard-working mother, all of whose loving thoughts and tenderness were concentrated on her son.[2] Like Arina Vlassievna, who loved her curt and unresponsive son with an all-sacrificing love, George Kelcey's mother endured patiently her son's impatient and irritating manners. The solicitous attitude of the mothers toward their restless and sullen sons only served to emphasize the cleavage and lack of understanding between them. In Crane's story, the conflict was not clearly formulated. There was religious opposition, which was of great importance; but no doubt the conflict went deeper and, as in *Fathers and Sons* and in *Rose of Dutcher's Coolly*, was insoluble. George Kelcey's mother "never understood the advanced things in life. He [George Kelcey] felt the hopelessness of ever making her comprehend. His mother was not modern."[3] Arkady's father, equally unable to understand his son, said:

"... I must confess, there's one thing I'm very sorry for: this was just the time when I hoped Arkady and I would become close friends, but it seems that I've dropped behind while he has forged ahead, and we can't understand each other."[4]

---

[1] Cf. the following letter by Crane: "My mother was a very religious woman but I don't think that she was as narrow as most of her friends or her family. ... I used to like church and prayer meetings when I was a kid but that cooled off and when I was thirteen or about that, my brother Will told me not to believe in Hell after my uncle had been boring me about the lake of fire and the rest of the sideshows. ..." Beer, *op. cit.*, pp. 49-50. Cf. also p. 327 n. 1.

[2] See Chap. X on Crane's debt to Zola, pp. 271 ff.

[3] *Work*, X, 76.

[4] *Fathers and Sons*, p. 48.

And he continued:

"Once I had a quarrel with our dear mother; she shouted and wouldn't listen to me. ... Finally I told her that she couldn't understand me, that we belonged to different generations. She was awfully cut up, and I thought: 'It can't be helped. It's a bitter pill, but it's got to be swallowed.' Well, now it's our turn and our successors can say to us: 'you are not of our generation, swallow the pill.' "[1]

Besides the similarities of theme between *George's Mother* and *Fathers and Sons*, Crane's novel is reminiscent of Turgenev's works in other respects also. George Kelcey was an irresolute, weak, and "superfluous" man, unfit for life. He may well be linked with Turgenev's heroes, who to varying degrees felt "superfluous"[2] in this world because of their inherent weakness, over-reflectiveness, and incapacity to act and to love; take, for instance, Rudin, Neschdanov, or Tschulkaturin. Like Tschulkaturin, the hero of *The Diary of a Superfluous Man*, George Kelcey was, at least from his own standpoint and despite his mother's affection, a man for whom no one really cared and whose presence on this earth was of no great consequence to anybody. With respect to women, George was as timid as Turgenev's hero, and while dreaming great dreams of attaining a woman's love, he was not capable of realizing his dreams. Like Tschulkaturin, he seems a failure in love as well as in other activities of life. When George fell in love with Maggie Johnson, he did little to let her know of his feelings. He remained an inactive daydreamer.

The shade of the girl was with him continually. With her he builded his grand dramas so that he trod in clouds, the matters of his daily life obscured and softened by a mist. ...
But then his courage flew away at the supreme moment. ... He could not approach the dread moment. He sank often from the threshold of knowledge. Directly after these occasions, it was his habit to avoid her to prove that she was a cipher to him.[3]

Both Crane's and Turgenev's hero, having failed in love and lacking self-reliance, had recourse to self-pity, keenly aware that they were failures and, therefore, useless. Tschulkaturin nursed his

---

[1] *Ibid.*, p. 58.

[2] Cf. the kinship of this type with the naturalistic one. In her decay Gervaise, for instance, felt "superfluous." See p. 264.

[3] *Work*, X, 46–7.

feeling of not being needed during years of traveling; George Kelcey sought refuge in drink which spelled degeneration to him.

During the next few days Kelcey suffered from his first gloomy conviction that the earth was not grateful to him for his presence upon it. When sharp words were said to him, he interpreted them with what seemed to be lately acquired insight. He could now perceive that the universe hated him. He sank to the most sublime depths of despair.[1]

George Kelcey was a failure type, a superfluous man, akin to Turgenev's heroes but independently portrayed, placed against the dismal Bowery slums. He was one of the many superfluous men, social outcasts that Crane may have met on his wanderings in the New York slums and later portrayed in his naturalistic stories. All of them shared with Tschulkaturin the sense of failure and superfluity.

Crane's story "A Dark Brown Dog" somewhat recalls Turgenev's tale "Mumu." Both stories treat of a little dog which was found and cared for. The new owners—in "Mumu"[2] a deaf and dumb giant of a man, Garassim, who was kind and as helpless as a child, and in Crane's story a small boy—became tenderly attached to their dogs, which instinctively returned the affection shown them. But in both stories trouble arose. The poor dogs disturbed the sleep of the households, and in a fit of bad temper the rich lady of "Mumu" decided that the pet should be killed. With unspeakable sorrow Garassim drowned his beloved dog himself. Crane's story also ended in tragedy. One day when the child's father returned, wild and furious with drink, to their poverty-stricken home in the slums, he beat the little dog and finally threw it out of the window. "The dark brown dog crashed in a heap on a roof of a shed five storeys below. From thence it rolled to the pavement of an alleyway."[3] The little boy, seated

---

[1] *Ibid.*, p. 48.

[2] "Mumu" first appeared in *Lippincott's Magazine*, VII (1871), 372–87 entitled "Mou-Mou." In 1884 it was reprinted in *Mumu and The Diary of a Superfluous Man* (New York, 1884).

[3] *Work*, XI, 124. Cf. also a similar episode in *Thérèse Raquin*, where Laurent killed the cat François by throwing it out of the window: "... il [Laurent] lui fit faire deux ou trois tours, puis l'envoya de toute la force de son bras contre la muraille noire d'en face. François s'y aplatit, s'y cassa les reins, et retomba sur le vitrage du passage." *Œuvres*, XXXIV, 214.

mute and dumbfounded by the side of the body of his dark brown friend, must have felt the same pain and suffered as much as Garassim, when he had drowned his only companion.

3. TURGENEV AND NORRIS

In four of his novels, *Vandover and the Brute*,[1] *Blix*, *The Octopus*, and *The Pit*, Norris portrayed weak and irresolute men sometimes set against strong and independent women; moreover, fate played a certain role in the lives of these characters. Since these elements, as we know, make up a common formula in Turgenev, it may be worth considering in detail whether Norris may in any way have been influenced by Turgenev. There is no reference whatever to Turgenev in Norris's works, or in letters which have been available to the present writer. No scholar of Norris, as far as I know, has considered a possible influence of Turgenev on Norris.

In *The Octopus*, Presley, Norris's alter ego, comes close to Turgenev's irresolute hero.[2] He was a failure, and like Rudin and others of Turgenev's characters, failed because of his temperament; he possessed a certain passivity and inability to act, together with a tendency to dream and ponder. In contrast to the other male characters of the novel, he was, like Rudin and Bazarov, a highly educated intellectual. Annixter, to be sure, had been graduated from college and was intelligent, but he was not intellectual. Presley had, like Rudin, "a nature more composite, a temperament more complex."[3] Like Turgenev, Norris stressed the lethargy and indecision of his hero:

Though morbidly sensitive to changes in his physical surroundings, he would be slow to act upon such sensations, would not prove impulsive, not because he was sluggish, but because he was merely irresolute. It could be foreseen that morally he was of that sort who avoid evil through good taste, lack of decision, and want of opportunity. His temperament was that of the poet; when he told himself he had been thinking, he deceived himself. He had, on such occasions, been only brooding.[4]

---

[1] For Vandover see Chap. XI. See also pp. 199 ff.

[2] This character was also modeled on Edwin Markham, whose "The Man with the Hoe" inspired, as is well known, Presley's poem "The Toilers."

[3] *Compl. Works*, I, 6.

[4] *Ibid.*, pp. 6–7.

Against Presley stood the forceful and active Annixter, his best friend—a contrast common in Turgenev's works. The weak Neschdanov in *Virgin Soil* had the strong Solomin for his friend, and the inactive Bersenev in *On the Eve* had the determined Insarov by his side. The irresoluteness of Presley was contrasted with the aggressiveness of Annixter. Norris wrote:

> The two men were diametrically opposed in temperament. Presley was easy-going; Annixter, alert. Presley was a confirmed dreamer, irresolute, inactive, with a strong tendency to melancholy; the young farmer was a man of affairs, decisive, combative, whose only reflection upon his interior economy was a morbid concern in the vagaries of his stomach. Yet the two never met without a mutual pleasure, taking a genuine interest in each other's affairs, and often putting themselves to great inconvenience to be of trifling service to help one another.[1]

As has been said, the indecision of Rudin and of others of the same type was greatest whenever love was concerned, because they were unable to love wholeheartedly; in like manner, Presley did not even realize until the end of the novel that he had been in love with Hilma, whose husband, Annixter, was killed in the clash between the farmers and the railroad; Presley had not been sincerely moved earlier for "his impulses were abrupt and of short duration."[2]

The Turgenev character whom Presley most resembles is Neschdanov, the anarchist, in *Virgin Soil*. This is most obvious in the latter part of *The Octopus*, where Presley turned anarchist. But right from the very beginning of the novel, he reminds one of Neschdanov; both were dreamers, poets, idealists, at heart romanticists confronted with a harsh and brutal reality. Both were sensitive aesthetes to whom reality with its misery and grimness was repulsive. This was Presley's reaction to his surroundings:

> These uncouth brutes of farmhands and petty ranchers, grimed with the soil they worked upon, were odious to him beyond words. Never could he feel in sympathy with them, nor with their lives, their ways, their

---

[1] *Ibid.*, p. 25.

[2] *Ibid.*, II, 338. Presley's inactivity and pleasure in theorizing were also evident whenever his great epic of the West was concerned. Cf. Warren Mason and his novel of Chicago life in *Rose of Dutcher's Coolly;* Mason and Presley are similar types. Presley's epic of the West was no doubt Norris's own *Epic of the Wheat*, on which he was at work.

marriages, deaths, bickerings, and all the monotonous round of their sordid existence.[1]

Neschdanov, likewise, was ill-adjusted to his task as a revolutionist and to his uncouth environment: "Oh, it is difficult, very difficult, to combine æsthetics and actual life!"[2] And again:

"Oh, and how I curse all the nervousness, the sensibility, the fastidiousness, which I have inherited from my aristocratic father! What right had he to call me into existence and furnish me with organs which are totally unfit for the sphere in which I am destined to move?—to make a bird, and then throw it into the water?—to make a democrat, a lover of the people, in whom the mere smell of that accursed whiskey causes disgust —almost sickness?"[3]

In *Virgin Soil* Neschdanov is called a "romantic realist."[4] That expression may be used with equal justice of Presley, for

it was his ambition to portray life as he saw it—directly, frankly, and through no medium of personality or temperament. But, on the other hand, as well, he wished to see everything through a rose-coloured mist— a mist that dulled all harsh outlines, all crude and violent colours.[5]

At first Presley had been in sympathy with the farmers and their revolutionary methods. It was only later that his attitude changed to one of antipathy. This puzzling transformation was perhaps in part inspired by *Virgin Soil*, in which Turgenev's attitude toward the anarchists was one of scepticism.[6]

---

[1] *Compl. Works*, I, 3.

[2] *Virgin Soil* (London 1878), p. 257.

[3] *Ibid.*, p. 262.

[4] *Ibid.*, p. 341.

[5] *Compl. Works*, I, 10. Presley may also be compared with Rosmer in Ibsen's drama *Rosmersholm*. Rosmer, too, was an idealist affected by the ideas of freedom of his day, who with his sensitive and delicate nature was not suitable for his task and reacted in the same way as Neschdanov did toward harsh and brutal reality. In Neschdanov, Rosmer, and Presley we have the same conflict between idealism and reality.

See also Sten Linder, *Ernst Ahlgren i hennes romaner* (Stockholm, 1930), p. 332. Linder rightly links Rosmer with the weak revolutionist Neschdanov.

[6] It should also be remembered that Étienne in *Germinal* underwent a similar development, probably under the inspiration of *Virgin Soil*. On the last page but one of the novel Étienne reflected: "Et il songeait à présent que la violence peut-être ne hâtait pas les choses. Des cables coupés, des rails arrachés, des lampes cassées, quelle inutile besogne ... Sa raison murissait, il avait jeté la gourme de ses rancunes." In like manner Presley realized that the violent methods

The atmosphere of anarchism, conspiracy, and revolt which pervades the latter part of *The Octopus* is somewhat reminiscent of that of *Virgin Soil*.[1] Through the influence of an anarchist saloonkeeper, Caraher, who "knew something of Mill and Bakounin," Presley leaned more and more toward anarchism. He threw away his former favorites, Homer, Milton, Tennyson and Browning, and substituted for them J. S. Mill, Malthus, Young, Pushkin, Henry George, and Bakunin.[2] After the armed clash between the farmers and the railroad he cried out: "'By God, I, too, I'm a Red!'"[3]

To rouse the people Neschdanov went out in order to speak to them, but he could not make himself understood, for he was too much of a poet, a daydreamer, and a theorist; Presley likewise spoke, but he, too, failed to rouse the masses, for he was bombastic, theoretic, and analytical. The same poignant sense of failure filled both Neschdanov and Presley. This was Presley's failure:

Presley ceased speaking. Weak, shaking, scarcely knowing what he was about, he descended from the stage. A prolonged explosion of applause followed, the Opera House roaring to the roof, men cheering, stamping, waving their hats. But it was not intelligent applause. Instinctively, as he made his way out, Presley knew that, after all, he had not once held the hearts of his audience. He had talked as he would have written; for all his scorn of literature, he had been literary. The men who listened to him, ranchers, country people, store-keepers, attentive though they were, were not once sympathetic. Vaguely they had felt that here was something which other men—more educated—would possibly consider eloquent. They applauded vociferously but perfunctorily, in order to appear to understand.

Presley, for all his love of the people, saw clearly for one moment that he was an outsider to their minds. He had not helped them nor their cause in the least; he never would.[4]

---

used by the farmers and himself were of no avail. It should be remembered, however, that the ending of *Germinal* foreshadowed a coming revolution; there was no such hint in *The Octopus*.

[1] Cf. also *Germinal*.

[2] *Compl. Works*, II, 23.

[3] *Ibid.*, p. 246. Throughout the novel Presley remained a comparatively inactive observer, and his attitude was similar to that of Reeves in *Jason Edwards*. In each book an Easterner, probably the author himself, visited the scene of conflict and played the role of an observer.

[4] *Ibid.*, p. 262. Presley's political speech may also be linked with a similar high-flown address delivered by Étienne in *Germinal* (cf. Biencourt, *op. cit.*, p. 217). Both speeches are similar in form and content, mainly made up of

Despite his conviction that he was a failure, Presley made a final attempt to further the cause of anarchism; he endeavored to kill Behrman, the railroad agent, by means of a bomb, but Behrman remained unscathed. Again Presley had failed:

After this, however, there had come to Presley a deep-rooted suspicion that he was—of all human beings, the most wretched—a failure. Everything to which he had set his mind failed—his great epic, his efforts to help the people who surrounded him, even his attempted destruction of the enemy, all these had come to nothing. Girding his shattered strength together, he resolved upon one last attempt to live up to the best that was in him, and to that end had set himself to lift out of the despair into which they had been thrust the bereaved family of the German, Hooven.[1]

But even this humanitarian effort came to nothing; chance was against him. "He had failed again. A superstitious fear assailed him that he was, in a manner, marked; that he was foredoomed to fail."[2] Norris hinted, however, that Hilma might eventually be able to make Presley stronger and more resolute, as did Tatiana with regard to Litvinov in *Smoke*.

Then suddenly, all the tired heart of him went out toward her. A longing to give the best that was in him to the memory of her, to be strong and noble because of her, to reshape his purposeless, half-wasted life with her nobility and purity and gentleness for his inspiration leaped all at once within him, leaped and stood firm, hardening to a resolve stronger than any he had ever known.[3]

---

questions directed against the bad social system. Norris seems to be indebted to both *Germinal* and *Virgin Soil* for the portrayal of Presley. Probably we may assume that Zola himself had *Virgin Soil* in mind when writing *Germinal*, for Étienne has some points in common with Neschdanov; he, too, failed in his task, and his bombastic address before the miners is reminiscent of Neschdanov when attempting to speak before the Russian farmers. We may perhaps venture the assumption that the weak, passive type of French naturalism was in part stimulated by Turgenev's weak type of hero. Both types may be called failures; the one was the victim of deterministic forces, the other of fatalistic ones. Note that Flaubert, Zola, and other French naturalists met Turgenev during his residence in Paris. We know that Turgenev even made suggestions for *Madame Bovary*. For the contact between Turgenev and French writers, see André Maurois, *Turgenev* (Stockholm, 1932) and E. Halpérine-Kaminsky, *Ivan Tourguéneff* (Paris, 1901).

[1] *Compl. Works*, II, 276–7.
[2] *Ibid.*, p. 298.
[3] *Ibid.*, p. 338.

Annixter, Presley's friend and opposite, although described with Dickensian humor, is related to those forceful and determined men whom Turgenev used as contrasts to his weak and irresolute heroes. Annixter has points in common with Bazarov;[1] his death was equally tragic, and may also be said to have been caused by chance. Although both were kind at heart, they exhibited a curt, irritated, and even offensive manner to their fellow men, and frequently hurt the feelings of others. Both had gone to college and were intelligent and promising young men. The following passage applies equally well to both:

He still remained one of the people, rough almost to insolence, direct in speech, intolerant in his opinions, relying upon absolutely no one but himself; yet, with all this, of an astonishing degree of intelligence, and possessed of an executive ability little short of positive genius. [2]

They were, moreover, somewhat eccentric, and had similar temperaments and similar attitudes toward women. They looked upon woman cynically, but nevertheless fell in love.[3] This is Annixter's attitude toward Hilma Tree:

To his surprise he found himself thinking of her after he had gone to bed that night, and in the morning when he woke he was bothered to know whether he had dreamed about Hilma's fine white arms over night. Then abruptly he had lost patience with himself for being so occupied with the subject, raging and furious with all the breed of feemales—a fine way for a man to waste his time. He had had his experience with the timid little creature in the glove-cleaning establishment in Sacramento. That was enough. Feemales! Rot! None of them in *his*, thank you.[4]

And again Annixter:

Women he distrusted with the instinctive distrust of the overgrown schoolboy. Now, at length, a young woman had come into his life. Promptly he was struck with discomfiture, annoyed almost beyond endurance, harassed, bedevilled, excited, made angry and exasperated. He was suspicious of the woman, yet desired her, totally ignorant of how to approach her, hating the sex, yet drawn to the individual, confusing the two emotions, sometimes even hating Hilma as a result of this confusion, but at all times disturbed, vexed, irritated beyond power of expression.[5]

---

[1] Cf. Mason in *Rose of Dutcher's Coolly*, pp. 324 ff.
[2] *Compl. Works*, I, 22.
[3] Cf. Mason's attitude toward Rose, p. 325.
[4] *Compl. Works*, I, 76.
[5] *Ibid.*, p. 219-20.

And this is Bazarov's attitude toward Mme Odintsova:

Indeed, a change had taken place in both young men from the very first days of their sojourn at Nikolskoye. Bazarov, who was obviously in Anna Sergeyevna's good graces, though she rarely agreed with him, began to reveal signs of uneasiness hitherto foreign to him: he was irritable, spoke reluctantly, looked sulky, and was fidgety and restless. . . . The actual reason for this "new turn" was the feeling that Odintsova inspired in Bazarov, a feeling which tormented and maddened him, but which he would have promptly denied with a sneering laugh and cynical invective if anybody had even remotely hinted at the possibility of what was actually happening to him. . . . His pulse quickened at the mere thought of her; he could easily have come to terms with his pulse, but something else had happened to him, something he never would have admitted, something he had always jeered at, and against which all his pride rose up in arms. When talking with Anna Sergeyevna he more than ever displayed a careless scorn for everything romantic, but when left to himself he was exasperated by the romantic fibre which he discovered in himself. . . . Or suddenly he would picture to himself those chaste arms entwining his neck, those proud lips responding to his kisses and those profound eyes gazing tenderly—yes, tenderly, into his, and his head would reel, he would forget himself for a moment until indignation would get the better of him. He caught himself at all kinds of "disgusting" thoughts, as though the devil were teasing him. At times he believed he could discern a change in Odintsova too, as if the expression she wore had someting unusual in it, as if perhaps . . . At this point he would generally stamp his foot or gnash his teeth and shake his fist in his own face.[1]

Bazarov and Annixter felt the same scorn for women; but gradually, although they did not at once admit that they were in love, the men changed. They were confused and bewildered by their feelings, and both were forced to revaluate their materialistic concepts of woman and love.

Just as the determined Annixter was contrasted with the irresolute Presley, so was the successful Jadwin of *The Pit* contrasted with the inactive Corthell. Corthell, like Vandover, has certain traits in common with Huysmans' decadent hero Des Esseintes;[2] he may also be linked with Turgenev's weak heroes, for, despite his outward success, Corthell gives the impression of a man who has failed. This was particularly obvious with relation to love. He was dominated by Laura just as Litvinov was dominated by Irina

---

[1] *Fathers and Sons*, pp. 93-5.
[2] See Chap. XI.

in *Smoke*. The following quotation is true of both Corthell and Litvinov:

> She had sent him away the first time, and he had gone without a murmur; only to come back loyal as ever, silent, watchful, sympathetic, his love for her deeper, stronger than before, and—as always timely—bringing to her a companionship at the moment of all others when she was most alone.
> Now she had driven him from her again, and this time, she very well knew, it was to be forever. She had shut the door upon this great love.[1]

For the complex portrait of Laura Dearborn, a deviation from his naturalistic type of woman, Norris may also have drawn on Turgenev for inspiration.[2] *The Pit* has some points in common with *Smoke*, and Laura at times recalls Irina; at least they were temperamentally akin. There is in both books the common triangle —a woman between two men;[3] in both novels the women were strong and forceful, whereas their lovers were weak and easily influenced by them. Laura was of the same superb and almost fatal beauty as Irina, and had the same magnetic ability to attract suitors. Like Irina she treated these suitors rather coldly and capriciously, but nevertheless liked to have them around. Both were of a passionate and proud disposition and exhibited a similar nervous temperament, with sudden changes from joy to grief; both were vaguely ambitious but did very little to realize their dreams. Furthermore, Laura was painted with the same sensitiveness and delicacy of touch which made Turgenev's women justly famous. She was essentially an esthetic type.

> Laura Dearborn's pallor was in itself a colour. It was a tint rather than a shade, like ivory; a warm white, blending into an exquisite, delicate brownness toward the throat. Set in the middle of this paleness of brow and cheek, her deep brown eyes glowed lambent and intense. They were not large, but in some indefinable way they were important. It was very natural to speak of her eyes, and in speaking to her, her friends always found that they must look squarely into their pupils.[4]

---

[1] *Compl. Works*, IX, 340.

[2] See also pp. 122, 343 n. 3, 403, 406 n. 2.

[3] Cf. also the triangle in *A Doll's House*, where Nora's admirer was the friend of her husband's. This was also the case in *The Pit*, whereas in *Smoke*, although the men knew each other, there was no friendship between them.

[4] *Compl. Works*, IX, 2.

And this is Irina:

She was a tall, slim girl, with a somewhat hollow chest and narrow un-
formed shoulders, with a skin of a dead-white, rare at her age, and pure
and smooth as china, with thick fair hair; there were darker tresses mingled
in a very original way with the light ones. Her features—exquisitely, almost too perfectly, correct—had not yet quite lost the innocent expression
that belongs to childhood; the languid curves of her lovely neck, and
her smile—half-indifferent, half-weary—betrayed the nervous temperament of a delicate girl; but in the lines of those fine, faintly-smiling
lips, of that small, falcon, slightly-narrow nose, there was something
wilful and passionate, something dangerous for herself and others. Astounding, really astounding were her eyes, dark gray with greenish lights,
languishing, almond-shaped as an Egyptian goddess's, with shining
lashes and bold sweep of eyebrow. There was a strange look in those
eyes; they seemed looking out intently and thoughtfully—looking out from
some unknown depth and distance. At school, Irina had been reputed
one of the best pupils for intelligence and abilities, but of uneven temper,
fond of power, and headstrong; one class-mistress prophesied that her
passions would be her ruin—*"vos passions vous perdront"*; on the other
hand, another class-mistress censured her for coldness and want of feeling, and called her *"une jeune fille sans cœur."* Irina's companions thought
her proud and reserved: her brothers and sisters stood a little in awe
of her: her mother had no confidence in her: and her father felt ill at ease
when she fastened her mysterious eyes upon him.[1]

Irina and Laura had a similar attitude toward love and marriage. We note that Irina laughed at the helplessness of her husband's love for her. When finally Laura agreed to become Jadwin's wife, she did so not because she loved him but because
of his great wealth and good social standing. It was implied in
Smoke that Irina never really loved her husband, and she certainly
treated him with indifference and coldness, just as Laura treated
Jadwin before their marriage. It is interesting to observe that in
both books it was the women who took the initiative. Note particularly that it was Laura who went up to Jadwin at the Opera,
and it was Irina who made arrangements to meet Litvinov. This
quality of forwardness is often found in Turgenev's women.
Moreover, each book has a happy ending: Litvinov found happiness at last with Tatiana by his side, and Jadwin and Laura became more intimately united, and emerged purified from their
matrimonial crisis.

---

[1] *Smoke* (Mod. lib. ed., New York, n. d.), pp. 49–50.

It should be noted, however, that there were important differences between Laura and Irina. Laura was at heart a virtuous daughter of New England, and did not get into sexual entanglements in the manner of Irina. Moreover, she was motivated by more idealistic principles, as is apparent in the episode of the intended elopements: Laura remained with Jadwin because she realized that she loved him, whereas Irina stayed with her rich husband, whom she did not love, because it was more convenient for her. Laura made her choice according to ethical standards, whereas Irina's decision was purely selfish.

To sum up: We know that Garland was acquainted with some of Turgenev's works and that he looked upon *Fathers and Sons*, for instance, with respect. Garland's indebtedness to the Russian writer is obvious, it seems, in his early work, in *Main-Travelled Roads*, *Jason Edwards*, *A Little Norsk*, *Prairie Folks*, and *Rose of Dutcher's Coolly* and is more extensive and goes deeper than Norris's. Garland may have drawn for inspiration particularly on *Fathers and Sons* and *Rudin*, and to a less degree on *A Sportman's Sketches*, *On the Eve*, and *Smoke*. In most of these books are found the common Turgenev formula: man is weak, woman is strong, and chance omnipotent. This theme may also, with slight variations, be found in *Jason Edwards* and *Rose of Dutcher's Coolly*. What seems to have attracted Garland most in Turgenev's work was the failure type of man. In Garland's early works there is a long line of failures: Grant McLane, Senator Ward, Jason Edwards, Bert, Elder Pill, Daddy Deering, and Warren Mason. These failed as a result of social conditions or of fate or because of a defect in their character, usually irresolution or inability to act.[1] Jason Edwards may be linked with Bazarov, because he was ultimately beaten by fate, whereas Mason, possessing an irresolute and vacillating temperament, is related to Rudin. In addition to the failure type, Turgenev may also have been stimulated by Garland's use of chance, his lyric description of the prairie, and his delineation of the conflict between the younger and the older generation as it is evidenced in *Rose of Dutcher's Coolly*.

This theme was also utilized by Crane in *George's Mother*, and

---

[1] Usually a combination of these factors contributed to the failure of the characters.

it is possible that he may have had Bazarov and Arina Vlassievna in mind when delineating the cleavage between George Kelcey and his over-solicitous mother. Moreover, Crane's superfluous men may be linked with those of the Russian writer; George Kelcey may be placed beside Tschulkaturin, the hero of *The Diary of a Superfluous Man*. The story "A Dark Brown Dog" has, finally, some points in common with Turgenev's "Mumu."

Norris's debt to Turgenev can be traced in at least two novels: *The Octopus* and *The Pit*. It is most apparent in the last-mentioned book, a fact which in part may account for its tone of refinement and lack of brutality. Four of Turgenev's novels, in particular, seem to have attracted Norris: *Rudin*, *Fathers and Sons*, *Virgin Soil*, and *Smoke*. Like Garland, Norris was in part indebted to Turgenev for the literary portrayal of the failure type of man. Presley failed in his task of promoting anarchism because, like Neschdanov, he was a dreamer and theorist; Annixter, who recalls Bazarov in his morose manner and in his cynicism, failed through the adversity of fate; Corthell, finally was a failure because of his inherent irresolution and weakness.[1] The part played by him in *The Pit* may be compared to that of Litvinov in *Smoke*, and Laura may be linked with Irina of the same novel.[2] In the works of our writers, determinism and literary fatalism were found side by side, a circumstance which in part may be due to the influence which the determinist Zola and the fatalist Turgenev exerted on their works.[3] The "poetic" realism of Turgenev, devoid of brutality and obscenity, may have been one of the factors that helped to counterbalance the influence of Zola on Garland and to some degree on Norris in his last novel. Turgenev's influence on Crane, on the other hand, appears not to have relieved the latter's naturalism, for *George's Mother*, which was possibly influenced by the Russian writer, is one of Crane's most naturalistic novels.

[1] Cf. Corthell and Des Esseintes. See pp. 312–14.
[2] Cf. pp. 122, 403 ff..
[3] See also Tolstoy, pp. 343 ff.

CHAPTER XIII

TOLSTOY AND STEPHEN CRANE

A few facts about the appearance and reception of Tolstoy's work in the United States have been noted in an earlier chapter.[1] In view of the Russian writer's popularity in the eighties and nineties, it seems reasonable to expect that to some extent he would have been a source of inspiration for our three writers. There is apparently no scholarly study of the influence of Tolstoy on these authors. The following analysis does not, in any way, aim at being an exhaustive treatment of the subject. On the contrary, it has been necessary to concentrate on Crane, who seems to owe a more substantial debt to Tolstoy than do Garland[2] and Norris.[3]

---

[1] See pp. 34 ff. Cf. also Gettmann, *op. cit.*, pp. 111 ff.

[2] For Garland's knowledge of Tolstoy, see p. 70. Garland's debt to Tolstoy seems to be less extensive than that to Turgenev and Ibsen. However, there are perhaps echoes of Tolstoy's concept of war, as expressed in *War and Peace*, in his story "The Return of a Private" in *Main-Travelled Roads*. In both writers we sense the meaninglessness and futility of war. Garland's first book of reminiscences, *Boy-Life on the Prairie*, recalls Tolstoy's descriptions of his early life in *Childhood* and *Youth*. The Russian's collection of short stories, *The Invaders*, may also have served as a model. Compare Tolstoy's use of fate striking mercilessly, in such stories as "Polikouchka" and "Khlostomir", with Garland's exemplification of fate in his short story "Daddy Deering" in *Prairie Folks*. Cf. pp. 323–4. Howells, ardent admirer of Tolstoy's art, linked a section of Garland's biography *Ulysses S. Grant* with Tolstoy's *Death of Ivan Ilyich*. On July 3, 1898, he wrote to Garland's brother Franklin: ". . . Give him [Hamlin Garland] my love, and say his chapter about Grant's last days was masterly; Tolstoy could not have done it better; it was like a passage out of Ivan Illitch . . ."

[3] For Norris's knowledge of Tolstoy, see p. 123. *The Octopus* probably owes some of its social sense and its way of describing rural life on a vast canvas to *Anna Karenina*. In addition, Levin and Annixter have points in common. Both passed through an emotional crisis during a night spent in the open air. Peace came with dawn when they realized that they were in love. Gradually the egoists grew to be altruists. Moreover, Vanamee's ruminations on the happiness of

We know that Crane had read *Sebastopol* and *War and Peace*, and that he ranked Tolstoy as "the supreme living writer of our time."[1] The effects of Crane's reading of Tolstoy are evident, it seems, in many of the American writer's tales of war, notably in *The Red Badge of Courage*, which has many points in common with Tolstoy's war narratives. Some of these, however, grow essentially out of the similarity of theme, and others represent incidental details; yet there are elements in Crane's war stories that suggest Tolstoy in the first place as a possible source of inspiration.

Let us first examine Crane's concept of war. It has been noted earlier that it deviated from Zola's, who looked upon war as a necessity, and that it was more closely related to the Russian's. Tolstoy was a pacifist, and to him, as to Crane,[2] war was meaningless slaughter. Neither Tolstoy nor Crane had any illusions about the glory of war. In Tolstoy's stories as well as in those of Crane, war was painted "without the brilliant and accurate alignment of troops, without music, without the drum-roll, without standards flying in the wind, without galloping generals."[3] Both authors depicted it as it was, "in blood, in suffering, and in death."[4] To Tolstoy and Crane the pain and bloodshed of war were even more

---

simple, primitive life in the country are reminiscent of Tolstoy's Rousseau-inspired concept of rural life in *Anna Karenina*. Finally, this novel may to an extent have been a source of inspiration for Norris's handling of the plot of *The Pit*, as well as for his treatment of Laura. As is well known, Tolstoy's novel opens and closes with a railroad accident, the first one being symbolic of the ultimate tragedy of Anna. Similarly *The Pit* opens and closes with a description of the Board of Trade Building, the first one in connection with the Helmick failure, which is symbolic of the final tragedy. For Norris's debt to *What Is Art?* see p. 162, and Marchand, *op. cit.*, pp. 11 ff.

[1] See p. 96.

[2] Cf. the following reference to Tolstoy in connection with Crane's own war experiences: "War was ridiculous but men went to war . . . 'What were we doing there at all? There was no definition. There was no use quoting Tolstoy. There was no Napoleon to say the right thing and lend a gilded finish to the occasion.'" Beer, *op. cit.*, p. 198. Crane gives evidence of a Kiplingesque glorification of battle in "The Clan of No-Name" and "The Price of the Harness."

[3] *Sebastopol* (New York, 1887), p. 27. Cf. in Crane's *War Memories*: "War is death, and a plague of the lack of small things, and toil." *Work*, IX, 219. See also *ibid.*, I, 87.

[4] *Sebastopol*, p. 27.

horrible, because they believed that war was not only unnecessary, but completely meaningless. Frequently Tolstoy asked the questions: "What's the use? What's the meaning?" "For what, then, had those legs and arms been torn off, those men been killed?"[1] There was no answer, however. Crane asked himself similar questions, but found no reply.

Lying near one of the enemy's trenches was a red-headed Spanish corpse. I wonder how many hundreds were cognizant of this red-headed Spanish corpse? It arose to the dignity of a landmark. There were many corpses, but only one with a red head. This red-head. He was always there. Each time I approached that part of the field I prayed that I might find that he had been buried. But he was always there—red-headed. His strong simple countenance was a malignant sneer at the system which was for ever killing the credulous peasants in a sort of black night of politics, where the peasants merely followed whatever somebody had told them was lofty and good. But, nevertheless, the red-headed Spaniard was dead. He was irrevocably dead. And to what purpose? The honour of Spain? Surely the honour of Spain could have existed without the violent death of this poor red-headed peasant? ... You came to another hemisphere to fight because—because you were told to, I suppose. Well, there you are, buried in your trench on San Juan Hill. That is the end of it, your life has been taken—that is a flat, frank fact.[2]

Despite the fact that war was horrible and without purpose, men went to war and were killed. Why? Neither Tolstoy nor Crane could give an answer. The soldiers "went because they went."[3] That was all.

Moreover, Tolstoy and Crane shared the concept that the actual happenings on the battlefield were not the logical results of careful planning on behalf of the generals; on the contrary, victories were "accidents, the outcome of a blind dash of unintelligent forces, rather than due to strategy and generalship."[4] Thus, what occurred on the battlefield had no connection with any previously determined plan. Things happened because incomprehensible forces were at work over which man had no control.

In order to illustrate the meaningless cruelty of war, Tolstoy . did not hesitate to depict in detail the sordidness and brutality of the soldier's life. In hospitals and on battlefields the reader

---

[1] *War and peace* (Mod. lib. ed., New York, n. d.), p. 382.
[2] *Work*, IX, 238–9.
[3] *Ibid.*, II, 241.
[4] Parrington, *op. cit.*, III, 328.

witnessed the terror and the bloodshed, the intense pain of war, in a number of heart-rending scenes, the vivid realism of which was perhaps only equaled by similar scenes in *La Débâcle*. Tolstoy recorded minutely and accurately the hissing of the bullets, the roar of the mortars, the piercing cries of the dying and the wounded, the nauseating smell of corpses, etc. It is probable that the Russian writer served to some extent as a model for the intense realism of Crane's tales of war. To exemplify this, it may perhaps suffice to compare the following two passages. The scene below is taken from *War and Peace*:

Some crows, scenting blood, flitted to and fro among the birches, cawing impatiently. For more than five acres round the tents there were sitting or lying men stained with blood, and variously attired. They were surrounded by crowds of dejected-looking and intently observant soldiers, who had come with stretchers. Officers, trying to keep order, kept driving them away from the place; but it was of no use. The soldiers, heedless of the officers, stood leaning against the stretchers, gazing intently at what was passing before their eyes, as though trying to solve some difficult problem in this spectacle. From the tents came the sound of loud, angry wailing, and piteous moans. At intervals a doctor's assistant ran out for water, or to point out those who were to be taken in next. The wounded, awaiting their turn at the tent, uttered hoarse groans and moans, wept, shouted, swore, or begged for vodka. Several were raving in delirium.[1]

Here is a similar scene taken from *Wounds in the Rain*:

The low white tents of the hospital were grouped around an old schoolhouse. There was here a singular commotion. In the foreground two ambulances interlocked wheels in the deep mud. The drivers were tossing the blame of it back and forth, gesticulating and berating, while from the ambulances, both crammed with wounded, there came an occasional groan. An interminable crowd of bandaged men were coming and going. Great numbers sat under trees nursing heads or arms or legs. There was a dispute of some kind raging on the steps of the schoolhouse. Sitting with his back against a tree a man with a face as grey as a new army blanket was serenely smoking a corncob pipe. The lieutenant wished to rush forward and inform him that he was dying.[2]

In both passages, which present an objective picture of how the wounded were taken care of, we note the same stress laid upon

---

[1] *War and Peace*, p. 758.
[2] *Work*, IX, 133. Cf. also *ibid.*, pp. 207, 234 and *ibid.*, pp. 88, 113.

the horror of war. Each writer depicted its bloodshed, its futility, its absence of glamour and heroic postures.

Another feature of Tolstoy's war stories was his new type of soldier, an ordinary individual[1] possessed of the usual shortcomings of the average man, whose sensations and emotions under fire were carefully analyzed. Turning to Crane, we observe that he, too, created a type of soldier that in some respects resembles Tolstoy's. To illustrate this, let us compare Volodia in *Sebastopol* with Henry in *The Red Badge of Courage*. In a burst of enthusiasm both Volodia, a second-ensign, and Henry enlisted as volunteers, dreaming happy dreams of bold deeds on the battlefield. However, their imaginary romance of warfare contrasted sharply with the stern reality of war itself. Since both were of a sensitive, impressionable, and meditative disposition, they began to reflect whether they would be able to fulfil the demands required of them or not. This was the main problem in both stories. When attempting to solve this problem by way of persuading themselves that they would not run away, their fear of being cowards[1] only augmented. The idea of failure tortured them constantly and would not leave their harassed minds. This is Volodia:

The feeling of this desertion in the presence of danger, of death, as he believed, oppressed his heart with the glacial weight of a stone. Halting in the middle of the place, he looked all about him to see if he was observed, and taking his head in both hands, he murmured, with a voice broken by terror, "My God! am I really a despicable poltroon, a coward? I who have lately dreamed of dying for my country, for my Czar, and that with joy! Yes, I am an unfortunate and despicable being!" he cried, in profound despair, and quite undeceived about himself.[3]

And this is Henry:

He felt alone in space when his injured comrade had disappeared. His failure to discover any mite of resemblance in their view-points made him more miserable than before. No one seemed to be wrestling with such a terrific personal problem. He was a mental outcast.[4]

---

[1] Occasionally Tolstoy has a tendency, it seems, to idealize the common soldier. See, for instance, *Sebastopol*, pp. 41–2. There is no such tendency in Crane.

[2] Cf. Maurice, whose fear was less a psychological problem than a normal reaction in the face of danger. When first under fire Maurice wanted to run away like a frightened animal.

[3] *Sebastopol*, pp. 174–5.

[4] *Work*, I, 44.

Both Volodia and Henry were kept awake at night, brooding, trying to persuade themselves that they would not be cowards when under fire. This is Volodia:

Left alone with his thoughts, Volodia at first felt a return of the terror caused by the trouble which agitated his soul. Counting upon sleep to be able to cease thinking of his surroundings and to forget himself, he blew out his candle and lay down, covering himself all up with his overcoat, even his head, for he had kept his fear of darkness since his childhood. But suddenly the idea came to him that a shell might fall through the roof and kill him. . . .

He rose and walked the room. The fear of the real danger had stifled the mysterious terror of darkness. He hunted and found to hand only a saddle and a samovar. "I am a coward, a poltroon, a wretch," he thought again, filled with disgust and scorn of himself. He lay down and tried to stop thinking; but then the impressions of the day passed again through his mind, and the continual sounds which shook the panes of his single window recalled to him the danger he was in. Visions followed. Now he saw the wounded covered with blood; now bursting shells, pieces of which flew into his room; now the pretty Sister of Charity who dressed his wounds weeping over his agony, or his mother, who, carrying him back to the provincial town, praying to God for him before a miraculous image, shed hot tears. Sleep eluded him; but suddenly the thought of an all-powerful Deity who sees everything and who hears every prayer flashed upon him distinct and clear in the midst of his reveries. He fell upon his knees, making the sign of the cross, and clasping his hands as he had been taught in his childhood. This simple gesture aroused in him a feeling of infinite, long-forgotten calm.

"If I am to die, it is because I am useless! Then, may Thy will be done, O Lord! and may it be done quickly. But if the courage and firmness which I lack are necessary to me, spare me the shame and the dishonor, which I cannot endure, and teach me what I must do to accomplish Thy will."

His weak, childish, and terrified soul was fortified, was calmed at once, and entered new, broad, and luminous regions. He thought of a thousand things; he experienced a thousand sensations in the short duration of this feeling; then he quietly went to sleep, heedless of the dull roar of the bombardment and of the shaking windows.[1]

And Henry:

He went slowly to his tent and stretched himself on a blanket by the side of the snoring tall soldier. In the darkness he saw visions of a thousand-tongued fear that would babble at his back and cause him to flee, while others were going coolly about their country's business. He admitted that he would not be able to cope with this monster. He felt that every

---

[1] *Sebastopol*, pp. 179–82.

nerve in his body would be an ear to hear the voices, while other men would remain stolid and deaf.

And as he sweated with the pain of these thoughts, he could hear low, serene sentences. "I'll bid five." "Make it six." "Seven." "Seven goes."

He stared at the red, shivering reflection of a fire on the white wall of his tent until, exhausted and ill from the monotony of his suffering, he fell asleep.[1]

Whereas Volodia freed himself temporarily from his fear by means of a prayer, Henry found no relief until sleep finally came.

When eventually under fire, they overcame their panic and emerged from the trial as victors, thus proving to be true heroes. This is Volodia's transformation:

Once at work, there remained no trace of that terror which the evening before showed itself so plainly. . . . As to Volodia, stirred by an enthusiastic satisfaction, he thought no more of the danger. The joy he felt at doing his duty well, at being no longer a coward, at feeling himself, on the contrary, full of courage, the feeling of commanding and the presence of twenty men, who he knew were watching him with curiosity, had made a real hero of him.[2]

And Henry's:

These incidents made the youth ponder. It was revealed to him that he had been a barbarian, a beast. He had fought like a pagan who defends his religion. Regarding it, he saw that it was fine, wild, and, in some ways, easy. He had been a tremendous figure, no doubt. By this struggle he had overcome obstacles which he had admitted to be mountains. They had fallen like paper peaks, and he was now what he called a hero. And he had not been aware of the process. He had slept and, awakening, found himself a knight.[3]

He saw that he was good. He recalled with a thrill of joy the respectful comments of his fellows upon his conduct.[4]

And again:

With this conviction came a store of assurance. He felt a quiet manhood, non-assertive but of sturdy and strong blood. He knew that he would no more quail before his guides, wherever they should point. He had been to touch the great death, and found that, after all, it was but the great death. He was a man.

So it came to pass that, as he trudged from the place of blood and wrath, his soul changed.[5]

---

[1] *Work*, I, 44–5. Cf. also *Work*, I, 30–1, 108–10.

[2] *Sebastopol*, p. 223.

[3] *Work*, I, 150.

[4] *Ibid.*, p. 197.

[5] *Ibid.*, p. 199.

Thus, the problem which had tortured the young soldiers' minds was solved in the same positive way, a problem which was vital because it was in the authors' own hearts.

There are dissimilarities, however, which deserve to be noted. As hinted, Henry gave way to his fright and ran away in the midst of the battle. Volodia, on the other hand, controlled his fear, stayed, and fought gallantly till the end. There is also a divergence in Tolstoy's and Crane's treatment of the fear motif, which may originate from the difference in scope between Tolstoy's short story and Crane's novel. If Tolstoy suggested the motif, which is probable, Crane expanded and deepened the problem of fear to comprehend various phases of Henry's mind, ranging from sheer nervousness to absolute panic and bottomless shame. Furthermore, Crane's portrayal of Henry was more intense, the feeling of frustration more marked, than in the case of Volodia. With Tolstoy the idea was to illustrate how a good soldier overcame his terror,[1] and with Crane this was also the central problem; in ad-

---

[1] The idea of flight caused by panic was a recurrent motif in *War and Peace*, where Nikolay Rostov was seized by a sudden fear and ran away. He soon overcame his weakness, however, and like Volodia proved a real hero in the moment of danger. *War and Peace*, pp. 244, 608. Crane, too, utilized this motif several times. The loud soldier in *The Red Badge of Courage* also conquered his battle fright and emerged a victor: "He was no more a loud young soldier. There was about him now a fine reliance. He showed a quiet belief in his purposes and his abilities." *Work*, I, 129.

Two American scholars [Lyndon Upson Pratt, "A Possible Source of *The Red Badge of Courage*," *American Literature*, XI (March, 1939), 1–10 and H. T. Webster, "Wilbur F. Hinman's *Corporal Si Klegg* and Stephen Crane's *The Red Badge of Courage*," *American Literature*, XI (November, 1939), 285–93] have made attempts to trace some of Crane's sources for his chief war novel. Pratt remarked that "if Chancellorsville contributed the general setting and rough plan of the novel, Antietam may well have provided at least two additional elements: the idea of Henry's panic and flight, and the heroism of the wounded color-bearer." P. 9. This statement is open to objection, since Pratt has not taken into consideration any literary sources which Crane may have used, such as *Sebastopol* and *War and Peace*. Webster is more convincing than Pratt, but his conclusion seems questionable: "But evidently, Crane got his conception of a commonplace, unromantic hero from Hinman, together with the theme of this raw recruit's development into the capable veteran. . . . In addition to this, Crane apparently adapted a good deal of the essential structure of his narrative from Hinman, as well as many incidents and details of army life." Pp. 291–2.

A close examination of *The Red Badge of Courage* on the one hand, and of

dition, however, he wanted to analyze all the various emotions felt in the process of conquering fear.

Since Tolstoy and Crane regarded war as a result of a series of events caused by uncontrollable forces, they looked upon the role played by the leaders, generals, etc. as of little consequence. "In historical events," asserted Tolstoy, "great men [Napoleon and Alexander]—so called—are but the labels that serve to give

---

La Débâcle, Sebastopol, and *War and Peace* on the other—neither Pratt nor Webster mentioned these books in their articles—makes it clear that the majority of the parallels adduced by the above-mentioned scholars can actually be found in the three novels just referred to, books which we know Crane was familiar with. If Crane ever read *Si Klegg,* which we do not know, he probably borrowed only external details, for it is not convincingly proved that Crane got his conception of the unromantic hero type from Hinman's portrayal of the common soldier, nor yet the theme of Henry's development into a real war hero. Webster, it seems to me, has ignored the psychological aspects of Crane's novel. He has not taken into consideration Crane's careful and intimate analysis of the emotions of his hero, but has paid too much attention to exterior details. This has led him to overemphasize Crane's possible debt to Hinman. Although Webster admits that *Si Klegg* and *The Red Badge of Courage* were basically different in tone, that the effects of the two books were "dissimilar"—*Si Klegg* being "a comic book"—he did not moderate the conclusion quoted above.

In a consideration of possible sources for Crane's stories of war, Bierce's *Tales of Soldiers and Civilians* (1891) and *Can Such Things Be?* (1893) should not be overlooked. For Crane's knowledge of Bierce, see p. 103. Spiller has rightly noted thematic similarities between Crane's work and Bierce's: "Poverty, innate cruelty, war, and death are the themes of all his [Crane's] best work as they were in Ambrose Bierce . . ." Spiller *et al., op. cit.,* p. 1021. Only a few more suggestions will be added here. Both Bierce and Crane painted the impact of war on the individual consciousness; moreover, to both, war was not an experience of pomp and grandeur, but of ugliness and death. Instead of recording elaborate and exact details they painted a few vivid impressions. In addition— perhaps the chief resemblance between the two writers—they did not exclude supernatural elements from their realistic and naturalistic narratives. Their preoccupation with terror suggests Poe, although their terror was "more realistically motivated." Harry T. Levin, "The Discovery of Bohemia" in Spiller *et al., op. cit.,* p. 1069. For Bierce's debt to Poe, see Arthur M. Miller, "The Influence of Edgar Allan Poe on Ambrose Bierce," *American Literature,* IV (May, 1932), 130–50; Carroll D. Hall, *Bierce and the Poe Hoax* (San Francisco, 1934); and George Snell, "Poe Redivivus," *Arizona Quarterly,* I (1945), No. 2, 49–57. Finally the authors' use of the supernatural recalls Maupassant. For Bierce's debt to Maupassant, see Haldeen Braddy, "Ambrose Bierce and Guy de Maupassant," *American Notes & Queries,* I (August, 1941), 67–8. What debt, if any, Crane actually owes to Bierce is hard to define, since both writers,

a name to an event, and like labels, they have the least possible connection with the event itself."[1]

And again referring to the leaders of the army, Tolstoy said:

> These men, drawn on by their own passions, were but the blind instruments of the most melancholy law of necessity; but they believed themselves heroes, and imagined that what they were doing was the noblest and most honourable achievement. They blamed Kutuzov, and declared from the very beginning of the campaign he had prevented them from conquering Napoleon; that he thought of nothing but his own sensual gratifications . . .[2]

Except for Kutusov, Tolstoy's attitude toward the officers was in the main critical; he was annoyed with their petty quarrels and their insatiable personal vanity. Zola, as we remember, also formed a low estimate of the qualifications of the generals, and blamed them ruthlessly for their mismanagement of the army. Crane had a similarly critical attitude to the war leaders.[3] If referred to at all, they were made to seem stupid or ineffective with few exceptions. As a rule, he neglected to mention them, which once made Joseph Hergesheimer write of *The Red Badge of Courage*: "Where

---

to an extent, may perhaps have been inspired by similar sources. Crane, may have looked to Poe as well as to Maupassant for inspiration. Moreover, there seem to be echoes of Tolstoy's war stories in Bierce's work. In addition to the unheroic treatment of war found in both writers, the main theme of "An Occurrence at Owl Creek Bridge" is reminiscent of that of an episode in *Sebastopol*. In both books, during a few seconds before their imminent death, Peyton Farquhar and Mikhaïloff—the one to be hanged, the other lying close to an exploding shell—saw in imagination a series of vivid pictures of their lives flash by. In the next moment one was dead, the other stunned. Finally, in "One of the Missing," Bierce, in the manner of Tolstoy (see pp. 357-9), explained the events as the result of a concatenation of a series of circumstances. The problem of Crane's possible debt to Bierce is obviously complicated, and worthy of investigation.

[1] *War and Peace*, p. 566. Cf. the following passage taken from *The Red Badge of Courage*: "They had taken themselves and the enemy very seriously and had imagined that they were deciding the war. Individuals must have supposed that they were cutting the letters of their names deep into everlasting tablets of brass, or enshrining their reputations for ever in the hearts of their countrymen, while, as to fact, the affair would appear in printed reports under a meek and immaterial title." *Work*, I, 86.

[2] *War and Peace*, p. 1011.

[3] Crane's attitude seems to have shifted later on; in "The Little Regiment," for instance, he drew a favorable portrait of a general.

was Lincoln bearing his benevolence like a tendered pardon to fault? Where was Grant with his half-consumed cigar? Where, above everything, was General Lee?"[1]

If Tolstoy and Crane looked upon the actions of the generals in a critical way, their attitude toward the enemy was far more positive.[2] Both regarded the enemies above all as human beings, frightened and like their own troops, at heart averse to killing, only doing their duty because they had to. This attitude was illustrated by Tolstoy in his description of the truce in *Sebastopol*, where French and Russian soldiers fraternized, talking and joking and exchanging souvenirs. The Russian officers even complimented the French officers on the bravery of their soldiers and *vice versa*, and deplored the tragedy of war.[3] The following quotation from *The Red Badge of Courage* indicates Crane's attitude:

The only foes he had seen were some pickets along the river bank. They were a sun-tanned, philosophical lot, who sometimes shot reflectively at the blue pickets. When reproached for this afterward, they usually expressed sorrow, and swore by their gods that the guns had exploded without their permission. The youth, on guard duty one night, conversed across the stream with one of them. He was a slightly ragged man, who spat skilfully between his shoes and possessed a great fund of bland and infantile assurance. The youth liked him personally.

"Yank," the other had informed him, "yer a right dum good feller." This sentiment, floating to him upon the still air, had made him temporarily regret war.

Various veterans had told him tales. Some talked of grey, bewhiskered hordes who were advancing with relentless curses and chewing tobacco with unspeakable valour; tremendous bodies of fierce soldiery who were sweeping along like the Huns. Others spoke of tattered and eternally hungry men who fired despondent powders.[4]

As to the delineation of individual enemy soldiers, we may call attention to the French drummer's boy in *War and Peace*, who was taken prisoner and treated with much sympathy and understanding by the Russian soldiers.[5] Crane has a similar incident in *The Red Badge of Courage*, in which a young soldier, who had fought bravely, was taken prisoner.

---

[1] *Work*, I, xvii.

[2] Zola, however, was hostile in his attitude toward the enemy in *La Débâcle*.

[3] *Sebastopol*, p. 119. See also *War and Peace*, pp. 157, 611.

[4] *Work*, I, 29–30.

[5] *War and Peace*, pp. 969 ff.

Another, who was a boy in years, took his plight with great calmness and apparent good nature. He conversed with the men in blue, studying their faces with his bright and keen eyes. They spoke of battles and conditions. There was an acute interest in all their faces during this exchange of view-points. It seemed a great satisfaction to hear voices from where all had been darkness and speculation.[1]

Crane retained his sympathetic view of the enemy in his later war stories; see, for instance, his portrait of the young enemy officer in his short story "Three Miraculous Soldiers."[2]

The problem of free will came particularly to the fore in the war narratives of Tolstoy and Crane. On the whole, both writers looked upon man as devoid of free will.[3] Tolstoy said of the Russian generals that they "were but the blind instruments of the most melancholy law of necessity."[4] Moreover: "Every action of theirs, that seems to them an act of their own free-will, is in an historical sense not free at all, but in bondage to the whole course of previous history, and predestined from all eternity."[5]

And again:

The acts of Napoleon and Alexander, on whose words it seemed to depend whether this should be done or not, were as little voluntary as the act of each soldier, forced to march out by the drawing of a lot or by conscription. This could not be otherwise, for in order that the will of Napoleon and Alexander (on whom the whole decision appeared to rest) should be effective, a combination of innumerable circumstances was essential without any one which the effect could not have followed. It was essential that the millions of men in whose hands the real power lay— the soldiers who fired guns and transported provisions and cannons— should consent to carry out the will of those feeble and isolated persons, and that they should have been brought to this acquiescence by an infinite number of varied and complicated causes.[6]

In *The Red Badge of Courage* Crane made it clear that the soldiers had little free will, and were pawns in the hands of forces they could not control. Henry Fleming was aware of the fact that his

---

[1] *Work*, I, 193.

[2] *Ibid.*, II, 57 ff. Cf. also *ibid.*, IX, 212–13.

[3] Cf. pp. 189–94.

[4] *War and Peace*, p. 1011. See also *ibid.*, p. 988.

[5] *Ibid.*, p. 566.

[6] *Ibid.*, pp. 564–5. In contrast to the non-religious Crane, Tolstoy identified the unknown force governing the universe with God.

enlistment, for example, was no action determined by his own will:

> But he instantly saw that it would be impossible for him to escape from the regiment. It enclosed him. And there were iron bars of tradition and law on four sides. He was in a moving box.
> As he perceived this fact it occurred to him that he had never wished to come to the war. He had not enlisted of his free will. He had been dragged by the merciless government. And now they were taking him out to be slaughtered.[1]

Moreover, the disorder on the battlefield served to emphasize the lack of free will on the part of the human mites fighting blindly and desperately:

> "Good Gawd," the youth grumbled, "we're always being chased around like rats! It makes me sick. Nobody seems to know where we go or why we go. We just get fired around from pillar to post and get licked here and get licked there, and nobody knows what it's done for. It makes a man feel like a damn' kitten in a bag. Now, I'd like to know what the eternal thunders we was marched into these woods for anyhow, unless it was to give the rebs a regular pot-shot at us. We came in here and got our legs all tangled up in these cussed briers, and then we begin to fight and the rebs had an easy time of it. Don't tell me it's just luck! I know better. It's this derned old—"[2]

Premonition of death is a recurrent theme in the works of Tolstoy and Crane. Take, for instance, Mikhaïloff's strange presentiment of death in *Sebastopol* before he went out on the bastion for the thirteenth time. "'I shall be killed, I'm sure,' he said to himself; 'I feel it. . . .'"[3] Similarly, the loud one in *The Red Badge of Courage* felt that he was to die when the battle began. "'It's

---

[1] *Work*, I, 48-9.

[2] *Ibid.*, p. 144. See also *ibid.*, pp. 148, 150, 158, 162. Cf. also the determinism of *La Débâcle*: ". . . maintenant, silencieux, irrités, ils traînaient la jambe, avec la haine du fusil, qui leur meurtrissait l'épaule, du sac dont ils étaient écrasés, ayant cessé de croire à leurs chefs, se laissant envahir par une telle désespérance, qu'ils ne marchaient plus en avant que comme un bétail, sous la fatalité du fouet." *Œuvres*, XX, 127.

[3] *Sebastopol*, p. 62. Other instances are afforded by Volodia and Kalouguine of the same novel, and Prince Andrey of *War and Peace*. Cf. a similar incident in *La Débâcle*, where Sapin had a presentiment of death and was killed in battle. *Œuvres*, XX, 222, 233-4. Cf. also "Der Fatalist" in Michael Lermontoff's *Ein Held unsrer Zeit* (Leipzig, n. d.).

my first and last battle, old boy.'"[1] The scene was made even more dramatic by the package of letters which the soldier handed over to Henry before going under fire. In Tolstoy's tale Mikhaïloff wrote a farewell letter to his father and gave it to his valet to keep and deliver after his death. In both stories, neither of the men was killed in the ensuing action.

In addition to the above-mentioned similarities between Tolstoy and Crane, there are also some minor resemblances that may be mentioned. Both contrasted, as did Zola, the peace of nature with the turmoil of war. Each of them compared the calm of the surrounding landscape with the horror and bloodshed on the battle-field. Take, for instance, the following scene in *Sebastopol*:

> Hundreds of mutilated, freshly bleeding bodies, which two hours before were full of hopes and of different desires, sublime or humble, lay with stiffened limbs in the flowery and dew-bathed valley which separated the bastion from the intrenchment, or on the smooth floor of the little mortuary chapel of Sebastopol. The dry lips of all these men murmured prayers, curses, or groans. They crawled, they turned on their sides, some were abandoned among the corpses of the blossom-strewn valley, others lay on stretchers, on cots, and on the damp floor of the field-hospital. Notwithstanding all this, the heavens shed their morning light over Mount Saponné as on the preceding days, the sparkling stars grew pale, a white mist rose from the sombre and plaintively swelling sea, the east grew purple with the dawn, and long, flame-colored clouds stretched along the blue horizon. As on the days before, the grand torch mounted slowly, powerful and proud, promising joy, love, and happiness to the awakened world.[2]

And in *The Red Badge of Courage*:

> As he listened to the din from the hillside, to a deep pulsating thunder that came from afar to the left, and to the lesser clamours which came from many directions, it occurred to him that they were fighting, too, over there, and over there, and over there. Heretofore he had supposed that all the battle was directly under his nose.
>
> As he gazed around him the youth felt a flash of astonishment at the blue, pure sky and the sun gleaming on the trees and fields. It was surprising that Nature had gone tranquilly on with her golden process in the midst of so much devilment.[3]

---

[1] *Work*, I, 56. Cf. the Swede in "The Blue Hotel." In this story the presentiment of death adds to the element of horror—related to that of Poe and Bierce—so often met with in Crane's writings.

[2] *Sebastopol*, pp. 110–11. See also *War and Peace*, pp. 131, 744.

[3] *Work*, I, 69–70. See also *ibid.*, pp. 98, 151, 189.

There is also the incident of the flag. In *War and Peace* Prince Andrey stood forth as a true hero when, seizing the staff of the falling flag, he bravely led his retreating comrades back into battle, most of whom were killed when following the flag.[1] The scene is reminiscent of a similar one in *The Red Badge of Courage*. Henry grabbed the battered flag from the dying colorbearer and led his wavering fellow soldiers back to the fight.

Both Tolstoy and Crane attempted to analyze the concept of heroism. The kind of false heroism or foolish bravery that Crane described in his short story "A Mystery of Heroism"[2] recalls Tolstoy's endeavor to investigate the nature of heroism in *War and Peace*. Both authors were baffled, and could give no definite answer. Heroism sprang perhaps from man's vanity, from his desire to make an impression on other individuals at any cost. Rostov, feeling discomfort and vague remorse after his gallant but silly exploit, inquired: "'Why, is this all that's meant by heroism? And did I do it for the sake of my country?'"[3] And Collins, the hero of Crane's story, reflected after a similar gallant feat: "He was, then, a hero. He suffered that disappointment which we would all have if we discovered that we were ourselves capable of those deeds which we most admire in history and legend. This, then, was a hero. After all, heroes were not much."[4]

The theme of Crane's story, "The Second Generation,"[5] reminds us of that of Tolstoy's *The Two Hussars*. Both stories deal with fathers and sons, the former brave and able men, the latter conceited bullies and cowards to boot.

Further, Pierre's frightened inactivity at the batttle of Borodino[6] may perhaps have served as an inspiration for Crane's portrayal of Peza in his war story "Death and the Child."[7]

As has already been hinted, Tolstoy believed that things happened as the result of a complicated concatenation of events, of incomprehensible forces. A murder, an execution, or a war was

---

[1] *War and Peace*, p. 255.
[2] *Work*, II, 95 ff.
[3] *War and Peace*, p. 611.
[4] *Work*, II, 102.
[5] *Ibid.*, p. 231 ff.
[6] *War and Peace*, pp. 712, 738.
[7] *Work*, XII, 241 ff.

not the logical outcome of one man's will, or the logical result of careful planning by a group of men. On the contrary, each event was the result of a haphazard, illogical combination of unknown forces, governed by the law of inevitability. This view was particularly well exemplified in the following episode taken from *War and Peace*.[1] During the French occupation of Moscow in 1812, Pierre Bezuhov got up one morning with the intent of murdering Napoleon, who, however, unknown to Pierre, was out of the city. A series of unexpected circumstances intervened, and Pierre was not destined to carry out his purpose. First he happened to pass a blazing house and rescued a child from the flames; second, he defended an insulted woman and became involved in a fight with French soldiers; third, at that moment a patrol of French Uhlans suddenly appeared and arrested Pierre, accusing him of incendiarism; fourth, as a result of his supposed crime, he was sentenced to death, but his life was spared by chance and he remained a prisoner of war until finally liberated by Russian guerilla troups. This is Tolstoy's description of the strange happenings that led up to the catastrophe:

> There was one idea all this time in Pierre's head. It was the question: Who, who was it really that was condemning him to death? It was not the men who had questioned him at the first examination; of them not one would or obviously could do so. It was not Davoust, who had looked at him in such a human fashion. In another minute Davoust would have understood that they were doing wrong, but the adjutant who had come in at that moment had prevented it. And that adjutant had obviously had no evil intent, but he might have stayed away. Who was it, after all, who was punishing him, killing him, taking his life—his, Pierre's, with all his memories, his strivings, his hopes, and his ideas? Who was doing it? And Pierre felt it was no one's doing. It was discipline, and the concatenation of circumstances. Some sort of discipline was killing him, Pierre, robbing him of life, of all, annihilating him.[2]

In "The Blue Hotel" Crane has a similar chain of circumstances to account for the accidental murder of the Swede. The Swede was a timid, nervous man, who on a cold winter's day got off the train in Fort Romper, Nebr., with the intention of getting a job. The owner of the Palace Hotel persuaded him to take a room for the night, despite the Swede's obvious fears of being killed in

[1] *War and Peace*, pp. 860 ff.

[2] *Ibid.*, p. 897.

what was to him the Wild West. A game of cards was played, and the Swede accused a man of cheating. A fight followed. The Swede was the victor, and as a result, his fright was gone; swaggering and boasting he left the hotel and entered a saloon, peopled by a gambler and a few other men. He aggravated the men by his aggressive and conceited manner, and suddenly the gambler knifed him "and a human body, this citadel of virtue, wisdom, power, was pierced as easily as if it had been a melon. The Swede fell with a cry of supreme astonishment."[1] Here follows Crane's motivation of the murder:

"We are all in it! This poor gambler isn't even a noun. He is kind of an adverb. *Every sin is the result of a collaboration.* We, five of us, have collaborated in the murder of this Swede. Usually there are from a dozen to forty women really involved in every murder, but in this case it seems to be only five men—you, I, Johnnie, old Scully; and that fool of an unfortunate gambler came merely as a culmination, the apex of a human movement, and gets all the punishment."

The cowboy, injured and rebellious, cried out blindly into this fog of mysterious theory: "Well, I didn't do anythin', did I?"[2]

Both Pierre and the Swede were victims, acted upon by a concurrence of forces[3] which made it impossible for them to behave in any other way.

To sum up: Crane's enthusiasm for Tolstoy's *Sebastopol* and *War and Peace* probably had a deeper justification than merely his interest in war narratives.[4] Crane's reading of these books certainly stimulated his interest in war, but Tolstoy's writings probably also confirmed and deepened his concept of human life and behavior. In Tolstoy, Crane found an author who surpassed Zola in the variety and penetration of his psychological analysis. The great part, for example, played by chance and circumstance in the life of the individual, which is found in most of Crane's

---

[1] *Work*, X, 129.

[2] *Ibid.*, pp. 131–2. Italics are mine. Cf. Bierce's story "One of the Missing in *Collected Writings* (New York, n.d.), pp. 30–40." See also p. 350 n. 1.

[3] In contrast to the characters of Zola and other naturalistic writers, it should be noted that Pierre and the Swede were the victims not of heredity and environment, but of a series of irrational circumstances. This is also illustrated in Crane's stories "Twelve O'Clock" and "The Five White Mice" dealing with Western material. *Work*, XII, 105–14; 157–75.

[4] Cf. Spiller's opinion, in Spiller *et al.*, *op. cit.*, p. 1021.

work, is paralleled in the writings of the Russian author. Both aimed at analyzing the motivations behind human conduct. Crane's indebtedness to Tolstoy is most obvious in his tales of war. Although Crane may have used other sources for *The Red Badge of Courage* and his various war narratives, it is clear that Tolstoy, to an extent, stimulated his concept of war, his use of an unromantic hero, together with minor narrative details, some of which may have been accidental. Moreover, in "The Blue Hotel" Crane successfully illustrated an idea, possibly derived from *War and Peace*, and applied it to native Western material.

CHAPTER XIV

THE INFLUENCE OF IBSEN

As has been pointed out earlier in this study, Henrik Ibsen's works became increasingly known in the United States in the eighteen nineties. His dramas were read and commented upon in literary circles. His technique and ideas were, therefore, likely to influence American writers. As far as the present writer has been able to find out, there is apparently no work on the influence of Ibsen on American fiction.[1]

Even before 1890, when the first volumes of William Archer's edition of Ibsen's plays were published, there were translations of some of his dramas available to American readers. In 1880 *A Doll's House* was translated into English and published in Copenhagen under the title *Nora*, and two years later the play was re-issued in London and New York. In 1888 three Ibsen plays were brought out simultaneously in England and America in one volume called *The Pillars of Society and Other Plays;* this volume included, besides the title play, *Ghosts* and *An Enemy of the People*. And an American edition of *The Lady from the Sea* came out in 1889. Then during 1890 and 1891 Archer brought out *Ibsen's Prose Dramas* in five volumes; these included *Lady Inger of Östrât, The Vikings at Helgeland, The Pretenders, Brand, The League of Youth, Emperor and Galilean, The Pillars of Society, A Doll's House, Ghosts, An Enemy of the People, The Wild Duck, Rosmersholm, The Lady from the Sea,* and *Hedda Gabler. Peer Gynt* was issued by William and Charles Archer in 1892; *The Master Builder* was published in London and New York in 1893; and *Little Eyolf* was printed in London and Chicago in 1895.

---

[1] For Ibsen and Herne, see Dorothy S. Bucks and Arthur H. Nethercot, "Ibsen and Herne's *Margaret Fleming:* A Study of the Early Ibsen Movement in America," *American Literature*, XVII (January, 1946), 311–33. See also Andersen, *op. cit.* Cf. pp. 42–6.

Finally, in 1897, *John Gabriel Borkman* came out in London and New York.

Scandinavian emigrants probably helped to introduce Ibsen to the American theatergoer.[1] As early as May 1882 *Ghosts* was played by Norwegian-Americans in Chicago and Minneapolis and other Midwestern cities.[2] In June of the same year *A Doll's House* was produced in English in Milwaukee, Wis.[3] In 1889 and 1890 the same drama was performed in Boston, New York, Chicago, and San Francisco, and *Pillars of Society*[4] was staged at the Amberg Theater in New York City in December, 1889.

Four major factors in Ibsen's plays seem to be of particular importance for the following discussion, namely, Ibsen's portrayal of woman, his attitude toward marriage, his exposure of the evils of society, and his emphasis on will and duty.

The most prominent characteristics of the Ibsen heroine[5] were her forcefulness and independence, her strength of mind, and her passionate but often wilful personality. Hjördis, Lona Hessel, Nora, Mrs. Alving, Rebecca West, and Hedda Gabler are of this type.[6]

Ibsen's purpose was above all to liberate woman as an individual; she should stand by man's side as his equal, with equal right to be regarded as a human being. She should be considered first as an individual, only secondly as a wife and mother. Moreover, he demanded a transformation of the conventional conception of marriage: the ideal marriage, he implied, should be first and foremost a union between free and independent equals. Thus, in *A Doll's House* he declared that it was woman's right to

[1] Cf. Hjalmar Hjorth Boyesen. See pp. 42–3.

[2] J. B. Halvorsen, *Bibliografiske Oplysninger til Henrik Ibsens Samlede Værker* (Copenhagen, 1901), p. 80.

[3] E. I. Haugen, "Ibsen in America: A Forgotten Performance and an Unpublished Letter," *Journal of English and Germanic Philology*, XXXIII (July, 1934), 396–420. Reprinted in an abbrevitated form in *Edda*, XXXV, (1935), 553–9.

[4] For title see p. 371 n. 1.

[5] We must bear in mind that Ibsen's women were not all strong and forceful, and that Ibsen frequently contrasted the dominating type with a weaker and more dependent one. In this study, however, our concern has been solely with the former.

[6] Turgenev has a similar type in Irina, Elena, Daria Mihailovna, and several others.

create a life that was morally and intellectually worthy of her; she was not, as the conventional view of a wife would have it, merely a doll, a plaything, a person of less importance than her husband. Practically all Ibsen's heroines of this type from Hjördis to Hedda Gabler, had the urge for personal freedom and independence.

In *Pillars of Society* and in *An Enemy of the People* he criticized the moral cowardice and the corrupt ways of society. In *Brand* he demanded that man give up everything to follow the voice of duty, and in *Peer Gynt* he attacked the liar and the hypocrite. Ibsen, the moral idealist, demanded of his fellow men truthfulness, will power, and self-sacrifice.

It should be remembered that Ibsen, by no means, stood alone in his demands for freedom, truth, and social justice. He was only one voice in a chorus of voices. These ideas were pivotal in nineteenth century liberal thought in Europe as well as in America.[1]

1. IBSEN AND GARLAND

One of the earliest and most zealous American disciples of Ibsen was Hamlin Garland, whose temperament and attitude toward life were of a kind readily to accept Ibsen's moralism and individualism. As a matter of fact, the Garland of the early nineties may be compared with Brand, for in his life he may be said to have lived up to Ibsen's ideals of will, truth, honesty, and duty. Brand's austerity was also found in the youthful American. Indubitably, Garland felt akin to Ibsen, the social critic, the champion of truth and right in society, the exposer of hypocrisy, pettiness, and shams.[2]

In 1888,[3] an important year in Garland's development as a writer, he seems to have been acquainted with Ibsen's *Pillars*

---

[1] Cf. L. T. Hobhouse, *Liberalism* (London, 1911).

[2] We call attention to Garland's advocacy of the single tax, woman's rights, and the amelioration of the conditions of the farmers in the Middle West. See pp. 71 ff. For the debate on the woman question, marriage, and divorce, see pp. 80 ff. Cf. also pp. 220–4.

[3] Garland was probably familiar with *A Doll's House* even before 1888, for in his short story "A Branch Road," which he claimed to have written in 1887, we find a variation of the *Doll's House* theme.

of *Society*, *Ghosts*, and *An Enemy of the People*, all included in
The Pillars of Society and Other Plays published in that year.
Garland's well-thumbed copy of the book, in the Garland Collection at the University of Southern California Library, is full of his
marginalia.[1] He wrote on the title page of his copy of *Pillars of
Society:* "A play that is life. One of the great plays of the world.
Unsurpassed by any modern work. The most radical departure
and the most vital modern life and thought. A play in which the
passion of love is subordinate—one force among many as in life.
In which the plot springs from the characters. Where the extraneous or factitious has no place to enter." *An Enemy of the
People* also appealed strongly to him, for he wrote: "*An Enemy of
Society*.[2] A Play in Five Acts. One of the most modern, radical
and unconventional plays in all literature. It is not a play—it is
life itself and yet would be thrilling upon the stage. Love plays no
part at all in this play. The 'heroine' is gone. We are absorbed
by other passions and other thoughts."

Garland's acquaintance with Charles E. Hurd,[3] and his friendship with James A. Herne[4] and other Ibsen enthusiasts, no doubt
augmented his interest in and admiration for the Norwegian playwright. In *Roadside Meetings* Garland told us that he became an
Ibsen convert. "French Impressionism and Russian Veritism
were still in debate when the doctrine of dramatic realism swept
upon us from the north, embodied in Henrik Ibsen's austere
plays, and I, being already instructed in northland literature by
Hurd of the *Transcript*, became its advocate."[5] And after his
first attendance of a performance of *A Doll's House* on October
30, 1889, Garland wrote: "I left the theater that afternoon converted to the new drama, and like all recent converts I began to
talk and write on Ibsenism as I had been talking and writing on
Impressionism and Veritism. It became another 'cause' for me."[6]

In the June, 1890, *Arena* Garland eagerly preached the gospel
of Ibsen in an article entitled "Ibsen as a Dramatist." Of the

---

[1] See p. 426.
[2] This is the title of the play in Garland's copy.
[3] See p. 67.
[4] See pp. 72–3.
[5] *Roadside Meetings*, p. 65.
[6] *Ibid.*, p. 66. Cf. p. 139.

six dramas[1] by Ibsen referred to in the article, Garland remarked that *An Enemy of Society*[2] was by far the best. It is interesting to observe that he found this play the most fascinating, the reason being, perhaps, that Ibsen here exposed the wrongs of society in a way Garland himself wanted to do.

In *Crumbling Idols* Garland again voiced his admiration for the works of the Norwegian dramatist, exhorting his compatriots to read and ponder over his plays, but he advised against imitation. Again it was Ibsen the reformer by whom Garland was stimulated. He also admired Ibsen's psychological realism, pointing out its universality and reminding his readers that "It might all have happened at Bar Haven or at Boomtown, Nebraska."[3]

In an unpublished notebook dated 1894 Garland jotted down the following passage under the heading of *The Master Builder*:

> The drama in America is in a transition stage. . . . In the transition period the plays of Ibsen are destined to have great influence. He is a liberation like Walt Whitman. He liberates from conventional forms in the drama as Whitman . . . of rhyme and meter.
>
> Ibsen . . . has made the drama the means of his most fearless and subtle moods.
>
> He is essentially a dramatist. "Peer Gynt" and "Brand" are dramas as well as poems. Where others of his contemporaries fly to the novel, he uses the dramatic form and his plays are all suited to the stage. He is a master of stage devices . . . Ibsen's plays face harder conditions here. The cost of production is greater, the rent of the theaters larger . . . and yet the time is rapidly nearing when they can be successfully produced.
>
> Meantime we owe much to the work of Miss Morgan.[4]

Of interest is also the following paragraph taken from Garland's unpublished lecture notes entitled "Current Plays," probably written in the early nineties:

> I do not point to any one dramatist as a model. I do not believe in models, the only criterion is life, yet Henrik Ibsen, the great Norwegian, has, it seems to me, taken front rank in depicting life in large forms on the stage. His "Enemy of Society," for example, is a picture of Society

---

[1] See p. 44.

[2] This is the title of the play in Garland's article.

[3] *Crumbling Idols*, p. 102.

[4] Anna Morgan, well-known Chicago actress, did much to increase the American interest in the modern drama in the nineties. See *Henry Fuller*, ed. by Anna Morgan (Chicago, 1929), p. 12.

everywhere in America, as well as the old world where the desire for dollars leads to a building up of a hollow deceitful convention. . . .

In Ibsen's dramas the winds of the present blow. The men think modern thoughts, the plots are such as rise naturally out of modern character and then the *denouement* follows in logical order. It is electrical to read such dramas, to hear them would be a privilege. Conventional heroes and heroines, the "funny man," the "villain" . . . all are lost sight of. He is deeply in earnest and his purpose is to depict modern life, modern passion in modern methods. A lack of either of these requisites would produce an abortion, together they produce a masterpiece.

The higher class of American dramas therefore must not be shambling, disconnected character studies, neither must they be sensational melodramas with thin "Realistic" tanks and horses, and lastly they must not imitate Ibsen or any other dramatist, but they must be studies of life, of social life, and must have breadth and compactness of form, cumulative interest, and depths and sincerity of purpose. . . .[1]

The influence of Ibsen, overlooked by scholars, is evident in most of Garland's early works. The sympathy for the subjugated woman and the interest in woman as an individual, which were displayed in such dramas as *Love's Comedy*, *Pillars of Society*, and *A Doll's House*, were also to be found in *Main-Travelled Roads*.[2] Like the unconventional Lona Hessel and the rebellious Nora, who revolted against society in order to be true to themselves and their ideals, Garland's heroines rebelled against men and conditions in order to become independent and free. In "A Branch Road," the first story of the collection, the heroine was the bitter, worn-out, but still young Agnes, the wife of a brutish farmer in the Middle West. Her married life was far from happy; her husband abused her and treated her contemptuously. Her life on the farm was but a sordid battle with her husband, to whom she was a mere plaything, as Nora was to Helmer. Then, however, Agnes's one-time suitor reappeared and spoke of freedom and independence in Ibsenian terms. " 'There's just one way to get out of this, Agnes,' " said her suitor, " 'Come with me. He don't care for you; his whole idea of women is that they are created for his pleasure and to keep house. Your whole life is an agony. Come! Don't cry. There's a chance for life yet.' "[3] Then followed a plea for a better married

---

[1] Cf. chap. viii, "The Influence of Ibsen," in *Crumbling Idols*, pp. 99–118.

[2] Cf. Garland's own experiences, see p. 71.

[3] *Main-Travelled Roads*, p. 63. Garland was once in love with a Western girl named Agnes, who, however, married a farmer and wasted away her life. See *A Son of the Middle Border*, pp. 121, 364 ff.

life, akin to that indicated by Ibsen in *A Doll's House*. The suitor suggested that, after a trip to the East and possibly to Europe, he would build her a house which would have pictures and books to read and discuss, a thing almost unheard of among the wives of the small Western farmers in those days, but an important point with Garland, who stood for intellectual sympathy between husband and wife. Agnes realized that the only way to be true to herself and develop herself as an individual was to leave her narrow-minded husband and to follow her lover. "He seemed to open a door for her, and through it turrets shone and great ships crossed on dim blue seas."[1] Thus the lover offered Agnes, to whom the development of the individual was, as it was to Nora, far more important than her duties as a mere housewife, the opportunity for self-expansion. But when this Western Nora was on the verge of leaving her husband and child, she realized in vivid contrast to Nora, whose indifference to her children was so severely denounced by critics, that she could not leave her baby. Swiftly she ran back to the house and returned to her waiting lover, carrying the babe in her arms. The lover was ready to welcome both mother and child with a gay "'The baby! Sure enough. Why, certainly! to the mother belongs the child.'"[2] Garland pleaded for the child's right to remain with its mother. The story makes clear that what interested Garland in *A Doll's House* was not the moral cowardice of Helmer or even the spiritual and temperamental differences between Nora and her husband—Agnes's husband was crude and prejudiced, but did not reveal the moral defects, which made Nora leave Helmer—but the fact that Nora was a woman who dared to rebel against a marriage which dwarfed her individuality, and seek personal independence.

The next story of the collection, "Up the Coulé," treated of a woman of the same defiant spirit as Nora, but without the force to begin a life of her own. Grant McLane's wife had once been a free woman with a career, but she was now merely a despondent, fretful, and overworked farmer's wife who deplored her present state and was discontented because she had not the slightest chance of intellectual companionship with her husband. She

---

[1] *Main-Travelled Roads* p. 66.

[2] *Ibid.*, p. 68.

wanted to break away, but she was chained to her family and had to remain.[1]

The third story "Among the Corn-Rows," contains the same theme: a rebellious woman anxious to get away from her family and to build up her own life. Like Agnes and Grant's wife, the young immigrant Julia Peterson was in bitter revolt against overwork. When a suitor appeared with an offer of marriage on equal terms—" 'You'll have half o' all I c'n make' "[2]—she decided to leave her parents, who treated her like a hired man, to follow the young American, who held down a claim in South Dakota. Julia reflected:

She was already living that free life in a far-off wonderful country. No more would her stern father and sullen mother force her to tasks which she hated. She'd be a member of a new firm. She'd work, of course, but it would be because she wanted to, and not because she was forced to. The independence and the love promised, grew more and more attractive. She laughed back with a softer light in her eyes when she saw the smiling face of Rob looking at her from her sun-bonnet.[3]

This story is, it seems, a variation of the *Doll's House* theme as Garland conceived it, illustrative of the doctrine of marriage as a partnership between equals. It was this message Garland wanted to convey to his readers.

The new type of woman to be found in the above-mentioned stories seems to be spiritually akin to Ibsen's independent heroines.[4] Ibsen, it is true, stressed the moral and intellectual differences between husband and wife perhaps more than Garland, with whom

---

[1] The grim, naturalistic story "Sim Burns's Wife" in *Prairie Folks* deals with a poor, overworked farmer's mate whose never-ending toil and loveless life made her revolt against married life. "I jest can't, and what's more, I *won't*," she declared. *Prairie Folks*, p. 103. She hated her husband, who was coarse and worn-out from too much drudgery, hated her mode of living, hated the squalor and poverty of the small Western farm. But she knew that revolt was futile; there was no way out for her. " 'I hate t' live. But they ain't no hope. I'm tied down. I can't leave the children, and I ain't got no money. I couldn't make a living out in the world. I ain't never seen anything an' don't know anything.' " *Ibid.*, pp. 112–13. She could not go away, but had to fight the battle to the bitter end; she illustrated the hopeless tragedy of the poor and uneducated woman.

[2] *Main-Travelled Roads*, p. 169.

[3] *Ibid.*, p. 172.

[4] For native prototypes, see pp. 71, 86 n. 1, 221.

the problem was also an economic one. Nevertheless, Garland probably used the Nora type as a model for his rebellious women —as his use of that type in his later books seems to indicate.

Jason Edwards,[1] the most naturalistic of Garland's books, also treated of the new woman and of marriage. Alice, the strong and determined heroine, had a successful career of her own. Matters were complicated, however, by the fact that, because her family was poor, she had to help support it. Such was the situation when a fairly wealthy man, Reeves, wanted to marry her. But Alice felt it her duty to stand by her parents and assist them according to her ability. Like Nora, she was altruistic and wanted to help her poor and overworked father.[2] Moreover, she did not desire to give up her independence to become a mere housewife. Resolved not to give up her career, she postponed the marriage. She loved her music and her studies and she wanted to earn her own living. "'I *want* to work. . . . I'm happier in my work. Let me have my freedom another'—,"[3] she said. Then, because the rent was raised, the Edwards decided to move to the Middle West and Alice accompanied them, thereby sacrificing both her love and her career. After four years of waiting, Reeves went West with the set purpose of bringing her East. But when he cried out triumphantly "'I'm master of you now,'"[4] he found her still unconquered; she was still a Nora fighting for personal independence. "'You are not,' she cried with a gesture of repulsion."[5] She persisted in her refusal, and the dialogue[6] between

---

[1] As has been said, the novel was but an adaptation of the play *Under the Wheel*. When the play was published the critics immediately linked Garland's name with that of Ibsen. An editorial in the *Chicago Tribune* said that "Boston produces an American Ibsen. Garland puts humble life on the boards undisguised." Quoted from the back cover of *Under the Wheel*. *The Review of Reviews* (London) found in the July *Arena*, 1890, a "remarkable feature, a modern play by Hamlin Garland entitled 'Under the Wheel.' It is a terribly realistic story; a terribly grim representation of the way in which human beings are ground 'under the wheel' of incessant and useless toil. Alice, the daughter, is a modern girl, somewhat of the Ibsen type." Quoted from the back cover of *Under the Wheel*. See also p. 75.

[2] *Jason Edwards*, p. 22.

[3] *Ibid.*, p. 34.

[4] *Ibid.*, p. 146.

[5] *Ibid.*

[6] *Ibid.*, pp. 148-9.

Alice and Reeves recalls that between Nora and Helmer in the third act of *A Doll's House*. There was the same tension between man and woman, and the denouement was somewhat similar. When finally Alice agreed to marry Reeves, she nevertheless regretted that their union would not be the ideal marriage, the marriage of the Ibsen type, a union between equals, since she had to give up her career. Her problem was not yet solved, only shelved.[1]

In a consideration of the influence of Ibsen on *A Member of the Third House*, attention must first be called to the fact that the novel has the revealing subtitle "A Dramatic Story." Indeed, the novel reads like a play;[2] the book consists of a series of more or less dramatic scenes, made up principally of dialogue, with but few descriptive passages.

The plot and some characters of the novel are reminiscent of those of *A Doll's House*. As Nora was associated with two men, her husband and Dr. Rank, who both loved her, in like manner Helene, the heroine of Garland's book, was involved with two men, Wilson Tuttle, to whom she was informally engaged, and Tom Brennan. The role played by Mrs. Linde, Nora's friend and confidante, corresponds to that of Helene's friend, Evelyn Ward; just as Mrs. Linde brought out, by means of contrast, the gay irresponsibility of Nora's character in the first part of the drama, Evelyn Ward threw the playfulness and childlike quality of Helene's personality into relief. It is implied that Nora's father had not been altogether unimpeachable as a business man; Helene's father was accused of bribery. However, the similarities between *A Doll's House* and *A Member of the Third House* are limited to the first two acts of the play. There is nothing comparable to the conflict between Nora and Helmer and the problem of marriage to be found in Garland's book. Rather, the novel is mainly an exposure of the lies and corruption of society, after the manner of *Pillars of Society*.[3]

The most interesting of the woman characters in the book is Helene, the daughter of the railroad giant, Lawrence B. Davis, a gay and childlike Nora who lacked a sense of responsibility.

---

[1] *Ibid.*, pp. 202–3.

[2] It was first written as a play. See Appendix, pp. 455–8.

[3] For title see p. 371 n. 1.

There was, however, no such development in her as there was in Nora; she remained the same pretty, innocent, helpless little creature throughout the book. Not even her father's ruin and suicide brought about any change in her. And she was treated with the indulgence usually bestowed on a child, like Nora and the wife of Consul Bernick. We remember the joyous Nora of the opening scene, bringing home a Christmas tree, happily occupied with her parcels, and stealthily eating macaroons.

Helmer (calls out from his room). Is that my little lark twittering out there?
Nora (busy opening some of the parcels). Yes, it is!
Helmer. Is it my little squirrel bustling about?
Nora. Yes!
Helmer. When did my squirrel come home?
Nora. Just now. (*Puts the bag of macaroons into her pocket and wipes her mouth.*) Come in here, Torvald, and see what I have bought.[1]

In like fashion Garland described Helene and her lover, who called her "a jovial little blue-jay,"[2] and both heroines were portrayed eating macaroons! But Nora was a generous and self-sacrificing woman, who had actually saved the life of her husband and had inherent possibilities for development; Helene, on the contrary, remained naïve and selfish.

The *Doll's House* atmosphere was well caught in the following passage, where Helene was first introduced to the reader:

Miss Davis chattered on like a jovial little blue-jay. She was pretty in a dainty, inconsequential sort of way, and was dressed in some light-colored, fluffy stuff that rustled as softly as a breeze in a poplar tree, and she looked deliciously comfortable. The little beads of perspiration on her white temples and chin seemed cool as the drops on a dainty vase.

"Ain't this heavenly?" she inquired, as she stirred the brown mixture with the long-handled, tiny spoon which went with the soda. "Don't you like to hear the spoon as it goes through? Grau-u!" She made a funny little noise to imitate the sound of the spoon. "This makes the fourth. Ain't you going to try one, Evelyn? I believe I could live on ice-cream sodas and macaroons! Couldn't you?

---

[1] *Eleven Plays of Henrik Ibsen* (Mod. lib. ed., New York, n. d.), p. 4. In the following pages the quotations are, if not otherwise stated, taken from this edition, which hereafter will be referred to as *Plays*. I follow this edition as regards titles and names of characters.

[2] *A Member of the Third House*, p. 10.

"For a limited time—yes," Tuttle replied, looking into the sunny shallows of her blue eyes. "However, I prefer to go on in a grosser way for the present—steaks and things like that."[1]

Moreover, when Tuttle spoke of politics, a subject in which he was tremendously interested, Helene instead of listening was reflecting on his beautiful eyes.

The next time we meet Helene and Tuttle is at a game of tennis, during which her playfulness and "natural coquetry" with him and with the other prospective lover, Tom Brennan, are reminiscent of Nora's coquetry with Dr. Rank. In both cases the flirtation brought forth a confession of love.[2]

During the trial of her father for bribery, Helene remained the child. She "clapped her hands as if it were a play."[3] Just as Helmer looked upon Nora as a child to be petted and spoiled, Tuttle was attracted by Helene's naïveté and helplessness during the trial. She "was irresistibly attractive . . . in her remorseful tenderness and her childish, helpless trust in him."[4] The final glimpse of Helene is caught when she visits her father, a ruined man making preparations for suicide:

"I can't eat, child. I'm too busy," Davis said . . . "Besides, you—you'll bother me."

"No, I won't. Just a cup of chocolate. I'm going to make it on that lovely little alcohol stove. Come, now; it will help you to sleep. And I'll roast some crackers"— . . .

Helene clapped her hands childishly. The novelty of camping down in this great house pleased her. "Oh, that'll be fun! And I know it'll do you good."[5]

Helene's childlike behavior, her most prominent characteristic, links her with Nora, the doll wife; her irresponsibility and self-interest make her stand out in marked contrast to Garland's gallery of forceful and altruistic women.

The second woman character, Evelyn Ward, was Helene's schoolmate and childhood friend, just as Mrs. Linde was Nora's. Evelyn was intelligent and resourceful, having something of the emanci-

---

[1] *Ibid.*, pp. 10–11.
[2] *Ibid.*, pp. 81 ff. *Plays*, pp. 48 ff.
[3] *Ibid.*, p. 161.
[4] *Ibid.*, p. 194.
[5] *Ibid.*, pp. 207–8. For further instances of Helene's nature, see pp. 210 ff.

pated woman about her. When her father confessed his guilt at the trial, she stood by his side, ready to help him. She had the sense of responsibility which Helene lacked. Evelyn, always regardful of others, recalled Mrs. Linde, who made sacrifices for her family, going so far as to marry a man she did not love. Mrs. Linde played the part of a confidante to Nora; in the same way, Evelyn Ward made Helene tell her everything, and managed to comfort and console her friend whenever the latter was in trouble.

Of the male characters, the Iron Duke, Lawrence B. Davis, resembles in many respects Consul Bernick in *Pillars of Society*. Like Bernick, who was a successful business man and the dominant figure in the commercial life of a small Norwegian town, the Iron Duke dominated the railroads in the Washington area. In both cases the conflict arose from a desire to build a new road. Like Bernick, Davis believed in his success, believed that what he did was for the good of the people; and like Bernick, who lied in order to realize his aims, Davis had recourse to bribery:

"I [Davis] don't care for the principle so much. My duty is to succeed. I believe we ought to succeed. Nobody can serve the public as well as we do. If we don't buy 'em I suppose somebody else will. But it's a different thing dealing with the senators. They're officials. It's a State-prison offense."[1]

Yet, both were afraid of scandal and public opinion; for both it was of extreme importance that their personal reputations should be without blame.

Davis treated his daughter with the same condescending indulgence that Bernick showed his wife. Neither had any confidence in women as equals. Bernick never thought of informing his wife about his business: "'My dear Betty, how can it interest you?'"[2] "'My dear Betty, it is an affair that does not concern ladies at all!'"[3] And again: "'Ah, my dear Betty, I knew you would not have been able to grasp the exact situation.'"[4] When Davis was threatened with the exposure of the bribery by which he had secured a franchise for his railroad scheme, he thrust his daughter

---

[1] *Ibid.*, p. 39.
[2] *Plays*, p. 404.
[3] *Ibid.*, p. 405.
[4] *Ibid.*, p. 406.

brusquely aside, saying: "'Go away; you can't understand it. This is a man's affair.'"[1]

Both Ibsen and Garland stressed the motivations[2] of their heroes. They were victims of conditions and their actions were, at least in part, justifiable. Bernick said:

Do you [Lona] suppose I acted as I did from selfish motives? If I had stood alone then, I would have begun all over again with cheerful courage. But you do not understand how the life of a man of business, with his tremendous responsibilities, is bound up with that of the business which falls to his inheritance. Do you realise that the prosperity or the ruin of hundreds—of thousands—depends on him? Can you not take into consideration the fact that the whole community in which both you and I were born would have been affected to the most dangerous extent if the house of Bernick had gone smash?[3]

Davis spoke in the same way:

"Senator, as man to man, I want to be perfectly frank with you. The loss of this charter may ruin my road. We've been building on our original line, changing grades, renewing bridges, and so forth, and we've borrowed largely this year—borrowed big money. If anything were to happen to make people—capitalists—lose confidence in the road, or in me, we'd be in the hands of a receiver in thirty days. It would be a terrible injustice to us, and especially to our small stockholders and employe[r]s. Just imagine the condition of things if we fail. Now, let's work together. Come,—what do you say?"[4]

Unlike Bernick, who was gradually brought to face his own lies and to confess them, Davis did not repent. His life, like Bernick's, was founded on lies, but he did not choose to recognize this; instead, when unable to find the solution in confession, he committed suicide.[5] Garland observed that Davis was not to be blamed, for what had happened was due to "the cursed conditions of things."

If the portrayal of Davis illustrated a character forceful and independent, whose end was as violent as many of Zola's characters,

[1] *A Member of the Third House*, p. 98.
[2] Note that Garland in his chapter on Ibsen in *Crumbling Idols*, pp. 106 ff., discussed Ibsen's "treatment of the moving forces of his characters" and quoted extensively from *Pillars of Society*.
[3] *Plays*, p. 439.
[4] *A Member of the Third House*, p. 130.
[5] *Ibid.*, pp. 200 ff.

Senator Ward may be said to be a naturalistic character turned into an Ibsen moralist. Both figures were, it seems, partially modeled upon Bernick. Rufus Ward, a drunkard by heredity but otherwise an able man and a member of the Senate, was tempted to accept bribes because of circumstances and his own weakness, but instead of deteriorating, he became conscious of the demand of duty to himself and to society, and in the manner of Bernick he acknowledged his guilt by means of public confession:

"Gentlemen and fellow citizens, I have a confession to make. ... I stand here after a week of sleepless debate, rising from a sickbed, with a duty to perform. The gentlemen on this committee know how the taint of corruption has been thrown upon me. Slander has been busy with me, and, since my testimony on Tuesday, my brain has about worn out with the trouble of it all. My own self-defense, if nothing more, demands that I should stand here and testify."[1]

Although financially and socially ruined by this act, Ward had found his true self and won respect by his firm stand against corruption.

And finally there is the young lawyer Wilson Tuttle, a born moralist and reformer, in some respects Garland himself. He recalls Dr. Stockmann in *An Enemy of the People*, although he lacked the warmth and impulsiveness that made Dr. Stockmann a real human being. Tuttle was the man behind the exposure of the Third House and the Senate and, like Dr. Stockmann, he stood alone against the people when, in a righteous cause, he was unable to present conclusive evidence. The following passage about Tuttle applies also to Dr. Stockmann: " 'I don't live here anyhow, but damned if I like to see the whole town jumpin' on a man's neck, 'specially when I'm sure he's right.' "[2] Both Stockmann and Tuttle were champions of truth and justice and the fact that they were in the minority only made them stronger and more eager to pursue their aims. " ... the strongest man in the world is he who stands most alone," are Dr. Stockmann's final words in *An Enemy of the People*.[3] The difference is, however, that toward the end of the novel society accepted Tuttle and rec-

---

[1] *Ibid.*, p. 171. Cf. Consul Bernick's confession. *Plays*, pp. 491-4.
[2] *A Member of the Third House*, p. 117.
[3] *Plays*, p. 288.

ognized the justice of his plea, whereas Dr. Stockmann's equally righteous cause remained unrecognized.

In *A Spoil of Office* Garland portrayed an independent and vigorous woman temperamentally akin to Lona Hessel and the Nora of the last act. Ida Wilbur was a radical and a leader of the woman's suffrage movement.[1] When not on lecture-tours, Ida was interested in modern literature, and was a member of a literary club that met at her house to dicuss such writers as Howells and Ibsen, the latter being translated for the club by a Norwegian-American.

Ida's views on women's rights are reminiscent of Ibsen's in *A Doll's House*. In her speech on "The Real Woman-Question," she defended "the right of women to live as human beings, to act as human beings, and to develop as freely as men."[2] And she went on to say "'I claim the right to be an individual human being first and a woman afterwards.'"[3] This echoes *A Doll's House*:

Helmer. Before all else, you are a wife and a mother.
Nora. I don't believe that any longer. I believe that before all else I am a reasonable human being, just as you are—or, at all events, that I must try and become one.[4]

Moreover, Ida was as staunch an advocate of women's claims in marriage as Garland believed Ibsen to be in *A Doll's House*. As has been said earlier,[5] Garland was above all impressed by the *Doll's House* theme as a means to the liberation of women. He was largely interested in the possibilities of improving women's social and legal position in marriage, and in the spiritual kinship and intellectual compatibility that Ibsen recommended between husband and wife, which he was to develop more fully in *Rose of Dutcher's Coolly*. Ida's declaration of women's independence

---

[1] Cf. the new woman, pp. 86 n. 1., 222–3.

[2] "A Spoil of Office," *Arena*, V (March, 1892), 515.

[3] *Ibid*. We must bear in mind that Garland at this period of his life was an eager social reformer, an advocate of Henry George's economic theories and a contributor to the radical *Arena*. See p. 67 ff. The novel was first run as a serial in that magazine. To Garland, Ibsen was first and foremost the reformer. Cf. also p. 222.

[4] *Plays*, p. 88.

[5] See pp. 366 ff.

in marriage savors of the rebellious Nora, who had courage enough to leave a husband who regarded her as a mere plaything. It was against Helmer's attitude that Ida actually turned, when she asserted:

"The time is surely coming when women can no longer bear to be dependent, to be pitied or abused by men. They will want to stand upright and independent, by their husbands, claiming the same rights to freedom of action, and demanding equal pay for equal work. She must be able to earn her own living in an *honorable* way at a moment's notice. Then she will be a free woman even if she never leaves her kitchen."[1]

Though independently conceived, Ida's kinship with the Nora type can hardly be questioned.

Rose in *Rose of Dutcher's Coolly*, Garland's most vivid woman, is also akin to the Nora type in certain respects. She demanded personal freedom and intellectual independence; she was physically and morally strong, and easily dominated the men she attracted.[2] Rose was not a woman of the common run, but spirited and individualistic like some of Ibsen's heroines. In addition, the view on marriage voiced by Rose in the novel is reminiscent of Ibsen's. Averse to being dependent upon the man, desirous of being his equal, she commented: "'I hate to think of marrying for a home, and I hate to think of marrying as a profession.'"[3] The ideal marriage as advocated by Ibsen and interpreted by Garland was illustrated by the marriage of Isabel Herrick with a friend, both modern, intellectual people. It was their happy relationship which finally inspired Mason to write an offer of marriage to Rose, who was waiting for "comradeship with a man of toil, of imagination, and hidden powers."[4] The letter reads as follows:

"I do not require you to cook for me, nor keep house for me. You are mistress of yourself; to come and go as you please, without question and without accounting to me. You are at liberty to cease your association with me at any time, and consider yourself perfectly free to leave me

---

[1] "A Spoil of Office," *Arena*, V (March, 1892), 516.

[2] Cf. also Turgenev's heroines. Rose was, moreover, set against an irresolute man, a device common in both Turgenev and Ibsen. See p. 316. As a child of nature Rose bears some resemblance to Björnson's *The Fisher Maiden* (1868) and to Tess, the heroine of Hardy's *Tess of the D'Urbervilles* (1891).

[3] *Rose of Dutcher's Coolly*, p. 286.

[4] *Ibid.*, p. 313. See also p. 326.

whenever any other man comes with power to make you happier than you are with me.

"I want you as comrade and lover, not as subject or servant, or unwilling wife. I do not claim any rights whatever over you. You can bear me children or not, just as you please. You are a human soul like myself, and I shall expect you to be as free and as sovereign as I, to follow any profession or to do any work which pleases you."[1]

Mason's letter with its plea for an intimate intellectual companionship between husband and wife, sharing a responsibility to each other and to society, may have been stimulated by Ibsen's exposure of an unworthy marriage in *A Doll's House*.[2]

It is perhaps no exaggeration to say that Ibsen was a basic factor in Garland's literary career and a fundamental source of inspiration for much of his work.

2. IBSEN AND CRANE

There is no reference to Ibsen[3] or his dramas in Crane's works, letters, and other material known to the present writer; nor has any scholar of Crane, as far as I am aware, ever considered a possible influence of Ibsen on the American writer. Nevertheless it seems probable that Crane was familiar with certain of the dramatist's works. Like Garland, Crane seems to have been sensitive to new literary currents and new ideas and he, too, may have come across some of Ibsen's plays. We need only call attention to the growing popularity of Ibsen in the United States in the nineties and to Crane's friendship with Garland.[4]

Crane may have derived some inspiration from Ibsen for at least one story, namely "The Monster" (1899). It is a long short story, made up of twenty-four episodic scenes or sections, and its theme is ostracism.[5] Crane's treatment of this motif is reminiscent of that

---

[1] *Ibid.* p. 333.

[2] Cf. the marrage debate, p. 81.

[3] Beer makes no mention of Ibsen in his biography of Crane.

[4] See pp. 44–6, 60–1, 95 n. 2.

[5] In the volume entitled *Whilomville Stories* (1900) treating of child life in Whilomville—the hero is a boy, Jimmie Trescott—Crane gives evidence of the same love of truth and hatred of meanness and distrust of mass opinion as is felt in "The Monster" and in Ibsen's social dramas. Ostracism is also the theme of the short story entitled "Shame," first published in *Harper's*

of Ibsen in *An Enemy of the People*. The scene of action is an obscure little town in the vicinity of New York, a setting very much like that of *An Enemy of the People*. In this little town Dr. Trescott lived a strenuous but peaceful life with his wife, his little son Jim, and Henry Johnson, a negro hostler. One night, when he returned home from a professional call, he found his house ablaze. Mrs. Trescott was rescued, but for a time it seemed that little Jim could not be got out of the burning building. He was eventually saved by the negro, however, who got so badly burned that, when he finally recovered through the efforts of Dr. Trescott, he had practically "no face."[1] Moreover, he had become a half-idiot, a monster, who scared everybody in town. Because the negro had saved the life of his son Dr. Trescott took care of him. As a consequence the doctor and his family were socially ostracized by the people of the small community.

The problem set by Crane was one of conflict between the individual and society, i.e. the same problem as in *An Enemy of the People*. In both works the individual stood for right, and society for power. The individual was supposed to be submissive to the authorities and public opinion but, like Dr. Stockmann, Dr. Trescott was not, and was isolated in consequence.

The two doctors, the heroes, have many points in common; both were skilful practitioners possessing an invincible sense of truth and justice; they were staunch idealists, conscious of their duty toward themselves and their fellow men. They never listened to the voice of the majority when they believed it to be wrong, nor had they recourse to devious ways or crooked manoeuvres. Unflinchingly, each fought for right and truth against the prejudice of an entire community. Their families were eventually excluded from society. In *An Enemy of the People* the first conspicuous sign of ostracism was perceived when the glazier did not dare to come to Dr. Stockmann's house to repair the windows. Then followed other blows in rapid succession: the notice to quit from the landlord, Petra's dismissal, Dr. Stockmann's own dis-

---

Monthly, C (January, 1900), 321–5, in which Jimmie Trescott is "made a social leper" because he went to a picnic with his lunch in a pail. Reprinted in *Whilomville Stories*. *Work*, V, 75–86.

[1] Cf. Bierce's words about some fallen soldiers in "On a Mountain": ". . . they had no faces." *Battle Sketches* (London, 1930), p. 7.

missal, and finally the loss of his practice and the great legacy. The Trescotts were ostracized in more or less the same way as the Stockmanns. When Jake Winter's girl fell ill after being frightened by the disfigured negro, the Winters did not call Dr. Trescott, their former family doctor. Moreover, the Hannigans were going to move out of their house next door to the Trescotts because the latter were considered morally dangerous; they were, in fact, enemies of society. Like Dr. Stockmann, Dr. Trescott gradually lost his practice. The last scene of the story showed the complete ostracism of the Trescott family. No guests attended the party at which Mrs. Trescott had expected fifteen. Dr. Stockmann's house was also bare of guests after his public speech.

Furthermore, when Dr. Stockmann received his dismissal from the Baths Committee, Peter Stockmann, the prompter of his discharge, excused himself in the following terms: "It gives us pain to do it; but, to speak frankly, we dared not do otherwise on account of public opinion."[1] In like manner, the four distinguished men of the community who visited Dr. Trescott in order to convince him that he was simply killing his practice through his "infernal pig-headedness" in not sending away the negro, expressed their personal sympathy. The reader is made to understand that they acted as they did because of their inability to oppose public opinion. " 'Now see here, Trescott, we like you, and we have come to talk right out about this business. It may be none of our affairs and all that, and as for me, I don't mind if you tell me so; but I am not going to keep quiet and see you ruin yourself. And that's how we all feel.' "[2] And again: " 'And there are a good many of us that admire you for it immensely,' interrupted Twelve; 'but that isn't going to change the minds of all those ninnies [i.e. the women].' "[3]

Like Ibsen, Crane launched fierce attacks on the mentality of small-town people, their narrowness, their hypocrisy, their complacency, their stupidity, and above all their moral cowardice. The ostracism of the Stockmanns resulted from the fact that almost nobody in the community dared to oppose the opinion of the majority. Old Judge Denning Hagenthorpe is in some respects a

[1] *Plays*, p. 274.
[2] *Work*, III, 99.
[3] *Ibid.*

faint echo of Peter Stockmann: both were smug and mighty leaders of the community; both were egoistic bachelors who played a somewhat similar role in questioning the advisability of Dr. Trescott's and Dr. Stockmann's stand for truth and right; both made vain attempts to keep the heroes from performing their duty to themselves and society. The old judge, for instance, looked upon Dr. Trescott's saving of the negro's life as an act of questionable charity.

In "The Monster" Crane seems to have adopted Ibsen's method of explaining the motive forces of his characters, and like Ibsen he achieved objectivity by presenting both sides of a problem. Ibsen used this method with particular success in the portrayal of Consul Bernick in *Pillars of Society*. In "The Monster" Crane used it, for example, in the scene depicting Reifsnyder's barber shop, where the various patrons took sides for and against Dr. Trescott. The general atmosphere of the story, with its mixture of satire, irony, wit, humor, and tragedy, is also reminiscent of *An Enemy of the People*. Contemporary critics, who saw in "The Monster" a tale of horror, failed to appreciate its full intent, for Crane may well have meant it to be chiefly a piece of social criticism more or less along the lines of Ibsen's drama.

Wilson Follett is correct, it seems, in saying that the story is "a sort of miniature Late Victorian anticipation of *Main Street*."[1] *An Enemy of the People* ends with an apotheosis of individualism, but "The Monster" closes on a note of resignation and pessimism. The concluding paragraph, with its whining wind and the snow beating upon the windows of the lonely Trescott house, only augments the effect of bitterness and ironic tragedy.

3. IBSEN AND NORRIS

That Norris knew of the works of Ibsen is clear from his occasional reference to the Norwegian. In an interview with David Belasco, the playwright, for example, he mentioned Ibsen's problem plays, and in writing up the conversation quoted "'Ibsen is a dramatist whom people read. Staged, his plays would fail surely and inevitably.'"[2] Again, in *The Responsibilities of the Novelist*,

---

[1] Introduction to *Work*, III, x.

[2] "Belasco on Plays," *Wave* (August 28, 1897). Reprinted in *Frank Norris of "The Wave,"* p. 157.

Norris mentioned Ibsen. Speaking of the deplorable state of the American drama, he asserted, "Vaudeville is all very well by itself, and one will even go so far as to admit that it has its place as much as an Ibsen problem play."[1]

Critics of Norris[2] have evidently been unaware of the influence which Ibsen exerted on his work, probably because of his larger and more obvious debt to Zola and French naturalism. But Norris, like Garland, sensitive to new ideas, new currents of thought, and new literary techniques, also came under the sway of Ibsen, whose forceful characters and ideas were to enrich his works. This indebtedness is felt to varying degrees in most of Norris's novels, but it is perhaps most evident in *A Man's Woman* (1900).

The influence of Ibsen's work on Norris seems to be of two kinds: the direct and apparent influence, which is seen in Norris's use of Ibsenian ideas and characters; and the less direct, less tangible influence, which is observed in his use of saga material. In some of his early plays Ibsen portrays his countrymen as devoid of strength and vitality.[3] Disgusted with their hypocrisy and moral shortcomings, Ibsen turned to the Old Norse sagas for inspiration, and set up a new ideal by incorporating saga material into such works as *The Vikings at Helgeland* and *The Pretenders*. Like Ibsen, Norris may have found in the sagas a new force, a new vitality, a new zest for life, for in some of his works the influence of Ibsen seems to be intertwined with impulses from the sagas. Norris also knew the saga material[4] and doubtless was often im-

---

[1] *Compl. Works*, VII, 223–4.

[2] There is no reference whatever to Ibsen and his plays in either Biencourt or Marchand. Marchand runs into difficulties in his attempt to explain *A Man's Woman* because of his unawareness of Norris's debt to Ibsen. Walker mentions Ibsen twice in passing. See *op. cit.*, pp. 98, 236.

[3] This attitude of Ibsen toward his compatriots is evident in such dramas as *Brand* and *Peer Gynt*.

[4] In *The Responsibilities of the Novelist* Norris mentioned the following poems and sagas: *The Song of Roland*, *The Nibelungenlied*, *The Romance of the Rose*, *Beowulf*, *Magnusson*, *The Heimskringla*, *The Grettir Saga*, pp. 46, 47, 50. Cf. also Norris's rendition of part of the *Grettir Saga* entitled "Grettir at Drangey," published in *Everybody's Magazine* (March, 1902) and included in *Compl. Works*, IV, 128–47. The story was perhaps based on William Morris's *The Story of Grettir the Strong* (1869). Morris was widely read in America in the nineties. See B. O. Flower, "William Morris and Some of His Later

mediately influenced by it; on the other hand, it is probable that some of the influence of the saga material came to him by way of Ibsen—or at least that his interest in it was stimulated by Ibsen, though we must be careful to avoid being dogmatic in this attempt at analysis. Norris was probably interested in the bold and primitive Vikings of the sagas because they fitted his Kiplingesque cult of the Anglo-Saxon race. Norris was lazy by temperament, and admired the savage force, the independence, the defiance, the iron will of the heroic characters of the sagas, poor in words but rich in deeds.

These two types of influence we found in Norris's works, sometimes the one, sometimes the other, sometimes both in the same piece of writing.

Moran of the Lady Letty has points in common both with *The Volsunga Saga* and *The Vikings at Helgeland.* Ibsen's drama was, as is well known, at least partly based on *The Volsunga Saga.*[1] There is one episode in Norris's novel which may have been inspired directly from the saga and not from Ibsen's drama, in which the same episode was somewhat differently handled. Wilbur, the hero of Norris's story, found Moran dressed in man's clothes, fast asleep on a derelict ship surrounded by a cloud of strangling gas, and only when picking her up did he discover that she was a woman. In like manner, Sigurd found Brunhilde, clad in helmet and byrnie, fast asleep in her fire-encircled castle, and only by ripping up her coat of mail with his sword did he find out that she was a woman.

Even if this episode seems to link *Moran of the Lady Letty* with *The Volsunga Saga*, it was perhaps Hjördis of *The Vikings at*

Works," *Arena*, XVII (December, 1896), 42–52. Cf. Karl Litzenberg, "William Morris as Critic of Old Norse Literature," *Edda*, XL (1940), 301–20. Concerning the influence of Old Norse sagas on English literature, see Jón Stefánsson's article "Oldnordisk indvirkning på engelsk literatur i det attende og nittende århundrede," *Nordisk Tidskrift* (1891), pp. 489–503. See also George Leroy White, Jr., *Scandinavian Themes in American Fiction* (Philadelphia, 1937) and Dorothy M. Hoare, *The Works of Morris and of Yeats in Relation to Early Saga Literature* (Cambridge, 1937),

[1] Kristian Elster, Jr., *Illustrert Norsk Litteratur Historie* (2nd ed., Oslo, 1934), p. 68. Cf. also Ibsen's own statement in W. Archer's Introduction to *The Vikings at Helgeland*, II, ix–x, in *The Collected Works of Henrik Ibsen* (11 vols., New York, 1906).

Helgeland rather than Brunhilde[1] that stimulated Norris's Valkyrie,[2] Moran. Repeatedly, Norris stressed the fact that Moran was a modern daughter of the Vikings, a primitive Norse type. Her father was a Northman,[3] a sea captain, and she herself a primitive, undaunted shield-maiden roving the seas. Both Hjördis and Moran were of the same type, blonde and unafraid Valkyries possessing the same recklessness and pride. They ate like men, drank like men, and fought like men. When their anger was roused, they plunged headlong into battle without stopping to reflect whether they were right or wrong. Moran took the same delight in fighting as did the shield-maidens of the sagas, and she turned Valkyrie when struggling in a hand-to-hand fight with Wilbur and the beachcombers on the coast of lower California. This is Moran:

It was very evident that the old Norse fighting-blood of her was all astir; brutal, merciless, savage beyond all control. A sort of obsession seized upon her at the near approach of battle, a frenzy of action that was checked by nothing—that was insensible to all restraint. At times it was impossible for him [Wilbur] to make her hear him, or when she heard to understand what he was saying. Her vision contracted. It was evident that she could not see distinctly. Wilbur could no longer conceive of her as a woman of the days of civilization. She was lapsing back to the eighth century again—to the Vikings, the sea-wolves, the berserkers.[4]

And again:

Her eyes were blazing under her thick frown like fire under a bush. Her arms were bared to the elbow, her heavy ropes of hair flying and coiling from her in all directions, while with a voice hoarse from shouting she sang, or rather chanted, in her long-forgotten Norse tongue, fragments of old sagas,[5] words, and sentences, meaningless even to herself. The fury of battle had exalted her to a sort of frenzy. She was beside herself with excitement. Once more she had lapsed back to the Vikings and sea-rovers of the tenth century—she was Brunhilde again, a shield-maiden, a Valkyrie, a berserker, and the daughter of berserkers, and like

---

[1] Cf. also an early poem by Norris entitled "Brunhilde" in *Occident*, XIX (November 21, 1890), 110.

[2] Since Wagner is sometimes mentioned in Norris's works, we may perhaps assume that his operas, for instance *Die Walküre* of the *Nibelung Tetralogy*, may have contributed to the creation of Norris's Valkyrie type.

[3] Note also Norris's use of the word "Norse" in the novel.

[4] *Compl. Works*, III, 276.

[5] This reminds one of Hjördis chanting "galder."

them she fought in a veritable frenzy, seeing nothing, hearing nothing, every sense exalted, every force doubled, insensible to pain, deaf to all reason.[1]

Like Hjördis, Moran wanted no weakling for a husband, only the strongest, the bravest of men was worthy of her.[2] Thus she did not love Wilbur until he had conquered her in a furious battle —a deed worthy of Sigurd, who had to kill a bear before he could enter Hjördis' room.

In the autobiographical *Blix*,[3] the heroine is a young, independent, modern woman, reminiscent of Nora in *A Doll's House*. Like Nora, who did not wish to trifle with a love she no longer felt, Blix renounced her tepid love for Condy. Her decision to give up the conventional life which she had been living recalls Nora's giving up of her family in order to begin a new life and to be true to herself. Blix, the spoiled society girl, decried San Francisco society because she found it too shallow and insincere:

"Mind, Condy," she concluded, "I'm not going to break with it because I have any 'purpose in life,' or that sort of thing. I want to have a good time, and I'm going to see if I can't have it in my own way. If the kind of thing that makes Jack Carter possible is conventionality, then I'm done with conventionality for good. I am going to try, from this time on, to be just as true to myself as I can be. I am going to be sincere, and not pretend to like people and things that I don't like; and I'm going to do the things that I like to do—just so long as they are the things a good girl can do."[4]

To this outburst the hero exclaimed: "'Why, this is a regular rebellion,'" and promptly came the heroine's retort, possibly Nora-inspired: "'No, sire ... it is a revolution.'"[5]

A far more considerable debt to Ibsen is felt in *A Man's Woman*,[6]

---

[1] *Compl. Works*, III, 286.

[2] Cf. p. 212.

[3] It is easily understood that Ibsen's new type of woman should have a particular appeal to Norris, who in his wife—the supposed heroine of the novel— saw the prototype of an unconventional, modern woman. His mother, too, was of this type. See p. 106.

[4] *Compl. Works*, III, 19.

[5] *Ibid.*, p. 21.

[6] For this novel, which was to deal with Arctic exploration, Norris needed a hero endowed with an indomitable will power and a granite firmness of purpose to be able to conquer the ice and to reach the Pole. In one of Ibsen's dramas he found an excellent model, namely Brand, who possessed many of the vir-

which seems to have been written partly under the influence of *The Vikings at Helgeland* and partly under that of *Brand*. We shall first compare Norris's novel with *The Vikings at Helgeland*.[1] The plot of the novel recalls somewhat Ibsen's drama of the Vikings. Sigurd and Gunnar were foster brothers and Vikings, who roamed the seas together in search of adventure and fame. In like manner, Bennett and Ferris, the best of friends, were portrayed as modern Vikings who, in the spirit of adventure, were pushing their way with undaunted courage through the Arctic Region with a view to performing a bold deed, namely to reach the North Pole. They "had lived together for so long, had fought out the fight with the Enemy shoulder to shoulder, had battled with the same dangers, had dared the same sufferings, had undergone the same defeats and disappointments."[2]

Out of his friendship for Gunnar sprang Sigurd's greatest sacrifice, the surrender of the woman he loved. By his strength and valor he was able to kill the white bear that guarded the entrance to her room, and then led Hjördis to believe it was Gunnar who had performed the feat. In much the same way did Ferris sacrifice his love for Lloyd Searight, whom Bennett also loved. In the Arctic night when their last hope of survival was gone, out of affection and pity for his best friend and in order to make death seem a little less hard for him, Ferris told Bennett that Lloyd loved him. It was not true, however; Lloyd had never told Ferris of her feeling for Bennett, although she loved him with all her heart. Finally, when the expedition was unexpectedly rescued, the falsehood was revealed to Lloyd, as the similar deception had been revealed to Hjördis. The deception deeply humiliated

---

tues necessary for a successful explorer. Norris's preoccupation with moral values in this novel may partially be accounted for by the fact that it was composed after Norris's acute attack of the South African fever. According to Norris, his wife gave him the idea of the novel. See Appendix, p. 461. See also p. 119.

[1] Typical saga elements are to be found also in *A Man's Woman*, although to a lesser degree than in *Moran of the Lady Letty*. Bennett, the hero, was described in terms of the sagas: "He appeared physically larger. It was no longer a man; it was a giant, an ogre, a colossal jotun hurling ice blocks, fighting out a battle unspeakable, in the dawn of the world, in chaos and in darkness." *Compl. Works*, VI, 24.

[2] *Ibid.*, p. 35.

Lloyd—the more so, because it was the man she loved who had humiliated her. "She had been hurt and to the heart, at a point where she believed herself most unassailable, and he who held the weapon was the man that with all the heart of her and soul of her she loved."[1] In the same way Hjördis was mortified by being deceived by the man she loved.

Besides similarities in plot between *A Man's Woman* and *The Vikings at Helgeland*, there are also likenesses in character portrayal. Like Moran and Blix, Lloyd belongs to the group of independent women met with in Ibsen's dramas. Lloyd resembles Hjördis, for, like Ibsen's heroine, she was a strong, proud Valkyrie; both had the same spirit of independence and valor. Like Hjördis, Lloyd was strong-willed and uncompromising and hated pettiness. Above all, both loved bold deeds; with them it was action that counted: "No matter how lofty the thoughts, how brilliant the talk, how beautiful the literature—for her [Lloyd], first, last, and always, were acts, acts, acts—concrete, substantial, material acts."[2] Hjördis knew her own strength, and she despised weakness whenever she encountered it, for instance in Dagny. Lloyd, too, was well aware of her physical as well as moral power. "Ah! she was better than other women; ah! she was stronger than other women; ... smiling proudly, almost insolently, in the consciousness of her strength, the fine steadfastness of her purpose."[3] Like Hjördis, Lloyd was passionate and, once her feelings was aroused, she was ready to sacrifice everything to accompany the man she loved. Hjördis and Lloyd wanted to be like men, to do men's work, and to take part in men's struggles. When Lloyd treated a dangerous typhoid case, she felt and behaved like a Valkyrie wrestling with a furious enemy: "All the exuberance of battle grew big within her breast. She was impatient to be there—there at hand—to face the Enemy again across the sick-bed, where she had so often faced and outfought him before."[4] It was but natural that such strong and spirited women should love only the strongest and the bravest of men,[5] men of

---

[1] *Ibid.*, p. 96.
[2] *Ibid.*, p. 49.
[3] *Ibid.*, p. 50.
[4] *Ibid.*, p. 105.
[5] Cf. p. 212.

unusual force, such as Sigurd and Bennett. The men themselves were well aware of the fact that they loved extraordinary women. Bennett declared:

I loved you because I believed you to be a woman, a great, strong, noble, man's woman, above little things, above the little, niggling, contemptible devices of the drawing room. I loved you because the great things of the world interested you, because you had no place in your life for petty graces, petty affectations, petty deceits and shams and insincerities.[1]

Hjördis' ambition was actually to be worthy of Sigurd, to encourage him, to accompany him everywhere, to stand by his side in time of peril. This is Hjördis:

I will follow thee [Sigurd] in harness of steel, whithersoever thou wendest ... Not as thy wife ... but like those mighty women, like Hildë's sisters, will I follow thee, and fire thee to strife and to manly deeds, so that thy name shall be heard over every land. In the sword-game will I stand by thy side; I will fare forth among thy warriors in the storm and on the viking-raid ...[2]

And again: "Plainly now I see my task in life: to make thee famous over all the world."[3]

Lloyd's aim was actually to be worthy of Bennett, to be his companion, and to urge him to bold deeds. She

had chosen a work to be done because he had set her an example. So only that she preserved her womanliness, she, too, wanted to count, to help on, to have her place in the world's progress. In reality all her ambitions and hopes had been looking toward one end only, that she might be his equal; that he might find in her a companion and a confidante; one who could share his enthusiasms and understand his vast projects and great aims.[4]

When Bennett suffered from typhoid fever, Lloyd realized that she was morally and intellectually the stronger, but what was more important, she discovered that duty demanded that she should stand by Bennett's side, as it had been Hjördis' duty to stand by the side of Sigurd. But unlike Hjördis, whose desire was to accompany Sigurd in battle, Lloyd was content to be left at home when her duty was fulfilled, and her husband once more sailed away to make a final attempt to find the Pole:

[1] *Compl. Works*, VI, 94.
[2] *The Vikings at Helgeland*, p. 90.
[3] *Ibid.*, p. 91.
[4] *Compl. Works*, VI, 147.

Hers was the woman's part. Already she had assumed it; steadfast unselfishness, renunciation, patience, the heroism greater than all others, that sits with folded hands, quiet, unshaken, and under fearful stress, endures, and endures, and endures. To be the inspiration of great deeds, high hopes, and firm resolves, and then, while the fight was dared, to wait in calmness for its issue—that was her duty; that the woman's part in the world's great work.[1]

Thus, Lloyd found that which she had been unconsciously seeking, her function in life, her duty. But as a truly Ibsen-inspired character, she had to struggle with herself, for the call demanded tremendous sacrifices of her. "When was it to end, this continual sacrifice of inclination to duty, this eternal abnegation, this yielding up of herself, her dearest, most cherished wishes to the demands of duty and the great world?"[2] These words of despondency had nothing of the glamour and valor which was typical of a proud and strong Valkyrie like Hjördis; they were rather the agonizing utterance of a frustrated and baffled soul in despair. In reality they had the ring of the sacrifices that Pastor Brand and his faithful wife, Agnes, had to make. For throughout *A Man's Woman*[3] there is evidence of a marked influence of *Brand*, particularly in the portrayal of Lloyd and Bennett.

---

[1] *Ibid.*, p. 209.

[2] *Ibid.*, p. 212.

[3] The novel falls naturally into two parts, the first comprising the two opening chapters (40 pages), the nucleus of which was written earlier and published separately as "End of the Beginning." This described the failure of Bennett's Polar expedition in a Zolaesque manner. The second part, by far the bulk of the novel (9 chapters; 205 pages) is of a different character. The violent action of the first part slows down, and in many respects the novel comes close to an Ibsenian drama of ideas. In the short story "End of the Beginning" published in the *Wave* of September 4, 1897 and reprinted in *Frank Norris of "The Wave,"* pp. 43–54, it is of interest to note that the roles of Bennett and Ferris are reversed, and Lloyd Searight bears the name of Helen Parry, which points to the assumption that Robert Edwin Peary's expedition in search of the North Pole may have been Norris's inspiration for this story, later worked out and used as the opening chapters of *A Man's Woman*. Cf. R. Peary's *Northward over the Great Ice* (1898). Of more interest, however, is the fact that there are no traces of the influence of *Brand* and Ibsen's ethics in the short story. When Norris undertook to write the novel, he not only reversed the roles of Bennett and Ferris, but he also created a new Bennett modeled on Brand. In the early version, i.e. the short story, Norris seems to have followed the saga motive of the falsehood rather than Ibsen's rendition of the saga in *The Vikings*

It was perhaps on Brand that Norris modeled Lloyd's sense of duty, her intensity of purpose, her imperious will, and her ultimate mastery of self.[1] By his indomitable will, Brand exercised so powerful an influence on Agnes, even shattering "her last idol shrine" that, having been forced to sacrifice everything, she was completely crushed. Similarly, Lloyd was defeated by the terrible will of Bennett. The following words uttered by Lloyd are with equal justice applicable to Agnes: "That insensate, bestial determination, iron-hearted, iron-strong, had beaten down opposition, had carried its point. Life and love had been crushed beneath its trampling without pity, without hesitation. The tragedy of the hour was done; the tragedy of the long years to come was just beginning."[2]

There are parallels between Brand and Lloyd: Brand inherited a fortune after his mother's death; Lloyd received a fortune after the death of her mother. Both, however, stripped themselves of all material wealth, Brand by building a new church and Lloyd by erecting a nursing agency. The following paragraph recalls Brand's activities: "And so it was that Lloyd came back to the house she had built, to the little community she had so proudly organized, to the agency she had founded and with her own money endowed and supported."[3] Brand as well as Lloyd were otherwise averse to giving away a mite of their fortunes, the former refusing to give anything to the poor people struck by cold and famine, and the latter refusing to give three cents to an old cripple dying of cancer. Like Brand, Lloyd was "animated by no great philanthropy, no vast love of humanity . . ."[4] Like Brand, Lloyd was strong-willed and obstinate; after Hattie's operation, for example, Lloyd observed: "'We *will* 'pull through,' yes, for I'll do

---

at *Helgeland*, for in Norris's early version and in the saga the hero and the heroine are engaged before the complications set in, while in the novel Norris seems to have followed Ibsen's adaptation of the saga motive.

[1] Norris often employed the terminology used by Ibsen, for instance, "the shifty mass of sophistries," "the conceptions of Duty and Will," "no compromise, no escape," "no compromise, no half measures," "It was no time for half measures and hesitation," "be true to one self," "mastery of self," "With the mastery of self had come forgetfulness of self," etc.

[2] *Compl. Works*, VI, 132.

[3] *Ibid.*, p. 140.

[4] *Ibid.*, p. 49.

it.'"[1] Like Brand, Lloyd had a keen sense of duty, and although a dangerous case might have killed her, she did not evade her duty. "'I cannot be false, I cannot be cowardly, I cannot shirk my duty,'" she asserted.[2] Like Brand's, her last struggle was one for the mastery of self, out of which she emerged the victor. Here is the serene and purified Lloyd of the last scene, having sacrificed all:

> Then Lloyd, standing alone on that heaving deck, drew herself up to her full height, her head a little back, her blue eyes all alight, a smile upon her lips. She spoke no word. She made no gesture, but stood there, the smile yet upon her lips, erect, firm, motionless; looking steadily, calmly, proudly into Bennett's eyes as his ship carried him farther and farther away.[3]

Bennett,[4] too, it seems, owes a considerable debt to Brand. The austere Norwegian environment had put its imprint on Brand, just as the Polar Region had marked Bennett. In both works, the conflict was set against a background of mountains, snow, ice, and piercing winds; the opening scene of Ibsen's drama shows Brand fighting like a fury against fog and snow on a mountain side, and the first chapters of *A Man's Woman* show Bennett and his men fighting for their lives in the Arctic night. Both Brand and Bennett were stern characters. Again and again Norris stressed Bennett's indomitable will, his determination to reach the Pole regardless of suffering, pain, and death. Both were intolerant of any weakness, any half measures, any compromises. This is Bennett:

> "To get forward, to get forward." Answering the resistless influence of their leader, that indomitable man of iron whom no fortune could break nor bend, and who imposed his will upon them as if it were a yoke of

---

[1] *Ibid.*, p. 58. Italics are Norris's.

[2] *Ibid.*, p. 129.

[3] *Ibid.*, p. 244.

[4] It should also be noted that Vandover in *Vandover and the Brute* was an obvious contrast to Ward Bennett, just as Peer Gynt was a contrast to Brand. Moreover, the character of Oswald in *Ghosts* has some points in common with Vandover. Both were artists of some talent, but through heredity and dissipation both had recurrent nervous attacks, and both had the same dread of becoming insane. In their physical and mental breakdown they eventually lost their art. Cf. a similar theme used in Zola's *Thérèse Raquin* and George Du Maurier's *Trilby*. See pp. 291–2.

steel—this idea became for them a sort of obsession. Forward, if it were only a yard; if it were only a foot. Forward over the heartbreaking rubble ice; forward against the biting, shrieking wind; forward in the face of the blinding snow; forward through the brittle crusts and icy water; forward, although every step was an agony, though the haul rope cut like a dull knife, though their clothes were sheets of ice. Blinded, panting, bruised, bleeding, and exhausted, dogs and men, animals all, the expedition struggled forward.[1]

Brand's will was as indomitable as that of Bennett, and the self-reliance of both was extraordinary. Soon, however, both realized that duty demanded sacrifices: Brand had to give up all that was dear to him, mother, child, and wife, everything, for his slogan was "All or Nothing"; and Bennett had to choose between the life of his dearest friend and that of the woman he loved. "How to meet this abominable complication wherein he must sacrifice the woman he so dearly loved or the man who was the Damon to his Pythias, the Jonathan to his David?"[2] And Norris went on:

Then Bennett realized with a great spasm of horror that for him there was no going back. All his life, accustomed to quick decisions in moments of supreme peril, he took his decision now, facing, with such courage as he could muster, its unspeakable consequences, consequences that he knew must harry and hound him all the rest of his life. Whichever way he decided, he opened his heart to the beak and talons of a pitiless remorse.[3]

Since he chose to save the life of the woman he loved, he suffered pangs of conscience which eventually began to weaken his will and determination. Crushed and humiliated, he had to fight as did Brand the last battle, the battle with self. Like Brand, he won self-mastery and emerged from the struggle free from pride. This is Brand, more of a human being and less an abstraction personifying will power:

> From to-day my life shall stream
> Lambent, glowing, as a dream.
> The ice-fetters break away,
> I can weep,—and kneel,—and pray![4]

---

[1] *Compl. Works*, VI, 19.

[2] *Ibid.*, p. 122.

[3] *Ibid.*, p. 123.

[4] Ibsen, *Samlede Værker* (10 vols., Copenhagen, 1898–1902), III, 259. The English translation is taken from P. J. Eikeland's *Ibsen Studies* (Northfield, Minn., 1934), p. 132.

And this is Bennett, purified and more submissive:

> By nature, by training, and by virtue of the life he lived Bennett had
> been a man, harsh, somewhat brutal, inordinately selfish, and at all times
> magnificently arrogant. He had neither patience nor toleration for natural
> human weakness. . . . His heart was callous; his whole nature and charac-
> ter hard and flinty from the buffetings he gave rather than received.
> Then had come misfortune. Ferris had died, and Bennett's recognition
> and acknowledgment of the fact that he, Ward Bennett, who never failed,
> who never blundered, had made at last the great and terrible error of his
> life, had shaken his character to its very foundations. This was only
> the beginning; the breach once made, Humanity entered into the gloomy,
> waste places of his soul; remorse crowded hard upon his wonted arrogance;
> generosity and the impulse to make amends took the place of selfishness;
> kindness thrust out the native brutality; the old-time harshness and impe-
> riousness gave way to a certain spirit of toleration.[1]

This transformation of Bennett may well have been conceived
under the direct inspiration of Ibsen's *Brand*.

In addition, certain ethical doctrines, already touched upon,
are to be found in *A Man's Woman* and in Ibsen's works, particularly in *Brand*. It may be worth while examining some of them
in detail.

One of Ibsen's leading ideas, as expressed in *Brand* and elsewhere, was his belief in a call.[2] To him everyone had a certain
mission or call in life to fulfil, and it was important that everyone
should pursue it since it was a gift of God to man.[3] Norris, too,
emphasized the call and asserted that Bennett's mission was to
reach the North Pole, Lloyd's to do her duty as a nurse and, after
her marriage, to stand by her husband and to encourage him in
his work. Nothing was allowed to interfere with the fulfilment
of the call.

Surveying the endless plains of snow and ice in the Polar Region,
Bennett knew that it was his task to conquer nature's resistance
and find the Pole. He did not want to give up what he knew was

---

[1] *Compl. Works*, VI, 205–6.

[2] "Call" stands here for calling, charge, mission, duty. The belief in a call
was, of course, a general idea and in no way limited to or emanating from Ibsen. It is clear, however, that Norris had *Brand* in mind when emphasizing
this concept.

[3] It is surprising to find that Norris stressed the fact that Bennett's call came
from God—Bennett was conceived as a Darwinian superman—but he was probably merely following Brand, whose call as a pastor was of divine origin.

his duty, although "it was easier to die than to live"; instead he pursued his task to the best of his ability. " 'The world wants men, great, strong, harsh, brutal men—men with purposes, who let nothing, nothing, nothing stand in their way,' " wrote Norris.[1]

When Bennett prevented Lloyd from doing her duty on a dangerous case, she was humiliated and almost crushed:

"Now I am helpless in your hands. You have conquered, and you can do with me as you choose. But if you make me do what is false, and what is cowardly, and what is dishonourable; if you stand between me and what I know is my duty, how can I love you, how can I love you?"[2]

Bennett, as has been said, had gone through an inner crisis and, like Brand, had emerged a different person. But Bennett was so humbled that his ambition was gone and he was unable to follow the voice of duty. Then Lloyd realized that her own call was to encourage her husband to follow his; she was to be his "inspiration, his incentive, to urge him to the accomplishment of a great work."[3] It was Bennett's work that counted. Lloyd recognized its supreme demands, and gave up her own career and her personal happiness in order to inspire her husband to do the great work, the duty given to him by God. This is her realization of her duty:

His work, his work, God made him for that; appointed the task, made the man, and now she came between. God, Man, and the Work—the three vast elements of an entire system, the whole universe epitomized in the tremendous trinity. . . . Duty once more stirred and awoke. It seemed to her as if some great engine ordained of Heaven to run its appointed course had come to a standstill, was rusting to its ruin, and that she alone of all the world had power to grasp its lever, to send it on its way; . . . She knew only that it was right that she should act. By degrees her resolution hardened. Bennett must try again.[4]

When, in a moment of weakness, Brand intended to leave the valley and its people, a member of his congregation asked him stay with them because it was his duty so to do. In the same way, a man called Adler came to Bennett and reminded him of his obligation to attempt once more to reach the Pole; like Brand Bennett remained true to his mission.

---

[1] *Compl. Works*, VI, 71.

[2] *Ibid.*, p. 129.

[3] *Ibid.*, p. 207.

[4] *Ibid.*, p. 218.

The demand of the call is the underlying principle which governs the other injunctions found in Ibsen's moral philosophy: truth, wholeness, and will.

As a result of having been forced by Bennett to shirk her duty, Lloyd experienced an emotional crisis. Her pride was wounded and her conscience was violated. Humbled by having to leave her patient against her will, she returned, crushed and desperate, to the nursing agency which she had erected, and which she supported. It was impossible for her to confess that the man she loved had caused her dereliction, so she resolved to take the easiest way, to avoid talking about the case and to trust to circumstances. Fate was favorable, and her failure was not discovered at the agency. But the voice of conscience soon began to speak, as it did eventually in Bernick. Unlike the characters in purely naturalistic works, who have no choice between alternatives, who are victims of forces beyond their control, Lloyd was an ethical being, able to choose between right and wrong. Her need to choose the right thing resulted in a sharp inner struggle:

> Abruptly she recoiled. Whither was she tending? If she supinely resigned herself to the current of circumstance, where would she be carried? ... Was it not her chance; was not this deception which others and not herself had created, her opportunity to recover herself, to live down what had been done—what she had been forced to do, rather? Absolute right was never to be attained; was not life to be considered rather in the light of a compromise between good and evil? To do what one could under the circumstances, was not that the golden mean?[1]

But Lloyd, like Brand, could not compromise:

> It was right that she should be true. She ought to do the right. Argument, the pleas of weakness, the demands of expediency, the plausibility of compromise were all of no avail. The idea "I ought" persisted and persisted and persisted. She could and she ought. There was no excuse for her, and no sooner had she thrust aside the shifty mass of sophistries under which she had striven to conceal them, no sooner had she let in the light, than these two conceptions of Duty and Will began suddenly to grow.[2]

Lloyd found herself in a typical Ibsenian situation, caught between two opposing concepts of justice: one, external, dependent

---

[1] *Ibid.*, pp. 152–3.

[2] *Ibid.*, p. 153.

on the approbation of society, the other, internal, dependent on the approval of the voice of conscience.[1] Since to Lloyd the latter was of the highest importance, she decided to confess her guilt:

> She knew what was right, and she had the strength to hold to it. Then all at once there came to Lloyd a grand, breathless sense of uplifting, almost a transfiguration. She felt herself carried high above the sphere of little things, the region of petty considerations. What did she care for consequences, what mattered to her the unjust comdemnation of her world, if only she remained true to herself, if only she did right? What did she care for what she gained? It was no longer a question of gain or loss—it was a question of being true and strong and brave. The conflict of that day at Medford between the man's power and the woman's resistance had been cruel, the crisis had been intense, and though she had been conquered then, had it, after all, been beyond recall? No, she was not conquered. No, she was not subdued. Her will had not been broken, her courage had not been daunted, her strength had not been weakened. Here was the greater fight, here was the higher test. Here was the ultimate, supreme crisis of all, and here, at last, come what might, she would not, would not, would not fail.[2]

After the pattern of Bernick she made a public confession, standing in the midst of those she had deceived. The dramatic contrast between the everyday chatter of the nurses and their friendly attitude toward Lloyd, and her somber mood and complete confession is reminiscent of Ibsen who, in *Pillars of Society*, depicted a similar contrast between the happy people who congratulated Consul Bernick and his own dark confession. Having delivered her speech, Lloyd left the stage, and the act closed: "Then she went out, and the closing of the door jarred sharply upon the great silence that had spread throughout the room."[3] Slowly Lloyd began to feel that her mind had been unburdened by the confession and once again she could continue her work, for she had done her duty and remained true to herself. "Was she not slowly getting back her strength by an unflinching adherence to the simple fundamental principles of right, and duty, and truth? Was not the struggle with one's self the greatest fight

---

[1] Cf. *Pillars of Society*, *A Doll's House*, *Ghosts*, and *An Enemy of Society*.

[2] *Compl. Works*, VI, 154. Cf. also Arthur Dimmesdale's confession in *The Scarlet Letter*. A study of related ideas and motifs in Hawthorne and Ibsen might perhaps prove fruitful.

[3] *Compl. Works*, VI, 160.

of all, greater, far greater, than had been the conflict between Bennett's will and her own?"[1] So completely had she succeeded in conquering her lower self that once again she was able to love the man who almost crushed her, for she had "succeeded, had conquered self, had been true when it was easy to be false, had dared the judgment of her peers so only that she might not deceive."[2]

Bennett underwent a crisis somewhat like Lloyd's in his attempt to find his true self, and with Lloyd's help he eventually succeeded and, once more following the demand of the call, set out to reach the Pole.

In Ibsen's dramas of ideas there is recurrent emphasis on the demand for wholeness.[3] Wholeness—for good or for evil—is always preferred to half measures. And wholeness demanded in turn characters with strong and powerful wills. Hjördis was of this type, possessing great vigor and will power. Norris also created a good many characters of marked will; attention has already been called to the similarities between Lloyd and Hjördis.

Bennett's forcefulness of will reminds us of Brand's. Both were men of single ideas and central purposes. Life in the Arctic Region had taught Bennett to have no use for compromises. With him as with Brand, it was the Kierkegaard-Ibsenian "enten—eller" (either—or) that counted. Bennett did not hesitate to leave one man to freeze and starve to death in the Polar Region in order to get forward, and without a moment's hesitation he killed Lloyd's horse with his hammer when the latter suddenly started to run away. When great things were at stake or when his will was set to one purpose, he did not stop to reflect on the consequences. In this respect he was like Brand, who also was unable to compromise. This is Bennett: "He had lost the faculty, possessed, no doubt, by smaller minds, of dealing with complicated situations. To resort to expedients, to make concessions, was all beyond him. For him a thing was absolutely right or absolutely wrong, and between the two there was no gradation."[4] If

---

[1] *Ibid.*, p. 182.   [2] *Ibid.*, p. 204.

[3] The quality and condition of devoting oneself completely and wholeheartedly to a certain task.

[4] *Compl. Works*, VI, 124. Cf. Brand's slogan: "All or nothing!" or the following words in the original: "Det, som du er, vær fuldt og helt, og ikke stykkevis og delt." (Literal translation: "Whatever you are be so fully and wholeheartedly, and not in part or in some measure.") Ibsen, *Samlede Værker*, III, 22.

Bennett had ever had recourse to half measures, he would not have stood forth as the splendid and heroic character he was.

Will power was a dominant characteristic of Hjördis and Lloyd, just as it was of Brand and Bennett. As Hjördis loved Sigurd because he was stronger than she, so did Lloyd love Bennett because his will was stronger than hers. Both Lloyd and Bennett were proud of their iron wills and were equally loath to yield to each other. The following lines from *Brand* applies also to *A Man's Woman:*

> First the Will
> Law's thirst for righteousness must still.
> You must first will! Not only things
> Attainable, in more or less;
> ⸻ ⸻ ⸻ ⸻ ⸻ ⸻ ⸻
> No, you must will with flashing eyes
> Your way through all earth's agonies.[1]

Although it might be impossible to fulfil one's duty, the main thing was to attempt, to *will*. This idea, expressed in *Brand*, is also found in *A Man's Woman*, for, although Bennett had failed in his Polar expedition, he had shown his fellow countrymen what a man of strong will could do. Lloyd said to Bennett's friend Ferriss: "'Oh, if I were a man! Ten thousand, a hundred thousand people are reading to-night of what you have done—of what you have done, you understand, not of what you have failed to do. They have seen—you have shown them what the man can do who says I *will*,[2] and you have done a little more, have gone a little farther, have been a little braver, a little hardier, a little nobler, a little more determined than anyone has ever been before.'"[3]

Although the atmosphere of rigor, austerity, and cheerlessness found in *Brand* is perceptible also in *A Man's Woman*, there are noteworthy differences between the two. In Norris's novel there is a conflict between two strong wills, whereas in *Brand* there is the portrayal of but one will and no comparable conflict; moreover, while Ibsen censured his compatriots rather severely, Norris's novel attempts to show that the Americans were destined to

---

[1] Ibsen, *Samlede Værker*, III, 89–90. Quoted by Eikeland, *op. cit.* p. 110.
[2] Italics are Norris's.
[3] *Compl. Works*, VI, 70.

find the North Pole because America possessed men of Bennett's stature, undaunted Darwinian supermen, who were able to perform deeds which demanded unsurpassed physical as well as moral strength. Finally, *Brand* ends on a tragic note, whereas in *A Man's Woman* the hero sets out for the Pole a second time, determined to fulfil his task. Such action and such an attitude was probably in conformity with Norris's inherent optimism, his national purpose, and, possibly, the dictation of the facts on which he based his novel.

A Man's Woman was, in many ways, a deviation from Norris's normal way of writing, and he felt that, to be true to himself and his art, he had to go back to the style of *McTeague*, as he told a friend of his.[1]

Norris's next novel, *The Octopus*, bears the stamp of Zola, that is true, but we recognize also the familiar signs of Ibsen. It is but natural to turn to Ibsen's social dramas when considering the influence of Ibsen on *The Octopus*.[2] For, like *Pillars of Society* and *An Enemy of the People*, *The Octopus* exposes the hollowness, hypocrisy, and corruption of society. A comparison between the novel and the two dramas reveals certain resemblances, some of which may be explained as the result of Ibsen's influence on Norris. The American writer's virulent satire upon the narrowness of the cultural life of San Francisco as represented by Mrs. Cedarquist may have been inspired in part by Ibsen's attacks on the smugness and hypocrisy of small-town life depicted, for instance, in *Pillars of Society*. The problem of *The Octopus*, as that of *An Enemy of the People*, was one of the individual against society. In

[1] See p. 119.

[2] The social criticism of *The Octopus* recalls that of Garland's *A Member of the Third House* (1892), which may also have influenced Norris's novel. There are some parallels between Magnus Derrick, on the one hand, and Lawrence B. Davis and Senator Ward, on the other, in *A Member of the Third House*. Lyman Derrick is somewhat reminiscent of Tom Brennan, the villain of Garland's novel. The scene depicting the attempt to bribe Senator Ward is reminiscent of a similar scene in *The Octopus*, in which the farmers try to win Magnus Derrick to their cause, by means of bribery. The description of their opposition to fraudulent means is closely paralleled. It should be remembered, however, that both Garland and Norris owe a considerable debt to Ibsen in these novels. Therefore, some of the parallels may be explained, first, as resulting from the use of similar themes, and, secondly, because the same dramas by Ibsen seem to have exerted an influence on both books.

Norris's novel the conflict was between might and right, represented by the P. and S.W. Railroad and the farmers of the San
Joaquin Valley; in *An Enemy of the People* Peter Stockmann stood
for might and Dr. Stockmann for right.

In his portrayal of Magnus Derrick, called the Governor, Norris probably owes something to Ibsen. Although fairly independently conceived, Magnus Derrick is, in many respects, rather
like Consul Bernick,[1] who to all appearances was a trustworthy
public leader whom everybody honored and respected, but who
had actually founded his career on a lie. In the end, however,
he atoned by repentance. Derrick was also a public leader, a
"prominent man," who loved "to preside, to dominate." "He
was . . . a fine commanding figure, imposing an immediate respect,
impressing one with a sense of gravity, of dignity, and a certain
pride of race."[2] Before he got entangled in the coalition formed
against the railroad, and the consequent fraudulent election and
bribery, he was portrayed as a strong, ethical[3] character who,
like Brand and Dr. Stockmann, did not tolerate any compromise. "None better than she [Mrs. Derrick] knew the iron integrity of her husband's character. None better than she remembered
how his dearest ambition, that of political preferment, had been
thwarted by his refusal to truckle, to connive, to compromise
with his ideas of right."[4] In the end, though only after insistent
pressure, Derrick failed to live up to his ideals. Thereafter his
power and authority, like those of Consul Bernick, were founded
on falsehood. Because the committee alone knew of his corruption,[5] Magnus Derrick was able to keep up appearances; similarly
Consul Bernick succeeded in playing the role of a disinterested
benefactor of society.

The resemblance between Bernick and Magnus Derrick extends
into the action. Genslinger threatened to print an article which
would disclose Derrick's bribery.[6] Similarly, Johan Tönnesen
threatened to use as proof of the Consul's guilt two letters
from Bernick which he possessed. Both Johan Tönnesen and

---

[1] Note the similarity between the name of Bernick and that of Derrick.
[2] *Compl. Works*, I, 59.
[3] Cf. Senator Ward of *A Member of the Third House*.
[4] *Compl. Works*, I, 172.
[5] *Ibid.*, II, 7. Cf. also the coalition in *Pillars of Society*.
[6] Cf. a similar device in *A Member of the Third House*, p. 64.

Genslinger, however, postponed the exposure. Consul Bernick had staked all his money on the branch-line, hoping to become a millionaire; Magnus Derrick, with a somewhat similar motive had invested all his money in the fraudulent election. Eventually, as Bernick's position became more and more hopeless, he found he could no longer endure the life of falsehood and hypocrisy. The voice of conscience beginning to speak in this liar and egoist, he realized that his life was wasted; existence itself became unbearable. A similar change took place in Magnus Derrick.[1]

The only way out for Consul Bernick was repentance and confession, and at the close of the drama, when the townspeople were about to pay tribute to him, he admitted his guilt. In *The Octopus* there was a similar scene of confession at the meeting in the Opera House. To make the contrast even more effective, both Bernick and Derrick were publicly praised before they confessed.[2] Afterwards the latter deteriorated in accordance with the naturalistic formula; the last glimpse of him revealed a half-witted dotard sitting at his desk aimlessly turning over and sorting his papers.

Of particular interest in the portraiture of these and other characters is the explanation of the motive forces behind their actions. We see things from their standpoint. Bernick was a product of circumstances. Norris's explanation was similar.[3] "Long-continued oppression, petty tyranny, injustice, and extortion had driven him [Magnus Derrick] to exasperation."[4] When legal means failed, he was forced to devious manoeuvrings. This was the only way for him, and he was, it seems, justified in his actions. This was also true, although to a less degree, of S. Behrman, Lyman Derrick, and above all of Shelgrim, the President of the P. and S.W. Railroad, whose justification echoes Consul Bernick's words. Shelgrim was "a giant figure in the end-of-the-century finance, a product of circumstance, an inevitable result of conditions, characteristic, typical, symbolic of ungovernable forces."[5] This

---

[1] *Compl. Works*, II, 112.

[2] *Ibid.*, p. 269. Cf. also Senator Ward's confession in *A Member of the Third House*.

[3] This technique underlining the author's objectivity is also used in *The Pit*. Cf. the same technique in *Germinal* with regard to Hennebeau.

[4] *Compl. Works*, I, 172.

[5] *Ibid.*, pp. 99–100. Cf. also the same view expressed by Hamlin Garland in *A Member of the Third House*, pp. 48–9, 71.

applies equally well to Bernick, who maintained that even pillars of society had no free will; they were nothing but the tools of society.

The scenes depicting the meetings of the farmers recall similar ones in *Pillars of Society* and *An Enemy of the People*. The fraudulent coalition between Consul Bernick, Vigeland, Rummel, and Sandstad concerning a railroad issue is paralleled by the Farmers' League in *The Octopus*. The opening scene of *An Enemy of the People*, describing the gathering in Dr. Stockmann's sitting room, probably inspired the opening of the third chapter[1] of *The Octopus*, which depicted the group assembled in Magnus Derrick's dining room. It was evening in both cases, and guests arrived. There was a dinner, and coffee and liquors were served, and cigars were handed around. Magnus Derrick and Dr. Stockmann were both portrayed as generous hosts. A common issue of great importance united the assembled people in each work. In *An Enemy of the People* the Baths were "the concern of every right-minded citizen,"[2] whereas in *The Octopus* the question at issue was the conflict between the farmers and the railroad. The group gathered at the Stockmanns' longed for a fine summer which would set everything right again, and the farmers longed for a fine summer and a bumper crop which would help them out. Further, Peter Stockmann suffered from weak digestion; Annixter's stomach was "out of whack." Hovstad the editor of the *People's Messenger* (*Folkebudet*), corresponds to Genslinger and the Bonneville *Mercury*. In each paper an article which was of extreme importance for those involved, and which would change conditions considerably, was about to be published. Dr. Stockmann's article was never printed, and Genslinger delayed the printing of his article to blackmail Magnus Derrick, only to sell him out later on.

There are other less extended similarities. One of the mottos in little Sidney Dyke's copy book seems to have been taken from this drama: "The P. and S.W. Is an Enemy of the State."[3] This sentence echoes Ibsen's title, and particularly Aslaksen's words to the effect that Dr. Stockmann was an enemy of the people.[4]

---

[1] *Compl. Works*, I, 91 ff.

[2] *Plays*, p. 179.

[3] *Compl. Works*, I, 213.

[4] *Plays*, p. 263.

Furthermore, Magnus Derrick echoed Aslaksen's words when he insisted upon moderation while the farmers were forming the League.[1] Aslaksen was always harping on "moderation." When the Stockmanns had been turned out of their house they found shelter with Captain Horster; Mrs. Dyke and her daughter in *The Octopus*[2] were invited to live with the Annixters at the Quien Sabe after the railroad had caused the collapse of their home. Finally, toward the end of *An Enemy of the People*, two ships were ready to sail, and in the last chapter of *The Octopus* the barque *Swanhilda*[3] was about to leave the port of San Francisco.

Norris's indebtedness to Ibsen is also evident in his last novel, *The Pit*, in which the bolero incident was probably inspired by the famous tarantella scene in *A Doll's House*.[4] Both Nora and Laura performed wild, reckless dances, the former with a tambourine in her hand and wearing the shawl of a Capri fishergirl, and the latter with castanets in her hands and wearing the costume of Bizet's *Carmen*, while their husbands accompanied them on the piano and the organ, respectively. Both women gave themselves up with reckless abandon to the fury of the dance. It is worth quoting the two scenes in full to show the similarity between them. This is Ibsen's scene:

Nora. ... You must give yourself up to me entirely this evening. Not the tiniest bit of business—you mustn't even take a pen in your hand. Will you promise, Torvald dear?

Helmer. I promise. This evening I will be wholly and absolutely at your service, you helpless little mortal. Ah, by the way, first of all I will just—

[*Goes towards the hall door.*

Nora. What are you going to do there?

Helmer. Only see if any letters have come.

Nora. No, no! don't do that, Torvald!

Helmer. Why not?

---

[1] *Compl. Works*, I, 269.

[2] *Ibid.*, II, 147.

[3] Cf. Svanhild, the heroine of *Love's Comedy*. Note also Norris's use of Scandinavian names for his heroes, such as Osterman and Broderson.

[4] Mrs. Charles N. Black, Norris's widow, informed me that, during the composition of *The Pit*, Mrs. Herne—ardent Ibsen enthusiast and actress by profession—occasionally visited the Norris family. This fact may have stimulated Norris's interest in Ibsen. Garland was also an intimate friend of Norris's at this time. See also *Walker, op. cit.*, p. 282.

Nora. Torvald, please don't. There is nothing there.

Helmer. Well, let me look. (*Turns to go to the letter-box.* Nora, *at the piano, plays the first bars of the Tarantella.* Helmer *stops in the doorway.*) Aha!

Nora. I can't dance to-morrow if I don't practise with you.

Helmer (*going up to her*). Are you really so afraid of it, dear.

Nora. Yes, so dreadfully afraid of it. Let me practise at once; there is time now, before we go to dinner. Sit down and play for me, Torvald dear; criticise me, and correct me as you play.

Helmer. With great pleasure, if you wish me to.

[*Sits down at the piano.*

Nora (*takes out of the box a tambourine and a long variegated shawl. She hastily drapes the shawl round her. Then she springs to the front of the stage and calls out.*) Now play for me! I am going to dance!

[Helmer *plays and* Nora *dances.* Rank *stands by the piano behind* Helmer *and looks on.*

Helmer (*as he plays*). Slower, slower!

Nora. I can't do it any other way.

Helmer. Not so violently, Nora!

Nora. This is the way.

Helmer (*stops playing*). No, no — that is not a bit right.

Nora (*laughing and swinging the tambourine*). Didn't I tell you so?

Rank. Let me play for her.

Helmer (*getting up*). Yes, do. I can correct her better then.

[Rank *sits down at the piano and plays.* Nora *dances more and more wildly.* Helmer *has taken up a position beside the stove, and during her dance gives her frequent instructions. She does not seem to hear him; her hair comes down and falls over her shoulders; she pays no attention to it, but goes on dancing. Enter* Mrs. Linde.

Mrs. Linde (*standing as if spell-bound in the doorway*). Oh!—

Nora (*as she dances*). Such fun, Christine!

Helmer. My dear darling Nora, you are dancing as if your life depended on it.

Nora. So it does.

Helmer. Stop, Rank; this is sheer madness. Stop, I tell you! (Rank *stops playing, and* Nora *suddenly stands still.* Helmer *goes up to her.*) I could never have believed it. You have forgotten everything I taught you.

Nora (*throwing away the tambourine*). There, you see. . . .

Helmer. Come, come, don't be so wild and nervous. Be my own little skylark, as you used.

Nora. Yes, dear. I will. But go in now and you too, Doctor Rank. Christine, you must help me to do up my hair.[1]

And now the bolero scene in *The Pit*:

Never had he seen her gayer. Her vivacity was bewildering.

"I wish," she cried, all at once, "I wish I had dressed as 'Carmen,'

---

[1] *Plays*, pp. 62–4.

and I would have danced for you. Oh, and you could have played the air for me on the organ. I have the costume upstairs now. Wait! I will, I will! Sit right where you are—no, fix the attachment to the organ while I'm gone. Oh, be gay with me to-night," she cried, throwing her arms around him. "This is my night, isn't it? And I am to be just as foolish as I please."

With the words she ran from the room, but was back in an incredibly short time, gowned as Bizet's cigarette girl, a red rose in her black hair, castanets upon her fingers.

Jadwin began the bolero.

"Can you see me dance, and play at the same time?"

"Yes, yes. Go on. How do you know anything about a Spanish dance?"

"I learned it long ago. I know everything about anything I choose, to-night. Play, play it *fast*."

She danced as though she would never tire, with the same force of passion that she had thrown into *Athalie*. Her yellow skirt was a flash of flame spurting from the floor, and her whole body seemed to move with the same wild, untamed spirit as a tongue of fire. The castanets snapped like the crackling of sparks; her black mantilla was a hovering cloud of smoke. She was incarnate flame, capricious and riotous, elusive and dazzling.

Then suddenly she tossed the castanets far across the room and dropped upon the couch, panting and laughing.

"There," she cried, "now I feel better. That had to come out. Come over here and sit by me. Now, maybe you'll admit that I can dance, too."

"You sure can," answered Jadwin, as she made a place for him among the cushions. "That was wonderful. But, at the same time, old girl, I wouldn't—wouldn't—"

"Wouldn't what?"

"Well, do too much of that. It's sort of overwrought—a little, and unnatural. I like you best when you are your old self, quiet, and calm, and dignified. It's when you are quiet that you are at your best. I didn't know you had this streak in you. You are that excitable to-night!"

"Let me be so then. It's myself, for the moment, whatever it is. But now I'll be quiet. Now we'll talk."[1]

As the quotations indicate, the two scenes opened and closed on a similar note, for while Nora entreated her husband to give himself up entirely to her, Laura implored Jadwin: "Oh, be gay with me to-night." Like Torvald, Jadwin was puzzled by his wife's strange behavior, and both men realized that there were unknown components in their wives' personalities. Helmer implored Nora to be his little lark again, and Jadwin declared that he liked the old Laura best when she was quiet, calm, and dignified. Nora's

---

[1] *Compl. Works*, IX, 297-8.

hectic wildness and high-strung joy in the tarantella episode was motivated by her agony of fear lest her crime should be discovered by her husband; there was, however, no such motivating factor behind the bolero incident in *The Pit*. Laura was agitated apparently for no reason.

The tarantella scene closed with the discovery of the fatal letter, and Nora made desperate and vain attempts to persuade Helmer not to open it. In *The Pit* Laura attempted futilely to persuade Jadwin not to open the door for his broker, who brought news of the wheat speculation which eventually was to be fatal. Both dancing episodes ended dramatically in disaster.[1]

In addition to the bolero incident, it is probable that Norris also derived some inspiration from the matrimonial conflict in *A Doll's House*. He made Jadwin leave Laura to devote himself almost entirely to his speculation in wheat at a time when she, on the verge of eloping with an artist, was most in need of him. Torvald, it will be remembered, left Nora without help when her need of him was greatest. Although the matrimonial conflict in *The Pit* seems to have been modeled on other sources,[2] it seems plausible that at least some suggestion for Norris's handling of the dramatic conflict between Laura and Jadwin, particularly the demand for spiritual affinity between husband and wife, came from *A Doll's House*.

Laura did not revolt against her husband as Nora did: when Laura was about to elope, she became conscious of her duty as a wife, and like Lloyd, decided to stand by her husband and inspire him to further deeds.[3]

There are suggestions of Ibsen's Hjördis, who wanted to stand by the side of the man in battle, in the words of Laura's sister Page: "'If my husband had a battle to fight, do you think I'd mope and pine because he left me at home? No, I wouldn't. I'd help him buckle his sword on, and when he came back to me I wouldn't

---

[1] Possibly Norris saw *A Doll's House* staged and, being impressed by the tarantella episode, he may have wanted to try his hand at something similar. His own scene does not lack anything of the dramatic quality inherent in Ibsen's.

[2] Jadwin and Laura are in part modeled on Norris's parents, who were divorced. See p. 118 n. 1. Laura is, moreover, reminiscent of Emma Bovary, Anna Karenina, and Irina of Turgenev's *Smoke*. Cf. pp. 339–41, 343 n. 3.

[3] Cf. the similarity between the final scene in *The Pit* and the one in *L'Argent*. See p. 304.

tell him how lonesome I'd been, but I'd take care of him and cry over his wounds, and tell him to be brave—and—and—and I'd help him.'"[1] Note that Page was speaking like Hjördis, as if the man were one of the gallant Vikings Hjördis conjured up when talking with Sigurd of the glory of battle, not a worn-out American business man.

To sum up: In *Crumbling Idols* Garland wrote that "Ibsen has helped us in our war against conventionalisms, but he must not dominate us."[2] It is true that Ibsen did not dominate Garland, but he was no doubt a potent factor in his career as a writer, particularly in the nineties.[3] The social dramas, *A Doll's House*, *Pillars of Society*, and *An Enemy of the People*, seem to have attracted him most. Many of his early works, most apparent perhaps in *A Member of the Third House* in its exposure of corruption, bear the stamp of Ibsen; some books contain ideas found in the Norwegian dramatist's plays, others present similarities in plot, characters, and incidents. Indubitably Ibsen influenced Garland in his struggle against romanticism and conventionalism. Moreover, and what is more important, Ibsen seems to have influenced Garland's concept of woman. The latter's free, independent, often rebellious, physically and mentally strong women who had few counterparts in American letters of the time, are similar to those found in Ibsen's dramas. Garland applied Ibsen's message of revolt, of freedom and independence to the overworked, subjugated Western woman. It is illuminating to follow Garland's type of Ibsen-inspired independent woman through his early work. There were, first of all, the rebellious farmers' wives in *Main-Travelled Roads*, who could not endure a marriage with men, utterly pevoid of understanding of their aspirations and ambitions. In *Jason Edwards* there was the Nora-inspired Alice, and in *A Spoil of Office* the radical Ida Wilbur, who made Nora's words her own. Finally there was Rose, strong and independent, who married a man who was her intellectual companion. In addition, Ibsen's and Garland's women were often desirous of the freedom and

---

[1] *Compl. Works*, IX, 384.

[2] *Crumbling Idols*, p. 118.

[3] Garland retained a keen interest in Ibsen throughout his life. It can be seen from his diaries that he frequently attended performances of Ibsen's dramas.

education which conventional society, or a husband lacking the will and capacity to understand women's problems, denied them. Like Ibsen's heroines, Garland's women had a keen desire to develop themselves, to get an education, to test their mental resources, as did Alice, Ida, and Rose. In the manner of Lona Hessel and Nora, these women wanted to be regarded first of all as individuals. Like Ibsen, Garland refrained from depicting women as lovers. "Life is to be depicted, not love-life," asserted Garland in his literary manifesto.[1] Moreover, his concept of the ideal marriage as a union between equals, morally as well as intellectually, recalls that propounded by Ibsen. Both Ibsen and Garland were first and foremost ethical thinkers; the concepts of freedom, justice, and truth were basic tenets in their philosophy of life. Ibsen's crisp, direct, realistic style may also have influenced Garland's simple and direct prose, for some of his stories consist mainly of dramatic dialogue. The influence that Ibsen's ideas, and above all his concept of woman, seems to have exerted on Garland may have counteracted the influence of naturalism. In his early works, characters possessing free will were set off against those who were victims of circumstances or other forces. Garland's adoption of Ibsen's concept and revaluation of man as a free ethical being was one of the factors conducive to his liberation from the conception of man propounded by naturalistic philosophers.

As a social critic Crane was inspired by Ibsen in at least one story. The treatment of ostracism in "The Monster" is reminiscent of that of *An Enemy of the People.* Dr. Trescott and Dr. Stockmann alike stood alone in their fight for truth and justice against the meanness and cowardice of the people of a small-town community; both Ibsen and Crane despised convention and liked to expose humbugs of all kinds. Each revealed the false idealism and hypocrisy of society.

Whereas Garland and perhaps also Crane felt more akin to Ibsen, the social critic, Norris seems to have found in the Norwegian dramatist primarily an individualist, an exponent of force and exuberant vitality, which appealed to him as a con-

---

[1] *Crumbling Idols,* p. 101. Note that Rose overcame the perils of sex and later married according to the Ibsen formula. See p. 209.

trast to his own indolence.[1] This may partly explain his interest in saga literature and in *The Vikings at Helgeland* with its forceful and proud characters. Such considerations probably also lay behind his indebtedness to *Brand*, in which Ibsen introduced to a sluggish generation a man of granite will power, of absolute adherence to duty and of complete self-sacrifice. Ibsen's concept of woman may well have influenced Norris. In his work there are independent women of strong will, for instance, Moran, Blix, and Lloyd, contrasted with weak, neurotic characters common among naturalists. In addition to *The Vikings at Helgeland* and *Brand*, *A Doll's House*, *An Enemy of the People*, and *Pillars of Society* seem to have attracted Norris. In his early works the likenesses to Ibsen are slight, but in *A Man's Woman* one realizes a considerable change in his concept of man and attitude toward life, and the change was probably due to the influence of Ibsen. Indeed, the novel reads like a problem play, in which the interest is focused on the ideas, and the characters are more or less reduced to abstractions. There is a vast distance between the naturalism of *McTeague* and the ethical doctrines of truth, wholeness, and will found in *A Man's Woman*. In *The Octopus*, which is essentially a *mixtum compositum* of various influences and ideas, naturalistic and anti-naturalistic modes of thinking were merged into a fabric of seemingly incongruous elements. The typical Ibsenian motifs of confession, of struggle with and mastery of self, found in *The Octopus*, are elements alien to pure naturalism. Perhaps the influence of Ibsen may account in part for this anomaly; Norris's acquaintance with Ibsen's works and the influence they had on him helped to bring about his alienation from the doctrine of naturalism, apparent in *A Man's Woman* and *The Pit*, to which he had adhered fairly closely in *McTeague* and *Vandover and the Brute*. Finally, it should be added that Norris's borrowings from Ibsen were not so well assimilated as similar material in Garland. Scenes, characters, ideas, words, and phrases found in Ibsen's dramas, seem to be easily recognizable in Norris's works. Nonetheless, whenever Ibsen was a source of inspiration, Norris utilized him with discrimination and talent.

---

[1] See Walker, *op. cit.*, p. 59.

CONCLUSION

When in the early nineties a few American authors began experimenting with naturalistic methods and techniques, works by Zola and other European naturalists and realists, introduced into the United States in increasing numbers in the eighties, indubitably helped to pave the way. Conditions in America at the time favored the new literary tendencies: industrialism had wrought great changes in American society; a new class, the proletariat, claimed attention; materialism had a strong grip on American life; and the closing of the frontier and its psychological implications challenged the earlier optimistic outlook. In addition, evolutionary doctrines helped to dissolve traditional conceptions of life and the universe.

The first American writers of any importance who were obviously influenced by naturalism were the young radicals, Garland, Crane, and Norris. Although different in temperament and background, they shared many beliefs about man and society, but there is no evidence that they felt that they belonged together for the advancement of a common cause. They were, however, aware of each other's works. Furthermore, Garland was well acquainted with both Crane and Norris, although at different periods, whereas Crane and Norris met only once. Moreover, Garland seems to have exerted a direct influence, both personal and literary, on Crane and Norris. To group them together here therefore seems justified.

Garland is, in my opinion, an important figure in the rise of American naturalism because some of his writings which exhibit traces of naturalism precede those of Crane and Norris. It would hardly be possible to give dogmatically an exact date for the first American naturalistic work. In the United States naturalism emerged but slowly and hesitatingly. Although traces of naturalism appear in *Main-Travelled Roads*, tentatively I have indicated the year 1892, when Garland brought out *Jason Edwards*, probably the first serious American novel to be obviously influenced by French naturalism. Garland's reading of Darwin and Spencer and of European naturalistic works stimulated his interest in the new literary movement. Books such as *Main-Travelled Roads*, *Jason Edwards*, *Prairie Folks*, and *Rose of Dutcher's Coolly* would probably not have been written as they stand without knowledge of European naturalism. Garland's experiences in the Middle West and in Boston—hard and bitter as he felt them—called for a realism of a harsher brand than Howells'. He exposed the dreariness, sordidness, and tragedy of farm life in the Middle West. He was largely interested in social problems, particularly the position of woman in marriage and society. For at least some of his inspiration he turned to Zola and other European writers and adopted them as models and guides. French naturalism, however, was hardly what Garland aimed at; on the whole, his writings owe more to Ibsen and Turgenev than to Zola. He refused to be labeled a realist or a naturalist; instead he preferred to be called a veritist. Nevertheless, it is justifiable to place him as an early exponent, however inconsistent, of American naturalism in its experimental phase. He was a direct forerunner of Crane and Norris.

Naturalism may have reached Crane through many channels. Since we have evidence that he read some of Zola's works, it is safe to assume that this reading was one way by which he arrived at a naturalistic outlook. Naturalism appears in particular in Crane's early works. The stamp of Zola is more evident in his stories of the slums, for instance *Maggie* and *George's Mother*, than in his tales of war or his Western sketches. Like Garland, he shows naturalistic tendencies in his concept of man and the universe, in his choice of theme, in his subject matter and treatment. His literary credo, like Garland's, was, however, akin to that of Howells. The forces that chiefly controlled man were, according to Crane as they were to Garland, society and fate. What gave to all Crane wrote a peculiar flavor was not so much his attitude of despair as his style. Like Garland, he was an impressionist, and his mosaic prose made up of vivid and striking pictures glitters and sparkles with gay colors and startling phrases. Unlike Garland, he was less an ethical thinker than an artist more interested in art as such than in reform. His work is perhaps best illustrated in his impressionistic pictures of New York with its forlorn characters and tenement areas which he exposed without mercy. The tone is dark and somber, touched with anguish. His work, although uneven, constitutes an important contribution to the emergence of the naturalism of the nineties.

One of the primary reasons for Norris's acquaintance with naturalism was his reading of Zola's novels. Norris's debt to French naturalism, especially to Zola, his avowed master, is fully evident throughout his writings, but is most apparent in *McTeague*—the most consistently naturalistic work of the period— *Vandover and the Brute*, and *The Octopus*. Some weakening of Norris's allegiance to Zola's naturalism is felt in *A Man's Woman* and *The Pit*, despite various elements of naturalism found in these novels. His works, particularly *The Octopus*, where naturalism and romanticism mingle, reflect his mind. This dualism, partly stimulated by the reading of Zola and certain contemporary English writers, runs through almost his entire production. Primitivism, joy of life, and worship of strength are elements encountered in his work. Interested in social issues, Norris was, however, no reformer; in this respect he was more akin to Crane than to Garland, the born reformer. Strictly speaking neither Crane nor Norris should be labeled a pure naturalist; perhaps the term *experimenters in naturalism* is more descriptive of their aims and methods. The three writers did not represent a naturalistic *movement*, but they were, in their way, pioneers of American naturalism, and their works constitute a bridge between the realism of Howells and the naturalism of Dreiser.

When considering the character of the naturalism found in the writings of the three Americans, we must bear in mind that in all probability it was Zola's naturalism, which contains no small amount of romantic elements, that influenced them most. This circumstance may in part explain the romantic exaggerations found in some of their works. The unreal accumulation of violent and sordid details, as in *Maggie*, may be explained as a probable debt to Zola. The grotesque proportions of McTeague may partly be explained as a literary borrowing from the Balzac-inspired Zola. There are other obvious affinities between the works of the three novelists and Zola's. To varying degrees their writings illustrate the determining forces of heredity and environment on the individual. Against a slum background in Boston, New York, and San Francisco, they placed some of their characters, often weak and passive, and let the milieu and hereditary tendencies operate on them. The result was usually despair, tragedy, or violent death. What may particularly have appealed to these writers was Zola's description of the milieu, and in this respect they probably learned some of their technique from the French writer. But there are significant dissimilarities between them and Zola. Most of Garland's characters, in contrast to the majority of Zola's, are ethical beings capable of moral judgments and decisions. The works of Garland and Crane lack Zola's epic breadth; whereas Zola indulged in elaborate descriptions, they usually gave hints or made suggestions. Norris, whose mind and art was most akin to Zola's, lacked Zola's zeal for reform. Moreover, while the French writer described a decaying society, Norris stressed the bigness of America, its fertility, and its great vitality. The naturalism of the three authors was more or less far from the brutal naturalism of Zola. It was mostly restrained, judiciously pruned, and modified.

One reason that the fictional output of the writers, including those works exhibiting elements of naturalism, was of such a varied nature, may be due to the fact that they were also inspired by authors whose way of writing differed from that of French naturalism. Turgenev stimulated the use of the failure type employed by Garland and Norris, and Crane's "superfluous" men may be linked with those found in Turgenev's works. Moreover, the mixture of determinism and fatalism found in the writings of the American authors may in part be explained as resulting from their debts to Zola on the one hand, and to Turgenev, and possibly to Tolstoy on the other.

Crane, in particular, seems to have been influenced by Tolstoy, chiefly in his tales of war where we have noticed similarities of treatment and concepts. In the realism of Turgenev and Tolstoy, illustrative of their deep psychological insight into the human mind and of their warmth and sympathy, the American writers may have found values which were lacking or less often met with in French naturalists with their emphasis on exposé and their comparatively superficial character drawing.

Another source of inspiration which may have helped to give

the peculiar flavor to American naturalism in its first phase, was Ibsen's dramas. In my opinion, they provide the key to some of Garland's thought and writings and they may also furnish a clue to certain attitudes of Crane and Norris. The moralism and the preoccupation with social problems and ethical values found in some of our three writers' works are reminiscent of the Norwegian's plays. I have tried to show that the stamp of Ibsen is apparent in various ways in most of Garland's early works; moreover, it is hard to believe that Crane's "The Monster" and Norris's *A Man's Woman* could have received their final form without a knowledge of Ibsen.

The various influences—many of the parallels adduced may be accounted for by similarities of temperament, similar sources of inspiration, and the general spiritual atmosphere of the period— helped to give the American naturalism of the nineties its heterogeneous character. It is different from French naturalism; it is varied and full of inconsistencies; strong, ethical characters are contrasted with weak, passive figures dominated by forces beyond their control; determinism is mingled with fatalism, pessimism with optimism, realism with lyricism, *Tendenz* with objectivity.

Although to a certain extent the writers depended upon Zola's novels—a circumstance which confirms the assumption that the American naturalism of the nineties was in part an offshoot of French naturalism—they were no mere imitators. They were, on the contrary, inspired, original writers who fashioned and created out of their material both life and living men and women. They succeeded in imparting to their works the stamp of their individual temperaments and, in spite of the influences from abroad, they remained distinctly American.

APPENDIX A

I. BOOKS OF HAMLIN GARLAND IN THE UNIVERSITY OF SOUTHERN CALIFORNIA LIBRARY

The following bibliography—365 items—includes books owned by Hamlin Garland now in the University of Southern California Library. When Garland died in 1940, he bequeathed to the University most of the books listed below. Later the University purchased from the Garland estate additional titles, particularly American literature items and association items. Although the collection comprises titles of biography, history, and literary criticism, its main emphasis is on belles-lettres. American writers are in the majority, but British and other European authors are also represented. The list includes such writers as Conrad, Gissing, Kipling, Shaw, and Ibsen. Of interest is Garland's collection of American literature from the last decades of the nineteenth century. Many of the volumes listed were autographed and inscribed to Garland in the eighties or nineties by the authors, among whom the following deserve to be mentioned: Stephen Crane, Edgar Fawcett, Harold Frederic, Mary Wilkins Freeman, E. W. Howe, W. D. Howells, Henry James, Joseph Kirkland, and Frank Norris. Of the poets listed Joaquin Miller, James Whitcomb Riley, and Walt Whitman should be noted. Of non-literary items the following seem of special interest: Véron's Æsthetics and Nordau's Conventional Lies. Several books in this collection are marked with notes and marginalia in Garland's handwriting. The items have been listed alphabetically by author and editor. Whenever a book contained an autograph or an inscription this has been included in the list.[1]

---

[1] I wish to express my sincere gratitude to Miss Hazel Rea and Mr. Lloyd Arvidson of the University of Southern California Library who have kindly corrected my list. Brackets [ ] about a date or a place of publication indicate that the material does not appear on the title page but is derived from other sources.

Adams, Henry. *Letters of Henry Adams, 1892–1918*. Ed. by Worthington C. Ford. Boston, 1938.

Adams, James T. *The Adams Family*. Boston, 1930.

A. E. (George W. Russell). *The Candle of Vision*. London, 1928.

Aldrich, Thomas Bailey. *The Poems of Thomas Bailey Aldrich*. Boston and New York, [1885]. (Autographed by author. Letter of author to Garland, January 21, 1888, concerning an article on Edwin Booth pasted in.)

Aldrich, Mrs. Thomas Bailey. *Crowding Memories*. Boston and New York, 1920.

Allen, James Lane. *A Kentucky Cardinal*. New York, 1899.

Bacheller, Irving. *From Stores of Memory*. New York, [1938].

—— *The Master of Chaos*. Indianapolis, [1932]. (Autographed by author.)

Badé, William Frederic, ed. *The Life and Letters of John Muir*. 2 vols. Boston and New York, 1924. (Both volumes are well marked.)

Baker, Josephine Turck. *Songs of Triumph*. New York, [1934]. (Inscribed to Garland by author.)

Barrie, James Matthew. *Farewell, Miss Julie Logan*. New York, 1932.

—— *Mary Rose*. New York, 1924. (The uniform edition of the plays of J. M. Barrie.)

—— *The Novels, Tales and Sketches of J. M. Barrie*. 11 vols. New York, 1909.

—— *Sentimental Tommy*. New York, 1896. (Inscribed: "Hamlin Garland with kindest regards from James Barrie. Nov. 1896.")

—— *Tommy and Grizel*. New York, 1900.

—— *A Window in Thrums*. New York, 1909. Vol. III of the *Works*, listed above. (Letter of author to Garland, December 16, 1923, pasted in.)

Becker, May Lamberton, ed. *Golden Tales of the Prairie States*. New York, 1932.

Bell, Lilian. *A Little Sister to the Wilderness*. Chicago, 1895. (Inscribed: "To Hamlin Garland with compliments and best wishes of the author. Lilian Bell. Chicago.")

Bennett, Enoch Arnold. *The Truth about an Author*. New York, [1911]. (Inscribed: "To Hamlin Garland—a book of shop with best wishes and many thanks for all his kindness in Chicago. Arnold Bennett. 17–11–11.")

Bradford, Gamaliel. *Saints and Sinners*. New York, 1932.

Brandes, Georg. *Voltaire*. Transl. by Otto Krüger and Pierce Butler. 2 vols. New York, 1930.

Brooks, Van Wyck. *The Life of Emerson*. New York, 1932. (Inscribed: "For Hamlin Garland with sincere regards. Van Wyck Brooks. March 17th, 1932.")

Brown, Howard Clark (Tokaniya). *The Stone Maiden*. Santa Fé, 1939.

Brownell, W. C. *An Anthology of His Writings*. New York, 1933. (Inscribed to Garland by author.)

—— *Criticism*. New York, 1914. (Inscribed: "Presented to Mr. Hamlin Garland in honor of his book, *Crumbling Idols*. C. Abison, Richmond, Indiana.")

Bryant, William Cullen. *A Forest Hymn*. New York, [1860].

Bucke, Richard Maurice. *Walt Whitman*. Philadelphia, 1883. (Author's autograph mounted on fly-leaf.)

Burke, Jane Revere. *Let Us in*. With a foreword by Edward S. Martin. New York, [1931]. (Inscribed to Garland by E. S. Martin.)

Burroughs, John. *Field and Study*. Boston and New York, 1919. (Inscribed to Garland by author, August 30, 1920. The volume is well marked.)

Burton, Richard. *Forces in Fiction*. Indianapolis, 1902. (Inscribed: "To Hamlin Garland whom I see once in a while and like all the while. From his Richd Burton.")

—— *Literary Likings*. Boston, 1898. (Inscribed: "To Hamlin Garland from his friend Richard Burton.")

Butler, Nicholas Murray. *Looking Forward*. New York, 1932. (Inscribed: "To Hamlin Garland, fellow member of the American Academy of Arts and Letters. Nicholas Murray Butler. January 26, 1932.")

Chamberlin, Joseph Edgar. *Nomads and Listeners*. Cambridge, Mass., 1937.

Chatfield-Taylor, H. C. *Chicago*. Cambridge, Mass., 1917. (Inscribed: "To Hamlin Garland with abiding friendship. H. C. Chatfield-Taylor. Christmas, 1933.")

—— *Two Women and a Fool*. Chicago, 1895. (Inscribed: "To Hamlin Garland with the sincere admiration of H. C. Chatfield-Taylor, April 1, 1895.")

Christman, W. W. *Songs of the Helderhills.* New York, 1926. (Inscribed to Garland by author.)

—— *Wild Pasture Pine.* Albany, N. Y., 1933. (Inscribed to Garland by author.)

Clark, Barrett H. *Eugene O'Neill: The Man and His Plays.* New York, 1929. (Inscribed: "To Hamlin Garland with the hope that he will agree with *some* of my enthusiasm. Cordially, Barrett H. Clark. New York, February 13, 1930.")

Clemens, Clara. *My Father: Mark Twain.* New York and London, 1931.

Clemens, Cyril. *Josh Billings, Yankee Humorist.* Webster Groves, Mo., 1932. (Inscribed: "To Hamlin Garland, Prince of Novelists with the homage of his humble admirer. Cyril Clemens, 8 January, 1933.")

—— *Petroleum Vesuvius Nasby.* Webster Groves, Mo., 1936. (Inscribed: "To Hamlin Garland, Prince of Authors, with the author's homage. Cyril Clemens. 1 May, 1936.")

Clemens, Samuel Langhorne. *Mark Twain's Autobiography.* Ed. by Albert B. Paine. 2 vols. New York, 1924.

Conrad, Joseph. *An Outcast of the Islands.* London, 1922.

—— *Victory.* New York, 1920. (Letter of author to Garland and photographs pasted in.)

Crane, Stephen. *George's Mother.* New York, 1896. (Inscribed: "To Hamlin Garland of the great honest West from Stephen Crane of the false East. New York City, July, 1896.")

—— *War Is Kind.* New York, [1899]. (Autographed by author.)

Davis, Richard Harding. *Gallegher and Other Stories.* London, 1891. (Inscribed: "To Hamlin Garland with thanks for pleasure received of Richard Harding Davis.")

Deland, Margaret. *The Kays.* New York, 1926. (Presentation edition limited to 250 copies.)

Deming, William Chapin. *Roosevelt in the Bunk House.* 2nd ed. Laramie, Wyo., [1927]. (Inscribed to Garland by author.)

Dennis, Ch. H. *Eugene Field's Creative Years.* New York, 1924. (2 copies.)

Dickey, Marcus. *The Maturity of James Whitcomb Riley.* Indianapolis, [1922]. (Inscribed to Garland by author.)

Ditmars, Raymond L. *The Making of a Scientist.* New York, 1937.

Drane, Dora. *Inevitable Voyage.* New York, [1935].

Dunsany, E. J. Moreton. *Plays of Gods and Men.* New York, 1923.

Eaton, Walter Prichard. *Echoes and Realities.* New York, [1918].

—— *Green Trails and Upland Pastures.* Garden City, N.Y., 1917. (Inscribed to Garland by author.)

Emerson, Ralph Waldo. *Nature, Addresses and Lectures.* New York, n.d. (Inscribed to Garland by John Burroughs, 1920.)

Farran, Don. *Ballad of the Silver Ring.* Muscatine, Iowa, 1935. (Inscribed to Garland by author.)

Fawcett, Edgar. *Divided Lives: A Novel.* New York, 1888. (Inscribed: "To Hamlin Garland, Esq., with kindest regards of Edgar Fawcett. New York, Nov., 1888.")

—— *Romance and Reverie.* Boston, 1886. (Inscribed: "To Hamlin Garland, Esq., with kindest regards of Edgar Fawcett. New York, November, 1888.")

Fearing, L. Blanche. *In the City by the Lake.* Chicago, 1892. (Inscribed: "Mr. Hamlin Garland. Compliments of the author. July 17, 1893.")

Ficke, Arthur Davidson. *Sonnets of a Portrait-Painter.* New York, 1914. (Inscribed: "To Hamlin Garland with the warm regards of Arthur Davidson Ficke. Dec., 1914.")

Field, Eugene. *The Complete Tribune Primer.* Boston, [1901].

—— *A Little Book of Profitable Tales.* New York, 1890. (Autographed by author.)

—— *A Little Book of Western Verse.* New York, 1890.

—— *Second Book of Verse.* New York, 1893.

—— *With Trumpet and Drum.* New York, 1892. (Autographed by author.)

Finley, John. *Thalia.* New York, 1929. (Inscribed to Garland by author.)

Fiske, Horace Spencer. *Ballads of Peace and War.* Boston, 1918. (Inscribed to Garland by author.)

Flint, Thomas. *The Diary of Dr. Thomas Flint.* Los Angeles, 1923.

Fornaro, Carlo de. *Carranza and Mexico.* New York, 1915. (Inscribed by author: "To Hamlin Garland, April 10, 1915.")

Foster, Stephen Collins. *The Stephen Collins Foster Memorial of the University of Pittsburgh.* Dedicated June 2, 1937. (Pamphlet.)

Fox, John, Jr. *A Cumberland Vendetta, and Other Stories.* New York, 1896. (Inscribed: "For Hamlin Garland with the cordial regards and best wishes of John Fox, Jr.")

—— *The Kentuckians: A Novel.* New York, 1898.

Frear, Mary D. *Lowell and Abigail.* New Haven, 1934.

Frederic, Harold. *The Damnation of Theron Ware.* New York, 1896.

—— *Seth's Brother's Wife.* New York, 1887. (Letter of author to Garland mounted at front.)

Freeman, Mary E. Wilkins. *"Doc" Gordon.* New York, 1906.

—— *Madelon.* New York, 1896. (Inscribed to Garland by author.)

Frost, Robert. *New Hampshire.* New York, 1923. (Letter of author to Garland pasted in.)

—— *North of Boston.* New York, 1915. (Inscribed: "Hamlin Garland from Robert Frost in some sort of return for several things beside a book actually presented.")

Fuller, Henry Blake. *The Chatelaine of La Trinité.* New York, 1892. (Letter of author to Garland mounted at front.)

—— *The Chevalier of Pensieri-Vani.* New York, 1892. (Inscribed to Garland by author.)

—— *The Cliff-Dwellers.* New York, 1893. (Inscribed by author: "This book to Hamlin Garland—being my first jump toward his side of the fence. December, 1895.")

—— *From the Other Side: Stories of Transatlantic Travel.* Boston, 1898. (Autographed by author.)

—— *Gardens of This World.* New York, 1929.

—— *The Last Refuge: A Sicilian Romance.* Boston, 1900. (Inscribed to Garland by author.)

—— *Not on the Screen.* New York, 1930.

—— *On the Stairs.* Boston, 1918.

—— *With the Procession.* New York, 1895. (Inscribed to Garland by author.)

Gale, Zona. *Birth.* New York, 1918.

—— *Frank Miller of Mission Inn.* New York, 1938.

—— *Old-Fashioned Tales.* New York, 1933.

—— *Portage, Wisconsin, and Other Essays.* New York, 1928. (Inscribed to Garland by author.)

—— *Preface to a Life.* New York. 1926.

—— *Yellow Gentians and Blue.* New York, 1927.

Galsworthy, John. *Swan Song.* New York, [1928]. (Letter of author to Garland dated 1925 pasted in.)

Garland, Hamlin. *Under the Wheel: A Modern Play in Six Scenes.*[1] Boston, 1890. (2 copies.)

—— *Main-Travelled Roads.* Boston, 1891.

—— *Main-Travelled Roads.* Cambridge and Chicago, 1893.

—— *Main-Travelled Roads.* With illustrations by Constance Garland. New York, 1930.

—— *A Member of the Third House.* Chicago, [1892]. (Inscribed: "This was first written as a play and afterward novelized for Schulte of Chicago. Hamlin Garland.") (2 copies. Different bindings.)

—— *A Spoil of Office.* Boston, 1892. (Inscribed: "To Lorado Taft who thinks he knows a heap more about women-folks than any blamed novelist. Hamlin Garland.")

—— *Jason Edwards: An Average Man.* Boston, 1892.

—— *Jason Edwards and A Little Norsk.* London, 1898.

—— *A Little Norsk: or, Ol' Pap's Flaxen.* New York, 1892.

—— *Prairie Folks.* Chicago, 1893. (2 copies. Different bindings.)

—— *Prairie Songs.* Cambridge and Chicago, 1893. (Inscribed: "Hamlin Garland's Library. Not to be loaned or taken away. Hamlin Garland.")

—— *Crumbling Idols.* Chicago, 1894.

—— *Rose of Dutcher's Coolly.* New York, 1895.

—— *Wayside Courtships.* New York, 1897.

—— *Ulysses S. Grant: His Life and Character.* New York, 1898.

—— *The Spirit of Sweetwater.* Philadelphia and New York, [1898]. (Inscribed: "The original name for this little book was 'Witches Gold' but Edward Bok cut away the first half of the story and named the remainder 'The Spirit of Sweetwater.' Hamlin Garland.")

—— *The Trail of the Goldseekers.* New York, 1899. (Inscribed: "Burton Babcock: To the companion of my miseries and joys on the famous trail from the 'Boss.' Hamlin Garland. Chicago, June 29, 1899.")

—— *Boy Life on the Prairie.* New York, 1899. (Inscribed: "To

[1] Works listed chronologically except for reprints and new editions which are placed under pertinent titles. This book is very rare.

Walter Ehrich. This copy of my record of boy life in Iowa in the '70's. Hamlin Garland. Colo. Sp., Aug. 6, 1901.")

Garland, Hamlin (*continued*). *Boy Life on the Prairie.* Rev. ed. New York, 1908.

—— *The Eagle's Heart.* New York, 1900.

—— *Her Moutain Lover.* New York, 1901.

—— *Her Mountain Lover.* New York, 1915.

—— *The Captain of the Gray-Horse Troop.* New York and London, 1902. (Inscribed: "First copy March 17, '02. For R. H. Garland from his son Hamlin.")

—— *Hesper.* New York, 1903.

—— *The Light of the Star.* New York and London, 1904. (Inscribed: "This story was suggested to me by a visit behind the scenes with Julia Arthur . . . Hamlin Garland.")

—— *The Tyranny of the Dark.* London and New York, 1905. (Inscribed: "To R. H. Garland, West Salem, Wis., from his son, the author. Hamlin Garland.")

—— *Witch's Gold.* New York, 1906.

—— *The Long Trail.* New York and London, 1907. (Inscribed: "A boy's story based on my record 'The Trail of the Gold-seekers.' Hamlin Garland.")

—— *Money Magic.* New York and London, 1907.

—— *The Shadow World.* New York and London, 1908.

—— *The Moccasin Ranch.* New York and London, 1909.

—— *Cavanagh, Forest Ranger.* New York and London, 1910.

—— *Other Main-Travelled Roads.* New York, [1910].

—— *Victor Ollnee's Discipline.* New York and London, 1911.

—— *The Forester's Daughter.* New York, 1914.

—— *They of the High Trails.* New York and London, 1916.

—— *A Son of the Middle Border.* New York, 1917.

—— *A Son of the Middle Border.* Ed. for school use by E. H. Kemper. New York, 1923.

—— *A Daughter of the Middle Border.* New York, 1921.

—— *A Pioneer Mother.* Chicago, 1922. (Inscribed: "To be returned to the home library. Hamlin Garland.")

—— *The Book of the American Indian.* New York and London, 1923. (Inscribed by author: "For my friend and neighbor A. G. Beaman. Hollywood, Oct. 3, 1932.")

—— *Trail-Makers of the Middle Border.* New York, 1926. (Inscribed: "This is a sort of preface to the series and should be considered Vol. I. Los Angeles, Sep., 1938. Hamlin Garland.")

Garland, Hamlin (*continued*). *The Westward March of American Settlement.* Chicago, 1927.

—— *Back-Trailers from the Middle Border.* New York, 1928. (Inscribed: "This is Vol. IV of the series. Hamlin Garland. Los Angeles, Sep. 13, 1938.")

—— *Roadside Meetings.* New York, 1930.

—— *Companions on the Trail.* New York, 1931.

—— *My Friendly Contemporaries.* New York, 1932.

—— *Afternoon Neighbors.* New York, 1934.

—— *Joys of the Trail.* Chicago, 1935.

—— *Iowa, O Iowa!* Iowa City, 1935.

—— *Forty Years of Psychic Research.* New York, 1936.

—— *The Mystery of the Buried Crosses.* New York, 1939. (2 copies.)

Gates, William D. *Buttonhole Talks.* Chicago, 1911. (Inscribed to Garland by author.)

Gessler, Clifford F. *Kanaka Moon.* New York, 1927. (Inscribed to Garland by author in 1932.)

Gilder, Richard Watson. *In the Heights.* New York, 1905. (Inscribed to Garland by author.)

Gilman, Lawrence. *Edward MacDowell.* New York, 1908. (Inscribed: "To Hamlin Garland with the appreciative regard of the responsible party. April 22, 1911. Lawrence Gilman." The volume is well marked.)

—— *Edward MacDowell.* London and New York, 1906. (Inscribed to Garland by author. The volume is well marked.)

—— *Edward MacDowell.* London, 1909. (Inscribed to Garland by author.)

Gissing, George. *The Whirlpool.* New York, 1897.

Glasgow, Ellen. *The Descendant.* New York, 1897. (Inscribed to Garland by author.)

—— *Phases of an Inferior Planet.* New York, 1898.

Gorges, Grace. *My Little Songs.* Florence, 1926. (Inscribed to Garland by author.)

Gosse, Edmund. *Aspects and Impressions.* London, 1922. (Inscribed: "Hamlin Garland from his friend the author.")

—— *Father and Son.* London, 1916. (Inscribed: "Hamlin Garland from his English friend Edmund Gosse. October 12, 1922.")

Grant, Robert. *Unleavened Bread*. New York, 1900. (Inscribed: "Hamlin Garland with the compliments of Robert Grant. Oct., 1901.")

Griffith, William. *Loves and Losses of Pierrot*. New York, [1924]. (Inscribed to Garland by author.)

Grinnell, George Bird. *Pawnee. Hero Stories and Folk-Tales*. New York, 1889. (The volume is well marked.)

Grossman, Edwina Booth. *Edwin Booth. Recollections by His Daughter*. New York, 1894. (Inscribed by author: "To Hamlin Garland. Nov., 1908.")

Grover, Edwin Osgood. *The Nature Lover's Knapsack*. New York, [1927]. (Inscribed to Garland by author.)

Guiney, Louise Imogen. *Roadside Harp*. Boston, 1893. (Letter of author to Garland mounted at front.)

Hagedorn, Hermann. *Ladders through the Blue*. Garden City, N.Y., 1925. (Inscribed to Garland by author.)

—— *The Rough Riders*. New York and London, 1927. (Inscribed: "For Hamlin Garland with affectionate regards! Hermann Hagedorn, 1927.")

Hale, William J. *Chemistry Triumphant: The Rise and Reign of Chemistry in a Chemical World*. Baltimore, 1932. (Inscribed to Garland by author.)

Hardy, Florence Emily. *The Early Life of Thomas Hardy, 1840–1891*. New York, 1928.

—— *The Later Years of Thomas Hardy, 1892–1928*. New York, 1930. (Inscribed: "For the hospitable Garlands. From Mr. and Mrs. Eldon C. Hill.")

Harris, Joel Chandler. *Free Joe*. New York, 1887. (Author's autograph mounted on fly-leaf.)

Harte, Walter Blackburn. *Meditations in Motley*. Boston, 1894. (Inscribed: "To my friend, Hamlin Garland, with all good wishes and the highest regard, W. B. Harte, 1894.")

Hawthorne, Julian. *Nathaniel Hawthorne and His Wife*. 2 vols. Boston, 1885. (Autographed by author.)

Hawthorne, Nathaniel. *Complete Writings*. 22 vols. Boston, 1900.

—— *Mosses from an Old Manse*. 2 vols. Boston, 1876. (Inscribed by Garland: "This is the edition which I recall reading

at the Cedar Valley Seminary about 1878. My first knowledge
of Hawthorne. It enormously moved and influenced me.")
Hawthorne Nathaniel. *Our Old Home*. Boston and New York,
[1863]. (The volume is well marked.)
Hazard, Lucy Lockwood. *The Frontier in American Literature*.
New York, [1927].
Hearn, Lafcadio. *Gibbeted*. Los Angeles, 1933.
Heiser, Victor. *An American Doctor's Odyssey*. New York, [1936].
Hellman, George S. *Washington Irving, Esquire*. New York, 1925.
Herrick, Robert. *The Master of the Inn*. New York, 1908. (In-
scribed: "Mr. and Mrs. Hamlin Garland with the regards of
Robert Herrick. Chicago, 3 November, 1908.")
Higginson, Ella. *The Flower that Grew in the Sand and Other
Stories*. Seattle, 1896. (Inscribed: "To Hamlin Garland with
high esteem. Ella Higginson, November, 1896.")
Hodge, Frederick Webb, ed. *Handbook of American Indians North
of Mexico*. 2 vols. Washington, D.C., 1907.
Hoover, Herbert. *The Challenge to Liberty*. New York and Lon-
don, 1934. (Inscribed to Garland by author.)
—— *Hoover after Dinner*. New York, 1933. (Inscribed to Garland
by author.)
Hough, Emerson. *The Passing of the Frontier*. New Haven, 1918.
—— *The Story of the Cowboy*. New York, 1897. (Letter of author
to Garland, October 1897, pasted in. The volume is well
marked.)
House, E. M. *The Intimate Papers of Colonel House*. Arranged by
Charles Seymour. Vols. III–IV. Boston, 1928.
Howe, E. W. *A Moonlight Boy*. Boston, 1886. (Inscribed to
Garland by author.)
—— *The Story of a Country Town*. Boston, 1884.
Howells, W. D. *My Mark Twain*. New York, 1910. (The volume
is well marked.)
—— *Stops of Various Quills*. New York, 1895.
—— *Suburban Sketches*. Boston, 1872.
—— *Venetian Life*. Boston, 1872.
Hubbard, Elbert. *Forbes of Harvard*. Boston, 1894. (Letter of
author to Garland mounted on fly-leaf.)
—— *Little Journeys to the Homes of English Authors: Alfred Ten-
nyson*. East Aurora, N.Y., 1900.

Huntington, Archer. *The Lace Maker at Segovia*. New York, 1928.

Ibsen, Henrik. *Letters of Henrik Ibsen*. New York, 1905. (Inscribed: "To my friend Hamlin Garland knowing his appreciation of Ibsen. James MacArthur.")

—— *Peer Gynt*. Transl. by W. and Ch. Archer. London and New York, 1892.

—— *The Pillars of Society and Other Plays*. Camelot series. Ed. by Ernest Rhys. London, [1888]. (The volume is well marked.)

James, Henry. *Daisy Miller*. Boston, 1883.

—— *English Hours*. Boston, 1905.

—— *The Private Life*. New York, 1893.

—— *The Reverberator*. London, 1888.

—— *The Spoils of Poynton*. Boston, 1897.

—— *Terminations*. New York, 1895.

James, Marquis. *Andrew Jackson: The Border Captain*. Indianapolis, [1933].

Johnson, Robert Underwood. *Heroes, Children and Fun*. New York, 1934. (Autographed by author.)

—— *Poems*. New York, 1902. (Inscribed: "To Hamlin Garland from his friend Robert Underwood Johnson. March, 1907.")

Johnson, Wolcott. *An Old Man's Idyl*. Chicago, 1905. (Inscribed to Garland by author.)

Johnston, Richard Malcolm. *Mr. Billy Downs and His Likes*. New York, 1892. (Inscribed: "Mr. Hamlin Garland with cordial regards. Richard Malcolm Johnston. Baltimore, January 30, 1893.")

Jones, Fortier. *With Serbia into Exile*. New York, 1916. (Inscribed; "To Hamlin Garland with all the admiration of an amateur for the master. Fortier Jones. Onteora, 1918.")

Jones, Howard Mumford. *Gargoyles, and Other Poems*. Boston, [1918].

Jones, Louise Seymour. *Put a Feather in Your Hat*. Los Angeles, 1938. (Inscribed to Garland by author.)

Judah, Mary Jameson. *Down Our Way*. Chicago, 1897. (Inscribed by author: "My dear Mr. Garland. Without you this book would never have been written. In it I have tried to be simple and direct and true—partly because knowing you I know how good it is to be these things. Dec. 1897.")

Keiser, Albert. *The Indian in American Literature.* New York, 1933. (Inscribed to Garland by author. Letter of author to Garland laid in.)

Kiernan, R. H. *Little Brother Goes Soldiering.* London, 1930.

Kipling, Rudyard. *The Day's Work.* New York, 1898. (Three letters of author to Garland mounted at front.)

—— *The Seven Seas.* New York, 1898. (Letter of author to Garland pasted in.)

Kirkland, Joseph. *The Captain of Company K.* Chicago, 1891. (Inscribed: "To my friend, colaborer and most dangerous rival Hamlin Garland with all good wishes, Joseph Kirkland. Chicago, Jan. 27, 1892.")

Kiser, Samuel Ellsworth. *The Land of Little Care.* Chicago, 1912. (Inscribed to Garland by author.)

Lampman, A. *Among the Millet and Other Poems.* Ottawa, 1888. (Inscribed: "Prof. Hamlin Garland with the best wishes of the writer. A. Lampman. June, '89.")

Leacock, Stephen. *Further Foolishness.* New York, 1916.

—— *Mark Twain.* New York, 1933.

Leonard, William Ellery. *Sonnets and Poems.* Boston, 1906. (Letter of author to Garland pasted in.)

—— *Tutankhamen and After. New Poems.* New York, 1924.

Lincoln, Joseph C. *Shavings.* New York, 1919. (Inscribed to Garland by author.)

Longfellow, H. W. *The Courtship of Miles Standish.* London, 1859.

Ludwig, Emil. *Napoleon.* Transl. by Eden and Cedar Paul. Garden City, N.Y., [1926].

MacKaye, Percy. *The Civic Theatre in Relation to the Redemption of Leisure: A Book of Suggestions.* New York, 1912.

—— *Epoch: The Life of Steele Mackaye.* 2 vols. New York, [1927].

—— *The Playhouse and the Play, and Other Addresses Concerning the Theatre and Democracy in America.* New York, 1909.

—— *The Present Hour: A Book of Poems.* New York, 1914.

—— *Tall Tales of the Kentucky Mountains.* Decorations by E. MacKinstry. London, 1930. (Letter of author to Garland mounted at front.)

—— *This Fine-Pretty World.* New York, 1924. (Inscribed to Garland by author.)

MacKaye, Percy (*continued*). *Yankee Fantasies; Five One-act Plays.* New York, 1912.

MacManus, Seumas. *Dark Patrick.* New York, 1939. (Inscribed to Garland by author.)

Main, Angelia Kumlien. *Bird Companions.* Boston, 1925. (Autographed by author.)

Malloch, Douglas. *The Woods.* New York, 1913. (Inscribed: "To my friend Hamlin Garland whom I have followed on main-travelled roads and whom I now invite to go with me to the woods. Douglas Malloch.")

Markham, Edwin. *The Man with the Hoe.* New York, 1899. (Inscribed: "To Zulime Garland and Hamlin Garland with the brotherly good wishes of Edwin Markham. Jan. 8, 1900.")

Marks, Jeanette. *The Sun Chasers: A Play in Four Acts.* Cincinnati, [1922]. (Inscribed to Garland by author.)

Marquis, Don. *Dreams and Dust.* New York, 1915.

Marshall, Archibald. *The Education of Anthony Dare.* New York, 1924.

Masefield, John. *The Daffodil Field.* New York, 1915.

—— *The Everlasting Mercy and The Widow in the Bye Street.* New York 1915.

—— *The Faithful.* New York, 1915.

—— *King Cole.* New York, 1921.

—— *A Mainsail Haul.* New York, 1913.

—— *The Story of a Round-House and Other Poems.* New York, 1915.

Matthews, Brander. *Aspects of Fiction, and Other Ventures in Criticism.* New York, 1896. (Inscribed to Garland by author.)

—— *A Confident To-Morrow: A Novel of New York.* New York, 1900. (Inscribed to Garland by author.)

—— *Pen and Ink: Papers on Subjects of More or Less Importance.* New York, 1888. (Inscribed to Garland by author.)

—— *The Story of a Story, and Other Stories.* New York, 1893.

Maulsby, O. W. *Rolling Stone: The Autobiography.* Los Angeles, 1931. (Inscribed.)

Mayfield, John S. *Sidney Lanier in Texas.* Dallas, 1932.

Melville, Herman. *Typee.* New York, 1932.

Metcalf, John Calvin and Wilson, J. S., eds. *The Enchanted Years, A Book of Contemporary Verse.* New York, 1921. (Autographed by Metcalf.)

Miller, Joaquin. *The Building of the City Beautiful.* Chicago, 1893.

—— *The Complete Poetical Works of Joaquin Miller.* San Francisco, 1897. (Inscribed to Garland by author.)

—— *Memorie and Rime.* New York, 1884. (Inscribed: "Good Gentle Garland, I'm yours, Joaquin Miller. Chicago, 1898." The volume is well marked.)

Mims, Edwin. *Sidney Lanier.* Boston, 1905. (Inscribed: "To Mr. Hamlin Garland with delightful memories of days in Southern California. May 1, 1934. Edwin Mims.")

Monroe, Harriet. *Valeria, and Other Poems.* Chicago, 1892. (Letter of author to Garland mounted at front.)

Morgan, Anna, ed. *Tributes to Henry B.* [Chicago, 1929]. (Privately printed.)

Neihardt, John G. *The Song of the Messiah.* New York, 1935. (Letter of author to Garland mounted at front.)

Nordau, Max. *The Conventional Lies of Our Civilization.* Chicago, 1887. (Post card of author to Garland, August 13, 1901, mounted at front.)

Norris, Frank. *McTeague.* New York, 1899. (Letter of author to Garland pasted in.)

—— *The Octopus.* New York, 1901.

Paine, Albert B. *The Bread Line: A Story of a Pauper.* New York, 1900. (Inscribed to Garland by author.)

—— *Jan the Romantic: A Story of France.* Philadelphia, [1929]. (Inscribed to Garland by author.)

—— *Mark Twain: A Biography.* 3 vols. New York, 1912. (Inscribed to Garland by author.)

——, ed. *Mark Twain's Letters, Arranged with Comment.* 2 vols. New York, 1917.

Parkman, Francis. *The Oregon Trail.* Illus. by Frederic Remington. Boston, 1892. (Letter of Remington to Garland mounted at front.)

—— *The Oregon Trail.* New York, 1930. (With an introduction by Hamlin Garland.)

Pattee, Fred Lewis. *The House of the Black Ring: A Romance of the Seven Mountains.* Harrisburg, Pa., 1927.

Payne, Will. *Jerry the Dreamer.* New York, 1896. (Inscribed: "To Hamlin Garland with sincere good wishes. Will Payne. Chicago, Dec. 30, '96.")

Pellew, George. *Jane Austen's Novels.* Boston, 1883. (Inscribed to Garland by author, March 9, 1888.)

Pelley, William Dudley. *Seven Minutes in Eternity with Aftermath.* n.p., [1934]. (Autographed by author.)

Perry, Bliss. *The Praise of Folly.* Boston and New York, 1923.

Peterson, Frederick. *Creative Re-Education.* New York, 1936. (Inscribed to Garland by author.)

Pickard, Samuel T. *Whittier-Land.* Boston, 1904.

Poole, Ernest. *The Harbor.* New York, 1915. (Inscribed to Garland by author.)

Priestley, J. B. *The Good Companions.* New York, 1929.

Quinn, Arthur Hobson. *American Fiction: An Historical and Critical Study.* New York, [1936].

Ralston, Jackson H. *What's Wrong with Taxation?* San Diego, 1931. (Inscribed: "To Hamlin Garland—Fellow Soldier in a common cause from Jackson H. Ralston. Palo Alto. Dec. 1931.")

Repplier, Agnes. *In Pursuit of Laughter.* Boston, 1936.

Richman, Irving B. *John Brown among the Quakers, and Other Selections.* Des Moines, 1894. (Letter of author to Garland pasted in.)

Riley, James Whitcomb. *Armazindy.* Indianapolis, 1894. (Inscribed to Garland by author.)

—— *Neghborly Poems.* Indianapolis, 1891. (Inscribed to Garland: "From your old Hoosier friend, James Whitcomb Riley. Indianapolis, Oct. 1891.")

—— *Pipes O' Pan at Zekesbury.* Indianapolis, 1889. (Poem in Riley's handwriting mounted at front.)

Roberts, Charles G. D. *Earth's Enigma.* Boston and New York, 1896. (Inscribed to Garland by author.)

Roberts, Elizabeth Madox. *Black Is My True Love's Hair.* New York, 1938.

Roberts, Kenneth. *Arundel.* New York, 1931.

—— *The Lively Lady.* New York, 1931.

Robinson, Corinne Roosevelt. *Service and Sacrifice.* New York, 1919. (Inscribed to Garland by author.)

Roosevelt, Theodore. *A Book-Lover's Holiday in the Open.* New York, 1916. (Inscribed to Garland by author. The volume is well marked.)

—— *The Strenuous Life.* New York, 1901. (Inscribed to Garland by author.)

—— *The Works of Theodore Roosevelt.* 24 vols. New York, 1923-6.

Rourke, Constance. *Audubon.* New York, [1936].

Ruskin, John. *The Queen of the Air.* Chicago, n.d.

Sampson, Alden. *Studies in Milton and An Essay on Poetry.* New York, 1913. (Inscribed to Garland by author.)

Sandoz, Mari. *Old Jules.* Boston, 1935.

Seton, Ernest Thompson. *The Preacher of Cedar Mountain.* New York, 1917.

—— *Sign Talk.* New York, 1918. (Inscribed to Garland by author.)

—— *The Trail of the Sandhill Stag.* New York, 1899. (Inscribed: "To Hamlin Garland from his friend Ernest Seton-Thompson.")

Seymour, George Steele. *Adventures with Books and Autographs.* Chicago, 1920. (Inscribed to Garland by author.)

Shaw, G. Bernard. *The Irrational Knot.* New York, 1905.

—— *Man and Superman.* New York, 1905.

—— *Plays, Pleasant and Unpleasant.* 2 vols. Chicago, 1898. (Photo and envelope pasted in Vol. I; inscribed card pasted in Vol. II: "Dear Hamlin Garland, Here you are! Yrs sincerely. G. Bernard Shaw.")

—— *Three Plays for Puritans.* Chicago, 1901. (Letter of author to Garland, May 3, 1899, pasted in.)

Shorter Oxford Dictionary, The. 2 vols. Oxford, 1933.

Sill, Louise Morgan. *In Sun or Shade.* New York, 1906.

Simonds, W. A. *A Boy with Edison.* New York, 1931. (Inscribed to Garland by author.)

Sinclair, Upton. *Mental Radio.* Pasadena, 1930. (Inscribed to Garland by author.)

Skinner, Constance L. *Adventures of Oregon.* New Haven, 1920. (Inscribed to Garland by author.)

—— *Pioneers of the Old Southwest.* New Haven, 1919. (Inscribed to Garland by author. Letter of author to Garland laid in.)

Smith, F. Hopkinson. *The Under Dog.* New York, 1911.

Smith, F. Hopkinson (*continued*). *The Veiled Lady, and Other Men and Women*. New York, 1911.

Stedman, Edmund Clarence. *Poems, Now First Collected*. Boston, 1897. (Letter of author to Garland mounted at front.)

—— *Poets of America*. Boston, 1885. (Letter of author to Garland mounted at front.)

Steed, H. Whickham. *Through Thirty Years, 1892–1922: A Personal Narrative*. 2 vols. New York, 1924.

Sterling, George. *Sails and Mirage, and Other Poems*. San Francisco, 1921. (Inscribed: "To my friend Hamlin Garland to help him remember California and this 'cool, grey city of love.' George Sterling. San Francisco, April 25, 1923.")

Stockton, Frank R. *The Girl at Cobhurst*. New York, 1898. (Letter of author to Garland pasted on fly-leaf.)

Strachey, Lytton. *Eminent Victorians*. London, 1921.

Stuart, Ruth McEnery. *A Golden Wedding, and Other Tales*. New York, [1893]. (Inscribed to Garland by author.)

Swift, Ivan. *Fagots of Cedar*. Goodhart, Mich., 1926. (Inscribed to Garland by author.)

Swinburne, Algernon Charles. *Poems*. New York, [1884].

Symonds, L. A. *The Life of Benevenuto Cellini*. New York, 1925.

Synge, J. M. *The Play-Boy of the Western World*. Boston, 1911.

Tarkington, Booth. *Alice Adams*. Garden City, N.Y., 1921. (Inscribed to Garland by author.)

—— *The Magnificent Ambersons*. New York, 1922.

—— *Mr. White, the Red Barn, Hell and Bridewater*. Garden City, N.Y., 1935. (Inscribed to Garland by author.)

Taylor, Ada White. *The Mystic Spell: A Metaphysical Romance*. Los Angeles, [1923].

Thanet, Octave (Alice French). *Otto the Knight and Other Trans-Mississippi Stories*. Boston, 1893. (Inscribed to Garland: "I hear such pleasant things of you here. Cordially your admirer, Alice French. New York, Oct. 30, '95.")

Theiss, Lewis E. *Piloting the U. S. Air Mail: Flying For Uncle Sam*. Boston, [1927]. (Inscribed to Garland by author.)

Tompkins, Juliet W. *Doctor Ellen*. Indianapolis, 1908. (Inscribed to Garland by author.)

Towne, C. Hanson. *Manhattan*. New York, 1909. (Inscribed to Garland by author.)

Traubel, Horace L. *With Walt Whitman in Camden.* 3 vols. New York, 1914.

——, ed. *Camden's Compliment to Walt Whitman.* Philadelphia, 1889.

——, Bucke, Richard Maurice, and Harned, Thomas B., eds. *In Re Walt Whitman.* Philadelphia, 1893.

Van Doren, Carl. *The American Novel.* New York, 1921. (Letter of author to Garland mounted at front.)

—— *Contemporary American Novelists, 1900–1920.* New York, 1922. (Inscribed to Garland by author.)

Van Dyke, John C. *The Meadows: Familiar Studies of the Commonplace.* New York, 1926.

Véron, Eugène. *Æsthetics.* Transl. by W. H. Armstrong. London and Philadelphia, 1878. (The volume is well marked.)

Ware, E. F. *Rhymes of Ironquill.* Topeka, Kan., 1889. (Letter of author to Garland mounted at front.)

—— *Some of the Rhymes of Ironquill.* 4th ed. Topeka, Kan., 1896. (Inscribed to Garland by author.)

—— *Some Rhymes of Ironquill of Kansas.* Chicago, 1892. (Letter of author to Garland mounted at front.)

Warren, Maude Radford. *The White Flame of France.* Boston, [1918].

Wayland, John W. *Whispers of the Hills.* New Market, Va., 1928.

Wharton, Edith. *Old New York.* New York and London, 1924. (Inscribed to Garland by author.)

White, William Allen. *God's Puppets.* New York, 1916. (Inscribed to Garland by author.)

—— *In the Heart of a Fool.* New York, 1918. (Inscribed to Garland by author.)

—— *Masks in a Pageant.* New York, 1928. (Inscribed to Garland by author.)

Whitlock, Brand. *On the Enforcement of Law in Cities.* Indianapolis, 1913. (Inscribed: "To Hamlin Garland from his friend Brand Whitlock. City Hall, Toledo. 8 April, 1913.")

Whitman, Walt. *Leaves of Grass.* Boston, 1881–2.

—— *Leaves of Grass.* Philadelphia, 1891. (Inscribed to Garland by author.)

—— *November Boughs.* Philadelphia, 1888. (Inscribed to Garland by author.)

Whitman, Walt. (*continued*). *Two Rivulets*. Camden, N.J., 1876.

Wiggin, Kate Douglas. *A Cathedral Courtship*. New York, 1895. (Inscribed: "To Hamlin Garland I give my most frivolous book to the least frivolous author I know. Kate Douglas Wiggin, 1896.")

Wilkinson, Marguerite. *The Great Dream*. New York, 1923. (Inscribed to Garland by author.)

Wister, Owen. *Lin McLean*. New York, 1898.

—— *Neighbors Henceforth*. New York, 1922.

—— *Red Men and White*. New York, 1896.

Wood, Grant. *Revolt against the City*. Iowa City, 1935.

Woolcott, Alexander. *Enchanted Aisles*. 2nd ed. New York, 1924. (Inscribed to Garland by author.)

2. OTHER BOOKS OF HAMLIN GARLAND

The following bibliography is compiled from various listings—now in the University of Southern California Library—of Garland's books made during his last years. It consists principally of belles-lettres. Of American writers of the eighties and nineties not recorded in Appendix A, 1, the following are worthy of note: G. W. Cable, Edward Eggleston, Bret Harte, and Jack London. There are furthermore additional titles by W. D. Howells, Joaquin Miller, and others. Among European writers Johan Bojer, Thomas Hardy, and Émile Zola deserve to be noted.

Dates of publication as well as the words "Autographed" and "Inscribed" have been set down whenever given in the listings. Such titles as have already been recorded in Appendix A, 1, have been removed from the present list.

Ade, George. *Artie*. 1896. (Autographed.)

—— *Circus Day*. (Autographed).

Aldrich, Bess Streeter. *The Lantern in Her Hand*. 1928. (Inscribed.)

Armstrong, Eliza. *The Teacup Club*. 1897. (Inscribed.)

Aylesworth, Barton O. *Thirteen and Twelve Others*. (Autographed.)

Bacheller, Irving. *Eben Holden*. 1900.

—— *A Man for the Ages*. 1919. (Inscribed.)

Barrie, James Matthew. *Courage.* 1922. (Inscribed.)

Baylor, F. Courtenay. *Behind the Blue Ridge.* 1887. (Autographed.)

Bell, Lilian L. *Hope Loring.* (Autographed.)

Bennett, Arnold. *The Human Machine.* (Inscribed.)

Bok, Edward W. *Why I Believe in Poverty.* 1916. (Inscribed.)

Bojer, Johan. *The Great Hunger.* 1920. (Inscribed.)

Bulfinch, Thomas. *The Age of Fable.* (Autographed.)

Bunyan, John. *The Pilgrim's Progress.*

Burnett, F. Hodgson. *Methods of Lady Walderhurst.* (Autographed.)

—— *Racketty-Packetty House.* (Autographed.)

Burton, Richard. *Dumb in June.* 1895. (Inscribed.)

Cable, George W. *Old Creole Days.* 1892. (Inscribed.)

Canby, Henry S. *Definitions.* (Inscribed.)

Cawein, Madison J. *Lyrics and Idyls. 1890.* (Inscribed.)

—— *An Ode.* 1918.

Connoly, James B. *The Seiners.* (Autographed.)

Crawford, Francis Marion. *The Heart of Rome.* 1903. (Autographed.)

Dana, Richard Henry, Jr. *Two Years before the Mast.*

Darrow, Clarence S. *Farmington.* 1904. (Inscribed.)

Dickens, Charles. *Great Expectations.*

Eaton, Walter Prichard. *Barn Doors and Byways.* 1913. (Inscribed.)

Eggleston, Edward. *The Hoosier Schoolmaster.* 1871. (Inscribed.)

Freeman, Mary E. Wilkins. *A New England Nun and Other Stories.* 1891.

Grayson, David (R. S. Baker). *Adventures in Contentment.* 1914.

—— *Adventures in Friendship.* 1914. (Inscribed.)

—— *The Friendly Road.* 1914. (Inscribed.)

Hardy, Thomas. *Desperate Remedies.*

—— *The Hand of Ethelberta.*

—— *Late Lyrics and Earlier.* 1922.

Harte, Bret. *Poetical Works.* 1890.

Herne, James A. *Shore Acres and Other Plays.* 1928.

Homer. *Odyssey.*

Hope, Anthony. *Phroso.*

Hough, Emerson. *Mississippi Bubble.*

Howells, W. D. *A Boy's Town.* 1890.

—— *A Chance Acquaintance.* 1898. (Inscribed.)

Howells, W. D. (*continued*). *The Lady of Aroostook.* 1884.
—— *New Leaf Mills.* 1913. (Inscribed.)
—— *An Open-Eyed Conspiracy.* 1897. (Inscribed.)
—— *Poems.* 1873. (Inscribed.)
—— *The Rise of Silas Lapham.* 1886. (Autographed.)
Irving, Washington. *A History of the Life and Voyages of Christopher Columbus.*
Janvier, Thomas A. *An Embassy to Provence.* 1893. (Inscribed.)
Kipling, Rudyard. *The Phantom Rickshaw.*
Kidd, B. *Social Evolution.* 1898.
Kirkland, Joseph. *The McVeys.* 1888.
Laughlin, Clara E. *James Whitcomb Riley.* 1916. (Inscribed.)
Lodge, Henry Cabot. *Early Memories.* 1920. (Inscribed.)
London, Jack. *Adventure.*
—— *A Daughter of the Snows.*
Mabie, Hamilton W. *Essays on Books and Culture.*
Macaulay, Thomas B. *Essays.*
Miller, Joaquin. *In Classic Shades and Other Poems.* 1890.
—— *Songs of the Mexican Seas.* 1887.
—— *Songs of the Sierras.* 1888. (Inscribed.)
—— *Songs of the Soul.* 1896.
Noyes, Alfred. *The Torch-Bearers.* 1922. (Inscribed.)
Osbourne, Lloyd. *The Queen versus Billy and Other Stories.* 1900. (Inscribed.)
Paine, Albert B. *Joan of Arc.* 1925. (Inscribed.)
—— *Tent Dwellers.* 1908.
Parker, Gilbert. *When Valmond Came to Pontiac.* 1895.
Quick, Herbert. *On Board the Good Ship Earth.* 1913. (Inscribed.)
Roberts, Charles G. D. *The Heart of the Ancient Woods.* 1900.
Seton, Ernest Thompson. *Animal Heroes.* 1905. (Inscribed.)
Shaw, G. Bernard. *Saint Joan.* 1924. (Inscribed to Mary Isabel Garland.)
Singmaster, Elsie. *Bennett Malin.* 1922. (Inscribed.)
Stevens, Thomas W. *The Daimio's Head.* 1912. (Inscribed.)
Sylvester, Herbert Milton. *Prose Pastorals.* 1887. (Inscribed.)
Thomas, Augustus. *The Print of My Remembrance.* 1922. (Inscribed.)
Tompkins, Juliet W. *Seed of the Righteous.* (Inscribed.)
Trollope, A. *Barchester Towers.*

Wagner, Harr. *Joaquin Miller and His Other Self.* 1929. (Inscribed.)

Wharton, Edith. *The Valley of Decision.* 1902.

Whitman, Walt. *Leaves of Grass.* 1876.

Wiggin, Kate Douglas. *Child's Journey with Dickens.* 1912. (Inscribed.)

Wilkinson, Marguerite O. *The Dingbat of Arcady.* 1922. (Inscribed.)

Young, Arth. H. *Authors' Readings.* 1897. (Inscribed.)

Zangwill, Israel. *The Bachelors' Club.* 1891. (Inscribed.)

—— *The Big Bow Mystery.* 1895. (Inscribed.)

—— *The Master.* 1897. (Inscribed.)

Zola, Émile. *Doctor Pascal.*

3. BOOKS OF HAMLIN GARLAND PRESENTED BY THE AUTHOR TO THE CLIFF-DWELLERS' CLUB OF CHICAGO

The following is a list[1] of the works of Hamlin Garland presented by him to the Cliff-Dwellers' Club, of which he was the first president. The inscriptions, published here for the first time, are both interesting and informative and offer additional knowledge of the background and the time of composition of some of the works listed. The items are arranged alphabetically by title.

Boy Life on the Prairie. New York, 1906. (Inscribed: "To the Cliff-Dwellers' Library. Hamlin Garland. I value parts of this book. It is all very close to the facts of my life in northern Iowa thirty-five years ago. Hamlin Garland.")

The Captain of the Gray-Horse Troop. New York and London, 1902. (Inscribed: "This book is based on my experiences among the northern Chyennes in the Summer of 1897. Hamlin Garland.")

The Eagle's Heart. New York, 1907. (Inscribed: "For the Cliff-Dwellers from the author, Hamlin Garland. January 19, 1909. Written in 1898, published first in the Saturday Post of Philadelphia.")

---

[1] Published by courtesy of the Cliff-Dwellers' Club.

438

Hesper. New York and London, 1903. (Inscribed: "This novel is based upon the 'Miners' War' in Cripple Creek but is in no sense a history of that turbulent dispute. Hamlin Garland.")

The Light of the Star. New York and London, 1904. (Inscribed: "For the Cliff-Dwellers. Hamlin Garland. January 16, 1909. A study of a phase of the present day American stage. Hamlin Garland.")

The Long Trail. Boston, 1907. (Inscribed: "For the Cliff-Dwellers. Hamlin Garland. Jan. 16. A story for boys or those of graver years who love the wilderness. Hamlin Garland.")

The Trail of the Gold-Seekers. New York, 1906. (Inscribed: "This book is a rough record of a rough experience. It makes no pretention to fine writing. Hamlin Garland.")

The Tyranny of the Dark. London and New York, 1906. (Inscribed: "'The Tyranny of the Dark' is based upon years of experiment in occult biology. Hamlin Garland.")

APPENDIX B

1. LECTURE SEASON OF 1885-6

The following circular dates from Garland's first years in Boston when he taught American and European literature at the Boston School of Oratory. The titles of the lectures reflect some of his early literary preferences, such as Victor Hugo and Friedrich Spielhagen. It has seemed worth while to reproduce this rare circular—now in the University of Southern California Library—because it sheds light upon the very beginnings of Garland's career as a student and teacher of literature.

LECTURE SEASON OF 1885-86

Studies in Literature and Expression
by
Hamlin Garland.

Teacher of English Literature, Boston School of Oratory.

1. Victor Hugo and His Prose Masterpieces.
2. Edwin Booth as a Master of Expression.
3. The Epic of the Age, the Novel—American and German.
4. Poets of the New Eldorado.

Victor Hugo and His Prose Masterpieces. ". . . The treatment of the subject was fresh and original, and the theory advanced as to the real intent and meaning of the characters in *Les Miserables* and *L'Homme qui rit* was supported and illustrated by passages from each, which were read with fine effect." Chas. E. Hurd, Literary Editor of the *Boston Transcript*.

The Epic of the Age—the Novel. (This lecture is based upon the saying of Friedrich Spielhagen, "The Epic of this Age is the Novel." It deals with the present schools of novelists in Germany and America, and their leanings as seen in the principal novels.)

Poets of the New Eldorado. (This lecture is an entirely new lecture, and deals with that unique era of "49" and of the poets and poetry now springing up to bloom in the "path of empire.")

"Professor Garland in this lecture works in a vein of gold. He gives a realistic and vivid picture of the age, time, and impulse that produced such types as Kit Carson and Tennessee's Partner. His analysis of the poems of Joaquin Miller and Bret Harte is as fresh, large, and generous as the atmosphere of the Sierras."

Moses True Brown.

2. LECTURE CIRCULAR

Gradually Garland expanded the scope of his lectures to include American literature from its very beginnings to his own time. The circular, now in the possession of Eldon C. Hill, Oxford, Ohio, should be of interest to the student of Garland's life and works, for it tells especially of his familiarity with American letters. Garland's approach to literary criticism was influenced by Taine, whose doctrines of race, milieu, and moment appear in No. 18 of the circular.

STUDIES IN LITERATURE AND EXPRESSIVE ART

by

Hamlin Garland

1888–89.

"Art for the multitude must be sincere and lifelike, true and tangible . . . and [it] is never greater than when it marches with the ideas and sentiments that influence a whole condition of society." Eugène Véron.

AMERICAN LITERATURE AND ART

1. Colonial Age.
2. Revolutionary Age.
3. First Age of the Republic.
4. The Landscape School. Studies of Bryant, Cole and Cooper. Art Beginnings.

5. The Transcendentalists. Emerson, Thoreau.
6. The Balladists. Readings from Whittier, Longfellow and Holmes.
7. Hawthorne and Poe. The Romance.
8. The Civil War. Its Effect on Thought. Literature of the War.
9. Walt Whitman. The Prophet of the New Age.
10. The Epic of the Age. The Novel. The American Novel.
11. Americanism in the Novel. William D. Howells and Henry James.
12. The Local Novelists. Their Significance as Precursors. Provincialism no Bar to a National Literature. The Spirit of the Age.
13. The Pioneers. Bret Harte and Joaquin Miller. *The New Eldorado*.
14. Some Representative Names. Joseph Kirkland and E. W. Howe: *Prairie West*. Geo. W. Cable, Joel Harris, Miss Murfree, Miss Baylor: *The South*. Miss Wilkins, Miss Jewett, Rose Cooke: *New England*. Unparalleled Vitality and Importance of the Movement.
15. Aristocracy of Democracy. The City in Fiction and the Drama. Sharpening Social Contrasts. Edgar Fawcett.
16. Poets from the Soil. Farm-Life. *Dialect*: James Whitcomb Riley, and Others.
17. Sidney Lanier and His Art. The Question of Future Verse-Form. The Modern Landscape School. Cosmic Feeling for Nature.
18. Summary of Principles and Results. Final Study of Race Elements, Momentum, Surroundings. Social Problems.
19. Logical Prophecy. The Future of Poetry and Fiction.

DRAMATIC STUDIES AND MISCELLANIES

1. Victor Hugo and His Prose Masterpieces.
2. The Rise of the Northern Minstrel.
3. Swinburne. Lecture and Reading from "Bothwell" and *Poems*.
4. Scenes from the Modern Novel. Howells, Kirkland, Harris, Miss Wilkins, Miss Baylor, and Others.
5. Lyrical Readings from Poe, Lanier, Shelley and Swinburne.

3. THE SEASIDE ASSEMBLY

The following brochure, now in the University of Southern California Library, is similar to the preceding one, except that item 9 is here called "The Literature of Democracy. The Genre and Landscape Poetry of Whitman." Compare this item with the extracts from Garland's lecture "The Literature of Democracy" in Appendix C, 1. It was during this lecture session that Garland met Stephen Crane who reported one of Garland's lectures for a New York newspaper.

THE SEASIDE ASSEMBLY

Avon-by-the-Sea, New Jersey.
Schools of Expression and Literature.
Eighth Session July 5–Aug. 28, 1891.
Wm. M. Alberti, Dean of School of Expression.

LECTURE-STUDIES IN AMERICAN LITERATURE AND EXPRESSIVE ART

by Professor Hamlin Garland

1. Colonial Age.
2. Revolutionary Age.
3. First Age of the Republic.
4. The Landscape School. Studies of Bryant, Cole and Cooper. Art Beginnings.
5. The Transcendentalists. Emerson, Thoreau.
6. The Balladists. Readings from Whittier, Longfellow and Holmes.
7. Hawthorne and Poe. The Romance.
8. The Civil War. Its Effect on Thought. Literature of the War.
9. The Literature of Democracy. The *Genre* and Landscape Poetry of Whitman.
10. The Epic of the Age. The Novel. The American Novel.
11. Americanism in the Novel. William Dean Howells and Henry James.
12. Local Novelists. Their Significance as Precursors. Provincialism no Bar to a National Literature. The Spirit of the Age.
13. The Pioneers. Bret Harte and Joaquin Miller. *The New Eldorado.*

14. Some Representative Names. Joseph Kirkland and E. W. Howe: *The Prairie West*. Geo. W. Cable, Joel Harris, Miss Murfree, Miss Baylor: *The South*. Miss Wilkins, Miss Jewett, Rose Terry Cooke: *New England*. Unparalleled Vitality and Importance of the Movement.

15. Aristocracy of Democracy. The City in Fiction and the Drama. Sharpening Social Contrasts. Edgar Fawcett.

16. Poets from the Soil. Farm-Life. *Dialect*: James Whitcomb Riley and Others.

17. Sidney Lanier and His Art. The Question of Future Verse-Form. The Modern Landscape School. Cosmic Feeling for Nature.

18. Summary of Principles and Results. Final Study of Race Elements, Momentum, Surroundings. Social Problems.

19. Logical Prophecy. The Future of Poetry and Fiction.

Terms: Single lecture   .50
5 lectures $2.00
10   " $4.00

H. Garland, Dean of School of Literature. Aug. 11–Aug. 25.

APPENDIX C

1. EXTRACTS FROM HAMLIN GARLAND'S LECTURE ON "THE MODERN NOVEL"

The following extracts from Garland's manuscript of a lecture, now in the University of Southern California Library, are published here for the first time. The forty-two pages taken from a notebook are undated, but on the cover of the notebook is written a quotation from Spielhagen which was used as an illustration of a lecture given during the lecture season of 1885 to 1886. The manuscript quoted below—to judge from such contents as Garland's critical attitude to Howells— certainly belongs to Garland's early manuscripts. His knowledge of and enthusiasm for the German writers referred to below was strong in the mid-eighties. The lecture is of interest because it shows Garland as a literary critic comparing and evaluating some contemporary American and European writers.

THE MODERN NOVEL IN GERMANY AND AMERICA.

Spielhagen	Howells
Heyse	Harte
Freytag	Cable
Auerbach	Craddock

"The Epic of the Age Is the Novel"—Spielhagen.

. . . I find the most marked tendency of the modern novel to be the deliberate study of the manifold relations of the various classes of society and especially of the middle and lower classes. *Andersen* writes of the Danish work-folk, *Björnson* of the peasants of Norway, *Auerbach* of children of convicts and clock-makers. . . . *Turgenev* pleads for the Russian serf, while *Thackeray, Dickens*, and *Eliot* [paint] the English laborer . . . *Hugo* pleads for humanity. (I find the most advanced and courageous thought of the time in the novel.) These writers are plebeian, their readers are legion for they write *for the poor*. The slave has become the peasant, the peasant the might, mind and muscle of his age. *They grow noble through their great deeds*. I observe the analysis becomes more and more psychological. Hugo, Eliot, Spielhagen, Björnson, Heyse, Freytag, Turgenev excel in the multiplicity and complexity of the characters . . .

Of later German novelists I place *Spielhagen* first, with Auerbach, Heyse, Hackländer, Freytag prominent. It is probable that a general vote would place *Howells* as first among *our* present writers with *James, Cable, Julian Hawthorne* as colleagues. I propose to institute a study of these men. It is very suggestive to contrast the contemporaneous novelists of these two countries who have so much in common.

I find in the Germans a deeper insight into the underworld whose presence is so near and yet so hidden to the superficial observer. I mean *the world of causes*. So many men see a world of bricks, mortar, business and bustle, but all things of a tender or spiritual nature seem to break in their grasp. I find also a superior earnestness in the German writers. Their views are broader. What they lose in art they make up in penetration. They have a broader culture. . . .

Taine says all the great literary works are born of certain mental revolutions. We have these deeper things around us today, yet how many men have we whose works under the broadest view may be said to live? How many fill the measurement for being of value? Does *Howells, James, Crawford, Fawcett, Julian Hawthorne*? Do any of these men touch the *deeper life of this nation*? Do they portray the inner causes which move this age? Let us be just but let us also attempt to get at some principle apart from patriotic pride in "our" writers.

Our writers spend too much time upon unmeaning detail, exteriors. . . .

Now, have we a novelist who *sees deep into the life* of our people, penetrating the externals and grasping currents of thought? I know of no one among us of whom it could be said as it has been said of *Spielhagen*, the next age may turn to his age to find its psychology.

I consider him the greatest writer of novels in Germany and perhaps in the first rank of all nations. Using him for a text allow me to enter a little in detail upon his great work *Problematic Characters* of which *Through Night to Light* is the conclusion.

He has been called and completely without reason the Dickens of Germany. . . .

Mr. Howells found no reason for believing in either of these great works (*What the Swallow Sang, Hammer and Anvil, Through Night to Light*) this is doubly unfortunate . . .

That which Mr. Howells denotes prolixity *may* be close analysis and deep, penetrative study to those who have time to read him.

There are but few scenes in literature so filled with a nameless terror . . . as the calm, icy old man Berger telling his story seated on the hillside at evening. And such a story! *It is the story of the disenchantment of youth. A youth in love* of course . . .

Conceive of Berger as one who has no God, believes in no good. One to whom the world is an empty flask, the past a horror, the future a baseless vision, one to whom comes no breath of spring, no scent of flowers, no song of bird, and *you feel those profound stirrings of the soul* which tell that genius is voicing the unutterable sorrows of humanity. *This chapter places Spielhagen among the masters.*

Spielhagen seems to be dominated with the idea of voicing the mental upheavals of his age.

There is also consummate art in the setting of this story. . . . What a contrast! . . . And we hear the multitudinous tramp of a world! . . . It is not a pleasant book, but it is a great one. I do not say the book is a pleasing one but it is suggestive. Surgery is not a delight. *Will you put Howells beside this man? Or Cable, or Crawford or James?* I tell you frankly we have no novel of society in our literature which can be put for a moment beside this work. We are superficial, we see only the surface. We see not the grandeur, the terror of human life. . . .

If we have a man who sees the wider significance of things, he is so excessively mental that he could no more depict a passion than make the wind visible. We have ten thousand statisticians to one poet. The emotional nature is dwarfed among our thinkers. John Fiske is the only man I know who could do the mental part of this age's novel and the emotional part he could *not* do. Howells in his *Undiscovered Country* started bravely upon a study of modern spiritualism but soon became convinced of his inadequacy and after dabbling around the edges drew off. He was a tenderfoot who had forgotten his compass. . . .

Sarah Orne Jewett with melodious prose paints the "Mash" and "Tom" and "Ed." E. W. Howe is painting with considerable poise impossible towns in the west. Cable depicts the Creole, Harris the negro quarters, Fawcett rococo furniture and Newport quadrilles, Craddock the Tennessee Mountains, while James and Hawthorne occupy their time in running from New York to Paris, and depicting . . . Americans, who are excessively vulgar and parvenu. . . .

We have said that a change more hopeful of a deeper study of our people is now in progress, that of local studies of character and scenery. . . . Bret Harte . . . he is a consummate artist . . . through it all runs a sensuous sympathetic delight. . . .

Miller is also a worthy worker in the western mountains. . . . Other men have attempted to work this field and failed from lack of sympathy. *These men are soaked in the aroma of their surroundings for it produced them! ! !*

Of course this local work is easier than any general work but [it] is a step in the right direction.

Cable's work in New Orleans merits much praise. H. H. [Helen Hunt Jackson] in *Ramona* has painted a powerful picture of the injustice of our government against the Indians. Her unquestionable earnestness gives a strong element to the work.

. . . Joel Chandler Harris . . . great value. . . .

Howe has assembled a company of impossible citizens in a Western town, missing the deeper significance of that which surrounds him. He writes with a taint of the journalist and a liking for head-lines and fat type. . . .

The trouble is we have no novelist who can feel the great mental revolution now going on around us.

Every great work of literature, says Taine, has been the utterance of some particular phase of mind, and you may set it down as a sovereign law that it will be so in the future. . . .

2. EXTRACTS FROM HAMLIN GARLAND'S LECTURE ON "THE LITERATURE OF DEMOCRACY"

I hereby present for the first time extracts from a lecture by Garland, the undated manuscript of which is now in the University of Southern

California Library. It consists of twenty-nine pages typed on an old-fashioned typewriter. The last page bears the name and address of the author. The manuscript voices Garland's admiration for Taine and Whitman and gives evidence of his belief in a literature for and about the people. The lecture also indicates his knowledge of European literature. Björnson, Ibsen, Auerbach, Freytag, Spielhagen, Gogol, Turgenev, Tolstoy, Daudet, Zola, and others are mentioned.

THE LITERATURE OF DEMOCRACY

M. Taine begins the last book of his great study of English literature with the most profound and eloquent statement of the principles which unquestionably underlie the modern age in Europe and in England, molding and sustaining its art and literature; and which possess the profoundest significance when applied to American thinking and American society. . . .

I assert that as in government so in art and literature there is progress. The zones of light march. I assert that the history of intellectual America for the last century is a history of the growth and dominance of ideas born on democratic social conditions. . . . [Here follow a great many quotations from the works of Walt Whitman.]

So great and rapid is the change in the condition and thought of this section of the Democratic world that in the last half of the nineteenth century, its mighty voice is saying—"give us ourselves as we are, delineate in your poems, paintings, novels and plays, our griefs and joys, our triumphs and possessions, and our growing comfort and security. Tell us of *the people* in France, in Germany, in Denmark, plead for our advancement in Russia and in Spain. Sound the call for the peoples' enfranchisement, the leveling of ranks. Advocate justice, mercy, equality before the law. Paint the customs, the multitudinous acts, emotions and concerns of the modern man till sympathy widens like a sea, till we shall indeed know each other as if face to face, till sharing each other's burden's we march shoulder to shoulder up the heights to brotherhood and liberty."

In answer to this call from the thinking classes of the people came splendid warriors like Hugo, satirists like Thackeray, humorists and sentimentalists like Dickens. Björnson and Ibsen in the

North, Auerbach, Spielhagen and Freytag in Germany, Tourgénief, Gogol and Tolstoy in Russia, Galdós and Valdés in Spain,
Balzac, Daudet and Zola, all belong to this mighty movement
which is to overturn all other values and ideals. On they march
like a conquering march.

In George Eliot the common people found their greatest delineator. . . . In the person of Hugo their greatest advocate.

. . . the writer who hopes to live must ally himself with the new
spirit of the age. He must base his art upon the lives of the people
not upon books. He must awake to the knowledge that new ideals
are in the ascendant, must see and express the growing beauty,
color and light which has already entered like the dawn . . . The
day will break by and by. Poet keep your face to the East.

I cannot conceive of a nobler task for the American poet than
to write for the average soul, interpreting and voicing for it the
deep emotions and daring aspirations which it can not itself express. The poet who does that will feel the rhythm of his verse
the heart beat of the millions. One little song that does this is
worth a thousand of the cold, ornate and imitative poems with
which our literature abounds from first to last.

No one it seems to me can study American imaginative production unbiased by patriotism without being convinced that it
has been almost entirely imitative throughout, exotic, cold, formal. . . .

The minds close down to the soil felt the influence first, for the
reason that the environment was new, stern and coercive, from
thence the American spirit has slowly spread into other departments
of thought, and poetry, the drama and painting have just begun
to adjust themselves to the new scale of values. Soon all will give
way. . . .

Before our poets and artists can be original they must develop
from the soil and become national, provincial, which is the very
quality which will alone save them from oblivion.

. . . Howells is incontestibly the leading figure in the rapid and
widespread realism of the last ten years, a movement which involves the best of the younger poets and novelists and which is the
most promising and original movement in the history of American
thought.

I turn first to the study of the principles so powerfully set forth by Whitman and to a consideration of his claims to the name "the poet of Democracy." Secondly to the study of the new school of novelists, the local novelists represented by Edward Eggleston, Geo. W. Gable, E. W. Howe, Miss Murfree, Joel C. Harris, and to the consideration of the realistic study of the city, as led by W. D. Howells, Edgar Fawcett and Henry James. . . .

Hamlin Garland

21 Seaverns Ave.

Jamaica Plain, Boston.

APPENDIX D

1. HAMLIN GARLAND AND THE FIRST INDEPENDENT THEATER ASSOCIATION

Garland's interest in the realistic drama was stimulated by his reading of Ibsen and his friendship with the Hernes. The folder, dated 1890 and now in the University of Southern California Library, is an early document of the First Independent Theater in the United States.

"TRUTH FOR ART'S SAKE"

A Prospectus of the First Independent Theatre Association. Issued by the committee of organization, Boston, Mass.

THE OBJECTS OF THE ASSOCIATION

Are first and in general to encourage truth and progress in American Dramatic Art. Second, and specifically, to secure and maintain a stage whereon the best and most unconventional studies of modern life and distinctively American life, may get a proper hearing. We believe the present poverty of Dramatic Art in America is due to unfavorable conditions, rather than to a lack of playwriting talent, and it is the purpose of the Association to remove as far as possible, the commercial consideration and give the Dramatist the artistic atmosphere for his work, and bring to his production the most intelligent and sympathetic acting in America.

THE SCOPE OF THE THEATRE

It is designed to be distinctively but not exclusively modern and American, and it will encourage the use of the wealth of native material lying at our hand. Its scope may be indicated thus:

I. Studies of American Society.
   (a) Social Dramas.
   (b) Comedies of Life.

II. Studies in American History.
   (a) Dramas of Colonial Times.
   (b) Dramas of the Revolution.
   (c) Dramas of Border History.
   (d) Dramas of the Civil War.

III. Famous Modern Plays by the Best Dramatists of Europe.

We believe that the above plan is sufficiently extensive to claim the support of all lovers of the Drama, while at the same time it maintains its distinctive character. We believe that with the encouragement of a fair trial for their plays, a part of the confessedly great talent of our novelists could be directed to the production of plays as modern and as American in flavor as our famous short stories.

METHODS OF WORK

The Association while it has in mind the great work done by a few unknown men in the Freie Buehne of Berlin, the Théâtre Libre of Paris, and the Independent Theatre of London, does not propose to model itself upon either of these organizations, but to take all helpfull hints and use them in its own way.

It is designed to have all enterprises conducted upon the co-operative principle as far as possible. A corporation will be formed to build within the coming year a small theatre, and to sell season tickets by subscription, very much as in the Freie Buehne. The season will last thirty weeks and will include the production of ten or twelve new plays. Tickets to admit subscribers three nights in the week and to be transferable. The unsold seats on subscribers' nights and the entire house on alternate performances will be open to the general public.

PLAYS

A Reading Committee will have entire charge of the selection of plays. To place all plays on equal footing, the MSS. must be submitted to the Secretary, in typewriting, unsigned, accompanied by the name of the author in a sealed envelope. If the play is accepted the envelope will remain unbroken till the last performance of the first week's trial. If the play is returned no one but the Secretary will know the name of its author.

It is designed also to extend the co-operative principle to the plays, the Association to retain an interest in the plays it produces.

A PLEA FOR ART

It seems to us that the most fitting city in America to begin the great work is Boston. Boston is at once the most conservative and the most progressive of cities. She has an autonomy that is lacking in most of our towns, and her influence on art is greater than any other American city. The establishment here of a theatre with "Truth for Art's Sake," as a motto would unquestionably result in the formation of similar enterprises in other places. We appeal to the art-loving population of Boston to assist us in the carrying out of this plan which we believe will result in the birth of a genuine, truthful, buoyant American Drama. . . .

> Edwin D. Mead
> B. O. Flower
> Sylvester Baxter
> Dr. Emil Blum
> Jas. A. Herne
> Mildred Aldrich
> Mary Shaw
> W. A. Brownell
> Ralph Adams Cram
> Henry A. Wyman, Chairman
> Hamlin Garland, Secretary

> > Address: Care *Arena*, Copley Square.
> > Committee.

Rapid Printing Company, Boston.

2. HAMLIN GARLAND AND *MARGARET FLEMING*

As another illustration of Garland's interest in the realistic drama, the following circular, now in the University of Southern California Library, is hereby reproduced.

A GENRE DRAMATIC PRODUCTION

Mr. and Mrs. Jas. A. Herne

in

MARGARET FLEMING

"An American Play without a Soliloquy."

at

Chickering Hall, Boston.

Week of May 4, 1891.

IN THE INTEREST OF AMERICAN DRAMA

It is generally admitted that the American drama is immeasurable below the work of American painters and novelists, and a despondent tone runs through much that is written upon the subject. We do not share this despondency. We believe with Mr. Howells, Mr. Perry and others of our critics in the comparative school, that literary ideals are relative, and that literature, and especially the drama follows intimately the changes in social life.

Without taking space to detail our reasons, we state our belief that we are on the eve of a great change in the drama commensurate with that already begun in the novel, that is, the change from the drama of plot and style to the drama of character and purpose.

The American public is large, and we believe there is a growing number of people to whom melodrama no longer appeals, and to whom farce comedy is a weariness, with its heartless as well as thoughtless caricature. This public is ready to welcome serious studies of American life.

We are convinced that this movement toward a higher dramatic art should be made—at least in its inception—along independent lines somewhat as in Paris and Berlin, maintaining, however, the same distinction as to choice of subjects that now exists between the French and American schools of novelists.

As a first modest trial of the independent art theatre we take genuine pleasure in calling attention to Mr. and Mrs. Herne's coming production of their latest play, "Margaret Fleming," at Chickering Hall, beginning May 4th. We do this the more readily because these thorough artists have been working alone and (in a literary way) unrecognized in the attempt to bring the accent of life upon the stage.

"Margaret Fleming" is not a perfect play, it could not reasonably be expected to be, but it has qualities which fit it to stand for the new idea, as Ibsen's "Young Men's Union" stood for the innovation in Norway, in 1869. It is absorbingly interesting, legitimately dramatic, has comedy as well as pathos, and mounts in the last act into an intellectual atmosphere unreached, so far as we know, in any other American play, and Mrs. Herne plays it with that marvelous art which conceals art, leaving the embodied character standing in place of the actress.

We thus publicly endorse Mr. and Mrs. Herne and their purposeful play, because they entirely merit our support, and also because we wish to oppose the pessimistic cry of "the decay of the drama." The drama changes but it never decays. There are scores of plays in America waiting the establishment of a theatre freed from necessity of compromise and whose production would be an honor and an inspiration, as we believe "Margaret Fleming" will prove to our stage.

B. O. Flower,
Hamlin Garland.

3. A READING OF *A MEMBER OF THE THIRD HOUSE*

The folder reproduced here, now in the University of Southern California Library, contains a program of a play written and read by Garland, which was never published but later converted into a novel under the name of A Member of the Third House. *The folder, probably dated 1891, lists also some newspaper clippings. It has been printed here since it adds to our knowledge of Garland's literary apprenticeship.*

AUTHOR'S READING
"A Member of the Third House"
A Play of To-Day
by
Hamlin Garland
(Copyrighted. All rights reserved.)

Mr. Hamlin Garland begs leave to announce the first public reading of his play at

CHICKERING HALL

Thursday, October 30th, at 2.30 P.M.

THE PROGRAMME WILL BE AS FOLLOWS:

Scene first.—Office of the Duke. "The gutter-snipe must rise."
Scene second.—Water-side. A game of tennis.
Scene third.—A casual call to buy a vote.
Scene fourth.—Committee Room B. The Joint Committee sitting.
Scene fifth.—In a *cul de sac*.

PERSONS CONCERNED IN THE SCENES.

Hon. Tom Brennan, Member of the Third House.
Lawrence B. Davis, the Iron Duke.
Helene Davis, his daughter.
Wilson F. Tuttle, the Scholar in Politics.
Senator Rufus Ward.
Mrs. Ward.
Evelyn Ward.
Samuel D. Fox, private Attorney for the Iron Duke.
Hon. Robert Binney, Attorney for Defence.
Attorney-General Russel, the Prosecution.
Hon. Pat Murnahan, }
Hon. Tim Sheehan, } Members of the House
Hon. Jacob Bloomb, representing the German vote.
P. Brooks Pierce.
James P. Smith, Chairman Joint Committee.

Members of Committee, Sergeant-at-Arms, Door Keeper, etc., etc.

Thursday, Oct. 30th, 2.30 P.M., sharp.
Reserved seats now on sale at Chickerings, 50 cents.
Wallace Spooner, Manager.

"Mr. Hamlin Garland read yesterday afternoon at Chickering Hall, before an audience made up chiefly of literary people, both authors and critics, his play entitled, 'A Member of the Third House.' He held the attention of the audience very closely, and the expressions and commendation should certainly be encouraging to a new playwright whose aim is to write plays for acting that shall show the life of our own times. Mr. Garland has certainly written a strong dramatic play. It has sufficient action to conform to the demands of the stage. It is powerful and sustained exposition of the eternal conflict between the power of money and the ideals of absolute righteousness."—*Boston Transcript*.

There was a very interesting difference of opinion upon the play as may be seen from the following candid comments:

The Boston Commonwealth: "It is a strong picture of the very worst influences that affect legislation. Direct, comprehensive."

The Boston Herald finds it "reportorial in style, lacking in humor and movement," whereas the *Post* expecting a "radical" play found it "theatrical as even a melodramatist could wish. Mr. Garland as a dramatist shows dramatic force and insight for character."

The Home Journal disagreed with both the *Post* and the *Herald*. "Mr. Garland has a conventional instinct for situation, but no power for developing character. Mr. Garland's play was pitilessly frank. His writing is often commonplace but often strong in its terseness and its fidelity to everyday life."

The Courier found it "ingeniously compounded in [an] argumentative way and administered with force and directness. Almost the same target which Mr. Hoyt has assaulted with small arms in his "Texas Steer" has also been assaulted by Mr. Hamlin Garland with heavier ordinance of his 'Member of the Third House.' Mr. Garland read his play very agreeably and well, and with an engaging earnestness of manner."

The Globe considered it "stirring, theatric, effective," and spent considerable space detailing its peculiar dramatic situations.

The Sunday Times thinks the author more interested in his theme than his characters, but adds: "Mr. Garland's play should be visited. It has, aside from its lesson, dramatic strength. Its art climaxes are theatrical, effective, and there are at least four characters that in the hands of capable actors would attract and hold the attention of an audience. Such a play, such an author are worthy all applause and encouragement. From such may come great plays—the American drama."

"A powerful play full of peculiarly dramatic situations."—
Boston Correspondent *Dramatic Mirror*.

"We found the play grand, not only in its moral purpose, but in its suitableness for stage presentation. Let us see this play properly staged and a blessing will fall upon us."—*American Art Journal*.

APPENDIX E

SOME OF THE BOOKS OF STEPHEN CRANE

The following bibliography is based upon a list in the Stephen Crane Collection in the Newark Public Library, Newark, N.J., and has not been published before. Since material on Crane's reading is scarce, it has seemed appropriate to include here the following brief record of books that once belonged to him.

Fielding, Henry. *Tom Jones.* London, 1880.
Frederic, Harold. *In the Valley.* London, 1891.
James, Henry. *The Bostonians.* London, 1886.
—— *Stories Revived.* London, 1885.
Kipling, Rudyard. *Many Inventions.* London, 1896.
—— *The Naulahka.* London, n.d.
Scott, Sir Walter. *Kenilworth.* London, n.d.

APPENDIX F

1. BOOKS OF FRANK NORRIS IN THE POSSESSION OF HIS WIDOW, MRS. JEANETTE (CHARLES N.) BLACK

The following bibliography includes some of the books which Frank Norris owned and which are now in the possession of his widow residing in San Francisco. Although the list is far from complete—in some cases it has not been possible to secure the place and date of publication—it is nevertheless significant. Among contemporaneous American authors we note volumes by Stephen Crane, Hamlin Garland, and Richard Harding Davis. Of the French writers listed Balzac, Flaubert, Prévost, and Zola ought to be mentioned. The works of Stevenson and Kipling are also on the list. Several of the books are inscribed in Norris's handwriting—note, for instance, the signature "The Boy Zola" in The Octopus—*others are autographed by the givers.*

Balzac, Honoré de. *Complete Works.* 19 vols. 1901.

Browning, Robert. *Works.*

Carlyle, Thomas. *Past and Present.* 1888.

Crane, Stephen. *George's Mother.* New York and London, 1896.

—— *The Red Badge of Courage.* New York, 1895. (Autographed by Frank Norris.)

—— *Wounds in the Rain.* New York, [1900]. (Autographed by Frank Norris.)

Davis, Richard Harding. *The West from a Car Window.* New York, [1892]. (Autographed by Frank Norris.)

Fielding, Henry. *Works.*

Flaubert, Gustave. *Madame Bovary.*

Garland, Hamlin. *The Captain of the Gray-Horse Troop.* New York and London, 1902. (Inscribed in Garland's hand: "To Frank Norris, March 18, 1902.")

—— *Prairie Folks.* Chicago, 1893. (Inscribed in Garland's hand: "To Mrs. Norris.")

Goethe, Johann Wolfgang. *Works.*

Harte, Bret. *Works.*

Horton, George. *The Tempting of Father Anthony.* Chicago, 1901. (Inscribed: "Chicago, September 23, 1901. To Frank Norris of the faithful, I present this book, which, I hope, is different. George Horton.")

Huneker, James Gibbons. *Melomaniacs.* New York, 1902. (Inscribed: "With the compliments of a Mr. James Gibbons Huneker confirmed Norris-maniac!")

Johnson, Samuel. *Rasselas: Prince of Abyssinia.*

Kipling, Rudyard, *Works.*

La Rochefoucauld, François, Duc de. *Maxims and Moral Reflections.* London, 1711. (Inscribed by Frank Norris: "Jeanette Black. Her book. August 1, 1899.")

Lark, The. Book I, Nos. 1–12, 1896. Book II, Nos. 13–24, 1897. (Inscribed: "To Frank Norris from his friend and admirer Frank Gelett Burgess, 1899.")

Macaulay, Thomas. *Little Masterpieces.* New York, 1898.

Montesquieu, Charles de S. *Persian Letters.* (Autographed by Frank Norris.)

Moore, Thomas. *Lalla Rookh.* (Inscribed by Frank Norris: "To Jeanette Black. Her book. November ninth, 1899.")

Norris, Frank. *Blix.* New York, 1899. (Inscribed: "Jeanette Black, her book. Frank Norris. September 8, 1899.")

—— *McTeague.* New York, 1899. (Inscribed: "To Jeanette Black. Very sincerely, Frank Norris. San Francisco, April 29, 1899.")

—— *A Man's Woman.* New York, 1900. (Inscribed: "To my wife Jeanette who gave me the idea of this story. Feb. 1900.")

—— *The Octopus.* New York, 1901. (Inscribed: "To my boss Jeanette Norris, most respectfully and as a testimony of sincere regard and deep admiration. Mr. Norris, Esq. (The Boy Zola)! Aug. 1901.")

Prévost, Marcel. *Lettres de Femmes.*

Saint-Pierre, J. H. Bernardin de. *Paul et Virginie.*

Schiller, Friedrich. *Works.*

Shakespeare, William. *Works.*

Sterne, Laurence. *Works.*

Stevenson, Robert Louis. *Works.*

Tennyson, Alfred. *Works.*

Thackeray, William M. *Works.*

White, William Allen. *The Court of Boyville.* New York, 1899.
(Autographed by Frank Norris.)

Zola, Émile.[1] *Pot-Bouille.* Paris, 1899.

—— *Le Rêve.* Paris, 1894.

—— *La Terre.* Paris.

—— *Le Ventre de Paris.* Paris, 1900.

2. FRANK NORRIS'S CHARACTER SKETCHES FOR *THE OCTOPUS*

The following manuscript notes in Norris's handwriting have never been published in their complete form, although one paragraph concerning Annixter was included in Franklin Walker's biography of Norris. The notes are now in the possession of Frank Norris's sister-in-law, Mrs. Kathleen (Charles G.) Norris, Palo Alto, Calif., and are printed here by her permission. It is interesting to observe how closely Norris adhered to his notes when he drew the characters of The Octopus. *One may compare these character sketches with those which Zola wrote in the preparation of his books. See, for instance,* La Terre *in* Œuvres, *XVI, 532–3.*

HILMA TREE. — Contrary Hilma and Angèle. Hilma always seen in sun. Angèle at night under moon. One hale, honest, radiant. The other mysterious, troublous, perplexing. Hilma the embodiment of day. Nineteen years old. A large girl. A certain amplitude of figure, of hips and shoulders that suggested the precocious maturity of a healthy, sane animal life. Her neck thick, slopes to her shoulders with full beautiful curves. Under her chin and ears the skin white as floss satin. Faint delicate brown on the nape of her neck, pale amber shadows under chin, on her throat, blending to sweet, warm flush of her cheeks. Mouth large. Lips always

---

[1] Mrs. Black informed me that other works of Zola that had belonged to Frank Norris were in her summer house in Arizona. The four books listed above were all bound in red, of which *Le Rêve* and *La Terre* had the following bookseller's seal: J. Tauzy and Co., 6 Port St. Booksellers, San Francisco. In the table of contents of the *Rougon-Macquart* series the following titles have been marked: *L'Assommoir, Nana, Germinal, La Terre, La Bête humaine, La Débâcle, Le Docteur Pascal.* Norris's copy of *La Terre* was well marked.

wet. Graceful charming outline of full wet lips and round white chin. Eyes, brown, opened wide on slightest provocation, disclosing the full disc of pupil. Eye lashes thick and dark—not long—rimmed her eyes with thin lines of black. Slightest movement of head and shoulders sent gentle undulations through all this beauty of soft outlines and smooth surfaces. The delicate amber shadows deepening or fading into the pretty rose color of her cheeks. Hair brown, thick, glossy, moist, lying in sweet-smelling masses low over her ears and nape, bitumen in shadow, vibrating with a sheen of tarnished gold in sun. Slow and deliberate in her movements. Her arms very large and white, pink finger tips. Her voice—a velvety huskiness, more of chest than throat. Great simplicity—statuesque evenness of contour. Straight lines of her carriage, single deep swell from waist to throat. Small contradictory suggestions of feminine daintiness. Her feet slim, the little steel buckles of her low shoes always brightly polished.

OSTERMAN. — About thirty. Singularly bald. Ears red and large, stuck out from either side [of] his head. His mouth large—a great horizontal slit beneath his nose. His cheeks a brownish red —cheek bones salient? His face that of a comic actor. A singer of songs. A poser, a wearer of clothes, always trying to draw attention to himself. Devotes his energy to small accomplishments. His desire of astonishing people, strong. Glib, ubiquitous, dexterous, voluble, strident, garrulous, a teller of funny stories, a cracker of jokes. Is mortgaged to S. Behrman. Continually striving to make a laugh. Never at a loss for an answer.

S. BEHRMAN. — Middle aged. Fat with a great stomach. Cheek and upper part of his neck run together to make a great tremulous jowl. Smooth shaven. *Blue gray* in color. Roll of fat over his collar. Sprinkled with sparse hairs. Black mustache. Round topped hat of stiff brown straw, highly varnished. "Light brown linen vest, stamped with innumerable interlocked horseshoes covered his protuberant stomach." Heavy watch chain of hollow links rose and fell with his difficult breathing, clinking against the vest buttons of imitation pearl. Never loses his temper. His fear of being shut in, an aversion to closed doors. "That may show obstinacy, but it don't [*sic*] show common sense."

BRODERSON. — An old man. Long beard, which he is in the habit of fingering. Does not understand the new agriculture. Cannot supervise, kills himself with overwork, no better than a higher order of farmhand. Out of his element in the West. Narrowminded, incapable of thinking of more than one thing at a time. Unable to let a subject drop. A slow thinker, conscientious to a powerful degree, losing himself in details, involving his conversation in a hopeless maze of inessential trivialities. Harassed by a morbid sense of justice. "Want [sic] to be fair and just to everybody." Scrupulously minute in his statements.

GENSLINGER. — About forty years old. Brown, dry, lean little man. Black hair. Wears glasses. His hands thin and osseous. Speaks with great rapidity and with nervous abrupt gestures. An alertness of manner that suggested the black and tan terrier. Prorailroad. Has a passion for statistics, for accurate information, figures, dimensions. Exact dates are his delight. Tape measure in his vest pocket. Compass on his watch chain. Almanac in hip pocket and table of metric system of weights and measures. Editor of *Bonneville Mercury*.

MRS. DERRICK (ANNIE). — Not far into the fifties. "Her brown hair still retains much of its brightness." Rather pretty. Her eyes large, easily assume a look of innocence and inquiry—a young girl's eyes. Look of uneasiness, almost of terror (of distrust and aversion) in her eyes when she is looking at the wheat field. Was teacher in seminary when married. Hated the droning heartbreaking routine of class room and music room. Ambitious to see Paris and Bay of Naples. *Marble Faun* and Trovadore her ideals. Reads *Marius* and Austin Dobson. Los Muertos frightens her.— She remembers the five hundred acres of the farm in Ohio—neatly portioned into lots. The direct brutality of ten thousand acres of wheat stunned her a little. "Something inordinate and unnatural" in this food of the People. This basic energy weltering there under the sun in all the unconscious nakedness of a sprawling primordial Titan. She easily obliterates herself. Is not made for the harshness of the world. Taught music and penmanship at the seminary, loathed the work. "The monotony of Los Muertos ate her heart hour by hour, year by year." No poetry in the rhythm of the seasons. Is very literary, conventional.

ANNIXTER. — Younger than Presley—about twenty-eight. A male cast of countenance. The jaw heavy, the lower lip thrust out. The chin masculine and deeply cleft. Stiff yellow hair, always in disorder. A little tuft of it always standing out from his crown like a feather on an Indian's scalp (lock). Continually seeking an argument. "In a way it is and then again in a way it isn't." *David Copperfield*. His stomach—eats dried prunes. A ferocious worker. Extremely inconsistent. Obstinate, contrary, dictatorial, wilful, perverse. Great executive ability. Very shrewd, far-sighted, suspicious. Admiration for Presley. The two great friends. Accepts no direct statement without modification. *A woman hater. Contradicts everything.* "Fool female girls" to take up a man's time. Suspicious that all women are "trying to get hold of him." Fear of involving himself in a petticoat mess. Clumsy when women are about. Talks about his "nature" and his stomach. His worst insult to call a man "a Pip." Spits with wonderful accuracy. Whit. Hates Derrick's cat. Belligerent, truculent, turbulent, irascible. "Hooks, nails and fetters." "Horse, foot and dragoon." "Lock, stock and barrell."

PRESLEY. — Thirty years old. Of a mixed origin. Composite. A character more than a type. Face almost swarthy. Dark brown eyes. His forehead that of [an] educated [person]. Certain unmistakable *lift* about it. Mouth and chin delicate and sensitive. Thin, loose lips. Wears corduroys, laced boots, sunbleached shooting coat. Incessantly smoking cigarettes. His "Song of the West." Searching for the *Epic*. Refinement gained at a loss of strength. Introspective. Morbid. Brooding instead of thinking. Eastern college. Post graduate. Love of Homer. Does not believe in style. Things without names, thoughts for which no man had yet invented words, terrible formless shapes, vague figures, colossal, monstrous, distorted, whirled at a gallop through his imagination. Hates the ranch and the People at first. Turns anarchist. Friendship with Caraher. Excitable, easily impressed. Impressionable, melancholic disposition, capable of extremes of exaltation. Almost prophetic —seer—an unbalanced mind. Could easily go insane.

LYMAN DERRICK. — About thirty or thirty-one. Physical resemblance to mother. Very dark. Protruding eyes, foreign appearance, unusual, unexpected. Little black mustache, that he pushes up from corners of the mouth with ball of thumb. The little finger extended. Little twitchy movement of fore arm to bring his cuff to view. A born politician. Distaste for ranching. State university. Three years [of] law school. Diplomatic, approachable, has talent for making friends. A genius for putting influential people under obligations. Has been sheriff's attorney and assistant district attorney. Moderate ambition. Unscrupulousness develops this. Belongs to the new school of politics as opposed to the old school. *Is bent upon being Governor of the State,* succeeding where his father failed.

HARRAN DERRICK. — Between twenty-three and twenty-five. Had the *fine carriage* that marked his father. The same *hawk-like prominent nose.* Duke of Wellington. Blond. High color in his cheeks instead of tan. Yellow hair that has an audacity to curl in forward direction in front of ears. Younger son of Magnus. Is overseer and head manager (superintendent) of Rancho de Los Muertos. Occupies himself with details of his father's plans. Stands for alternate system of farming as opposed to Magnus's no-system.

ANGÈLE. — Eighteen years old. Contrast with Hilma. The embodiment of night. Hair of gold hanging in two straight plaits on either side [of] her face, making three-cornered her round white forehead. Her wonderful eyes. Violet blue, heavy lidded with their astonishing upward slant toward the temples. The slant that gave a strange Oriental cast to her face. Perplexing, enchanting. The almost Nubian, Negroidal, Egyptian fullness of the lips. The strange balancing movement of her head upon her slender neck. The same movement slow, weaving that one sees in a snake at poise. "Never had he seen a girl more radiantly beautiful, never a beauty so strange, so troublous, so out of all accepted standards." Pallid gold and pale carnation. She is the symbol of the wheat.

MAGNUS DERRICK. — Sixty years old. All of six feet. *Erect* as an officer of cavalry. A sense of gravity. Imposing respect. Smooth shaven. Thin lipped. Broad chin. Prominent hawk-like nose, thin like later portraits of the Duke of Wellington. Thin.

Erect. Thick, grey hair, that had a tendency to curl in forward direction toward the temples. Top hat of gray, wide brim. Frock coat. Cane with yellow ivory handle. A politician of the old school. Unsuccessful candidate for governor. An old time gambler. The reckless, haphazard spirit of '49. Unscientific. Has no genius for detail. The prominent man. Presides wherever he is. Dominates. "Certain grandiose lavishness of disposition." Does things on a grand scale. Patriarchal. Always ready to take chances. Haphazarding on the hope of colossal returns. Considers farming a gamble. Unwilling to husband resources of land. Great affection of Harran. Stands with one hand in the breast of his frock coat.

BIBLIOGRAPHY

i. MANUSCRIPT MATERIAL

Hamlin Garland

The extensive Hamlin Garland Collection in the Doheny Library of the University of Southern California, Los Angeles, includes unpublished manuscripts, diaries, notebooks, lecture notes, letters to and copies and originals of letters from Garland, books, and some marginalia. Citations of manuscripts, letters, and lecture notes in the text refer to this collection unless otherwise noted. The Garland-Gilder correspondence is available in the New York Public Library. A few Garland letters are to be found in the Newberry Library, Chicago, Ill. This library also has significant unpublished material on Joseph Kirkland and Henry B. Fuller.

Stephen Crane

The Stephen Crane Collection in the Newark Public Library, N.J., has clippings and memorabilia. The Stephen Crane Collection at Dartmouth College, N.H., includes some unpublished letters and other material of interest. Mr. Ames W. Williams' private collection of Crane material is made up of unpublished letters, books, uncollected articles, and some marginalia. The manuscript of Crane's story "The Five White Mice" is in the Henry E. Huntington Library.

Frank Norris

A few unpublished letters of Frank Norris are available in the Hamlin Garland Collection in the Doheny Library and in the New York Public Library. The manuscript of the character sketches for *The Octopus* is in the possession of Mrs. Kathleen (Charles G.) Norris. Professor Franklin Walker's private collection of Norris material includes letters, notes on interviews, and memorabilia.

2. EDITIONS USED

(Deviations from this list are duly noted in the text.)

Hamlin Garland[1]

"Under the Wheel," *Arena*, II (July, 1890), 182–228.
Main-Travelled Roads. Chicago and New York, 1898.
Jason Edwards. Boston, 1892.
A Member of the Third House. Chicago, [1892].
A Little Norsk. New York, 1892.
"A Spoil of Office,"[2] *Arena*, V (January–May, 1892), 253–68, 376–400, 495–522, 619–44, 749–74 and *ibid.*, VI (June, 1892), 104–32.
Prairie Folks. Chicago, 1895.
Crumbling Idols. Chicago and Cambridge, 1894.
Rose of Dutcher's Coolly.[3] Sunset ed. New York and London, [1899].
Wayside Courtships. New York, 1897.

Stephen Crane

The Work of Stephen Crane. Ed. Wilson Follett. 12 vols. New York, [1925–7]. Referred to as *Work*.

Frank Norris

The Complete Works of Frank Norris. 10 vols. Garden City, N.Y., 1928. Referred to as *Compl. Works*.

Émile Zola

Œuvres complètes. Ed. François Bernouard. 50 vols. Paris, [1927–9]. Referred to as *Œuvres*.

Henrik Ibsen

Eleven Plays of Henrik Ibsen. Introduction by H. L. Mencken. Mod. Lib. ed. New York, n. d. Referred to as *Plays*.

---

[1] Works listed chronologically according to first appearance in book form. Brackets [ ] about a date or a place of publication indicate that the material does not appear on the title page but is derived from other sources.

[2] This novel has not been available in book form.

[3] The title page has erroneously *The Rose of Dutcher's Coolly*.

470

3. PERIODICALS

Ainslee's (Magazine). New York, 1898–1926.
America. Chicago, 1888–91.
American. Philadelphia, 1880–1900.
Arena. Boston, (New York), 1889–1909.
Atlantic Monthly. Boston, 1857+.
Bookman. New York, 1895–1933.
Century (Magazine). New York, 1870–1930.
Chap-Book. Chicago, 1894–8.
Cosmopolitan. New York, 1886–1925.
Critic. New York, 1881–1906.
Dial. Chicago, 1880–1929.
Forum. New York 1886–1930.
Harper's Monthly (Magazine). New York, 1850+.
Harper's Weekly. New York, 1857–1916.
Independent. New York, (Boston), 1848–1928.
Literary World. Boston, 1870–1904.
Literature. New York, 1897–9.
Living Age. Boston, 1844+.
McClure's Magazine. New York, 1893–1929.
Munsey's Magazine. New York, 1889–1929.
Nation. New York, 1865+.
North American Review. Boston, (New York) 1815–1940.
Outlook. New York, 1870–1935.
Philistine. East Aurora, N.Y., 1895–1915.
Popular Science Monthly. New York, 1872+.
Scribner's Magazine. New York, 1887–1939.
Wave. San Francisco, 1887–1901 [?].

4. BOOKS

(This bibliography includes all the works quoted and other
works consulted.)

ADAMS, HENRY. *The Education of Henry Adams.* Mod. Lib. ed. New York,
[1931].
ADAMS, JAMES TRUSLOW. *The Epic of America.* Garden City, N.Y., [1941].
AHLSTRÖM, GUNNAR. *Det moderna genombrottet i Nordens litteratur.*
Stockholm, 1947.
—— *Georg Brandes' Hovedstrømninger: En ideologisk undersökning.*
Diss. Lund, [1937].
ÅHNEBRINK, LARS. *The Influence of Émile Zola on Frank Norris.* In
Essays and Studies on American Language and Literature, V. Upsala
and Cambridge, [1947].
ALLEN, GRANT. *The Woman Who Did.* London, 1895.

ALLEN, JAMES LANE. *Summer in Arcady*. New York and London, 1896.
ALLEN, RALPH BERGEN. *Old Icelandic Sources in the English Novel*. Diss. Philadelphia, 1933.
AMERICAN GUIDE SERIES. *Hamlin Garland Memorial*. [Mitchell, S.D.], 1939.
ARRIGHI, PAUL. *Le Vérisme dans la prose narrative italienne*. In *Études de littérature étrangère et comparée*, IV. Thèse. Paris, 1937.
BALZAC, HONORÉ DE. *Eugénie Grandet*. Paris, 1892.
—— *Le Père Goriot*. Paris, 1892.
BEACH, J. W. *The Twentieth Century Novel*. New York, 1932.
BEARD, CHARLES A. and BEARD, MARY R. *The Rise of American Civilization*. New York, [1945].
BEER, THOMAS. *The Mauve Decade*. Garden City, N.Y., [1926].
—— *Stephen Crane: A Study in American Letters*. Garden City, N.Y., 1927.
BELLAMY, EDWARD. *Looking Backward, 2000–1887*. New York, [1917].
BENNEWITZ, HILDEGARD. *Die Charaktere in den Romanen Joseph Conrads*. Diss. Greifswald, 1933.
BERGER, IDA. *La Description du prolétariat dans le roman naturaliste allemand*. Paris, 1935.
BESANT, WALTER. *The Art of Fiction*. Boston, 1884.
BIENCOURT, MARIUS. *Une Influence du naturalisme français en Amérique: Frank Norris*. Thèse. Paris, 1933.
BIERCE, AMBROSE. *Can Such Things Be?* New York, 1893.
—— *In the Midst of Life*. New York, 1898.
—— *Tales of Soldiers and Civilians*. New York, 1891.
BIERHOFF, ERICH. *Das Verhältnis zwischen "hérédité," "milieu" und "moment" in Zolas Romanen*. In *Arbeiten zur Romanischen Philologie*, XI. Diss. Münster, 1934.
BING, JUST. *Litteraturens inre utveckling under det nittonde århundradet*. Stockholm, 1924.
BJØRNSON, BJØRNSTJERNE. *Samlede værker*. Mindeutgave. 5 vols. Christiania and Copenhagen, 1910–11.
BLANCK, JACOB. *Merle Johnson's American First Editions*. New York, [1947].
BLANKENSHIP, RUSSELL. *American Literature*. New York, [1931].
BORCHERS, LOTTE. *Frauengestalten und Frauenprobleme bei Henry James*. Diss. Berlin, 1929.
BOUTCHIK (BUČIK), VLADIMIR. *La Littérature russe en France*. Paris, [1947].
BOWERS, DAVID F., ed. *Foreign Influences in American Life*. Princeton, N.J., 1944.
BOYESEN, HJALMAR HJORTH. *The Mammon of Unrighteousness*. New York, 1891.
BOYNTON, PERCY H. *A History of American Literature*. New York, 1919.
BRADBROOK, M. C. *Ibsen, the Norwegian: A Revaluation*. London, 1946.

472

BRENEL, HJALMAR. *Etiska motiv i Henrik Ibsens dramatiska diktning*. Diss. Uppsala, 1941.

BROOKS, VAN WYCK. *New England: Indian Summer, 1865–1915*. New York, 1940.

BROWN, E. K. *Edith Wharton: Étude critique*. Thèse. Paris, 1935.

BROWN, SYDNEY BARLOW. *La Peinture des métiers et des mœurs professionnelles dans les romans de Zola*. Thèse. Montpellier, 1928.

BRUNETIÈRE, F. *Le Roman naturaliste*. Paris, 1897.

BRUNS, FRIEDRICH. *Die amerikanische Dichtung der Gegenwart*. Leipzig and Berlin, 1930.

BUDKE, WILLI. *Die Darstellung der Frau bei Thomas Hardy unter besonderer Berücksichtigung Schopenhauers*. Diss. Greifswald, [1933].

CAHAN, A. *Yekl: A Tale of the New York Ghetto*. New York, 1899.

CALVERTON, V. F. *The Liberation of American Literature*. New York, 1932.

CARGILL, OSCAR. *Intellectual America: Ideas on the March*. New York, 1941.

CAZAMIAN, MADELEINE L. *Le Roman et les idées en Angleterre: L'Influence de la science (1860–1890)*. In *Publications de la faculté des lettres de l'université de Strasbourg*, XV. Thèse. Strasbourg and Paris, 1923.

CESARI, PAUL. *Les Déterminismes et les êtres*. Thèse. Paris, 1938.

CHOPIN, KATE. *At Fault*. St Louis, 1890.

—— *The Awakening*. Chicago, 1899.

CLAUS, HORST. *Studien zur Geschichte des deutschen Frühnaturalismus*. Diss. Halle, 1933.

CLEMENS, SAMUEL L. and WARNER, CHARLES DUDLEY. *The Gilded Age*. New York and London, [1915].

COMMONS, J. R. *Races and Immigrants in America*. New York, 1920.

COMTE, AUGUSTE. *La Philosophie positive*. Paris, 1880.

CONRAD, JOSEPH. *The Nigger of the Narcissus*. London, 1897.

COOPER, FREDERIC TABER. *Some American Story Tellers*. London, 1912.

COWIE, ALEXANDER. *The Rise of the American Novel*. New York, [1948].

COX, ROY ALAN. *Dominant Ideas in the Works of Guy de Maupassant*. In *The University of Colorado Studies*, XIX, No. 2. Boulder, Colo., 1932.

CRANE, STEPHEN. *Men, Women and Boats*. New York, [1921].

—— *The Red Badge of Courage*. Mod. Lib. ed. New York, [1925].

—— *The Work of Stephen Crane*. Ed. Wilson Follett. 12 vols. New York, [1925–7]. [*Work*.]

CRAVEN, AVERY and JOHNSON, WALTER. *The United States: Experiment in Democracy*. Chicago, [1947].

CRAWFORD, F. MARION. *The Novel: What It Is*. London and New York, 1896.

CROSS, WILBUR L. *The Development of the English Novel*. New York, 1899.

CURTI, MERLE. *The Growth of American Thought*. New York and London, [1943].

DAINTREY, LAURA. *Gold.* New York, 1893.
DANGELZER, JOAN YVONNE. *La Description du milieu dans le roman français de Balzac à Zola.* Thèse. Paris, 1938.
DARWIN, CHARLES. *The Origin of Species and The Descent of Man.* Mod. Lib. ed. New York, n.d.
DAUDET, ALPHONSE. *Jack.* Paris, 1889.
—— *Sapho.* Paris, 1888.
DAVID-SAUVAGEOT, A. *Le Réalisme et le naturalisme dans la littérature et dans l'art.* Paris, 1890.
DE MILLE, GEORGE E. *Literary Criticism in America: A Preliminary Survey.* New York, 1931.
DEFFOUX, LÉON. *Le Naturalisme.* Paris, 1929.
DELAND, MARGARET. *John Ward, Preacher.* Boston and New York, 1888.
DOSTOEVSKY, FEODOR. *Arma människor.* Stockholm, [1920].
—— *The Brothers Karamazov.* Mod. Lib. ed. New York, n.d.
—— *Crime and Punishment.* Liv. Lib. ed. Cleveland and New York, [1947].
—— *The Idiot.* Mod. Lib. ed. New York, [1935].
DOUCET, F. *L'Esthétique d'Émile Zola et son application à la critique.* Thèse. The Hague, [1923].
DOWNS, BRIAN W. *Ibsen: The Intellectual Background.* Cambridge, 1946.
DREISER, THEODORE. *Sister Carrie.* Mod. Lib. ed. New York, [1917].
DU MAURIER, GEORGE. *Trilby.* New York, 1894.
DUDLEY, DOROTHY. *Forgotten Frontiers: Dreiser and the Land of the Free.* New York, 1932.
DUMESNIL, RENÉ. *L'Époque réaliste et naturaliste.* Paris, 1945.
EIKELAND, P. J. *Ibsen Studies.* Northfield, Minn., 1934.
EGGLESTON, EDWARD. *The Circuit Rider.* New York, 1874.
—— *The Hoosier School-Master.* New York, 1889.
—— *Roxy.* New York, [1878].
ELIAS, ROBERT H. *Theodore Dreiser: Apostle of Nature.* New York, 1949.
EMERSON, RALPH WALDO. *Essays.* New York, [1945].
FARMER, ALBERT J. *Le Mouvement esthétique et "décadent" en Angleterre (1873–1900).* Thèse. Paris, 1931.
FAULKNER, HAROLD UNDERWOOD. *American Economic History.* New York, 1924.
—— *American Political and Social History.* New York, 1946.
—— *The Quest for Social Justice, 1898–1914.* In *A History of American Life,* XI. New York, [1946].
FAWCETT, EDGAR. *A Man's Will.* New York, 1888.
FAŸ, BERNARD. *Civilisation américaine.* Paris, [1939].
FIRKINS, INA TEN EYCK. *Henrik Ibsen: A Bibliography of Criticism and Biography with an Index to Characters.* New York, 1921.
FIRKINS, OSCAR W. *William Dean Howells: A Study.* Cambridge, Mass., 1924.
FISCHER, FRIEDRICH. *George Bernard Shaw als Dramatiker und sein Verhältnis zu Henrik Ibsen.* Diss. Weimar, 1917.

474

FISCHER, WALTER. *Die englische Literatur der Vereinigten Staten von Nordamerika.* In *Handbuch der Literaturwissenschaft,* IV. Wildpark-Potsdam, [1929].

FLAUBERT, GUSTAVE. *Correspondance.* 4 vols. Paris, 1920.

—— *Madame Bovary.* Paris, 1884.

—— *Salammbô.* Paris, 1887.

FOERSTER, NORMAN, ed. *American Critical Essays: XIXth and XXth Centuries.* London, [1930].

FOGELQVIST, TORSTEN. *Henrik Ibsen i hans förhållande till samhälle och samhällsproblem. Några sociala synpunkter.* In *Verdandis småskrifter,* CXL. Stockholm, 1914.

FORD, FORD MADOX (HUEFFER, F. M.). *Portraits from Life.* Boston and New York, 1937.

—— *Thus to Revisit.* London, 1921.

FRANC, MIRIAM ALICE. *Ibsen in England.* Boston, 1919.

FRANKE, CARL. *Émile Zola als romantischer Dichter.* Diss. Marburg a. L., 1914.

FREDERIC, HAROLD. *The Damnation of Theron Ware or Illumination.* New York, 1896.

—— *In the Sixties.* New York, 1897.

—— *The Lawton Girl.* New York, 1899.

—— *Seth's Brother's Wife.* New York, 1897.

FREEMAN, MARY E. WILKINS. *A New England Nun and Other Stories.* New York, 1891.

FREIHOW, HALVDAN WEXELSEN. *Henrik Ibsens "Brand": Litterær-psykologisk studie.* Oslo, 1936.

FRENCH, ALICE. *Knitters in the Sun.* New York, 1887.

—— *Stories of a Western Town.* New York, 1893.

FRIEDMAN, I. K. *By Bread Alone.* New York, 1901.

—— *Poor People.* Boston, 1900.

FRIERSON, WILLIAM C. *L'Influence du naturalisme français sur les romanciers Anglais de 1885 à 1900.* Thèse. Paris, 1925.

FULLER, HENRY, B. *The Cliff-Dwellers.* New York, 1893.

—— *With the Procession.* New York, 1895.

GARLAND, HAMLIN. *See* Appendix A and Editions Used, pp. 421-3, 469.

GARNETT, EDWARD. *Friday Nights.* New York, 1922.

—— *Turgenev: A Study.* London, [1917].

GARNIER, MARIE-REINE. *Henry James et la France.* In *Bibliothèque de la revue de littérature comparée,* XLIV. Paris, 1927.

GEORGE, HENRY. *Progress and Poverty.* New York, 1889.

GETTMANN, ROYAL A. *Turgenev in England and America.* In *Illinois Studies in Language and Literature,* XXVII, No. 2. Urbana, Ill., 1941.

GHENT, WILLIAM J. *Our Benevolent Feudalism.* New York, 1902.

GIBSON, WILLIAM M. and ARMS, GEORGE. *A Bibliography of William Dean Howells.* New York, 1948.

GISSING, GEORGE R. *The Emancipated.* London, 1890.

—— *The Nether World.* London, 1889.

GISSING, GEORGE R. *New Grub Street.* London, 1892.
—— *The Unclassed.* London, 1884.
GLASGOW, ELLEN. *The Descendant.* New York and Lodon, 1900.
GONCHAROV, IVAN ALEXANDROVITCH. *Oblomov.* London and New York, [1946].
GONCOURT, EDMUND and JULES DE. *Germinie Lacerteux.* Paris, 1875.
GOSSE, EDMUND. *Ibsen.* London, 1907.
—— *Studies in the Literature of Northern Europe.* London, 1879.
GRAN, GERHARD. *Henrik Ibsen: Liv og verker.* 2 vols. Christiania, 1918.
GRANT, ROBERT. *Unleavened Bread.* New York, 1900.
GRESIK, GERTRUD. *Giovanni Vergas Kunst und ihre Beziehungen zur Dichtung des französischen Realismus und Naturalismus.* Diss. Breslau, 1940.
GRIFFITH, BENJAMIN. *Balzac aux États-Unis.* Thèse. Paris, [1931].
GRÖNBECH, V. *Dostojefski og hans Russland.* Copenhagen, 1948.
GÜNTHER, IRMGARD. *Die Einwirkung des skandinavischen Romans auf den deutschen Naturalismus.* In *Nordische Studien,* XIV. Greifswald, 1934.
GUNDEL, SVEN. *Dansk Digtning fra Halvfjerdserne til Nutiden: Naturalismens Historie i Omrids.* Copenhagen, 1933.
HALL, ERNEST JACKSON. *The Satirical Element in the American Novel.* Diss. Philadelphia, 1922.
HALPÉRINE-KAMINSKY, E. *Ivan Tourguéneff d'après sa correspondance avec ses amis Français.* Paris, 1901.
HALVORSEN, J. B. *Bibliografiske Oplysninger til Henrik Ibsens Samlede Værker.* Copenhagen, *1901.*
HANS, WILHELM. *Schicksal und Wille: Ein Versuch über Ibsens Weltanschauung.* München, 1906.
HARDY, THOMAS. *Far from the Madding Crowd.* London, 1893.
—— *Jude the Obscure.* London, 1903.
—— *The Return of the Native.* London, 1884.
—— *Tess of the D'Urbervilles.* London, 1891.
HARE, R. *Russian Literature from Pushkin to the Present Day.* London, 1947.
HARKINS, E. F. *The Schemers.* Boston, 1903.
HART, JAMES D. *The Oxford Companion to American Literature.* New York, [1944].
HARTWICK, HARRY. *The Foreground of American Fiction.* New York, 1934.
HATCHER, HARLAN. *Creating the Modern American Novel.* New York, 1935.
HAYES, CARLTON J. H. *A Generation of Materialism, 1871–1900.* New York, 1941.
HAZARD, LUCY LOCKWOOD. *The Frontier in American Literature.* New York, 1941.
HENKIN, LEO. *Darwinism in the English Novel.* New York, 1940.
HERRICK, ROBERT. *The Gospel of Freedom.* New York, 1898.
—— *The Web of Life.* New York, 1900.

476

HERRON, IMA HONAKER. *The Small Town in American Literature.* Durham, N.C., 1939.

HICKS, GRANVILLE. *The Great Tradition.* New York, [1935].

HICKS, JOHN D. *The Populist Revolt.* Minneapolis, 1931.

HILL, ELDON C. *A Biographical Study of Hamlin Garland from 1860 to 1895.* Unpublished diss. Ohio State Univ. Columbus, Ohio, 1940.

HILL, JAMES J. *Highways of Progress.* New York, 1910.

HLAUSCHEK, HELMUT. *Der Entwicklungsbegriff in den theoretisch-programmatischen Schriften des frühen Naturalismus.* Diss. Wien, 1941.

HOARE, DOROTHY M. *The Works of Morris and of Yeats in Relation to Early Saga Literature.* Cambridge, 1937.

HOFSTADTER, RICHARD. *Social Darwinism in American Thought, 1860–1915.* Philadelphia, 1945.

HOPPE, HANS. *Impressionismus und Expressionismus bei Émile Zola.* In *Arbeiten zur Romanischen Philologie,* I. Diss. Münster, 1933.

HOWE, E. W. *The Story of a Country Town.* New York, 1927.

HOWELLS, MILDRED, ed. *Life in Letters of William Dean Howells.* 2 vols. New York, [1928].

HOWELLS, WILLIAM DEAN. *Annie Kilburn.* New York, 1889.

—— *Criticism and Fiction.* New York, 1891.

—— *A Hazard of New Fortunes.* New York, 1890.

—— *Heroines of Fiction.* New York, 1901.

—— *The Minister's Charge.* Boston, 1887.

—— *A Modern Instance.* Boston, 1882.

—— *My Literary Passions.* New York, 1895.

—— *The Rise of Silas Lapham.* Boston, 1885.

—— *The World of Chance.* New York, 1893.

HUBER, ROBERT. *Ibsens Bedeutung für das englische Drama.* Diss. Marburg a. d. L., 1914.

HUNT, THEODORE. *Le Roman américain, 1830–1850.* Thèse. Paris, 1937.

HUXLEY, T. H. *Evolution and Ethics and Other Essays.* New York, 1894.

HUYSMANS, J.-K. *A Rebours.* Paris, 1922.

IBSEN, HENRIK. *Eleven Plays of Henrik Ibsen.* Introduction by H. L. Mencken. Mod. Lib. ed. New York, n. d. [*Plays.*]

—— *Samlede Værker.* 10 vols. Copenhagen, 1898–1902.

JAMES, HENRY. *The Princess Casamassima.* London, 1886.

—— *What Maisie Knew.* Chicago, 1897.

JOHNSON, ROB. U. and BUEL, C. C., eds. *Battles and Leaders of the Civil War.* 4 vols. New York, 1887-9.

JONES, HOWARD MUMFORD. *The Theory of American Literature.* Ithaca, N.Y., 1948.

—— and LEISY, ERNEST E. *Major American Writers.* New York, 1935.

JOSEPHSON, MATTHEW. *Zola and His Time.* London, 1929.

JÜRGENSEN, HANS. *Henrik Ibsens Einfluss auf Hermann Sudermann.* Diss. Heilbronn a. N., [1903].

KASTEN, HELMUT. *Die Idee der Dichtung und des Dichters in den literarischen Theorien des sogenannten "deutschen Naturalismus."* Diss. Würzburg, 1938.

KAZIN, ALFRED. *On Native Grounds: An Interpretation of Modern American Prose Literature.* New York, [1942].

KELLEY, CORNELIA PULSIFER. *The Early Development of Henry James.* In *Illinois Studies in Language and Literature*, XV, Nos. 1–2. Urbana, Ill., 1930.

KERST, HENRI, ed. *Romanciers Américains contemporains.* In *Cahiers des langues modernes*, I. Paris, [1946].

KIHLMAN, ERIK. *Ur Ibsen-dramatikens idéhistoria.* Helsinki, 1921.

KING, GRACE. *Tales of a Time and Place.* New York, 1892.

KIPLING, RUDYARD. *The Works of Rudyard Kipling.* Service ed. 26 vols. London, 1914–19.

KIRKLAND, JOSEPH. *The McVeys.* Boston and New York, 1888.

—— *Zury: The Meanest Man in Spring County.* Chicago, 1887.

KOCH, SIGFRID VON. *Farmertypen nach dem amerikanischen Roman.* Diss. Hamburg, 1933.

KÖNINGSBERGER, SUSANNE. *Die Romantechnik von William Dean Howells.* Diss. Berlin, 1933.

KRAG, ERIK. *Leo Tolstoi.* Oslo, 1937.

KRIKORIAN, YERVANT H., ed. *Naturalism and the Human Spirit.* New York, 1944.

KRUTCH, JOSEPH WOOD. *The Modern Temper.* New York, [1929].

LANSON, GUSTAVE. *Historie de la littérature française.* Paris, 1920.

—— *Méthodes de l'histoire littéraire.* Paris, 1925.

LAVRIN, JANKO. *Tolstoy: An Approach.* London, 1944.

LEACH, HENRY GODDARD. *Scandinavia and the Scandinavians.* London, 1915.

LEGOUIS, ÉMILE and CAZAMIAN, LOUIS. *A History of English Literature.* New York, [1940].

LEON, DERRICK. *Tolstoy: His Life and Work.* London, [1944].

LERMONTOFF, MICHAEL. *Ein Held unsrer Zeit.* Leipzig, n.d.

LEVIN, POUL. *Den naturalistiske Roman.* Copenhagen and Christiania, 1907.

LEWIS, ALFRED HENRY. *Sandburrs.* New York, 1900.

LILJEGREN, S. B. *The Revolt against Romanticism in American Literature as Evidenced in the Works of S. L. Clemens.* In *Essays and Studies on American Language and Literature*, I. Upsala, 1945.

LINDER, STEN. *Ernst Ahlgren i hennes romaner: Ett bidrag till det litterära åttitalets karakteristik.* Diss. Stockholm, [1930].

—— *Ibsen, Strindberg och andra: Litteraturhistoriska essäer.* Stockholm, 1936.

LONDON, CHARMIAN. *The Book of Jack London.* 2 vols. New York, 1921.

LONDON, JACK. *The Call of the Wild.* New York, 1903.

—— *A Daughter of the Snows.* New York, 1905.

—— *The Son of the Wolf.* Boston, 1900.

478

LOTE, G. *La Doctrine et la méthode naturalistes d'après Émile Zola.* In *Zeitschrift für französische Sprache und Litteratur*, LI, 193–224, 389–418. Jena and Leipzig, 1928.

MACMILLAN COMPANY. *Hamlin Garland: A Son of the Middle Border.* [New York], n.d.

McWILLIAMS, CAREY. *Ambrose Bierce: A Biography.* New York, 1929.

MARCHAND, ERNEST. *Frank Norris: A Study.* Stanford Univ., Calif., [1942].

MARCOSSON, ISAAC F. *Adventures in Interviewing.* New York, 1923.

MARTIN, EDWARD W. *History of the Grange Movement.* San Francisco, 1874.

MARTINO, P. *Le Naturalisme français (1870–1895).* Paris, 1930.

MASSIS, HENRI. *Comment Émile Zola composait ses romans.* Paris, 1906.

MATTHIESSEN, F. O. *Henry James: The Major Phase.* New York, 1944.

MAUPASSANT, GUY DE. *The Complete Short Stories of Guy de Maupassant.* New York, [1903].

—— *Pierre et Jean.* New York, [1936].

MAUROIS, ANDRÉ. *Turgenev.* Stockholm, [1932].

MEISSNER, PAUL. *Der Bauer in der englischen Literatur.* In *Bonner Studien zur englischen Philologie*, XV. Bonn, 1922.

MEREDITH, GEORGE. *The Egoist.* London, 1889.

MICHAUD, RÉGIS. *The American Novel To-Day.* Boston, 1928.

MILLETT, FRED B. *Contemporary American Authors.* New York, 1944.

MOORE, GEORGE. *Confessions of a Young Man.* London, 1888.

—— *A Drama in Muslin.* London, 1886–7.

—— *Esther Waters.* London, 1894.

—— *Impressions and Opinions.* London, 1895.

—— *A Modern Lover.* London, 1883.

—— *A Mummer's Wife.* London, 1893.

MORRIS, WILLIAM. *The Collected Works of William Morris.* 24 vols. London, 1910–15.

MORRISON, ARTHUR. *Tales of Mean Streets.* London, 1894.

MORTENSEN, JOHAN. *Från Röda Rummet till sekelskiftet.* Stockholm, [1918].

MUCHNIC, HELEN. *Dostoevsky's English Reputation (1881–1936).* In *Smith College Studies in Modern Languages*, XX, Nos. 3–4. Northampton, Mass., 1939.

—— *An Introduction to Russian Literature.* Garden City, N.Y., 1947.

MULLER, HERBERT J. *Modern Fiction: A Study of Values.* New York and London, 1937.

MYERS, GUSTAVUS. *History of the Great American Fortunes.* Mod. Lib. ed. New York, [1910].

NEUSCHÄFFER, WALTER. *Dostojewskijs Einfluss auf den englischen Roman.* In *Anglistische Forschungen*, LXXXI. Heidelberg, 1935.

NEVINS, ALLAN. *The Emergence of Modern America, 1865–1878.* In *A History of American Life*, VIII. New York, [1944].

NIEMANN, LUDWIG. *Soziologie des naturalistischen Romans.* In *Germanische Studien,* CXLVIII. Berlin, 1934.

NORDAU, MAX. *Die Conventionellen Lügen der Kulturmenschheit.* Leipzig, 1884.

—— *Entartung.* Berlin, 1893.

NORRIS, CHARLES G. *Frank Norris, 1870–1902.* New York, [1914].

NORRIS, FRANK. *The Complete Works of Frank Norris.* 10 vols. Garden City, N.Y., 1928. [*Compl. Works.*]

—— *Frank Norris of "The Wave."* San Francisco, 1931.

ODELL, GEORGE CLINTON DENSMORE. *Annals of the New York Stage, 1891–1894.* Vol. XV. New York, 1949.

PARRINGTON, VERNON LOUIS. *Main Currents in American Thought.* 3 vols. in one. New York, [1930].

PATTEE, FRED LEWIS. *The Development of the American Short Story.* New York and London, 1923.

—— *The New American Literature, 1890–1930.* New York and London, [1930].

PATTERSON, J. G. *A Zola Dictionary.* London, 1912.

PAXSON, F. L. *The Last American Frontier.* New York, 1910.

PAYNE, WILL. *The Story of Eva.* Boston and New York, 1901.

PERRY, RALPH BARTON. *Puritanism and Democracy.* New York, [1944].

PETERS, RUDOLF. *Der Bauer im französischen Roman von Marivaux bis zur Gegenwart.* Diss. Strassburg, 1914.

PETTERSEN, HJALMAR. *Henrik Ibsen bedømt af samtid og eftertid.* Oslo, 1928.

PHELPS, WILLIAM LYON. *The Advance of the English Novel.* London, 1919.

PHILLIPS, DAVID GRAHAM. *The Great God Success.* New York, 1901.

QUINN, ARTHUR HOBSON. *American Fiction: An Historical and Critical Survey.* New York and London, [1936].

—— *A History of the American Drama from the Civil War to the Present Day.* New York, [1945].

RALPH, JULIAN. *People We Pass.* New York, 1896.

RAMOND, F. C. *Les Personnages des Rougon-Macquart.* Paris, 1901.

RAUSCH, LOTTE. *Die Gestalt des Künstlers in der Dichtung des Naturalismus.* Diss. Giessen, 1931.

REMMERS, KÄTHE. *Die Frau im Frühnaturalismus.* Diss. Warendorf, 1931.

RIIS, JACOB A. *How the Other Half Lives.* New York, 1890.

—— *A Ten Years' War. An Account of the Battle with the Slum in New York.* Boston, 1900.

RILEY, WOODBRIDGE. *American Thought from Puritanism to Pragmatism.* New York, 1915.

RIVES, AMÉLIE. *Barbara Dering.* Philadelphia, 1893.

ROBERTS, R. ELLIS. *Henrik Ibsen: A Critical Study.* London, 1912.

ROBINSON, [U. V. FEILITZEN]. *Ibsen och äktenskapsfrågan.* In *I tidens frågor,* V. Stockholm, 1882.

RÖHL, HANS. *Der Naturalismus.* Leipzig, 1927.

ROSS, CRYSTAL RAY. *Le Conteur Américain O Henry et l'art de Maupassant.* Thèse. Strasbourg, 1925.

480

ROUTH, H. V. *Towards the Twentieth Century.* Cambridge, 1937.

RUSK, RALPH LESLIE. *The Literature of the Middle Western Frontier.* 2 vols. New York, 1925.

SALTUS, EDGAR. *Eden.* Chicago, 1888.

SALVAN, ALBERT J. *Zola aux États-Unis.* In *Brown University Studies,* VIII. Providence, R.I., 1943.

SAUERACKER, JOHANNA. *Bourget und der Naturalismus.* In *Sprache und Kultur der germanischen und romanischen Völker.* C. Romanistische *Reihe,* XIII. Breslau, 1936.

SCHLESINGER, ARTHUR MEIER. *The Rise of the City, 1878–1898.* In *A History of American Life,* X. New York, [1946].

SCHNEIDER, HERBERT W. *A History of American Philosophy.* New York, 1946.

SCHREINER, OLIVE. *The Story of an African Farm.* New York, 1888.

SHACKLETON, ROBERT. *Stories of the East Side.* New York, 1900.

SHAW, BERNARD. *The Quintessence of Ibsenism.* London, 1891.

SHERMAN, STUART P. *The Genius of America.* New York and London, 1923.

SHIPLEY, JOSEPH T. *Trends in Literature.* New York, 1949.

SIMMONS, ERNEST J. *Leo Tolstoy.* Boston, 1946.

SMITH, BERNARD. *Forces in American Criticism: A Study in the History of American Literary Thought.* New York, 1939.

SOUGNAC, JEAN. *Sarah Orne Jewett.* Thèse. Paris, 1937.

SPEARE, MORRIS E. *The Political Novel: Its Development in England and in America.* New York, 1924.

SPENCER, HERBERT. *First Principles.* New York, n.d.

SPIELHAGEN, FRIEDRICH. *Beiträge zur Theorie und Technik des Romans.* Leipzig, 1883.

SPILLER, ROBERT E. *et al. Literary History of the United States.* 3 vols. New York, 1948.

STANTON, ELIZABETH CADY *et al. History of Woman Suffrage.* 6 vols. New York, 1881–1922.

STEPHENSON, G. M. *A History of American Immigration.* New York, 1926.

STEVENSON, ROBERT LOUIS. *The Strange Case of Dr. Jekyll and Mr. Hyde.* New York, n.d.

—— *The Wrecker.* New York, 1898.

TAINE, HIPPOLYTE. *Histoire de la littérature anglaise.* Paris, 1873.

TAUPIN, RENÉ. *L'Influence du symbolisme français sur la poésie américaine (de 1910 à 1920).* Thèse. Paris, 1929.

TAYLOR, WALTER F. *The Economic Novel in America.* Chapel Hill, N. C., 1942.

—— *A History of American Letters.* New York, [1936].

TENNANT, P. F. D. *Ibsen's Dramatic Technique.* Cambridge, [1948].

THIBAUDET, ALBERT. *Histoire de la littérature française de 1789 à nos jours.* Paris, [1936].

THOMASSEN, EJNAR. *Rysk litteratur under 200 år.* Stockholm, [1948].

TIANDER, KARL. *Turgenjev i dansk Aandsliv.* Copenhagen and Christiania, 1913.

TINDALL, WILLIAM YORK. *Forces in Modern British Literature, 1885–1946.* New York, 1947.

TOLSTOY, LEO. *Anna Karenina.* Liv. Lib. ed. Cleveland and New York, [1946].

—— *Hvad är konsten?* Stockholm, [1898].

—— *The Kreutzer Sonata.* New York, 1890.

—— *Sebastopol.* New York, [1887].

—— *War and Peace.* Mod. Lib. ed. New York, n.d.

TOWNSEND, EDWARD W. *Chimmie Fadden, Major Max, and Other Stories.* New York, 1895.

TOWNSHEND, HARVEY G. *Philosophical Ideas in the United States.* New York, 1934.

TRENT, W. P. *et al.* *A History of American Literature.* 4 vols. Cambridge and New York, 1918–21.

TURGENEV, IVAN. *Annuschka.* Upsala, [1885].

—— *Fatalisten och andra berättelser.* Upsala, [1886].

—— *Fathers and Sons.* Moscow, 1947.

—— *Faust.* Helsinki, 1892.

—— *Mumu and The Diary of a Superfluous Man.* New York, 1884.

—— *A Nest of the Gentry.* Moscow, 1947.

—— *On the Eve.* London and New York, 1906.

—— *Rudin.* Helsinki, [1922].

—— *Senilia: Dikter på prosa.* Upsala, [1883].

—— *Smoke.* Mod. Lib. ed. New York, n.d.

—— *A Sportman's Sketches.* 2 vols. London, 1895.

—— *Vårflöden.* Helsinki, [1923].

—— (TOURGÉNIEF, I. S.). *Virgin Soil.* London, 1878.

TURNER, FREDERICK JACKSON. *The Frontier in American History.* New York, [1920].

VAN DOREN, CARL. *The American Novel, 1789–1939.* New York, 1946.

VANWELKENHUYZEN, GUSTAVE. *L'Influence du naturalisme français en Belgique de 1875 à 1900.* In *Académie royale de langue et de littérature françaises,* IV. [Brussels], 1930.

—— *J.-K. Huysmans et la Belgique.* Paris, 1935.

VÉRON, EUGÈNE. *L'Esthétique.* Paris, 1921.

VIZETELLY, E. A. *Émile Zola: Novelist and Reformer.* London, 1904.

WALCUTT, CHARLES CHILD. *Naturalism in the American Novel.* Unpublished diss. Univ. of Michigan, Ann Arbor, 1937.

WALKER, FRANKLIN. *Frank Norris: A Biography.* Garden City, N.Y., 1932.

—— *San Francisco's Literary Frontier.* New York, 1939.

WARD, MRS. HUMPHRY. *Robert Elsmere.* London and New York, 1888.

WARREN, SIDNEY. *American Freethought, 1860–1914.* New York, 1943.

WEBER, CARL J. *Hardy in America: A Study of Thomas Hardy and His American Readers.* Waterville, Me., 1946.

482

WELLEK, RENÉ and WARREN, AUSTIN. *Theory of Literature*. London, 1949.

WHARTON, EDITH. *The Greater Inclination*. New York, 1899.

WHITE, GEORGE LEROY, JR. *Scandinavian Themes in American Fiction*. Diss. Philadelphia, 1937.

WHITE, HERVEY. *Quicksand*. Cambridge, Mass., 1900.

WHITLOCK, BRAND. *The 13th District*. Indianapolis, [1902].

WHITMAN, STEPHEN FRENCH. *Predestined*. New York, 1901.

WHITMAN, WALT. *Complete Prose Works*. London, 1920.

WILKINS, MARY E. *See* FREEMAN, MARY E. WILKINS.

WILLIAMS, AMES W. and STARRETT, VINCENT. *Stephen Crane: A Bibliography*. Glendale, Calif., 1948.

WILLIAMS, HAROLD. *Modern English Writers*. London, 1925.

WILSON, HARRY LEON. *The Spenders*. Boston, 1902.

WRIGHT, C. D. *The Industrial Evolution of the United States*. New York, 1924.

WRIGHT, H. G. *Studies in Anglo-Scandinavian Literary Relations*. Bangor, 1919.

YOUNG, ARTHUR N. *The Single Tax Movement in the United States*. Princeton, N.J., 1916.

ZOLA, ÉMILE. *Œuvres complètes*. Ed. François Bernouard. 50 vols. Paris, [1927–9]. [*Œuvres*.]

5. ARTICLES

(Only the most significant items are listed.)

ANDERSEN, ANNETTE. "Ibsen in America," *Scandinavian Studies and Notes*, XIV (February–May, 1937), 63–109, 115–55.

ARMS, GEORGE. "The Literary Background of Howells's Social Criticism," *American Literature*, XIV (November, 1942), 260–76.

BECKER, GEORGE J. "Realism: An Essay in Definition," *Modern Language Quarterly*, X (June, 1949), 184–97.

BENTZON, TH. (BLANC, MARIE THÉRÈSE). "Un Radical de la prairie: Hamlin Garland," *Revue des deux mondes*, CLVII (January, 1900), 139–80.

BURTON, RICHARD. "The Healthful Tone for American Literature," *Forum*, XIX (April, 1895), 249–56.

CARTER, EVERETT. "William Dean Howells' Theory of Critical Realism," *ELH*, XVI (June, 1949), 151–66.

CLAUDE, SIMPSON. "Hamlin Garland's Decline," *Southwest Review*, XXVI (January, 1941), 223–34.

COWLEY, MALCOLM. "Naturalism's Terrible McTeague," *New Republic*, CXVI, (May 5, 1947), 31–3.

—— "'Not Men': A Natural History of American Naturalism," *Kenyon Review*, IX (Summer, 1947), 414–35.

CRANE, HELEN R. "My Uncle, Stephen Crane," *American Mercury*, XXXI (January, 1934), 24–9.

DICKASON, DAVID H. "Benjamin Orange Flower, Patron of the Realists," *American Literature*, XIV (May, 1942), 148–56.

EDWARDS, HERBERT. "Howells and the Controversy over Realism in American Fiction," *American Literature*, III (November, 1931), 237–48.

—— "Zola and the American Critics," *American Literature*, IV (May, 1932), 114–29.

FIFE, ROBERT HERNDON and ANSTENSEN, ANSTEN. "Henrik Ibsen on the American Stage," *American-Scandinavian Review*, XVI (April, 1928), 218–28.

FLANAGAN, JOHN T. "Hamlin Garland, Occasional Minnesotan," *Minnesota History*, XXII (June, 1941), 157–68.

—— "Joseph Kirkland, Pioneer Realist," *American Literature*, XI (November, 1939), 273–84.

FLOWER, B. O. "Uninvited Poverty," *Arena*, V (March, 1892), 523–7.

FRIERSON, WILLIAM C. and EDWARDS, HERBERT. "Impact of French Naturalism on American Critical Opinion 1877–1892," *PMLA*, LXIII (September, 1948), 1007–16.

GARLAND, HAMLIN. "Ibsen as a Dramatist," *Arena*, II (June, 1890), 72–82.

—— "Meetings with Howells," *Bookman*, XLV (March, 1917), 1–7.

—— "Stephen Crane as I Knew Him," *Yale Review*, N.S. III (April, 1914), 494–506.

—— "The Work of Frank Norris," *Critic*, XLII (March, 1903), 216–18.

GOLDSTEIN, JESSE SIDNEY. "Two Literary Radicals: Garland and Markham in Chicago, 1893," *American Literature*, XVII (May, 1945), 152–60.

GRATTAN, C. HARTLEY. "Frank Norris," *Bookman*, LXIX (July, 1929), 506–10.

HANIGHEN, F. C. "Huysmans' Influence in America," *Revue de littérature comparée*, XIII (1933), 173–86.

JONES, CLAUDE. "Stephen Crane at Syracuse," *American Literature*, VII (March, 1935), 82–4.

JONES, HOWARD MUMFORD. "The Influence of European Ideas in Nineteenth-Century America," *American Literature*, VII (November, 1935), 241–73.

KIRKLAND, JOSEPH. "Tolstoï, and the Russian Invasion of the Realm of Fiction," *Dial*, VII (August, 1886), 79–81.

LOEWENBERG, BERT J. "Darwinism Comes to America, 1859–1900," *Mississippi Valley Historical Review*, XXVIII (1941), 339–69.

NYE, RUSSEL B. "Stephen Crane as Social Critic," *Modern Quarterly*, XI (Summer, 1940), 48–54.

PRATT, LYNDON UPSON. "The Formal Education of Stephen Crane," *American Literature*, X (January, 1939), 460–71.

—— "A Possible Source of *The Red Badge of Courage*," *American Literature*, XI (March, 1939), 1–10.

484

SPENCER, BENJAMIN T. "The New Realism and a National Literature," *PMLA*, LVI (December, 1941), 1116-32.

WALCUTT, CHARLES CHILD. "Frank Norris on Realism and Naturalism," *American Literature*, XIII (March, 1941), 61-3.

—— "Harold Frederic and American Naturalism," *American Literature* XI (March, 1939), 11-22.

—— "Naturalism and the Superman in the Novels of Jack London," *Papers of the Michigan Academy of Science, Arts and Letters*, XXIV, Part IV (1938), 89-107.

—— "The Three Stages of Theodore Dreiser's Naturalism," *PMLA*, LV (March, 1940), 266-89.

WALKER, FRANKLIN. "Frank Norris at the University of California," *Univ. of California Chronicle*, XXXIII, No. 3 (July, 1931), 320-49.

WEBSTER, H. T. "Wilbur F. Hinman's *Corporal Si Klegg* and Stephen Crane's *The Red Badge of Courage*," *American Literature*, XI (November, 1939), 285-93.

WICKHAM, HARVEY. "Stephen Crane at College," *American Mercury*, VII (March, 1926), 291-7.

INDEX

490

French literature, 16; in America, 38–41

Freytag, Gustav, 69, 148, 444–5, 448–9

Friedman, I. K., 60n

Frierson, William C., 29n, 127n

Froissart, Jean, *Chronicles*, 107

Frontier, 4–5, 12; closing of, 1, 6, 14–15; significance of, 6

Frost, Robert, 420

Fuller, Henry B., 50, 58n, 122n, 365n, 420, 468; *The Cliff-Dwellers*, 58n, 123; *With the Procession*, 58n

Galdós, Benito Pérez, *see* Pérez Galdós, Benito

Gale, Zona, 420

Galsworthy, John, 421

Garborg, Arne, 30

Gardener, Helen H., 80n, 81n

Garland, Franklin, 73

Garland, Hamlin, 15, 20, 40n, 43n, 51, 54n, 55n, 58, 59n, 60–1, **63–89**, 94–5, 104, 106, 123–4, 128, 132–3, 135–6, 139–40, 145, 152, 154–6, 160–2, 165, 181–2, 186, 205–10, 214–15, 218–20, 221–5, 228–49, 315, 317–28 *passim*, 341, 363–6, 382, 401n, 403n, 407–8, 410–16, 421–3, 442–4, 447–8, 450–1, 453, 455–7, 460, 469; on Grant Allen, 67n; Americanism, 135, 143–4; and *Arena*, 75–6, 78; and Balzac, 449; beast in man, theme in the work of, 214–15; birth, 63; on Björnson, 68n; in Boston, 65–70; boyhood, 63; on Chicago, 50; claim-holder, 65, 84; and Cliff-Dwellers' Club, 437–8; and Crane, 61, 86, 89, 94–5, 103, 152–3; on critics, 137, 148; on Darwin, 66; death, 89n, demand for originality, 135; democracy in literature, 147–8, 448–50; on Dickens, 68n; documentation, 169–71; doing odd jobs, 65; education, 64ff; on Eggleston, 52; essayist, 68; evolutionist, 66, 69; family moves, 63, 65; and B. O. Flower, 75–6, 82, 84n, 86; on Frederic, 56n, 70; free will, rejection of, 184ff; on Heine, 69n; and Herne, 72–3, 86; and Howells, 69, 70, 82, 86, 87n, 88n, 136, 139, 142; on Howells, 132–3; and Ibsen, 75, 86n, 147–8, **363–78**, 415, 426, 448; on Ibsen, 44, 136–7; on impressionism, 149–50; and Independent Theater Association, 72–3, 451–5; influence of Ibsen on,

363–78; influence of Tolstoy on, 343; influence of Turgenev on, 317–28; influence of Zola on, 233–49; on Kirkland, 70; lecturer, 61, 67, 89, 439–50; library, 415–37; literary credo, 135–50; marriage, 89n; mood of bitterness, 71–2; on naturalism, 69, 141–3; and nature, 63; new woman, 221–4, 366–78; and Norris, 61, 109, 123n, 124n; on Norris, 61n, 117, 123; objectivity, 145–6; parents, 63; purpose in the novel, 146; quoted, 8, 12–14, 50, 63, 67n, 69n, 70–5, 88, 89n, 90, 95n, 205n, 317–18; reformer, 71, 84–7, 89, 136, 141, 146; revolts against the literary supremacy of New England, 50, 137; and Riis, 3n; on romanticism, 148; romanticist, 88–9; scope, 144; setting, use of in the work of, 177–82; sex, treatment of, 204–10; single-taxer, 67, 89; on socialism, 74; on Spencer, 7–8, 66; teacher, 66, 439, 443; theme, 166–8; and Tolstoy, 70, 136, 148, 343, 448–9; on Tolstoy, 58; tramps through Eastern states, 65; trip to the West, 70–2; and Turgenev, 70, 75, 144n, 148, **317–28**, 444–5, 448–9; on Turgenev, 58; on veritism, 126–7, 138–41; meets Whitman, 71n; and Zola, 75, 135, 139–40, 141n, 142, 148, **233–49**, 437; on Zola, 132–3

READING, 64–70, 73–5; dime novels, 64; *The Hoosier School-Master*, 64; Ibsen, 44, 68n, 74; *McTeague*, 61; Taine, 65, 440; Tolstoy, 70; Turgenev, 70; Zola, 69

WRITINGS, *Afternoon Neighbors*, 317; "The Alliance Wedge in Congress," 78n; "Among the Corn-Rows," 368; *Back Trailers of the Middle Border*, 317n; *Boy Life on the Prairie*, 88, 343n; "A Branch Road," 214, 363n, 366; *The Captain of the Gray-Horse Troop*, 61, 172; "Color in the Wheat," 72; *Companions on the Trail*, 61, 63n, 317n; quoted, 123n; *Crumbling Idols*, 44n, 50n, 86–7, 129n, 135, 138–9, 163, 206n, 221, 317, 365, 374n; quoted, 14, 135–7, 140–2, 144–9, 161, 205, 365, 407–8; "Curious Places," 170; "Daddy Deering," 323, 343n; *A Daughter of the Middle Border*, 63n; "The

500

ADDITIONS AND CORRECTIONS

p. 12, l. 33: slowy *read* slowly
p. 29, l. 19: *delete* essence and
p. 29, l. 32: often *read* occasionally
p. 35, l. 34: J. F. Hapgood *read* I. F. Hapgood
p. 38, l. 9: *delete* in
p. 39, l. 24: seemed *read* seems
p. 46, l. 13: *read* During the following years American magazines
p. 49, l. 22: *read* a growing shift away from
p. 52, l. 18: poor-house *read* poorhouse
p. 57, l. 31: *Transcript read Boston Evening Transcript*
p. 68, l. 35: *Worse read Worsé*
p. 70, l. 16: He was later *read* Later he became
p. 73, l. 19: Katharine *read* Katherine
p. 73, l. 27: *read* To a certain extent, Garland no doubt stimulated Herne's interest in the modern realistic drama, for at the time
p. 74, l. 11: *read* in 1935 to Eldon C. Hill
p. 76, l. 4: needed . . . . *read* needed. . . .
p. 80, l. 8: *read* illustrate, for instance, *Main-Travelled Roads, Jason Edwards*
p. 80, l. 33: law *read* laws
p. 103, l. 27: of his "Occurrence *read* of "An Occurence
p. 108, l. 9: and "The Son *read* and "Son
p. 116, l. 14: *Moran read Moran of the Lady Letty*
p. 122, l. 15: *Nibelungen read Nibelungenlied*
p. 145, n. 4: *add* Italics are Garland's.
p. 147, l. 12: Touqueville *read* Tocqueville
p. 149, l. 17: effect. . . *read* effect . . .
p. 157, l. 2: smaller *read* small
p. 158, l. 36: *delete* instead
p. 188, l. 10: the back trail *read* the "back-trail"
p. 202, n. 2: *add* Italics are Norris's.
p. 210, l. 31: *read* frankly, for instance, in
p. 214, l. 18: "A Branch-Road" *read* "A Branch Road"
p. 225, l. 7: women *read* woman
p. 229, l. 6: man's ability to create *read* man's ability eventually to create
p. 248, l. 33: *read* occasionally destroyed
p. 296, l. 2: diningroom *read* dining room
p. 301, l. 18: Bcause *read* Because

p. 327, l. 32: possiby *read* possibly
p. 327, l. 38: teme *read* theme
p. 334, l. 5: æsthetics *read* aesthetics
p. 339, l. 26: esthetic *read* aesthetic
p. 345, n. 1: *peace read Peace*
p. 357, l. 27: batttle *read* battle
p. 378, n. 2: marrage *read* marriage
p. 394, l. 32: him stay *read* him to stay
p. 422, l. 6: *Moutain read Mountain*
p. 449, l. 17: verse the heart beat *read* verse, the heartbeat
p. 454, l. 10: immeasurable *read* immeasurably
p. 464, l. 27: Trovadore *read* Trovatore